The Psychoanalytic Study
of the Child

VOLUME XVIII

The Psychoanalytic Study

of the Child

VOLUME XVIII

INTERNATIONAL UNIVERSITIES PRESS, INC.

New York   New York

CONTENTS

Contributions to Psychoanalytic Theory

JAY KATZ—On Primary Gain and Secondary Gain 9

SEYMOUR L. LUSTMAN—Some Issues in Contemporary Psychoanalytic Research 51

LEO RANGELL—The Scope of Intrapsychic Conflict: Microscopic and Macroscopic Considerations 75

LEO RANGELL—Structural Problems in Intrapsychic Conflict 103

JOSEPH SANDLER, ALEX HOLDER, and DALE MEERS—The Ego Ideal and the Ideal Self 139

JOSEPH SANDLER and HUMBERTO NAGERA—Aspects of the Metapsychology of Fantasy 159

Aspects of Normal and Psychological Development

SIBYLLE K. ESCALONA—Patterns of Infantile Experience and the Developmental Process 197

ANNA FREUD—The Concept of Developmental Lines 245

ELIEZER ILAN—The Problem of Motivation in the Educator's Vocational Choice 266

M. MASUD R. KHAN—The Concept of Cumulative Trauma 286

MARGARET S. MAHLER—Thoughts About Development and Individuation 307

FRED PINE and MANUEL FURER—Studies of the Separation-Individuation Phase: A Methodological Overview 325

ANNE-MARIE SANDLER—Aspects of Passivity and Ego Development in the Blind Infant 343

BENJAMIN SPOCK—The Striving for Autonomy and Regressive Object Relationships 361

Clinical Contributions

DOROTHY BURLINGHAM in cooperation with ARTHUR T. BARRON—A Study of Identical Twins: Their Analytic Material Compared with Existing Observation Data of Their Early Childhood ... 367

K. R. EISSLER—Notes on the Psychoanalytic Concept of Cure 424

LISELOTTE FRANKL—Self-Preservation and the Development of Accident Proneness in Children and Adolescents 464

EDITH LUDOWYK GYOMROI—The Analysis of a Young Concentration Camp Victim 484

HUMBERTO NAGERA—The Developmental Profile: Notes on Some Practical Considerations Regarding Its Use 511

JANICE NORTON—Treatment of a Dying Patient 541

BERNARD ROSENBLATT—A Severe Neurosis in an Adolescent Boy .. 561

SARA KUT ROSENFELD and MARJORIE P. SPRINCE—An Attempt to Formulate the Meaning of the Concept "Borderline" 603

RUTH THOMAS in collaboration with LYDIA FOLKART and ELIZABETH MODEL—The Search for a Sexual Identity in a Case of Constitutional Sexual Precocity 636

Contents of Previous Volumes 663

CONTRIBUTIONS TO PSYCHOANALYTIC THEORY

ON PRIMARY GAIN AND SECONDARY GAIN

JAY KATZ, M.D. (New Haven)

Early in the development of a psychoanalytic theory of symptom formation, Freud introduced the concepts primary gain and secondary gain,[1] and over the years, he repeatedly sought to clarify their meaning and their relationship to each other. Primary gain presented less of a problem; once defined it needed little modification. Secondary gain, however, was a more troublesome concept. Its definition never became clearly delineated and, instead, required frequent alterations, lengthy explanations, and numerous caveats to avoid misunderstanding. Two factors may have contributed to the divergent treatment accorded to these concepts:

1. Historically, primary gain was a novel construct which had few, if any, roots in traditional psychiatric thought and thus was less subject to contamination by precedent. Secondary gain, on the other hand, had an extensive history. Under a variety of labels it had been ascribed to patients of many centuries "to whom [their] illnesses [were] sources of enjoyment, and who [had] neither the wish nor the intention of being bettered" (Tuke, 1892, p. 853). In these pre-psychoanalytic formulations, of course, no distinction was made between conscious and unconscious intentions, although the former seemed strongly implied. Because of such ancient roots, contemporary formulations about secondary gain could more readily revert in

---

[1] My interest in this topic stems from an analysis of an agoraphobic business man. In supervision with Dr. R. P. Knight the question frequently arose whether particular behavior patterns could be identified as belonging to the primary gain or the secondary gain. Often it seemed difficult to make such a differentiation, and we explored the possibility of introducing "tertiary gain" as an auxiliary concept. My discussions with Dr. Knight led me to pursue this subject further, and this is gratefully acknowledged.

Presented, in part, before the Western New England Psychoanalytic Society on February 22, 1963.
Yale Law School and Department of Psychiatry, Yale University School of Medicine.

meaning or suggest connotations which on careful scrutiny turn out to be inconsistent with the over-all postulates of psychoanalytic theory.

2. In psychoanalytic writings primary gain has always been viewed as an important theoretical concept, while secondary gain has been segregated as a technical concept, of little, if any, theoretical significance (Brenner, 1955, p. 207; Fenichel, 1945, p. 462). This unexplained distinction removed secondary gain from constant theoretical scrutiny and, in turn, precluded a re-examination of secondary gain in the light of any advances in psychoanalytic theory. Furthermore, the absence of an ongoing theoretical scrutiny allowed the meaning of secondary gain to become contaminated by non-analytic formulations—a fate which can befall all concepts which are not constantly re-examined in the light of theory—thereby reinforcing the regressive pull already exerted by ingrained historical preconceptions. Moreover, treating primary gain as a theoretical concept and secondary gain as a technical one obscured the relationship between the two constructs.

The purpose of this paper is twofold: (1) to present a review of the literature and (2) to attempt a systematic metapsychological re-examination of primary and secondary gain in order to assess the place of these concepts within our present psychoanalytic framework. Except for Freud's writings the review of the literature is selective. Contributions have been chosen which highlight problem areas requiring further elucidation.

FREUD'S FORMULATIONS

Freud's interest in primary and secondary gain can be traced from his earliest case histories to the posthumously published *Outline of Psychoanalysis*. This presentation has been organized around the twenty-fourth lecture of *A General Introduction to Psychoanalysis* (1916-17), and the "Fragment of an Analysis of a Case of Hysteria" (1905), including its important footnote added eighteen years later (1923).

In *A General Introduction to Psychoanalysis,* after twenty-three lectures on the psychology of errors, dreams, symptoms, resistance, and libido theory, Freud, before turning to a discussion of primary and secondary gain, intimated that his audience might have preferred "illustrations from life instead of theories" (p. 386):

> I have ascribed to you a wish that I had begun the subject of the neuroses with a description of the neurotic's behavior, and of the ways in which he suffers from his disorder, protects himself against it, and adapts himself to it . . . there are reasons against beginning with this aspect. *The danger is that the unconscious will be overlooked, the great importance of the libido ignored, and that everything will be judged as it appears to the patient's own ego.* Now it is obvious that his ego is not a reliable and impartial authority. The ego is after all the force which denies the existence of the unconscious. . . . We are forewarned against being misled by what the ego tells us. According to its evidence it would appear to have been the active force throughout, so that the symptoms arise by its will and agency; *we know that to a large extent it has played a passive part,* a fact which it then endeavors to conceal and to gloss over [p. 388; my italics].

Freud's warning was prompted by a growing realization that unless he first succeeded in demonstrating the ramifications and implications of unconscious mental processes, concepts like secondary gain could easily be misunderstood. For a failure to heed the psychological distinction between conscious and unconscious intentions could only lead to the employment of such constructs in their prepsychoanalytic meaning, thus turning a general acceptance of a psychoanalytic concept like secondary gain into a Pyrrhic victory. Despite his caution, this is what happened. Freud noted repeatedly that the study of war neuroses demonstrated to the medical world "the importance of psychoanalysis in neurotic disturbances" and made popular "our psychological conceptions such as the 'gain from illness' and the 'flight into illness' " (1925, p. 54), but that there was "no reason to see in these approaches" any "reconciliation or any appeasement of opposition" (1919, p. 208).[2] For the "insight [through psychoanalysis] into the causation of war neuroses led to a [painful form] of treatment. . . . It seemed expedient to treat the neurotic as a malingerer and to disregard the psychological distinction between conscious and unconscious intentions, although he was known not to be a malingerer" (1920a, p. 213).

2 See also Freud (1932, p. 182).

Freud also emphasized in his introductory warning that the ego "to a large extent [plays] a passive part in symptom formation." But what are the implications of the existence, whatever the extent, of an active component? Is the active component the degree of the ego's opposition to the instinctual derivative seeking discharge? Or does it also connote an ego activity which attempts to shape symptom formation so that it can be put to some specific reality use? Is symptom formation initiated by reality factors or instinctual pressures and is the ego's participation in this process a conscious or unconscious ego activity? Freud's warning seems to be that it must not be equated with conscious activity, but he does not categorically rule out some conscious participation.[3]

Freud then begins his discussion of primary gain. He noted that in traumatic neuroses, especially the war neuroses, "we are particularly impressed by a self-seeking, egoistic motive, a straining toward protection and self-interest" (1916-17, p. 390). The egoistic motives alone could "perhaps" not have produced the disease, but they support it once it has been formed. Therefore, in addition to an "internal *advantage through illness,*" the ego may gain under certain conditions a "tangible external [or 'accidental'] advantage more or less valuable in reality" (p. 391). Freud here divided primary gain into two components—an internal one and an external one—and the latter he urged must not be equated with secondary gain. He illustrated the external component of primary gain by an example:

> . . . a woman who is brutally treated . . . by her husband . . .
> takes refuge in a neurosis, if her disposition admits of it. This
> will happen if she is too cowardly or too conventional to console
> herself secretly with another man, if she is not strong enough to

[3] Years later, Freud returns to this problem: "when we were young students at the hospital . . . we were told [that hysterics] produce their symptoms in order to make themselves interesting. . . . *It is extraordinary how these old profundities recur!* . . . *Some element of this doctrine . . . must of course be correct,* though they regard this fragmentary explanation as the complete one. The instinct of self-preservation will attempt to turn every situation to its own account: the ego will try to get some advantage even out of being ill. . . . But indeed, when one thinks of the facts of masochism, of the unconscious need for punishment and of the neurotic tendency to self-injury, all of which seem to imply the existence of instinctual impulses which run counter to self-preservation, *one comes to question even the general validity of [this] platitude . . .*" (1932, p. 182; my italics). Freud, while first stating that there must be something correct in such doctrines, then has second thoughts and questions the entire proposition.

defy all external reasons against it and separate from her husband, if she has no prospect of being able to maintain herself or of finding a better husband, and last of all if she is still strongly attached sexually to this brutal man. Her illness becomes her weapon in the struggle against him, one that she can use for her protection, or misuse for purposes of revenge. She can complain of her illness [p. 391].

Freud was aware of the pitfalls inherent in his example and attempted to dispel them. He stressed that he did not wish to imply that the ego either desires or creates the neurosis: "Perhaps it means merely this: that the ego is pleased to accept the neurosis which it is in any case unable to prevent, and that if there is anything at all to be made out of it, it makes the best of it" (p. 391). In a later paper Freud stressed the unconscious aspects of such gains even more by pointing to the patient's ignorance about the motives for falling ill, including the gains he derives from them. One can only combat "the influence of these trends by compelling the ego to take cognizance of them" (1926b, p. 222).[4] Thus analytic treatment is required to convince a patient of his intention to be ill.

Yet, in his clinical illustrations of primary gain, Freud speaks of "cowardice,"[5] "conventionality," "lack of strength," "sacrifice of other members of the family," and "concealment of professional incompetence." What does he wish to communicate to his readers by the use of such words? Perhaps they must first be disentangled. When Freud is addressing himself to the patient's exploitations of his family and his incompetence, Freud may not, in the light of his exposition, mean conscious exploitation; rather, Freud implies that the vicissitudes of the patient's personality development contribute to the unconscious use to which symptoms are put and that specific environmental conditions shape the employment of symptoms. But we are left with cowardice, conventionality, and lack of strength. Such labels, on first impact, can obscure the fact that unconscious motives are at work and may, instead, create the impression that

4 See also Freud (1905, p. 45) and (1909a, p. 232).
5 In the discussion of Miss Lucy R., Freud stated: "The hysterical method of defence . . . lies in the conversion of the excitation into a somatic innervation; and the advantage of this is that the incompatible idea is repressed from the ego's consciousness. . . . the mechanism which produces hysteria represents on the one hand an act of moral cowardice and on the other a defensive measure which is at the disposal of the ego" (Breuer and Freud, 1895, p. 122f.).

the advantage through illness is the result of conscious motivations. Freud clearly would have rejected such implications. However, Freud's choice of such words may have been shaped by his value orientation. Since these value-freighted words recur in discussions on secondary gain, it will be more profitable to examine first Freud's development of this concept.

The " 'secondary advantage' through illness":

. . . supervenes later than that born with the symptom, so to speak. When such a mental organization as the disease has persisted for a considerable time it seems finally to acquire the character of an independent entity; it displays something like a self-preservative instinct; it forms a kind of pact, a *modus vivendi*, with the other forces in mental life, even those fundamentally hostile to it, and opportunities can hardly fail to arise in which it once more manifests itself as useful and expedient, thus acquiring a secondary function which again strengthens its position [1916-17, p. 392].

Freud illustrated secondary gain by another clinical example: a capable worker, crippled by an accident and no longer able to work, learns to "exploit his mutilation" by becoming a beggar. ". . . if you were to remove his disability you would deprive him for a time of his means of subsistence, for the question would arise whether he would still be capable of resuming his former work. When a secondary exploitation of the illness such as this is formed in a neurosis we can range it alongside the first and call it a *'secondary* advantage through illness' " (1916-17, p. 393). Why did Freud view the begging as an exploitation rather than as the best possible adaptation the cripple could make to the accident? And why did Freud not suggest that the traumatic impact of the accident created the need for a new intrapsychic equilibrium, determined by the patient's life history and present circumstances and which led to a permanently regressive adaptation? Yet, in speaking about "a self-preservative instinct," *"modus vivendi,"* and "secondary function which again strengthens its position," he must have had more in mind than is conveyed by "exploitation." Does Freud imply that the worker would be unwilling to give up his new life as a beggar even if a promise of recovery and rehabilitation could be made? He might have felt that such a promise should not even be necessary. We know from

Jones (1955) and Freud's letters (Jones, 1955, p. 464) that Freud had very strong moral feelings and, as Hartmann (1960) put it, that he "admired independent, autonomous morality and despised moral weakness and the tendency to compromise" (p. 16). Freud's value orientation seems to prescribe not only that it is better to be a capable worker than a beggar but also that if confronted with the chance of becoming a capable worker again, it is more "honorable" to take such a course. Freud had little patience with cowardice, conventionality, or lack of strength because he valued highly the heroic aspects of our rendezvous with destiny.[6] He once contrasted man and camel encountering a lion on a steep mountain path. With flight impossible, man would give himself up for lost,

> . . . not so the camel. He takes one leap with his rider into the abyss. . . . The remedies provided by neurosis avail the patient no better . . . perhaps because . . . symptom-formation is after all an automatic process which may show itself inadequate to meet the demands of life, and involves man in a renunciation of his best and highest powers. The more honourable choice, if there be a choice, is to go down in fair fight with destiny [1916-17, p. 393].[7]

What problems does Freud's unexplored value orientation raise? If it could be demonstrated that a patient must cherish similar values in order to benefit from psychoanalytic treatment, one might argue that Freud is not speaking here about moral judgments but about significant clinical observations which, in turn, would have important technical implications. Freud might also have expressed by such

6 But there are other values: "It may be true that not every neurotic whom we meet is worth the expenditure of an analysis; but there are some very valuable individuals among them as well. *We must set ourselves the goal of bringing it about that as few human beings as possible enter civilized life with such a defective mental equipment.* And for that purpose we must collect much experience and learn to understand many things" (Freud, 1926b, p. 222; my italics).

7 Freud, in a discussion of treatment without fee, remarked that a poor man once he has become neurotic can only be treated with difficulty. The neurosis "renders him too good a service in the struggle for existence; the secondary gain from illness which it brings him is much too important. He now claims by right of his neurosis the pity which the world has refused to his material distress and he now can absolve himself from the obligation of combating his poverty by working" (1913, p. 133). Again Freud suggests that the poverty-stricken neurotic is not making "the more honourable choice," but at the same time he also introduces the important question of what happens when the neurosis renders the patient "too good a service in the struggle for existence." Thus the impact of external reality on the maintenance of secondary gain needs further scrutiny. See also Freud (1920b, p. 158).

words his "surprise and dismay [that] so many people obey only
outer pressures instead of developing their own moral standards"
(Hartmann, 1960, p. 15). Thus he might have wanted to say something about normal superego development and the concomitant relative freedom from sociocultural pressures. But in the present context
Freud neither qualifies the use of words like "cowardice" nor identifies them as conceptual statements or value preferences. Had he
identified them as such, it might have become clearer that his description of the two gains also included statements about the kind of life
men *ought* to lead. Freud was aware of the moral issues. In an earlier paper he wrote: "Thus the mechanism which produces hysteria
represents on the one hand an act of moral cowardice and on the
other a defensive measure which is at the disposal of the ego . . . a
greater amount of moral[8] courage would have been of advantage to
the person concerned" (Breuer and Freud, 1895, p. 123). Since such
terms as cowardice, conventionality, and exploitation contain hidden
value preferences, they must not be considered evidence of neurosis,
for such an employment would only interweave character descriptions of undefined neurotic implications[9] with health values. Yet,
when the moral values contained in such words remain of low visi-
bility, they can readily be mistaken for symptoms of ill health. Then,
as Hartmann (1960) recently wrote, the "equation of mental health
values with moral values may come to mean an equation also of
moral 'badness' with mental dysfunction. This aspect, though commonly considered to be an advance in tolerance, betrays a relation
to pre-Freudian thinking. . . . Freud had stated emphatically that
neurotics should not be considered morally inferior to so-called
normal human beings" (p. 70). Thus in the absence of articulated
value preferences, statements about secondary gain can easily become
a judgmental evaluation of the patient's inability (or unwillingness)
to face up to his neurotic conflict. Any definition of secondary gain

    [8] Freud, in a later paper, gave a meaning to "moral" which perhaps he had in mind
all along: "we are dealing with what may be called a 'moral' factor, a sense of guilt
which is finding its satisfaction in the illness and refuses to give up the punishment of
suffering" (1923, p. 49).
    [9] For example, Freud wrote: "the permanent character-traits are either unchanged
prolongations of the original instincts, or sublimations of those instincts, or reaction
formations against them" (1908a, p. 175). See also Waelder's recent discussion (1960,
p. 200).

must clearly state the extent to which it includes preferences about human behavior or must avoid such judgments altogether.

In a later passage in the twenty-fourth lecture Freud briefly touches on the issue of health values:

> There are indeed cases in which the physician himself must admit that the solution of a conflict by a neurosis is the one most harmless and most tolerable socially . . . there is *other* misery in the world besides neurotic misery—real unavoidable suffering— that necessity may even demand of a man that he sacrifices his health to it, and . . . such suffering in one individual may often avert incalculable hardship for many others. Therefore, although it may be said of every neurotic that he has taken '*flight into illness*,' it must be admitted that in many cases this flight is fully justified [p. 390].

While Freud distinguishes other misery from neurotic misery, he does not go on to identify when "real unavoidable suffering," which is reality oriented, is nonneurotic and under what conditions it becomes neurotic.[10] One surely can maintain that suffering under certain external conditions is "fully justified," but is flight into illness ever "justified" or "unjustified"? Is it not, as Freud himself has put it, "an automatic process"? What may be missing here is a detailed consideration of the problem of adaptation. Freud was aware of the issue of adaptation, as is implied in the following statement: "there are cases [where] the solution of a conflict by a neurosis is the one . . . most tolerable socially." In a later paper Freud added, "It has . . . long been known that the . . . disappearance [of this gain from illness] in consequence of some change in real external circumstances, constitutes one of the mechanisms of a cure of the symptom" (1914, p. 53).

At the same time a phrase like "advantage through illness," when used as a conceptual term, should highlight the need for a clear delineation of the values contained in a scientific observation since the words themselves convey a value judgment. For example, Freud's

10 Freud made such a distinction in another paper: if sexual freedom is limited too much by society, the "number of strong natures who openly oppose the demands of civilization will increase enormously, and so will the number of weaker ones who, faced with the conflict between the pressure of cultural influences and the resistance of their constitution, take flight into neurotic illness" (1908b, p. 192).

first obsessional patient (whom he must have treated prior to 1895) was troubled by innumerable scruples, among them a compulsion to iron all paper money to prevent the spread of bacterial disease. Freud, who at that time "already had a vague suspicion of the connection between neuroses and sexual life" (1909c, p. 197), inquired into his sexual activities. The patient answered that this was no problem for him since he had opportunities to spend the night with young girls and on such occasions would masturbate them. Freud then asked: " 'But aren't you afraid of doing [them] some harm, fiddling about in [their] genitals with your dirty hand?' " The patient "flared up: 'Harm? Why, what harm should it do . . . they've all of them enjoyed it. . . .' " He took Freud's "remonstrance in very bad part, and never appeared again." Freud went on:

> I could only account for the contrast between his fastidiousness with the paper florins and his unscrupulousness in abusing girls . . . by supposing that the self-reproachful affect had become *displaced*. The aim of this displacement was obvious enough: if his self-reproaches had been allowed to remain where they belonged he would have had to abandon a form of sexual gratification to which he was probably impelled by some powerful infantile determinants. The displacement therefore ensured his deriving a considerable advantage from his illness [1909c, p. 198].

What does Freud mean here by "advantage"? Why is the sexual play the advantage from illness rather than the fastidiousness with money? It is not at all clear perhaps because another question needs answering first: what is the "illness"? Is it the innumerable scruples, or the absence of concern over his sexual activities, or the lack of interest in heterosexual intercourse, or the powerful infantile determinants, or is it the sexual activity with the girls, despite the patient's inability to identify this behavior as his illness? Whatever the illness, it becomes clear that the advantages bring in their wake numerous disadvantages and that the "advantages" may have to be bought at a considerable price. Thus the words advantage and gain may convey an implication which, once the totality of the neurotic conflict is kept in view, turns out to be one-sided. Also does "advantage or disadvantage from illness" say more than how a patient experiences a particular symptom? The compulsion to iron all paper money and the sexual play with girls are felt differently by the patient and thus may say a great deal about their respective availability to analytic scrutiny. But conceptually do not both symptoms, like all symptoms, imply a combination of "advantages" and "disadvantages"? Freud in his discussions of Little Hans addresses himself to these points:

> One day while Hans was in the street he was seized with an attack of anxiety. He would not yet say what it was he was afraid of; but at the very beginning of this anxiety-state he betrayed to his father his motive for being ill, *the advantage he derived from it*. He wanted to stay with his mother and to coax with her [1909b, p. 114; my italics]. 'Little Hans' refused to go out in the street because he was afraid of horses. . . . *Which part of it constituted the symptom?* Was it his having the fear? Was it his choice of an object for his fear? Was it his giving up of his freedom of movement? Or was it more than one of these combined? *What was the satisfaction which he renounced?* [1926a, p. 101; my italics].

Freud, in an earlier paper, had commented on the question of flight into illness in an intriguing but different fashion. He wondered what might happen if eventually society would be aware of the meaning of symptoms; for example, that anxious overtenderness conceals hatred. He speculated that this will make "the gain from illness illusory" and people then "will have to be honest, confess to the instincts that are at work in them, face the conflict, fight for what they want, or go without it; and the tolerance of society, which is bound to ensue as a result of psycho-analytic enlightenment, will help them in their task" (1910, p. 150). This suggests another question: to what extent is secondary gain created or maintained by the people who surround the patient? Freud was aware that flight into illness might be "the mildest possible outcome" of a neurotic conflict and that the demands by society that a patient face his conflict might "cause a mischief greater than neurotic illness" (1910, p. 150). However, Freud felt that "The gain from illness . . . is nevertheless on the whole and in the end detrimental to individuals as well as to society. The unhappiness that our work of enlightenment may cause will after all only affect some individuals. The change-over to a more realistic and creditable attitude on the part of society will not be bought too dearly by these sacrifices" (1910, p. 150).

The discussion of secondary gain in the introductory lectures was the first detailed reconsideration of the position Freud had taken in "Fragment of an Analysis of a Case of Hysteria." There Freud distinguished between *"motives of illness"* and *"liability* to being ill . . . the material out of which symptoms are formed" and maintained that the "motives have no share in the formation of symptoms, and indeed are not present at the beginning of the illness. They only appear secondarily to it; but it is not until they have appeared that the disease is fully constituted" (1905, p. 42). Eighteen years later, Freud added a footnote to this point. He corrected his earlier proposition that motives of illness are absent at the onset of illness and noted that, in fact, his observation that childhood motives contribute to the outbreak of illness had already contradicted it.[11] In this footnote Freud introduced

> . . . a distinction between the *primary* advantage derived from the illness and the *secondary* one. The motive for being ill is, of course, invariably the gaining of some advantage. . . . But in every neurotic illness a primary gain has also to be recognized. In the first place, falling ill involves a saving of psychical effort; it emerges as being economically the most convenient solution where there is a mental conflict (we speak of a 'flight into illness'[12]) . . . This element in the primary gain may be described as the *internal* or psychological one, and it is, so to say, a constant one. But beyond this, external factors (such as . . . the situation of a woman subjugated by her husband) may contribute motives

[11] "The motives for being ill often begin to be active even in childhood. A little girl . . . has now discovered a means of enticing out her parents' love. . . . When such a child has grown up . . . [she will be able to make use] of a means which she had found effective in her years of childhood" (1905, p. 44f.). And it "is worth emphasizing that his [the Rat Man's] flight into illness was made possible by his identifying himself with his father. The identification enabled his affects to regress on to the residues of his childhood" (1909c, p. 199).

[12] The expression "flight into illness" was first introduced by Freud in "Some Remarks on Hysterical Attacks" (1909a, p. 232). In the same paper, he also made explicit the distinction between primary and secondary gain, but called them "primary purpose" and "secondary purpose." The specific term "secondary gain from illness" was introduced in 1913 (p. 133). Much earlier, in 1894, Freud had introduced the term "flight into psychosis": "the ego has fended off the incompatible idea through a flight into psychosis. . . . The ego breaks away from the incompatible idea; but the latter is inseparably connected with a piece of reality, so that, in so far as the ego achieves this result, it, too, has detached itself wholly or in part from reality. In my opinion, this latter event is the condition under which the subject's ideas receive the vividness of hallucinations" (p. 59f.). Here Freud postulated that symptom formation (and the related primary gain) brings about a strikingly new relationship to the environment.

for falling ill and these will constitute the *external* element in the primary gain [1905, p. 43].

In the same footnote Freud commented that the remainder of the original 1905 paragraph applied to the secondary gain:

A symptom comes into the patient's mental life at first as an unwelcome guest; it has everything against it; and that is why it may vanish so easily, apparently of its own accord, under the influence of time. To begin with there is no use to which it can be put in the domestic economy of the mind; but very often it succeeds in finding one secondarily. Some psychical current or other finds it convenient to make use of it, and in that way the symptom manages to obtain a *secondary function* and remains, as it were, anchored fast in the patient's mental life [1905, p. 43].

Freud's metapsychological position with respect to primary and secondary gain reveals that: primary gain must account for (1) mental conflict which requires structural and dynamic propositions; (2) saving of psychical effort, an economic proposition; (3) childhood experiences, a genetic proposition; and (4) external factors, an adaptive proposition. He included mainly adaptive propositions under secondary gain, if "secondary function" is meant to indicate that eventually the symptom finds additional reality ties. In addition, Freud made the following points: (1) A symptom cannot become a permanent illness unless secondary-gain mechanisms come into play (1905). A symptom may be or become a "disease" without the presence of secondary-gain mechanisms (1916-17). Thus Freud leaves us with two positions about the relationship of symptoms to disease. (2) Secondary gain comes into operation "once the disease has persisted for a considerable time" and "serves to strengthen [the disease's] position." The distinction between the external component of primary gain and secondary gain may therefore, at least in part, be based on a time factor. A number of questions arise: Can symptoms become established without secondary gain? Must a distinction be made between symptom and illness? Do all symptoms or illness eventually acquire secondary-gain aspects? Are the differences between secondary gain and the external component of the primary gain sufficiently clear-cut to allow for a meaningful distinction in theory and practice? If secondary gain is necessary to maintain the

symptom, how are such gains related to the gains arising out of
original defensive effort?[13] Might a complete metapsychological
analysis of primary and secondary gain obliterate the distinction
between the two concepts?

Freud concluded the discussion of "gain through illness" in the
case of Dora by turning to therapeutic considerations:

> Motives that support the patient in being ill are probably to be
> found in all fully developed cases. But there are some in which
> the motives are purely internal—such as a desire for self-punish-
> ment, that is penitence and remorse. It will be found much easier
> to solve the therapeutic problem in such cases than in those in
> which the illness is related to the attainment of some external
> aim [1905, p. 46].

At the time Freud must have believed that psychoanalytic technique
was better suited to dealing with internal than external resistances.
He later reversed his position. In *The Ego and the Id,* while commenting on the negative therapeutic reaction, Freud wrote that this
resistance "reveals itself as the most powerful of all obstacles to
recovery, more powerful than the familiar ones of narcissistic inacces-
sibility, a negative attitude towards the physician, and clinging to
the gain from illness" (1923, p. 49). He reiterated this in "The
Economic Problem of Masochism": "The satisfaction of this unconscious sense of guilt is perhaps the most powerful bastion in the
subject's (usually composite) gain from illness—in the sum of forces
which struggle against his recovery . . . all that matter[s is] that it
should be possible to maintain a certain amount of suffering" (1924,
p. 166). Secondary gain from illness, like primary gain, has two
components—an external one and an internal one. Most intriguing
is Freud's afterthought, in parenthesis, "usually composite." Can
these two components be easily separated in clinical practice?[14]

---

13 See also Freud (1887-1902, pp. 199 and 212).

14 In *An Outline of Psychoanalysis* Freud suggested such a question: ". . . the
deeper our knowledge of the mental life of neurotics penetrates, the more clearly two
new factors force themselves upon our notice . . . they [do not] arise from the patient's
ego. They can both be included under one description of 'need to be ill' or 'need to
suffer'; but they are of different origins, though in other respects of a similar nature.
The first of these two factors is the sense of guilt . . . the portion of the resistance
contributed by a [severe] superego. . . . It is not so easy to demonstrate the existence of

What is the relationship of all the resistances opposing recovery to the secondary gain resistance motivated by "external advantages"?[15]

In *Totem and Taboo* Freud made a suggestion which opens up a new area of inquiry with respect to primary and secondary gain. In discussing systems of thought, such as the animistic theory of the universe, Freud refers to the secondary revision of dreams:

> The secondary revision of the product of the dream-work is an admirable example of the nature and pretension of a system. There is an intellectual function in us which demands unity, connection and intelligibility from any material. . . . Systems constructed in this way are known to us not only from dreams, but also from phobias, from obsessive thinking and from delusions. . . . In all these cases it can be shown that a rearrangement of the psychical material has been made with a fresh aim in view; and the rearrangement may often have to be a drastic one if the outcome is to be made to appear intelligible from the point of view of the system. Thus a system is best characterized by the fact that at least two reasons can be discovered for each of its products: a reason based upon the premises of the system (a reason, then, which may be delusional) and a concealed reason, which we must judge to be the truly operative and the real one . . . an inhibition upon movement . . . (an . . . agoraphobia) will gradually become more complete and more detailed, when once that system has succeeded in installing itself as a representative of an unconscious wish and of the defence against the wish [1913-14, p. 95f.].[16]

yet another form of resistance. . . . There are some neurotics in whom . . . the instinct of self-preservation has actually been reversed. They seem to have nothing in view but self-injury and self-destruction" (1940, p. 74ff.). Interestingly enough, in this last legacy, Freud omits for the first time a discussion of secondary gain in its traditional usage.

15 What is the "equation" for isolating secondary gain? "The primary motive force in the therapy is the patient's suffering and the wish to be cured that arises from it. The strength of this motive force is *subtracted* from by various factors—which are not discovered till the analysis is in progress—above all . . . the 'secondary gain from illness' " (1913, p. 143; my italics).

16 Freud returned to this in *Inhibitions, Symptoms and Anxiety:* ". . . the ego [shows an] impulsion . . . to incorporate [the symptoms] into its organization. . . . The ego now proceeds to behave as though it recognized that the symptom had come to stay and that the only thing to do was to accept the situation in good part and to draw as much advantage from it as possible. It makes an adaptation to the symptom—to this piece of the internal world which is alien to it—just as it normally does to the real external world. . . . The presence of a symptom may entail a certain impairment of capacity, and this can be exploited to appease some demand on the part of the super-ego or to refuse some claim from the external world. In this way, the symptom gradually comes to be the representative of important interests; it is found to be useful in

If intelligibility is demanded from symptoms as it is from dreams, the relationship between secondary (symptom) revision and secondary gain requires scrutiny. To what extent is the behavior, now labeled as secondary gain, also a rationalization of the symptom in order to make sense out of it? For example, when Little Hans said that he wanted to stay home and coax with mother, is he also trying to explain to himself and others why he cannot go out? Such rationalizations may easily impress people as proof that a significant conscious gain is derived from the symptom, when instead it may merely indicate a patient's need to "explain" something that is difficult for him to understand. Does the degree of revision also depend on the severity of the underlying conflict which initially led to symptom formation? If so, the secondary revision—which can assume proportions of systematized delusions—may make a significant contribution to the struggle against recovery. Thus, there are at least three aspects to secondary gain, two intrapsychic ones due to secondary revision and the unconscious sense of guilt and an external one due to the symptom's impact on the environment.

Freud's views on primary and secondary gain not only underwent considerable evolution but also were discussed by him from two vantage points. On the one hand, Freud considered secondary gain part of the technical issue of resistance about which, in his earlier writings, he expressed some annoyance.[17] Later, though, when the external component of secondary gain became one aspect of the composite gains from illness, and not even the crucial one, the annoyance disappeared. On the other hand, Freud discussed primary

asserting the position of the self and becomes more and more closely merged with the ego and more and more indispensable to it. It is only very rarely that the physical process of 'healing' round a foreign body follows such a course as this. *There is a danger, too, of exaggerating the importance of a secondary adaptation of this kind to a symptom, and of saying that the ego has created the symptom merely in order to enjoy its advantages.* It would be equally true to say that a man who had lost his leg in the war had got it shot away so that he might thence forward live on his pension without having to do any more work.

"In obsessional neurosis and paranoia the forms which the symptoms assume become very valuable to the ego because they obtain for it, not certain advantages, but a narcissistic satisfaction. . . . The systems which the obsessional neurotic constructs flatter his self-love . . . he is specially . . . conscientious. . . ."

"All of this results in . . . the '(secondary) gain from illness' which follows a neurosis. This gain comes to the assistance of the ego in its endeavour to incorporate the symptom and increases the symptom's fixation" (1926a, p. 98ff.; my italics).

17 See Freud (1887-1902, pp. 220 and 235).

and secondary gain from the vantage point of psychoanalytic theory, but did not return to an extensive reconsideration of both concepts after 1923. One can only speculate what might have happened if he had revised his formulations in terms of his new theoretical insights beginning with *The Ego and the Id*.

FORMULATIONS BY OTHERS

Since Freud no original contributions have been made to the discussion of primary and secondary gain. However, a brief review of subsequent writings on this subject may prove useful if only to highlight the thesis that without theoretical scrutiny concepts like secondary gain can "regress" to their prepsychoanalytic status. In any event, the absence of such scrutiny has kept secondary gain uninfluenced by new or deeper theoretical insights.

Primary gain has been hailed as "the central concept of modern psychopathology" (Eissler, 1951, p. 227). It has been defined as the gains accruing to an individual from the relief of guilt and anxiety through symptom formation as well as from the disguised instinct gratification present in the symptom. Some confusion about its definition has arisen since some writers have stressed either exclusively or primarily only one or the other component of the primary gain.[18]

Primary gain, if defined only from the vantage point of relief from anxiety and guilt, represents a purely intrapsychic process which is unconsciously elaborated and has no referent in external events. Metapsychologically, such a definition says something about structure (e.g., the relations of id, ego, and superego), economics (e.g., the vicissitudes of the amount of excitation), and dynamics (e.g., conflicts and ego aims), but nothing *explicitly* about genetics and adaptation.[19] However, if instinct gratification through symptom formation is included in the definition of primary gain, interaction with the

18 For example, see Nunberg (1955): "*primary* gain . . . is derived from the disguised instinct gratification in the symptom" (p. 300); or Glover (1949): ". . . primary gain . . . can be defined roughly as the relief from unconscious stress obtained by means of the defence mechanisms that are mobilised in default of successful repression" (p. 128).

19 See Glover: ". . . the psychoneurotic attempts an endopsychic solution of his conflicts, a solution in which the environment is involved only in respect to secondary gain" (1949, p. 132).

external world and thus adaptive propositions must be considered as an aspect of the primary gain.

The conciseness and precision in the definition of primary gain does not apply to secondary gain. Brenner, for example, states:

> The secondary gain is merely a special case of the ceaseless efforts of the ego to exploit the possibilities for pleasurable gratification which are available to it. *Once a symptom has been formed,* the ego may discover that there are advantages which the symptom brings with it. To take an extreme example, the combat soldier in wartime who develops an anxiety state has a realistic advantage over his fellows: he is evacuated to the rear, where the danger of being killed is less. To be sure, such an example is not the best, though so obvious on the surface, since the development of the anxiety state itself may be unconsciously influenced by the knowledge that it will lead to removal to safety. However, *there are many cases in which there is no question of such a possibility and in which the neurosis comes to have a certain value to the individual only after its development* [1955, p. 207; my italics].

Brenner's definition of secondary gain emphasizes the advantages which may accrue subsequent to symptom formation; yet, in his example of the combat soldier Brenner is aware that the distinction between the advantages of primary and secondary gain origins become hazy. Here an external state at least participates in symptom formation since the symptom *will be* of "value." A number of questions arise: Must a definition of primary gain include the abolition or diminution of anxiety mobilized by the ego's relative weakness in the face of external danger? Would careful scrutiny of the advantages attributed to secondary gain reveal that they participated, at least to some extent, in the events leading to a primary gain? If so, what remains of the difference between primary and secondary gain?

Brenner's discussion prompts another question. Do the advantages from symptom formation only serve ego interests? Fenichel notes: "Secondary gains are certainly effective in hysteria, too, but are never so integrally bound up in the personality as is the narcissistic gain from the reaction formations in the character in compulsion neurotics" (1945, p. 310). Fenichel's reference to "narcissistic gain" suggests that secondary gain may also serve superego interests.[20]

[20] See also Laforgue (1938, p. 290) and Waldhorn (1960, p. 498).

Once superego considerations are introduced the "gain" derived from a need for punishment must be distinguished from "gains" derived from the external world.

Alexander also stresses the advantages subsequent to symptom formation in his formulation of secondary gain, but then he has second thoughts:

> Being incapacitated by illness may have certain advantages. Among the most transparent is financial compensation for accidents. Illness may serve also as a legitimate excuse to avoid unpleasant duties and discard pressing responsibilities. It provokes sympathy and attention and assures the sufferer a privileged position. These advantages retard recovery and make therapy particularly difficult.
>
> *They are secondary consequences of neurotic illness* and do not belong to its dynamic structure or to the motivation which produces neurosis. This is particularly true of financial compensation for accidents. It is, however, extremely difficult to draw a sharp line between earlier dependent longings of patients and their secondary exploitation of illness to satisfy passive dependent needs. . . .
>
> The concept of secondary gain must be applied with great precaution. Any adult person who prefers support from others to the productive use of his own powers is unduly dependent. This infantile trait is always a significant, and frequently the most significant, factor in his neurosis. The important consideration is that the emotional and financial gains derived from illness contribute to the prolongation of illness [1948, p. 213; my italics].

Alexander brings genetic propositions ("infantile traits, earlier dependent longings") to the discussion of secondary gain. But he addresses himself primarily to the impact of reality factors without sorting them out. Illness, for example, may result in a partial regression to an earlier developmental level and thus alter patterns of interaction with significant persons in the environment. Here secondary gain will be affected by the degree of regression and the responsiveness of the environment. Then there is the reality of society which provides compensations for injuries and illnesses. In the context of such social reality the question arises whether the "exploitation of illness" may not for particular patients represent a "better" adaptation to reality than they had previously been able to make. To answer such questions, criteria for adaptation and maladaptation

are needed.[21] One of the difficulties with Alexander's formulation is
that he postulates both that secondary gain does not "belong to the
dynamic structure of the neurosis" and that there is a relationship
"between earlier dependent longings . . . and . . . secondary exploitation of illness." Alexander is aware of the problem—"no sharp line
can be drawn."

Hendrick discusses secondary gain, at least in part, as an exploitation of the neurosis and this leads him to the conclusion that

> "Secondary gain" is the result of the effort *to win from the neuro-*
> *sis itself a "bonus,"* consisting in additional pleasures which could
> not be obtained without it. Thus the primary gain of a hysterical
> symptom, as has been shown, is the solution of the tension
> between an unconscious sexual wish and the need for punish-
> ment. But, once established, the hysteric *utilizes* his paralyzed arm
> *as an excuse to do no work,* his nausea as reason *for special atten-*
> *tion* in the preparation of his food, his tantrums as a threat to
> people who do not do what he wants them to do. Gradually,
> especially if the neurosis is severe and the ego potentiality small,
> *he will discover one childish means after another* by which he may
> get people to do what he likes and not to do what he does not like
> [1958, p. 236; my italics].[22]

While not explicitly stated, one gets the impression from Hendrick
that secondary gain operates on a conscious level.[23] If so, it remains

21 In this context it may prove useful to distinguish between adaptations which are
largely predicated on defensive needs and those which are not. The former are more
likely to happen when the defensive struggle against the impulse component of the
symptom continues after symptom formation. If, on the other hand, the symptom
becomes integrated in the ego, the new adaptations may under favorable environmental
circumstances be free from conflict. One might say that the symptom may lead either
to "defensive" or to "autonomous" adaptations.

22 See also English and Finch (1954, p. 197).

23 It is often difficult to evaluate statements about secondary gain. In textbooks like
Fenichel's (1945) and Glover's (1949) comments about secondary gain are scattered over
hundreds of pages and only if they are evaluated *in toto,* do they suggest that the
authors consider secondary gain as predominantly, if not exclusively, an unconscious
phenomenon. I have chosen examples from Glover's textbook (1949) and italicized the
relevant words: "[patients] *unwittingly* extract a good deal of advantage from both
family and friends" (p. 127); "there is a natural tendency to *confuse* secondary gain
with conscious malingering" (p. 128). But there are doubts: "[secondary gain] is dictated *more often* by unconscious ethical motivations" (p. 128). It is not made clear
when it is conscious and what is meant by "ethical motivations." Then there is the
problem with choice of words: e.g., "it . . . enables the patient to exercise a *direct*
influence on his immediate family" (p. 127); "[a] release from the *responsibilities* of
adapting to existing or threatened crises" (p. 127); "[the patient] *exploits* already
established conversion symptoms" (p. 143); "the patient . . . *succeeds* in entrenching

unclear whether it does so exclusively or only in part. Gardner (1947) goes a step further: "These are the *secondary*—conscious—gains to the act of stealing as distinguished from the *primary* gains through 'instinctive' expressions" (p. 439).[24]

Nunberg (1955) takes exception to the frequently made comment that secondary gain does not belong to the dynamic structure of the neurosis:

> The synthetic function of the ego is not first manifested in the secondary gain through illness, but even earlier. . . . With the secondary gain through illness, the synthesis is increased as a compensatory measure. At the outbreak of the illness, the synthetic function fails at first. Soon, however, it gives impetus to the symptom formation and then dominates the course of the illness to such an extent that, in extreme cases, it helps the repressed instincts to break through (obsessional neurosis). After the formation of the symptom, however, the synthesis fails again, but it becomes active once more by the indirect route of the secondary gain through illness. Under the influence of the neurotic conflict, on the one hand, and of the threatening danger of the disintegration of the ego, on the other, the synthesis is driven to increased activity [p. 300].

Nunberg postulates a relationship between primary and secondary gain—both are the result of the synthesizing function of the ego. He sees both symptom formation and the establishment of illness as "narcissistic injuries" for which the ego has to compensate, and this becomes the focus of his inquiry and not the external advantages. In a clinical vignette of a phobic husband,[25] Nunberg does not

---

himself in a favoured . . . position" (p. 313). It all could be read as if conscious intent is implied—one of the difficulties may be that these statements are made from the vantage point of the observer-analyst, but this is not spelled out.

24 See also Fenichel (1941): "The resistances due to secondary gain . . . are more likely to be accessible to the conscious will" (p. 33). For a preanalytic formulation see Tuke (1892): "One form of nervous case in which [treatment] is sure to be unsuccessful, is that of the comfortable, well-feeding, well-nourished, and thoroughly selfish, nervous patient, to whom her illnesses are sources of enjoyment, and who has neither the wish nor the intention of being bettered. Cases of this kind are not rare" (p. 853).

25 "A phobic patient suffered from agoraphobia. His anxiety gradually increased to such an extent that he could no longer go to his place of business and consequently was unable to work. His wife had to support him. The symptom appeared first, and his inability to work followed. But the patient became satisfied with the symptom, believing that his wife's supporting him was a proof of her love for him, that it was a sacrifice she made out of love. He accepted and assimilated his illness under the condition that it offered him narcissistic gratification" (Nunberg, 1955, p. 298).

emphasize the "advantages" of not working or the indulgences by the wife; instead, he conceptualizes the advantages as an unconscious attempt by the patient to make sense out of them, to assimilate them into his personality structure.

It is striking throughout most of the literature on primary and secondary gain that, while "gain" or "advantage" is part of both definitions, different though unarticulated connotations are given to these words. What is the difference between the "value" the neurosis has after its development (secondary gain) from the "value" inherent in its development (primary gain)? Why does a patient "prefer to keep his neurosis"? Is it only, or at all, related to the secondary gains? May this not be too superficial an interpretation of the "obvious" use to which symptoms are put?[26] Is it not possible that the resistance to give up the neurosis represents, at least in part, a further defensive effort by the ego to protect the individual from a re-emergence of the dreaded id impulses (primary gain) which initially had led to symptom formation? Glover suggests such a possibility: "Secondary gain is also a second line of defence during analysis. Having breached the first line [primary gain] we are in a suitable position to tackle this more superficial defence" (1955, p. 148). But what is meant by "more superficial defence"? Does it connote secondary in a temporal sense without any implication as to its strength; does it imply shallow, that is, easy to penetrate; or is it a topographical statement? For example, Jones and others have stated that secondary gain resistances lie predominantly in the conscious and preconscious (Jones, 1910, p. 354; Fenichel, 1941, p. 33; Menninger, 1958, p. 106). But later Jones modified his position somewhat: "[They] are usually, but not always, unconscious; more strictly they are preconscious" (1918, p. 574).

In another passage Glover writes: "Even in the [therapeutically accessible cases] where the factors of prognosis, etiological depth and accessibility to ordinary analytic techniques correspond closely, the groupings may be upset by, for example, the factor of 'secondary gain' alone" (1955, p. 226). Here Glover seems to imply that the strength of the resistance due to secondary gain may be greater than the

---

26 Glover (1949) writes: "Although the main function of the symptom is to deal with unconscious conflict . . . once it is well established *it usually enables the patient to exercise a direct influence on his immediate family or his friends, or on his social environment in general*" (p. 127).

resistance due to primary gain. This prompts another question: Is it possible that some of the so-called secondary gains may over time result in "positive" achievements for the individual? If so, then the analysis of secondary-gain resistances can be impeded by a patient's fears that the "positive" achievements may inadvertently become jeopardized.

The word "advantage" itself adds to the confusion since it carries the connotation of increased "profit" and "leverage" and, therefore, its use can easily hide unarticulated value judgments. And in labeling one aspect of the symptom picture as bringing advantages, the concomitant disadvantages usually receive insufficient attention. In addition, the impact of other mental mechanisms which may come into play, e.g., regression, are not sufficiently considered. For example, is the "advantage" the discarding of pressing responsibilities, the expectation of financial compensations, or the attempt at integration at a regressed level? Here all the disadvantageous manifestations of the ego's inability to cope with both the inner and outer world at a higher developmental level must also be included in the analysis. Fenichel suggests this:

> A factor common to all phobias is regression. In childhood, dangers could be overcome by seeking the protection of seemingly omnipotent adults in the environment, and in a sense, all phobic patients behave like children whose anxieties are allayed by a comforting mother whose presence dispels fear. . . . That the gains of regression are secondary is often not recognized. The individual is not striving for the "helplessness" of childhood but for the relative security of being protected by grown-ups. This neurotic helplessness which the patient feels as loneliness and lack of human contact is due to a remobilization of infantile instinctual conflicts [1944, p. 279f.].

Consequently, are the resistances to treatment due to the advantages which have accrued or are they a result of the underlying precarious mental balance? None of these questions can be answered until the theoretical clarification of primary and secondary gain has advanced considerably.

Discussion

The major questions involved in such a clarification include: (1) Is symptom formation influenced by reality pressures and does

it have an immediate impact on the environment? If adaptive propositions are required for a complete metapsychological analysis of
primary gain, what differences remain between the external component of primary gain and the secondary gain? (2) Do childhood
experiences, personality structure and dynamics, in addition to
environmental factors, contribute to the development of secondary-
gain mechanisms? Does their impact on secondary gain differ from
that on primary gain? (3) Must the concepts of primary and secondary gain be maintained to distinguish between the gains from symptom formation (movement toward illness) and illness (symptomatic
state)? Alternatively, what are the differences between the "value"
the neurosis has after its development (secondary gain) from the
"value" inherent in its development (primary gain)? (4) What is the
relationship of primary-gain resistances to secondary-gain resistances? How can secondary-gain resistances be distinguished from
other resistances, especially those motivated by the unconscious sense
of guilt and the need to suffer (the negative therapeutic reaction)?
(5) Do words like "advantage" and "gain" hide unarticulated value
judgments and, if so, what is their impact on theoretical formulations
and technical interventions? (6) If the concepts of primary and secondary gain need to be modified, how can the clinical observations
which led to their introduction be more profitably conceptualized?

THE TWO GAINS FROM THE VANTAGE POINT OF SYMPTOM FORMATION

Traditionally, the distinction between primary and secondary
gain is based on assigning one gain to symptom formation and the
other to the symptomatic state. Therefore, it may prove useful to
review briefly, and somewhat schematically, the course of symptom
formation. A symptom comes into being as one of the possible consequences of internal conflict. Once a symptom is formed, anxiety
diminishes and the force of the instinctual impulse pressing for
discharge is at least temporarily decreased. Such a formulation
emphasizes the intrapsychic aspects of symptom formation, and the
concomitant primary gain is the result of both the reduction in
anxiety and the resolution of this conflict. But external events can
contribute to symptom formation, at least if they find a connection
with instinctual drives. Moreover, the anxiety evoked by instinctual
impulses pressing for discharge is in part the result of opposition

from external objects.[27] Thus, external conditions can participate in symptom formation, and a primary gain may also accrue from a reduction in fear of the environment. Furthermore, a symptom has been defined as a compromise formation which expresses drive and defense simultaneously. The instinct gratification contained in the symptom may change the relationships with objects in the environment, and this too can result in environmental gains. Therefore, primary gain accrues from anxiety and fear reduction as well as from gratifications in relation to the environment; it has an internal and external component, and requires that adaptive propositions be included in any metapsychological analysis of primary gain.[28] It is important to recognize that intrapsychic and environmental factors may have from the beginning a simultaneous impact on the way in which symptom formation proceeds and consequently bring about both internal and external gains. Initially, however, it may be less apparent how a person will utilize and elaborate the symptom and the external gains. Thus, the external component of the primary gain may only express what *may happen* with certain patients, under certain circumstances, and over a period of time. One might say that it represents the ground plan for the possible ensuing secondary gain.

By tracing the fate of a symptom, once formed, it becomes apparent that the initial conflict which led to symptom formation is continued in the defense against the instinct component of the symptom. Here there are two possible outcomes. The ego may try to incorporate the symptom into its organization.[29] Inasmuch as the presence of a symptom entails a certain amount of ego impairment and necessitates a realignment—or more precisely, a secondary

27 ". . . an instinctual demand often only becomes an (internal) danger because its satisfaction would bring on an external danger—that is, because the internal danger represents an external one. On the other hand, the external (real) danger must also have managed to become internalized if it is to be significant for the ego. It must have been recognized as related to some situation of helplessness that has been experienced" (Freud, 1926a, p. 167ff.).

28 Rapaport has traced in great detail the historical development of the psychoanalytic theory's conceptions of reality (1960, p. 57). This paper is also an attempt to rediscuss primary and secondary gains in the light of the "third, fourth, and fifth conceptions of reality."

29 Freud stated that the symptom may "[maintain] its existence outside the organization of the ego" (1926a, p. 97). The statement cannot be taken literally; it probably alludes to the relationship of the symptom to the self-concept and says something about the degree to which a symptom can remain ego alien or alien to the self.

realignment—vis-à-vis the superego and environment, the ego, as it does in symptom formation, will attempt to make the best of a bad bargain. For example, the ego will use the impairment to appease superego demands or to refuse some claim from the external world. "In this way," Freud stated, "the symptom gradually comes to be a representative of important interests; it . . . becomes more and more closely merged with the ego and more and more indispensable to it" (1926a, p. 99). Such "healing round a foreign body" (1926a, p. 99) occurs infrequently. The second outcome is more likely. The ego is forced into further defensive efforts because the impulse component of the symptom continually renews its demand for satisfaction. This may bring other mechanisms of defense into play; for example, regression in phobia. The agoraphobic patient may be able to walk in the streets only with someone he knows. Thus, once a symptom is formed the ego attempts to make an intrapsychic adaptation and to bring about an external realignment. The view that the ego's defensive efforts are an essentially never-ending process, starting with symptom formation and continuing once a symptom is established, reinforces the possibility that the "gains from illness," too, are an elaboration, both defensively and adaptively, of the "gains from symptom formation." By disregarding the continuous nature of this process and by focusing too exclusively on the "obvious" advantages a patient derives from his illness, it was possible to look at secondary gain as virtually unrelated to the entire neurotic process. This brief survey suggests, however, that the traditional distinction between the terms primary gain and secondary gain could be maintained on the basis of a temporal factor.

THE METAPSYCHOLOGY OF THE TWO GAINS

Traditionally, metapsychological discussions of primary gain have emphasized the advantages accruing to an individual from the resolution of intersystemic conflicts. In an analysis of such conflict resolutions, structural, economic, and dynamic propositions have usually been employed. I have already mentioned that Freud also included genetic propositions once he realized that "motives for being ill [arising out of the childhood situation are] in existence before the outbreak of the illness" (1894, p. 43). Adaptive propositions, on the whole, have been omitted from a metapsychological analysis of primary gain. Discussions of secondary gain, on the other hand, have stressed motives for being ill arising out of the infantile situation and the interaction of the individual with his family and society. Since secondary gain has rarely been considered of sufficient theoretical interest, the vast amount of clinical data has been presented in a descriptive fashion, often with insufficient realization that the statements were descriptive and not conceptual in nature.

Rapaport and Gill (1959) have stated that systematic studies in metapsychology must distinguish between empirical and metapsychological propositions. With respect to primary and secondary gains the empirical propositions can be directly verified by observations about the various benefits which accrue to a patient from symptom formation or illness once it is established. At this level of analysis a distinction between the two gains can be made on the basis of a temporal factor.

Rapaport and Gill have persuasively argued that a systematic metapsychological analysis of any concept must include not only dynamic, economic, and structural, but also genetic and adaptive propositions. Such a complete analysis has not been attempted and thus has precluded a theoretical comparison between the two gains. I shall now try to discuss primary and secondary gain from each of the five metapsychological points of view. Again, this presentation can by no means be considered exhaustive.

Primary Gain

The *dynamics* of symptom formation leading to primary gain are characterized by an urgency of drive discharge which interacts with inhibiting and channeling forces. Since more mature mental dynamics are characterized by a delay in discharge and since primary gain accrues from the ego's ability, in the face of anxiety, to make a compromise, one might say that a primary gain results when primary-process functioning is impeded by the ego's defensive activities.[30] The severity of the underlying conflict will have an important

[30] The instinct gratification contained in the symptom, on the other hand, would be an expression of primary-process functioning. If the symptom also has an adaptive potential and leads to a "fitting into" the environment, then the instinct gratification will acquire characteristics of secondary-process functioning. The relationship, if any, between primary and secondary process and primary and secondary gain has never been considered. Pious (1962) suggested that "there is an equivalence to the concepts

impact on how the gains are utilized in the subsequent defensive and integrative efforts. Dynamic assumptions about primary gain, however, have insufficiently stressed that psychological forces alter not only the internal environment but also the relations to the external environment. Anna Freud, in discussing intellectualization, has shown that a defense against instinctual danger also has a reality-oriented aspect (1936, p. 173), and Hartmann repeatedly stated that a "mechanism of defense against instinctual drives may at the same time be regarded as an adaptation process" (1939, p. 14). Thus the dynamic assumptions about "primary gain" lead to adaptive propositions.

The *economics* of primary gain must account for the deployment of cathexes. Since symptom formation results in a compromise, the instinctual-drive energy now manifests itself in two ways: it may still press for discharge from the id, and it may also seek pleasurable gratification due to the presence of the drive derivative in the symptom. Thus the ego may have to expend a portion of the psychic energy at its disposal vis-à-vis the id and the symptom. In addition, the ego invests some of its own energy in the symptom, and both instinctual and ego cathexes are directed via the symptom to objects in the environment. Immediately upon symptom formation the ego's defensive efforts continue in relation to the symptom and, at the same time, ego cathexis may be utilized to obtain further environmental gratifications. It is likely, therefore, that the economics of primary gain, and also secondary gain, have to account for the hypercathexes necessary to restrain drive discharge from both the id and the symptom in addition to the cathexes employed in the service of environmental gratification. I have not limited this discussion to primary gain in order to illustrate that similar metapsychological considerations may apply for an analysis of primary and secondary gain.

Since motivations from childhood and subsequent experiences contribute to symptom formation, the *genetic* assumptions must account for the impact of such experiences on primary gain. The

of primary and secondary process, if these are considered ideals in Kris's terms, and that a careful scrutiny of the concept of 'gain' would reveal a hierarchy starting from that statement of the neurotic situation which is closest to the primary process and extending to the statement which is closest to the secondary process."

kind of external and internal conditions which lead to qualitatively and quantitatively differing gains are undoubtedly affected by infantile factors.

From the *structural* point of view we can assume that id, ego, and superego relationships are altered as soon as symptom formation is initiated. Id, and at times superego, demands impair ego functioning, with the ego losing some of the "territory" it has wrested from the two. But the ego becomes reconstituted, in an autonomous or regressed form, depending in part on how the symptom is integrated in the inner and outer world. Thus, the primary gain which results from the diminution of anxiety may be obtained at the expense (primary loss) of ego autonomy, no matter what integrations eventually ensue.

From the vantage point of *adaptation,* the ego's relationship to the environment is altered as soon as the defensive struggle against the instinctual impulse begins. Such new relationships can be viewed as efforts to increase adaptation in the wake of the internal conflicts which initiated the process, but it may not turn out that way. The kind of adaptation made during symptom formation will be influenced by a variety of factors; for example, by the kind of acceptance the emerging symptom encounters in and continues to receive from the external world and by the extent to which outside influences participated in symptom formation. Whether the outcome will be adaptive or maladaptive may depend on how the environment interacts with the person having the symptom.

Adaptation in this paper is used in two ways: as a metapsychological concept and as a descriptive statement. I have tried to make clear each time in which sense I use it. As an unmodified descriptive term and of course as a metapsychological proposition it is not to be equated with a good environmental fit; rather it leaves unexplored whether the outcome will be adaptive or maladaptive.

Secondary Gain

With respect to secondary gain, the huge quantity of clinical material that is available begs for a metapsychological analysis. Hartmann and Kris (1945) have stated that *genetic* assumptions "describe why, in past situations of conflict, a specific solution was adopted; why the one was retained and the other dropped, and what

causal relation exists between these solutions and later developments" (p. 17). The clinical phenomena labeled secondary gains
must include an analysis in terms of their genetic antecedents. It is
unlikely that such genetic considerations will differ for primary and
secondary gain.

Secondary gains, for example, through narcissistic satisfaction or
the appeasement of superego demands, may alter the *dynamic* and
structural relationships between ego, superego, and id. The outcome
may be greater ego strength or weakness. Either possibility will be
affected by the adaptive possibilities of the secondary gains.

The *economics* of secondary gain must account for the further
countercathectic efforts necessary subsequent to symptom formation
as well as for the additional discharge of cathexis vis-à-vis the environment. Ego cathexis may have to be utilized for defensive purposes but may also be directed to other ego functions such as reality
testing since the person has to rearrange his relationship to reality.
The cathexes employed for reality testing may serve the defensive
function of preventing deeper regression, but they may also serve
the integrative function of making possible the establishment of new
relationships with the environment.

Despite focus on the impact of secondary gains on the environment, little effort has been made to analyze the clinical data from
the *adaptive* point of view. Hartmann (1939) has commented that
"the distinctive characteristics of a psychoanalytic investigation is not
its subject matter but the scientific methodology, and the structure
of the concepts it uses" (p. 5) and that "our increased interest in . . .
formulations about mental health which use 'adjustment to reality'
as a criterion" (p. 3) require investigations of the problem of adaptation. Any established symptom requires analysis in terms of its
adaptation disturbances as well as its positive adaptation values. If,
as Hartmann feels, adaptation is guaranteed by "man's primary
equipment, the maturation of his apparatuses . . . and the ego-regu-
lated actions which . . . counteract the disturbances in and actively
improve the person's relationship to the environment" (p. 25), then
it may also follow that in neurotic disturbances, while altering the
process and outcome of adaptation, the same inborn and acquired
guarantees continue to be operative and will influence the kind of

adaptation that is achieved. Thus it is misleading to view "secondary gains" only as a result of accidental environmental circumstances; instead, they must also be analyzed as "mutual regulations" (Erikson, 1953, p. 199) between a neurotic individual (his equipment and life history) and his society.

From the vantage point of optimal functioning, a neurotic symptom initially leads to a maladaptation, yet the picture may change. Hartmann, for example, points out that "an attitude which arose originally in the service of defense against an instinctual drive may, in the course of time, become an independent structure and . . . through a change of function turn a means into a goal in its own right" (1939, p. 26). While Hartmann's concept of change of function refers to such issues as ego autonomy, it possibly can be analogized to the fate of a symptom. The symptom's instinct component may be defended against ("neutralized") so effectively and the symptom may turn out to be so useful to an adaptation of a particular individual to a particular environment, that one could speak here too of a means having been turned "into a goal in its own right." Thus in the life history of secondary gains, due to their constant interaction with mental structures and the outside world, many changes may occur.

For example, Erikson (1956, p. 77) has stressed that at times, especially in adolescence, it may be necessary for a person temporarily to become a patient in order to take time out before he commits himself to an adult role. How the environment meets this situation will be crucial for the integration of the individual. Thus a symptom may allow a person to find, for a while, a much-needed identity as a patient. Also, if members of a family accept the patient's symptoms, or in fact have unwittingly helped to bring them out for neurotic reasons of their own, then such symptoms may eventually allow the patient an adaptation to his neurotic environment. And if removal from such an environment is impossible, the adaptive value may be considerable. If society through provisions for workmen's compensation, welfare funds, and large insurance settlements creates an environment where there may be advantages to being sick for at least certain people, the extent to which illness becomes a "fitting into" the environment requires much further scrutiny. Surely social structure influences the adaptive possibilities of a particular form of behavior. While a descriptive approach to the study of secondary gain has been able to list the "advantages" which a patient derives from his illness, it has tended to overlook the adaptive aspects of such advantages. Such an approach has also contributed to an insulation of "gains" from their genetic and dynamic setting and, instead, has tended to view them almost as independent goals. The concept of adaptation suggests that the "advantages through illness" are the result of complex mutual regulations between the individual and society—of more or less successful and unsuccessful attempts by patients to find an appropriate niche in their environment.

Criteria are needed to distinguish adaptation from maladaptation, but to establish such criteria requires a model for analysis. Criteria will differ if ones sees, for example, in secondary gain (1) a reversal of the normal developmental progression involving the intrapsychic representation of the external world, or (2) an attempt toward a new adaptation (Gill and Brenman 1959, p. 208). If one uses the first model, secondary gain is by definition maladaptive since internal conflicts are in part dealt with by obtaining gratifications from the outside world; i.e., extrapsychic instead of intrapsychic representations. The second model, on the other hand, permits secondary gain to be an adaptive or maladaptive proposition. Whether it is one or the other may depend on the extent of the regression to an earlier organization, the degree of the environment's acceptance of the patient's symptoms, and the dynamic and structural rearrangements which the symptoms entail. Pertinent to such an inquiry will be an analysis of the relative autonomy of the ego prior and subsequent to symptom formation. One may also have to inquire whether external conditions can be so frustrating yet so unalterable for an individual that the adaptations which a person makes can be analogized to Kris's concept of "regression in the service of the ego" (1952) as adaptations in the service of the ego.

Primary and Secondary Gain

A systematic metapsychological analysis of primary and secondary gain suggests that no new conceptual issues arise as one moves from primary to secondary gain. To be sure, adaptive considerations may become more prominent over time in the analysis of "secondary gain," but they do not differ essentially from those already present in primary gain. The time factor alone does not seem to require a metapsychological distinction between the two gains since genetic propositions already account for temporal distinctions. However, should it turn out to be clinically useful to distinguish between gains from symptom formation and the symptomatic state, then it still does not necessarily follow that they have to be separately treated metapsychologically. Yet, even if this should happen, it will be clearer from now on that the two gains are not as separate as they have been viewed traditionally; instead, they at least have much in common. For, many of the aspects traditionally assigned to secondary gains, for example, the interaction of the person with his environment, already play a significant role in symptom formation. Moreover, the analysis of primary and secondary gain from the other metapsychological points of view suggests that structural alterations, shifts in cathexes, dynamic relationships, and genetic influences are similar for both gains. Thus it appears more useful to speak of one continuous gain than to maintain the distinction between a primary and secondary gain.

Two questions remain: (1) Does the term "gain" itself create problems by focusing too exclusively on the advantages from symptom formation, thus detracting from the concomitant disadvantages? (2) Does the more basic psychoanalytic concept of adaptation better account for most of the observations which have traditionally been included under secondary gain? If the term gain should prove expendable, we shall have to inquire how the clinical observations which led to the introduction of primary and secondary gain can be more profitably conceptualized. But before turning to these questions it may be helpful to interpose a few brief comments on primary- and secondary-gain resistances.

PSYCHOANALYTIC TECHNIQUE AND THE TWO GAINS

The technical approach to a patient's "secondary-gain" resistances will be influenced by the theoretical formulations of "secondary gain." If environmental conditions are considered crucial and "secondary gain" is seen as a more or less deliberate (conscious or preconscious) attempt to exploit them, then such resistances may eventually have to be brought to the patient's attention so that he can choose between maintaining his "favored" position or continuing his analysis. If, on the other hand, "secondary-gain" resistances are also seen as a further elaboration of primary-gain resistances[31] and thus as an expression of the ego's total integrative and defensive effort, then the technical problem of when and how to interpret them becomes more complex though more consistently analytic in nature.

"Secondary-gain" resistances have perhaps been given too much weight in the analysis of all the resistances to the therapeutic effort. In his later writings, Freud attached less importance to secondary-gain resistances—they are not even mentioned in *An Outline of Psychoanalysis*—and instead he singled out the unconscious sense of guilt and the need to be ill[32] as more crucial impediments to analytic work. Thus Freud's emphasis shifted from external factors to "deep-going modifications in [the] instinctual economy" (1940, p. 78). And in pointing to the composite nature of all these resistances, Freud suggested another area of inquiry, namely, the interrelationship of these resistances.

The present attitude toward secondary-gain resistances is not unlike the attitude toward resistances in general prior to the publication of *The Ego and the Id*. Until then many analysts felt that resistances were a nuisance, which must be overcome as quickly as possible in order to get to earlier childhood data which would in turn lead to both insight and cure. Today, however, the analysis of resistances is a constructive part of every analysis and is considered crucial for a meaningful exploration of the patient's earlier conflicts. "Secondary-gain" resistances, nevertheless, have retained an

[31] In the search for factors which influence "secondary-gain" resistances the impact of the original defensive effort has been insufficiently considered. Surely such a relationship is difficult to work out clinically: "It would be . . . an enticing task to trace, in a concrete case, the interaction of those processes which assimilate the external and internal stimuli and lead to average adaptiveness and normal adaptation . . . [or] to trace such interactions in many problems of character development, in that aspect of the personality which we call 'ego interests,' and so forth. For instance, the influence of special talents on the distribution of narcissistic, object-libidinal and aggressive energies, their role in facilitating certain forms of conflict solution, and in determining the choice of preferred defenses, are clinically important but insufficiently studied problems" (Hartmann, 1939, p. 10).
[32] It is possible that some of the manifestations of these resistances can be easily mistaken as belonging to secondary-gain resistances.

aura of "nuisance" value and thus may have been used too readily to explain the analyst's frustrations about slow therapeutic progress. It may prove useful to pay greater attention in clinical work to those secondary-gain resistances which disappear readily because their analysis is continuous with the rest of the analysis, and thereby learn to differentiate the resistances which are more easily amenable to psychoanalytic technique.

The "advantages" which the patient derives from his illness have often been given prognostic significance. Yet, it has been recognized that similar environmental situations present more formidable obstacles to the therapeutic effort in some patients than in others. The reasons for this have remained unclear. The prognoses have not always turned out to be correct, since they largely rested on the "obvious gains" which the patient derived from his life situation, rather than on all the intrapsychic and external factors, including their dynamic interplay, which led to such "gains." And there may be other factors. For example, Freud in commenting on the secondary revision of the product of the dream work, remarked: "There is an intellectual function in us which demands unity" (1913-14, p. 95). Thus secondary revision attempts to bring the dream in line with our waking thoughts. A symptom, as Freud recognized, creates a condition analogous to the dream situation, for the ego will similarly attempt to make sense out of the "foreign body" that has become established within the psychic apparatus. This can lead to system formations of varying complexity, and such systems will seek to make connections with and find support in the external world. Thus the prognostic significance of "secondary gain" may also be affected by the way in which the advantages have been rationalized and systematized. For example, a fear of going places which led to "sacrificing" other members of the family and "exacting" proofs of their love may have a different prognosis if it is *also* "explained" or "justified" more or less ego-syntonically, in terms of malevolent spirits which populate the heavens and which punish people if they enjoy themselves while away from home. (It is usually difficult to ascertain both the extent and the ego syntonicity of such fears without prolonged analysis.) It is beyond the scope of this paper to suggest alternatives to the traditional conception of primary- and

secondary-gain resistances in the light of the preceding metapsychological analysis. If such an analysis has merit, our views on primary-
and secondary-gain resistances will require extensive reformulation.

VALUE PREFERENCES AND THE TWO GAINS

The value judgments which have infiltrated into discussions on
secondary gain are primarily moral ones. In clinical illustrations
patients have been labeled as "compensation neurotics," or "childish
hysterics," or "beggars," or "neurotic housewives," and the impression has often been created that the patients deliberately cling to a
"favored" position. Rarely has the possibility been discussed[33] that
the state of adaptation conveyed by these labels may be an indication
of the severity of the underlying conflict; of the external adjustments
necessitated by the conflicts; and, thus, of the only conflict resolution possible for the patient. At times the moral implications have
received unwitting reinforcement in the analytic situation when
poorly understood resistances slowed the therapeutic process. In
looking for "explanations," the "obvious" external advantages the
patient "derived" from his neurosis have been given undue weight
and with insufficient scrutiny of what Hartmann calls "value testing." "We could call moral values more authentic . . . when, in an
individual, or in a culture, they are not only represented in ideas
on ethics but also are recognizable as dynamic factors in the moral
aspects of a personality or a culture. . . . The individual tests moral
values against the psychological background of his acts of moral
valuation. This testing is to be distinguished from assigning these
values a place in any hierarchy of moral values" (Hartmann, 1960,
p. 50f). These potential blind spots are not restricted to evaluations of secondary gain; good clinical terms like passivity, hysteria,
aggression, or narcissism can contain hidden moral evaluations
(Hartmann, 1960, p. 72). "Secondary gain" is similarly enlisted in a
service not countenanced by psychoanalysis when, for example, the
compensation neurotic in the context of a therapeutic encounter is
evaluated as a social inferior and not as a product of a complex
interaction of constitutional, developmental, defensive, and social
forces. It is difficult, especially when analytic work with patients

[33] A notable exception is Eissler (1951).

reaches a prolonged plateau, to sort out one's moral judgments about patients, their evil inclinations, and their selfish interests. Hartmann (1960) has noted that Freud "took pains to keep clinical apart from moral valuation" (p. 17), and this can be documented in Freud's writing. Nevertheless, with respect to secondary gain, Freud did not consider it necessary to identify the impact of his own health and social values on his formulations. Perhaps this made it impossible for secondary gain, unlike primary gain, to fit completely into his over-all theoretical scheme. Freud may have been aware of this when he wrote that "I should like to advise you . . . not to underestimate the practical importance of the advantage through illness and yet not be too much impressed by its theoretical significance" (1916-17, p. 393). It is doubtful that Freud intended to suggest that secondary gain is of *little* theoretical significance (Brenner, 1955, p. 207; and Fenichel, 1945, p. 462); instead he may have expressed a warning: should his discussion of secondary gain run counter to the over-all psychoanalytic scheme, something must be missing which required further elucidation. And what needed elucidation was well put by Hartmann: "Science cannot decide on what aims one 'ought' to strive for and what values should be considered supreme. . . . We have to accept the difference between normative statements on the one hand, and descriptive and theoretical statements on the other" (1960, p. 51). Medawar (1959), writing from the perspective of a geneticist, makes a telling point. It has been said that

> . . . less intelligent parents have larger families because they are less well informed about birth control . . . because they are less well able to see the material disadvantages of having more children than can be well provided for . . . I do not like it to put it this way because it seems to import a moral judgment which, valid or not, has no bearing on the argument. Someone might insist that it was *right* for all parents to have all the children they were capable of having, and that the unintelligent live up to that precept because, being more innocent than learned but worldly people, they have a clearer perception of what is right or wrong [p. 76].

Although acceptance of the implications of unconscious conflicts extricated "primary gain" from the web of moral judgments, secondary gain took its place. Further and more systematic reflections of moral values, along the lines of Hartmann's recent challenging and pioneering comments (1960), may eventually clarify such blind-spots.

Since labels such as "gain" and "advantage" connote value judgments, it might have facilitated analytic inquiry if more neutral terms had initially been coined. A renewed search for such terms, however, may not be necessary. Psychoanalytic theory has repeatedly emphasized that the ego constantly endeavors to make the best possible bargain when confronted with competing instinctual, superego, interdynamic ego, and reality pressures. Thus the striving for gains is an aspect of any ego operation. But such gains are in a sense Pyrrhic victories, since the ego has to make compromises and thus to some extent loses out. A real gain would be achieved if the ego were able to deal with the competing interests by analyzing the situation and gaining insight, or by intuitively altering circumstances, making it unnecessary to resort to the compromise of symptom formation. Therefore, what has been called primary gain is at least a limited gain. Similarly, secondary gains have also maladaptive implications, since without symptom formation the hypothetical normal individual would be able to maintain more meaningful relationships with objects in the outside world. Thus it seems that the concepts primary and secondary gain overemphasize one aspect of the process of symptom formation and illness and reiterate a proposition about a well-known aspect of ego activity, namely, that it constantly strives for an acceptable conflict resolution. Therefore, the concepts primary and secondary gain in focusing on the advantages have neglected the corresponding disadvantages. Clearly, an analysis of gains must proceed side by side with an analysis of losses;[34] in this light, the concept "gain" proves to be too limited. One must, therefore, ask oneself whether a specific theoretical concept is needed to account for such gains or losses or whether the existing theoretical formulations are adequate to conceptualize the clinical phenomena labeled primary and secondary gain.

The substitution of one word for another, however, cannot solve the basic confusion. Indeed, the very concepts used here—for example, "autonomy" and "adaptation"—although they describe cer-

---

[34] It is more than likely that in clinical practice such an analysis takes place and that only in theoretical writing the gains have been more emphasized than the losses.

tain states of ego functioning, also imply a standard of optimal ego functioning and an imperative to achieve that level because it is "healthy" or "valuable" to do so. But this kind of value judgment based on the *utility* which maximum capacity and control offer each patient—Hartmann (1960) calls it a "health value" (p. 55)—is quite different from a moral judgment which scales persons in orders relative to some moral code or intuitive response. The analyst who expresses his approbation or disapproval for maximum ego functioning chooses a value different for his patient from an analyst who—consciously or unconsciously—judges his patient "moral, immoral, or amoral" without reference to the patient's unique (and perhaps limited) ability to cope with his particular circumstances. No matter what language is used to describe levels of development, the task remains for each analyst to sort out the kind of approval or disapproval: that is, to distinguish "value" as psychological utility or disutility to his patient from "value" as moral worth of his patient.

It appears that the five metapsychological points of view already provide a sufficient framework for the analysis of the gains and losses inherent in symptom formation and illness. In using such a framework, analysts would systematically study the structural, economic, dynamic, and adaptive changes which a neurosis brings about, and how these changes are influenced by the patient's life history. Such a detailed inquiry will place the clinical observations now called primary and secondary gain in clearer context. It will highlight the complexity of the issues which need to be resolved, but analysis constantly teaches us that what is analytic is rarely very simple. The concepts primary and secondary gain can be abandoned without loss. Instead, in any analysis of the clinical phenomena which led to their introduction attention will shift to a separate analysis of the alterations in specific ego functions, ego-id-superego relationships, energy distributions, and object relationships. In suggesting that the two constructs be abandoned, it is not the clinical phenomena themselves that are being questioned; rather it is the nature of their conceptualization. Perhaps after one has sufficiently analyzed symptoms from all these metapsychological vantage points, one can begin to synthesize all the components into a unified picture and do this with the realization that no general statement about gains or losses can be made. With such a new approach it should be possible to pin-point the clinical observations which struck Freud and other observers and to integrate them into the over-all psychoanalytic scheme. The coercive and manipulative aspects of illness which have troubled so many commentators may prove more amenable to psychoanalytic scrutiny by utilizing the five metapsychological points of view than by all-inclusive, and therefore vague, references to secondary gain. This approach may contribute to psychoanalytic formulations about both the unity and complexity of psychic functioning, and may also facilitate the further refutation of the age-old notion that neurosis is a sign of moral weakness.

SUMMARY

A systematic analysis of symptom formation reveals that the ego's defensive efforts against instinctual impulses entails simultaneous changes in the relationship between self and the environment. Thus primary gain has both an intrapsychic and external component, and adaptive propositions must be included in a metapsychological analysis of symptom formation.

Once symptom formation has led to illness, attention has traditionally been focused on the gains derived from the patient's interaction with his environment. Such an analysis has rarely gone beyond the descriptive level. Also, the dynamic, economic, structural, and genetic aspects of the gain from illness as well as its relationship to the underlying conflict which led to symptom formation have been insufficiently studied. Moreover, little attention has been paid to intrapsychic changes subsequent to symptom formation, e.g., the "secondary revision" of symptom and the constant interplay between internal and external adaptations. Thus secondary gain too has an intrapsychic and external component.

A complete metapsychological analysis of primary and secondary gain indicates that a distinction between the two gains may no longer be necessary. The time factor which intervenes between symptom formation and the subsequent course of a symptom does not require a metapsychological distinction between "two" separate gains.

Labels like "gain" and "advantage" have complicated analytic inquiry since by their very meaning they convey a judgment. Also they neglect to emphasize the corresponding losses. An understanding of the clinical phenomena previously subsumed under primary and secondary gain may more profitably be pursued by studying separately the adaptive, genetic, economic, structural, and dynamic changes which occur in the development of a neurosis.

Such a reformulation will require a reconsideration of the resistances which have been ascribed to primary and secondary gain.

BIBLIOGRAPHY

Alexander, F. (1948), *Fundamentals of Psychoanalysis*. New York: Norton.

Brenner, C. (1955), *An Elementary Textbook of Psychoanalysis*. New York: International Universities Press.

Breuer, J. & Freud, S. (1895), Studies on Hysteria. *Standard Edition*, II. London: Hogarth Press, 1955.

Eissler, K. R. (1951), Malingering. In: *Psychoanalysis and Culture*, ed. G. B. Wilbur & W. Muensterberger. New York: International Universities Press.

English, O. S. & Finch, S. M. (1954), *Introduction to Psychiatry*. New York: Norton.

Erikson, E. H. (1953), Growth and Crises in the "Healthy Personality." In: *Personality in Nature, Society and Culture*, ed. C. Kluckhohn & H. Murray. New York: Knopf.

—— (1956), The Problem of Ego Identity. *J. Amer. Psa. Assn.*, IV.

Fenichel, O. (1941), *Problems of Psychoanalytic Technique*. Albany: The Psychoanalytic Quarterly.

—— (1944), Remarks on the Common Phobias. *Collected Papers*, II. New York: Norton, 1954.

—— (1945), *The Psychoanalytic Theory of Neurosis*. New York: Norton.

Freud, A. (1936), *The Ego and the Mechanisms of Defence*. New York: International Universities Press, 1946.

Freud, S. (1887-1902), *The Origins of Psychoanalysis*. New York: Basic Books, 1954.

—— (1894), The Neuro-Psychoses of Defence. *Standard Edition*, III. London: Hogarth Press, 1962.

—— (1905), Fragment of an Analysis of a Case of Hysteria. *Standard Edition*, VII. London: Hogarth Press, 1953.

—— (1908a), Character and Anal Erotism. *Standard Edition*, IX. London: Hogarth Press, 1959.

—— (1908b), 'Civilized' Sexual Morality and Modern Nervous Illness. *Standard Edition*, IX. London: Hogarth Press, 1959.

—— (1909a), Some General Remarks on Hysterical Attacks. *Standard Edition*, IX. London: Hogarth Press, 1959.

—— (1909b), Analysis of a Phobia in a Five-Year-Old Boy. *Standard Edition*, X. London: Hogarth Press, 1955.

—— (1909c), Notes Upon a Case of Obsessional Neurosis. *Standard Edition*, X. London: Hogarth Press, 1955.

—— (1910), The Future Prospects of Psycho-Analytic Therapy. *Standard Edition*, XI. London: Hogarth Press, 1957.

—— (1913), On Beginning the Treatment. *Standard Edition*, XII. London: Hogarth Press, 1958.

—— (1913-14), Totem and Taboo. *Standard Edition*, XIII. London: Hogarth Press, 1955.

—— (1914), On the History of the Psycho-Analytic Movement. *Standard Edition*, XIV. London: Hogarth Press, 1955.

—— (1916-17), *A General Introduction to Psychoanalysis*. New York: Permabooks, 1953.

—— (1919), Introduction to Psycho-Analysis and the War Neuroses. *Standard Edition*, XVII. London: Hogarth Press, 1955.

—— (1920a), Memorandum on the Electrical Treatment of War Neurotics. *Standard Edition*, XVII. London: Hogarth Press, 1955.

—— (1920b), The Psychogenesis of a Case of Homosexuality in a Woman. *Standard Edition*, XVIII. London: Hogarth Press, 1955.

—— (1923), The Ego and the Id. *Standard Edition*, XIX. London: Hogarth Presss, 1961.

—— (1924), The Economic Problem of Masochism. *Standard Ediiton*, XIX. London: Hogarth Press, 1961.

—— (1925), An Autobiographical Study. *Standard Edition*, XX. London: Hogarth Press, 1959.

—— (1926a), Inhibitions, Symptoms and Anxiety. *Standard Edition*, XX. London: Hogarth Press, 1959.

—— (1926b), The Question of Lay Analysis. *Standard Edition*, XX. London: Hogarth Press, 1959.

—— (1932), *New Introductory Lectures on Psycho-Analysis*. London: Hogarth Press, 1937.

—— (1940), *An Outline of Psychoanalysis*. New York: Norton, 1949.

Gardner, G. E. (1947), The Primary and Secondary Gains in Stealing. *Nerv. Child*, VI.

Gill, M. M. & Brenman, M. (1959), *Hypnosis and Related States*. New York: International Universities Press.

Glover, E. (1949), *Psycho-Analysis*. London: Staples Press.

—— (1955), *The Technique of Psycho-Analysis*. New York: International Universities Press.

Hartmann, H. (1939), *Ego Psychology and the Problem of Adaptation*. New York: International Universities Press, 1958.

—— (1960), *Psychoanalysis and Moral Values*. New York: International Universities Press.

—— & Kris, E. (1945), The Genetic Approach in Psychoanalysis. *This Annual* I.

Hendrick, I. (1958), *Facts and Theories of Psychoanalysis*. New York: Knopf.

Jones, E. (1910), The Action of Suggestion in Psychotherapy. *Papers on Psycho-Analysis*. London: Baillière, Tindall and Cox, 1920.

—— (1918), War Shock and Freud's Theory of the Neuroses. *Papers on Psycho-Analysis*. London: Baillière, Tindall and Cox, 1920.

—— (1955), *The Life and Work of Sigmund Freud*, II. New York: Basic Books.

Kris, E. (1952), *Psychoanalytic Explorations in Art*. New York: International Universities Press.

Laforgue, R. (1938), *Clinical Aspects of Psycho-Analysis*. London: Hogarth Press.

Medawar, P. B. (1959), *The Future of Man*. New York: Mentor Book.

Menninger, K. A. (1958), *Theory of Psychoanalytic Technique*. New York: Basic Books.

Nunberg, H. (1955), *Principles of Psychoanalysis*. New York: International Universities Press.

Pious, W. L. (1962), Personal communication.

Rapaport, D. (1960), *The Structure of Psychoanalytic Theory*. New York: International Universities Press.

—— & Gill, M. M. (1959), The Points of View and Assumptions of Metapsychology. *Int. J. Psa*, XL.

Tuke, D. H. (1892), *A Dictionary of Psychological Medicine*. London: J. & A. Churchill.

Waelder, R. (1960), *Basic Theory of Psychoanalysis*. New York: International Universities Press.

Waldhorn, H. F. (1960), Assessment of Analyzability: Technical and Theoretical Observations. *Psa. Quart.*, XXIX.

SOME ISSUES IN CONTEMPORARY PSYCHOANALYTIC RESEARCH

SEYMOUR L. LUSTMAN, Ph.D., M.D. (New Haven)

> Man is the *Interpreter of nature;* Not
> *the Spectator merely, but the Interpreter.*
> —WM. WHEWELL

The intent of this paper is to call attention to the changing research atmosphere within the United States, and to relate this to psychoanalysis and some of the methods used by psychoanalysts in their research work. Although there are a myriad of factors which produce what one can call the research atmosphere or climate of the scientific enterprise, I will focus on the three which I feel have had the most pervasive and formative impact.

The first of these is the incredible fact of nuclear energy, which has re-emphasized the position of physics as a prototypic science. To many, this has endowed paragon virtue to one aspect of that endeavor, i.e., the experiment. The second factor is the equally astonishing manner in which these awesome uses of nuclear energy were developed. The model of the Los Alamos project and its results have indelibly demonstrated the promise of the "crash program." One sees its current expression in large programmed research efforts of huge teams in predetermined "crucial areas." It is unfortunately difficult for laymen both to differentiate and understand the relationships between such applied researches and the researches of basic science.

The third factor is the ever-increasing financial support of research by the Government (Swain, 1962). This stewardship of huge sums of money makes it possible to direct and even divert the course

From the Yale University Child Study Center and Department of Psychiatry.

of science. As Abelson (1963a) pointed out, "In almost any enterprise, the agency furnishing the monetary support has, or can seize,
the predominant role in decisions affecting the way in which the
money is spent. In applied research such control is desirable and even
necessary. In fundamental research it is often well to give the investigator wide latitude to determine his own course." (See also Abelson,
1963b.)

A special problem for the multiplicity of theoretical systems
which comprise the behavioral sciences lies in the fact that the func-
tionaries who make decisions require standards of what is and what
is not "scientific." As Hartmann (1958) has stated, "The methodological demands on science are generally made from the vantage point
of its most advanced field." This has meant a return to an empiricism
based on methods of physics, but unlike physics—antitheoretical.
The importance of this to psychoanalysis is blatant and is a matter
to which I will return shortly.

It is my thesis that these three factors, concordantly, have determined and will continue to determine the direction and rate of
scientific growth. While it is apparent that all areas of basic and
applied science are affected, our concern must be with the behavioral
sciences, since they have the closest relationship to and impact upon
psychoanalysis.

The aid to behavioral scientists from the National Institute of
Mental Health has had a relatively short, but quite proud history.
Support to scientists and students training for scientific careers had
a salutary effect on research, many benefits of which have already
become available to the nation. The initial over-all policy was
broadly defined in terms of supporting creative and potentially
creative people. This emphasis on people never ignored specific
project research, which was also bounteously supported. Science and
scientists were accepted for what they are—calculated risks. There
was an implicit faith in the gains of the basic sciences, and the ultimate applicability of such knowledge was never in doubt. Psychoanalysts and psychoanalytic projects were included in these grants.

In this atmosphere, the individual scientist was free to pursue
his curiosity without need to justify this by standards of expediency,
immediate applicability, or artificially imposed standards of scientific

purity. In the course of these developments there has been an unprecedented expansion of the university research facilities, for which the major source of funds remains the Government. By the nature of the granting specifications, scientists also had to be attached to universities almost exclusively.

For a variety of reasons, including abuse, there now appears to be imminent changes in the over-all policies of support. With a sense of palpable urgency, the emphasis has turned to practical results in the immediate public interest. Echoing Los Alamos in its confidence in the combined brainpower of teams, trouble areas are delineated for scientific annihilation. Through a combination of available funds and high-pressure recruitment, large teams of scientists are assembled and assigned projects. Monotopical research institutes have been formed, and there is even the possibility that entire university departments will be committed to one problem.

This course has administrative advantages and will—I have not the slightest doubt—lead to rather immediate public benefits. My concerns are with the inevitable intrusion into the functioning and training of individual basic scientists. To the extent that such planning prizes team commitment, excludes the "high risk" basic scientist who works alone, and the sciences which tend to work best in relative isolation, longer-range concerns are great and justified. Although many scientists (Abelson, 1963a, 1963b; Ingle, 1963; Wolfle, 1963) have expressed grave concern for the basic scientists in all fields, this is particularly true of psychoanalysts and psychoanalysis.

For one thing, the recruiting problems alone can be accomplished only by depleting less well-supported—though no less important—areas. This has already extended into the recruiting of students on the doctoral level where the glamour and the "future" of an area, in addition to the immediate stipends, takes precedence over the curiosity of the individual student. In terms of research training of future basic scientists, precious little concern has been manifested about the advisability of conducting such research training programs in project-committed research departments. Of greatest import is that all postdoctoral programs, in which I include psychoanalysis, will be ultimately faced with the results of the quality and quantity of earlier selection and training.

Psychoanalytic Research Growth

The above-described era of national scientific development has witnessed a corresponding progressive institutionalization of psychoanalytic research. To describe this it will be useful to follow the three divisions of analytic research suggested by Kris (1947).

The first, and most important, remains the basic model of research with psychoanalytic data obtained by the psychoanalytic method. By tradition, this has been and continues to be done in private practice. However, this approach has been enriched by more complex modifications which require institutional structuralization for their continued growth. I refer to such endeavors as simultaneous analysis of mother and child, the psychoanalytic study of the family, studies on pregnancy, and developmental studies. Such efforts require more staff, more extensive data-recording and data-reducing techniques, more time to think and confer than is possible in an exclusively private-practice setting.

The second area of psychoanalytic research has an even greater need for institutional structure. That is the area of psychoanalytic observation that has been so particularly fruitful in infancy and early childhood. This crucial avenue of research has flourished within such settings as the Yale Child Study Center, Boston University, Masters Children Center, University of Colorado, and others. Its contributions to psychoanalytic theory have been rich and extensive. However, it must be noted that if this method is to continue, psychoanalysts must have access to obstetrical services, the newborn nursery, the pediatric well-baby clinic, the nursery school, and specially trained and skilled colleagues. This represents the greatest extent to which psychoanalysis has developed a multidisciplinary team approach to such problems as the longitudinal study of development. That such research could flourish outside of universities seems unlikely.

The third area, which will concern us the least, is the area of "experimental" psychoanalysis. This exists for the most part as distantly derived work going on in departments of psychology. It uses or misuses psychoanalytic theory, but not method. While there are some notable exceptions, if one reads this literature, one can only agree with Hartmann (1959) who stated "On the whole, this field of research has not so far decisively contributed toward a clarification or systematization of psychoanalytic theory. As a rule, these studies do not go beyond what has been demonstrated in analysis before; they have often not achieved new insights nor stimulated research. The main body of evidence does not rest on these studies, but on the wealth of empirical data gathered by the analytic method in the analytic situation." However, all share hopeful attitudes toward some work in this area (Klein, 1954, 1958; Luborsky and Shevrin, 1962).

It is thus apparent that to the extent that national policy affects institutionalized research, psychoanalysis must consider the possible fate of its research programs. In one sense, the major issue may be defined as the superimposition of judgmental control on the energies of individual scientists. Such judgmental control is wielded by an increasing number of "study sections" as the review boards are called. Their task is no easy one, and one can sympathize with their attempts to juggle money, projects, and people, while desperately seeking standards.

Psychoanalysis does not fare well in these boards. Perhaps some of the fault lies in the fact that few analysts serve on these boards. This, in part, stems from a tradition of comparative isolation and willingness to admit to ignorance which makes it difficult for psychoanalysis to judge other sciences. Another factor which must be pointed out is the degree of involvement within psychoanalysis by which many psychoanalysts make themselves unavailable for such "chores." One could question the soundness of thus limiting psychoanalytic responsibility and scope. At any rate, it is unfortunately true that N.I.M.H. boards are staffed not by psychoanalysts but primarily by social scientists who tend to apply the nineteenth-century criteria of physics to psychoanalytic theory. In addition, the nature of psychoanalytic research is primarily more fundamental than applied, and cannot readily fit into the "decreed crucial areas."

It is an unfortunate fact that psychoanalytic projects get serious consideration only if there is a methodologist from another discipline on the staff. It is also an unfortunate fact that psychoanalytic career scientists stand in career jeopardy. By this I do not mean that psychoanalysts have any difficulty finding or keeping academic posts—quite the contrary. However, it is becoming increasingly difficult to maintain such posts and function as psychoanalysts.

Our age is characterized by a great fear of, and a great faith in, science. Since applied science produced the fear, it is to applied science that many turn with a perceptible and understandable sense of urgency. It is uncomfortably true that the technological advances of the physical sciences have so far outdistanced the technology of the behavioral sciences, that the world can be destroyed at a time when it is still very difficult completely to understand how two people get along—let alone nations. As a matter of fact, none of us can say whether this lag between the physical and behavioral sciences will be our epigraph or our epitaph.

However, I hold that this lag has almost nothing to do with methodology in a basic sense. Without in any way minimizing the genius of some of the representatives of the physical sciences, I feel that their impressive growth and accomplishments are primarily related to the characteristics of the phenomena which comprise the field—a field which permits of isolation and control of few manageable variables, and which gave rise to the method of experiment. In contrast, the advance in the behavioral sciences has been slower not because they have attracted fewer geniuses, but rather because the incredible complexity of the field defies meaningful isolation and control of few manageable variables.

To think otherwise is to divide method from phenomenon and results in the futile researches in which the literature abounds. In its frustrations, it has also led to a generation of methodological critics.

The hue and cry for fastidious method and meticulous theory seem not to recognize that method and theory cannot be superimposed, regardless of fit, but must be precisely geared to the phenomenon under study—that is, if it is to be meaningful even though not neat. This congruence of empirical data, method, and theory can come only from an internal development which reflects "the nature of the beast" in all its bewildering complexity.

It is quite possible to feel self-righteously methodologically anointed and to develop theoretical propositions which lend themselves to experimentation and prediction—*only* if one is exquisitely selective and limited. For example, if one accepts the equivalence of species (which I do not) and then goes to a presumably simple animal, say, the pigeon, and addresses himself to a very limited aspect of that pigeon's life, e.g., its response to operant conditioning, he can develop a theory which is close to the empirical data of experimentation. However, the attempt to apply this to the complexity of man, his development, his behavior, his ideals, his poetry, leaves one with a theory that is "for the birds."

As Hartmann (1958, 1959) has repeatedly stressed, psychoanalysis is not adverse to borrowing techniques from other disciplines. However, the phenomenological field studied by psychoanalysis is so different, so formidably complex, so inextricably multivariable in nature, that it has been virtually impossible to superimpose available techniques without serious loss of meaning. It is interesting to note that Shakow and Rapaport (1963) point out that the premature preoccupation with rigor, and the eagerness to mimic the older sciences, have rendered all of psychology a major disservice. The "measuring rage" and the "axiomatic furor" (Rapaport, 1960) has made psychology's theorizing about man one of proud, genteel, fastidious sterility.

Yet it is this nineteenth-century criterion of science which is brought to bear on psychoanalytic theory. It centers on the old demand for agreement with the empirical data (whatever those are presumed to be) of experiment. It seems most striking, and perhaps regressive, that philosophers and psychologists criticize psychoanalytic theory thus, at a time when physics in its increasing sophistication has begun more and more to doubt its measurements and its theoretical statements. The explicit causality demanded of psychoanalytic theory continues at a time when "indeterminancy" has caused physicists to take a much humbler position with respect to its concepts of causality.

Moreover, the critics of psychoanalytic theory seem unaware that psychoanalysis has two theories and that what can be asked of one is presented as the criticism of the other. I refer to Rapaport's useful distinction between the clinical theory and the general theory of psychoanalysis. The former is very specific, limited, deals with matters such as the neuroses, transference, defense, technique, etc., and

is very close indeed to the empirical data of the psychoanalytic
method. It is true that this area of theory is ignored by critics. In
part this stems from the layman's ignorance of this vast body of
clinical, empirical data and its related theory and method. As
Waelder (1962) states, "Understandably enough, the critic of psychoanalysis is inclined to discuss those matters with which he has a
measure of acquaintance, such as Freud's philosophy or the more
abstract concepts of theory, and to shun the discussion of observations in analysis and their interpretations. . . . The opponents of
psychoanalysis will probably steer away as soon as possible from the
data with which he is not familiar and return to generalities about
which it is easier to sermonize. The psychoanalyst [who becomes
involved in such debates] cannot prevent this from happening, but
he can make it somewhat less easy for his opponent."

The metapsychological theory of psychoanalysis represents the
highest order of abstraction of a general theory of man. It is by now
better systematized through the efforts of Hartmann, Kris, Loewenstein, Waelder, Rapaport, Gill, and others. This theory is a theory
of high generality. Like all theories of high generality (even in
physics), many aspects are considerably removed from empirical data.
Like all theories of high generality, it cannot be judged by criteria
of logic and agreement with observed fact alone. It requires additional criteria by which its scientific utility can be judged. As with
physical theories of high generality (Frank, 1957), additional criteria
of efficiency or simplicity, and "dynamic" or heuristic value must also
be used.

Simplicity can only be judged in relationship to the complexity
of the field. Thus, the admitted complexity of the psychoanalytic
theory is far simpler than dividing man up into separate theories of
perception, cognition, learning, developmental theory, personality
theory, etc. Furthermore, this comprehensiveness permits crucial
interrelationships not feasible with a multitheoretical approach.

Perhaps the most profound aspect of the function of theory is its
dynamic or heuristic value, its ability to provoke new questions and
to extend into unknown territory. On this ground, even the most
vitriolic critics express appreciation. There is no *general* theory of
man available which remotely approximates the utility of psycho-

analytic theory when the criteria are comprehensiveness, logical consistency, explanatory power, coherence, economy of concept, heuristic value, and agreement with the domain of empirical data with which it deals. This only states the relative merits of the theory and makes no claim for a theory without serious problems and drawbacks. For example, there are some who feel one of the most serious of these is the absence of a learning theory of its own—one which does not fractionate the psychoanalytic theory. However, it is a dynamic theory and both theory and method will grow.

Since every psychoanalyst knows this, I find mere criticism, even though edged with financial threat, insufficient to account for the defensiveness of many analysts. To the extent that this stems from a wish for progress, it is a progressive force. To the extent that it leads some research analysts to abandon the analytic method for the comparative methodological safety of laboratory research, and to the extent that it leads others to not-so-creative borrowing, it is regressive.

However, the most distressing aspect is the willingness of some analysts to relinquish their research obligations and prerogatives. Any scientific area belongs ultimately to the researchers who move it forward—not to the practitioners who apply its subsidiary benefits. As Hartmann (1958, 1959) points out, this is most complicated for analysis because the paradigm of treatment as the prerequisite for meaningful research makes the two functions go hand in hand. But the research problems can be solved only by analysts and no amount of turning to "Hessian troups of methodologists" or "methodolotry" will suffice.

I believe one of the factors which brings about defensiveness in the analyst is one he shares with his critics. The burdens shared by all scientists in these urgent days exaggerate the very old methodological defensiveness of the behavioral scientist vis-à-vis the physical scientist. At this stage of scientific development, the behavioral scientist must be capable of tolerating a significant degree of ambiguity. That this is difficult can be attested to by the struggles within psychology. Without looking to its history, psychology seems more determined than ever to achieve respectability through mimicry. This longing for rigor is reflected in the vitriolic tone of critique, and unfortunately in the decisions of study sections.

Psychoanalysts and their critics share the same problems faced by all individual scientists. As a research method, analysis is slow, painstaking, and very individual. This is difficult in an agitated and apprehensive atmosphere. To put it another way, it is the problem of how the individualistic scientist can afford to follow his curious nose when that nose may be cataclysmically destroyed. This is not the problem of psychoanalysis alone. It confronts every individual scientist who continues to work within the heritage of individual scholarly curiosity, without regard for expediency, popularity, or immediate applicability. To this one can only say that fortunately—for some scientists, like Freud—there is no other alternative.

PSYCHOANALYTIC RESEARCH METHODS

University-housed psychoanalytic research is experiencing considerable pressure to alter both its theoretical conceptualizations and its methods of doing research. The possibility exists that this important setting for research development may be lost, or that serious changes in method and theory may be imposed in order to compete for funds. In view of the pressures being exerted on psychoanalytic research, it becomes obligatory for analysis to maintain a critical self-inventory of its methods.

In the hope of moving in this direction, I will follow the advice of Einstein (1934): "If you want to find out anything [from physicists] about the methods they use, I advise you to stick closely to one principle: Don't listen to their words, fix your attention on their deeds." I will therefore not talk about concepts, constructs, intervening variables, hypotheses, validation, basic postulates, etc.—this ground has been well discussed by others (Benjamin, 1950, 1961; Escalona, 1952; Frenkel-Brunswik, 1954; Freud, 1920; Hartmann, 1958, 1959; Kris, 1947; Kubie, 1952; Rapaport, 1960). Instead I will focus on modes of research as they appear in the literature of psychoanalysis. Therefore, this is not a systematic description of all possible research mediations of psychoanalytic theory and method, rather it is impressions of what psychoanalysts consider their methods.

For my own purposes, I find it helpful to think of primary and second-order methodological concerns. The primary methodological concerns have to do with the method of data collection, and the second-order concerns have to do with recording, reducing, otherwise treating and analyzing those data.

PRIMARY METHODS

In an over-all sense, the principal methods are those of experiment, observation, and treatment. Such a classification is in some ways arbitrary. It can be pointed out that overlap can be considerable. There will always be observational components in experiments and experimental aspects in primarily observational studies; moreover, observational technique is an integral part of treatment. However, it is always possible to blur the boundaries of any useful polarity. I hold this classification is useful, particularly because of the possibility of conjoint use of methods which demand methodological clarity (Janis, 1958). With the exception of Gill and Brenman's (1959) research use of hypnosis, experimentation is noteworthy in analytic literature by its absence. A great deal of external criticism stems from what is felt to be the lack of *experimental* sophistication in analysis. *Experimental* sophistication and *scientific* sophistication are not synonymous. Actually it is precisely the presence of *scientific* sophistication which prevents analysts from distorting and diluting their area of study through the use of *available* experimental techniques developed by neighboring disciplines.

Psychoanalytic treatment hours are not experiments. While it is true that control of frequency, place, time, use of the couch, and the relative anonymity of the analyst lend an aura of constancy, this does not approach the experiment if we follow Feibleman (1960): an "experiment is controlled observation of what happens when some segment of the natural world is forced to an alternative in which it will be as easy to obtain a negative as well as a positive answer. . . . It must be isolated, analytic, repeatable, crucial, and heuristic." In the sense that isolation refers to the elimination of *all* uncontrolled variables, the crucial question is not: can psychoanalysis be compressed into an experimental mold? It is rather: to the degree that the scientific *modus operandi* is dictated by the characteristics of the phenomenological domain, is the experiment as we know it, not applicable to the phenomenological domain of psychoanalysis?

The experiment is not the only approach to science—it is the one which was uniquely made possible by the characteristics of such physical sciences as physics. There is no self-generated experimental paradigm similar to the physical experiment in the behavioral sciences relating to man—there is only a self-conscious borrowing which demands such sacrifice for fit that it produces the rigor of rigor mortis. Most attempts to overcome this in relation to man, such as statistical probability, randomness, statistical controls, while helpful in many ways, are not indigenous to the data of psychoanalysis and still have a patched-on quality when applied.

Clinical Psychoanalysis

The basic paradigm of method is clinical psychoanalysis. Intrinsically geared to the level of the phenomena of the unconscious, the psychoanalytic method is the result of empirical data and intuitive genius. It has not the clarity of the experiment because it does not deal with few variable phenomena. If change in this method is to come about, I predict that it *too* will arise from the soil of empirical data as viewed by genius. It will bear no resemblance to the experiment of physics, and because of its uniqueness will perhaps be forthcoming from those who are unencumbered by the current standards of science and that philosophical myth, "the scientific method." Such developments would help us with the many methodological problems we face such as circularity, prediction, etc.

The clinical paradigm of Freud has many great advantages. Principal among these is the degree to which the motivations of the clinical situation replace the superficiality which plagues constructed experiment and observation. Of greater import is the fact that not only does one obtain the significant behavioral data, but that related thoughts, feelings, slips, dreams give them meaning, dimension, and perspective not available through other methods.

Within the clinical paradigm the closest psychoanalysis can come to experimental manipulation is to take advantage of the experiments in nature. Catastrophe, maternal deprivation, the sensory deprived, and the like, have all been richly used within analysis. These are areas in which many competent research workers from other disciplines have made contributions. In some instances, psychoanalysts entered the field after others had established it. Actually the method is an extension of the classical approach of psychoanalysis, which was the use of the neurosis to understand normal man. This leads to the usual criticism of moving from pathology to a theory of normal man, a criticism which implies not only a difference between the two but an invalid way of functioning. The validity is less crucial a question than the utility of this classic psychoanalytic approach.

Freud was not the only scientist who capitalized on pathology. Paul Weiss (1961) was most articulate in his use of deformity and "experiment in nature" to understand growth. His statement could have been written by a psychoanalyst, and describes very well the methodological uses of this pattern. ". . . Changes in the standard pattern of formative processes lead to deviations from the standard form: Deformations end up as 'deformities.' In this sense, 'deformities' become valuable clues to the inner workings of formative processes. . . . Pathology and developmental biology must be re-integrated so that our understanding of the 'abnormal' will become but an extension of our insight into the 'normal,' while, *pari passu*, the study of the 'abnormal' will contribute to the deepening of that very insight."

Psychoanalytic treatment *is* the basic method of psychoanalytic research. As clinical research, at bedrock it is the method of the expert observer and judge. The reliability of the research depends upon the reliability of the analysis. The controls on this are better within psychoanalysis than any other treatment method, because of the extensive personal analysis of the analyst, the rigor of his training, and his continuing self-analysis. In addition, the method of supervisory consultations can be used as a control if uncertainty exists.

This method has been extended via "parameters" to research on the analytic process itself, the use of the method to investigate development, character, symptom formation, creativity, the child, the psychotic, interaction between family members, etc. It needs no review here.

As ways of working with this method in research, Freud left us at least three basic models: (1) the compilation of cases of similar research utility—either from the individual analysts's personal experience or through pooling of efforts; (2) the classic single-case method of the case histories; and (3) the focus on large numbers of part aspects of the individual or individuals, such as the dream, slips, jokes, behavioral patterns, or symptoms.

The second model, i.e., the classic single-case method, is by far the most prominently used in the literature and has most certainly had the richest impact on analytic theory. In addition to its classical use as a case report, it has methodological applicability to phenomena within the same patient which can be compared. Examples are elements such as developmental changes, change brought about by treatment, or comparison of two differing patterns of behavior, thinking, or dreaming. The major advantage lies in the fact that having defined the sample upon which the research is being done in this way, the two components to be compared are then matched. Matching and control are major problems in all behavioral science research, and while techniques are available to minimize sampling errors, they require such great numbers that they are of little use to psychoanalysis as a research tool. It is even possible via this stochastic model (Chassan, 1961) to apply appropriate statistics.

One further aspect of case reporting bears some mention. While all reports make some effort to review the literature on the theoretical point they wish to make, very few make a careful compilation of similar *clinical* reports in the literature. This is not in keeping with the usual use of the literature in other areas of medicine, and does not do justice to the wealth of accumulated clinical data which could be used to add a numerical dimension to the report.

Even though appreciative of the basic contributions of the single-case method, many people decry the absence of large numbers of cases in psychoanalytic research. For some problems this criticism seems exaggerated and ignores the number of observations. But it must be noted that there is a growing demand within psychoanalysis itself for larger compilations of case material. Usual psychoanalytic practice does not very often permit such accumulations of a significant number of cases. However, in a research sense, particularly with a career psychoanalytic investigator, it should be possible for one man to take into psychoanalytic treatment a significant larger sample of cases which represent the problem in which he is interested. Though possible, this may not be a wise procedure for the research, the patients, or the analyst. The obvious solution has been an increased growth in collaborative research within psychoanalysis, particularly the model set by the Hampstead Child-Therapy Clinic.

One model of collaborative research left by Freud (1909) was that of Little Hans. This has become the model for supervision, and for some it remains a research-collaboration model. As a research method, I do not think it is the best for the following reasons. Supervision is a teaching device and as such introduces contaminations of its own. But assuming that these can be controlled, the greatest risk remains that of "consensus of opinion" research, in which the *senior* member is the one who never sees the data at first hand. To the extent that expert judgment is a method, unless some technique of establishing reliability is introduced, I do not feel that a supervisor adds any reliability to the case in a collaborative sense. He functions as a control on technique, but his distance from the data makes him a discussant. It is a curious fact, consistent with the model of Little Hans, that although the vast majority of supervised cases in the United States are adults, the vast majority of published supervisor-supervisee collaborations exists around the child.

There have been numerous outgrowths of other methods of collaboration. Each of these strives for independent analysts working together. One model has been the simultaneous analyses of mother and child, another model has been the study-group method started by E. Kris, and recently described by Rosen (see Pfeffer, 1961). Another model is that of M. Kris et al., in the psychoanalytic study of a family. As described by Rosen, the study-group method is essentially the extension of the continuous case conference for research purposes. It is openly acknowledged that this sharing of data runs the same "consensus of opinion" risk, but assumes that fully trained analysts can better deal with this. Bibring highlights the issues by pointing out that although there are advantages to such groups, such as pooling of data and the stimulation of alternate hypotheses, there are the disadvantages of dilution of responsibility, group suggestibility, too early presenting of ideas and formulations, and the possible inhibition of the development of ideas (see Pfeffer, 1961). In addition, all such collaborative ventures indicate the need for clarification of such problems as individual styles in technique, problems in technique arising from the research aspects of the venture, comparability of case material, and "contamination." They also focus on the second-order concerns of the problems of very large amounts of data.

Freud's third model of compilation of part aspects of individuals or the individual is also extensively used. One major development in this direction is the development of "indexing" or categorizing of psychoanalytic data, which makes it possible to gather together large numbers of similar dreams, fantasies, incidents, and the like. I will speak of this later on.

A major future concern for psychoanalytic methodologists must be a complete exploration of all the methodological benefits and difficulties in the stochastic model of research, the compilation and comparability of cases as treated by different analysts, the limitations of part-phenomenon study, the complexities of simultaneous analyses ranging from mother-child to entire families, etc.

OBSERVATION

The use of observational techniques is made necessary by the unavailability of psychoanalytic data in certain areas. These particular areas have great theoretical importance such as the neonate, the infant, early childhood, and to a lesser extent, the psychotic. Again this model for research derives from Freud, and he used it most clearly in his description of the child's play in *Beyond the Pleasure Principle* (1920), which he related to the theoretical concept of the repetition compulsion.

Methods of observation differ sharply from analysis, even in the hands of trained psychoanalysts. The data obtained are on a different level of conceptualization than analytic data and should not be used the same way. In some ways the problem is akin to using the manifest dream without any free associations. The data are always closer to surface manifestations, and always present risks in speculation. The danger of such observational data lies in the fact that observation is of events only; *everything* else is interpretation. Thus, observational research can almost always be interpreted in many ways. Alternate theories as well as alternate hypotheses must be considered. The greatest danger is that one may "lend too much depth" to the observation in order to use the data to support one hypothesis rather than another.

One way in which psychoanalysts have tried to deal with some of these problems is the development of a team. As stated above, this is the area where collaborative research has been at a premium. The essential principle has been the use of many observers with the idea that if viewed from a number of different perspectives, a core of reliable data will emerge from which validity can be inferred. The difficulties of this approach in practice have to do with the multidisciplinary aspects of the team and the differing degrees of sophistication relevant to analysis, as well as the differing conceptual frameworks within which the observations are made. At the same time, it must be stated that it has been an incredibly useful development in psychoanalytic research; and in some instances, longitudinal studies have merged into child analysis. Here, as nowhere else in analysis, one has the opportunity for particularly vivid and collaborative evidence of reconstructions.

Metapsychological Essays

Although all clinical papers in psychoanalysis make the attempt to bring the data into relevant relationship to psychoanalytic theory, it is the metapsychological essay which ultimately becomes the repository for systematized psychoanalytic theory. As a rule, these papers deal primarily with theoretical concepts, and are characterized by having no directly stated inductive or deductive reference to or from clinical data. This is even so in those instances where vignettes of clinical material are used in an illustrative manner. For the most part, the tasks of such essays have been to initiate new theoretical possibilities, to trace the historical development of particular concepts, to debate and extend theoretical issues, and to systematize theory. Their models are Freud's Chapter VII of *The Interpretation of Dreams* and his metapsychological papers.

As a general group of papers—or way of working—they meet with a great deal of resistance from both within and without psychoanalysis. Most of the criticism from outside analysis is rooted in the Anglo-American tradition of empiricism. As Gordon W. Allport (1955) has so lucidly pointed out, Anglo-American psychology is rooted in the Lockean tradition. It conceptualizes the mind as a *tabula rasa,* is molecular in content, accepts species equivalence, and "its representatives are found in associationism of all types, including environmentalism, behaviorism, stimulus-response psychology, and all other stimulus-oriented psychologies, in animal and genetic psychology, in positivism and operationism, in mathematical models, in short, in most of what is cherished in our laboratories as 'true scientific' psychology."

In addition to its empirical bias, these critics share with some psychoanalysts an antitheoretical bias which is rooted in a misunderstanding of the function and indispensability of theory. Because of the distance from data, such essays are labeled "pure speculation," as if that is not an important, even crucial, facet of science. The significance of theory to psychoanalysts and the dangers of sequestering practice from theory have been vividly presented by Hartmann, Kris, and Loewenstein (1953) and Rapaport (1960).

For those who worship physics, it is important to point out that the science of psychoanalysis, like the science of physics—as methodologically conceived by Einstein—has two sources for its concepts. One is empirical and the other is theoretical. Ultimately one goes nowhere without the other.

To Einstein (1934) the theoretical component was a free invention of the human intellect. "The way from the empirical data to the postulates of deductively formulated physical science is a frightfully difficult one. Here, rather than anywhere else, the scientist's genius exhibits itself. The way is so difficult that no methods whatever must be barred; no source of meaning whatever, imaginative, theoretical, of whatever kind, are to be excluded. It appears that nature covers up her basic secrets; she does not wear her heart on her sleeve. Thus only by the freest play of the imagination, both the intuitive and the non-intuitive, formal, theoretical imagination, can the basic concepts and postulates of natural science be discovered." (See also Northrop, 1959.)

Einstein continues with the plea, "There is no logical path to these laws; only intuition resting on sympathetic understanding of experience can reach them. . . . A theorist who undertakes such a labor should not be carped at as 'fanciful', on the contrary, he should be encouraged to give reign to his fancy, for there is no other way to the goal."

To the empiricist who, as Rapaport (1960) puts it, can find "no new method, i.e., ways of experimenting, in contradistinction to designs of experiment," one can only quote Professor H. H. Price who, according to McGlashan (1962), said, "One should not be too strongly deterred by the fear of talking nonsense. . . . If the Logical

Positivists had been alive in the early part of the seventeenth century, physics would never have got itself started."

At their best, metapsychological essays are organizing, conceptualizing, systematizing, clarifying, and play their most crucial role in their heuristic function. At their worst, they are dogmatic, repetitive, appeal to hierarchical authority, and are misused as data to settle issues. Logic and creative thinking alone can ignite a spark, show a direction; they are not empirical data and should never be so confused. There is always the empirical aspect of science, which in response to inspiration arrays itself for or against a hypothesis.

SECOND-ORDER METHODOLOGICAL CONCERNS

The most primary of such concerns has to do with the recording of data. Whether the empirical data come from psychoanalytic treatment or observation, they remain the most basic building block of the scientific endeavor.

The recording of such data is no simple matter in psychoanalysis, because one has to record the patient, the participant observer, the transference and countertransference relationship between the two, and at the same time manifest a great awareness of what the very fact of recording does to the data. On the whole, recording of data (Kubie, 1952; Pfeffer, 1961; Shakow, 1960) has ranged from movies to tapes, to immediate postinterview dictation, to writing of notes at night, to reliance on memory. I consider it peculiar that analysts who every day deal with the vagaries of memory would trust their own memories in terms of scientific data.

Assuming that, for scientific purposes, the analyst makes regular notes following every session, I would think it crucial that such notes include the phenomenological aspects of the hour, rather than exclusively psychoanalytic formulations about it. Hartmann (1959) has repeatedly pointed to the dangers of reporting concepts as observations.

From this basic core of psychoanalytic data, many analysts are now seeking methodical means of ordering the material. In some research projects this has taken the form of monthly summaries, yearly summaries, inventories, etc. The form it takes cannot be ascertained without knowledge of the purpose of the research.

The usual technique in a single-case report has been to describe the material, using one or another point of view to highlight its theoretical pertinence. Thanks to the clearly stated efforts of Rapaport and Gill (1959) one can now be much more methodical in clinical description (in those instances where it is felt to be crucial) by recognizing that any phenomenon to be described psychoanalytically must be described from all metapsychological points of view, i.e., dynamic, economic, structural, genetic, and adaptive. Attention to this could in itself bring more order to clinical reporting. At the same time it must be noted that such methodical reporting was not used by Freud, and runs the risk of inhibiting the spontaneity and creativity in some workers.

Yet with all this, there are other concerns manifesting themselves among research analysts, having to do not only with the consolidation of material for intra-case analysis but also with inter-case analysis. Led by Anna Freud and the Hampstead Index effort, there are currently many experiments dealing with methods of categorization and indexing of psychoanalytic data. The success of this approach with large masses of psychoanalytic material coming from large numbers of patients remains to be demonstrated. By that I refer to problems of compressability, fragmentation, and the loss of meaning when taken out of context.

Here too, one can only hope that future research efforts of a pilot nature will highlight the uses and difficulties of such efforts both to reduce and to consolidate large masses of psychoanalytic material. Yet to be. solved are methods of correlating data of disparate origin—such as one has in multidisciplinary longitudinal studies, which include psychoanalysis.

SUMMARY

The attempt has been made in this paper to describe some changes in the current scientific atmosphere of the United States and to trace their possible impact upon psychoanalysis and psychoanalytic research. There appears to be a revitalization of a Lockean tradition of empiricism within study sections of the national Government, which has so much direct influence on university-housed research. To the extent that a great deal of psychoanalytic research has become so institutionalized, some thought must be given to the future of these programs.

I have tried to indicate that the nature of the phenomenological field with which psychoanalysis deals makes it impossible to compress psychoanalysis into the mold of a nineteenth-century concept of physics and the physical experiment. Pressures to alter analytic research are considerable, and make it obligatory for analysis to maintain a critical self-inventory of its methods. In this direction I have tried to describe those aspects of modes of scientific work which present themselves in the psychoanalytic literature as the psychoanalytic research methods of analysts.

In concluding, I feel very keenly that psychoanalysis as a research method must develop internally through the efforts of psychoanalysts, and that no amount of borrowing will be to any significant avail. Toward this direction the logical step would be for psychoanalytic institutes to develop and finance their own full-time research sections to take over as much institutionalized psychoanalytic research as possible.

The other alternative, which is not mutually exclusive of institutionalized research, is more complex and must be explored. It can be approached as one small segment of the larger issue of the function and status of the university in modern life. It calls for a sober reappraisal of the mutual obligations and mutual impact of the university and the "outside world" (government, industry, and the community) upon each other. To date this is a matter which has concerned educators far more than scientists.

There can be no doubt that the gradual emergence of the university from its classical monastic seclusion has had an enormously beneficial effect on all concerned. One major function of the university must remain that of a reservoir of highly skilled, specialized talent for the practical problems of government, industry, and the community. It is by now obligated to so remain a vital force in civilization.

And yet, one must seriously question the developing concept of the itinerant consultant—which is the lot of many professors of science. I do not know if it possible to have it both ways—perhaps it is a matter of degree—but it must be possible to function as such a reservoir without completely relinquishing the concept of university as a community of highly individual, independent, free scholars.

If we focus on psychiatry, besieged by service needs, community needs, national mental health, etc., the problem of basic research can seem a luxury rather than a crucial urgency. This is further complicated by the multidisciplinary nature of the enterprise as well as by the multitheoretical characteristics of the field. It can be a bewildering morass which should concern all psychiatrists.

From the viewpoint of the incomplete nature of the research results of *all* theoretical systems, methods, and disciplines, great humility on the part of all thoughtful scientists seems appropriate. Practically, it may call for eclectic departments of psychiatry. This does not mean departments composed of eclectics. At this stage of scientific progress, most scientists would agree that this blunts the probe and blurs the exploration.

I refer rather to an over-all eclecticism arising from a community of experts representing their own disciplines with integrity, dedication, and security. In such a department, psychoanalysis can stand, contribute, and grow alongside neurophysiology, biochemistry, neuropharmacology, and the social sciences. In the unconditional freedom of the university tradition, each specialist must be free to immerse himself in the complexities of his own research area.

He must also be free to collaborate—not by assignment but by inner direction. If there is to be fruitful, multidisciplinary collaboration, it would best arise spontaneously from such an intellectual climate rather than from a calculated financial need. It cannot be programmed for it depends too much on the ripeness of the moment, the people, the methods, and the communication.

I do not intend to demean the multidisciplinary studies which have already been done. For one thing, they have forced helpful clarifications and sharpened awareness of similarities and differences. This is no inconsiderable service. To my mind, they raise the consideration that our knowledge is still insufficient to launch many such teams. The progress of science might be best served by pushing individual theory to its limits. I remain convinced that when the time is at hand for basic research collaboration between disciplines, the best of it will come as highly individual, inspired spurts rather than from premeditated calculation. Perhaps the best one can do to enhance the probability is the preservation of the most fertile soil, i.e., the provocative skepticism of university heterogeneity. In such a structure, whether through intrigued interest or irritated awareness, multidisciplinary communication and teaching occur.

Psychoanalysis *and* the university will both lose something very important if the community of free scholars, and the communication so made possible within the university, is altered. The future development of both begs for a tolerant re-evaluation by men of vision.

BIBLIOGRAPHY

Abelson, P. H. (1963a), Congress and Research. *Science,* CXXXIX.
—— (1963b), Government Support of Research. *Science,* CXXXIX.
Allport, G. W. (1955), *Becoming.* New Haven: Yale University Press.
Benjamin, J. D. (1950), Methodological Considerations in the Validation and Elaboration of Psychoanalytic Personality Theory. *Amer. J. Orthopsychiat.,* XX.
—— (1961), Knowledge, Conviction, and Ignorance. *J. Med. Educ.,* XXXVI.
Chassan, J. B. (1961), Stochastic Models of the Single Case as the Basis of Clinical Research Design. *Behav. Sci.,* VI.
Einstein, A. (1934), *The World as I See It.* New York: Covici Friede.
Escalona, S. (1952), Problems of Psychoanalytic Research. *Int. J. Psa.,* XXXII.
Feibleman, J. K. (1960), Testing Hypotheses by Experiment. *Perspectives in Biol. & Med.,* IV.
Frank, P. (1957), *Philosophy of Science.* Englewood Cliffs: Prentice-Hall.
Frenkel-Brunswik, E. (1954), Psychoanalysis and the Unity of Science. *Proc. Amer. Acad. Arts & Sci.,* LXXX.
Freud, S. (1900), The Interpretation of Dreams. *Standard Edition,* IV. London: Hogarth Press, 1953.
—— (1901), The Psychopathology of Everyday Life. *Standard Edition,* VI. London: Hogarth Press, 1960.
—— (1905), Jokes and Their Relation to the Unconscious. *Standard Edition,* VIII. London: Hogarth Press, 1960.
—— (1909), Analysis of a Phobia in a Five-Year-Old Boy. *Standard Edition,* X. London: Hogarth Press, 1955.
—— (1913), The Claims of Psycho-Analysis to the Interest of the Non-Psychological Sciences. *Standard Edition,* XIII. London: Hogarth Press, 1955.
—— (1920), Beyond the Pleasure Principle. *Standard Edition,* XVIII. London: Hogarth Press, 1955.
Gill, M. & Brenman, M. (1959), *Hypnosis and Related States: Psychoanalytic Studies in Regression.* New York: International Universities Press.
Hartmann, H. (1958), Comments on the Scientific Aspects of Psychoanalysis. *This Annual,* XIII.
—— (1959), Psychoanalysis as a Scientific Theory. In: *Psychoanalysis, Scientific Method and Philosophy,* ed. S. Hook. New York: New York University Press.
—— & Kris, E., Loewenstein, R. M. (1953), The Function of Theory in Psychoanalysis. In: *Drives, Affects, Behavior,* ed. R. M. Loewenstein. New York: International Universities Press.
Ingle, D. J. (1963), Congressional Support for Medical Research. *Perspectives in Biol. & Med.,* VI.
Janis, I. (1958), *Psychological Stress: Psychoanalytic and Behavioral Studies of Surgical Patients.* New York: Wiley.
Klein, G. (1954), Need and Regulation. In: *Nebraska Symposium on Motivation,* ed. M. R. Jones. Lincoln: University of Nebraska Press.

—— (1958), Cognizant Style and Motivation. In: *Assessment of Human Motives*, ed. G. Lindzey. New York: Rinehart.

Kris, E. (1947), The Nature of Psychoanalytic Propositions and Their Validation. In:_ *Freedom and Experience*, ed. S. Hook & M. Konwitz. Ithaca: Cornell University Press.

Kris, M. (1957), The Use of Prediction in a Longitudinal Study. *This Annual*, XII.

Kubie, L. S. (1952), Problems and Techniques of Psychoanalytic Validation and Progress. In: *Psychoanalysis as Science*, ed. E. Pumpian-Mindlin. Stanford: Stanford University Press.

Luborsky, L. & Shevrin, H. (1962), Artificial Induction of Day-Residues: An Illustration and Examination. *Bull. Phila. Assn. Psa.*, XII.

Lustman, S. L. (1962), Defense, Symptom, and Character. *This Annual*, XVII.

McGlashan, A. (1962), Psyche Unbound. *Lancet*, II, No. 7251.

Northrop, F. S. C. (1959), Einstein's Conception of Science. In: *Albert Einstein, Philosopher, Scientist*, ed. P. A. Schilp. New York: Harper & Bros.

Pfeffer, A. Z. (1961), Panel report: Research in Psychoanalysis. *J. Amer. Psa. Assn.*, IX.

Ramzy, I. (1963), Research Aspects of Psychoanalysis. *Psa. Quart.*, XXXII.

Rapaport, D. (1960), *The Structure of Psychoanalytic Theory* [Psychological Issues, Monogr. 6]. New York: International Universities Press.

—— & Gill, M. (1959), The Points of View and Assumptions of Metapsychology. *Int. J. Psa.*, XL.

Schrödinger, E. (1957), *Science, Theory and Man*. New York: Dover.

Shakow, D. (1960), The Recorded Psychoanalytic Interview as an Objective Approach to Research in Psychoanalysis. *Psa. Quart.*, XXIX.

—— & Rapaport, D. (1963), *The Influence of Freud on American Psychology* [Psychological Issues, in press]. New York: International Universities Press.

Swain, D. C. (1962), The Rise of a Research Empire: N.I.M.H., 1930-1950. *Science*, CXXXVIII.

Waelder, R. (1960), *Basic Theory of Psychoanalysis*. New York: International Universities Press.

—— (1962), Psychoanalysis, Scientific Method, and Philosophy. *J. Amer. Psa. Assn.*, X.

Weiss, P. (1961), Deformities as Cues to Understanding Development of Form. *Perspectives in Biol. & Med.*, IV.

Wolfle, D. (1963), University Responsibility. *Science*, CXL.

THE SCOPE OF INTRAPSYCHIC CONFLICT

Microscopic and Macroscopic Considerations

LEO RANGELL, M.D. (Los Angeles)

The theory of psychoanalysis has from the beginning been a conflict theory. In broad strokes, the sequence of Freud's thinking went through a number of crucial stages with regard to the nature of the basic etiologic conflict (Nemiah, 1962). The earliest phase, as reviewed by Rapaport (1960), was conceived as occurring "between the memory of the traumatic event and the dominant ideational mass of the person, or as the conflict of the ideas and affects present in the traumatic situation with the moral standards of society." The latter having been internalized and taken over by the patient as his own, the conflict was seen at once as an intrapsychic one, although a step removed from having been inner vs. outer. It was early conceived in topographic terms, i.e., between unconscious memories, ideas and affects, and the essentially conscious inner dictates of morality. The dynamic and economic points of view were implicit in the assumptions made, and were soon made manifest.

The intrapsychic locus of the conflict thus existed long before the structural point of view. In the next development, the conflict was seen as between "the wishful impulse" and the endopsychic censorship, or as between the primary and the secondary processes (Freud, 1900). Later, the intrapsychic components opposing each other consisted of libidinal vs. ego-preservative instincts, both forces residing within the instinctual drives (Freud, 1911, 1914). We know that with the elaboration of the structural point of view (Freud, 1920, 1923), as well as with both the revised theory of anxiety (Freud,

An earlier version of this paper was presented at the panel on "The Significance of Intrapsychic Conflict," Fall Meeting of the American Psychoanalytic Association, New York, December 8, 1962.

1926) and the dual-instinct theory (Freud, 1920, 1923), the intra-psychic conflict took its final and present form as an intersystemic one, a structural conflict between the instinctual drives of the id and the defensive forces, the anticathexes of the ego. The struggle had long before this already been conceived of as taking place mainly at the unconscious level. Jones (1955) refers in a broader way to a striking and characteristic dualism in Freud's basic thinking, a fact which has been noted by Hartmann and many others.

Theory always brought with it, sometimes too rapidly, its results. The various phases described were accompanied by a series of pendular shifts with regard to the applicability of the new points of view and of the insights gained, not only by nonanalysts, such as parents and teachers eager with each new phase for its help, but also as reflected in the goals and techniques used by analysts in treatment as well. Anna Freud (1956) has outlined the phases of such applications and expectations. Since it was the pathogenic nature of intra-psychic conflicts which was the first to be exposed, the desideratum was considered to be to avoid or at least to minimize all conflict. The means of bringing this about prophylactically progressed, with the successive conceptual stages, from sexual enlightenment, to complete tolerance of sexual and derivative autoerotic activity, to abandoning all discipline so that there could be no difficult superego to be internalized, to permitting and even encouraging all aggressive behavior. In the face of the resulting chaos and the failure to achieve the desired goal, Anna Freud concluded by recommending that the mother can lend her own resources and ego strength to the child only until the time when he has matured enough to have incorporated these into himself. In this way the child's ego equipment could be optimally developed to deal in as rational a manner as possible with the inevitable developmental anxieties and conflicts of human life. The latter were not to be avoided.

Subsequently, with the recognition of the role played by such conflicts as a spur to maturational processes and to the entire line of developmental progression, the existence of conflict came to be seen as a necessary and even as the most desirable of psychological phenomena to assure the course of effective development. Anxiety, conflicts, and the need to resolve them were seen as the motive force and the *sine qua non* of all progression, without which satiety, stagnation, and emotional arrest would be the inevitable results.

Actually, as is usually the case with such pendular swings, the truth lies somewhere between the two extremes. The classic causes of fixation, as Fenichel (1945) has pointed out, occur with either excessive satisfaction or with excessive deprivation. Provence and Ritvo (1961), testing a hypothesis advanced by Ernst Kris that in the infant comfort serves to build object relationships while discomfort stimulates differentiation and structure formation, studied a group of institutionalized infants deprived of normal maternal care. These authors found that more than discomfort alone, it was discomfort-comfort contrast of a certain degree which was important for stimulating differentiation and the formation of psychic structure. The "ordinary devoted mother," to borrow Winnicott's term (1945), ministered to her child in close proximity to the peak intensity of the discomfort, which was followed then by an experience of fuller gratification and a greater degree of comfort than was the case in the institutionalized infant. In the latter case, protracted discomfort occurring over a long period of time and without relief, resulted in disorganization and disruption of the infant's capacity for ego functioning. While the ego apparatuses and repertories for action appeared on time in the maturational timetable, they were clumsily used, poor in adaptation, and lacking in richness or subtlety. The crucial role of early object relationships in providing such favorable attention to the needs of the infant was stressed. In the same panel on object relations in which the above work was presented, Rubinfine (1962), elaborating on observations made by Escalona (1953), described mothers who were overzealous in anticipating and preventing frustration on the parts of their infants, thus permitting no build-up of tension to take place, and interfering particularly thereby with the discharge of aggression. In both sets of subjects quoted, those with a steady diet of excessive tension and those without the chance of developing a sufficient amount, the results were affects which were muted, shallow, and hollow, and an incomplete and stilted register of emotions.

A nodal contribution, which resulted in a major change in our viewpoint toward conflict, was Hartmann's classic monograph (1939a)

in which he described and gave due place to the conflict-free ego
apparatuses and their roles and destinies in psychic functioning.
Present from the beginning as part of the constitutional endowment, they contain a potential for meeting the "average expectable
environment" and are to serve an indispensable role in adaptation.
While "the ego certainly does grow on conflicts," Hartmann writes,
"these are not the only roots of ego development" (p. 8). In order to
fulfill its role as a *general* developmental psychology, psychoanalysis
must encompass and explore thoroughly that prolific "ensemble of
functions" which develop and exert their effects outside the realm
of mental conflicts, the "peacetime traffic" within the ego borders
as well as the history of its conflicts. One of our major tasks is also
"to investigate how mental conflict and peaceful internal development mutually facilitate and hamper each other" (p. 11). Of course,
Freud's interest in the phenomena of a "general psychology," such as
in dreams (1900), wit (1905) and everyday life (1901), had long ante-
dated this—although, it is true, at first largely from the point of
view of conflict-solving behavior.

In a series of illuminating articles which followed (Hartmann,
1950, 1952, 1955; and with Kris and Loewenstein, 1946), this entire
area was amplified in many necessary derivative directions. We
learned subsequently of the differentiation between primary and
secondary ego autonomy, and how in the latter large portions of
the ego previously in the service of defense and conflict may acquire
secondary conflict-free autonomy following "a change in function."
Rapaport (1951, 1958), among others, elaborated later on the nature
of autonomous structures; and Spitz (1957) on the phenomenon of
"change of function," drawing parallels between such occurrences
on the psychological and on the embryological and physiological
levels.

With these contributions, and with the entire literature which
they triggered, there came an enormous expansion in our understanding of the life of the ego, which was thus to catch up with the
previous emphasis given to the role of instinctual drives. Ego action
was seen now in fresh perspective, not only with respect to these
newly appreciated conflict-free regions, but also, in conjunction with
the impetus given concurrently by Anna Freud's detailed investiga-

tions into the mechanisms of defense (1936), with a more intensive understanding of its role within the conflict situation itself. With these, the processes of adaptation received new dimensions of understanding.

Hartmann (1939a) decisively pointed out, and it bears repetition here, that "It would be an error to assume that the contrast of conflict situation and peaceful development corresponds directly to the antithesis of pathological and normal" (p. 12). Such is of course by no means the case, nor is the dichotomy conflict-free vs. conflictful, by similar error, to be equated with congenital vs. experiential. Rather, all three divisions are scrambled together, in mutual and complementary fashion. Thus, for example, conflict or conflict-free activity can be associated with either the normal or the pathological. "Conflicts are part of the human condition" and absence of conflicts can be associated with failure (Hartmann, 1939a, p. 12). And ontogenetically, apparatuses destined for each sphere are included within the congenital givens, as well as being subject to the facilitations or the deterrences which are to come from subsequent environmental fates. Thus there are inborn defense thresholds (Rapaport, 1951, 1953), as well as the innate conflict-free apparatuses referred to above, all with their own "primary ego energy" to provide their own motive power.

There are spectra in all of these, as we come to see in discussions of most of our psychological phenomena (such as sublimation, conversion, nosology, etc.) so that we may extricate ourselves at once, for example, from the fruitless nature-nurture controversy, or the other similar dichotomies named, in all of which Freud's original description of the complementary series is to be applied.

Thus the same spectrum and mutuality applies in the reciprocal interaction and overlap which take place continuously between the conflict-laden and the conflict-free spheres of activity themselves. Conflict-free apparatuses may attract to themselves, or else have thrust upon them, conflicting forces, such as in somatic compliance. Similarly, areas of conflict may become conflict-free or secondarily autonomous as described above. Yet, as with all spectra, there are components which belong and operate in a polar fashion at each end. Thus, while some functions or organs are in the central band,

there are nevertheless some which are prone to be free of conflict
throughout their developmental histories, while others are more
destined to operate within areas of conflict and of mounting tension.

I

I would now like to turn to the nature of the intrapsychic conflict itself, approaching it from two different positions. We might
regard the first as a microscopic view; it examines the intricate components which make up the interior of the phenomenon and their
sequential relationships, in a manner which I have described (1959)
as micropsychophysiology. The second would be a macroscopic view,
of how we are confronted with the ingredients and the consequences
of conflict in a global way in the clinical and the therapeutic situation, and of what our task consists in that setting.

When applying the microscopic interior view, we should consider the following. Because of the tendency for fusion and synthesis
among psychic products, it is necessary, for clarity, to distinguish
the various components which take place within the entire arc which
comprises the conflict situation and to separate the events which
occur prior to, during, and following what can be called the actual
period of conflict itself. This would entail delineating as separate
entities, for example, frustration, the build-up of tension, the occurrence of anxiety, and what relation these bear to the actual conflict
situation, and then the defensive cathexes, inhibitions, symptom
formations, or hierarchy of symptom formations which may result.
It is my contention that too often such statements as "the patient is
overwhelmed by tension—or by anxiety—or by conflict" are loosely
interchanged, without clarity. I take it as an opportunity, if not an
assignment, to attempt to clarify such issues.

Hartmann (1939a) points out that "It would be meaningless to
call every disruption of equilibrium a conflict. This would rob the
concept of all precision. Every stimulus disrupts the equilibrium, but
not every stimulus causes conflict" (p. 38). Hartmann then reminds
us of four different mental states of equilibrium which concern
psychoanalysts in relation to our regulation principles. There is the
equilibrium between the individual and his environment, the equi-

librium of instinctual drives (vital equilibrium), the equilibrium of mental institutions (structural equilibrium), and the equilibrium between the synthetic function and the rest of the ego (p. 39). To my mind, not all of these are of equal and central weight when we come to examine the question of intrapsychic conflict. It is the third of these, the structural equilibrium, which is most regularly involved and of most universal interest by the time a state of intrapsychic conflict is attained; I will comment in further detail below, however, on the important aspects of the equilibrium within the ego itself, as well as on the question of the equilibrium between the instinctual drives.

Freud has given us the model for separating contiguous and closely related events, and for the establishment of the proper sequential relationships between them, in his classic study on anxiety (1926), when he separated and clearly demonstrated the relationship between inhibitions, symptoms, and anxiety. Any further elaboration in this area has had to be built upon this base.

The chain of events which leads to, includes, and stems from the significant intrapsychic conflict situation comprises the following sequence:

1. Since we must arbitrarily select a starting point, let us start with a hypothetical state of psychic equilibrium, with a person at ease, content, at rest, not particularly "bothered" by anything. He is well *defended* and averagely satisfied with how *adapted* he is at that moment. (Such states are, to be sure, most often transitional and not too long-lasting in daily waking life.) You will remember also that in accordance with our constancy and nirvana principles, it is not called for that such a state be tension-free; rather a condition of optimum tension exists, indeed one "characteristic for the organism," as has been pointed out by Fenichel (1945). Actually, all four of Hartmann's specific equilibria enumerated above are in a relative state of quiescence to achieve this dynamic-economic state, although it is the intrapsychic reverberations (Hartmann includes the environment) which are decisive and which, from my point of view, we will be especially compelled to watch.

2. This existing equilibrium, between the psychic structures as well as at the other levels, is impinged upon by a precipitating factor.

This may be either from an external stimulus (influx) or from within, somatic or psychic. The latter may come from any one of various possible directions, for example, from an increase in intra-systemic instinctual tension, or a relaxation of a defensive ego anti-cathexis. While a common instance is that of an increase in instinc-tual pressure, either libidinal or aggressive, it is possible, in accord-ance with Hartmann's principle of autonomy, that an increase in intrasystemic tension can originate *ab initio* from other than the instinctual-drive organization, for example, from the exercise of an ego judgment, or the arousal of a superego attitude toward a specific existing instinctual urge. Writing on hierarchy and autonomy, Rapa-port (1960) states: "these more neutralized derivative motivations will be autonomous from—i.e., can be activated without being trig-gered by—the underlying less neutralized motivations. For instance, they may discharge when their autonomously accumulated energy reaches threshold intensity."

3. When such a stimulus encroaches, a new imbalance is created, and a new economic condition prevails. From whatever source it originates, when it reaches a sufficient magnitude, it is the ego which is confronted with this new situation.

4. There are a great variety of possibilities from this point on, some of trivial psychoeconomic import, not going many steps beyond this. For the sake of pursuing, however, what follows in the case of an appreciable and significant disturbance of the psychoeconomic condition, I will select one of the possibilities, in fact, one of the quite typical outcomes, and pursue this along its possible course. It should be borne in mind that this is selective and of course extremely schematic, as is inevitable in any such stripping process which attempts to arrive at "model" activities.

The "typical" situation I have chosen is one in which, from whatever source it originates, whether activated directly or by stimu-lation from any of the other sources mentioned, an instinctual temptation is aroused. This may be a new instinctual pressure, or a necessary recontemplation of an old one. At once, however, the ego is now confronted with this instinctual demand, while facing a superego and possible external figures ready to pass judgment. (The superego is a *sine qua non* in this intrapsychic process, the external figure may be an added burden.) Between these and after it judges the nature of these forces, the ego will have to make a decision.

5. In our literature it is frequently stated, quite summarily, that at this point the ego uses anxiety as a signal. While this is certainly true, we must interpose first a few vital steps, indispensable links in the sequential chain, which take place at this juncture as preparatory stages before the anxiety signal can ensue—steps which it is my impression are usually glided over in our descriptions of this process.

The ego is now subjected, automatically, to the experience of this new balance of intersystemic forces and to their mutual interaction. Not automatic, however, is the dosage. The ego, in control, permits only a slight amount of discharge of the instinctual tension, sampling the gratification which ensues, and ready for the consequences thereof. The latter is forthcoming immediately, and again automatically, but again in controlled dosage, in proportion to the cautious instinctual pleasure which had been permitted. This is not yet *the* intrapsychic conflict but a miniature controlled sample of the conflict which might ensue if the entire dose were to be permitted. We might call it a minor preliminary phase. Hartmann and Loewenstein (1962) have called a similar process "tentative temptation," but one which they refer to in a more limited and special way. "Here the ego allows itself a small dose of gratification which then serves to set in motion the forces of the superego."

6. The ego samples all of these. The analogy which Freud (1926) made between signal *anxiety* and inoculation comes to mind and applies to this phase as well. This is like a skin test, a preliminary small dose of the antigen, to test the reactions of the host. Just as thought is experimental action, so this entire interaction is experienced, in controlled amount, in an experimental way and in a signal manner. The experience, which was an experimental conflict, is to conflict what thought, which is experimental action, is to action. Neither is yet the end result.

The concept of the signal can, it seems to me, be extended forward to explain, with profit, this phase as well. The experimental action, the controlled gratification, is a signal action, as is the return signal of the superego's reaction. The ego receives, judges, and reacts to this series of preliminary signals.

7. The reaction is crucial, the estimate of the danger. The ego is the recipient, on the basis of the above, of either an automatic reaction of anxiety or else of a sense of safety. On the basis of this, the ego judges that there either is or is not a danger situation, and if so whether it is mild or severe.

8. If the latter is deemed mild or nonexistent, the ego can act accordingly toward the instinctual demands, and allow lenient gratification. During the course of everyday life such an outcome occurs frequently, with action or other behavioral discharge taking place without even the production of a significant intrapsychic conflict. Up to this point the latter cannot yet be said to have occurred. The scanning, judging, and filtering functions of the ego, which constitute a continuous action during the process of waking life, have performed their tasks without too much challenge. We might say, in Hartmann's sense, that the equilibrium—or rather, the equilibria have been disturbed, but a conflict did not ensue.

9. However, the result may not be the above, but instead the ego may judge that there is indeed an appreciable danger involved if the instinct in question were to be yielded to, danger from the superego or from the external world (castration or loss of love), or from the strength of the instincts themselves. This is now the true stage of the anxiety signal. As a result of having experienced a small sample of a significant danger, and of being able to judge and anticipate what its full impact would be, signal anxiety is automatically experienced, a new level of signal, and the crucial one in this train of events. This may range in intensity from mild and easily controlled, to severe and barely controlled, or may presage the imminence of panic or of the traumatic state, as in Schur's (1953) series of controlled to uncontrolled anxiety. Incidentally, lest this point be overlooked, it should be made explicit that the outcome here depends not only on the particular current stimulus in question, either its quantitative or qualitative aspects, but more importantly on the extent to which this has access to and arouses a traumatic chain of memory traces, i.e., the pull from the repressed, as well as the push from above. It is, as always, the situation in depth, based on the ontogenetic history, which is crucial.

10. Only now does a significant increment of conflict ensue. I

say "increment" to differentiate it from the quiescent conflict which existed as a baseline even before the present stimulus appeared. This increase is that specifically related to the new disturber (and its ability to arouse latent ones).

As will become clearer with what follows, this present spurt of conflict is only one phase of the conflict's total later history, and can be designated as "major phase one" of the conflict (there has been previously the "minor" phase referred to above, i.e., the experimental, controlled, signal phase). It is anxiety—or more correctly, the danger which this anxiety heralds—which caused this new and major increment in conflict, just as this same anxiety will be the motive for defense. The motive must precede (this phase of) the conflict, and the conflict must precede the later defense. At this stage, and as a result of the estimate of danger occasioned by the degree of signal anxiety, the ego is "in conflict" as to what to do next.

It might at this point occur to you to intercede, as it did indeed to several discussants on first hearing this material, with the question, "But doesn't conflict *cause* anxiety, rather than the other way around?"[1] It might thus be thought, for example, that it is the perceived or experienced conflict between the superego and the id which causes the ego to feel the anxiety. To this I would say first that the superego's demonstrated opposition to the instincts has so far mostly been kept in check. At best it can be argued that only a minor and experimental conflict has at yet ensued, as stated above, with a more major one perceived as potential *if* certain things were allowed to happen (i.e., instinctual gratification). It is for this reason that I said above that *the* (i.e., significant) intrapsychic conflict has not yet taken place. However, speaking more strictly, it might be said that even in the controlled minor and experimental interchange, what has been demonstrated and experienced so far has not been an existing *conflict* but a series consisting of act and punishment (in small doses). The potential doer and the reactive punisher have been defined, but they have not yet locked grips, i.e., there is not yet a *conflict* between them, with forces deployed one to the other. Moreover, as I will show in another paper (1963b), it is even a question

[1] Drs. Arlow and Schur both posed this question in discussing this point during the panel discussion at which this paper was presented (see Nemiah, 1963).

whether the superego is in conflict with the id in the usual instance at all, or whether it is not rather in conflict only with the ego, in response to a certain attitude of the latter toward the id. In this sense, it might properly be said that the ego has by now suffered a small amount of experimental intersystemic conflict, felt by it from the direction of the superego as a result of its already slight gratification of the id. In this sense the anxiety can be said to be a *result* of this already-discovered conflict. But speaking strictly again, what *actually* caused the anxiety was not the conflict but the *danger* which was revealed as lurking in the superego.

So, at the most, a small experimental and only minor conflict has revealed the danger, which provoked the signal anxiety. As a result of the latter, and depending on its extent, a major increment now occurs, what we may call a first phase of the major conflict. The ego is now "in conflict" as to what it should do next.

This is a good point at which to consider another issue which makes for confusion and which needs clarification at once. The term "conflict" has two different meanings which need to be distinguished in this discussion. One is, according to Webster, "competition or opposing action of incompatibles—antagonism, as of divergent interests." Another is "a battle, a fight, struggle, hostile encounter." What I have just outlined about the ego's conflict applies to it in the first of these meanings, in the sense of competing alternatives, and the obligation to effect a choice. It is in fact this meaning which occurred to me first as the usual one, which an analyst thinks of when he speaks of the ego as being in conflict. However, the second has of course just as much validity and even a longer historical tradition in our field.

In my opinion, this differentiation has not been pointed out or at least is usually neglected or insufficiently kept in mind in the psychoanalytic literature on intrapsychic conflict. Historically, it was the opposition-of-forces type which first held exclusive sway in our early theoretical formulations. While the participants in the struggle changed a number of times, the form of it endured. However, the alternative-competition or decision type of conflict described above entered the scene with the tripartite structural model and the role assigned to the ego as mediator and integrator between the other two systems. Although such a function came into play at once, this new distinction in types of conflict was not, to my knowledge, made explicit. This division of meanings of our main term, however, is indispensable and must clearly be borne in mind when we follow the changing interrelationships which take place.

To return now, after this necessary digression, to the plight of the ego, it is to be noted that its problem at this point is an intra-systemic one. This point is the center of a separate accompanying paper (1963b) in which I elaborate in greater detail on the struc-tural questions with regard to intrapsychic conflict. Possessed now of an awareness of cause and expected effect, of impulse and antici-pated punishment, the ego is confronted with an internal, intra-systemic decision-dilemma, as to what to do, which to choose, how to find a way out.

I should like to pause still further at this stage to make a number of other relevant observations which come to light here. It may be noted, for example—and this is also a point which, it is my impres-sion, is frequently not appreciated—that the severity of the conflict, at least this segment and form of it, is not necessarily proportional to the severity of the anxiety. Thus, I believe it would be accurate to state that the decision-conflict at this point is most intense, not with the most intense anxiety, but rather in the middle of the spectrum of intensity of the latter. Such a conflict-dilemma is at its height when the forces comprising it are most nearly balanced, while the issue is more easily decided in one direction or the other when the balance is uneven. Thus in mild signal anxiety, this conflict is mini-mal, in favor of instincts. But similarly when the anxiety is severe or there is even the verge of panic, it is not the conflict which reaches a high peak but rather the ego's doubts with regard to its own re-sources. In other words, in the face of the severity or imminence of the threat, the ego's concern is not which way to go, but whether it is able to go in the direction it knows it must, i.e., repress, or other-wise defend. The ego is now not so much in a state of conflict as in a state of impending impotence, or at least of relative insufficiency. Can it stave off the threatening pressures? It is faced now with the possibility of the signal becoming an actual danger, to the point of psychic helplessness.

A corollary of the above is that the severity of the (ultimate) outcome is also not necessarily proportional either to the severity of the anxiety or to the intensity of the conflict. There may be the most anxiety in a phobic, the worst conflict in an obsessional, and the most severe total pathology in a psychotic. The determining factor is the relative strength and resourcefulness of the ego in the face of the particular balance of threats.

Thus, an example of the most intense and raging conflict of this (dilemma) nature is that behind a severely obsessional state, rather than in more severe psychopathological conditions. Ambivalence, indecision, an almost precise and devastating balance are the rule, sometimes with simultaneous and at times with alternating opposing actions, representing in turn each arm of the conflicting forces. Indeed, the ego here must be strong to contend with such formidable adversaries, and this is often the case in the obsessional neurotic, who may appear in many ways as if made of iron. In more regressed and malignant states, however, as in schizophrenic or other psychotic episodes, while the pressures may be more severe, and the threats more overwhelming, it is the disorganization of the ego and its relative insufficiency in the face of these primitive archaic and violent forces, at the level to which regressions have taken place, which form the core of the psychopathology at this phase, rather than a greater intensity of the conflictual state.

11. I will now return to an examination of the continuing succession of events. We have seen until now how signal anxiety brings on conflict, which then behooves the ego to act, to choose, to look for a solution—of course, at the least price. What follows now are the sequelae of this phase of conflict, the attempts at its resolution.

In a favorable situation, with the threat the least, the forces impinging not too great, and the sufficiency of the ego resources quite equal to the task, mastery is achieved with the least sacrifice and the most satisfactory and simple solution. Anna Freud (1962) quotes, as a good prognostic sign, the child who, when frustrated, can simply say, "Okay." (I add: In a way which we do not have to worry about!) In contrast to the situation described above in which signal anxiety was not forthcoming at all, as a consequence of which the ego was able to permit lenient discharge, the present situation generally calls, even in a most favorable instance, for at least a certain amount of defense, of denial, repression, or other. This is seen to institute the next phase of conflict, although here in a benign and adequate way, either an increment or at least a reaffirmation of the existing *inter*systemic conflict between the ego and the instincts. Now the form of the conflict changes to the opposition type, with counter-cathectic ego energy being called for and sacrificed at the ego-id border. We can call this the "second major phase" of the conflict emanating from the original traumatic stimulus which I hypothesized. It supersedes and outlasts the first "decision" phase, and will continue, after the latter may have come to rest, until a final point of relative stability is achieved.

12. Under less favorable circumstances, however, things continue to happen, and the instincts will not be so easily put off. I would like to single out, en route to symptom formation, a next intermediate phase which the ego undergoes in its successive and continuing steps toward an attempt at resolution. This is a phase, quite regular in its occurrence, which is often passed over quickly, and which I feel deserves the dignity of separate attention commensurate with its clinical importance. It is the state of dammed-up tension, occasioned by the fact that, while the blockage of discharge is exerted, the instinctual pressures will not abate. The intersystemic, opposition type of conflict continues in an unstable form. The resulting tension state, from a continuing increase and a damming-up of this instinctual pressure, plays, I believe, a regularly significant part in the ensemble of derivative sequelae which follow the suffering of conflict.

Intersystemic conflict thus results in increasing intrasystemic tension, which in turn exerts intersystemic effects. Tension continues to harass the ego, which, depending on its intensity and the relative strength of the ego to absorb or resist or otherwise handle it, may remain as an enduring state, or may be transitory, to be superseded by more definitive symptoms, or else may, in more favorable situations, recede.

I will again digress briefly, this time because we touch here upon certain aspects of the theory of anxiety. It was this stage within the parade of intrapsychic dynamic events which I believe led Freud to his theory of "actual neurosis" and of the direct transformation of repressed libido into anxiety. And it was his correct observation of the existence of this phase which caused him to retain this theory of direct toxic transformation even after he changed to his second, signal theory of anxiety (1926). In my unitary concept of anxiety (1955), I feel that I resolved Freud's "non-liquet" statement with regard to these two conflicting theories, by retaining the existence of this tension state, but not with it his explanation of transformed libido. This state of tension does exist, as stated here, but it is not anxiety.

Although I have spoken in favor of its presence, I have differentiated this state from the actual-neurotic anxiety of which Freud spoke, and with which Fenichel tends to concur. In my view, the dammed-up state is one sequel stemming from anxiety, as in the sequence which I have shown above, or anxiety may then again follow from it (see below) in circular fashion. But the two are not the same, and in each case the anxiety, when it occurs, serves the same function, i.e., the recognition and signal of danger. When anxiety follows this tension state, and is admixed to it, the danger which it forebodes is that of the dammed-up state continuing, or getting worse, and of the ego being overrun by the instincts.

There are a number of other points of difference between my view and the original concept of actual-neurotic anxiety, chiefly in that the latter implies an absence of ego or even of mental participation and a direct physiological transformation to anxiety. This latter view is concurred in by Blau (1952) and equivocally by Benjamin (1961) but is disputed by most other students of the problem of anxiety, as Brenner (1953), Schur (1953), Greenacre (1941), Spitz (1950), and Kubie (1941). A number of the latter, however, fail to assign any place to the dammed-up state in the spectrum of psychic events.

I return from this brief and unavoidable digression into anxiety theory. This tension state has its own derivative effects, which stem directly from this dynamic and economic situation rather than from any other part of the total complex arc, or the composite collection of them all. Certain subjective experiences of the patient, which may be part of his final total symptom complex, may derive from these intrasystemic instinctual pressures themselves. They may come out in such expressions as "I feel like busting out all over," or "I'm going to burst out of my skin," or even by another derivative step of incipient somatization, "I just feel itchy and tense all over." One patient put it, "I feel like a Cadillac engine in a Ford body." Such feelings, sometimes spoken and most often not, may be quite universally behind all the more varied symptoms of severe and more definitive neurotic disorder, due precisely to an insufficiency of the ego in the face of continuously pressing instinctual demands. Fenichel (1945) is of the same opinion when he states that "actual-neurotic symptoms form the nucleus of all psychoneuroses" (p. 192). Fenichel divides the symptoms attributable directly to this tension state into negative and positive ones (p. 168 ff.). The negative symptoms, which consist of general inhibitions of ego functions, are due to a decrease of available energy as a result of the energy consumed in the service of defense. The positive symptoms are traceable to the instinctual pressures themselves, and consist of "painful feelings of tension, of emergency discharges, including spells of anxiety and rage, and producing sleep disturbances due to the impossibility of relaxation." I would say that the latter are already indirect effects.

13. The above phase, although I have belabored it to give it its due place, is most often a transitional one, to be followed by further attempts at a more stable and a more livable-with resolution of the unstable and continuing conflict state. I cannot discuss in equal detail all the possible succeeding steps toward conflict resolution, but will have to pass over the rest by merely stating them. This is due not only to limits of space, for such an undertaking would necessitate the space of a book, but also because these next moves involve the traditional center of psychoanalytic exploration, have been the phases most copiously studied in the past, and are not the center of our interest at this time. They involve the well-known methods of symptom formation, including regression (to previous points of fixation), and the entire range of compromise formations which arise as end products. In a wider sense and over a more sustained view they also lead in the direction of character formation. Although these more stable resolutions are still along the line of conflict solving, in the interest of selectivity I have here enlarged only upon those relatively earlier phases which have usually not been highlighted and on the several dynamic details which to my mind have not been spelled out clearly before—see, e.g., Nemiah's review (1962).

II

For my focus of interest, it should be noted that the process of conflict formation itself continues alongside of and subsequent to the various sequelae which its presence has initiated. Thus, as noted above, the tension state itself may become a source of anxiety, with a new layering of conflict resulting and demanding solution on its own account. Similarly, there may be defenses against defenses, or a symptom may be defended against, or an entire neurosis may represent a new threat to the ego. These may be for reasons related to the original etiologic conflict, or the motives and the anticipated dangers now may be of quite a different caliber, but in either case they then trigger off a repetition of the entire process, which may then again be repeated, either in whole or in part, etc.

The above process, however, is not limited to psychopathologic events, but may similarly be responsible for the achievement of highly effective psychic formations. Thus, Rapaport (1953) has eloquently described such a process of increasingly complex hierarchic development in the formation of derivative motivational drives and of increasingly complex ego defenses. The same layering process is at the root of the "taming of affects" described by Fenichel (1941) and of the increasingly subtle shadings of affect discharge which become possible with the attainment of maturity, as described by Jacobson (1952, 1953) and by Rapaport (1953). This continuous process of conflict solution, derivative conflict, and derivative solution results in the increasing neutralization and modulation which accompany the course of psychic development. Along with neutralization, increasing ego autonomy, and the use of increasingly effective sublimatory discharge channels, these processes, to quote Jacobson (1952), "change the quality of drives, bind mobile energy, and by producing various combinations of high- and low-speed discharge processes result in the complex affect experiences of some of our most sublime pleasurable states."

Rapaport (1960), writing on motivations, states "clinical evidence shows that the defense motives are themselves subject to defense formation, and indeed whole hierarchies of such defense and derivative motivations layered one over the other must be postulated to explain even common clinical phenomena. Knight, and Gill have demonstrated this for the relationships of aggression, homosexuality, and paranoia. This hierarchic layering of structures is conceived to be the means by which the neutralization of instinctual-drive cathexes is brought about. These multiple structural obstacles transform the peremptory instinctual drives into delayable motivations by setting the structural conditions under which the pleasure principle must operate."

The process of decomposing, which demonstrates the stratification in the developed state, can further be compared and viewed with profit against the background of the ontogenetic development. It will be remembered that the earliest months of life, in gross description, are characterized psychically by the experiencing of frustration, tension, unpleasure and pleasure, but not yet anxiety or conflict. The psychic apparatus, such as it is, is directed toward a unified purpose, that of discharge, under the complete sway of the pleasure principle. With the advent of anxiety—and it does not matter for our purposes whose timetable we adhere to as to when this supervenes—there is added the capacity to anticipate and to delay, resulting in the acquisition now of conflict, but at this stage between inner (needs) and outer (sources of supply).

Perhaps we can say that the true intrapsychic conflict arises only with what Spitz (1957) calls the third organizer of the psyche, the achievement of the ideational concept of the negative and the affirmative. Although there were barriers to discharge long before this, such as the inborn defense thresholds, or the stimulus barrier, these can by no means be said to have constituted the nature of a true conflict. "The tacit assumption that the stimulus barrier represents such an opposing force is misleading. . . . The stimulus barrier is neither an obstacle, nor does it express refusal. It is a manifestation of a maturational state, namely, that at birth the sensorium is not yet cathected. . . . The stimulus barrier does not belong in the same conceptual category as negation and affirmation" (Spitz, 1957, p. 105). With the acquisition of apparatus for the latter, "beyond doubt the most spectacular intellectual and semantic achievement in early childhood" (p. 99), a new level of ego integration is reached which heralds the advent of symbolization, abstract thinking, and concept formation, and converts passivity to activity. While this new state brings with it the triumphant ability to refuse, deny, and oppose the environment, it also means, concomitantly, the same ability to oppose and countermand inner forces; indeed it brings with it an increased necessity to do so. The entire scope is enlarged, and with the increased range of ego functioning comes also greater exposure to danger, and hence a greater need, and with it a greater ability, to defend. Now there is possible, and exists, a true intrapsychic conflict.

This ontogenetic acquisition, in stages, of frustration, tension, anxiety, and conflict, has its counterparts, as described, and is recapitulated in the stratification which exists in the end result of psychic development. In regression, or in states of slow-motion psychopathology, they can be seen again in their separate states.

There are a good many further problems in relation to intrapsychic conflicts which center on the structural composition of such conflicts and the various possibilities which exist. These are of a sufficient order of magnitude and are sufficiently cohesive so that I have decided to deal with them in a separate paper (1963b).

III

The above presents the complexity of the procession of intrapsychic events in which conflict plays a part. It helps the accuracy of our understanding clearly to elucidate and to bear in mind that conflict itself is only a part of the process; that it comprises crucial links in the chain, but is not the entire process. We are apt, in the grosser clinical setting, which will be discussed below, to speak loosely of a patient being "overwhelmed by conflict," when we might more properly mean "by the unbearable tension from instinctual pressure, or by severe anxiety at the prospect of impending danger, or by an unconscious premonition of a hopelessly ineffective ego in the face of forces against which it will wither." These are all close together, to be sure, and intermingle, but it would benefit us conceptually to separate the successive components. Conflict plays an important part in all, but it is sometimes at the center, and sometimes at the periphery of the presenting segments from this etiologic chain.

The above events, although they have been teased apart and presented as a discreet succession of psychic phenomena, can and usually are compressed in time so that they may take but a moment to exert their effects. As befits the variability of human behavior, however, the temporal characteristics of this process may range from almost instantaneous action at one end to prolonged, stabilized, and almost static behavioral processes at the other. Thus, for example, we all know how in daily waking life the entire gamut from initiating stimulus to a final end point of one kind or another can take place rapidly and repeatedly, most often entirely subliminally, but at times with such telltale surface derivatives that an analyst, or sometimes even the subject, can be aware of the process. The rapidity with which such psychic processes operate are familiar to us in dream formation, where we know how a seemingly long and complex dream can occur in but a moment following the application of an experimental waking stimulus. Or the same can be attested by Fisher's experiments (1954, 1956) in which the tachistoscopic signal is incorporated instantaneously into a ready and complicated psychic functioning. Or it is known to us in reports, such as I have heard from a patient, of how, in a moment during which death is expected, the crucial events in almost an entire life history can flash before a person. My patient was lying in a trench during the Battle of the Bulge and caught sight of an enemy soldier with a bayonet in full view above him. He lived to tell me later what went on in his mind during but a moment.

When I thought of what examples I might present to illustrate some of the theoretical sequences outlined here, I chose two instances at opposite ends of the temporal spectrum. One was at the short-lived end just talked about, and consisted of an episode in which a patient, talking comfortably to a few friends, had a question, or really just a remark, directed at him, which almost instantly caused him to feel a flush. Although so brief—and I chose it because of its benignity and universality—an analysis of the intervening phases into which the resulting process could be broken down, which took place in the moment between stimulus and response, would show some fifteen or twenty separable components along the lines outlined above. To elaborate on the details of these would take another complete presentation, just as the analysis of the simplest of dreams can take a chapter.

At the other end of the spectrum, both in time as well as in severity of outcome, I thought of a woman patient who had been living for the last eight or ten years between the horns of an interminable dilemma, caught in the gripping throes of an illicit love affair. Since her nature and her history did not make her particularly facile at such an activity, the dilemma was correspondingly more meaningful and rocked her very foundations. The forces of the commanding and all-embracing intrapsychic conflict were strong on each side and fairly evenly balanced, which accounted for its tenacity and long duration. As I knew this patient I could observe many of the phases which I have described, this time not all telescoped together, but living out their filtered effects in discreetly visible segments of time. Thus one could observe either in the one hour or over a period of days or weeks how the patient would be dominated at one time by the victory and excitement of the instinctual drives, at another by the ascendancy of the nagging, tormenting, and threatening superego, and at still another overtaken by the state of sometimes controllable and sometimes uncontrollable anxiety. Some of these states were quite transitory, others lasted longer, and some were fused in various combinations. Again to illustrate the details would take time of an order which I do not have. Many other such cases could be adduced.

In a recent paper "Beyond and Between the No and the Yes" (1963a), I spoke of the realm of the ambivalent and the undecided, of those who spend their lives in this in-between region. I described between the No and the Yes the world of the "Nyeh" (meaning "Who cares?" and accompanied, as it is spoken, by a shrug of the shoulders), and gave clinical examples. Different from the true obsessional or even the ambivalent, it portrays a type of character who has developed a certain specific, albeit I believe common, character attitude toward conflicting forces.

In opposite vein from the interior view of the discreet components of intrapsychic conflict, I would like to balance these now by pointing out that at the other end of the spectrum, as in the final clinical state, we see a tendency not to dissect and to separate, but to fuse and to combine, so that the clinical picture we see is more likely to be a composite behavioral mass, composed of the various ingredients cohered together. This is what I meant at the start as a macroscopic as contrasted to a microscopic view of the ingredients and products of the conflict state.

The presenting picture might by this time be expressed by a nondescript cover-all, "I don't know, I just feel nervous," or "I just feel terrible," or "all in"—characterizations which are not necessarily evasive but are indicative of this agglutinization process. I recently described (1955), as a case in point, the multiplicity of background factors which lay behind the façade in a patient who could only describe that he felt "weird." This was again seen to be a composite compounded out of many separate ingredients which would take pages to include. The free associations of any analytic hour demonstrate this.

In keeping with the ego's synthetic function, what we are confronted with clinically is not only the symptom, which is already a compromise of impulse and defense, but a total clinical picture which might contain within it still-pressing instinctual tensions, derivatives and equivalents of anxiety itself, evidences of superego actions, and intricate secondary elaborations. The clinical picture is much like the dream, kaleidoscopic in its contents and distorted in its syntax. Besides the secondary gain of symptoms, I have described (1954b) a tertiary gain, relating to changes in body image and the concept of the self. There are probably other elaborations, as complex and as hierarchic as is the development of the psychic apparatus itself.

All this is what the patient does, with and around and on top of his conflicts. Our task as analysts is to reverse the direction, to separate, to decompose, and thus to be able to analyze. In spite of his resistance, the patient welcomes this, at least with that part of his ego which is in therapeutic alliance with us. To get at the intrapsychic conflicts, and the succession of events around them, aimed eventually at the infantile neurosis, comprises the center of our task. The uncovering of the successive events, the accurate reconstruction not only of their subtle contents, but of their syntactical interrelationships, is what our *modus operandi* consists of and what we offer to the patient, "with which to build a better life." With every degree to which we accomplish this reordering, the patient receives added hope of eventual complete understanding and mastery.

This brings me to a final point of interest. It often happens that

constructs arise, valuable and informative ones in themselves, which
are in a sense midway and intermediate formations in this psychic
unfolding, whether one thinks of it in terms of the direction from
origins toward the final presenting picture, or in the reverse, the
direction from the presenting clinical façade working backward, as
we do therapeutically, toward origins. Such constructs, which usually have abundant validity as empirical phenomena as well as widespread theoretical significance, may then be used misleadingly as a
central *explanatory* concept, presumably of irreducible import. As
examples, I would mention the very useful concepts of the self, the
self- (and object) representations, ego identity, and other closely
related phenomena, which have received a great deal of attention
in our recent literature. Broad and lucid investigations of these
psychic formations, in particular by Jacobson (1954, 1963) and by
Erikson (1950), have enriched our understanding of many aspects
of human behavior. However, there is also a tendency on the parts
of many to use such concepts without proper perspective.

Both the concept of the self and that of ego identity are in themselves complex psychic achievements, each culminating from a combination of maturational factors, conflict solutions, and conflict-free
experiences and activities. Each then in turn can serve as a nub
which contributes further either to conflictful or to conflict-free
activities, and from which emanate either bland or charged affective
experiences. They thus result from as well as contribute to complex
psychic derivatives. The major writers in these fields, referred to
above, have described extensively the weblike genetic and structural
determinants going into the formation of "the self" or "an identity"
as well as the complexities which follow from them and which depend upon their status and composition.

I can demonstrate, however, as an example of the misuse of these
concepts, the use of "disturbances in ego identity" as an ultimate
explanatory concept for a multiplicity of clinical states. While the
recognition of this type of disturbance was a valuable addition which
enriched our knowledge of psychopathology, this concept has been
used excessively and, to my mind, inappropriately, to *explain* the
origins of many symptoms, character defects, and conflict states.
Thus, not only did I recently hear a well-known psychoanalytically
influenced author in a public interview diagnose the troubles of

the modern American character as due to deficiencies in their ego identity, so that "they do not know who or what they are or what they want to be," but many analysts also offer similar explanations as the basis for many of our present-day "borderline" or character problems. At times this is done, as Waelder (1961) points out, as a defense against, or at least at the expense of, libidinal conflicts.

The same mechanism is reminiscent of the differences between psychotherapy, which stops at intermediate formulations, and psychoanalysis, which addresses itself toward the nuclear infantile conflicts as its ultimate goal (Rangell, 1954a).

I would contend instead that such ego disturbances are as much the results as they are the causes of psychopathology. Thus a disturbance in identity, just as a disturbance in the concept of the self, or of the body image, evolves first as an *outcome* of intrapsychic conflict rather than being a satisfactory explanation of the cause of it. It is then likely to serve as a further stimulus to maladaptive functioning. An age-specific "crisis" of ego identity is an intrapsychic conflict (or combination of conflicts) composed of elements specific to the instinctual and ego problems of that particular age, such as occurs notably at adolescence. Erikson (1950) frequently refers to such identity *conflicts,* and Jacobson (1963) has stressed at length such interaction.

Of greater cogency are explanations whose scope encompass the broad range of the relevant intrapsychic conflicts and which take into account the nature of the forces and the structures of which these are composed. Thus, explanations for many of the stubborn and frustrating cases on today's scene might include, among other elements, specific new types of crippling suffered by the psychic systems of persons brought up in a particular segment of today's cultural soil. I would also predict such findings as that they may not know whom to love or hate, so that instinctual object is only hesitantly attached to instinctual aim. The identifications of which the ego is a precipitate may have been spotty, shifting, and unreliable, leaving these characteristics behind in the patient's ego itself. But above all, the motives for defense are often not clear and crisply known, so that such a patient is apt to ask clingingly, "Should I be afraid? Am I supposed to feel guilty, or to be ashamed?" Such stamps cannot fail to have a profound effect upon and to bring about new qualities of intrapsychic conflict. These certainly leave their mark on the identity and the self, but secondarily, and these then further influence the course of events.

As a general formulation, however, it can be said that the etiologic core of a piece of psychopathology lies in an otherwise insoluble intrapsychic conflict, or group of conflicts, associatively linked through a series of less and less distorted derivatives to the infantile neurosis.

The goal of treatment is not the removal of all conflict or even of the potential for conflict, which is part of the human condition, but rather of the pathogenic conflicts and their derivatives, and of the entire sequential processes of which they are in the center. "Conflict-free," Erikson (1962) writes, "is a miserly way of characterizing our access . . . to the world of deeds." It is rather "an ego state of active tension" for which one strives. This, according to Jones (1942), results in the "gusto" of the healthy individual. Civilization, Freud (1930) has pointed out, owes its advances largely to the price of frustration, conflict, and neurosis. All students of the normal mind, as Jones (1942), Hartmann (1939b), Reider (1950), and Anna Freud (1959), concur in the fallacy of equating normality with the conflict-free. Gill (1963), discussing whether defenses can disappear after an analysis, writes, "In a hierarchical conception, the defenses are as much the woof of personality functioning as the drives and drive derivatives are its warp." Anna Freud (1962) emphasized the valuable and widespread use of regression, not only in the service of the creative and noble in human accomplishment, but in the daily lives of "little people."

Actually, the goal is to achieve optimum conditions for both the conflictful and the conflict-free spheres of operation, and the possibility for a mutually enhancing relationship between them. The ego should be free to benefit from the advantages accruing from each, which Kris described as stemming from peaks of comfort and discomfort in the developing infant. By various combinations of such experiences, as well as the "lowgrade discharges with lower peaks, but more steady and sustained" which Jacobson describes, there can result the "sublime pleasurable states" of the adult which have been described by Jacobson, Rapaport, Fenichel and other psychoanalytic students of affect.

BIBLIOGRAPHY

Benjamin, J. D. (1961), Some Developmental Observations Relating to the Theory of Anxiety. *J. Amer. Psa. Assn.*, IX.

Blau, A. (1952), In Support of Freud's Syndrome of 'Actual' Anxiety Neurosis. *Int. J. Psa.*, XXXIII.

Brenner, C. (1953), An Addendum to Freud's Theory of Anxiety. *Int. J. Psa.*, XXXIV.

Erikson, E. H. (1950), *Childhood and Society*. New York: W. W. Norton.

—— (1962), Reality and Actuality. *J. Amer. Psa. Assn.*, X.

Escalona, S. (1953), Emotional Development in the First Year of Life. In: *Problems of Infancy and Childhood* [Transactions of the Sixth Conference], ed. M. J. E. Senn. New York: Josiah Macy, Jr., Foundation.

Fenichel, O. (1941), The Ego and the Affects. *Psa. Rev.*, XXVIII.

—— (1945), *The Psychoanalytic Theory of Neurosis*. New York: Norton.

Fisher, C. (1954), Dreams and Perceptions. *J. Amer. Psa. Assn.*, II.

—— (1956), Dreams, Images and Perception. *J. Amer. Psa. Assn.*, IV.

Freud, A. (1936), *The Ego and the Mechanisms of Defense*. New York: International Universities Press, 1946.

—— (1956), Emotional Factors in Education. Address delivered at Western Reserve University, Cleveland, Ohio.

—— (1959), The Concept of Normality. Address delivered at the University of California at Los Angeles.

—— (1962), Regression as a Principle in Mental Development. Delivered as the C. F. Menninger Memorial Lecture at Topeka, Kansas.

Freud, S. (1900), The Interpretation of Dreams. *Standard Edition*, IV & V. London: Hogarth Press, 1953.

—— (1901), The Psychopathology of Everyday Life. *Standard Edition*, VI. London: Hogarth Press, 1960.

—— (1905), Jokes and Their Relation to the Unconscious. *Standard Edition*, VIII. London: Hogarth Press, 1960.

—— (1911), Formulations on the Two Principles of Mental Functioning. *Standard Edition*, XII. London: Hogarth Press, 1958.

—— (1914), On Narcissism: An Introduction. *Standard Edition*, XIV. London: Hogarth Press, 1957.

—— (1920), *Beyond the Pleasure Principle*. London: Hogarth Press, 1922.

—— (1923), *The Ego and the Id*. London: Hogarth Press, 1935.

—— (1926), Inhibitions, Symptoms and Anxiety. *Standard Edition*, XX. London: Hogarth Press, 1959.

—— (1930), Civilization and Its Discontents. *Standard Edition*, XXI. London: Hogarth Press, 1961.

Gill, M. M. (1963), *Topography and Systems in Psychoanalytic Theory* [Psychol. Issues, Monogr. 10]. New York: International Universities Press.

Greenacre, P. (1941), The Predisposition to Anxiety. In: *Trauma, Growth, and Personality*. New York: Norton, 1952.

Hartmann, H. (1939a), *Ego Psychology and the Problem of Adaptation*. New York: International Universities Press, 1958.

—— (1939b), Psycho-Analysis and the Concept of Health. *Int. J. Psa.*, XX.

—— (1950), Comments on the Psychoanalytic Theory of the Ego. *This Annual*, V.

—— (1952), The Mutual Influences in the Development of Ego and Id. *This Annual*, VII.

—— (1955), Notes on the Theory of Sublimation. *This Annual*, X.

—— & Kris, E., Loewenstein, R. M. (1946), Comments on the Formation of Psychic Structure. *This Annual*, II.

—— & Loewenstein, R. M. (1962), Notes on the Superego. *This Annual*, XVII.

Jacobson, E. (1952), The Speed-Pace in Psychic Discharge Processes and Its Influence on the Pleasure-Unpleasure Qualities of Affects. Paper read at the Panel on the Theory of Affects, rep. L. Rangell. *Bull. Amer. Psa. Assn.*, VIII.

—— (1953), The Affects and Their Pleasure-Unpleasure Qualities, in Relation to the Psychic Discharge Processes. In: *Drives, Affects, Behavior*, ed. R. M. Loewenstein. New York: International Universities Press.

—— (1954), The Self and the Object World. *This Annual*, IX.

—— (1963), *The Self and the Object World* [*J. Amer. Psa. Assn.*, Monogr. II]. New York: International Universities Press, in press.

Jones, E. (1942), The Concept of a Normal Mind. *Int. J. Psa.*, XXIII.

—— (1955), *The Life and Work of Sigmund Freud*, II. New York: Basic Books.

Kris, E. Quoted by S. Provence & S. Ritvo (1961).

Kubie, L. S. (1941), A Physiological Approach to the Concept of Anxiety. *Psychosom. Med.*, III.

Nemiah, J. C. (1962), The Development of the Concept of Intrapsychic Conflict in Freud's Writings. Paper read at panel on "The Significance of Intrapsychic Conflict" at the meeting of the American Psychoanalytic Association, New York.

—— (1963), Panel report: The Significance of Intrapsychic Conflict. *J. Amer. Psa. Assn.*, XI.

Provence, S. & Ritvo, S. (1961), Effects of Deprivation on Institutionalized Infants: Disturbances in Development of Relationship to Inanimate Objects. *This Annual*, XVI.

Rangell, L. (1954a), Similarities and Differences between Psychoanalysis and Dynamic Psychotherapy. *J. Amer. Psa. Assn.*, II.

—— (1954b), A Tertiary Gain of Symptoms. Paper read at the meeting of the American Psychoanalytic Association, New York.

—— (1955), On the Psychoanalytic Theory of Anxiety: A Statement of a Unitary Theory. *J. Amer. Psa. Assn.*, III.

—— (1959), The Nature of Conversion. *J. Amer. Psa. Assn.*, VII.

—— (1963a), Beyond and Between the No and the Yes. In: *Counterpoint: Libidinal Object and Subject* [A Tribute to René A. Spitz on His 75th Birthday], ed. H. S. Gaskill. New York: International Universities Press.

—— (1963b), Structural Problems in Intrapsychic Conflict. *This Annual*, XVIII.

Rapaport, D. (1951), The Autonomy of the Ego. *Bull. Menninger Clin.*, XV.

—— (1953), On the Psychoanalytic Theory of Affects. *Int. J. Psa.*, XXXIV.

—— (1958), The Theory of Ego Autonomy: A Generalization. *Bull. Menninger Clin.*, XXII.

—— (1960), On the Psychoanalytic Theory of Motivation. Unpublished manuscript.

Reider, N. (1950), The Concept of Normality. *Psa. Quart.*, XIX.

Rubinfine, D. L. (1962), Maternal Stimulation, Psychic Structure, and Early Object Relations; With Special Reference to Aggression and Denial. *This Annual*, XVII.

Schur, M. (1953), The Ego in Anxiety. In: *Drives, Affects, Behavior*, ed. R. M. Loewenstein. New York: International Universities Press.

Spitz, R. A. (1950), Anxiety in Infancy: A Study of Its Manifestations in the First Year of Life. *Int. J. Psa.*, XXXI.

—— (1957), *No and Yes: On the Beginnings of Human Communication*. New York: International Universities Press.

Waelder, R. (1961), Discussion remarks. Center for Advanced Psychoanalytic Studies. Princeton, N. J.

Winnicott, D. W. (1945), Primitive Emotional Development. *Collected Papers*. New York: Basic Books, 1958.

STRUCTURAL PROBLEMS IN INTRAPSYCHIC CONFLICT

LEO RANGELL, M.D. (Los Angeles)

In my first paper on intrapsychic conflict (1963), I attempted to assess the scope of intrapsychic conflict in human psychology, tracing briefly the historical changes and leading up to our present thinking. I then attempted to have us observe the course of an intrapsychic conflict, in somewhat stripped and "model" form, in what I called a microscopic view of the processes which take place from the time of the advent of the precipitating stimulus to its final resolution in one form or another. This was contrasted with a macroscopic view of what we see clinically and in the therapeutic situation in the manifest surface derivatives of this composite process.

This was a broad approach which traversed a long psychogenetic arc. While certain sections of this arc were selected for more detailed examination, other areas were dealt with only tangentially. Among the latter was the question of the structural characteristics of intrapsychic conflict. The present paper represents an amplification, extension, and a more detailed exposition on this particular segment of the problem. It is accorded separate treatment in the hope that the ambiguities inherent in excessive condensation can thus be avoided.

Such a more extensive treatment is also indicated to take into sufficient account the valuable new views put forth on this specific aspect by Hartmann and by Hartmann and Loewenstein. The former, in his detailed inquiry into the structure and functions of the ego (1950), and the latter, in their similar investigation more recently on the superego (1962), have pointed to the possibilities of intrasystemic conflicts within these respective agencies. The need for a proper perspective and orientation toward such conflicts came up for extensive discussion in the course of the panel on intrapsychic

conflict (see Nemiah, 1963). Hartmann, Loewenstein, and Schur
stressed that such intrasystemic conflicts may play a significant role
and be rather widespread, whereas I, supported by Arlow, suggested
certain restrictions and qualifications of this concept. This discussion
was ended by the time curfew, without, in my opinion, the opportunity for proper clarification. In addition, it was agreed that further
clarification was needed of such terms as "competition" vs. "conflict" which had been introduced into the discussion.

For these reasons, it appeared to me that a more extensive and
detailed consideration of this range of problems was in order. The
present paper is a result of my own continued thoughts on this subject, enriched by the above discussion, and after the luxury of a more
leisurely consideration of the relevant data, the theoretical problems,
and the issues involved.

I

Before embarking on my main arguments, I would like to begin
with a clarification of the terms and recapitulate a distinction I made
in the previous paper (1963) between two different types and meanings of conflict. These are (1) an opposition type, of forces battling
against each other, in hostile encounter, and (2) a dilemma type, the
need for a choice between competing alternatives. Traditionally, before the advent of the structural point of view, intrapsychic conflict
referred always to the first of these meanings, that of the opposition
between forces. Although the forces which opposed each other underwent a number of changes in our theoretical formulations, the form
had persisted. Although the second type of conflict came into play
with the advent of the tripartite structural model, with the role of
the ego as a mediator and integrator between the other two systems,
this differentiation in forms of conflict was not explicitly spelled
out. Actually even before the structural point of view, a choice
conflict had confronted the ego, or its historical precursors in our
theory, in its position between the instincts, or originally the wish
impulse, and the external world, but this was also far from clearly
stated. Incidentally, while generally overlooked in psychoanalytic
formulations, this type of "choice behavior" is what is meant routinely by the experimental psychologists in their studies of conflict,

in which the experimental animal, for example, is confronted by food together with shock or another noxious stimulus. At any rate this added variation in the form of intrapsychic conflict is to be noted as a specific addition to psychoanalytic theory which came with the structural theory, and the concurrent modifications of anxiety and instinct theories. This division of meanings of the term "conflict" must be borne in mind and is indispensable for a clear understanding of the various relationships and vicissitudes of conflict which I will trace and discuss.

I will now focus my attention on the structural problem in relation to intrapsychic conflict, the question of the locus of the conflict, and what is in conflict with what. To start my inspection of these questions, I begin with Fenichel's (1945) summary statements—he was writing, it should be remembered, about the neuroses—to the effect that "The general formulation [is that] the neurotic conflict takes place between the ego and the id." Later he added: "The superego may participate on either side in the neurotic conflict, but the formulation [still] remains valid," i.e., the conflict takes place between the ego and the id. Fenichel then arrived at the two possible formulae, of (1) the ego and the superego vs. the id, and (2) the ego vs. the id plus the superego. The latter, which he sees as occurring especially "in compulsion neuroses, and, to an extreme degree, in depressions" is clearly meant by Fenichel not as an "indecision type of conflict"—the distinction between the two types of conflict which I have described above is, as far as I can see, not made—but as a "two-front" opposition conflict. He said, "All the defense mechanisms usually employed in the fight against instincts may also become directed against the 'anti-instincts' originating in the superego. In such cases, the ego develops a double countercathexis, one against the instincts and another one against the superego."

A few years after Fenichel's summary formulations of the intersystemic conflicts, which were the only types he considered, Hartmann (1950), in a detailed investigation of the development and functions of the ego, was the first to postulate and to lay special emphasis on the possibility of intrasystemic conflicts within that agency. Pointing out that "ego interests" and many partly independent ego functions have been neglected in analysis because of their unessential role in the etiology of neurosis, Hartmann feels that such factors become more relevant when we turn to general psychology. Many ego functions oppose each other, he observes, and there are many contrasts within the ego. "Because these contests are clinically not of the same relevance as those between the ego and the id, or the ego and reality, etc., we are not used to thinking of them in terms of conflict. However, we may well describe them as intrasystemic conflicts and thus distinguish them from those other, better-known conflicts that we may designate as intersystemic." As examples of such contrasts, Hartmann lists the ego's tendency to oppose drives, while also having as a main function to help them toward gratification; its role in arriving at insight, but also in rationalizing; its promotion of objective knowledge, coupled with its participation in the conventional prejudices of the environment; and its pursuit of independent aims, while also considering the demands of other structures. Hartmann then states that "we have not yet trained ourselves to consider the ego from an intrasystemic point of view." On another occasion, Hartmann (1963) gives as a further example the conflict within the ego in the analytic situation between the wish to maintain its defenses intact and also to form a therapeutic alliance which would oppose this.

In a recent paper Hartmann and Loewenstein (1962) make similar observations in a parallel study in depth of the superego. Pointing out that "a state of peaceful coexistence between the various aspects of the superego" does not often exist, they state, "Contradictions between conscious and unconscious morality, between the demands of the ego ideal and the moral taboos, and between various parts of the individual value systems are frequent, and may be the rule. Contrasting tendencies in the superego do exist and can be compared to the intrasystemic conflicts in the ego. Still another analogy with the ego suggests itself . . . [Just as there are ego distortions, there can be superego distortions, etc.]."

II

With these nodal formulations as general background, I should now like to proceed to a detailed examination of the intersystemic relationships. Beginning with Fenichel's formulations, and extending our investigation of the structural conditions over a wider area as we are doing, to include not only the neuroses but all other types of functioning, normal and abnormal, I would make the following additional observations. First, it is well known that the formula given by Fenichel above as the significant one (i.e., "the general formulation," that between the ego and the id) is crucial not only in pathology but over the wider normal spectrum as well. The continuity between normal and pathological with regard to such basic mechanisms has been demonstrated from the beginning and is one of our basic propositions, shown by Freud in many works. The ego has a certain amount of defensive anticathectic energy deployed against a low level of instinctual pressure at all times, even in a state of quiescence, resulting in a certain optimum tension, or in fact in an amount of tension "characteristic for the organism" (Fenichel, 1945).

The same, however, is also true for the "double-front" conflict, which, by the way exists in both senses I have described, the "opposition" as well as the "either-or" or alternative type of conflict. Such a two-front concern, and in both senses, though it is present in a more acute and severe form in the pathological states mentioned by Fenichel, such as obsessional ones where the superego is especially highly charged, is also present to a much lesser degree in more benign and quiescent conditions. Thus, just as there is a certain constant tension from the ego to the id, the same is also true in the direction toward the superego. This baseline state of vigilant alertness toward the superego is due, first, to the fact that the ego never gives in completely to the dictates of the prohibitive agencies, so that it must at all times remain wary of their reactions (this includes the external world as well as the superego). Secondly, there always exists the danger of a change in the latter's rules, which might make the ego's presently acceptable relationship to the instincts no longer to their liking. Thus, while one of the ego's fronts is directed toward the instincts, the other is cathected *at all times* toward the superego (and the external world), this being a derivative and residual of the original inner-outer conflict. It is only under unfavorable conditions, e.g., when the tension between them becomes heightened or especially changeable, that there may then exist what Hartmann and Loewenstein (1962) call "a kind of ataxia—between the two systems."

This constant and baseline double-front cathexis applies in both senses of conflict which must always be considered and taken into account. Thus, there is a need for the ego not only to oppose and ward off real or potential guilt feelings which may emanate from the superego, but to be ready to make a choice between instincts and prohibitions, and to change the existing balance or status between them. During periods of increasing activation of the latter, there is an exacerbation not only of the vigilance and of the *defensive* activity at this border toward the superego, but of the "competition-conflict" state within the ego, which must concern itself again more acutely with the comparative relationships between the *two* opposing forces which press it.

To add to the two formulae given by Fenichel, it is also necessary to include certain other intersystemic possibilities which can occur when we consider a more extensive range of data and a wider arc of possible actions. Thus, for example, a third possible formula would be the superego vs. the ego and the id, in instances in which the ego elects to grant the id its wishes, taking its chances as to whether or not it may have to pay for this later, for example, by guilt feelings. Hartmann and Loewenstein (1962) refer to a similar ego action as a mechanism of "tentative temptation."

To complete the gamut, as another possible intersystemic type of conflict some authors speak of the superego being at times directly in conflict with the id. Thus Hartmann (1955) mentions that there are certain instances in which "the gates between id and superego are wide open." I would rather say, however, if we take the ego's assigned function as mediator seriously, that in the great preponderance of cases, the ego is sufficiently in control to stand effectively between these two systems. The ego's functions being what they are, the ego stands squarely in the midst of the conflict and can never really be left out of it, so that the conflict becomes one between the ego and the id or the superego or both. Through various changes and expansions in theory, the id and the superego continue to act generally upon the through the ego, rather than upon each other or directly upon external reality.

There are no doubt, however, certain exceptional states in which the pathways between id and superego do open into more direct contact. Such might be the case in certain states of ego exhaustion, for either psychological or even organic reasons, or of the ego being overwhelmed and rendered temporarily impotent, as in certain

STRUCTURAL PROBLEMS IN INTRAPSYCHIC CONFLICT 109

severe psychotic states. Perhaps then the energies do merge and intermingle, with the total organism being engulfed, flooded either simultaneously or else alternately with a voluminous surge of instinctual
cathexis, both libidinal and aggressive, and counteraggressive and
destructive thrusts by a punitive superego. The hapless ego, unable
to stem the tide or to introduce any order into the chaos, is inun-
dated with all the rest. Strictly speaking, as I pointed out previously
(1963), there is really no conflict present in the true sense of the
word during this period. There is no choice involved, and, without
an ego to exercise some control, there is really no combat conflict
present either. It is rather an orgy followed by a punishment, or the
two together, both having full access and allowed full sway. It is true
that pure cases of this are hard to observe. A mania, followed by a
depression, may be a close and related example, but this is a special
form with other characteristic economic conditions and really does
not quite fulfill the above requirements. Here the ego, though battered and disorganized, is nevertheless holding on, and the conflict
takes the form of opposing and giving in to both, but alternately and
exclusively over longer periods of time. When each has had enough,
or both id and superego have been spent, the ego, if it still survives,
may begin to "restitute" itself. For a while, though, it is like a country which has been occupied beginning to get on its own feet again.

Thus the intersystemic oppositional encounters can occur in a
variety of combinations. It can be illuminating to our subject to
make some quantitative and comparative observations as well as
qualitative ones. While the superego can typically, as described
above, be in opposition to the ego, and in certain instances which
have been mentioned can possibly be in more direct opposition to
the id as well, the ego, in accordance with our major insights into
the nature of intrapsychic conflict, can be classically locked in intersystemic conflict with either or both of its other two structural partners. Probably the most common dynamic and structural interplay,
however, both in the psychopathological spectrum and in the normally maintained intersystemic balance, is the state of conflict between the ego and the id. For this reason Fenichel accords it the
major role in his summary formulation in reviewing the psychoanalytic theory of neurosis. I do not think that this emphasis is due
basically to the historical sequence of the development of our science,

starting as it did with the neuroses, but that this view is confirmed
and maintained by our subsequently wider orientation and experience, over a broader clinical front as well as after the inclusion of
normal psychology. Such economic relationships derive ultimately
from the nature of the forces involved, the unitary forward urge of
the instinctual id and the central role of the ego in judging, guarding, and guiding this force. In a quantitative sense a dominant function of the ego is its permanent management of instinctual pressure.
There is of course a more active, volatile, and "hotter" conflict going
on at this border in the case of pathology, and a "colder" war, more
quiescent and composed, operating with more neutralized instinctual
as well as ego energies, in the "normal" intersystemic balance.

To make a further quantitative comparison, I would say that the
ego-id opposition is the more usual and constant one, while the intersystemic ego-superego tension is, comparatively speaking, more likely
to be one of vigilant alertness rather than of constant interim interaction. The typical situation for the ego would probably be, under
usual circumstances, to have a small but steady detachment of countercathectic energy deployed at the border of the id, but relatively
speaking only a watchful eye perched toward the superego, ready
but not equally in *action* as is the case toward the id. Even in the
case of pathology, where there is more activity on both of these
fronts than there is in the relatively quiescent normal states, Fenichel
has pointed out how much less frequently an ego-superego conflict
endures than is the case between ego and id. It would thus appear
that the superego is more apt to do its work and then rest than is the
more constantly and easily arousable instinctual reservoir of the id.
It is, however, as Schafer (1960) correctly points out, "ever on duty."
There are nevertheless unusual cases in which this economic ratio
and mode of action is reversed.

Fenichel's observation, that there is a general optimum tension
"characteristic for the organism," can no doubt be further broken
down with regard to the more specific internal components. It is
likely that this includes a characteristic amount and quality of intersystemic tension among all three of the psychic structures, as well as optimum and characteristic intrasystemic tensions within each of them.
Hartmann and Loewenstein (1962) point out specifically, for example, for the superego that "the scope of these [ego-superego] tensions

tend to become a characteristic of the individual," and that "what matters above all is the degree to which the two agencies can collaborate, while at the same time preserving the optimum tension between them." Such a characteristic and optimum balance exists between each pair of the three corners of the structural interplay. Internal and external impingements that are there in copious and ever-changing combinations result in the various fluctuations and vicissitudes of these optimal intersystemic balances, which are then translated into adaptive or maladaptive responses.

III

I would like to turn now from the intersystemic relationships to consider the situation of the possible intrasystemic conflicts which have been introduced and referred to above. While Hartmann and Loewenstein contributed these new suggestions as part of broader studies centering on the contents and functions of the ego and superego, I will focus more centrally on these specific observations concerning types of conflict, and try to follow in detail the resulting implications. In doing so, we will find, I believe, that while leading to new discoveries, these valuable new insights also bring with them certain problems which need to be considered and which call for a number of concomitant clarifications and decisions.

I would like to approach the relationships between intrasystemic components from several different directions. As a first observation, I would point out that the description of the "decision-making" type of conflict, which I have spelled out, is in harmony with the concept of intrasystemic conflict, in that its locus of action is certainly entirely intrasystemic. Although the factors which have brought about the need for decision have impinged from intersystemic directions, the resulting dynamic change following ego absorption of these stimuli is an intrasystemic one within the confines of the ego system itself. In fact, as stated above, it has not been sufficiently appreciated that such an intrasystemic state of being "in conflict" came into being at once with Freud's description of the tripartite structural model, with the role of mediator being assigned to the ego. This intrasystemic role existed despite the fact, as Hartmann (1950) states, that "the intrasystemic correlations and conflicts in the ego have hardly ever been

consistently studied." Moreover, the frequent description of clinical
states as "a split in the ego" attests further to the recognition of such
an intra-ego condition.

Considering first the situation of the ego, it will be seen to be
different in crucial respects from what prevails in the other two
systems. Although the concept of multiple functions of the ego has
been considerably stressed (Waelder, 1930), and the fact that these
diverse functions operate in different and not entirely harmonious
directions has been increasingly known, Hartmann is correct that an
appreciation that these internal component functions, or contents,
can be in conflict has been lagging. In point of fact, the ego, being
the recipient of messages from its two flanking systems, demands from
one and warnings or prohibitions (if not permission) from the other,
and having taken into itself these requests and dictates, now has a
problem or conflict within, and may, in instances where no easy
decision or solution is forthcoming, become, at least for a time, a
house divided within itself. In this sense there is, to be sure, with
great ubiquitousness, an intrasystemic conflict within the ego. After,
and as a result of, a choice, and concomitant with its decided course
of action, there may then ensue an intersystemic conflict as well,
now one of the opposition type, against the id, or against the superego, or against both. In many instances, courses are mapped out
through which the ego manages deftly to be in conflict with neither,
having chosen actions or attitudes which can satisfy both contending
parties.

To consider further the intrasystemic state within the ego, it is
certainly possible that, just as the ego is divided within itself between
elements representing the id and others representing the superego
(or external reality), so there may be similar intrasystemic ego conflicts about other contrasting or conflicting pairs within it. Thus the
critical ego may be called upon to decide between internal, conflicting and contradictory self-interests, or between interests of security
and dependence vs. the tendency toward independence, or between
opposing and contradictory ego value factors. In all such cases, we
know that there is a specific and indeed major ego function, or rather
series of functions, which have to do with scanning, judging, and
then deciding whether the objects or contents which are thus put
to the test are external to it, in other systems, or other functions or

contents within the borders of its own system. Or perhaps we may think that it is the matrix of the ego, the interstitial connecting portions which remain after all of its multiple other specific functions are accounted for and taken away, which is charged with this final function of deciding. (I wish to make it clear that I do not have in mind any physical or organic matrix here, lest it be thought that the language used suggests this.) Or perhaps we think of it as part of the organizing, or integrating, or synthesizing function of the ego to render such a final decision. Whether we think of it as a separate function, or as a global and integrating one connecting all the others,[1] it is plainly our common usage and intent to assign such a "deciding" and coordinating function within the ego—and I might add, only within the ego.

This leads to the following thoughts. If we accept this to be the case, how does this reflect on the concept of possible intrasystemic "conflicts" within either of the other two systems? Hartmann and Loewenstein (1962) quite correctly point to contrasting and contradictory elements, or even pairs, existing within the superego, or within the ego ideal, or between the ego ideal and the superego (considering these both within the same system). Examples of these have been quoted above. Such contrasting tendencies, these authors suggest, "can be compared to the intrasystemic conflicts in the ego."

But to pursue this idea further, if we consider the only two possible modes of conflict as described above, we might well ask the following. With regard first to the "alternative" type of conflict formation, to which I am momentarily limiting my discussion, does the superego include within its scope a specific function of choosing or deciding (whether such a function resides in a special segment or in the matrix of the superego, as described above for the ego)? Would not such an activity or a responsibility be a prerequisite for the ability to "be in conflict?" Hartmann and Loewenstein (1962) ask a similar question about whether the function or capacity of "knowing" can reside in any other system but the ego, a question which, I might indicate in advance, they answer in the negative. Is this the same with regard to "deciding," and is this too a function left squarely and exclusively to the much overworked ego? Clearly an

[1] This discussion will be further continued below.

answer to the question of possible superego conflicts hinges to a large measure on how the first issue is resolved.

Thus, when contrasting or contradictory views exist, either between the ego ideal and superego, or from opposite values within the superego itself, is it the superego within which an intrasystemic conflict resides, or are all the contents presented to the ego, to add only to the complexity of *its* ultimate problem of synthesis and choice? There are many ways in which one can look at this. Can it perhaps be that there is first an intrasystemic conflict within the superego, which is either solved there *or else* transferred *in toto* to the ego, for it to have the problem and to decide? Or is it solved in steps, partially in one, and then finished in the other? Or does the superego always first "decide" and then present only its decision, the final choice, to the ego? Certainly I do not feel that the latter corresponds with clinical evidence.

Many of these questions are difficult to answer, and depend on the definitions and the historical usages with which these concepts must be consistent. Indeed, it may be felt, and with some justification, that it does not matter much and that all emerging phenomena can be explained either way. Nevertheless, if one wishes theoretical rigor and consistency, one has no choice but to pursue even what may become a thin line as far as it will go. I cannot offer unequivocal answers but merely wish to confront the questions which arise and which need to be followed through. Our increasing knowledge leads to further probing which brings with it these perplexities. I would like at this point to try not to give a definitive answer to the basic question I have posed but to approach the solution in another way, namely, to describe in succession two alternative ways of looking at this situation. We could then see with each possible answer what falls into place as evidence for the view, what elements, if any, are solved by it, whether any new or secondary problems arise, and whether any inconsistencies come into play with any established viewpoints. We might then be in a better position to arrive at a consensus.

IV

As a first alternative, I propose that we consider what would appear to be, from a total view, an entirely logical position: that the function of choice or consistency is left squarely and exclusively to the domain of the ego. In favor of this easily defended view, I believe that it is consistent with our historical as well as our present attitudes toward the various structural divisions and the functions comprising them to reserve the most definitive, and by this way of thinking the only, function of "deciding," as Hartmann and Loewenstein (1962) say about "knowing," to the ego. This then would make *ego*, and only the ego, the psychic structure which can be undecided, or "in conflict," in the sense which we are now speaking. It would follow from this view that the superego would offer whichever of its elements are sufficiently cathected to the ego, for the *ego's* use and consideration and choice. If such elements of the superego and the ego ideal are all of one persuasion, the task of the ego is relatively simple. It at least knows what the terms are, from the side of the moralizing and directing agency. If, however, the latter presents to the ego a composite of incompatibilities, it is the ego which faces the additional burden, having to amalgamate these with the further values and interests existing within its own borders.

With this view, one could also say, indeed one would have to say, that there can be contrasting or even contradictory elements within the superego without their being in conflict with each other. They neither oppose each other nor does the system have to make a choice, for they can exist, side by side, with each demanding its due, and both can come out. In accordance with a generally held proposition, the superego in this respect would be said to share a specific characteristic with the id, just as it has many other qualities in common with it: if "There are no contradictions within the id," there are none within the superego. It could further be reasoned that contrasting and even contradictory elements not only exist but make up the very essence of the total system superego, and are responsible for the variability and flexibility and even unpredictability of its responses. Thus ambivalence could occur not only from instinctual contradictions but also from opposite superego attitudes, existing side by side in a nonexclusive relationship. If such contradictions are passed on to the ego, whether from the id or the superego, it would be the work of the ego to decide, to choose, or to synthesize, either eliminating one or the other of the contradictory elements, or to fuse, amalgamate, or compromise in some way. We have indeed in the past not assigned such a task, or such a function, to either the id or the superego.

This is in harmony with the view expressed by Hartmann (1960) that the *scrutiny* of moral values, or what "we might designate as *value testing*," in the service of the integration and organization of action, "is, very likely, a function of the ego" (p. 51). As further "evidence" and substantiating reasoning for this point of view, one would adduce the other known areas in common between the superego and the id. Thus the superego is known to operate with and to have at its disposal aggressive instinctual energy as well as libidinal energy (albeit it can and does operate also with neutralized energy). There is, moreover, the statement by Freud, in a passage which emphasizes the developmental continuity between the superego and the id: "Whereas the ego is essentially the representative of the external world, of reality, the super-ego stands in contrast to it as the representative of the internal world, of the id" (1923, p. 36). Thus it could be argued that the superego would share essential characteristics with the id, including in this connection its basic tolerance for contradictions.

At this point I would like to interject in a descriptive way that we can visualize the following as taking place during superego functioning. The superego can be thought of as enduring in a relatively passive way the cathexis of its "opinion" function. The latter, I submit, occurs automatically, and certain ingredients of its opinion repertoire are awakened and charged, in accordance with the meanings to it of the current act, or intention, of the instinctual push, or the reality event, or the ego decision. This repertoire consists of a spectrum of attitudes, or value judgments, which exist side by side, but any one of which, or more usually any complex combination, may be cathected at any one time or by any one event. The automatic nature of this arousal mechanism is similar in quality to the automatic occurrence of signal anxiety in the ego. These "opinions" are in fact to the superego what signal anxiety is to the ego. The nature and content of this automatic choice, as to which component or combination of superego opinions will be cathected, depend, of course, on the entire ontogenetic history and on the state of associative readiness of the various components in the same way as the previous history and former sensitizations will determine whether and which stimuli can elicit signal anxiety in the ego. Schafer (1960), in his excellent review of the characteristics of the superego, makes similar reference to the use of the signal concept in superego functioning and that the superego "can discriminate degrees of evil and react accordingly."

To be sure, then, the direction-giving, or the prohibiting, or above all the enforcing functions of the superego require the greatest degree of activity on its part, for which an appropriate amount of aggressive energy, either neutralized or unneutralized, lies at its disposal. The controversial nub which enters the picture here is whether, in addition to these active functions just named, there is also the activity of choosing one out of a number of possibly contradictory opinions or values, or of effecting a mean between them. According to the point of view being expounded at this juncture, such a function is *not* included in this repertoire, so that the subsequent activity response is stimulated by the entire range of the value spectrum which has been aroused and activated. The nature and amount of such subsequent activity can be extremely variable, both from a total point of view and selectively for each of the functions named—directing, prohibiting, enforcing, etc.

In general, in this view, the process of superego activation is such that its opinions are passively aroused, without its further shaping them, after which it does what it can actively with them, which may be much or little. This process would not include or allow for its "being in conflict," although its contents may be such as to turn out to be mighty confusing to the ego.

V

Thus far the point of view whose tenets and implications I have been tracing and following through and which seems to be restricting intrasystemic conflict to the ego applies only to the dilemma or choice sense of the meaning of conflict. We should now include, within the scope of this purview, conflict in the more traditional sense, that of opposition. Just as intersystemic conflicts have been traditionally composed of the mutual opposition of forces, so, as a corollary, opposition conflicts have always been thought of as intersystemic—until the recent suggestions of the intrasystemic locus. Let

us therefore extend our scope and see how our alternative views fare
in covering this possibility as well.

I therefore turn now to the interesting and significant question
whether the "opposition" type of conflicts can occur intrasystemically. I have developed the theme and offered the proposition that
the intrasystemic "alternative-choice" type of conflict does exist very
definitely and even characteristically within the ego, while for the
time being I have regarded its existence in the superego or the id as
more dubious. We are nevertheless faced with the question whether
the original opposition type of conflict does not in fact exist intrasystemically—in any of the systems, or in all of them, or selectively, as the
first type, in one or more. Or is the possibility of intrasystemic conflict
limited to the dilemma or choice type? It is indeed the direct-contact
opposition type of conflict which I believe Hartmann, Loewenstein,
Jacobson (1963), and other writers have had in mind exclusively in
proposing and giving examples of intrasystemic conflicts. These authors speak uniformly of such conflicts as being *between* the contrasting pairs rather than in the superego, or ego, *about* them. Hartmann
(1950), in fact, states the matter quite explicitly, as "ego functions
opposing *each other*" [my italics]. In the absence of any statements
of qualifying or contrary nature, we can only assume that the *form*
of the conflict was carried over from the intersystemic model as one
between opposing forces. Thus when Hartmann or Jacobson speak
of contradictory self-interests or of conflicting values within the
system ego, or when Hartmann and Loewenstein list ego ideals
which conflict with each other, or superego values or judgments
which are in direct contrast and therefore in mutual opposition,
they mean, I believe, that the energic forces of one of each pair are
directly pitted against the forces of the other, each one tending thus
to negate or obliterate the other. Either the stronger of the two, or
in some cases a compromise and resultant of both, emerges as the
force which will then be presented in the intersystemic confronta-
tion. This is in fact, I submit, what has routinely been meant by
most authors who write about intrapsychic conflict, not having had
in mind the distinction which I have been making here.

Do such intrasystemic confrontations and oppositions actually
take place? In considering first the case of the id, while some authors
refer quite commonly to instinctual conflicts, for example, between

the libidinal and the aggressive drives, or between many other possible pairs of polar opposites (Alexander, 1933; Anna Freud, 1936),
it is the more general conception, it seems to me, as stated most
explicitly by Fenichel, that instinctual drives exist side by side and
are directed only toward discharge, rather than in any way toward
each other. "Instincts contradictory in aim, without . . . reinforcement by the defending ego, would not conflict with each other. Within the realm of the id there is no conception of contradiction, logical
order is here nonexistent. Instincts contradictory in aim can be
satisfied one after the other, sometimes even simultaneously." This is
Fenichel's rejoinder (1945), with which I agree, to the idea advanced
by some that heterosexuality can oppose homosexuality, or sadism
be in conflict with masochism, or passivity with activity, etc. (Alexander, 1933). "An instinctual conflict . . . is always a structural conflict as well; one of the conflicting instincts represents the ego . . .
[or is] strengthened for purposes of ego defense (Fenichel, 1945, p.
130). Note here that the ego, another system, chooses one instinctual
stream, and opposes another, *which keeps pressing*. It is the latter
force, continuing against the ego, which makes for the conflict.

Alexander (1933) has given the most explicit description of what
he calls instinctual as contrasted to structural conflicts. He cites, in
addition to the dichotomies named above, many other pairs of instinctual opposites, such as expulsive-receptive, masculine-feminine,
exhibitionistic-voyeuristic, etc. But his subsequent descriptions
patently indicate the structural participation when, in each instance,
he speaks of "[one] striving [being] rejected because it is incompatible with another, *ego-acceptable* one which determines the *ego's*
actual attitude" (my italics). It is the ego which is clearly one of the
contending arms in the conflict. Similarly, while Anna Freud (1936)
also gives a place, as does Alexander, to "conflicts between opposite
[instinctual] tendencies," she attributes these to "the *ego's* need for
synthesis," includes these under a heading of "defense *against instinct*" (my italics), and points out that the ego wards off one or the
other of the opposing impulses or else arrives at a compromise between them.

In this context, however, we must consider the concept of drive
fusion, which does visualize a coming together and thereby a mutual
influencing of one drive by the other. But fusion is a complementary

and harmonious blending, rather than a conflict, or due to a conflict. "That this takes place regularly and very extensively is an assumption indispensable to our conception" (Freud, 1923). Correspondingly, in the regressive state of defusion, the two components again exist side by side, and press for independent and separate discharge, accounting for the strength and hence the danger emanating from each.

Hartmann, while describing such direct conflicts as occurring intrasystemically between contiguous tendencies within the ego and within the superego, has nevertheless given some support to the above view in the case of the id, stating that such a view about the relationship between contrasting instinctual tendencies can be argued with merit (Hartmann, 1963). Thus, in summary, with regard to id components, I support the view which holds that neither a conflict of choice nor one of opposing forces can be held to exist within the id in accordance with our total prevalent concept of the psychological functioning of this agency.

I will now turn to the superego, which in this connection I propose to discuss separately from the ego, since it is likely that crucial differences might again exist between the two, and that different considerations might apply. We now face a slight variation of the question we asked before regarding the superego. Whereas previously I was concerned with whether the superego had the capacity to be in conflict over contrasting elements existing within it, I am now asking whether the *elements* can be in conflict *with each other*. With regard to the id, my answer has been that this cannot be so, i.e., that here the instinctual drives do not oppose *each other*. Can this be otherwise for superego elements? Can one value within the superego attack or defend against another? Does a function of defense, or of directional assertion, lie within the element itself. Or, for that matter, does a function of defense exist within the superego?

To answer these questions in order, I would venture first that there is no reason why we should assume or assign a more definitive function along these lines to *an element* of the superego than we feel to exist in an instinctual drive. There is not that much autonomy or complexity within the single value judgment or moral edict to direct itself against another, nor for that matter to defend itself against a force from another. This might be done by the entire system, or structure, or aggregate of functions, which can direct itself against, or oppose another system, and which has the energy and the functions with which to do so. But can this be done by one of its parts? It would stretch what we think to be the function of a part to assume that it can, and I believe that it would fit better with our way of thinking to answer in the negative. A certain amount of complexity, of differentiation, and of structural development is necessary for the capacity to engage in psychic conflict. Spitz (1959) points out that conflict in the human is "in terms of highly structured intrapsychic components" (p. 79).

An intrasystemic opposition conflict, however, is conceivable in still another way. If the parent structure is able to, or indeed must, choose between contrasting or contradictory elements within it, and the rejected element or elements *keep pressing* for discharge, or for attention cathexis, from the matrix of the system, or from its aggregate functions, there would then be the background for another opposition type of conflict—intrasystemic in locus—between the parent body and one of its parts. This would be a replica in miniature of what takes place intersystemically, when the ego, after *choosing* one between id and superego, then often finds itself in an *opposition* conflict with the other.

With regard to the superego I have for the time being proceeded on the assumption that order, and therefore choice, is not among its functions. The same reasoning could apply simultaneously with regard to defense. Can the superego employ a defense against an undesirable element within it? We come again to the same principle as before, whether the superego can perform a function ordinarily thought of as reserved for the ego—in this case the function of defense. I would suggest that whatever answer we pursue for one question, i.e., that of an organizing type of function within the superego, would apply similarly to the other, i.e., the question of defense. Thus pursuing my present line of argument, just as an organizing and synthesizing function is being reserved for the ego, and denied in the id and superego, so the function of defense would also be solely an ego function and activity. Hence, intrasystemic conflict of either type, of choice or of opposition, does not occur in either the id or the superego. This would follow from the assumptions made thus far, which I consider to be consonant with other parts of our present theoretical formulations.

On the other hand, with regard to the disputed and controversial functions which I have been examining in connection with id and superego, the entire concerted view of our literature converges much more uniformly about my views of these functions within the ego. Both the functions of deciding and of instituting defense reside squarely in the middle of the spectrum of the ego's activities, thus giving to it a central role in situations of conflict. Since we envisage unequivocally that the ego encompasses, and is centrally responsible for, the maintenance of order, logic, and consistency; of being the mediator between the various and frequently incompatible influences impinging upon it from all directions, not only from id and superego but continuously from the external world as well, and from multiple and variable components within each—the ego must and does have commensurate power and resources to deal with these. Since the power of defense and opposition is centrally and unbegrudgingly vested in it in order to achieve these functions, and the energy to carry these out is part of its armamentarium, it is easy to conceive, and makes for clarity and consistency, that the ego can apply such power and use such energy in all and any directions, wherever needed or wherever it can be of utility. This would apply, and would be possible in the case of the ego, in the case of intrasystemic divisions and oppositions, as well as in intersystemic ones.

Applying the same schema to the ego which I have just used for the other systems to encompass all possible mechanisms for the formation of intrasystemic conflicts, I would say that the following obtains. The same reasoning would apply here as elsewhere with regard to the individual elements themselves, i.e., they can neither choose, nor oppose, nor defend, and hence can hardly in themselves be "in conflict." This would apply to the individual "ego interests" or specific ego functions or activities. Thus I cannot see, as Hartmann says, that ego components can "oppose each other." However, the ego itself can be "in conflict" about any contradictory or inconsistent parts within it just as about any incompatible forces outside of it. As a result of such conflict, it can and does make a choice or compromise. It may then encounter continued pressure from a rejected internal element, as it does from a denied or thwarted external one. Defensive energy can then conceivably be deployed against such pressure, setting up in this way an oppositional type of intrasystemic conflict.

Thus it is entirely logical and consistent with the roles and functions which we have assigned to the individual systems to consider that the ego can suffer as well as create conflicts within its borders as well as between itself and other parts. In this way, intrasystemic conflicts can come to abide within the ego involving any of its multiple functions or its varying contents or interests, with defensive anticathectic energy being employed at the borders toward any such incompatible elements, whenever such is necessary to bring about or maintain effective thinking, behavior, or even affects. The ego has the function, the responsibility, and the power to experience, create, and solve such multiple, varied, and widespread conflict situations. Such intra-ego processes complement parallel intersystemic ego activities in the service of achieving increasing neutralization, the advance and dominance of secondary-process modes of thinking and action, and the achievement of order, logic, modulation, and subtlety, all of which are an expression of the firm dominance of an effective ego extending its influence and its power over a willing and cooperative and not-too-rebellious id and superego.

In the interest of greater precision and after more careful thought I would add the following about the ego's choice or decision-making function. While we have thus far not been quite exact in defining the relationship of this activity to its contiguous ego functions, I would have us now take a clearer stand and to recognize that this function is actually separate from, although closely related to, the functions of organization or synthesis. Closer attention results frequently in our decomposing various functions or contents which on a grosser view we are apt to consider as one. Thus *to choose* is not the same as to organize, and neither are the same as to synthesize. Actually even to decide is somewhat different from choosing, although one may follow closely upon the heels of the other. Hartmann (1947) has asked for the same exactitude when he suggested than an organizing function be separated and delineated from the synthesizing function as Nunberg (1931) described it. Hartmann pointed out that organization may at one time consist of synthesis and integration, while it may at another emphasize primarily a differentiating process. The latter has recently been singled out and described in

more elaborate detail by Hacker (1962) as a most important discriminatory function of the ego. While this process is characterized as
almost synonymous and sometimes interchangeable with selection,
deciding, and choosing, I would have us note that though contiguous
and interdependent, these functions are still not the same. The
ability to discriminate is a precondition for the capacity to choose,
but the former may exist without the latter. Peto (1960, 1961) has
suggested and described a closely related but still different function
of the ego which he calls fragmentation. This function aims at
splintering apart various complexes, also serves differentiation, and
is postulated as a precondition for the operation of defenses.

The function of effecting a choice in the face of a dilemma, of
making a decision in the case of competing alternatives, is an activity
which I think should be spelled out on its own and given a central
and prominent place in the multiple ensemble of ego functions.
While such activity has certainly been implicit in general usage,
it has heretofore been assumed in a rather nondescript and imprecise way as part either of the ego's mediating role or of its general
organizing tendency. In keeping with our procedure of being ever
more precise as we subject each specific item to closer and more
individual inspection, I would suggest separation of this specific
function and recognition of its importance not only as a discreet but
as a crucial and indispensable link. The sequential chain in which
it plays a part runs: filtering, scanning, judging, deciding, *choosing*
—and then executing its choice and decision, via defense, or adaptation, motility, etc. All of these are subsidiary methods which aid and
enhance the more global functions of coordination, synthesis, and
organization. While these functions are all closely interwoven and
part of one continuous action, we come to know their individuality
by virtue of one or the other undergoing an exceptional development, either in a positive or in a negative direction. Thus any particular aspect of these sequential functions can become either especially highly developed or singularly deficient. Each separate ego
function, as Hartmann has pointed out, can undergo its own selective
development, both maturationally and experientially. Thus we see
people who have good judgment but are slow or even paralyzed in
decision-making, and others who can effect choices with dispatch

but on the basis of incomplete appraisal or poorly conceived judg-mental action.

It is to be noted that this function of choice is not limited to conflict situations; it is operative just as assiduously in furthering conflict-free interests and activities, such as any kind of coping, or most decisively in problem solving. The latter can operate with essentially neutralized energy—and may in the individual case be a highly developed and effective capacity quite independently of any involvement in intersystemic or intrasystemic conflict. In fact, the onset of the latter may blunt its effective operation in the former sphere. This special capacity of "decision-making" has of late come in for a great deal of attention in its many important and derivative aspects on the social front. Studies relative to its various manifesta-tions are of active interest to experimental psychologists as well as to sociologists and political scientists. From the psychoanalytic orienta-tion, we are concerned with the locus of its origins and its micro-scopic aspects, as a discreet and central and important ego function.

Following this digression, I would further summarize: by adher-ing to the propositions which I have chosen above, I come to the conclusion that intrasystemic conflicts of both the "opposition" and the "choice" types can and do exist within the ego, but it is not possible to support the existence of either of these within either of the other two systems.

Another line of thought leading in the same direction is that anxiety too, which is after all to the greatest degree responsible for conflict (and is—at least in the types of conflict to which we have hitherto paid the most attention—in reciprocal relationship with it [see Rangell, 1963]), resides only in the ego, and neither in the id nor in the superego. The same is true for the related series of anxiety derivatives or equivalents, the other motives for defense, as guilt, shame, disgust, etc. The function of *being in* conflict—over contra-dictory forces—is furthermore so close to the function of *feeling* conflict that it is eminently logical that these both reside within the same agency. (Although we refer to the "feeling" of conflict, of course the whole process may be, and usually is, unconscious.) Thus the agency which experiences anxiety, and which is the seat of the affects, and which has the functions of knowing and judgment and cognition in general, all of which are so much part of one close and continuous process,[2] is by the same token the seat of conflict, whether the latter is entirely encompassed within its borders, or extends from it to other parts. For such conflict to be able to reside similarly within another agency would presuppose that the latter would be similarly endowed with a motive, such as anxiety, or a need for synthesis or organization, all of which we consider as functions of the ego and not of either of the other structures.

It would follow from the pursuit of the present line of reasoning that an intrapsychic conflict must involve the ego, although it may come from and emanate toward some other part as well (the exceptional instances in which the ego can be bypassed or at least its role diminished have been described previously). At least such conflict cannot be complete within another system.

VI

However, I have until now in one sense been taking the role of the Devil's advocate. I have done so both because the position taken stood on a logical base, and because it led to a number of insights and conclusions which I think are incontrovertible and will stand. However, now that I have presented the logical sequelae of a strict and formalistic view, one which I believe stemmed from certain of our accepted and established propositions, I would like to show where I think we must bend and change our views to a certain degree. I have developed these thoughts thus far based on the assumption of a strict division between ego and superego in respect to certain crucial functions. Further thoughts, however, show that the matter is not thereby put to rest—on the contrary, certain objections arise which make it necessary that we now consider an alternative view. These objections stem from two sources, one clinical-empirical and the other theoretical.

First, on a clinical and experiential basis, it does not seem that "there are no contradictions within the superego," as is true for the id. This does not seem to fit what we actually see. If we speak, in some cases of psychopathy, of a "corrupt superego," which can tolerate with ease mutual contradictions, and in other cases of psychosis

---

[2] I have described this process in its "microscopic" aspects in my accompanying paper (1963).

of "an archaic superego" (Hoedemaker, 1955; Wexler, 1952), which also encompasses within it regressively defused and violently contrasting elements, and in still other instances, in certain character types, of "lacunae in the superego," do we not imply that in the "normal" development the superego does not tolerate such divisiveness within itself? I believe that clinically this is true. Rather than presenting to the ego a group of conflicting values, which we would expect and discern quite routinely from the assumptions we have made above, it appears more usual that the superego is more nearly "of one mind" in its value judgments. It does not seem to me that this can all be attributed to subsequent ego activity, but that an effort or striving toward uniformity and cohesiveness is more likely operative in both systems.

The same can be gleaned on certain theoretical grounds. Much evidence points to the fact that there is no such strict cleavage between ego and superego as I have here assumed, and that my formulations, although stemming from commonly accepted tenets, are predicated on a degree of purity which actually does not exist. The fact is that there is to a large degree a continuum in functioning between ego, ego ideal, and superego, as brought out by many writers (Freud, 1920, 1921, 1923; Jacobson, 1963; Bing et al., 1959), so that the cleavage between ego and superego is not as sharp as that between the ego and the id. The functions of judging, value-giving, establishing directions, and others bridge across from one to the other. Thus, in spite of the developmental continuity between superego and id, the superego has more separateness from the id than it has in common with it. It is after all a superordinate structure, not only to the id but in many ways even to the ego. The superego is, moreover, in its basic origins the internalized morality of the external world, so that its relationship to reality can never be disregarded. Complete contrariness, a haven for contradictions, and an utter disregard for external reality can thus be said to exist with consistency only in the id, but neither in the ego nor in the superego.

I believe that these considerations are of sufficient cogency to necessitate a change in my position. It cannot be so clean-cut that all psychic elements are in a state of total haphazard disarray and in mutual contradictions until and only until they reach and are acted upon by the ego. I believe that such an economic and dynamic state can be said to be characteristic of the id, but I do not believe that it is either useful or correct to hold that a similar state is characteristic for the superego—after all man's most highly developed and civilized agency, his "higher nature" (Freud, 1923), upon which his dignity, morality, and higher ethical values depend (Freud, 1920, 1923).

I would therefore conclude the following: we must assume some concern with order and consistency to exist within the superego; from this it follows that there is, at least to a certain degree, an organizing and synthesizing function within the superego and the ability to exercise a choice in order to effect this; therefore the superego *can* suffer internal intrasystemic conflicts when such cohesiveness and uniformity are either disrupted or nonexistent. These assumptions would be consonant with many of the facts enumerated above and would resolve and clarify some inconsistent areas. The superego would carry some of these functions along in its development *out of* the ego (Freud, 1920, 1921, 1923), including to some degree the functions of defense and of choice to carry on and resolve the above-named inner conflicts. Thus a sharp cleavage in its functions from the ego would be seen *not* to exist, which is consonant with Freud's descriptions of the superego as a differentiated grade "within the ego," and is in keeping with the efforts of some authors (Bing et al., 1959) actually to merge its functions, via the ego ideal, with the ego.

I would further vouchsafe, however, that we must now make some quantitative and economic comparisons of such activities within the superego as compared to the ego. Although there is this continuum and overlap in function, there is still a distinct difference in centrality and degree which makes for the differences between the two systems. While a synthetic and integrating function is a central activity within the ego, it is only secondary and peripheral to the superego, which is still basically concerned with its value and direction-giving functions. The former is subordinate to and only in the service of the latter in the superego. While the ego has the task of synthesizing elements from throughout the psychic apparatus, the superego does so only, if at all, to the extent that this is necessary within its own borders, and to perform its own central functions. When such intrasystemic incompatibilities or conflicts fail to be solved within the superego, it is most likely the case that they are then passed on to the ego for further and final action, in a manner which Hacker (1962) refers to as "a fluid division of labor between superego and ego." In this connection I would agree with Hartmann and Loewenstein (1962), and with Bak (1952), who, commenting on the pathology of schizophrenia, point out that "what is often called the 'disintegration' of the superego in schizophrenia—is at least partly traceable to the deficiencies in the ego." These authors attribute the central role in the pathology of schizophrenia "to the impairment of certain ego functions."

These conclusions bear out the suggestion of Hartmann and Loewenstein (1962) that intrasystemic conflicts can indeed exist within the superego. Unlike their formulation, however, such conflict would be envisaged as existing not between the contrasting elements but rather in two stages. First there is the conflict within the superego itself *about* such incompatible elements, due to a violation of its need for order and consistency, and second a conflict between the total superego and the internal element which it has decided to reject. The quantitative differences with respect to the degree and centrality of such activities which I have pointed out in superego as compared to ego functioning may correspond with Hartmann and Loewenstein's apparent reservations when they state that such contrasting tendencies in the superego *"can be compared to"* (my italics) the intrasystemic conflicts in the ego, in a paper in which they stress in another connection that analogies and precursors are not necessarily the same thing as the final product. Thus the processes may be similar in both systems, but different in efficiency and degree.

Other quantitative comparative variations and spectra also obtain. There are different degrees of the intrapsychic conflicts themselves, in conjunction with the different forms which I have been noting. Thus the intersystemic, opposition-type, anxiety-based conflicts which have heretofore been the cornerstone of our psychoanalytic interest are the most highly structured, the most definitive, and no doubt the most etiologically significant intrapsychic conflicts —certainly as far as psychopathology is concerned. But in the widest framework of our general psychoanalytic psychology, there is a spectrum of forms, of motives for, and degrees of, intrapsychic conflicts. Thus there are at the very start in the built-in apparatuses at least the potential for, if not actual, conflicts—the opposite instinctual

tendencies, the instincts and the built-in defensive thresholds (Rapaport, 1953), the constitutional id and ego apparatuses, or the primary
enmity of the ego in relation to the drives (Anna Freud, 1936). In
all of these the familiar problem of the differences between precursors and the final product, and of when the forerunners become
the real thing, stalks here as elsewhere. By no means do any of the
above as yet comprise conflict, as psychoanalysts think of the latter,
any more than the early shadows of ego equipment are the ego, or
the earliest internal prohibitions are yet the superego. Much more
complex differentiation and structuralization have to take place to
have the ingredients of true intrapsychic conflict. Hartmann (1939)
has pointed to the same principle and need for caution when he
warns that not every disruption of equilibrium can be considered
a conflict, without the latter term losing all precision of meaning.
For conflict, one needs an opposing force, not just an obstacle. Spitz
(1957) inserts caution in a similar direction in noting that the early
stimulus barrier likewise does not represent a true opposing force,
rather "it is a manifestation of a maturational state, namely, that at
birth the sensorium is not yet cathected."

As structures develop, and the forces line up in their ultimate
relationships, there still exists a hierarchy of motives for and types
of conflict. Thus I would say that an intrasystemic conflict, of any
of the types which I·have been describing, is not apt to have the
same scope, or the same depth, or the same reverberations as does an
intersystemic one of our more familiar and traditional variety. In
general, I think the same would be true about the choice or competitive type of conflicts as compared with the opposition types;
namely, the former do not have the force, tenacity, or serious implications of the latter. That this is not *always* true, though, can be appreciated if one calls to mind certain cases of obsessional neurosis, or
even perhaps certain obsessive characters. With regard to a spectrum
of motives, a conflict based on the need for synthesis, or on inevitable,
innate, opposing tendencies, is not of the same caliber or magnitude
as one based on anxiety, certainly not of the same neurosogenic
quality. Conflicts based on the need for synthesis are less global and
significant to the entire organism than the usually more disruptive
conflicts based on danger and anxiety.

There is thus a hierarchy of motives and of conflicts and of results, just as there is of psychic development itself. The anxiety-provoked, intersystemic conflict situations, with the broad range of interstructural participation as we have known them, is still the ultimate destiny of the usual and typical psychic dilemmas to which man is heir. Indeed, with the development of the complex psychic apparatus which is man's distinctive stamp, it is not likely that a process which has already reached a conflict stage will remain confined to the simpler units without becoming enmeshed in the more complex interrelationships which lie ready and able to take over. Actually, as I have gone into previously in more specific detail (1963), there is a simultaneous and reciprocal interaction between them all. Intrasystemic tensions create intersystemic effects which in turn influence new intrasystemic conditions, etc.

Thus clinically and experientially it is difficult, if not well-nigh impossible, to furnish a satisfactory example of an intrasystemic conflict, without it being easy to show how each arm of the conflicting forces has become intertwined with intersystemic implications. This was conspicuously evident in the panel discussion on intrapsychic conflict, when one considered any of the interesting clinical vignettes which were offered (see Nemiah, 1962). In the same vein is Fenichel's statement (1945) that an apparent instinctual conflict is always a structural conflict as well. In an internal conflict within the ego it can almost always be shown that one of the contending elements is an ego representative of the instincts, or of the superego. This is the case, for example, in the formulation sometimes made in the Kleinian system, or by some who work with psychotics, of a conflict between incompatible introjects or contradictory identifications within the ego. To cite another striking example, in the very interesting clinical report of a case of strephosymbolia, which was ingeniously traced to an intrasystemic disturbance of the synthetic function in the ego (Rosen, 1955), it was abundantly evident that within the conflicting forces were intense oedipal instinctual wishes, prematurely aroused and with catastrophic potential consequences to the patient. From the complex genetic determinants, it was ascertained that the auditory and phonetic aspects of words were associated with and meant for this patient the mother, while the visual and idiographic elements involved stood for the father. The ultimate effect of the failure of the necessary synthesis of these by the ego, however, was the achievement of an *instinctual* wish, i.e., to keep the parents apart—and hence oedipal fulfillment for the patient.

I agree with Loewenstein (1963) when he says that one does not have to find "a pure case" of something in order to demonstrate its existence. Indeed, it is the unusual instance in psychic life to be able to do this. We see not "pure" instincts but only the most filtered derivatives, or pure defense without instinct showing through, etc. Thus empirical clinical statements made above are meant not to deny the existence of the simpler forms but to show that in the developed organism the achieved complexity can also not be denied from playing its inevitable part.

To overlook these comparative and quantitative considerations and the hierarchic and mutual interplay of forces which are at work can lead to erroneous and incomplete theoretical formulations. Thus Jacobson (1963), in an otherwise comprehensive and full-bodied work which takes notable cognizance of the intricate genetic interrelationships between all of the psychic structures in forming the workable concept of the self, makes the rather surprising generalization that shame, inferiority feelings, and identity problems are not induced by intersystemic but by intrasystemic conflicts—a formulation which I would energetically dispute on empirical-clinical as well as theoretical grounds. One would not have to look far to see the artificiality and the indefensibility of such a limitation. Jacobson's own subsequent clinical examples disprove its validity. Elsewhere Jacobson attributes castration fear to "an intrasystemic (ego) tension," in contrast to superego fear which "is expressive of an intersystemic tension" (Jacobson at times uses "tensions" and "conflicts" interchangeably and somewhat loosely). These generalizations are not at all clear and are difficult to understand. They fail to take into account, for example, in the case of castration anxiety the indispensable contributions of instinctual pressures as well as the dangers which emanate not only from the superego but from the external world.

Such formulations tend to take a new piece of insight—in this case, that of intrasystemic conflicts—and to overdo its role. In this connection, Arlow points out, in agreement with me, that too great an extension of the role of intrasystemic conflicts would lead in the direction of minimizing the importance of drives and of other intersystemic contributions (see Nemiah, 1963). What we might conceive of as a trend from this would be the tendency to impart to each of the individual structures the functions of all the others. Thus, as our knowledge increases in scope, depth, and detail, and we see the greater intricacies and complexities within each structure or function, we might tend to ascribe to each the abilities of the whole. In such a way, the superego would come to acquire the capacity for unity and synthesis completely within itself, instead of depending largely upon the ego for these. Another such example is the idea of id inhibitions as existing within the id, instead of the inhibiting forces being thought of as being part of the ego or at least of what will become the ego. There thus grows with development a tendency to see a complete homunculus within each unit, as though each could almost tolerate being split off and still survive. I can visualize, for example, that carrying the above intrasystemic process further, as we know more and more about smaller and smaller units, one might postulate that there are conflicts not only within the system but within each specific smaller element. Thus, with regard to each value judgment of the superego, or each goal in the ego ideal, or each interest in the ego, it could be said that there can be a struggle between contiguous attitudes of varying shades of intensity, such as "this is good, vs. this is less good, not so good, neutral, a little bad, worse," etc. Perhaps I am carrying this argument too far to make a point. However, one may also say that only such a hierarchy and multilayering of conflicts can explain a system as complex as the psychic apparatus, and indeed this may be so. But at some point, I believe, we will benefit from insisting on some simplicity and limitations and on establishing the irreducible. The concept of conflict needs to fulfill certain definite criteria, and I have indicated what I consider some of these irreducible conditions to be.

Actually, what the above trend does is to carry the concept of autonomy much further than, and I am sure far beyond, what Hartmann (1939) had in mind when he introduced this useful term. The autonomy of the ego from conflicts and from drive influence was a true and an extraordinarily useful discovery, but Hartmann and Loewenstein (1962) themselves point out that autonomy is only relative and never absolute. "There can be no question of 'absolute' independence in this or in the other forms of autonomy we know in psychoanalysis." While this is true even for the ego, which is in our way of thinking the most complex of the structural systems, with the widest and most all-inclusive range of functions, I would venture that it must be even more true of the superego, which is considerably more limited in its scope, function, and diversity. Thus, while autonomous action can properly be achieved on a wide front by the ego, with its complex ensemble of functions and its own store of energy, such is probably quantitatively less possible of achievement by the superego. The latter remains throughout too dependently interrelated with other activities, particularly with many of the ego functions, for the process of autonomy to develop far in this direction. Nor do the superego's functions warrant it. Values and ideals are not independently viable without actions or behavior, or at least intentions toward the latter, to go with them. On the other hand, perception, motility, security interests, etc., can be more sufficient unto themselves. This is in consonance with the conclusions of Hartmann and Loewenstein (1962), that while the superego can become reasonably autonomous from the original objects and from drives, "its normal functioning is constantly bound to certain actions of the ego," from whose influence it cannot, nor should it, be separated. Just as these authors feel that the superego does not, as the ego, have constitutional, inborn elements—"present knowledge does not provide us with any cogent reason to speak of inheritance in the case of the superego"—so I believe the superego has less chance than the ego to become as autonomous. But this is in accord also with the reasoning I have advanced with regard to conflict—that by the same token the superego, though to some degree it possesses the ingredients necessary to encompass conflict within its borders, is quantitatively less able to do so than is the ego.

I must pose one further question which may have occurred to many by this time. That is, are we carrying this division too far, and are we asking for a precision in concepts beyond the point of either its usefulness or our ability to make such fine distinctions? This is a legitimate question, and comes more into focus when one considers the conclusions and final assertions made by many of the writers in this area. Many of the nuclear concepts are characterized as much by overlap as they are by separateness. Thus, as Fenichel (1945) points out, "the concepts of instinct and defense are relative;

the two are always interpenetrated" (p. 130), or "It is not the case of one definite defensive attitude fighting against one definite impulse; there are always variations, an active struggle, and mutual interpenetration" (p. 475). The ego operates with energy derived from the id, deinstinctualized and neutralized energy, as well as primary energy of its own (Hartmann, 1955). The superego also utilizes instinctual energy, notably aggressive, but also libidinal. It is also, as conceptualized by Freud (1921) genetically a "differentiated grade within the ego," or "a precipitate in the ego—[or a] modification of the ego [which] retains its special position (Freud, 1923, p. 34). Many writers have noted the similarity between functions of the ego ideal and the ego, as well as the intricate interrelationships and overlapping between the interests and activities of the ego, ego ideal, and superego. Both of the latter arise genetically from the ego, as well as from the external object relationships. Bing, McLaughlin, and Marburg (1959) actually regard the ego ideal as " 'anatomically' a part of the ego," while Hartmann and Loewenstein (1962) prefer to consider it, as most do today, as part of the superego system. Hartmann, Kris, and Loewenstein (1946) have pointed out the common origin of all of the subsequent structural divisions from a common unified and undifferentiated matrix. Thus one can see the fluidity of the borders, at least from genetic considerations.

It is true, therefore, that both genetically and functionally we should be aware of common origins, original unity, continuity, overlap, and interpenetration. However, this does not militate against the eventual existence of separate entities, with separate functions, of specialized and limited scope. I have pointed out before, in considering other psychoanalytic subjects (in discussing, for example, psychoanalysis vs. psychotherapy [1954], or nosological problems [1960], etc.), this dilemma between continuity and separateness, this frequent problem of the continuous spectrum. In each instance it is necessary and helpful to be aware of both, of the common line which binds as well as the borders which separate. Thus Jacobson (1963), in explaining why we need to postulate a superego as separate from rather than as just another part of the ego, points out that "Freud's last systemic distinctions are based on significant inner experiences. . . . It is not accidental that in times of conflict we may hear the voice of temptation, the id, the voice of reason, the ego, and the voice of conscience, the superego."

VII

In summary, with regard to the various structural problems which come up in connection with intrapsychic conflict, I have surveyed the range of intersystemic possibilities, as well as the question of an intrasystemic locus for such conflicts. The latter was seen to occur quite regularly within the ego, in connection with the ego's function as mediator and decision-maker. In fact, it was suggested that the function of making a choice and effecting decisions between contending elements, both outside and inside its borders, be explicitly spelled out as a central and major ego function which is not the same as its organizing or synthetic function. Such activity operates over a spectrum from essentially conflictful spheres to more neutralized and relatively conflict-free problem-solving activity.

I further concluded that the superego is a locus for intrasystemic conflicts, but relatively less so and in only a secondary way as compared with the ego. An accompaniment of this conclusion was the proposition that the superego must therefore also have some choice and organizing functions, but again less centrally and less dominantly than the ego. These comparative relationships are to be stressed and recognized. While the ego can achieve quite some autonomy, from conflict, drives, and even from the superego, the superego can do so to a much lesser degree. On the other hand, while the superego as well as the id can initiate conflict, the ego largely suffers it. Although I have described certain variations and exceptions, in general from wherever conflict may come, it is largely fought in the ego's land. The id, the pressor, is usually objected to; the ego is the objector; the superego is the warner. Sometimes the objector objects to the warner. But always the objector also has a "dilemma conflict" in addition, having to decide whether and what to do. This part of the action is always within the ego's own, and only the ego's borders. The ego then has action at its flanks as well, at one or both borders facing its neighbors.

One thought keeps presenting itself to me as I come to the end of what I have to say about this subject, a thought which I fear may speak against the most basic points which I have made. That is, it may be, following Freud, that the basic and irreducible conflict is between life vs. death *instincts!* Maybe so—analysts seem divided on this point. But perhaps, as a last statement, I would say that if this is so—and I myself tend to give the general idea of this dichotomy much respect—these two relentless forces are, in relation to each other, partners, rather than in conflict! Each can, and will, have its say. And it is not the clash between *them* that results in the phenomena with which analysts spend their working days.

BIBLIOGRAPHY

Alexander, F. (1933), The Relation of Stuctural and Instinctual Conflicts. *Psa. Quart.,* II.

Bak, R. C. (1952), Discussion of Dr. Wexler's Paper. In: *Psychotherapy with Schizophrenics: A Symposium,* ed. E. B. Brody & F. C. Redlich. New York: International Universities Press.

Bing, J. F., McLaughlin, F., & Marburg, R. (1959), The Metapsychology of Narcissism. *This Annual,* XIV.

Fenichel, O. (1945), *The Psychoanalytic Theory of Neurosis.* New York: Norton.

Freud, A. (1936), *The Ego and the Mechanisms of Defense.* New York: International Universities Press, 1946.

Freud, S. (1920), Beyond the Pleasure Principle. *Standard Edition,* XVIII. London: Hogarth Press, 1955.

—— (1921), Group Psychology and the Analysis of the Ego. *Standard Edition,* XVIII. London: Hogarth Press, 1955.

—— (1923), The Ego and the Id. *Standard Edition,* XIX. London: Hogarth Press, 1961.

—— (1926), Inhibitions, Symptoms and Anxiety. *Standard Edition,* XX. London: Hogarth Press, 1959.

Hacker, F. J. (1962), The Discriminatory Function of the Ego. *Int. J. Psa.,* XLIII.

Hartmann, H. (1939), *Ego Psychology and the Problem of Adaptation.* New York: International Universities Press, 1958.

—— (1947), On Rational and Irrational Action. In: *Psychoanalysis and the Social Sciences,* I. New York: International Universities Press.

—— (1950), Comments on the Psychoanalytic Theory of the Ego. *This Annual,* V.

—— (1955), Notes on the Theory of Sublimation. *This Annual,* X.

—— (1960), *Psychoanalysis and Moral Values.* New York: International Universities Press.

—— (1963), In Panel on "The Significance of Intrapsychic Conflict," rep. J. C. Nemiah. *J. Amer. Psa. Assn.,* XI.

—— & Kris, E., Loewenstein, R. M. (1946), Comments on the Formation of Psychic Structure. *This Annual,* II.

—— & Loewenstein, R. M. (1962), Notes on the Superego. *This Annual,* XVII.

Hoedemaker, E. D. (1955), The Therapeutic Process in the Treatment of Schizophrenia. *J. Amer. Psa. Assn.,* II.

Jacobson, E. (1954), The Self and the Object World. *This Annual,* IX.

—— (1963), *The Self and the Object World* [*J. Amer. Psa. Assn.,* Monogr. 2]. New York: International Universities Press, in press.

Loewenstein, R. M. (1963), Discussion remarks at panel on "The Significance of Intra-psychic Conflict," reported by J. C. Nemiah. *J. Amer. Psa. Assn.* XI.

Nemiah, J. C. (1963), In Panel on "The Significance of Intrapsychic Conflict," rep. J. C. Nemiah. *J. Amer. Psa. Assn.,* XI.

Nunberg, H. (1931), The Synthetic Function of the Ego. *Int. J. Psa.,* XII.

Peto, A. (1960), The Fragmentizing Function of the Ego in a Masochist. Paper read at meeting of the American Psychoanalytic Association, Atlantic City, N.J.

—— (1961), The Fragmentizing Function of the Ego in the Psychoanalytic Session. Paper read at meeting of the American Psychoanalytic Association, Chicago, Ill.

Rangell, L. (1954), Similarities and Differences between Psychoanalysis and Dynamic Psychotherapy. *J. Amer. Psa. Assn.,* II.

—— (1960), Problems of Nosology from the Psychoanalytic Standpoint. Abstracted in Panel on "An Examination of Nosology According to Psychoanalytic Concepts," rep. N. Ross. *J. Amer. Psa. Assn.,* VIII.

—— (1963), The Scope of Intrapsychic Conflict: Microscopic and Macroscopic Considerations. *This Annual,* XVIII.

Rapaport, D. (1953), On the Psychoanalytic Theory of Affects. *Int. J. Psa.,* XXXIV.

Rosen, V. H. (1955), Strephosymbolia: An Intrasystemic Disturbance of the Synthetic Function of the Ego. *This Annual,* X.

Schafer, R. (1960), The Loving and Beloved Superego in Freud's Structural Theory. *This Annual,* XV.

Spitz, R. A. (1957), *No and Yes: On the Beginnings of Human Communication.* New York: International Universities Press.

—— (1959), *A Genetic Field Theory of Ego Formation.* New York: International Universities Press.

Waelder, R. (1930), The Principle of Multiple Function: Observations of Over-Determination. *Psa. Quart.,* V, 1936.

Wexler, M. (1952), The Structural Problem in Schizophrenia: The Role of the Internal Object. In: *Psychotherapy with Schizophrenics: A Symposium,* ed. E. B. Brody & F. C. Redlich. New York: International Universities Press.

THE EGO IDEAL AND THE IDEAL SELF

JOSEPH SANDLER, Ph.D., ALEX HOLDER, Ph.D., and
DALE MEERS, M.A.
(London)

This paper has been prompted by the need to resolve a number
of practical problems which have arisen in the course of indexing
psychoanalytic case material in the Hampstead Index. Faced with
the need to classify observations relating to ideal formation in children, it has been found impossible to distinguish sharply between
the operation of an "ego ideal" and the superego system, although
a number of features which are commonly referred to as constituents
of the ego ideal are not fully included within the concept of the
superego. Accordingly, the model of superego functioning (Sandler,
1960; Sandler et al., 1962), and that of the representational world
(Sandler and Rosenblatt, 1962), used as a theoretical basis for indexing superego material, have been extended in an attempt to take
into account the different facets of the concept of the ego ideal as
described at different times by Freud and in some of the subsequent
psychoanalytic literature.

Briefly, the view has been taken that various elements of what
might be referred to as the ego-ego ideal-superego system have to
be considered both in isolation and in their interaction. In particu-

The investigation reported here has been aided by a joint grant from the Foundations' Fund for Research in Psychiatry, New Haven, Connecticut, and the Psychoanalytic Research and Development Fund, Inc., New York, and by a grant from the
National Institute of Mental Health, Bethesda, Maryland.

The material used has been collected at the Hampstead Child-Therapy Clinic, a
therapeutic and research center financed by the following foundations: The Field
Foundation, Inc., New York; The Ford Foundation, New York; The Foundations'
Fund for Research in Psychiatry, New Haven, Connecticut; The Anna Freud Founda-
tion, New York; The Grant Foundation, Inc., New York; The Estate of Flora Haas,
New York; The Old Dominion Foundation, U.S.A.; The Psychoanalytic Research and
Development Fund, Inc., New York; and the National Institute of Mental Health,
Bethesda, Maryland.

lar, we have found it valuable to distinguish the notion of the ideal
self from that of the ideal object, and to consider our clinical material
from the point of view of the factors determining the content of
the ideal self at any given time.

The term "ego ideal," first introduced by Freud in 1914, has
undergone a number of subtle changes in meaning during the course
of the development of psychoanalytic metapsychology. Since the publication of *The Ego and the Id* (1923b) the predominant usage of the
term has been as a synonym for the superego, although in relatively
recent years a number of attempts have been made to differentiate
the ego ideal from the superego (e.g., Piers and Singer, 1953; A. Reich,
1954, 1960; Novey, 1955; Lampl-de Groot, 1962), to regard it either
as a separate mental structure or as a descriptive term referring to
some, but not all, of the functions of the superego. Most of the recent
formulations have been concerned with the need to distinguish
between the benevolent and critical aspects of the superego (cf.
Schafer, 1960), or with the differences between the ontogenetic development of ideals on the one hand and the conscience on the other.

Much of the present ambiguity attached to the term (leading
inevitably to a degree of theoretical confusion) derives from the
different shades of meaning attached to it by Freud, and it is the
purpose of this paper to examine some of these variations in meaning, beginning with Freud's own writings. At present "ego ideal"
is an omnibus term, and it seems clear that a number of rather
different concepts are subsumed under it. We cannot speak of
the ego ideal without specifying the sense in which it is used. In
order to attempt a theoretical clarification, the notion of the ego
ideal will be examined in the final part of this paper from the point
of view of previous Hampstead Index work on the superego (Sandler, 1960; Sandler et al., 1962) and the representational world
(Sandler, 1962; Sandler and Rosenblatt, 1962).

FREUD'S VIEWS ON THE EGO IDEAL

Freud introduced the term "ego ideal" in his paper "On Narcissism" (1914). He pointed out that impulses undergo repression if
they come into conflict with the individual's cultural and ethical
ideas. The person recognizes these ideals as a standard for himself

and submits to their claims. "Repression . . . proceeds from the ego; we might say with greater precision that it proceeds from the self-respect of the ego." Freud goes on to say that such repression may occur before the objectionable ideas have entered consciousness. The individual "has set up an ideal in himself by which he measures his actual ego. . . . For the ego the formation of an ideal would be the conditioning factor of repression."

Freud saw here the development of the ideal as being in direct continuity with the original narcissistic state. "The subject's narcissism makes its appearance displaced on to this new ideal ego, which, like the infantile ego, finds itself possessed of every perfection that is of value. . . . What he projects before him as his ideal is the substitute for the lost narcissism of his childhood in which he was his own ideal."

Freud specifically distinguishes in this paper between the ego ideal and the "special psychical agency which performs the task of seeing the narcissistic satisfaction from the ego ideal is ensured and which, with this end in view, constantly watches the actual ego and measures it by that ideal." (In an editorial note to this paper Strachey points out that the later concept of the superego evolved from a combination of this special agency and the ego ideal as described at this juncture.) Freud is quite clear here on the existence of a distinction between the "narcissistic ego ideal" and the "institution of conscience" which is basically "an embodiment, first of parental criticism, and subsequently of that of society." He also refers to the conscience as a "censoring agency."

In the *Introductory Lectures* (1916-17) Freud maintained the position he had taken in 1914. The ego ideal was seen as being created by man *for himself* "in the course of his development," and this is done "for the purpose of recovering thereby the self-satisfaction bound up with the primary infantile narcissism, which since those days has suffered so many shocks and mortification." Distinguished from the ego ideal we have the conscience. "We recognise in this self-criticising faculty the ego censorship."

The next reference to the ego ideal comes in 1921 in *Group Psychology and the Analysis of the Ego* where Freud then states that the melancholias show us "the ego divided, fallen apart into two pieces, one of which rages against the second . . . the piece which

behaves so cruelly is not unknown to us. . . . It comprises the conscience, a critical agency within the ego, which even in normal times
takes up a critical attitude towards the ego." However, Freud goes
on to say:

> On previous occasions we have been driven to the hypothesis
> that some such agency develops in our ego which may cut itself
> off from the rest of the ego and come into conflict with it. We
> have called it the "ego ideal," and by way of functions we have
> ascribed to it self-observation, the moral conscience, the censor-
> ship of dreams, and the chief influence in repression. We have
> said that it is the heir to the original narcissism in which the
> childish ego enjoyed self-sufficiency; it gradually gathers up from
> the influences of the environment the demands which that en-
> vironment makes upon the ego and which the ego cannot always
> rise to; so that a man, when he cannot be satisfied with his ego
> itself, may nevertheless be able to find satisfaction in his ego ideal
> which has been differentiated out of the ego.

In a comment on this passage Freud refers to his papers "On
Narcissism" (1914) and "Mourning and Melancholia" (1917) for previous discussions of the "critical agency," and he gives the impression in the text (quoted above) of *Group Psychology* that the term
"ego ideal" had been previously applied to the conscience. This is
not in fact correct, for nowhere in "Mourning and Melancholia"
does Freud refer to the ego ideal, and he specifically calls the "critical agency" the conscience. In "On Narcissism," moreover, the
conscience was quite specifically distinguished from the ego ideal.
It would appear that in *Group Psychology* Freud now condensed his
two former concepts into one, extending the term "ego ideal" to
cover the agency of conscience as well as the ideal *which the individual has set up for himself*. Although, no doubt influenced by his
earlier consideration of melancholia, the ego ideal is seen as critical
and punitive, it is still linked with the formulations in the paper
"On Narcissism." For example, we read: "It is even obvious, in many
forms of love choice, that the object serves as a substitute for some
unattained ego ideal of our own. We love it on account of the
perfections we have striven to reach for our own ego, and which
we should now like to procure in this roundabout way as a means
of satisfying our narcissism."

Two years later, in *The Ego and the Id* (1923b) Freud proposed his structural theory. The ego ideal is now referred to as the super-ego, and Freud remarks that the considerations which led to the assumption of a differentiation within the ego have been stated in the paper "On Narcissism" and in *Group Psychology*. But, as Strachey points out in his introduction to *The Ego and the Id,* the distinction between the ideal itself and the agency concerned with its enforcement has been dropped. We can also detect a greater stress being laid by Freud on the critical and punitive aspects of what was now the superego.

Few other references to the ego ideal occur in Freud's writings. In "Remarks on the Theory and Practice of Dream-Interpretation" (1923a), written just prior to *The Ego and the Id,* Freud stated that "we should keep firmly to the fact that the separation of the ego from an observing critical, punishing agency (an ego ideal) must be taken into account in the interpretation of dreams as well." Another, and rather significantly different use of the term came nine years later, in the *New Introductory Lectures* (1932), where Freud, for the first time since the introduction of the structural theory, seems to imply a distinction between the superego and the ego ideal. He states: "We have now to mention another important activity which is to be ascribed to the superego. It is also the vehicle of the ego ideal, by which the ego measures itself, towards which it strives and whose demands for ever-increasing affection it is always striving to fulfil. No doubt this ego ideal is a precipitation of the old idea of the parents, an expression of the admiration which the child felt for the perfection which it at that time ascribed to them." It is worth noting that this formulation of the ego ideal is not identical with that given in "On Narcissism." In 1924, in "The Economic Problem of Masochism," Freud had spoken of the ego's "perception that it has not come up to the demands made by its ideal, the superego." In the same paper he comments that "the superego, a substitute for the Oedipus complex, becomes a representative of the real external world as well and thus also becomes a model for the endeavours of the ego." It would appear that Freud here viewed the ego-ideal aspect of the superego in terms of the oedipal parents as *ideal figures* for the child. Thus the introjected parents who constitute the superego are regarded both as ideal models for the child and also as an internal

self-observing and critical agency. This formulation would correspond to that given in "On Narcissism" only if we assumed that
the ideal which the child "projects before him . . . the substitute for
the lost narcissism of his childhood . . ." is *identical* with the ideal
parental figures which have been introjected as part of the process
of resolving the oedipus complex. However, the term "ideal" in
Freud's later formulations is presented quite unambiguously as referring to the parents *as models,* while in the 1914 presentation the
term "ideal" is an ideal created by the child for himself, an ideal
form of *himself,* representing a state which he strives to attain in
an effort to regain the earliest condition of narcissistic perfection.[1]

We can conclude from the above discussion that Freud made use
of the term "ego ideal" in a number of varying senses during the
course of his writings from 1914 onward.

1. In "On Narcissism" (1914) and *"Introductory Lectures"*
(1916-17) the term was used to refer to the individual's ideal for himself, constructed as a consequence of his efforts to regain infantile
narcissism. It was here distinguished from the self-observing and
critical agency, the conscience.

2. In *Group Psychology* (1921) the term was used to cover the two
ideas which had been distinguished in the earlier phase. It now
included what had been referred to as the conscience.

3. In "Remarks on the Theory and Practice of Dream Interpretation" (1923a) the term was used in the same sense as the "superego,"
as a mental structure. In *The Ego and the Id* (1923b), the two terms
are indeed used synonymously.

4. In the *New Introductory Lectures* (1932) the superego is referred to as the "vehicle of the ego ideal." This usage was foreshadowed in 1924 in "The Economic Problem of Masochism" where
Freud notes that "the ego reacts with feelings of anxiety . . . to the
perception that it has not come up to the demands of its ideal, the

---

[1] This distinction is by no means merely an academic one. Attention has been
drawn by various authors (e.g., A. Reich, 1954; Hartmann and Loewenstein, 1962)
to the difference between idealization of the parents and early self-idealizations, but
these authors stress the importance of the difference from the point of view of the
genetic development of the ego ideal, whereas the view which we take is that the term
"ego ideal" covers a number of aspects which should also be *functionally* differentiated
at all ages.

superego." The use of the term "ideal" here refers to the ideal parents as embodied in the superego.[2]

LATER WORK ON THE EGO IDEAL

Freud did not in his later work conceive of the ego ideal as distinct from the superego. From 1923 he used the two terms synonymously, and where he spoke of the ego ideal in relation to the superego it was in the sense of the superego's function of maintaining and enforcing standards on the ego. In a very recent paper on the superego, Hartmann and Loewenstein (1962) uphold this view, and speak of the "ego-ideal aspect" of the superego, regarding pre-oedipal self and object idealizations as precursors of this aspect of the superego system. This formulation of Hartmann and Loewenstein is a consistent and legitimate one, but it carries with it the possible disadvantage that because Freud's early concept of ego ideal includes something other than his later concept of superego, a very wide spectrum of functions has to be subsumed under the term "superego," with the consequence that such statements as "conflict with the superego," or "tension between ego and superego" may be theoretically and clinically imprecise unless carefully qualified.[3] As Novey (1955) remarks: "The concept of the superego has been considerably hampered by its unwieldy nature. Because of this there has gradually crept into the psychoanalytic literature a splitting of this concept into a superego and an ego ideal."

It is worth while examining briefly some of the ways in which this "splitting of the concept" has been formulated.

Jones (1935) speaks of the topographical prolongation of the ego ideal into the unconscious, and equates the unconscious part of it with the superego. He goes on: "The love component, so evident with the more conscious ego ideal, is with the unconscious superego quite subordinate to fear and severity."

[2] Freud may have been making the unspoken assumption here that the ego's ideal standards for itself (the 1914 meaning of "ego ideal") are identical with the inner representation of the ideal parents.

[3] It was the existence of problems of this sort, arising in the course of indexing clinical material in the Hampstead Index, that prompted the formulations of the Superego Group of the Hampstead Clinic (Sandler, 1960; Sandler et al., 1962) in which a distinction was made between the introjection of parental authority (resulting in the superego introjects) and various other ego mechanisms (such as identification).

A differentiation between superego and ego ideal, based on the antithesis between the two types of instincts, was proposed by Nunberg (1932), who said: "When instinct gratification is renounced out of fear of losing the love object, this object is absorbed by the ego and cathected with the libido; it becomes a part of the ego. In contrast to the ideal ego, it is called ego ideal. Out of love for this ideal, man clings to it and submits to its demands. Whereas the ego submits to the superego out of punishment, it submits to the ego ideal out of love." He goes on to refer to the ego ideal as "an image of the loved objects in the ego," in contrast to the superego which is "an image of the hated and feared objects." Nunberg relates this distinction to the shift in emphasis in Freud's writings from the libidinal to the more sadistic aspects of the ego ideal (superego), and comments that it is difficult in practice to separate these concepts sharply from each other.

Annie Reich (1954) distinguishes between the superego, "the later and more reality-syntonic structure," and the ego ideal, "the earlier, more narcissistic one." She sees the ego ideal as being based on "identifications with parental figures seen in a glorified light," while the superego represents the "identifications resulting from the breakdown of the oedipus complex." She further suggests that the "ego ideal expresses what one desires to be; the superego, what one ought to be."

In a more recent paper (1960) Annie Reich extended the idea of "primitive" and "archaic" ego ideals—primitive identifications with idealized infantile objects. She demonstrates the role of persistence of these early ego ideals in later pathology. What characterizes these early ego ideals is the feeling that the person is himself the admired, omnipotent, and idealized object. There is a magical fusion of self and object representations; he feels "as though he *were* his own ego ideal."

Jacobson (1954) regards the ego ideal "as part of the superego system, as a pilot and guide for the ego," but also sees its formation as a *precursor* to the establishment of the superego system proper. She refers to "processes [which] transform the magic images of the self and of the love objects into a unified ego ideal and, by internalization of the parental prohibitions and demands, establish superego identifications and self-critical superego functions." She adds: "This double face of the ego ideal, which is forged from ideal concepts of the self and from idealized features of the love objects, gratifies indeed the infantile longing of which we said that it is never fully relinquished: the desire to be one with the love object."

Piers and Singer (1953) relate the experiencing of shame to tension between ego and ego ideal, and guilt to the outcome of tension between ego and superego.[4] These authors consider it to be immaterial whether one wishes to regard the ego ideal merely as one particular aspect of the superego, or as a psychological formation entirely separate and independent from the latter. The superego sets *boundaries* for the ego, the ego ideal *goals*. Piers and Singer see the ego ideal as possessing four major attributes. It contains a core of narcissistic omnipotence. It represents the sum of the positive identifications with the parental images. It contains layers of later identifications, more subject to change than the earlier ones. Finally, it contains the goals of the drive to mastery (Bühler's *Funktionslust*).

Novey (1955) suggests that the term "ego ideal" should not be used as a synonym for the loving or punishing superego, as the superego is based on the resolution of oedipal conflicts. He says: "The concept of the ego ideal is of use to define that particular segment of introjected objects whose functional operation has to do with proposed standards of thoughts, feeling, and conduct acquired later than the Oedipal superego, but having its roots in the early pregenital narcissistic operations against anxiety. This operative unit seems to play a separate role in character formation and functioning. It is clearly related to the superego but has different origins and a different function from it." Novey regards the ego ideal as being rooted in primitive parental identifications, but in the mature individual it is also dependent upon later significant persons. It is "a distinct psychic institution related to the ego and superego."

Recently Lampl-de Groot (1962) has proposed a clear differentiation between the ego ideal and the superego. The superego is considered to be equivalent to conscience, and is viewed as an essentially restricting and prohibiting agency. The ego ideal, on the contrary, has a different function, in that it is from early life a need-

4 Cf. also Devereux (1950).

satisfying agency, and retains a degree of functional independence from the superego, although the two agencies normally work together harmoniously. The content of the ego ideal is "I am like my omnipotent parents," whereas the superego's content may be expressed as "I will live up to the demands of my parents."

Finally, Hartmann and Loewenstein (1962) link the ego-ideal aspect of the superego with positive aims, and contrast it with the moral restrictions and prohibitions which constitute another aspect. Although these are two sides to the superego, they are not always in harmony; yet in the developing normal individual they achieve a high degree of integration.

While the brief survey given above shows a number of alternative approaches to the problem of defining the ego ideal, there are certain common elements in all the approaches described. Perhaps the most striking is the recognition that Freud's later formulation of the ego ideal, in which it is equated with the structural superego, is insufficient to cover the phenomena to which the concept was earlier applied. In "On Narcissism" the ego ideal did not include the conscience, and its libidinal rather than its aggressive components were stressed. This situation has been dealt with by subsequent writers either by broadening the concept of the superego as presented in *The Ego and the Id,* or by retaining the latter concept and applying the term ego ideal to one or other elaboration of Freud's original ego-ideal concept.

There can be little doubt, on clinical and theoretical grounds, that some such step is necessary, and all the authors quoted earlier have made significant contributions in this area. However, it should be remembered that any new formulation of the ego ideal as distinct from the superego will not fully embrace all the meanings attributed to it by Freud at various times. Freud's 1914 ego ideal is different from his 1923 ego ideal, and even when the ego ideal is seen as an aspect of the superego system (e.g., Hartmann and Loewenstein, 1962) the resulting superego concept has had telescoped into it Freud's 1914 view of the ego ideal. In post-Freudian literature on the ego ideal, the term has been used either as a synonym for the structural superego or to refer to some development of the first formulations in "On Narcissism."

The Ego and the Self

Part of the difficulty which has been experienced by many authors in regard to the concept of the ego ideal has arisen from the fact that Freud used the same term to denote both the *ego* and the *self*. James Strachey, in his editorial introductions to "On Narcissism" and *The Ego and the Id,* points out that the meaning which Freud attached to *das Ich* underwent a gradual modification. "At first," says Strachey, "he used the term without any great precision, as we might speak of 'the self.' " Strachey also points out, in his introduction to the later paper, that it "seems possible to detect two main uses: one in which the term distinguishes a person's self as a whole . . . from other people, and the other in which it denotes a particular part of the mind characterised by special attributes and functions." He adds: ". . . in some of his intervening works, particularly in connection with narcissism, the 'ego' seems to correspond rather to the 'self.' " In a footnote, Strachey remarks that in a few places in the *Standard Edition, das Ich* has been translated by "the self."

Hartmann (1956)[5] has suggested that, in the second decade of this century, the term "ego" as used by Freud became interchangeable with "one's own person" or the "self." He further remarks that this usage tends to obscure the fact that, particularly where the problem of narcissism is concerned, two quite different sets of propositions are involved. One refers to the functions and cathexes of the ego as a system (as distinct from the cathexes of different parts of the personality), the other to the opposition of the cathexis of one's own person to that of other persons (objects).

If we follow this formulation of Hartmann's, and distinguish between the ego and the self (self-representation and self-image), a distinction which is also maintained by others (e.g., Jacobson, 1954; Spiegel, 1959), then we can consider the term "ego ideal" to carry the following set of meanings in Freud's writings:

1. The superego in the sense of that specialized set of ego functions which we call the "conscience."

[5] Cf. also Hartmann (1950) and Edith Jacobson (1954).

2. Certain ego functions which were at one time considered to be functions of the superego (e.g., self-observing and defensive functions).

3. The ideal self-representation or ideal self-image.

4. Ideal parental introjects which serve as models for the self (the term "superego" has been used synonymously with "ego ideal" in this sense).

The Ego Ideal and the Representational World

It would appear from the preceding discussion that the term "ego ideal" can embrace a selection of rather different, though related elements, and that no precise agreement exists on what particular combination of elements should be referred to as the ego ideal. Freud and subsequent writers have all made use of the term to refer to various constellations within a larger system which includes functions and contents belonging to both the ego and the superego.

The lack of precise agreement in the literature has been reflected in the practical difficulties we have had in attempting to index clinical material derived from child analyses under the heading "ego ideal." In attempting to order our clinical observations on the conscious and unconscious ideals of children of different ages, we have been forced to the conclusion that these are for the most part so overdetermined that we could not differentiate an ego-ideal system or structure as functionally distinct from the ego and the superego. In Freud's later usage the ego ideal is identical with the superego; and in his own writings and in those of other psychoanalysts, the concept has included, as we have previously shown, both ideal object and ideal self-representations. A child's ideal object may be embodied in one or other aspect of his superego introjects, or in the inner representation of some external person. It may also contain elements derived from reaction formations to unwanted impulses of his own. We can frequently detect elements of the child's own self-representation or elements of his ideal self externalized or projected onto the object. The ideal self may in turn gain its content from a variety of sources, and need not be a mirror image of the ideal object or introject.

In our clinical work it is also necessary to take into account the fact that ideal self and object representations exist from early in life, well before the formation of the superego proper. A further difficulty in indexing has arisen from the fact that the content of the child's ideal self can vary from time to time, from one situation to another, although the ideals carried by the parental introjects remain relatively stable. It is well known, for example, how a gang leader or teen-age idols may replace the adolescent's parental introjects in determining the content of the ideal self (although parental ideals exert a profound and significant influence).

In our work with the analytic material of child patients in the Hampstead Index we have found it convenient to view the superego in terms of what has been called the *representational world* of the child (cf. Hartmann, 1950; Jacobson, 1953, 1954; Sandler, 1960, 1962). A fuller account of the concept of the representational world will be found elsewhere (Sandler and Rosenblatt, 1962). Briefly, it is the universe of representations,[6] of ideational and affective content, which the developing child constructs, on the basis of the sensory experiences arising from the drives and from the interaction between his own body and the outside world. At first it is extremely rudimentary, and the representations which are constructed by the developing ego are linked with experiences of need satisfaction, but later the child creates representations of many other things, activities, feelings, and relationships. He differentiates a self-representation from object representations, and learns to distinguish between "inner" and "outer" experiences. As time goes on, certain representations (linked with unwanted instinctual wishes) are repressed, and remain unconscious, while other aspects are permitted access to consciousness and motility. A specialized part of the representational world consists of words and symbols and provides the furniture for the ego activity of thinking. The representational world is not at all synonymous with the ego, although it is one of the functions of the ego to create and organize the representational world.

Relevant to the present discussion is the idea of the *shape* of a representation of self or object—the particular form or character

6 The term "representation" covers, for the time being, both the organized and enduring "schema" (cf. Sandler, 1962), which is always unconscious, and the various images (conscious and unconscious) which arise on the basis of the schema.

assumed by that representation at any given moment, determined by the pressures of the id, the requirements of the external world, and the standards and demands of the introjects. Introjection in this context is the elevation of the parental representations (or aspects of these) to special status. It occurs when the child acts in the absence of a parental authority figure as if the parent were actually present. It is the investment of object representations with an authority or status which they did not previously possess. The relationship of this type of introjection, associated with the resolution of the oedipus complex, to superego formation has been discussed in detail elsewhere (Sandler, 1960). Introjection can take place without resulting in identification.

Identification, as distinct from introjection, can be defined as the changing of the shape of one's self-representation on the basis of another representation as a model. Identification is not bound to introjection, and in its most primitive form represents a fusion, in whole or in part, of self- and object representations. Later, it can take place as a conscious or unconscious copying of aspects of the "shape" of an object representation, and duplicating it in the self-representation, with the distinction between self- and object representations being maintained.

Identifications of one sort or another take place early in life, but the analysis of pregenital identifications forms an important part of analytic work with both children and adults. After the formation of the superego through the introjection of parental authority, there can occur identification with features of the introjects as well as with aspects of nonintrojected objects. The capacity to identify with objects (via object representations) continues through life, irrespective of whether these objects are persons in the subject's environment or introjects.

The self-representation is built up on the basis of the child's experiences of his own body through its interaction with the external world, and through identifications with his objects.[7] One of the shapes which the self-representation can assume is that which we can call the *ideal self,* i.e., that which, at any moment, is a desired shape

---

[7] The object representation includes all the distortions through projection, etc., which the child has made during the course of his development.

of the self—the "self-I-want-to-be." This is that shape of the self which, at that time, in those circumstances, and under the influence of the particular instinctual impulse of the moment, is the shape which would yield the greatest degree of well-being for the child. It is the shape which would provide the highest degree of narcissistic gratification and would minimize the quantity of aggressive discharge on the self.[8]

The ideal self at any moment is not necessarily simply that shape of the self which represents instinctual impulses as being fulfilled[9] but will be determined as well by the child's need to gain the love and approval of his parents or introjects, or to avoid their disapproval. In this sense the ideal self is at any moment a compromise formation, a compromise between the desired state of instinctual gratification and the need to win the love of, or to avoid punishment from, authority figures, internal or external. The ultimate criterion at any given time is an economic one. If the threat of punishment or of loss of love is greater than the libidinal or aggressive gains obtained through direct wish fulfillment, then the child will abandon his wish-fulfilling ideal in favor of one which is more acceptable to his objects, internal or external. It is clear, however, that in any given situation there might be a conflict of choice between various shapes of the ideal self.

The special economic gain obtained through constructing the ideal self on the basis of *identification* deserves mention. If the parental injunction is "behave as I do," then the formation of an ideal self which is modeled on the object provides a double gain. In the first place it represents compliance with the wishes of authority and the child gains a feeling of being loved; in the second place, the child feels identified with his admired object, and can love and admire himself as he does the object.

We are now in a position to distinguish between several types of ideals, all of which have been included by Freud and other writers

8 While this paper is primarily concerned with the elaboration of the concept of the ideal self, it is of some interest to note that in different situations the *ideal object*, the wished-for object, may also change. We can also speak of an *ideal relationship* at any particular time, the "relationship-I-would-now-like-to-exist."

9 From a genetic point of view the earliest shape of the ideal self is probably a wish-fulfilling one exclusively. The consideration of the genetic development of the ideal self does not form part of this paper.

in the concept of "ego ideal." The first we can refer to as the "ideal object," where the child possesses an admired, idealized, and omnipotent object. The second represents those ideals which are held up to the child by his parents or introjects in the form of the ideal ("good," "well-behaved") child. This ideal, conveyed to the child by his parents, need not be identical with the ideals or behavior of the parents themselves. It represents the parents' ideal of a desirable and loved child, as perceived by the child. The child may be aware of these parental ideals, yet they need not have been integrated into the content of the child's self or ideal self. Whether they are or not depends on the child's ego development and on the economic loss or gain involved. Both these types of ideal appear to be included in the sense in which Freud spoke of the superego as the vehicle (*Träger*) of the ego ideal (1932).

Finally, we have the set of ideals which constitutes the content of the ideal self, and this is the sense in which Freud spoke of the ego ideal in his first formulation, in the paper "On Narcissism" (1914), and even in *Group Psychology* (1921), although in the latter paper he had, in contrast to his 1914 formulation, included the "conscience" in the ego ideal.

Clearly the content of the ideal self on the one hand, and that of the ideal object or ideal child (as transmitted by the object) on the other, need not necessarily be the same, though they are often closely related. The child has a strong motive for identifying in his ideal self with the idealized features of his authority figure, whether real person or introject, for by identification he can transfer some of the libidinal cathexis attached to the object to the ideal self. Object love is transformed into secondary narcissism, with resulting potential increase in well-being and self-esteem. By identifying in his ideal self with the "good" child image of his parents or introjects, he can feel loved and admired by them.

The ideal self is far more fluid and flexible than the ideals held up to the child by his introjects, although it will contain a solid core of identifications with the admired parents of his earliest years. In the well-adapted individual the content of the ideal self will undergo continuous modification in the light of the person's experiences of reality. In states of regression, the content of the ideal self will approximate more closely to aspects of the idealized pregenital objects.

In normal development parental ideals which have previously been taken over will be modified and displaced in a reality-syntonic fashion and will be integrated with the ideals taken over from other figures throughout life—such figures as friends, teachers, and colleagues; indeed, from any admired object. Ideals may also be derived from feared objects, through a mechanism similar to "identification with the aggressor."

The sources of the content of the ideal self can be categorized as follows:

1. Identification with aspects of loved, admired, or feared objects. These objects may be introjects (after the formation of the superego proper), or may be at any time persons in the individual's environment.

2. Identification with the image of the "good" or "desirable" child as conveyed by the objects.

3. Identification with previous shapes of the individual's own self. By this is meant the construction of ideals based upon the wish to attain "ideal" states previously experienced in reality or in fantasy.[10]

To these sources we should perhaps add the influence of the individual's reality knowledge. The capacity to take reality into account in the construction of the ideal self of the moment is a most important one from the point of view of development and adaptation. Reality knowledge here includes knowledge of one's own potentialities and limitations as well as knowledge of the environment.

At any one moment and in any situation the ideal self will be a resultant of the operation of all the factors mentioned. It will contain temporary and *ad hoc* elements to varying degree, but will also contain a more stable core, for the most part unconscious, based upon the ideals created in childhood. In particular, the ideals based on and maintained by the relationship to the introjects will play an important part in normal and pathological mental life. Conflict of choice between various shapes of the ideal self, especially between

10 The topic of regression in relation to the ideal self is relevant here, but will form the subject of another study.

those derived at various stages of development, will also play a significant role in determining pathology.

When we have spoken in the preceding passages of the formation of the ideal self we have been guilty of an oversimplification. The formation of the ideal self has been described as if in fact the individual is easily capable of changing the shape of his self-representation to conform to his ideal, but we know from clinical experience that this is often far from being the case. To the picture presented above, we have to apply the same modification as was made by Freud in the theory of dreams, when he amended his statement that the dream was a wish fulfillment, to the view that it was an *attempted* wish fulfillment. In the same way the construction of an ideal self, and the efforts to attain it, constitute an attempt to restore, sometimes in a most roundabout way, the primary narcissistic state of the earliest weeks of life. But the effort to attain the ideal self is not always successful. If the individual cannot change the shape of his self so as to identify it with his ideal self, then he will suffer the pangs of disappointment, and the affective states associated with lowered self-esteem. As Edith Jacobson (1954) has pointed out, self-esteem is a function of the discrepancy between the self-representation and the wishful concept of the self, which we refer to here as the ideal self. This is also the basic assumption made by Annie Reich in her paper on "Pathologic Forms of Self-Esteem Regulation" (1960), which covers and applies clinically a number of the ideas presented here.

The establishment of an ideal self within the representational world of the child provides him with a potential source of well-being. Some of the libido attached to the objects can now be transferred to the ideal and the child can become more independent of the love, praise, and encouragement of his objects, attempting to avoid disappointment and frustration by living up to his ideal self ("identification with the ideal self").[11]

11 It is of some interest that there are ways in which the ideal self can be "gained" other than by identification. In a form of "narcissistic object choice," parts of the ideal self are externalized (projected) onto an object, which then becomes the vehicle of desired aspects of the self (rather than "idealized parts of the self"). By forming a relationship with the object, the externalized parts of the ideal self are regained through a love which results in narcissistic gratification through a concealed union with the ideal self. Probably such a mechanism enters very frequently into object

We would stress that the system of ideal selves (like the representational world in general) has elements in all three of the systems *Ucs.*, *Pcs.*, and *Pcpt-Cs.* As the child develops, the various shapes of his ideal self become modified and supplemented. Some aspects will be defended against, and may reappear in modified form. Regression to earlier forms of the ideal self may show itself in a number of clinically important states, and in the severest form of regression we can see a state of magical omnipotence in which self, ideal self, and ideal object are fused into one.

Finally, a short comment on shame and guilt might be in place. A number of authors (e.g., Piers and Singer, 1953), have related shame to tension between the ego and the ego ideal, and guilt to tension between ego and superego. In the present frame of reference it is possible to suggest, more specifically, that the affect of shame arises when the individual perceives himself (or believes himself to have been perceived by others) as having failed to live up to ideal standards which he accepts, whereas guilt is experienced when his ideal self differs from that which he feels to be dictated by his introjects. Shame might be related to "I cannot see myself as I want to see myself or as I want others to see me." Guilt, on the other hand, would be associated with "I do not really want to be what I feel I ought to be." This distinction is of clinical significance in relation to the formulation of appropriately worded interpretations and the aim to which they are directed.

BIBLIOGRAPHY

Devereux, G. (1950), In Panel: The Interaction of Social and Deep-Psychological Factors. *Bull. Amer. Psa. Assn.*, VI.
Freud, S. (1914), On Narcissim: An Introduction. *Standard Edition*, XIV. London: Hogarth Press, 1957.
—— (1916-17), *Introductory Lectures on Psycho-Analysis*. London: Allen & Unwin.
—— (1917), Mourning and Melancholia. *Standard Edition*, XIV. London: Hogarth Press, 1957.
—— (1921), Group Psychology and the Analysis of the Ego. *Standard Edition*, XVIII. London: Hogarth Press, 1955.

relationships, for we need only think of the way in which a woman may gain the penis, which forms part of her ideal self, through a love relationship with a man.

If the object which acts as a vehicle for the ideal self in reality differs markedly from the ideal, then what might be called an illusional or even delusional relationship ensues.

—— (1923a), Remarks on the Theory and Practice of Dream-Interpretation. *Standard Edition*, XIX. London: Hogarth Press, 1961.

—— (1923b), The Ego and the Id. *Standard Edition*, XIX. London: Hogarth Press, 1961.

—— (1924), The Economic Problem of Masochism. *Standard Edition*, XIX. London: Hogarth Press, 1961.

—— (1932), *New Introductory Lectures on Psycho-Analysis*. London: Hogarth Press, 1933.

Hartmann, H. (1950), Comments on the Psychoanalytic Theory of the Ego. *This Annual*, V.

—— (1956), The Development of the Ego Concept in Freud's Work. *Int. J. Psa.*, XXXVII.

—— & Loewenstein, R. M. (1962), Notes on the Superego. *This Annual*, XVII.

Jacobson, E. (1953), Contribution to the Metapsychology of Cyclothymic Depression. In: *Affective Disorders*, ed. P. Greenacre. New York: International Universities Press.

—— (1954), The Self and the Object World: Vicissitudes of Their Infantile Cathexes and Their Influence on Ideational and Affective Development. *This Annual*, IX.

Jones, E. (1935), Psycho-Analysis and the Instincts. In: *Papers on Psycho-Analysis*. London: Baillière, Tindall & Cox, 4th ed., 1938.

Lampl-de Groot, J. (1962), Ego Ideal and Superego. *This Annual*, XVII.

Novey, S. (1955), The Role of the Superego and Ego Ideal in Character Formation. *Int. J. Psa.*, XXXVI.

Nunberg, H. (1932), *Principles of Psychoanalysis*. New York: International Universities Press, 1955.

Piers, G. & Singer, M. B. (1953), *Shame and Guilt*. Springfield: Thomas.

Reich, A. (1954), Early Identifications as Archaic Elements in the Superego. *J. Amer. Psa. Assn.*, II.

—— (1960), Pathologic Forms of Self-Esteem Regulation. *This Annual*, XV.

Sandler, J. (1960), On the Concept of Superego. *This Annual*, XV.

—— (1962), Psychology and Psychoanalysis. *Brit. J. Med. Psychol.*, XXXV.

—— Kawenoka, M., Nerath, L., Rosenblatt, B., Schnurmann, A., & Sigal, J. (1962), The Classification of Superego Material in the Hampstead Index. *This Annual*, XVII.

—— & Rosenblatt, B. (1962), The Concept of the Representational World. *This Annual*, XVII.

Schafer, R. (1960), The Loving and Beloved Superego in Freud's Structural Theory. *This Annual*, XV.

Spiegel, L. A. (1959), The Self, the Sense of Self, and Perception. *This Annual*, XIV.

ASPECTS OF THE METAPSYCHOLOGY
· OF FANTASY

JOSEPH SANDLER, Ph.D. and HUMBERTO NAGERA, M.D.
(London)

A year or two ago a number of analysts and child psychotherapists working on the Hampstead Index were faced with the need to create a workable classification of observed clinical material relating to the superego concept as it was developed by Freud and in subsequent psychoanalytic writings. This led to a formulation of the superego (Sandler, 1960; Sandler et al., 1962) which stressed, among other things, its function as a source of well-being and self-esteem, and its general role in the regulation of narcissistic supplies. On the basis of these formulations and their interaction with actual clinical observations recorded in the Index, it became clear that one of the main mechanisms used by certain children to deal with lowered narcissistic cathexis of the self was the creation of daydreams in which the child could restore his diminished self-esteem through the creation of ideal and satisfying situations in which he played a cen-

The investigation reported here has been aided by a joint grant from the Foundations' Fund for Research in Psychiatry, New Haven, Connecticut, and the Psychoanalytic Research and Development Fund, Inc., New York.

The material used has been collected at the Hampstead Child-Therapy Clinic, a therapeutic and research center financed by the following foundations: The Field Foundation, Inc., New York; The Ford Foundation, New York; The Foundations' Fund for Research in Psychiatry, New Haven, Connecticut; The Anna Freud Foundation, New York; The Grant Foundation, Inc., New York; The Estate of Flora Haas, New York; The Old Dominion Foundation, U.S.A.; The Psychoanalytic Research and Development Fund, Inc., New York; The Taconic Foundation, New York.

The fantasy research group of the Hampstead Index includes the following psychoanalysts, child psychotherapists, and students: Mrs. L. Neurath, Mrs. M. Kawenoka, Mrs. H. Kennedy, M. Goldblatt, Professor I. Janis, Miss S. Baker, Miss A. Schnurmann, A. Holder, Miss E. First, D. Meers, H. Nagera, and J. Sandler.

This paper was presented at a meeting of the British Psycho-Analytical Society, on 6 June, 1962, and formed the basis for a contribution to the Symposium on Fantasy at the 23rd Psycho-Analytical Congress, Stockholm, July, 1963.

tral and often heroic role. (This applies, of course, to adults as well; cf. A. Reich, 1960.) The mechanism was provisionally called "compensation in fantasy," and it was a natural step to turn to the fantasy material recorded in the Index in order to explore it further. A small research group was set up in order to examine and elaborate the classification of our indexed fantasy material, so that fantasies of different types and fulfilling different functions could be differentiated.

Up to this point the fantasies of the child patients had been classified for convenience according to their "manifest themes." The Index Manual for fantasies provided the following instructions for manifest themes:[1]

> The text or content of conscious fantasies only are indexed under what the therapist judges to be the main theme. . . . The manifest theme card should contain (a) the content (text) of the fantasy; (b) the context in which the fantasy was understood and interpreted (i.e., the latent meaning).

For each card containing such fantasy material a second card, listing the heading under which the latent theme was indexed, was also prepared.

An example of a "fantasy" card from the Index follows. It is quoted here merely as an illustration of the type of material recorded on the cards, and will thus be out of its fuller context.

Name: J.   Age: 10   Therapist: Miss S. Baker

FANTASIES: MANIFEST THEME: Vegetarianism
          LATENT THEME: Oral Incorporation of Father's Penis

> J. said it was dangerous to eat meat because the animal inside might retaliate and start eating your inside. He expressed concern about the health of the therapist and the paternal grandmother (who are meat eaters). He then related a complicated fantasy that the dead animals might retaliate against the *relatives* of the meat eaters. He also worried because he had once been made to eat liver at his nursery school. He felt that this should not deserve retaliation because it was involuntary; he also said that it was all right to eat things which had been harmless when they were alive (Weekly Report: 2.12.60).

---

[1] Because of differences in American and British spelling, the Hampstead Index lists this under "Phantasy."

The therapist verbalized the secrecy surrounding father's relationship with K., and linked this with J.'s anxiety about K. (the father's girl friend) having meals at their home (known to be disapproved of by all the relatives), together with his fear of K.'s becoming pregnant which he knew was similarly forbidden. The meals were therefore dangerous, like eating wild animals who might retaliate on the relatives, as in a public scandal father might lose his job and therefore be unable to feed the children adequately (Weekly Report: 9.12.60).

J. brought material linking his vegetarianism with his defenses against the wish to take and eat the father's penis (Weekly Reports: 18.3.61, 25.3.61). When the therapist verbalized his wish to eat meat, J. agreed but said it was difficult because he lived in a vegetarian family; nevertheless he would not care whether his father objected to his eating meat or not (Weekly Report: 31.3.61). The direct material on the vegetarianism has come in relation to J.'s masculine wish to eat meat in order to have a big penis, but this was long preceded by J.'s fears of eating meat arising from his feminine identification with the pregnant mother.

In addition to manifest and latent themes, the Fantasy section of the Index contained a subsection with the general heading "Characteristics." The cards indexed here did not record the actual content of the fantasies, but statements made by the therapists referring to the frequency of fantasies in the child, the form in which the fantasies were usually expressed, the functions of the child's fantasies, and any other significant features relevant to fantasy production.

The existing system of classification, into manifest and latent themes, was devised in order to bring together fantasy material of a similar sort. Thus, investigators who were interested, for example, in "rescue" fantasies, or in fantasies involving animals, could readily find the appropriate material.

For a number of reasons the existing system was found to be not completely satisfactory. These reasons can be summarized as follows:

1. The indexed material often referred not only to verbally expressed daydreams but also to other verbal communications of the child—for example, observations, reported happenings (e.g., when a child would recount a story which he had previously read), sexual theories of one sort or another, as well as a certain amount of trans-

ference material relating to the child's speculations about the therapist. Under the existing system of classification practically any piece
of verbal communication could be indexed in the fantasy section if
the therapist indexing the case felt that it was appropriate.

2. In addition to this, material was permitted which was not
expressed verbally, but communicated in the form of activities such
as dramatization and painting. This extended the permissible range
of manifest fantasy material to practically every derivative of the
child's unconscious mental life. In practice, however, such derivatives
were on the whole indexed elsewhere, e.g., in the "Defense" and
"Treatment Situation and Technique" sections of the Index, unless
the therapist wished to highlight the content of the child's material.

3. The fantasy, as recorded by the therapist, often contained a
mixture of the patient's actual material and the therapist's psychoanalytic insight into the material. It was often impossible to extract
the content of the child's communication from the reported data.
Instead, in a certain number of cases, it was impossible to disen-
tangle the child's material from the therapist's interpretations.

4. In the recorded fantasy material no clear differentiation was
made between the various elements which might enter into the manifest fantasy. The role of instinctual drives, unconscious wishes,
affects, repressed memories, preconscious thoughts, and, in particular,
of unconscious repressed earlier fantasies which enter into the formation of the manifest derivative could usually not be isolated from
the material recorded on the card, and at times not from the more
extensive weekly reports to which the cards referred.

5. The classification of latent themes in the fantasy material was
not at all systematic, and employed such headings as "abortion,"
"bisexuality," "accidental conception," "doing and undoing,"
"masochism," "sacrifice of parents," "penis-feces equation," "guilt
over soiling," and "treatment." Drives, content, pregenital fixations,
affects, and defenses all found their place in the potentially endless
list of latent fantasy themes.

6. A special difficulty seemed to be present in the indexing of
childhood sexual theories. This difficulty had been apparent for some
time, and the placing of this group in the fantasy section was provisional. Nevertheless, the question of whether a given sexual theory
was a fantasy or not was frequently raised.

It will occasion no surprise when we say that this state of affairs gave rise to some misgivings over the use of the term fantasy, and the research group set itself the task of formulating a more precise set of definitions so that the material contained in the Fantasy section could be ordered more suitably. As the term was used in practice, almost any derivative of the instinctual drives could qualify as a fantasy, or as pointing to a fantasy.

As a first step toward clarification, a review of Freud's writings on the subject was undertaken, and this paper includes an attempt to summarize his views on the subject. This constitutes part I of the paper. Part II consists of a number of theoretical propositions put forward in an effort to extend Freud's views on fantasy. Finally, in part III, a discussion of the varying uses of the term "fantasy" will be presented.

In order to make our task somewhat easier, and to minimize controversial issues as far as possible, we shall not be concerned here with the *dating* of fantasies, nor with their specific *content*.

I. Freud's Views on Fantasy

Freud had a great deal to say on the topic of fantasy, and his views on the subject show a progressive development from 1895 onward. As with many of his concepts, however, he had used the term in a number of different meanings on different occasions, and this necessitates a careful consideration of the full context wherever the term appears. He used the word "fantasy" to refer to conscious daydreams as well as to their unconscious analogues. At times "fantasy" was used more generally, to refer to all unconscious mental processes, as well as to unconscious thoughts. It was applied to normal as well as pathogenic phenomena, and served too to designate psychic reality in contrast to actual events. In addition, the content of psychotic delusions was referred to as fantasies. But in spite of minor inconsistencies in the use of the term, a clear and coherent theory of conscious and unconscious fantasy does emerge.[2]

---

[2] A recent paper by David Beres (1962) considers some of the problems arising in connection with Freud's use of the concept of fantasy. We find ourselves largely in agreement with his views, and some of the formulations in this paper are extremely close to those expressed by Beres.

It is worth noting that the theory of fantasy was developed very largely before the introduction of the structural theory in 1923, and its systematic formulation in structural terms was not attempted by Freud.

The metapsychology of fantasy was initially elaborated by Freud in connection with conscious daydreams, and we will begin our presentation by examining his statements relating to the metapsychology of daydreams. This will be followed by a description of the extensions which Freud found necessary in order to understand the nature and function of unconscious fantasy.

THE METAPSYCHOLOGY OF DAYDREAMS

In *Studies on Hysteria* Breuer and Freud (1895) put forward the view that the essential basis of hysteria is the existence of hypnoid states, and that daydreaming, which could be pathogenic if excessive, occurred in such a semihypnotic state.[3] The experiencing of a trauma during such a state of dissociation rendered the appropriate discharge of affect impossible, and a "pathogenic memory" could be implanted. In referring to Anna O., the authors said: "She embellished her life in a manner which probably influenced her decisively in the direction of her illness, by indulging in systematic day-dreaming, which she described as her 'private theatre' " (p. 22). The authors later refer again to "harmful daydreaming."

Later Freud abandoned the view that an actual trauma, such as a sexual seduction, was the pathogenic agent in hysteria, and shifted the emphasis to the content and fate of the fantasies themselves.

The material which now follows has been ordered under a number of different headings, and a strict historical sequence will not be adhered to:

Fantasies as Distinct from Other Mental Processes

In *The Interpretation of Dreams* (1900), Freud said that daydreams are not normally confused with reality while they are taking

---

[3] This formulation appears to be a compromise between Breuer and Freud. Freud later abandoned Breuer's notion of the central role of hypnoid states in favor of a more dynamic conception of mental conflict, though he always attributed great importance to daydreams and the daydream state.

place. However, later (1907) he pointed out that in delusions fantasies have gained the upper hand, that is, have obtained *belief* and have acquired an influence on action. This quality of belief is also attached to hallucinations and to dreams (during dreaming).

Fantasies have two sets of determinants. One is conscious and manifest to the subject. The other is unconscious and is revealed through analysis. The fantasy is the outcome of a struggle, and represents a compromise between these two sets of determinants.

Freud distinguishes between the fantasy on the one hand, and the instinct and wish on the other. The fantasy is a *wish-fulfilling* product of the imagination.

In "Two Principles" (1911), Freud referred to fantasy as a type of *thought:* "With the introduction of the reality principle one species of thought-activity was split off; it was kept free from reality-testing and remained subordinated to the pleasure principle alone. This activity is *phantasying,* which begins already in children's play, and later, continued as *day-dreaming,* abandons dependence on real objects" (p. 222). Freud's view that fantasying is a type of thinking is expressed in a number of other places (e.g., 1922). In 1921 he pointed out that daydreaming is freely wandering fantastic thinking as opposed to intentionally directed reflection, i.e., nonfantasy thought.

Thoughts, which include fantasies, differ from dreams in that in the latter only the concrete subject matter of thought is visually represented, not the relation between the various elements, the specific characteristic of thought. Fantasy, therefore, is more than thinking in pictures, for it includes relations, and hence is closely connected with verbal development.

We know, too, from *The Ego and the Id* (1923) and subsequent writings, that mental content such as fantasies is not to be confused with aspects of the unconscious ego such as mechanisms of defense.

The Function of Fantasy

Fantasies are, for Freud, fulfillments of secret and repressed wishes and protect the ego from anxiety arising from undischarged instinctual tension. They may be compared to a dream in waking life, and the term "daydream" is thus appropriate. Because reality is on the whole unsatisfying we develop a life of fantasy in which we make up for the insufficiencies of reality by the production of wish fulfillments. In 1897, in a letter to Fliess, Freud referred to fantasies as "defensive structures, sublimations and embellishments of the facts, [which] . . . at the same time serve the purpose of self-exoneration." In the case studies of Little Hans (1909b) and the Rat Man (1909c) he again speaks of defensive, self-justificatory fantasies. In his fantasies about his infancy the individual tries to erase the memory of his autoerotic activities. Thus he may fantasy seductions and assaults in place of memories of such activities.

Fantasies may be a substitute for play. When play has to become secret it may be carried on in fantasy. The fantasy allows the repressed memories to become conscious in distorted form. In fantasies that accompany satisfaction the sexual object is raised to a degree of perfection not readily found again in reality. The function of fantasy, says Freud as late as 1930, is to help make oneself independent of the external world by seeking satisfaction in internal psychic processes. It gives the ego time to modify external circumstances in order to attain instinctual discharge.

Thus the function of fantasy is to create a wish-fulfilling situation which allows a certain amount of instinctual discharge—a discharge which would not be permitted in the existing circumstances of external reality—and which also corrects and modifies that reality in the imagination.

In regard to the relation between fantasy and masturbatory activities (in the wider sense) Freud (1908a) points out that there was a time when the masturbatory act was compounded of two parts. One was the evocation of a fantasy, and the other some form of active self-gratificatory behavior. "Originally the action was a purely auto-erotic procedure for the purpose of obtaining pleasure for some particular part of the body, which could be described as erotogenic. Later, this action became merged with a wishful idea from the sphere of object-love and served as a partial realization of the situation in which the phantasy culminated" (p. 161).

The Dating of Fantasy

Freud is quite explicit in linking the emergence of fantasy with the development of the reality principle. Before that all mental functioning is pleasure-directed, whereas reality-directed thinking appears only with the reality principle. He made this point in "Two Principles of Mental Functioning" (1911) where he speaks of fantasying as a species of thought activity which splits off as the reality principle is introduced. In the *Introductory Lectures* (1916-17) Freud states the position very clearly. Out of external necessity the ego has to pursue the reality principle and renounces temporarily or permanently various of the objects and aims of its desire for pleasure. This is very hard to endure and cannot be accomplished without some kind of compensation. Consequently, a mental activity—fantasy— in which these relinquished sources of pleasure are permitted, has been evolved. Here they are free from the demands of reality and the reality principle. Longings are transformed into ideas of fulfillment. Dwelling upon a wish fulfillment in fantasy brings satisfaction, although the knowledge that it is not reality remains unobscured. Through fantasy man can be alternately a pleasure-seeking animal and a reasonable being. Freud remarks that the realm of fantasy is like a reservation or nature park which has been reclaimed from the encroachments of the reality principle.

Later Freud brought this into line with the structural theory. In 1924, he speaks of a world of fantasy, a domain which has become separated from the external world at the time of the introduction of the reality principle. This domain has since been kept free from the exigencies of life. It is not inaccessible to the ego, but is only loosely attached to it. It is from this world of fantasy that the neurosis draws the material for its new wishful constructions, and it usually finds that material along the path of regression to a more satisfying real past. Again, in 1930 Freud speaks of the intention to make oneself independent of the external world by seeking satisfaction in internal psychical processes. In turning to such internal processes the connection with reality is further loosened; satisfaction is obtained from illusions, which are recognized as such, without the discrepancy between them and reality being allowed to interfere with enjoyment. The region from which these illusions arise is the life of the imagination. At the time when the development of the sense of reality emerged, this region, i.e., the imagination, was expressly exempted from the demands of reality testing and was set apart from the purpose of fulfilling wishes which were difficult to carry out. The psychotic takes a further step and applies these delusions (fantasies) to reality.

There is thus no doubt that Freud links the emergence of fantasy as a distinct mental activity in the child with the development of a sense of reality. This specifically excludes such phenomena as the hallucinatory gratification of the infant from what Freud called fantasy. Since the sense of reality is one of the hallmarks of the ego, it seems to us clear that *fantasying* as Freud saw it could be considered an ego function, and he did not speak of fantasy as existing before the emergence of an ego capable of differentiating reality from other forms of experience.

The Component Parts of Fantasies

The relation between memories and fantasies is a subject with which Freud was concerned throughout his psychoanalytic writings. In 1897, in a letter to Fliess (1887-1902), Freud defined fantasies as psychical facades constructed in order to bar the way to memories. At the same time fantasies serve the purpose of modifying and purifying the memories. They are built up out of previous impressions, which are only subsequently employed; thus they combine past experiences, as well as things heard about past events.

In *The Interpretation of Dreams* (1900), Freud pointed out that daydreams share a large number of their properties with night dreams, and suggested that their investigation might, in fact, have served as the shortest and best approach to an understanding of night dreams. Like dreams, they are wish fulfillments; they are based to a great extent on infantile impressions, and they benefit by a certain degree of relaxation of censorship. The wish that is at work has rearranged the material and has formed it into a new whole. Daydreams stand in much the same relation to the childhood memories from which they are formed, says Freud, as do some of the baroque palaces of Rome to the ancient ruins whose pavements and columns have provided the material for the more recent structures.

In 1907 the relation of fantasies to memories is again discussed. Fantasies are seen as transformed and distorted derivatives of memories of youthful love, which have been prevented from making their way into consciousness in an unmodified form. They have an element of "today" about them. Freud refers to fantasies as the product of a compromise in the struggle between what is repressed and what is dominant in the present. As a result of this compromise, memories are turned into fantasies.

However, childhood memories themselves show the influence of the same struggle which results in daydreams. In "Leonardo" (1910b) Freud emphasized that childhood memories, unlike conscious memories of later life, are not fixed at the moment of being experienced, but are elicited only at a later age when childhood is already past. In the process they are altered and put into the service of later trends so that they usually cannot be sharply differentiated from fantasies.

In "Creative Writers and Day-dreaming" (1908b), the driving force of the fantasy is considered to be an unsatisfied wish; and Freud points out that every single fantasy is the fulfillment of a wish, the correction of unsatisfying reality. The two main groups of wishes concerned are the ambitious and the erotic ones. In fantasies the actual link with the real object is diminished when the growing child stops playing, but this link is in fact retained in the fantasy.

In the same paper, Freud said that fantasies are not unalterable but accommodate themselves to the subject's new impressions of life and change with every change in his situation. They receive what might be called a "date stamp" from every new impression. Freud points out that the fantasy hovers between three moments in time: (1) some current impression which arouses one of the subject's major wishes; (2) it then harks back to a memory of an early experience (usually an infantile experience in which this wish was fulfilled); (3) the fantasy now creates a situation relating to the future which represents a fulfillment of the wish.

It follows from all this that the daydream, like the nocturnal dream, draws upon elements of recent and present experience as well as on past repressed memories. To this we must add the modification and elaboration of these memories in previous daydreams, now repressed. But the consideration of the role of repressed fantasies will be left to the section on unconscious fantasy, as will a short discussion of primal memories and fantasies, those attributed to phylogenetic inheritance.

UNCONSCIOUS FANTASIES

Thus far we have considered only Freud's statements relating to the metapsychology of conscious daydreams. But the notion of unconscious fantasies is a central one in psychoanalytic theory, and the elucidation of their nature and function presents a rather difficult task.

In *The Interpretation of Dreams* (1900) Freud points out that the frequent occurrence of conscious daytime fantasies brings the "structures," i.e., the daydreams, to our knowledge; but just as there are fantasies of this kind, so too are there many unconscious ones which have to remain unconscious on account of their origin from repressed material.

At this juncture we would like to call attention to a point which is of the utmost importance in Freud's writings on unconscious fantasy, one which we believe to have been the source of a great deal of confusion in the post-Freudian literature on this subject. It is simply this: When Freud spoke of unconscious fantasies he meant *two quite distinct classes* of fantasy, and in his writings it is necessary to examine carefully the context in which his statements occur in order to determine which of the two classes he is describing. The first group comprises fantasies which arise predominantly from the repression of conscious and preconscious daydreams and which, as a consequence of the act of repression, enter the system Unconscious. There they are subject to the laws of functioning which characterize the system Unconscious, in short, to the primary processes. The second group contains fantasies which are formed in and remain in the system Preconscious; that is, they are subjected to modification and elaboration according to the secondary process. Yet both these groups of fantasies are not conscious, i.e., *they are unconscious in a descriptive sense*. They do not have the attention cathexis of consciousness attached to them.

This poses a semantic problem. Should we refer to fantasies which belong to the system *Ucs.* as *U*nconscious fantasies and to all fantasies which do not have the property of consciousness as unconscious fantasies? Or should we rather reserve the term unconscious fantasy for all fantasies which reside in the system Unconscious, and call the remaining nonconscious fantasies preconscious fantasies? The latter suggestion may seem preferable to the former, but if we make this distinction, it should be borne in mind that Freud has stated quite clearly that the censorship can operate between the system *Cs.* and the system *Pcs.* as well as between the system *Ucs.* and the *Pcs.* He says: "The *Ucs.* is turned back on the frontier of the *Pcs.* by the censorship, but derivatives of the *Ucs.* can circumvent this censorship, achieve a high degree of organization and reach a certain intensity of cathexis in the *Pcs.* When, however, this intensity is exceeded and they try to force themselves into consciousness, they are recognized as derivatives of the *Ucs.* and are repressed afresh at the new frontier of censorship, between the *Pcs.* and the *Cs.* Thus the first of these censorships is exercised against the *Ucs.* itself, and the second against its *Pcs.* derivatives. . . . In psycho-analytic treatment the existence of the second censorship, located between the systems *Pcs.* and *Cs.*, is proved beyond question" (1915b, p. 193).

It follows that preconscious fantasies cannot be described as possessing the capacity for entry into consciousness without hindrance. Preconscious fantasies as well as those belonging to the *Ucs.* can be subjected to repression, *and may perhaps never acquire the property of consciousness.* It was, of course, the existence of problems of this sort that provided some of the impetus for the creation of the structural theory.

We shall therefore ask the reader to keep in mind the fact that when Freud speaks of unconscious fantasies he may be referring to either one of these types of fantasy. Fortunately, it is not difficult to decide when he is speaking of one and when of the other type, and in what follows we shall for the time being use the term unconscious fantasy to designate fantasies belonging to the system *Ucs.*, and shall make it clear whenever the term is to be used in reference to preconscious fantasy.

The Origin of Unconscious Fantasies

Clearly Freud considered one source, if not the major source, of unconscious fantasies to be conscious memories and daydreams which have been repressed. Thus in 1907, he remarks that repression acts upon feelings, but we can be aware of these only in their association with ideas; therefore if erotic feelings are repressed, the memories of the object of those feelings are forgotten.

In his classic paper on "Hysterical Phantasies" (1908) Freud remarks that either unconscious fantasies have been formed in the *Ucs.;* or, as is more often the case, they were once-conscious fantasies, daydreams, and have since been purposely forgotten and have become unconscious through repression. Their contents may afterward either have remained the same or have undergone alteration, so that the present unconscious fantasies are derivatives of the once-conscious ones.

What of these unconscious alterations of fantasy content? In his paper on "Repression" (1915a) Freud indicates that repression does not hinder the instinctual representative—i.e., the fantasy—from continuing to exist in the Unconscious, from organizing itself further, putting out derivatives, and establishing connections. He further says that the instinctual representative develops with less interference and more profusely if it is withdrawn by repression from conscious (and we must add preconscious) influence. It proliferates in the dark, as it were, and takes on extreme forms of expression which, when they are translated and presented, not only are bound to seem alien, but frighten by giving the picture of an extraordinary and dangerous strength of instinct. This deceptive strength of instinct is the result of an uninhibited development of fantasy and of the damming up consequent on frustrated satisfaction.

If we take into account Freud's remarks in the paper on "The Unconscious" (1915b), we can summarize the sources of unconscious fantasy which we have considered so far:

1. Repressed memories and daydreams.
2. Fantasies which have been subjected to elaboration in the system *Ucs.* according to primary-process laws.
3. Daydream derivatives of unconscious fantasies which have gained consciousness in a new form and which have again been repressed.
4. Derivatives of unconscious fantasies which have been elaborated in the system *Pcs.*, but which have been repressed into the *Ucs.* before they have reached consciousness.
5. To these we must add the possibility of the so-called primal fantasies, a subject which we will consider presently.

It is of some interest to note, as Freud pointed out in the *Introductory Lectures* (1916-17), that daydreams can be tolerated in the *Pcs.* and *Cs.* as long as the amount of libido attached to them is below a certain quantitative level. If the amount of libido attached to the daydreams becomes too great, as occurs under conditions of frustration, the cathexis of the daydreams becomes so intense as to impel them toward realization; then conflict arises, the daydream fantasies are subjected to repression, and are exposed to the attraction exerted from the side of the *Ucs.* The libido now travels back to the fixation points in the *Ucs.*, and a different outlet for the pent-up libido has to be found, for example, through art. If it is not found, symptoms may develop.

In "The Unconscious" (1915b) Freud mentions that object cathexes exist in the repressed fantasies in the *Ucs.*, and that it is these which are re-created in the transference.

A characteristic feature of unconscious fantasies, and one which is all important for an understanding of unconscious mental functioning, is that unconscious fantasies possess *psychic reality* in contrast to material reality (Freud, 1916-17). Whereas conscious daydreams are known to be unreal, this knowledge does not apply to unconscious fantasies, which are treated as if they were in fact real events. Thus repressed memories and repressed daydreams have the same status in the *Ucs.*

We now turn briefly to the controversial problem of primal unconscious fantasies, that is, fantasies which have never been conscious and which are phylogenetic or inherited.

The notion that fantasies may be inherited was put forward in the *Introductory Lectures* (1916-17) and in the "History of an Infantile Neurosis" (1918), written in 1914 and revised in 1918. Freud felt that it might be necessary to postulate such inherited fantasies in order to account for the universality of material relating to childhood seduction, to the phallic mother, to the witnessing of the primal scene, to the family romance, and to the threat of castration, even in the absence of relevant real experiences. However, he had himself considerable doubt as to the validity of the assumption of inherited memories, and drew attention to the fact that children may react subsequently in their fantasies to very early experiences which were not understood at the time. He put forward an alternative view in regard to the universal occurrence of primal-scene material in the analysis of neurotics. Based on the child's experience, for instance, of seeing animals copulate, a wish is constructed to see the parents in intercourse, and this wish gives rise to a fantasy which is later remembered. He remarked, however, that the whole problem of inherited fantasies was far from clear. We would like to add that in the ensuing forty-five years it has become no clearer.

We return briefly to the question of fantasies belonging to the system *Ucs.* and those which show the influence of the system *Pcs.* The distinction between these two types of descriptively unconscious fantasy is vital because upon it hinges the possibility of successfully translating what Freud has had to say about fantasies into structural terms. It is quite clear that logical thinking, of the sort which characterizes conscious thoughts, can influence the form of unconscious fantasies. But the influence of organized and formal modes of thought can only be assumed to have occurred previously outside the system *Ucs.*, either in the construction of conscious daydreams, or in the formation of preconscious derivatives which do not succeed in reaching consciousness.

Freud (1911) made a statement which is crucial to this issue; he said: in the realm of fantasy, repression remains all-powerful; it brings about the inhibition of ideas in *statu nascendi* before they can be noticed by consciousness, if their cathexis is likely to occasion a release of unpleasure. Again, in his introduction to Varendonck's book on *Daydreams* (1921), he referred to the fact that even strictly directed thinking can occur without the cooperation of consciousness, that is to say, preconsciously.

The Role and Fate of Unconscious Fantasies

Unconscious fantasies, in particular repressed daydreams, play a major part in determining the form and content of later daydreams, which are now further derivatives, but they also occupy a crucial role in the formation of neurotic and certain psychotic symptoms, and in determining the content of dreams. Indeed they enter into all the derivatives of unconscious mental life which are permitted to find expression in consciousness or in motility.

It is convenient to deal with the material in this section under a number of different headings. Here the term "fantasy" will be used to denote unconscious fantasy in the system *Ucs.* unless otherwise specified.

Fantasies and Pathology

It will be remembered that Freud attributed importance to the state of daydreaming as a predisposing element in hysterical illness (Breuer and Freud, 1895). He further emphasized the importance of daydreams as the basis of hysterical symptoms (1887-1902).

The higher mental structures which constitute fantasies, when repressed together with the associated perverse impulses, give rise to the higher determination of the symptoms resulting from the memories and to new motives for clinging to the illness. He also pointed out that the defensive fictions of paranoia are fantasies which penetrate to the surface in a distorted form imposed by compromise.

In *The Interpretation of Dreams* (1900) Freud spoke of the hysterical woman's fantasy of seduction by a doctor as the emergence into reality of a fantasy. In the same work he says that hysterical symptoms are attached in the first instance to fantasies, and that the forerunner of the hysterical attack is a repressed daydream fantasy. He also spoke of fantasies entering into phobias and other symptoms. In "Hysterical Phantasies" (1908a) Freud spoke of unconscious fantasies which express themselves in symptoms and attacks. In both paranoia and hysteria the unconscious fantasies may be the same. In paranoia they become conscious and acquire belief; in hysteria they become conscious through the devising of attacks and assaults. Behind these hysterical attacks lie conflicting fantasies, heterosexual and homosexual. In the paper on "Hysterical Attacks" (1909a), he speaks more explicitly of the attack being the outcome of fantasies translated into the motor sphere, projected onto motility, and portrayed in pantomime. Indeed, much earlier (1887-1902, p. 278), he had already referred to hysterical vomiting as a consequence of a wish-fulfilling fantasy of having a baby together with the wish to cease to be attractive.

The relation of fantasies to delusions was discussed in 1907, and to obsessional symptoms in the paper on the Rat Man (1909c).

The neurosis draws its material from the world of fantasy for its new wishful constructions, and it usually finds that material along the path of regression to a more satisfying real past. In the psychosis the internal world is put in place of reality, while in neurosis, on the contrary, we find it attached to a piece of reality which has a symbolic meaning (1924).

Both reality and fantasy play their part in the formation of a neurosis. If what is presented in reality is too close to what is most intensely longed for in daydreams, the neurotic flees from it. Conversely, daydream fantasies are indulged in most readily where there is no danger of seeing them realized (1905).[4]

Finally, as in the dream, as we shall see presently, the relation between an unconscious fantasy and its expression as a symptom is similar to the relation which obtains between the latent dream thoughts and the manifest content of the dream.

We have spoken so far of the fate of unconscious fantasies as if these fantasies could lead a life of their own. This can be misleading unless we remember that the motive behind the fantasy is the instinctual drive with which it is cathected and which it has attempted to satisfy. Freud was quite clear on the point that the degree of resistance to an unconscious fantasy is a function of the degree to which it is invested with instinctual cathexis.

Fantasies and Dreams

So far we have followed Freud in speaking of fantasies which exist in the system Unconscious, and which owe their origin in the main to the repression of previously experienced conscious daydreams. We know too, from Freud, that the conscious (and we may add, preconscious) daydream represents, like the nocturnal dream, an attempt at fabricating a wish-fulfilling or need-satisfying situation. An examination of the role of the various types of fantasy in the formation of the dream has made it evident that the unconscious fantasy, in so far as it exists in the system *Ucs.*, functions not as a wish fulfillment as it did originally in the daydream *but as an unsatisfied wish* which has taken a particular form imposed upon it by

4 This gives us some insight into a possible distinction between the processes which characterize normal and neurotic persons. The normal person may translate his fantasy into action under propitious circumstances, i.e., when he is offered the opportunity to gratify his wish-fulfilling daydream in external reality. The neurotic, on the other hand, may react to the same opportunity for gratification in reality by flight accompanied by repression of the previously tolerated fantasy.

the daydream when it was conscious. The wish-fulfilling daydream creation becomes transformed, when it is repressed, into a desire for the fantasied situation, a desire which increases in proportion to the instinctual drive with which it is cathected. This leads us to the conclusion, implicit in Freud's writings on unconscious fantasy, that the unconscious fantasy is fundamentally an elaborated and *unsatisfied* unconscious wish.

Dreams are, for Freud, the royal road to the Unconscious, and repressed unconscious fantasies are clearly shown in the analysis of a nocturnal dream. There are some dreams which consist merely in the repetition of a preconscious or conscious daytime fantasy (1900). More often, however, the ready-made fantasy forms only a portion of the dream. The fantasy is treated in general like any other portion of the latent material, but it may often remain recognizable as an entity.

Different fantasies, like any other components of the dream thoughts, may be compressed and condensed, superimposed on one another, and so on. Freud points out that thus we can get the whole range from where they constitute the complete manifest content of the dream, to the case in which they are represented in the dream by one of their elements only or by a distant allusion. The fate of fantasies present in the dream thoughts is determined by the advantages which they offer in regard to the requirements of the censorship and secondary revision and by the possibilities for condensation. The less the fantasy derivative resembles the original mental content associated with the drive, the more likely it is to be brought to consciousness.

Maury's dream of being guillotined when a piece of wood struck his neck is explained by Freud as an unconscious fantasy which was utilized for the creation of an apparently long dream. The fantasy is then remembered as the dream. Freud uses this example to explain the apparent rapidity of mental processes in the dream. Furthermore, the labor of building up a façade (through secondary revision) for the dream is spared if a ready-made fantasy is available for use in the dream thoughts.

Symbolic representations in dreams are the expressions of certain unconscious fantasies, deriving probably from the sexual impulses, which find expression not only in dreams but also in hysterical phobias and other symptoms.

It is of interest that as late as 1925, Freud described the dream as a piece of fantasy, working on behalf of the maintenance of sleep.

Fantasies and Creativity

When fantasies receive an instinctual hypercathexis, the outcome need not necessarily be the formation of symptoms. In his paper on "Creative Writers" (1908b) Freud refers to the way in which unconscious fantasies can find expression in stories. These are similar to daydreams, but creative productions also exist in which the writer is recognizable as the self. The artist represents his wishful fantasies as fulfilled; but they become a work of art only when they have undergone a transformation which modifies the offensive elements and conceals their personal origin (1913). In the *Introductory Lectures* (1916-1917) Freud points out that fantasy can find a way to reality through art. This explains why the artist has not far to go to become neurotic. In his work he expresses a stream of pleasure which temporarily adjusts things for him. Again in *Civilization and Its Discontents* (1930), Freud comments that at the head of all the satisfactions through fantasy stands the enjoyment of works of art.

As long ago as 1900, Freud suggested that what was new and essential in the creations of such men as Goethe came without premeditation and as an almost ready-made whole. In this Freud is presumably referring to the result of mental activity in the system *Pcs*.

In regard to the value of fantasy for reality adaptation, a subject which was later elaborated upon by Hartmann and others, Freud (1910a) pointed out that the successful man is one who succeeds in turning fantasies into reality. If this fails, he may withdraw into fantasy, the content of which is transformed into symptoms if he falls ill. Or he may find another path leading from fantasies to reality, e.g., through artistic gifts. If he cannot find such a path, the libido, keeping to the source of the fantasies, will follow the path of regression, will revive infantile wishes, and end in neurosis. Neurosis takes the place of monasteries, said Freud, which used to be the refuge of all whom life disappointed.

Other Derivatives of Fantasy

Unconscious fantasies, as the ideational content of unsatisfied instinctual wishes, find a path to consciousness and motility in a multitude of ways. Only one of these is conscious daydreaming, and we have mentioned some of the others; but there are many more. Freud has shown, for example, how recalled memories screen repressed unconscious fantasies. Similarly, acting out and the reliving of object relationships in the transference have been described by Freud as being derivatives of repressed fantasies. Jokes and humor allow a discharge of forbidden instinctual wish fantasies; and so do the play, dramatizations, and artistic creations of our child patients. (In regard to play, it is of some interest that Freud's writings imply a distinction between two sorts of play. The first is the early play of childhood from which fantasies could be derived. Fantasies can, in one sense, be considered as internalized play. The second, or later type of play, is that in which unconscious wishes are expressed, in censored and symbolic form.)

Summary of Freud's Writings on Fantasy

1. Conscious fantasy, or daydreaming, is a reaction to frustrating external reality. It implies the creation of a wish-fulfilling situation in the imagination, and thereby brings about a temporary lessening of instinctual tension. Reality testing is discarded; the ego nevertheless remains aware that the imaginative construction is not reality, without this knowledge interfering with the gratification thus achieved.

Conscious fantasy differs from hallucinatory wish fulfillment in that the daydream is not normally confused with reality, whereas the hallucinatory gratification cannot be distinguished from reality.

2. Fantasies which are *descriptively* unconscious can be divided into two main classes: (i) those which are formed in the system *Pcs.*, and which parallel the formation of conscious daydreams, except that they do not possess the quality of consciousness; and (ii) those which are relegated by repression to the system *Ucs.* To the repressed daydreams in the system *Ucs.* we must add the proliferated derivatives of fantasies and memories which have been formed according to the laws of the primary process, as well as derivatives which have

reached the systems *Pcs.* and *Cs.*, subjected to secondary-process elaboration, and then repressed. For the sake of completeness, we can add the hypothetical primal or inherited fantasies.

3. Once a conscious or preconscious fantasy has been repressed into the system *Ucs.*, it functions exactly like a *memory of instinctual satisfaction* and can provide the ideational content of the instinctual drives. Fantasies in the system *Ucs.*—perhaps we can say, unconscious fantasies proper—are *not* wish fulfillments, but are now *the ideational content of instinctual wishes*. They deserve the name of fantasy only inasmuch as they are *derived* from the content of conscious or preconscious fantasies. Fantasies belonging to the system *Ucs.* and those in the systems *Pcs.* and *Cs.* may be similar in their ideational content. They can be contrasted in the descriptive, dynamic, and topographical senses.

4. Unconscious fantasies can find expression in new conscious and preconscious daydreams; but they can also find expression and gratification in any one of a large number of other forms, none of which necessarily qualifies for the designation "fantasy."

II. Some Extensions of Freud's Views on Fantasy

1. As already mentioned, the term "unconscious fantasy" is capable of more than one interpretation in Freud's writings, and its unqualified use may lead to confusion. Freud himself did not always specify the exact sense in which he used the term, although this could usually be elicited from the context in which the term occurred. Unconscious fantasy (in the *descriptive* sense, i.e., fantasy which is not-conscious) includes fantasy in the system *Ucs.* as well as that in the system *Pcs.*, and there appears to be a clear theoretical distinction between the two types.

Fantasy in the Ucs. (the term "unconscious fantasy" is often used to denote only this type) was seen as dominated by primary- rather than secondary-process functioning. Moreover, this type of fantasy *does not constitute a wish fulfillment;* rather it provides the *ideational content of unsatisfied wishes*—a wished-for but not-attained experience. In the *Ucs.* the fantasy functions like a *memory* of a real gratifying experience which, when cathected or recathected by the drives, provides the content of the wish in the *Ucs.*

Preconscious fantasy (descriptively, this is also a form of unconscious fantasy) can constitute an attempt at wish fulfillment, in exactly the same way as conscious daydreams. (At times such fantasies may be repressed before they are permitted to reach awareness, their content being added to the content of the *Ucs.* (Freud, 1915b).

In the system *Pcs.* we can distinguish between (a) the preconscious fantasy as a wish fulfillment—the *Pcs.* fantasy proper; (b) the preconscious fantasy as the content of an unfulfilled preconscious wish. In this case the preconscious wish is a wish derivative of an unsatisfied wish in the *Ucs.* and will press toward some form of discharge. One of the forms in which it may obtain fulfillment is as a preconscious or conscious fantasy.

A clinical example may make this a little clearer. A patient, in the course of his associations, produces the daydream of being seduced by a certain actress. He is given the interpretation that this is the fulfillment of a wish to be seduced by the analyst. This interpretation is a reconstruction of a preconscious (but descriptively unconscious) wish which had been formed during the course of the analysis, and had then been warded off. As it came closer to consciousness it was not permitted to proceed, and attained expression and satisfaction through a further derivative (the daydream brought in the material). The preconscious transference wish was itself, however, a derivative of a wish in the *Ucs.* to be seduced by the mother. This latter wish naturally met with more resistance than the preconscious transference wish derived from it. The content of the *Ucs.* wish (the *Ucs.* fantasy) was in its turn derived from a childhood fantasy, a wish-fulfilling oedipal daydream, created as the fulfillment of a wish to have active intercourse with the mother. This was subjected to repression at the time of the resolution of the oedipus complex. With repression, the wish-fulfilling oedipal daydream was transformed into the content of an unsatisfied wish to be seduced by the mother, and strove for satisfaction under the pressure of the instinctual drives which it once satisfied in the childhood daydream, and with which it is now cathected.

This sequence can be summed up as follows:

(a) Numerous precursors, leading to the
(b) Oedipal wish to have intercourse with the mother.

(c) This wish was satisfied through the (*Pcs.* or *Cs.*) daydream of being seduced by the mother.

(d) The (*Pcs.* or *Cs.*) fantasy content was subjected to repression.

(e) The fantasy content now became the content of a wish in the *Ucs.*

(f) When activated in the transference, this unconscious wish was transformed into a preconscious wish to be seduced by the analyst.

(g) This preconscious wish (probably) resulted in a preconscious fantasy of being seduced by the analyst.

(h) As the preconscious fantasy was not acceptable, it was itself warded off, and the wish was finally fulfilled through the creation of a conscious daydream of seduction by an actress.

This example is, of course, a highly condensed and schematic one.

2. The ideas presented so far are incomplete in that Freud's statements on the subject were largely prestructural, and the difficulties which the structural theory was intended to solve are inherent in the presentation. Freud did not return to the subject of fantasy in any comprehensive way after the formulation of the structural theory (1923), and a number of gaps remain to be filled in from the rest of his writings.

In some respects this task is not very difficult, as Freud made a number of additions to the theory of *dreams* in his later writings, and these can be extended to fantasies. In particular, he brought anxiety dreams and punishment dreams into line with the theory of wish fulfillment—dreams which were originally considered to be exceptions to the theory.[5]

It is well known that anxiety fantasies and punishment fantasies exist which resemble anxiety and punishment dreams in their content. In the short statements which follow, the word "fantasy" has been added in brackets where "dream" occurs in Freud's description, and it can be seen that the definitions fit fantasies as well as dreams.

Anxiety fantasies: Freud pointed out that the censoring agency (the ego) may be caught unawares when the dream [fantasy] content

[5] The same holds true for the fantasies which parallel so-called "counter-wish" dreams (1900) and which show the fulfillment of masochistic trends.

is so outrageous that it had not been anticipated. Where such dreams [fantasies] affront the censorship, the ego experiences the affect of anxiety. Anxiety indicates the failure of the censorship to control or distort the dream [fantasy] contents (1917, 1925). In the *New Introductory Lectures* (1932), Freud modified his statement that the dream is a wish fulfillment to "the dream is an attempted wish fulfillment," and this must surely be true of fantasies as well.

Punishment fantasies: Freud says that "Even punishment-dreams [fantasies] are wish fulfillments, but they do not fulfill the wishes of the instinctual impulses, but those of the critical, censuring and punishing functions of the mind" (1932, p. 43). In a footnote added to *The Interpretation of Dreams* (1900) in 1930, Freud refers to punishment dreams (and we may extrapolate this to fantasies). He says: "Since psycho-analysis has divided the personality into an ego and a super-ego . . . , it has become easy to recognize in these punishment dreams fulfilments of the wishes of the super-ego" (p. 476).

3. With the transmutation of the systems *Pcs.-Cs.* into the structural concept of the ego, the term "unconscious" came to be used more descriptively. This change brought with it a certain shift of emphasis. In the topographical view the systems *Pcs.* and *Cs.* were conceived as being relatively superficially placed in the mental apparatus. The ego, however, was now seen as having areas which were deeply unconscious. These unconscious parts of the ego do not coincide with the repressed; they represent aspects of its structure, functions, and operations which, like the id and parts of the super-ego, are well removed from the "sense organ" of consciousness.

These considerations would imply that unconscious fantasies may be highly organized and structured, by virtue of the activities of the unconscious ego, and are capable of sharing the properties of the conscious daydream with the exception of the quality of consciousness.

However, before accepting this proposition, it is worth while examining its significance in relation to the various meanings which the term "fantasy" can assume in the present context. Particularly important is the differentiation between "fantasy" as representing a particular sensorimotor *content,* and "fantasy" as a mental *function* (fantasying); a distinction which is often lost or obscured in the discussion of this topic.

The Function of Fantasying

Freud saw this mental process as the effort to attain the fulfillment of an unsatisfied wish through the creation of an imagined wish-fulfilling situation, in which the wish was represented as being fulfilled (usually in a disguised form). Frustrating reality is known, but is temporarily put aside. This process, involving a knowledge of what is "real" and what is "unreal," can without difficulty be considered, from the structural point of view, as a *function* of the ego. It represents a technique whereby the ego temporarily avoids unpleasure or disappointment by holding reality in abeyance. Fantasying may represent the formation of a compromise between instinctual wishes and the demands of the superego, and in general lends itself well to defensive use.

As fantasying in this sense can be considered an ego function, it makes use of secondary (as well as primary) processes, and as an activity can reach a high degree of organization. It is a form of *thinking,* which may be differentiated from reality-oriented thinking in that it involves a turning away from frustrating reality, although it may itself subserve adaptation (as in the creation of tentative fantasy solutions to problems; fantasies which may later be fulfilled by the manipulation of reality).

Fantasying involves a *fantasy work* which closely parallels the dream work, although the influence of secondary-process functioning is more evident in the former. The fantasy work of the ego will include much of what in dreaming constitutes secondary elaboration or revision. As in the process of dreaming, the fantasy work makes use of both repressed and nonrepressed mental contents (recent memories, percepts, the content of past fantasies and other derivatives, etc.), and will often make use of elements of reality knowledge in the elaboration of the fantasy. (This might be thought of as corresponding to the use of the day's residues in dream formation.)

The product of this process—the fantasy content—may be (descriptively) either conscious or unconscious.[6]

6 It might be legitimate to add "preconscious" here, if one wished to designate unconscious content which is not repressed, but only temporarily latent; however, from a descriptive point of view even temporarily latent contents are unconscious. Certainly degrees of consciousness or unconsciousness exist, and we do not have a satisfactory nomenclature for these.

Fantasy Content

The products of the ego's *fantasying function* represent organized, structured, and often highly symbolic fantasies. Their form is imposed on them by the organization of the ego, and by its defensive requirements.

Fantasy content produced in this way may receive an attention cathexis and be perceived as a conscious daydream; it may remain outside consciousness, but be only temporarily latent, with the possibility of being brought into consciousness unchanged; or it may arouse an anxiety signal even after it has been formed, and be repressed. This repression would involve (i) the withdrawal of any attention cathexis which might have been directed toward it, or which was in the process of being directed toward it; and (ii) the construction of anticathexes directed against that fantasy content in that particular form. *Repression of fantasy content may therefore take place without the content ever having been conscious.*

The motives for such repression are numerous. We can include such factors as the heightening of the instinctual cathexis attached to the content, the increase in the dangerous quality of the fantasy content when reality tends to correspond to it, the tendency for the content to find expression in motility, and so on.

Once repressed, the fantasy content becomes potential wish content. It is added to the conglomerate of repressed contents which have, in a variety of different ways, become associated with the instinctual drive in question. Drive cathexis can then be displaced from one content to another, contents can be condensed, etc.; in short, they will be subject to the primary process. If drive cathexis is not withdrawn from a piece of repressed content, or if it is withdrawn and reapplied, it will be urged toward consciousness or motility, but can be permitted discharge only in the shape of a further derivative.

We come now to an important point. When in this way a fantasy becomes part of repressed id-cathected content[7] (a better formulation

[7] The term "id-cathected content," though clumsy, is used here in place of "id-content," as there is some controversy over the consideration of repressed content (in the sense in which it is used here) as part of the id. Id-cathected content refers to mental representations which have become cathected by instinctual energies alone, as the result of the reactivation of memory traces. If this id-cathected content receives

might be id representation) it takes its place alongside other repressed mental contents *which need not have originated in fantasies.* Such contents include memories of all sorts; non-fantasy imaginative contents such as reality-oriented thoughts; word representations (words as "things") and indeed, sensorimotor images of every conceivable variety.[8] In general, any experience that leaves a memory trace can, with the recathexis of that trace by the id drives, constitute wish content. Moreover, if the path to direct discharge of this content via the ego is blocked, such content will possess "psychic reality," as the labeling of content as "unreal" is an ego function. Any unconscious elaboration of these contents, *as far as the id is concerned,* will follow the primary process.

At this point an apparent paradox emerges. There is clear evidence, particularly from the theory of dreams (1900) that the content of a fantasy can retain a high degree of organization and coherence *even after the fantasy has been repressed.* Yet the id, by definition, is unorganized and incapable of organizing the mental content cathected by the instinctual drives (except via primary-process functioning). The capacity for secondary-process organization of content belongs to the ego.

It seems necessary, therefore, to distinguish between the capacity of the ego *to organize* mental content (as it does in perception, organized memory, reality-oriented thinking, as well as in fantasy), and the *organized form* imposed on the mental content, an outcome of the ego's work. *Once formed by the ego, fantasy content which becomes id-cathected content (wish content) may retain all or part of the organized qualities which have been imposed on it.* This is obviously also true for repressed memories, for a memory derives from (conscious or unconscious) perception, an ego function which produces, in the percept, highly organized mental content. (We speak here of the state of affairs which exists after the ego has reached a fair degree of development, because unorganized impressions which are registered before the beginnings of an ego, in the so-called undifferentiated state, must be excepted, the organizing of mental content being by definition one of the functions which we call "ego.")

---

an ego cathexis as well as an id cathexis, it will be referred to as "ego-cathected" or as "ego-modified content."

8 We do not propose to discuss the question of affective content, since this complicated subject deserves separate treatment. However, if the reader is willing to accept the notion of repressed affects, then they could be included here.

4. In this presentation the question of the dating of fantasy has not been considered. It has been assumed throughout that the processes described occur in a child or adult in whom an ego capable of differentiating the products of the imagination from real percepts has developed. Before the operation of the reality principle, the infant may be assumed to obtain partial and temporary gratification when reality does not provide satisfaction, through the process of *hallucinatory wish fulfillment.* By this is implied the perceiving (sensing would perhaps be better) of the experiences previously associated with the reduction of instinctual tension, as if these experiences were arising anew from the sensory end of the primitive psychic apparatus. Hallucinatory gratification, as described by Freud, is distinct from fantasy, which is an ego activity occurring when some degree of reality testing and the capacity for *imagining* (as distinct from perceiving) has developed. It is clear, however, that hallucinatory gratification is a basic precursor of later fantasying. The difference between the two reflects the difference between primary and secondary process.

III. Aspects of the Use of the Term "Fantasy"

In this paper we have attempted to describe the concept of fantasy as we have understood it in Freud's work, and to integrate it to some extent into the structural theory. The impetus for this attempt has come from the need to classify and categorize fantasy material in the Hampstead Index, a project in which the structural point of view has been largely utilized.

The material presented here also constitutes an effort to make the task of communication easier, not only within a single analytic group, but between people of differing viewpoints. The terms "fantasy" and "unconscious fantasy" mean different things to different workers; yet in the course of scientific argument there often arise situations in which it is assumed that because the word used is the same, its meaning is constant.

Broadly speaking, there are two approaches to the notion of fantasy which can be discerned in psychoanalytic writings. The first is that which regards the content of all unconscious mental processes, even the most primitive content, as fantasy. This is the approach which is adopted by Melanie Klein and which was made explicit by Susan Isaacs in her well-known paper on fantasy (1948). There she states quite clearly (1) that fantasies are the primary content of unconscious mental processes; (2) that they are, in the first instance, the psychic representatives of the libidinal and destructive instincts, and early in development become elaborated into defenses as well as wish fulfillments and anxiety contents; (3) that the earliest fantasies are experienced in sensations, later they take the form of plastic images and dramatic representations. Isaacs makes it clear that she extended Freud's concept of fantasy and unconscious fantasy so as to give the term a wider meaning. The metapsychological implications of her view have been discussed by Glover (1945), and we will restrict ourselves to the comment that in her usage of the term "fantasy," the distinction between fantasying as an ego function and hallucinatory gratification is lost. In Kleinian usage, the term has become a synonym for the psychic representatives of the drives.

The second approach to fantasy regards fantasying as an ego function, and fantasy as only one type or source of conscious or unconscious mental content. This is the approach which is inherent in Freud's writings, which we have attempted to define and extend in this paper. It involves a narrower concept of fantasy than the first, and is less simple; it involves a recognition, for example, of a double meaning of the term unconscious fantasy, and of a distinction between content derived from fantasies on the one hand, and the function or process of fantasying on the other. The distinction between fantasying as an ego function not present from birth and hallucinatory wish fulfillment is an important one, although the latter process can be regarded as a precursor of fantasying, a function which is only gradually developed with maturation and experience.

We can assume that the laying down of memory traces of sensory experiences associated with drive tension and discharge occurs from very early in life, and that these memory traces, when recathected by drive energies, can give rise to memory images which represent instinctual gratification. Thus the infant who has experienced the satisfaction of oral needs will, when he is hungry, temporarily hallucinate the experiences which have been associated with relief of hunger as well as the accompanying pleasure. This serves to provide a partial and transitory satisfaction, which breaks down when the drive tension increases. To the pleasurable and satisfying contents associated with drive reduction can be added those associated with unpleasure and even trauma, and which can reach hallucinatory intensity.

The hallucination of which we speak is not distinguishable from a real sensory experience. It possesses psychic reality, for the ego has not yet acquired the capacity to *disbelieve,* to invest psychic contents with the knowledge of their psychic unreality. We can assume that the infant gradually begins to differentiate between hallucinatory revival and fresh impressions, particularly as a result of those circumstances where the hallucinated content does not receive a reinforcement from the side of reality. Primary-process functioning begins to be controlled by the secondary process, the id by the developing ego. Hallucinatory wish fulfillment is given up, although we can surmise that the child's perception of the outer world will for a long time remain colored by gross apperceptive distortions.

With the progress of reality testing and the development of the reality principle, a realm of trial perception and trial action becomes established, and we can now speak of the ego's function of imagination, a function which can, as we know, create both conscious and unconscious (the terms are used in their descriptive sense) fantasy content. Imagination can operate side by side with perception, and although the one function constantly influences the content produced by the other, they are not identical. Thought, and in particular that special form of thought which we refer to as fantasy, is now possible. Fantasy is, for Freud, a wish-fulfilling product of the *imagination,* quite different from hallucinatory wish fulfillment, for which "fantasying" would in any case appear to be too mild and weak a term. The products of the latter process are perceptual rather than imaginative, and are at the start indistinguishable from sensations arising from the real world.

Fantasying, then, can be regarded as an ego function, producing organized, wish-fulfilling, imaginative content, which may or may not become conscious. It involves a temporary laying aside of reality, although elements of reality can be utilized in the creation of the fantasy. Once formed by the ego, the fantasy content, which may show a high degree of organization and symbolization, can be repressed and subjected to primary-process functioning alone. Fantasy thinking differs from reality-oriented thinking precisely in the fact that the demands of reality are partially or wholly ignored. It does not aim at changing reality in order to obtain satisfaction; rather it involves the creation of an imagined alternative and satisfying state. It arises as a consequence of the frustrations inevitably imposed by reality, and although the ego remains aware that the imaginative construction is not reality, partial and immediate gratification is achieved.

There are, of course, many thoughts which occupy an intermediate position between fantasy and reality-oriented thoughts, and the two cases represent the extreme ends of a continuum. Moreover, fantasying, although it involves a turning away from immediate frustrating reality, can be utilized as an important aspect of scientific and artistic creativity. It should be added that these remarks on fantasying do not preclude the possibility that, in certain circumstances, reality can subsequently be changed so as to bring about a realization of the fantasy.

In our view, the following considerations would have to be taken into account in any consideration of fantasy.

(a) As ideational contents (representations) may originate from a number of sources (early unorganized sensations, organized thoughts, percepts, memory images, fantasies, etc.), it would appear to be inappropriate to use the term "fantasying" for the primary-process elaboration of these into the content of instinctual wishes. It is only when the ego takes a hand in the organization of content into wish-fulfilling imaginative products, that we should speak of fantasy formation.

(b) It would appear to be correct to speak of the content of the system *Ucs.* as unconscious fantasy only when that content has been derived from repressed fantasies. In using the term "unconscious fantasy" it should always be made clear whether the term is used to refer to those contents of the *Ucs.* which have been derived from fantasying, or in its broad descriptive sense.

(c) We regard the process of fantasying as an ego function, resulting in organized, wish-fulfilling, imaginative content, which may or may not be consciously perceived. The fantasy may then be a derivative, a compromise constructed by the ego between that wish and the demands of the superego. Reality knowledge may be partially or completely suspended in the formation of this derivative, or it may be utilized and influence the fantasy to a high degree. The fantasy content may be repressed soon after it has been created, or defended against in other ways.

(d) The fantasy is only one of many derivatives which the ego can construct.

(e) The possibility exists that some fantasies represent wish fulfillments, when the wish in question arises neither from the id nor from the superego, but from the ego itself.

It follows that we have a situation in which the ego may create a fantasy using, in distorted and censored form, id-cathected content which was derived, let us say, from a repressed memory. (Such a memory may, of course, have been distorted in its content at the time when it constituted a percept, by preconscious and unconscious wishes.) On the other hand, id-cathected repressed fantasy content may find expression in such ego-modified derivatives as apperceptions, artistic creations, dramatic productions, free associations, delusions, etc.

This can be expressed schematically in the following way:

Id-cathected content Derived from repressed:		*Content of derivatives Expressed in:*
Memory images		Perceptual images
Reality-oriented		(appercepts)
thoughts		Wishes
Dream images		Action
		Reality thinking
Fantasies	Repression	Dreams
Etc.	⟵	Play
(We include also		Free associations
primal memories)	Return of the	Screen memories
	⟶	Distorted recollections
	repressed	Manifest transference
		content
		Symptoms
		Delusions
		Scientific theories
		Hypnagogic phenomena
		Artistic and literary
		creations
		Daydream fantasies
		Etc.

In this scheme we distinguish between

1. *Id-cathected content,* subject to the primary process alone, which forms the content of instinctual wishes. This content consists of images arising from memory traces when these traces are re-cathected by the drives. Inasmuch as they possess only a drive cathexis, the ego function of judging whether they constitute real or imagined contents does not operate, and they possess "psychic reality."

2. *Ego-modified content.* Because repressed content is not permitted direct discharge, it can achieve this only through the formation of derivatives. We can assume that in order to circumvent the censorship, some degree of modification and organization of the id-cathected content must have occurred before the ego permits drive discharge. It can also be assumed that the content of the derivative has received, in addition to the drive cathexis which impels it toward discharge, ego cathexes of varying degree.

It can be argued that many of the derivatives listed above are very similar to fantasies, and deserve to be labeled as such. To do so would obscure, we believe, some of the essential character of the fantasy, and would lead to a generalization of the term which would then cover all derivatives and thus conceal the significant theoretical and important clinical distinctions.

It is certainly true that many nonfantasy derivatives occur simultaneously, or in close association, with wish-fulfilling fantasies; but others do not, being rather *alternatives* to fantasy. In the course of psychoanalytic treatment we often interpret a derivative as being the outcome of an underlying fantasy. Even when this is not correct, the patient can bring material which appears to confirm this interpretation. What has happened is that, *through the interpretation,* we provide *alternative derivatives* (fantasies, thoughts, and wishes). This is one important step in the process of therapy, leading ultimately to further insight and the "making of the unconscious conscious."[9]

The importance of fantasies in mental life cannot be overestimated. In this study we have attempted to bring out something of the confusion which attends the use of the terms "fantasy" and

[9] Psychoanalytic therapy, particularly with children, can be understood in terms of the changes which occur in derivatives, and the substitution of new derivatives for old ones. A study based on this approach is in progress.

"unconscious fantasy," and to offer a number of thoughts, based on Freud's work, which may lead to a clarification of the scientific and semantic problems involved. Although we have emphasized the distinction between the ego function of fantasying and other ego functions, and between fantasy content and other ideational content, we have hesitated to introduce any new terms, but there can be little doubt that the "blanket" terms need to be supplemented in some way so that the different concepts subsumed under the terms can be more clearly differentiated.

The present project was begun to solve the practical problem of classifying "fantasies" in the Hampstead Index. As a consequence of the considerations expressed in this paper, we have begun to devise a classification which is based on the differentiation of the various types of derivative, as well as on the dynamic meaning of the derivative content. From the point of view of the derivatives, fantasy is only one of many such derivatives, although repressed fantasies may dominate the content of derivatives other than fantasy. This classification shows a great deal of promise, for there is an indication that the delineation of the various derivatives will throw light on the differences in instinctual and ego development in different children. The door appears to be open for an investigation, through child analysis and observation, of the natural history of derivatives, and this may in turn lead to greater diagnostic and therapeutic precision.

BIBLIOGRAPHY

Beres, D. (1962), The Unconscious Fantasy. *Psa. Quart.*, XXXI.
Breuer, J. & Freud, S. (1895), Studies on Hysteria. *Standard Edition*, II. London: Hogarth Press, 1955.
Freud, S. (1887-1902), *The Origins of Psychoanalysis*. New York: Basic Books.
—— (1900), The Interpretation of Dreams. *Standard Edition*, IV & V. London: Hogarth Press, 1953.
—— (1905), Fragment of an Analysis of a Case of Hysteria. *Standard Edition*, VII. London: Hogarth Press, 1953.
—— (1907), Delusions and Dreams in Jensen's *Gradiva*. *Standard Edition*, IX. London: Hogarth Press, 1959.
—— (1908a), Hysterical Phantasies and Their Relation to Bisexuality. *Standard Edition*, IX. London: Hogarth Press, 1959.
—— (1908b), Creative Writers and Day-Dreaming. *Standard Edition*, IX. London: Hogarth Press, 1959.
—— (1909a), Some General Remarks on Hysterical Attacks. *Standard Edition*, IX. London: Hogarth Press, 1959.

—— (1909b), Analysis of a Phobia in a Five-Year-Old Boy. *Standard Edition*, X. London: Hogarth Press, 1955.

—— (1909c), Notes upon a Case of Obsessional Neurosis. *Standard Edition*, X. London: Hogarth Press, 1955.

—— (1910a), Five Lectures on Psycho-Analysis. *Standard Edition*, XI. London: Hogarth Press, 1957.

—— (1910b), Leonardo da Vinci and a Memory of His Childhood. *Standard Edition*, XI. London: Hogarth Press, 1957.

—— (1911), Formulations on the Two Principles of Mental Functioning. *Standard Edition*, XII. London: Hogarth Press, 1958.

—— (1913), The Claims of Psycho-Analysis to Scientific Interest. *Standard Edition*, XIII. London: Hogarth Press, 1955.

—— (1915a), Repression. *Standard Edition*, XIV. London: Hogarth Press, 1957.

—— (1915b), The Unconscious. *Standard Edition*, XIV. London: Hogarth Press, 1957.

—— (1916-17), *A General Introduction to Psychoanalysis*. New York: Garden City Publishing Co., 1943.

—— (1917), A Metapsychological Supplement to the Theory of Dreams. *Standard Edition*, XIV. London: Hogarth Press, 1957.

—— (1918), From the History of an Infantile Neurosis. *Standard Edition*, XVII. London: Hogarth Press, 1955.

—— (1921), Introduction to J. Varendonck's *The Psychology of Day-Dreams*. *Standard Edition*, XVIII. London: Hogarth Press, 1955.

—— (1922), Some Neurotic Mechanisms in Jealousy, Paranoia and Homosexuality. *Standard Edition*, XVIII. London: Hogarth Press, 1955.

—— (1923), The Ego and the Id. *Standard Edition*, XIX. London: Hogarth Press, 1961.

—— (1924), The Loss of Reality in Neurosis and Psychosis. *Standard Edition*, XIX. London: Hogarth Press, 1961.

—— (1925), Some Additional Notes upon Dream-Interpretation as a Whole. *Standard Edition*, XIX. London: Hogarth Press, 1961.

—— (1930), Civilization and Its Discontents. *Standard Edition*, XXI. London: Hogarth Press, 1961.

—— (1932), *New Introductory Lectures on Psychoanalysis*. New York: Norton, 1933.

Glover, E. (1945), Examination of the Klein System of Child Psychology. *This Annual*, I.

Isaacs, S. (1948), The Nature and Function of Phantasy. *Int. J. Psa.*, XXIX.

Reich, A. (1960), Pathologic Forms of Self-Esteem Regulation. *This Annual*, XV.

Sandler, J. (1960), On the Concept of Superego. *This Annual*, XV.

—— et al. (1962), The Classification of Superego Material in the Hampstead Index. *This Annual*, XVII.

ASPECTS OF NORMAL AND PSYCHOLOGICAL DEVELOPMENT

PATTERNS OF INFANTILE EXPERIENCE AND THE DEVELOPMENTAL PROCESS

SIBYLLE K. ESCALONA, Ph.D. (New York)

In this paper I shall report on a small fragment from a body of research material dealing with behavior and development during the first year of life.[1] From detailed observations of young babies and their families, I hope to derive greater understanding of the manner in which the patterning of life experience reflects the developmental process, and at the same time determines the course of development. By the term patterning of life experience I refer to the infinite number of behavior episodes that take place hour by hour, day by day, and month by month. In other words, I refer to *what* babies do, *when* they do it, *how* they do it, and under *what circumstances* behavior takes particular forms and intensities. I expect to demonstrate that what infants experience as they are fed, clothed, bathed; the nature of their perceptual and motoric encounters with the world about and with their own bodies, and most importantly their transactions with the mother and with other people—the nature of these events is influenced by the baby's established reaction tendencies (which may be biologically given or acquired), and by the mother and outer circumstances generally—the actual reality to which they must adapt.

The relationship between intrinsic characteristics of the organism, built-in maturational sequences, and environmental forces and conditions, as all of these affect developmental course has received much discussion. My view of the old "nature-nurture" problem is rather different from the most customary ones. A discussion of how I conceptualize developmental events will be developed as data are presented, and in the last section of this paper.

[1] This research project was made possible (in part) by a grant from The Foundation's Fund for Research in Psychiatry.

However, a brief reference to the theoretical frame of reference, which of course determined my use of the data, is appropriate. While my conception of development derives from many sources, two influences were of paramount importance. These are psychoanalytic ego psychology, especially some of Hartmann's formulations (1939), and Piaget's work on the development of thought (1936). The method of approach leans heavily on Piaget, while the substantive content of the inquiry is largely drawn from psychoanalytic formulations.[2]

Piaget demonstrated the manner in which formal aspects of early experience (sensorimotor schemata) lead to adaptations that take into account properties and relationships of the real physical world that, once they find mental representation, constitute the basic elements of thought. In other words, such functions or "operations" as anticipation, intentionality, means-end relationships, the constancy of the object world, spatial and temporal coordinates, and the like are, in a manner of speaking, "learned" on a sensorimotor level, at first without a counterpart in terms of corresponding ideas or structures on a psychological level. Further, he postulates, and with good empirical support, that the later development of intelligence proper, in terms of symbols, images, and an expanding cognitive apparatus, is predicated on such early body learning.

Psychoanalysis similarly assumes that ego functions, and in fact all aspects of psychic organization, have their roots in early and essentially somatic experience. Psychoanalytic exploration has rarely extended to a concrete assessment of patterns of infant behavior, as these may reflect successive stages in the development of ego functions, cognitive or otherwise.

My data suggest the possibility that what Piaget proposes for cognition is true of all adaptive aspects of mental functioning: namely, that the emergence of such functions as communication, modulation of affect, control over excitation, delay, and aspects of object relation, and hence identification, all are the result of a de-

[2] A discussion of the psychoanalytic literature on early development and on the nature-nurture problem would exceed the scope of the present paper. I wish to mention, however, that my formulations were stimulated, and in part anticipated, by a number of psychoanalytic writings. These include publications by Benjamin (1950, 1959), Spitz (1955), Spitz and Wolf (1949), and the well-known series of articles by Hartmann, Kris, and Loewenstein (e.g., 1946).

velopmental sequence in sensorimotor terms, before they can emerge as ego functions in the narrower sense.

THE SUBJECTS AND BACKGROUND INFORMATION

I shall draw on information concerning four healthy infants, all of whom were studied at twenty-eight weeks of age. They are among the subjects of an earlier study conducted by Mary Leitch, myself, and a group of associates, under the auspices of the Menninger Foundation and the U.S. Public Health Service.[3] The original investigation provided descriptive information about 128 healthy children who lived with their families in a Midwestern town. It included a history of the infant's development up to the time he became a research subject, a detailed account of his behavior in a large variety of situations at the time of the study, and as much information as could be obtained about the mother, the family, and the social matrix in which they lived. The subjects ranged in age from four weeks to thirty-two weeks. Each was studied at only one point in his development since our interest was to describe individual differences within the normal range for a large number of children.

The four subjects to be presented were among those selected for a particularly intense analysis at a later date. In order to learn what impact on immediate adaption may be discerned for a particular biologically given characteristic, I selected the small sample so as to include the most active and the least active babies in the total group. Activity level was defined in terms of the forcefulness and frequency of bodily movement shown by these babies under a great variety of circumstances. At the time the original observations were made, each infant was assigned an "activity rating" which classified him as "very active," "moderately active," or "markedly inactive." (Both hyper- and hypoactive infants were excluded from the sample.) The present study, then, compares and contrasts the behavior of children of the same age, always pairing one markedly active baby with a markedly inactive one. Such a "contrast analysis" has been prepared for sixteen pairs of infants, two pairs at each age from four to thirty-two weeks in monthly intervals. Only four of these subjects, both pairs at the twenty-eight-weeks age level, will be used on this occasion.

3 USPHS Grant #MH-27. See Escalona, Leitch, et al. (1952).

For present purposes the organization of the contrast analyses need not be described in detail. Under a great variety of categories I listed side by side, on the same page, each baby's behavioral response to comparable circumstances. The categories run the gamut from such headings as "Bodily Need States" (hunger, fatigue) or "Body Manipulations" (dressing, diapering, bathing, etc.) through the baby's behavior in response to things and to people. His responsiveness to stimuli in all of the various perceptual modalities was included as well as a good many other areas. It was necessary to distinguish between quantitatively and qualitatively different stimulus conditions within each category. For instance, smiling at a baby from a distance is not the same as smiling and talking to him from close by. A stationary toy nearby is not the same as being handed the same toy by the mother. Nor is feeding from a propped bottle comparable to being held and nursed at the breast. Similarly, even stimulus conditions closely resembling each other cannot be compared if the babies are in different states at the time (Escalona, 1962). An infant is not inconsistent if he fails to respond to playful advances while fatigued, but reciprocates delightedly while awake and comfortable. It is no wonder, then, that these contrast analyses became formidable documents. They are suitable reading matter only for those who approach them with a specific interest in the minutiae of infant behavior.

The subjects will be referred to by name. They are Harry, the most active twenty-eight-week-old in the sample, compared to Sybil, the least active one in the group. And Grace, the second most active, compared to Peter, the second least active among our twenty-eight-week-olds. It may be well to introduce the four by a brief reference to what they have in common—in other words, by a brief reminder of what six-month-olds are like. By this age babies relate to the world about in a large number of ways. They are able to sit, roll, crawl or creep, and sometimes to pull themselves to an erect position. They reach for things and manipulate them in various ways. They bring toys to the mouth, transfer them from hand to hand, look at them, wave them, bang them, drop them at will, and occasionally can already retrieve a lost object. They are quite discriminatory in that mother is distinguished from all others, novelty and strangers are responded to as such—sometimes with apprehension, at other times with special fascination. Twenty-eight-week-olds have expressive physiognomies. They can smile faintly, broadly, apprehensively, and provocatively. They produce the relatively indistinct pleasurable sounds known as cooing, and usually have gone beyond this to the enunciation of simple or multisyllabic sounds such as Dada, technically known as babbling. Many twenty-eight-week-olds unmistakably convey their feelings by loud squeals, which may be joyous, irritable, or angry. Many six-month-olds perform simple feats of imitation, and all can actively participate in the universal game of peek-a-boo. In short, at twenty-eight weeks of age babies do more than to respond in a differentiated manner to what befalls them. They already make things happen, displaying intentionality, choice, resistance, and eager participation in turn.

In more or less rudimentary form we can observe in six-month-olds the operation of many ego functions. Anticipation, memory, voluntary and hence purposive use of the musculature, communicatory behavior, and something approaching the simplest form of problem solving, such as obtaining a desired toy out of reach by pulling at a string to which the toy is visibly attached.

For my purposes it is fortunate that these four babies not only are of identical age, but to developmental testing they proved to be at very comparable levels of behavior organization. On the Cattell Infant Intelligence Scale their I.Q.s were 113, 116, 112, and 131 respectively. Harry (the most active one, henceforth also designated as A_1) was unusually advanced with respect to gross motor coordination. On this test as well as on the Gesell Schedules it turned out that in most other ways he functioned at the bright normal level, as did the other three. For the others test results were as follows: Grace $(A_2) = 116$; Sybil $(I_1) = 112$; Peter $(I_2) = 113$.

Some characteristics of the mothers are also favorable to my purpose. Harry and Sybil (A_1 and I_1) had mothers who deal with their babies in very different ways. Harry's mother was warm, attentive, and playfully stimulating. She touched him freely and seldom lost contact with him during his waking hours. Sybil's mother, on the other hand, took excellent care of her baby whom she valued highly, but did so in a remarkably impersonal manner. She touched Sybil seldom except during caretaking procedures, and even these were often carried out expertly but with an absolute minimum of social play. She left the baby to her own devices unless and until the baby needed something. Since Sybil was not at all irritable, the number of intense direct contacts between those two was much smaller than is ordinarily the case. When we turn to the comparison between Grace (A_2) and Peter (I_2) things are different. Both these mothers not only were warm and loving, but both tended to be actively stimulating (by ordinary standards somewhat overstimulating) with their babies. They were responsive to them at all times, and constantly intruded upon their children's awareness by forceful means.

It is thus possible to compare the active Harry who has an active mother with the inactive Sybil who has a minimally active mother. But we can also compare the active Grace with the inactive Peter, both of these babies in the hands of very active mothers. And further, the two inactive babies, Sybil and Peter, can be compared in light of the fact that the former has a mother who keeps her distance, whereas the latter has an exceedingly intrusive mother.

As I follow these four infants through some of the most typical and recurring kinds of situations, my aim will be twofold. I wish to describe the different ways in which they made contact with, or became aware of, their own bodies, their mothers, different attributes among things, surrounding space, and all that makes up the infant's world of experience. Secondly I wish to point to the developmental relevance of these experiences. As a baby stretches his limbs and encounters resistance from the bars of the crib he experiences both a "something other than the own body" and a heightened awareness of the boundary of his body, where the toe ends and the crib starts. This experience and a thousand similar ones presumably mediate the separation of self from a surround that is not part of the self. Or, as another example, if perception of the mother often brings a sharp change in how the baby feels (from neutral feeling to strong pleasure, from crying to contented calm, from autistic containment to focused perception of things about, etc.), these experiences may be presumed to contribute to the ways in which he learns to recognize mother as a constant part in an otherwise still fairly fluid field. It also must feed into the particular qualities of feeling and of expectation that he learns to extend toward mother. In this manner two fundamental developmental processes—the establishment of body-ego boundaries and the beginnings of the first object relationship—can be viewed as being influenced by each and every small event of the sort I mentioned. It is possible to assume that development consists of *nothing but* the aggregate of all the relevant experiences occurring at the relevant times. I assume that all of the infant's encounters with "reality" (including the own body) are relevant to the development of many different ego functions at the same time, and that the same ego functions can differentiate and emerge from markedly different constellations of experience.

BEHAVIOR COMPARISONS UNDER VARIOUS CONDITIONS

I turn now to a comparison among the four subjects in terms of prominent behavior tendencies as a function of differences in the situation to which children were responding, and as a function of one organismic characteristic, namely, activity level. I shall discuss the results of each comparison in terms of a few among the emerging ego functions to which the behavior in question may be relevant.

Self-initiated Activity while Alert and Content

Six-month-olds typically spend a good deal of their time awake and "playing" whether in a crib, play pen, baby chair, or on the floor. Frequently toys are in the vicinity, and usually others are in the room who do not address themselves to the baby, though they keep an eye on him. All four babies were observed in this condition of spontaneous activity for appreciable periods of time.

Table I reflects some of the observed differences in the behavior of the two pairs. In order to interpret Table I and all that follow it is necessary to keep in mind that these tables represent summaries of more detailed analyses. Each of the four infants was repeatedly observed during spontaneous activity, and each single behavior episode was recorded throughout. From a tabulation of the frequency and duration of such behavior activations as various types of body movement, various types of vocalization and so forth, a rating could easily be made as to whether the behavior in question was frequent, moderately frequent, occasional, or rare. From a large number of such comparative ratings I included in the table only those that reflected conspicuous differences, and those that have a bearing on the ego functions under discussion.

The first four categories deal with body movements. It is to be expected that Harry and Grace (A_1 and A_2) would be the ones who showed a greater tendency to bounce, creep, roll, and toss, and to pull themselves to upright postures. The fact that Sybil and Peter were more given to gentle and modulated motion of body segments is equally to be expected. One also notes that all of the babies grasped objects, picked them up, moved them about, or merely fingered them. It was the inactive member of each pair who spent much of his time running his fingertips or palms over toys or furnishings. This occupied all of their attention and looked to us as though it were as vivid a way of focusing on things, as lifting and moving toys was for Harry and Grace, neither of whom became more than transiently interested in merely tactile exploration.

Even these few observations suggest that markedly active and markedly inactive infants may traverse different routes in achieving awareness of a separation between the body-self and surrounding space; and similarly, of the fact that the outer environment contains space-filling objects. Harry and Grace experienced large objects chiefly as barriers to movement, and as something to hold on to in support of pulling or dragging their bodies into a different position. Sybil and Peter experienced larger objects primarily as a sort of periphery, something noted at some distance from head and trunk, yielding sensations in only the outer portions of the body. It is possible that the separateness of the self from the crib is impressed upon the infant when he is physically close to it, and registers not only the impact of the wood on his skin surface but also the kinesthetic sensations as he strains, pushes, or pulls against it. Or perhaps the actual separateness between body and thing, the localization of thing-related sensations in hands and feet only, may facilitate the differentiation of self from nonself. Probably, these are two of the many ways in which infants learn the separation. It remains to be seen whether or not it makes a difference whether articulations of this sort occur predominantly in one mode or in another.

Table I contains another bit of information that is important, especially in the light of material that is to follow. The various behavior items listed in the table differ, among other things, in complexity. Multisyllabic babbling is a recent developmental acquisition. For twenty-eight-week-olds, it is among the most mature behaviors of which they are capable. The same is true with respect to the pattern of pulling themselves to upright, kneeling or standing postures, a feat performed by a minority among the six-month-olds.

For each baby it is of interest to learn what are the conditions under which he is likely to function at what is for him the most mature level, and under which conditions he is apt to content himself with easy, well-learned kinds of behavior activation. During spontaneous activity it was the active member of each pair who babbled a good deal more than did his inactive partner. It was also the more active babies who pulled themselves to vertical positions, a complex behavior which in these instances the inactive babies had not yet achieved.

The underlying developmental process to which observations of this kind are relevant concerns the mother's role in facilitating the emergence of specific ego functions. The active Harry performed at his peak level of maturity when left to his own devices, and his inactive partner Sybil did not. One might relate this to the fact that Harry's mother aroused and stimulated him a lot, and Sybil's "laziness" could be thought related to the fact that her mother failed to push and excite her. On the other hand, the inactive Peter was constantly prodded and actually taught by his mother, and yet failed to carry this over into those periods when he was left to himself. The hypothesis arises that at this age, social stimulation is a necessary condition for the emergence of relatively mature behavior in motorically inactive children, whereas this is not the case for markedly active ones.

A close inspection of Table I, and of several others, will show that the differences between pairs are all in the same direction, but that the relative frequencies noted for specific behavior activations are not constant for either the active or the inactive children. Thus multisyllabic babbling was rare in A_1 and absent in I_1, yet it was frequent in A_2 and rare in I_2. Had comparison been made between A_1 and I_2, there should have been no difference, as both these babies babbled only rarely. Nonetheless, I consider these differences worth noting for the following reasons. I do not suggest that active children have certain specific behavior propensities (other than a tendency toward vigorous bodily motion), and that inactive ones show a different set of behavior characteristics. Rather, I suggest that, depending on many other variables as well, certain formal characteristics of

Behavior during Spontaneous Activity

Behavior	Comparative Prominence			
Forceful, coordinated whole body activation	A_1 A_2	frequent frequent	>	I_1 rare I_2 occasional
Upright posture, pulls self to kneeling or standing	A_1 A_2	frequent moder. frequent	>	I_1 absent I_2 absent
Forceful, coordinated body segment activation	A_1 A_2	frequent frequent	>	I_1 occasional I_2 absent
Gentle, coordinated body segment activation	A_1 A_2	rare occasional	<	I_1 frequent I_2 frequent
Multisyllabic babbling	A_1 A_2	rare moder. frequent	>	I_1 absent I_2 rare
Moving objects in space	A_1 A_2	frequent frequent	>	I_1 occasional I_2 occasional
Fingering objects	A_1 A_2	absent moder. frequent	<	I_1 moder. frequent I_2 frequent

the behavior of active and inactive babies differ consistently. In the analysis of a much larger number of pairs it has become apparent that the difference among inactive and vigorously active infants may manifest itself in terms of rather varying behavior entities. Up to this point in my analysis of the larger body of data (which is not reported in this paper) it has been true that whatever differences do appear, are in the same direction. I have found no instance in which an inactive baby showed a complex behavior more frequently than did an active one—under the condition of spontaneous activity. I therefore assume that if different babies had been chosen for comparison, for instance, if A_2 had always been compared with I_1, the behavioral items that differentiated between them would have been somewhat different, but the character or formal attribute of the differences would have been the same. It is for this reason, among others, that a comparison of the entire group of active infants, with the entire group of inactive ones, proved unrewarding.

Behavior during Bodily Need States

Among the vital recurring experiences of infants are those in which their state changes with hunger or fatigue or due to other causes of which we, as outside observers, know that they arise from within the body. The change toward cessation of discomfort or positive well-being may or may not be experienced by the infant in the context of perception of the mother. Freud (1900) postulated that the earliest awareness of an environment as separate from the self arises during need states (hunger) when the infant experiences a sense of tension or discrepancy or disharmony in the presence of hunger and the absence of the source of food.

Table II reflects the behavioral response of the subjects to the condition of fatigue.[4] Fatigue is more difficult to understand than hunger. It brings bodily discomfort, as is well known to parents. Yet, while mothers can often help a baby go to sleep, they cannot provide gratification of the bodily need. Only the baby himself can do that, and not by voluntary means. In thinking about Table II it must also be remembered that twenty-eight-week-olds have gone beyond the earliest phases of awareness of an outer world. However indistinctly, they know mother as a source of food, comfort, pleasure, and—as I hope to show—of other things as well.

Table II shows that the impact of fatigue upon the babies' behavior was greater for the more active Harry and Grace than for their less active counterparts. They went in for crying, screaming, and squealing, while the inactive Sybil and Peter whimpered or cried transiently and softly. Further, once it had begun the distress associated with sleepiness was unremitting for the more active babies, whereas it was only intermittent, alternating with a condition of drowsiness without distress for the less active Peter and Sybil. This matter of how intensely discomfort is felt seems unrelated to the ease with which these babies fell asleep. The inactive Sybil and the active Grace both had something of a sleeping problem. We were told that not only while we happened to observe but on most occasions they had to fuss for close to an hour before they could finally go to sleep. In both families getting the baby off to sleep was viewed as the only difficult part of taking care of the baby. Peter was the only one who generally, as well as when we saw him, went easily to sleep within ten minutes of first registering fatigue.

---

4 Fatigue is used instead of hunger primarily because these infants were fed before hunger distress had developed. Both they and their mothers were accustomed to regular mealtimes. In addition, our observations of prefeeding behavior were contaminated by the chance circumstance that for three of the babies, observation began shortly before feeding time. Therefore, prefeeding behavior reflected stranger anxiety at least as much as it reflected hunger.

SUMMARY TABLE II

Behavior during Fatigue

Type of Behavior		Changes with Fatigue		
A. Body movement				
a. Amount	A_1	Marked increase	I_1	Moderate increase
	A_2	Moderate increase $>$	I_2	Marked *decrease*
b. Continuity	A_1	Continuous	I_1	Intermittent
	A_2	Continuous $>$	I_2	Continuous *decrease*
c. Loss coordination	A_1	Marked	$= I_1$	Marked
	A_2	Moderate $>$	I_2	Absent
B. Intensity unpleasure	A_1	Extreme	I_1	Moderate
	A_2	Extreme $>$	I_2	Minimal, transient
C. Vocalizations				
a. Screaming or	A_1	Marked, intermittent	I_1	Absent
squealing	A_2	Marked, intermittent $>$	I_2	Absent
b. Crying	A_1	Marked, continuous	I_1	Mild, intermittent
	A_2	Marked, intermittent $>$	I_2	Mild, brief
c. Whimpering	A_1	Absent	I_1	Marked, intermittent
	A_2	Absent $<$	I_2	Moderate, brief
d. Cooing	A_1	Absent	$= I_1$	Absent
	A_2	Absent $<$	I_2	Moder. toward end
D. Duration fatigue	A_1	Moderate	$< I_1$	Very long
state	A_2	Very long	$> I_2$	Brief

Clearly, the range of feeling and behavioral alteration commonly experienced with fatigue was greater for the more active among our babies. For all of them, the fatigue discomfort brought contact with the mother. Harry was held, patted, and spoken to. Crying loudly he threw himself at the mother who tried to comfort him, as he buried his face in her neck. This was one time when almost physical merging with the mother seemed, if anything, to heighten his distress. Grace's mother rocked and swung her baby. She sang to her, she patted her, she held her tight, and all to no avail. Finally there was nothing for it but to put the baby down and let her squeal, cry, "cradle rock," and toss about. Sybil's mother also patted and stroked her baby, at one time even holding her for a while. This was one situation in which the mother considered that the baby needed her. Unlike the other two, Sybil always responded by calming down while being soothed. When she seemed comfortable the mother put her down; mild but definite distress recurred, and the mother would resume patting her; and so it went for forty minutes. This baby did experience mother as a comforting presence even while fatigued. Peter would probably have gone to sleep without maternal help. However, he also felt his mother's touch and heard her voice as he changed from mild fussiness to contented drowsiness.

Does it make a difference to the emerging mother-child relationship if vivid perception of mother is—to the infant—associated with distress as much as with relief or pleasure? Does mother demarcate herself in the infant's awareness the more sharply the higher the tension and affect level, so that the very fact of being aroused at the time registers the more strongly the sight and sound and feel of her? Do children who alternate with sharp transitions between high pleasure and high unpleasure the more readily perceive the entity of self? Or do the higher levels of excitation, more frequently experienced, tend to blur boundaries and to flood the child with diffuse sensation? By these questions I mean to point again to at least one of the ways in which observations of this sort are relevant to major aspects of ego development.

It may be said in passing that what was true for fatigue was equally true for need gratification, namely, the situation of being fed. All four of these subjects enjoyed the eating situation, and all four maintained close perceptual contact with their mothers during it. But for both Grace and Harry the situation was far from tranquil. They were so eager that they threw their whole bodies toward breast, bottle, or spoon. Their excitement led to random movements that caused interruptions, whereupon they might squeal or briefly cry. After partial satiation, when feeding went more smoothly, both became very playful. They touched their mothers, vocalized happily, and did not lose interest in their surroundings until toward the very end of feeding. Not so the inactive Sybil and Peter, both of whom were so engaged in the feeding process that they seemed unaware of —certainly unresponsive to—their mothers and all else. They looked most content and came much closer to the image of blissfulness and peace frequently evoked in the literature. Here too, multiple and conflicting intense behavior activations were seen in the more active children, whereas it was the less active ones to whom feeding, by the mother, constituted a single episode obviously calming and pleasant as to quality. In so far as the gratification through sucking is concerned, it was the inactive ones who had the more intense experience, at the expense of significant interaction with the mother. Again I ask: are the early ego differentiations aided if life consists of fewer clear-cut episodes occurring with a high degree of regularity? Or are frequent, complex, markedly variable episodes of arousal an effective stimulus for an early orientation to the existence of an outer world?

Social Intrusions into the Infant's Awareness

In a further effort to find out how these babies experienced their mothers, and rather direct contacts with other people generally, I turn now to those situations in which someone approaches them actively in order to do something for or with them. These situations include being dressed, diapered, and bathed. They include mild, moderate, and strong social approaches (by which I mean playful contact-making efforts for their own sake, not as part of routines); they include the physical examination, the psychological test, and a few others.

In Tables III and V some of the results are summarized. One must remember that these percentages do not refer to the number of times we saw a baby show pleasure or some other response to a person's approach. With the exception of the physical examination and the psychological test, we saw such things as diapering, or a playful approach, many times for each baby. I included only those situations for which a conspicuous, regularly present mode of response could be observed.

Table III describes the proportion of social intrusions that usually evoked affect in the baby, and the kind of affect. For all babies the majority of social intrusions typically elicited some definite sign of affect. This was somewhat more true for the active member of each pair. Sybil and Peter registered neither pleasure nor unpleasure in response to several such situations (40 per cent and 34 per cent, respectively), whereas Harry and Grace remained neutral to only very few types of situations. Further, for the less active babies, these intrusions brought either pleasure or no change. In the active babies some among these situations typically evoked unpleasure, and in the case of Grace simultaneous occurrence of smiling and whimpering

SUMMARY TABLE III

Affective Response to Intrusions from the Environment, Mediated Socially

Affect	Subject	% Situations*		Subject	% Situations*
Pleasure	A_1	36	<	I_1	60
	A_2	45	<	I_2	66
Unpleasure	A_1	36	>	I_1	—
	A_2	18	>	I_2	—
Mixed	A_1	—		I_1	—
	A_2	18	>	I_2	—
Neutral	A_1	27	<	I_1	40
	A_2	18	<	I_2	34
TOTAL N SITUATIONS	A_1	11		I_1	10
	A_2	13		I_2	12

* Each situation was observed repeatedly (ranging from four times to over a hundred times). Thus percentages do *not* reflect number of times each affect was observed. They reflect the proportion of *situations* in which the stated affect occurred very frequently or invariably.

was observed. It is generally thought that young infants depend for pleasure and relief upon their mothers, whereas they experience unpleasure from within. And indeed, all of the four babies experienced most, if not all, of the acute pleasure that came their way as mediated by, or at least associated with, the presence of another human being. Yet, it may make a difference that for the more active babies, mothers regularly bring unpleasure as well. Whatever difference this may make to the child's emerging feeling toward his mother, it is certain that these discomforts with her do not disturb the primary positive orientation. All of these four babies showed strong selective ties to their mothers. They all smiled at sight of her, turned toward her and no one else for comfort, and in every way demonstrated the most vivid pleasure of which they were capable during contacts with her.

So far I have referred to only one way in which these babies experienced differently the direct approach of mother or another person; namely, that the active ones had more occasion to experience mother in association with unpleasure as well as pleasure, and that for them the approach of a person evoked some sort of affective response even more often than it did for the inactive ones. These crude comparisons fail to reflect important quantitative as well as qualitative differences in the experience of these babies.

One important factor is the frequency with which these categories of social intrusion occur. For instance, all infants are diapered frequently. To Harry this was invariably irritating, even if he was in excellent spirits just before and immediately afterwards. Sybil, on the other hand, usually remained impassive; she gazed at mother and seemed content enough, but never smiled or frowned. Grace and Peter always seemed to derive positive enjoyment as a by-product of being diapered. By not responding in any particular way, Sybil, as it were, missed out on not one but hundreds of occasions which brought pleasurable excitement to Peter and Grace. Whereas poor Harry could not escape the frequent unpleasure involved in this necessary procedure.

With respect to many of these situations, the frequency of their occurrence depends on the mother's behavioral style. For instance, both Harry and Grace disliked being tickled. Peter either ignored or mildly enjoyed it. For Sybil, on the other hand, it was one of the few kinds of stimulation that invariably brought what was for her a maximal pleasurable response. The mothers of Harry and Grace had the good sense seldom to play with their babies in this fashion. Peter, who responded little one way or another, had a mother who could not keep her hands off him. He actually showed more intense pleasure at being spoken to, at mother's sight, and at firm touch than he did when mother tickled him. This did not prevent the mother from providing the sensation very very often, clearly because *she* enjoyed it. Yet Sybil, who responded to this kind of stimulation with particular pleasure, had a chance to enjoy it only on the very rare occasions when her mother happened to feel playful.

More important is the mother's influence on the pattern of the baby's experience in consequence of the manner in which she tends to approach her baby socially. As is fully summarized in Table IV, all these babies responded with positive pleasure to playful approaches from their mothers, and in fact from anyone. Both Grace and Sybil were generally left to their own devices as long as they appeared content. It was only when these mothers detected signs of irritability, or when they expected the baby to be uncomfortable, that they initiated social interactions with their babies. For Grace, an irritable baby, this was a very frequent event. For the placid Sybil it was a rare one. Harry and Peter were played with because their mothers enjoyed doing so, and when they were perfectly content as much as otherwise. This means that for Grace and Sybil the more vigorous social interactions often took place at times when they were tense and experiencing some degree of unpleasure which, more often than not, turned to pleasure as mother entered their awareness in this way. Peter and Harry experienced these pleasurable encounters very often when this did not involve a change in feeling state for them. In a manner of speaking they did not need their mothers at these times, and there was for them less occasion to apperceive mother as that which restores an active sense of well-being.

These observations are an example in support of my notion, referred to earlier, that the infant's experience and hence his behavior are determined by intrinsic and extrinsic factors not to varying proportions, but in interaction. The differences just enumerated are not a function of activity level, nor are they a function of the mother's behavioral style, yet they are systematically related to both. It is the combination of the infant's responsiveness when the particular situation occurs, and the dosage in which mothers provide the situation, that yields a picture of a variety of patterns in the interactions between mother and child: from the highly responsive Sybil who made the most of the minimal social stimulation she received, to the markedly responsive Peter who got more social stimulation than he could possibly respond to; and, from Harry whose responsiveness was highly differentiated and whose mother gauged her contacts to the behavioral clues he provided, to Grace whose mother also was responsive to the baby's state, but who persisted in vigorous play even when the baby screamed from fatigue and was in no condition to respond.

Different Intensities of Social Stimulation

Table IV deals with how these babies characteristically responded to social advances, whether these were made by the mother or by another person. As is true in other areas, all four of the infants had at their disposal much the same repertoire of social response. All smiled, chuckled, cooed, laughed, and turned toward the partner. But it is equally true that the conditions that ordinarily elicited minimal or strong responses were different for the more active children as compared to the less active ones.

SUMMARY TABLE IV

Behavioral Response to Various Degrees of Social Stimulation

Stimulus Situation	Active	Inactive
Persons in sight, not attending to baby, baby content	Smiling, vocalizing persistently, turning toward. Some smiling regard only.	Smiling regard as at "pleasant spectacle."
Minimal social stimulation, as in smiling or speaking from distance	Intensification social response. Squealing, cooing, babbling, very intense gazing, moving toward.	Intense smiling prolonged. Occasionally brief cooing.
Moderate and strong social stimulation Baby content	Squealing, cooing, babbling, moving as above. In addition, laughing and touching partner.	I_1 smiling, babbling, laughing, touching mother. I_2 intense smiling, brief cooing. Occasionally babbling, touching mother, chuckling. Occasionally ignoring social stimulation.
Strong social stimulation Baby discontent	Reduction or cessation of crying. Sometimes smiling, squealing, cooing. Sometimes vigorous approach while crying loudly. Social stimulation never ignored.	I_1 sometimes cessation crying. Sometimes avoidance, behaviorally ignoring social stimulation. I_2 (did not occur).

The content of Table IV may be summarized as follows.

All four of these infants reacted to the mere sight of a person, even if the person neither looked at them nor responded to them in any way. The less active babies smiled in a pleased fashion, much as they might at a toy or at patches of sunlight. The active babies responded more strongly, and also in a more distinctly social manner. They not only smiled but cooed and gurgled, and persisted as if they were trying to get a response (which they often succeeded in doing). With mild social stimulation, such as looking at the baby

from a distance in a friendly fashion, or speaking briefly in his direction, all the babies intensified the same kind of response as they had
made at the mere sight of a person. The inactive ones smiled more
broadly, and in a more specifically social way. Occasionally they
cooed pleasurably. But they were still far from responding strongly.
And when the adults turned their attention elsewhere, Sybil and
Peter ceased responding and made no effort to prolong the social
interaction. Harry and Grace became even more animated and persistent than they had been at sight of a person. They added squeals
and babbling, using every means likely to evoke further attention
from the adult.

The difference in response to mild as compared to fairly strong
or very strong social stimulation was great for the inactive ones, and
barely noticeable for the others. By strong social stimulation I refer
to those situations in which the adult focuses his attention on the
baby and energetically invites him to respond. Always the adult
comes close to the baby, usually he speaks to him (or makes playful
noises), and very often also touches him. Under this condition Harry
and Grace really could not add much to the signs of delight and the
vigor of response already elicited by minimal social stimulation. Except for occasional laughter, and for touching the mother in connection with turning-toward responses (made possible by her proximity),
their behavior did not vary with the difference in the intensity of
stimulation. Not so Sybil and Peter, who showed what they could do
only when social stimulation became fairly strong. They now behaved exactly as Grace and Harry had to much lesser stimulation.
They babbled, chuckled, touched their partners, and generally did
more than their share to keep the social interaction going. One way
of stating what we saw is to say that in the active children the threshold for the release of strong and pleasurable social responses was
much lower than for the relatively inactive ones, who responded
strongly only when strongly stimulated.

This observation runs parallel to what was reported in relation
to spontaneous activity. Spontaneous activity also is a situation in
which external stimulation is minimal. Under that condition it was
the active babies who produced some of their most mature behavior
integrations. The idea was advanced that, at this age at any rate,
inactive babies may require the incentive of specific stimulation in

order to activate more complex patterns of behavior. The data summarized in Table IV provide partial support, although only some of the most intense social responses are also the most recent developmental acquisitions (laughter, babbling). If one assumes that the very act of responding to a social partner facilitates the development of more sustained and increasingly communicative interpersonal contact, one might speculate that progress in this realm is more dependent on the amount of social stimulation provided among the inactive babies than is the case with active ones.

Table IV contains one other interesting piece of information. Both Peter and Sybil could behaviorally ignore strong social stimulation, whereas neither Grace nor Harry were ever seen to do so. For Peter, who was played with such a lot, it was true that vigorous response occurred only with strong social stimulation. But at other times when mother juggled him, kissed him, and spoke to him in lovingly provocative ways, the baby contented himself with placid smiles, no different from those he showed when there was no particular stimulation at all. One felt that it would have been beyond him to meet all of the mother's demands for playful response. In Sybil we saw much the same thing, but only if the strong social approach occurred while the baby was discontent. As the mother tried to divert the crying baby, Sybil would look away from the mother, perhaps focusing on a nearby object with a blank expression, or would close her eyes and cry all the louder. I do not know if Peter would have had the same capacity, for he was never seen in acute distress! But I do know that neither Harry nor Grace were ever able to ignore their mother's advances, no matter what their mood. When their mothers tried to soothe and divert them while the babies cried, the youngsters responded in one of two ways. Either they stopped crying, began to smile, and the episode turned into one of pleasurable social interaction. Or else, they continued to cry, sometimes showing heightened distress as the mother increased the intensity of her approach. Unlike their inactive counterparts, however, they were at these moments wholly oriented toward the mother. They gazed at her unhappily, or actively sought body contact, either clutching her tightly or, as Harry especially tended to do, burying their faces in her neck while screaming.

This observation is relevant to the same issue that was raised before, namely, the degree to which the infant's behavior is dependent upon what the mother does and does not do in her dealings with him. The preceding data suggested that the behavior of the active babies was less closely dependent upon maternal or other external stimulation than was true of the inactive babies. Yet when it comes to the capacity to deal with strong social stimulation, we note a reversal. It was the relatively inactive babies who showed what might be thought of as greater independence, in protecting themselves against the disruptive influence of overstimulation, at least when such overstimulation was of a distinctly social nature.

Different Intensities of Object Stimulation

The whole matter of how the outer world—not just the people it contains—presents itself in the infant's experience and begins to guide his behavior is at the core of what I mean in speaking of emerging ego functions. It is precisely the acts of attending to something "out there," remembering things perceived before, discriminating among different kinds of perceptions, learning that there is a connection between something you do and a change in the outside world (shaking a rattle produces a noise, extending the arm toward something leads to the sensation of grasping) that constitute the earliest mental activity.

It follows that everything we can learn about the way in which infants change their behavior as a function of an aspect of the world about (instead of as a diffuse manifestation of body needs and body states) may be viewed as material documenting the process of ego development. For this reason very detailed comparison was made of the behavior of the subjects as it was directed toward objects, and their coordinated manipulation. Table V is limited to a summary of one small aspect of such comparison. It describes those behavior activations which occurred when the mother or someone else actively stimulated the baby's awareness of things about. It is the counterpart to Table I, in which the babies were compared when not specifically stimulated. As in other areas, Harry and Grace excelled Sybil and Peter in the more vigorous behavior activations. The point at issue is not the amount but the *kind* of thing these babies were more apt to do when the outside world intruded. Note that fretting, panting, and squealing are diffuse behaviors. These simple vocalizations were shown more frequently by the active Harry and Grace, than by Peter and Sybil. While an adult actively presented toys, all of the babies also showed more complex behaviors, such as babbling or manipulating objects in a purposive manner. These more mature patterns were shown about equally often by the active and inactive infants. This result is the reverse of what was noted for spontaneous activity. In that situation of exposure to things, it was the more active babies who excelled in producing more mature behavioral patterns.

SUMMARY TABLE V

Prominent Behavior in Response to Environmental Intrusions

Shown More Or Only by A	Shown More Or Only by I
Whole body strong movement*	Body segment gentle movement*
Body segment strong movement*	Looking as primary activity*
Vocalizing*	
Crying	Manipulating two objects at once
Fretting	
Panting	
Squealing	

* Very marked difference.

The notion that inactive and active babies show somewhat opposite behavioral tendencies when conditions of lesser and greater intensity of stimulation are compared is supported by one further finding reflected in Table V. The behavior pattern of manipulating two objects at once is among the most complex of which twenty-eight-week-olds are capable. It was Sybil and Peter who showed this under the rousing influence of active intrusion from the outside, whereas neither one of them had shown such mature behavior when left to their own devices. It is interesting supplementary information that the less active babies also related to objects about by intense visual regard. Yet this behavioral difference was not manifest when comparison was made during spontaneous activity (Table I).

The results of Tables IV and V are parallel. Both indicate that the behavior of the more active children does not greatly alter when the intensity of external stimulation is great, as compared to when it is small. Under strong stimulation the more active ones may even be prevented from displaying their developmentally most advanced coordinations, as a result of high levels of excitation. The relatively inactive ones, on the other hand, show a sharp difference in behavior under mild and intense stimulus conditions respectively. Their most advanced behavior integrations occur only under more intense stimulation—just when the active ones are apt to fall back on simpler schemata.

Assuming that differences of this kind are often found, they become relevant to the issue of the manner in which the mother's behavior, and the social environment generally, determines the course of some aspects of early ego development. An infant learns by doing. The more he applies whatever he is capable of at the time by way of orienting and adapting his behavior to what he perceives, the more does the very act of practicing push him toward the next step: from looking at an object to grasping it, to looking at it while holding and moving it, to letting go of it on purpose, to remembering it sufficiently to have some awareness of its existence though he no longer sees or feels it, to the capacity to look for it and retrieve it; that is, from the simplest and briefest direct perceptual contact toward increasingly differentiated, ordered sequences of goal-directed behavior. Consequently, the more opportunity and incentive the baby has to engage in these behaviors, the more or the better he is learning. We know that a lack of suitable stimuli has a retarding effect—as in children who are relatively isolated from things and people, or prevented from moving their bodies with appropriate freedom. We think that mothers who encourage babies by providing appropriate scope and by combining pleasurable social episodes with encounters with the world of things are promoting developmental progress in their babies. The observations I have cited may add another dimension. The same maternal interventions which for some infants encourage the activation of developmentally important behavior patterns may make no difference or even be a hindrance for other infants (vigorous stimulation). And a condition which is optimal for the emergence of significant learning experiences for some infants fails to provide these experiences for others (spontaneous activity).

The above remarks are limited to immediate situational contexts, as these may have variable effects upon the activation of behavior patterns that play an important role in the development of some early ego functions. How infants respond to any kind of stimulation, and whether they can utilize appropriate stimulation as nutriment for developmental progress, probably depends on other and more stable aspects of experience. These four subjects, like all healthy infants, showed spontaneous pleasure in and an active readiness for activities related to mastery. Differences in response of the sort described in this paper are of interest only as applied to children whose total life experience and biological equipment provide the primary conditions for adequate developmental progress.

Table V indicates no more than that active subjects tended to produce relatively simple behaviors more prominently than did inactive ones, under conditions of fairly strong stimulation. In addition, it was noted that (as reflected in Tables I and V) the inactive babies tended to produce some fairly complex behaviors when stronger stimulation was provided, while they had failed to show these behaviors under minimal stimulation. These gross comparisons are hardly a sufficient basis for the speculation that social stimulation will have different effects upon developmentally relevant behaviors in active infants as compared to inactive ones. The comparisons presented in Table V are an oversimplified reflection of complex facts. Actually, I began by tracing the behavior changes in each infant as he experienced a series of different kinds and degrees of stimulation. I was struck by the different pattern of interaction between behavior and external situation as observed in the more active and less active members of each comparison pair. A few of the primary observations will be cited to convey a concrete picture of the learning processes that underlie the schematic presentation in the tables.

In all four subjects I could make comparisons of their use of objects while alert and left alone with them, and during the psychological test. The latter situation is one in which the examiner uses every means of inciting the baby toward action with the toys. This is done by talking to the baby, offering toys provocatively, offering variety, and never allowing the baby to settle into stereotyped activity. In a more concentrated fashion, it is precisely what mothers do when they devote themselves to play with children of this age. The difference between Harry and Sybil (the extremes on the activity continuum) were greater than those between Grace and Peter but in the same direction. Harry and Sybil both registered excitement as the test progressed. Harry lunged toward offered toys with his whole body, or at least with both arms. He squealed and panted, and at times his motions became jerky and less well coordinated as a result of visible muscle tension. Sybil did not reach comparable heights, but showed more excitement than we saw at any other time. She flushed, moved more, and showed occasional uncharacteristic large tremors of hand and arm. During the test Sybil showed five behavior patterns that were never seen during spontaneous activity. One of them was a sign of excitation (mouthing), but the others consisted of visual-motor coordinations, namely, banging an object purposively, touching one object with another, holding and moving an object while regarding it intently, and holding one object while mouthing another. During spontaneous play she had limited herself to occasional mouthing or waving of a toy, to visual regard without manipulations, or to fingering in the absence of visual regard. Six-month-old infants are at a point in their development where two new sorts of integration take place. One consists of apprehending the same object simultaneously in various modalities, as in touching or moving it while also intently regarding it. Behavior patterns of this kind promote visual-motor coordination in that the hand learns to be guided by visual clues, and the baby experiences the visual consequences of motoric action. They also promote a more distinct awareness of the thing and its properties than is possible through a single modality. Things that look small are things that can be moved with little muscular effort; a thing that looks round requires a different hand and finger posture to be grasped than a thing that looks square, a bell will produce a noise if grasped by the handle but not if grasped at the opening, etc. Sybil was actively learning things like these only with special stimulation.

Harry, on the other hand, showed during spontaneous activity all of the kinds of behavior integration that he also showed during the test. It is possibly for this reason that parents and pediatricians often think of active babies as brighter or more advanced than fairly inactive ones, an assumption which is not supported by the facts.

Another observation further supports the notion that the more stimulating test condition did not bring forth, for our active subjects, their maximal level of integrated functioning. Soon after the test had started both Harry and Grace became so intensely involved in their actions with the toys that responsiveness to the social aspects of the situation disappeared. In contrast to their usual behavior, they did not look at the examiner or smile and vocalize in response to her close presence. Nor did they turn toward mother, who also was close by. Sybil and Peter, on the other hand, were exceedingly responsive to the examiner, watching her as she handed toys, smiling at her delightedly as they performed, interrupting object play to smile and coo at mother and examiner alike. One example will illustrate the difference. When Peter inadvertently dropped a toy he did not follow it with eyes or arms. Instead he turned at once to the examiner as if expecting her to restore it. Grace, when the same thing happened to her, turned in the direction of the disappearing object and sometimes stretched her arms as if trying to maintain contact or to retrieve it. Yet Grace's mother unceasingly restored toys (more than Peter's did), and on other occasions Grace was distinctly more capable of intentional social communication than was Peter. To maintain active involvement with things and with people at the same time is a more differentiated mode of functioning than to be absorbed in one or the other exclusively. It was the less active babies who, under special stimulation, achieved this level of integration.

THE EMERGENCE OF RELATIVE INDEPENDENCE OF ACTION

The material so far has dealt with four different aspects of behavioral difference among relatively active and relatively inactive infants. These may be summarized as follows:

1. For all four infants strong pleasure was evoked in situations during which the baby was in direct perceptual contact with the mother or another person. All four infants experienced unpleasure in nonsocial situations. However, unpleasure did occur also in situations of close contact between mother and baby. The difference between active and inactive infants was that the former experienced unpleasure while in contact with the mother in more situations than did the latter. In addition, the inactive babies experienced a somewhat larger number of interactions with the mother during which

no marked affect was shown, whereas this was a rare situation for the active ones.

2. All four infants demonstrated differentiated responsiveness to external stimuli at about the same level, and were capable of equally complex behavior integrations. However, under conditions of minimal or mild stimulation the active infants responded in a more differentiated manner than did the inactive ones. When external stimulation was more intense this difference disappeared, there was then little difference between the active and inactive infants with respect to the complexity of their behavioral response. In fact, under strong stimulation the active infants sometimes functioned below their optimal level of maturity, whereas this variety of primitivization was not noted in the inactive infants.

3. In response to very intense social stimulation both of the inactive infants at times ceased responding, as though they were able to erect a "stimulus barrier." Neither of the active infants showed the capacity behaviorally to ignore strong social stimulation, as though they were more vulnerable to strong external stimuli, regardless of their level of excitation at the time.

Up to this time these observations were discussed as they may have a bearing on the following aspects of ego development: (1) the separation of self from nonself; (2) the gradual emergence of an awareness of space and of physical objects in space; (3) the development of a strong tie to the mother, especially variations in the quality and intensity of feelings, sensations, and anticipations that delineate the mother in the child's awareness.

There is one other aspect of early ego development that may be affected by experiential differences of the sort I have described. One of the adaptive consequences of the entire process of ego formation is that the infant changes from primarily *re*active patterns of behavior to active ones. At first, behavior is reactive to internal and external stimulation of all sorts. But gradually the infant behaves in such a way as to alter the environment, or alter the situation in which he finds himself. For instance, focusing upon a toy is primarily a reaction or response to a visual stimulus. But reaching for a toy and bringing it to the mouth are also active. They alter the relationship between the perceived stimulus and the child.

Such a capacity actively to alter the content of experience is predicated upon maturational advances in neuromuscular coordination and other areas. It is also inextricably interwoven with the emergence of intention and volition, of anticipation, of sustained attention and other ego functions, however transient and primitive these still may be at the age of twenty-eight weeks. Viewed in terms of consequences for immediate adaptation, this growing capacity to act upon the environment might be described as "behavioral autonomy." The infant's moment-by-moment behavior is the less dependent upon whatever stimulation may befall him, the greater his behavioral autonomy, i.e., his capacity to alter aspects of the environment. Since the external environment is greatly influenced by what mothers do for and with their children, greater behavioral autonomy in this sense makes for a lesser degree of dependence upon the mother as well. A baby who can retrieve a lost toy is less dependent upon mother's willingness to restore it; and one who can rock himself to sleep is less dependent on mother's availability to soothe him. From the mother's point of view, this variety of infantile "independence" is a mixed blessing. A mother's control over her baby rests with her ability to alter his behavior at will. In fact, when a mother refers to her baby as being "difficult" to care for, she often means that his behavior cannot be regulated by her manipulations. Thus this matter of behavioral autonomy is important as a component of the changing interaction between mother and child, as well as being a component of the child's changing transactions with the physical environment, including the own body.

The material summarized in the tables suggests that the two active infants showed relatively greater behavioral autonomy in relation to the world of things than did their inactive counterparts. Yet it was the inactive member of each pair who showed greater independence in relation to the social environment. Or rather, this was true when social stimulation was intense, but not under conditions of minimal and mild social stimulation.

It appears to me that the same behavioral proclivity—the tendency to respond readily and strongly to stimulation—has somewhat opposite consequences for an infant's relative independence in relation to objects and in relation to persons. The difference lies not in the baby but in that to which he is responding. For the active Harry and Grace, the mere perception of toys and physical objects was an incitement to behavioral arousal. Yet, this same tendency to be compelled toward response made these active babies more vulnerable in relation to stimulation that emanates from other human beings. Physical objects do not make demands. A rattle is indifferent to being dropped, it does not initiate renewed contact when it is ignored. A mother does not similarly accommodate. If she is intent on calming the baby, or on feeding him, or on getting him to smile, the infant's failure to respond leads to redoubled effort on her part. Thus the same characteristic that left the inactive baby somewhat dependent on external circumstances with respect to inanimate objects facilitates a kind of power to resist social stimulation.

In terms of the infant's experience these occurrences are probably not felt as social encounters resembling a power struggle until just about the age of our subjects, somewhere close to the six- and seven-month level. Earlier, these phenomena are best described in terms of thresholds for response, the degree to which perception impels bodily action. On the other hand, it is likely that infants come to know the mother as a separate entity, someone the child can depend on, can persuade and can resist—largely through experiences of the kind I have described. It can be speculated that a predisposition for one or another pattern of exercising autonomy—and therefore for some defense systems rather than others—is acquired during the early months of life. If so, my observations suggest that initial activity level may play a role: not because relatively weak impulse toward massive body movement in and of itself constitutes an Anlage for passive stubbornness, but because relatively inactive children are likely to have more experiences in which their capacity to withhold response is perceived as antagonism and resistance by the social environment.

An example of one among the infinite number of ways in which such behavioral tendencies may come to influence the quality of relationship between mother and baby will be given. Toward the end of feeding both Harry and Grace (active) took unmistakable steps to terminate the feeding. They turned their heads away, spat out the nipple, arched their backs, and vocalized irritably. It was they who altered the situation in which they found themselves. Sybil conspicuously, and Peter to a slight degree, also determined when the feeding was to end. Sybil made no sound or movement, nor did her body visibly tense. But she clamped down her lips so tightly that the mother could not insert the nipple—and that was that. Peter simply failed to suck, allowing the nipple to move about in his mouth incidental to vocalizing motions. The kind of difference in behavioral style that *may* be foreshadowed is that between the somewhat older child who defies the mother by continuing to act as he wished (for instance, touching the forbidden ashtray), and the child who refuses to carry out an action despite mother's forceful urging (for instance, to drink his milk or to say "thank you").

BODILY SELF-STIMULATION

Behavioral differences other than those already reported exist, and might be related to a variety of ego functions. However, I do not mean to limit myself to an exploration of differences among active and inactive infants, nor do I consider activity level to be of greater importance than many other variables. I shall therefore pursue the problem of the interaction between infant characteristics and characteristics of the maternal environment in relation to another sort of infantile behavior, namely, the dominant modes of bodily self-stimulation.

From birth onward infants behave in ways which result in self-stimulation. As the hand happens to touch the mouth sucking ensues, and in the course of random arm movements newborns stroke or scratch their own skin. A bit later, and well before the age of six months, infants engage in rocking or bouncing motions, and they may pull at their own ears and hair.

One of the interesting things about bodily self-stimulation is that the very same behavior sometimes has a soothing effect, whereas at other times it is clearly excitatory. As early as age four months babies are seen not only to comfort themselves by sucking (as even newborns do) but also to suck or chomp so vigorously as to create increasingly high states of excitation. From about age five months onward, some babies "cradle rock" in rhythmic fashion when distressed or tired, and this may lead to a reduction in bodily tension and to a more contented state of mind. Yet they may also start to rock while alert and unoccupied (one is tempted to say bored) and work themselves up to high peaks of excitation. In young infants tactile self-stimulation is very common, but it is difficult to say whether it tends to be excitatory or soothing. Most often it appears along with other signs of increasing tension as, for instance, in the universal and more lasting pattern of rubbing the eyes when tired. Yet some infants can be seen to "entertain themselves" by stroking, scratching, or pinching portions of their skin with every appearance of mild pleasure, but no distinct signs of heightened tension.

Psychoanalytic theory has dealt with these phenomena under the general heading of infantile autoerotism. Primarily, any one of these activities has been seen as linked to libidinal excitation. There has been relatively little emphasis upon the role of these experiences in facilitating awareness of the own body and its boundaries.[5] Nor has infantile autoerotic activity been discussed with respect to the degree to which it may enable infants to achieve some functional independence of the mother, a point I will develop below. Further, infants differ strikingly from one another as to which particular type of self-stimulation is preferred, and we know very little about the origin of such differences. Postulating that the mouth zone, or the skin, or the proprioceptors related to kinesthetic sensations may be erotized, it remains to be seen whether or not the subsequent developmental course is influenced by the choice of one rather than another autoerotic modality.

Table VI summarizes the patterns of bodily self-stimulation observed in the four six-month-old subjects. Note that Grace (A) and Sybil (I) went in for a good deal of rocking and bouncing. Harry (A) only moderately so, and Peter (I) not at all.

It has occurred to me (as it has to others) that in stimulating their own bodies infants provide for themselves sensations which previously they have experienced at the hands of their mothers. Babies are rocked, patted, and stroked, and subsequently rock and touch themselves. If this is so, mother's mode of dealing with her baby should bear a relationship to the type of infantile autoerotic activity preferred by the baby. The facts bear out the assumption, but again the relationship is not as simple as has just been described.

[5] The point has been made both by A. Freud and by Hartmann but has not received much elaboration in the literature.

Patterns of Bodily Self-Stimulation

Type of Self-Stimulation	Subject	Frequency and Context
Kinesthetic: Rocking, bouncing	Harry (A_1)	Moderately frequent. Intense with unpleasure, gentle with pleasure.
	Grace (A_2)	Very frequent, usually intense. Often with pleasure, also fatigue or distress.
	Sybil (I_1)	Frequent, usually gentle secondary activity with mild pleasure. With unpleasure moderately vigorous.
	Peter (I_2)	Not observed or reported at any time.
Tactile: Scratching, rubbing pinching, patting	Harry (A_1)	Did not occur (except single occasion rubbing foot along opposite leg, fatigued).
	Grace (A_2)	Occasional but *only with unpleasure*, then moderately prominent.
	Sybil (I_1)	Very frequent, *always with pleasure*.
	Peter (I_2)	Occasional, secondary, no affect.
Nonnutritive Oral:	Harry (A_1)	*Finger sucking rare*, fatigue only. *Object* mouthing *frequent* in *spontaneous* play (gentle mouthing, sucking, seldom chomping). *Frequent* with *test* (vigorous chomping, intense sucking, engulfing).
	Grace (A_2)	*No finger sucking. Object* mouthing *frequent* in *spontaneous* play (gentle mouthing, rarely sucking or engulfing). *Frequent* with *test* (vigorous chomping, sucking).
	Sybil (I_1)	Very rare, gentle object mouthing only.
	Peter (I_2)	When *fatigued frequent object* sucking, *rare* finger sucking. *Spontaneous* play *frequent* (intense chomping, licking, engulfing, rubbing toy along gum). With *test moderate* (secondary licking, chomping).

To return to the data. Harry was occasionally rocked or swung by his mother, almost always as part of a soothing maneuver when he was very distressed. We could not observe a strong response on his part; it did not seem that passive motion had marked specific effects upon his state. As seen in Table VI, he rocked with only moderate frequency. What he really went in for was mouthing behavior.

Grace, on other hand, was swung and rocked a very great deal, both in play and as a means of soothing her. And it was Grace, among

the four, who provided for herself a very great deal of the same kind
of stimulation; she did more rocking and bouncing both with pleasure and with distress than did any of the others.

Peter's mother, on the other hand, played with her baby inces-
santly, but rarely in the kinesthetic mode. He was said to never have
been rocked—nor did we see him swung about—and he never once
generated comparable sensations for himself.

Sybil was rocked and swung rarely. But in contrast to Harry,
she was seen to respond very strongly when it did occur. For instance,
it was a combination of being held firmly and rocked that finally
put her to sleep (as usual, the mother said). Also, when Sybil became
fussy mother frequently put her in a "jumper swing" or pushed
her around in the carriage, knowing that it was the motion that
soothed and apparently pleased the baby.

To anticipate the tentative formulation which seems to cover
the facts, and for which additional documentation will be given
shortly: it appears that babies in this age range select those patterns
of bodily self-stimulation which generate sensations in the same
modalities that have characterized intense contacts with the mother
in the past, when it was she who provided the stimulation. In other
words, I think that the frequency and intensity with which Grace's
mother induced passive motion in her baby had a lot to do with
Grace's tendency to rock and bounce.

Sybil's behavior provided especially clear-cut patterns. As shown
in Table VI, tactile self-stimulation was most prominent in her.
She often touched her thigh or belly in stroking or pinching motions,
or rubbed her skin, or dug her fingers deeply into the soft portions
of abdominal tissue. Whenever this behavior was observed, it was
in association with pleasurable animation. Interestingly enough, she
showed such behavior not only when left to her own devices but
also while receiving social and tactile stimulation from the mother
or from one of the observers. In her case the choice of this modality
cannot have been the function of the sheer frequency with which
mother provided stimulation of this sort. As was reported, Sybil's
mother was somewhat distant and seldom touched her baby. But,
as has also been reported, Sybil showed a strong social response *only*
on those occasions when touch was added to other approach modalities. These occasions may have been infrequent, but they were

nonetheless peak moments of pleasure and excitement in Sybil's contacts with her mother. To a lesser degree the same state of affairs existed in respect to kinesthetic sensations. They were not offered with great frequency, but Sybil was markedly responsive to them.

An interesting variation was seen in connection with Grace's behavior in the tactile modality. Table VI indicates that she did stimulate her own skin at times, but *only at moments* of *distinct unpleasure*. Grace's mother often touched her, though generally in the context of routine procedures. It was not a prominent mode of soothing her or of playing with her, and for a good reason. When in a good mood and touch was not prolonged, Grace did not respond to it one way or another. But when it was at all prolonged, or when she was somewhat irritable, touch always evoked unpleasure in Grace. At the time we studied Grace, she provided for herself tactile stimulation only in the same affective context in which she experienced it from the mother, namely, when uncomfortable and distressed. The situation was similar for Harry, who also either ignored touch or responded with some displeasure. His mother was keenly aware of his irritability to touch, even warning the observers to be cautious in this respect. And Harry was neither seen nor reported to engage in tactile self-stimulation.

For Peter, in whom this behavior was infrequent and not linked to an affective state, the constellation was different again. Despite the fact that being touched was not seen to elicit pleasure, the mother so much enjoyed it that she constantly ran her fingers along his body, and tickled or stroked him. Such tactile stimulation did not interfere with his positive responses to mother, but it certainly did not enhance them. Despite the fact that he so constantly experienced touch from the mother he rarely touched himself. I am inclined to think that we are dealing with the inverse of what was true for Sybil. While tactile stimulation was offered with high frequency, it was not responded to strongly and therefore did not play a significant role in his experience of contact with the mother.

All of this suggests that in order for a particular modality to become the focus of intense and pleasurable contact with the mother, two conditions must be met. In the first place, the mother must offer the particular kind of body stimulation. Secondly, the infant's response to this variety of stimulation must be pleasurable and excitatory. It seems to me that if Peter's skin had been more reactive, his mother's pleasure in touching him would likely have transformed itself in Peter's experience to pleasurable feelings associated with tactile sensations and thus to autoerotic activity in this form. Conversely, Grace's skin was exceptionally reactive which made this type of stimulation unpleasurable, despite the relative infrequency with which mother offered this type of stimulation.

Nonnutritive Oral Behavior

Among the autoerotic activities of infancy oral behavior holds a special place. In part this is because mouth activations in situations unrelated to eating are a prominent and universal behavior manifestation. All theories of human development have had to account for it in one way or another. Secondly, psychoanalytic theory postulates an intrinsic relationship between the oral zone as the primary locus of excitation, and the earliest phase of psychosexual development. It is well to remember that the psychoanalytic concept of orality did not arise from a desire or necessity to account for the behavior of infants and young children. The concept was formulated because oral sensations, oral imagery, and oral fantasies proved to be a component of mature sexuality.

In my judgment the psychoanalytic concept of orality does not stand or fall with what can be learned about the *overt oral behavior* of infants. Even if babies and young children did not show a universal tendency to use their mouths for all sorts of things other than eating, such a circumstance would not do away with the clinical phenomena which, for better or worse, Freud designated as oral. In presenting some material on the different role which mouth activity played in the experience of these four babies, I therefore do not intend to establish a direct connection with the central psychoanalytic formulations. For the time being I would like to regard this component of behavior much like others, as a way of tracing the ebb and flow of excitation, of pleasure and unpleasure, of contact and involvement with things and people about.

Table VI shows that none of these four subjects were given to sucking their own hands and fingers except transiently. This is a bit unusual, though it is generally true that finger sucking is less conspicuous at the six-month level than it usually is both earlier and later. In three of the four babies (all but Sybil) finger sucking occurred, but only briefly while they were fatigued.

Yet in three of these four babies oral behavior was frequent and intense. They tended to put objects to the mouth. These they would lick, suck, chomp at, and bite or engulf (insert deeply into the mouth) or rub against their gums with force. With greater or lesser frequency all three of them also mouthed portions of their mother's body. If one were to look only at what these babies did and how intensively, one would have to say that appreciable differences did not exist between them with respect to oral behavior.

Yet if one scrutinizes *when* they tended to engage in oral behavior and the manner in which environmental situational factors influenced mouthing behavior, then conspicuous differences do emerge. Grace and Harry, the two active babies, showed a somewhat similar pattern. Both included a great deal of oral behavior in their transactions with things about during spontaneous activity. For both would mouth or suck a toy briefly, or chomp or chew at it for a moment. During spontaneous activity these were not intense episodes. They tended to be integrated with other modes of apprehending the object. They would look at it, bring it to the mouth, remove it, manipulate it, bring it to the mouth, etc. At no time did either child become so absorbed in the sensations excited in the mouth as to lose interest in other properties of the thing—or in the immediate environment. In fact, it is plausible to assume that under this condition of spontaneous activity mouth contacts mediated perceptual awareness of what the object was like, so to speak. By touching, looking, lifting, pushing, and mouthing, the properties of the thing (rough, smooth, large, small, round, angulated, etc.) were impressed upon awareness more strongly than would be possible within any one modality. That is to say, mouth contacts facilitated separation between the self that now looks, now touches, and now sucks and the object upon which these activities converge.

In both Harry and Grace oral behavior changed conspicuously under more excitatory conditions, that is, during the psychological test and at times when the mother actively played with the child, using objects. When Grace and Harry dealt with objects while responding to greater intensity of stimulation gentle mouthing and sucking became rare. Instead, intense sucking, forceful chomping and chewing, and engulfing became prominent. While so engaged these babies now became oblivious of all else. What appeared to be the focus of awareness were the strong sensations generated within and about the mouth. To judge by the behavioral context, mouth contacts now tended to submerge the independent characteristics of the toy, as the object was assimilated to excitatory mouthing intense enough to be described as "passionate" and "violent" by the recording observers.

For the relatively inactive Peter the situation was quite different. His oral behavior with objects was, if anything, even more intense and prolonged than that of Grace or Harry. But it occurred during spontaneous activity, when he and accessible objects were left to their own devices. He then picked up toys and chomped or chewed at them with total absorption. He also often took an object (a toy, or shoe or piece of blanket, whatever came to hand) and rubbed it against his gums in energetic motions. Of course, he also looked at things, and used them in other ways. But in him there appeared to be an alternation between episodes during which he acted upon things and experimented with their potentialities, and moments when objects were used to act upon himself by intense oral stimulation. If my hypothesis is correct, mouthing during spontaneous activity precluded the awareness of things as independent of the self, much as I thought to be the case for Grace and Harry during the excitatory test situation.

A parallel to what I reported about other aspects of how these children interacted with inanimate objects, Peter's behavior during the test and other more stimulating situations changed as had that of Grace and Harry, but in the opposite direction. During the test Peter still showed a good deal of oral behavior, but far less than during spontaneous activity. Further, the intense chomping and biting as well as the engulfing and rubbing against the gums disappeared almost entirely. Instead, he sucked, licked, or gently mouthed objects. All of these episodes were transient, none absorbed all of his attention, and mouthing certainly did not get in the way of other modes of relating to the objects.

Peter's oral behavior differed from that of the others in additional ways. During spontaneous activity he very often looked at an object, and then approached it with his mouth to lick or suck. This happened with stationary objects such as the edge of the crib, but it also happened with small things that could have been grasped and brought to the mouth, and which at other moments he did manipulate. It seems to me that approaching an object "mouth first," and sucking at it while the body is necessarily brought very close to the object, would again tend to diminish the experienced distance between the thing and the child, whose boundaries merge as the child maintains contact only through mouthing. If so it would fit in to know that such behavior was seen transiently in Grace (under the same condition as in Peter, namely, spontaneous activity) and not at all in Harry, who was the most advanced developmentally.

Peter was also the only child for whom oral activation was a conspicuous part of social interaction. He was the only one of the four who often contacted his mother's body with his mouth. He bit her finger (with her enthusiastic support), he brought his mouth to her cheek, her hand and her clothing. Not infrequently he did the same with an observer's hand, sometimes in a manner so like that shown toward things that it seemed doubtful whether or not he perceived the hand as part of the other person's body.

Sybil's lack of oral behavior is something of an oddity. She showed herself capable of the required behavior integrations. That is, she occasionally brought an object to the mouth and briefly sucked at it while most of her attention was elsewhere. Sometimes she briefly held an object against her lip (as she held it against cheek or thigh at other times). But such mouth contact did not stimulate in her the schema of active mouthing as it did in the others. A few times she brought her mouth against the crib edge or the mother's hand, but with minimal activation of the mouth musculature.

I do not know how to account for this unusual behavior pattern in a baby who gave every sign of normal reactivity in other spheres. But it may be relevant that Sybil was the baby who engaged in an unusual amount of tactile self-stimulation. It almost seems as though for her the equivalent of oral activity took place in the tactile sphere. It is more than likely that at some time after our acquaintance with Sybil, she discovered the pleasures of oral play, but we shall never know.

In relation to oral behavior the mother's role is often thought about in connection with her tendency to interfere with what we know to be a powerful, spontaneous impulse, or to indulge it. So far as I could learn none of these four mothers had taken steps to prevent finger or object mouthing in their babies. Harry's mother thought he was too young, and expected him to show this behavior later on. Peter's mother had been surprised at his lack of interest in thumb sucking and joked that she guessed he preferred the taste of objects. Grace's mother had a few times removed the baby's fingers from her mouth which, she said, had not bothered the baby. She fully approved of the fact that Grace, as she put it, "chews everything in sight."

It will not surprise the reader to learn that Peter's was the only mother who played oral games with him. She kissed him, blew at him, playfully pretended to bite him, and was once seen to run her tongue over his fingertips. (Incidentally, she was oral in her imagery as well; a person whose speech was peppered with references to "swallowing," "biting," "good enough to eat," and similar meta-phors.) She actively encouraged his oral behavior. His wet approaches were hailed as kisses, and she gladly surrendered her hand "to see how hard you can bite."

Harry's and Grace's mothers would drop an occasional kiss on top of the baby's head, but made no other use of their own mouth in making direct contact with the babies. Sybil's mother was not seen to kiss her baby, though she may well have done so when not observed. However, I feel certain that she would never have indulged either herself or her baby in the oral mode.

In thinking about possible relationships between oral behavior on the baby's part and aspects of the mother-child relationship it is to be remembered that six-month-olds have a history of intense oral sensations. Sucking and swallowing have occurred at moments of high arousal (hunger). They have been associated with changes in body state (cessation hunger, relaxation), and they were experi-enced while mother was perceived. Young infants do not know that it is mother who *gives* them food, but they feel food coming in, and feel their mouth activate, while they also feel mother's touch, see her, and perhaps smell her. By the age of twenty-eight weeks these experiences have become a part of them, and it is not surprising that some sort of oral activity is an important component of behavior in all young children, though to different degrees.

These considerations, which suggest some sort of learning in the process of organizing behaviors involving the mouth, in no way contradict the assumption that there exists a biologically rooted tendency (drive, instinct) for sucking and other oral behaviors which, in consummation, gratify a need. In a biological framework I assume that drives or needs can be recognized as inborn partly by the fact that they are supported by anatomical and physiological structures of the organism. The mouth zone does indeed lend itself to activation in early life by more than one biological characteristic. Not only are hunger and food intake by mouth a primary given in human existence. The mouth zone is also especially sensitive in newborns and in infants (Bridger, 1962). Further, some of the reflexes that govern early motor behavior inevitably lead to hand-mouth contacts. The flexion-extension patterns of the limbs together with the so-called tonic-neck reflex which leads to a lateral rotation of the head, together with that component of the rooting reflex which leads newborns to activate the mouth musculature in response to lateral stimulation—all these together provide organic support for sucking and mouthing needs, though these needs are postulated on the basis of quite a different sort of observation.

What is more puzzling in the context of ego development is the capacity of the same behavior activation to fulfill quite different functions. The more autistically oriented autoerotic kind of mouthing which tends to screen the child off from awareness of external stimuli has received much attention in psychoanalytic psychology. Other theories of child development have placed more emphasis on what might be called the adaptive functions of oral behavior. These are the occasions, described earlier, when the mouth is used somewhat like a sense organ, but also somewhat like a part of the motor apparatus; namely, to mediate perceptual registration, to aid in the recognition and the discrimination of inanimate objects, and also to provide experiences in which the separateness of the acting subject and the acted-upon object can be felt with clarity.

In this respect oral activity appears to me to occupy a special position in the developmental process. Other body activations that also lend themselves to autoerotic activity (whether tactile, kinesthetic, or genital) are not especially well suited to exploration of the outer world. Once they are activated, their usual effect is to withdraw attention from the environment. Not so with oral activity which, in infants between roughly four and fourteen months, is equally well suited to self-contained activity as to outwardly directed action. It is intriguing to observe that in an infant's mouth-encounters with the world about, these two different potentials mingle and even lead to conflict. We often saw Peter, for instance, focus on something like a piece of furniture with alert attention. Then he moved his body toward it and as soon as his mouth contacted the object the sucking and licking schema took over. Having set in motion the resulting body sensations they absorbed all of his attention. For a while, he neither fingered the object nor took time out to look at it. Similar observations were made typically in Grace and Harry during the psychological test. As toys were offered they evoked, with the aid of the examiner, fairly complex adaptive actions, such as transferring an object from hand to hand, or ringing a bell. When an incidental motion brought the grasped toy toward the face, the oral schema asserted itself as these babies gave themselves to sporadic orgies of chewing or engulfing. (At such moments a toy must be removed from the baby's hand and reoffered if he is to use it in another way.) Most comically, we saw this conflict in Grace when, while obviously thirsty, she was offered water from a cup. As the rim contacted her lips the chomping pattern took over, water spilled, but she got none of it, and cried in frustration. She was obviously unable to let go of the rim until the mother forcibly removed it. In reoffering, the mother made certain that water touched the baby's lips at the same moment as the rim, and then Grace was able to drink in a coordinated manner.

There can be little doubt that when both are possible, the autoplastic kind of oral activity is the more primitive, whereas the alloplastic use of oral sensitivity tends to "exercise" rudimentary ego functions and serves developmental advance. This is not to say that reality-oriented mouthing is necessarily the more adaptive. For instance, the more autoplastic mouthing during the test had adaptive virtues for the excitable Harry and Grace. It provided intervals of rest from external stimulation and apparently helped them to maintain tolerable levels of excitation. These episodes of intense mouthing did not prevent optimally mature functioning in relation to the same objects in between times. In fact, I speculate that it was these intervals of "rest" that made the more complex behaviors possible. This is similar to my speculation concerning the way in which Sybil's and Peter's capacity to withdraw from strong social stimulation played a role in protecting them from the acute distress which the more active babies experienced under comparable circumstances.

It may be said that each of the four infant[6] subjects, by means of such body stimulation as they selectively employed, secured for themselves two sorts of important experience: on the one hand, the self-contained, body-sensation-centered mode of oral, tactile, or kinesthetic self-stimulation which, among other things, mediates a heightened awareness of the own body, and which, under some conditions, serves to protect the child against unduly strong stimulation from without; on the other hand, the employment of the oral mode in mediating awareness of aspects of the environment. In this situation the special sensitivity of the oral zone facilitates keener perception than would otherwise be possible, much as adults use their fingertips rather than the palm when they wish to obtain a vivid experience of textural quality, as in feeling the softness of velvet.

In leaving the topic of the significance of autoerotic activities for the development of early ego functions, it is desirable to state the broader developmental context. For what was said applies only to certain stages of development. In earliest infancy all sensory modalities are intact and functioning, but it is the near receptors that mediate both excitatory and soothing sensations. Assuming an undifferentiated organism in which a split does not exist between attention directed "outwardly" or "inwardly," one can accept a suggestion made in the psychoanalytic literature; namely, that in the beginning the entire skin surface, the skin and tissue in and about the mouth, and the proprioceptive systems all are actual or potential erogenous zones. The distance receptors (auditory, visual) are ill suited to the production of self-generated bodily sensations. Both vision and sound may become eroticized, of course, but only later in development. To begin with it is the distance receptors

---

6 Sybil is included despite the relative absence of oral behavior. As previously described, she tended to explore objects by prolonged gentle touch, while she was also the baby who was most prone to engage in tactile self-stimulation.

which mediate experiences leading to awareness, recognition, and the like—the very experiences which first establish a separation between self and nonself. It is not chance that those behaviors which unmistakably reflect something like anticipation, like memory, like intentionality, and like problem solving all normally occur at that time in development when we know that the distance-receptor systems have matured. Neurologists and psychologists alike recognize that it is only during the second half of the first year of life that the distance receptors begin to play a dominant role in the infant's adaptation.

What has been said about the dual role of oral activity, on the one hand in the service of mediating body sensations and excluding awareness of outer reality, and on the other hand in the service of a primitive and literal form of reality testing, holds good for only one phase of development. It applies to the transitional stage during which a shift in dominance occurs from primarily the near-receptor systems to primarily the distant ones. The role of oral behavior in the total developmental process is quite different during later phases of early childhood.

SUMMARY AND THEORETICAL IMPLICATIONS

I have presented an approach to the investigation of early developmental processes which focuses on patterned aspects of the infant's *experience* as the matrix of growth. At the outset I stated that I hoped to trace the influence of various environmental as well as biologically given factors upon the course of development. Yet I also said that I did not expect to find a constant effect of any one of these variables upon developmental outcome. In this last section I shall try to formulate some tentative ideas about the nature of the relationship between determining influences and the course of development.

The key word is experience; not the outer stimuli as such, not the infant's reaction tendencies, not both of these in simple summation, but the manner in which these factors alter what the baby feels with his senses, what he does with his body, and the content and quality of successive events in his life. Both the universals of development and the extraordinary variations may be said to *consist* of experience. A person can be said to do, or feel, or think, or be anything only as these verbs are taken to refer to the events that constitute his subjective experience. What I call experience is a series of events ordered on a time-space continuum, unified by virtue of the fact that they occur in a single organism that remains the same.

By definition experience is something subjective. The method of using observational data in order to construct specific constellations of experience on the basis of overt behavior under known circumstances is fraught with hazards. A word is in order on the methodological issue. I proceed on the assumption that it is possible to obtain objective information on external situational influences and conditions on the one hand, and concurrent behavior on the other. In saying that a startle occurred in response to an auditory stimulus we already make an inference about events not accessible to direct scrutiny. It is reasonable to do so, because the same response can be elicited with regularity by the same stimulus. In principle our observations are put to the same use when we infer from behavioral regularities under known circumstances constellations and qualities of experience.

However, a regular and predictable link between outer stimulus and behavioral response is not the only basis for inferences concerning infantile experience. Nor can it be established accurately with complex behaviors of the kind I have discussed. Another legitimate basis on which to construct models of experience lies with the intrinsic similarity between object and subject which is the unique feature of the observation of human beings by other human beings. Human communication is based on this similarity, and despite its limitations it does work by and large. The nervous system of the baby is much the same as that of the observer, and they are exposed to many of the same outer and inner stimulus conditions. The investigator's experience and that of the baby have much in common. We, the observers, know how touch or light are registered in awareness; we know the sensations designated as excitement, drowsiness, pleasure, and distress. In other words, empathy enters the process, and so does the hazard of adultomorphic speculation. The corrective for this source of error lies in adhering for one's data to overt behavior on the one hand, and to demonstrable stimulus conditions on the other. All statements about possible relationships between factors that determine experiences, and specific behavior organizations that result, must be based on the consistency and regularity of behavioral phenomena.

In presenting behavioral data on four infants of the same age, the aim has been to highlight differences in their response to similar or nearly identical stimulus conditions. It was assumed that almost every experience on the baby's part forms a link in the chain that constitutes developmental progress. Therefore, the observed behavior differences were discussed in relation to those developmental transitions known or thought to be central during the first year of life. In the case of six-month-olds these were the emerging separation of self from nonself, the awareness of differential characteristics of the environment, the early forms of acting upon the environment in an adaptive manner, and the developing relationship with the mother. The data suggest that the same developmental transitions may be accomplished by different routes, depending upon the infant's established reaction propensities, and the mother's mode of dealing with the child. The data also suggest that differences in organismic characteristics, such as activity level or perceptual sensitivity, may determine the impact of external stimulation upon the child's experience. For instance, in six-month-old infants who are markedly responsive, strong stimulation from the mother is arousing, but does not usually lead the infant to engage in the most mature behavior integrations of which he is capable. In fact, it may lead him to activate simpler, already well-established schemata. However, the same kind of external stimulation is a necessary condition for the emergence of the relatively most mature behaviors in markedly inactive babies of this age. Thus both respond to maternal stimulation, in both the resulting behavior activations have a bearing on the establishment of some early ego functions, but the immediate effect is in an almost opposite direction as a function of activity level. This is what is meant by postulating the infant's experience as the crucial intervening variable.

Similar observations were reported with respect to patterns of bodily self-stimulation. Infants differ in the type of body stimulation which they conspicuously show. The data suggest that infants provide for themselves the kind of bodily sensation which mothers have provided for them at moments of intense and pleasurable interaction. In this area, too, the facts are such that knowing how the mother tends to stimulate her infant does not predict the preferred modality for autoerotic activity in the baby. Nor is there a consistent relationship between that modality to which the infant proves most reactive and the modality he chooses for conspicuous self-stimulation. Again, in order for the infant to have had the constellation of experience that I believe determines the choice of autoerotic activity, the stimulation must have been provided, and he must have responded in a certain way.

Bodily self-stimulation was discussed also from the point of view of how it mediates reality-oriented behavior, how it screens the infant from external stimuli, and how it serves moment-by-moment adaptation. Thus not only may autoerotic behavior in some infants be used chiefly in the context of autistic withdrawal, whereas at a given point in their development other infants may use it chiefly in the context of exploring reality. The same infant, during the same stage of development, will activate oral behavior in the context of markedly different experience. When and how he uses oral behavior to mediate one or another kind of awareness can then be seen as influenced by the external situation, by established reaction tendencies, and by other variables.

The central theme throughout this presentation has been to make plausible the notion that very different actions on the part of mothers (or other environmental variations) may have very similar consequences in terms of their impact upon the child's experience, as reflected in behavior; and conversely, that similar or identical external stimulation may have varying and opposite consequences— in terms of the direction in which they alter behavior. Two categories of variables, environmental and organismic, converge and reciprocally interact in shaping the moment-by-moment and year-by-year experience of the growing child. The fact that all healthy children do come to recognize an environment that exists independently of their action; the fact that all learn to regulate motor actions in a purposive manner; the fact that all develop a selective tie to the mother— these and other universalities are seen as a necessary consequence of closely similar biological equipment, and a high order of regularity in the encounters with animate and inanimate objects in the human habitat, what Hartmann (1939) calls the average expectable environment. Ego functions necessarily emerge and differentiate in the course of these successive encounters and adaptations. What all normal children have in common is the result of experience just as much as differences are the result of experience. And all experience, whether it leads to walking which is universal, or to a tendency for abstraction and ideational defenses which is particular, is the result also of biological organismic characteristics. The assumption of a reciprocal relation among influences which in their totality make up the child's experience should make unnecessary the distinction between maturation and learning when these terms are applied to aspects of the developmental process. It should facilitate the recognition that the laws of development—the relationship between behavioral patterns and supporting psychic structures on the one hand, and experiential antecedents on the other—are the same for normal development as for pathology. For instance, to conclude with a clinical example, contradictory findings about the genesis of some varieties of infantile psychosis are reconcilable in this manner. Children who suffer from this illness have in common the lack or distortion of a mutual relationship with a mother person. They do not respond to their mothers in the ways I described for my four normal subjects. Clinical evidence shows that in some instances this deficiency arises because there was no mother who responded to the baby as normal mothers do—an environmental deficiency. But the illness also occurs in children who were raised by normally responsive mothers who provide all that other children receive. But the child is so constituted that he cannot participate in the usual patterns of interaction, probably due to an inborn deficit yet to be specified. But if the patterning of behavioral events is used as a clue for the child's experience, the different clinical histories prove alike in the only crucial area. The child deficient in the capacity to respond is just as motherless as is the normally equipped child without a mother. The controversy as to whether infantile autism is "due to" inadequate mothering or "due to" inborn deficit loses its significance. It is a result of a lack in experiences which may come about through extreme variations in either intrinsic or extrinsic determinants, or both. But autistic psychosis in childhood is not directly caused by a maternal deficit or by a deficit in the child. It is caused by the absence of those vital experiences in early childhood which we regard as the necessary condition for ego synthesis.

BIBLIOGRAPHY

Benjamin, J. D. (1950), Methodological Considerations in the Validation and Elaboration of Psychoanalytic Personality Theory. *Amer. J. Orthopsychiat.*, XX.
—— (1959), Prediction and Psychopathological Theory. In: *The Psychopathology of Childhood*, ed. L. Jessner & E. Pavenstedt. New York: Grune & Stratton.
Bridger, W. H. (1962), Sensory Discrimination and Autonomic Function in the Newborn. *J. Amer. Acad. Child. Psychiat.*, I.
Escalona, S. K. (1962), The Study of Individual Differences and the Problem of State. *J. Amer. Acad. Child Psychiat.*, I.
—— & Leitch, M., et al. (1952), *Early Phases of Personality Development: A Non-Normative Study of Infant Behavior* [Monographs of the Society for Research in Child Development, Inc., Vol. XVII, Serial No. 54]. Evanston, Ill.: Child Development Publications, 1953.
Freud, S. (1900), The Interpretation of Dreams. *Standard Edition*, IV & V. London: Hogarth Press, 1953.
Hartmann, H. (1939), *Ego Psychology and the Problem of Adaptation*. New York: International Universities Press, 1958.
—— & Kris, E., Loewenstein, R. M. (1946), Comments on the Formation of Psychic Structure. *This Annual*, II.
Piaget, J. (1936), *The Origins of Intelligence in Children*. New York: International Universities Press, 1952.
Spitz, R. A. (1955), The Primal Cavity: A Contribution to the Genesis of Perception and Its Role in Psychoanalytic Theory. *This Annual*, X.
—— & Wolf, K. M. (1949), Autoerotism: Empirical Findings and Hypotheses on Three of Its Manifestations in the First Year of Life. *This Annual*, III/IV.

THE CONCEPT OF DEVELOPMENTAL LINES

ANNA FREUD, LL.D. (London)

The diagnostic Profile which we have set up serves the systematic assessment of childhood disturbances by seeing the picture of any given child against the background of a developmental norm into which the state of his inner agencies, his various functions, conflicts, attitudes, and achievements have to be fitted. In our psychoanalytic theory such developmental sequences are laid down so far as certain circumscribed parts of the child's personality are concerned. With regard to the development of the sexual drive, for example, we possess the sequence of libidinal phases (oral, anal, phallic, latency period, preadolescence, adolescent genitality) which, in spite of considerable overlapping, correspond roughly with specific ages. With regard to the aggressive drive we are already less precise and are usually content to correlate specific aggressive expressions with specific libidinal phases (such as biting, spitting, devouring with orality; sadistic torturing, hitting, kicking, destroying with anality; overbearing, domineering, forceful behavior with the phallic phase;

Like last year's article on "Assessment of Childhood Disturbances," this paper is extracted from a more extensive study of child development as a preliminary communication. Together with the "Diagnostic Profile" it forms the basis of an investigation in the Hampstead Child-Therapy Clinic. This investigation, under the title of "Assessment of Pathology in Childhood," is supported by Public Health Service Research Grant No. M-5683, MH (1), from the National Institute of Mental Health, Washington.

The individual lines of development have been discussed in detail with the Diagnostic Research Committee of the Hampstead Child-Therapy Clinic, and I have incorporated suggestions and amendments made by John Bolland, Liselotte Frankl, Ilse Hellman, Martin James, Maria Kawenoka, Humberto Nagera, Joseph Sandler, Ruth Thomas, Doris Wills.

Material for the Lines has been provided by the Hampstead Child-Therapy Clinic, an institution maintained at present by The Field Foundation, Inc., New York; The Anna Freud Foundation, New York; The Grant Foundation, Inc., New York; The Estate of Flora Haas, New York; The Old Dominion Foundation, New York; The Psychoanalytic Research and Development Fund, Inc., New York; The Taconic Foundation, Inc., New York.

inconsiderateness, mental cruelty, dissocial outbursts with adolescence, etc.). On the side of the ego, the analytically known stages and
levels of the sense of reality, in the chronology of defense activity and
in the growth of a moral sense, lay down a norm. The intellectual
functions themselves are measured and graded by the psychologist by
means of the age-related scales of the various intelligence tests.

On the other hand, it is true that we need more for our assess-
ments than these selected developmental scales which are valid for
isolated parts of the child's personality only, not for its totality.
What we are looking for are the basic interactions between id and
ego and their various developmental levels, and also age-related
sequences of them which, in importance, frequency, and regularity,
are comparable to the maturational sequence of libidinal stages or
the gradual unfolding of the ego functions. Naturally, such sequences
of interaction between the two sides of the personality can be best
established where both are well studied, as they are, for example,
with regard to the libidinal phases and aggressive expressions on
the id side and the corresponding object-related attitudes on the ego
side. Here we can trace the combinations which lead from the
infant's complete emotional dependence to the adult's comparative
self-reliance and mature sex and object relationships, a gradated
developmental line which provides the indispensable basis for any
assessment of emotional maturity or immaturity, normality or
abnormality.

Even if perhaps less easily established, there are similar lines of
development which can be shown to be valid for almost every other
area of the individual's personality. In every instance they trace
the child's gradual outgrowing of dependent, irrational, id- and
object-determined attitudes to an increasing ego mastery of his internal and external world. Such lines—always contributed to from the
side of both id and ego development—lead, for example, from the
infant's suckling and weaning experiences to the adult's rational
rather than emotional attitude to food intake; from cleanliness
training enforced on the child by environmental pressure to the
adult's more or less ingrained and unshakable bladder and bowel
control; from the child's sharing possession of his body with his
mother to the adolescent's claim for independence and self-determination in body management; from the young child's egocentric

view of the world and his fellow beings to empathy, mutuality, and companionship with his contemporaries; from the first erotic play on his own and his mother's body by way of the transitional objects (Winnicott, 1953) to the toys, games, hobbies, and finally to work, etc.

Whatever level has been reached by any given child in any of these respects represents the results of interaction between drive and ego-superego development and their reaction to environmental influences, i.e., between maturation, adaptation, and structuralization. Far from being theoretical abstractions, developmental lines, in the sense here used, are historical realities which, when assembled, convey a convincing picture of an individual child's personal achievements or, on the other hand, of his failures in personality development.

PROTOTYPE OF A DEVELOPMENTAL LINE: FROM DEPENDENCY TO EMOTIONAL SELF-RELIANCE AND ADULT OBJECT RELATIONSHIPS

To serve as the prototype for all others, there is one basic developmental line which has received attention from analysts from the beginning. This is the sequence which leads from the newborn's utter dependence on maternal care to the young adult's emotional and material self-reliance—a sequence for which the successive stages of libido development (oral, anal, phallic) merely form the inborn, maturational base. The steps on this way are well documented from the analyses of adults and children, as well as from direct analytic infant observations:

(1) The biological unity between the mother-infant couple, with the mother's narcissism extending to the child, and the child including the mother in his internal "narcissistic milieu" (Hoffer, 1952), the whole period being further subdivided (according to Margaret Mahler, 1952) into the autistic, symbiotic and separation-individuation phases with significant danger points for developmental disturbances lodged in each individual phase;

(2) the part object (Melanie Klein), or need-fulfilling, anaclitic relationship, which is based on the urgency of the child's body needs and drive derivatives and is intermittent and fluctuating,

since object cathexis is sent out under the impact of imperative desires, and withdrawn again when satisfaction has been reached;

(3) the stage of object constancy, which enables a positive inner image of the object to be maintained, irrespective of dissatisfactions and frustrations;

(4) the ambivalent relationship of the preoedipal, anal-sadistic stage, characterized by the ego attitudes of clinging, torturing, dominating, and controlling the objects;

(5) the completely object-centered phallic-oedipal phase, characterized by possessiveness of the parent of the opposite sex, jealousy and rivalry with the parent of the same sex, protectiveness, generosity, curiosity, bids for admiration and exhibitionistic attitudes; with girls a phallic-oedipal (masculine) relationship to the mother precedes the oedipal relationship to the father;

(6) the latency period, i.e., the postoedipal lessening of drive urgency and the transfer of libido from the parental figures to contemporaries, community groups, teachers, leaders, impersonal ideals, and aim-inhibited, sublimated interests, with fantasy manifestations giving evidence of disillusionment with and denigration of the parents ("family romance," twin fantasies, etc.);

(7) the preadolescent prelude to the "adolescent revolt," i.e., a return to early attitudes and behavior, especially of the part-object, need-fulfilling, and ambivalent type;

(8) the adolescent struggle around denying, reversing, loosening, and shedding the tie to the infantile objects, defending against pregenitality, and finally establishing genital supremacy with libidinal cathexis transferred to objects of the opposite sex, outside the family.

While the details of these positions have long been common knowledge in analytic circles, their relevance for practical problems is being explored increasingly in recent years. As regards, for example, the much-discussed consequences of a child's separation from the mother, the parents or the home, a mere glance at the unfolding of the developmental line will be sufficient to show convincingly why the common reactions to, respectively, the pathological consequences of, such happenings are as varied as they are, following the

varying psychic reality of the child on the different levels. Infringements of the biological mother-infant tie (phase 1), for whatever
reason they are undertaken, will thus give rise to separation anxiety
(Bowlby, 1960) proper; failure of the mother to play her part as a
reliable need-fulfilling and comfort-giving agency (phase 2) will cause
breakdowns in individuation (Mahler, 1952) or anaclitic depression
(Spitz, 1946), or other manifestations of deprivation (Alpert, 1959),
or precocious ego development (James, 1960), or what has been called
a "false self" (Winnicott, 1954). Unsatisfactory libidinal relations to
unstable or otherwise unsuitable love objects during anal sadism
(phase 4) will disturb the balanced fusion between libido and aggression and give rise to uncontrollable aggressivity, destructiveness, etc.
(A. Freud, 1949). It is only after object constancy (phase 3) has been
reached that the external absence of the object is substituted for, at
least in part, by the presence of an internal image which remains
stable; on the strength of this achievement temporary separations can
be lengthened, commensurate with the advances in object constancy.
Thus, even if it remains impossible to name the chronological age
when separations can be tolerated, according to the developmental
line it can be stated when they become phase-adequate and nontrau-
matic, a point of practical importance for the purposes of holidays
for the parents, hospitalization of the child, convalescence, entry into
nursery school, etc.[1]

There are other practical lessons which have been learned from
the same developmental sequence, such as the following:

that the clinging attitudes of the toddler stage (phase 4) are the
result of preoedipal ambivalence, not of maternal spoiling;

that it is unrealistic on the part of parents to expect of the preoedipal period (up to the end of phase 4) the mutuality in object
relations which belongs to the next level (phase 5) only;

that no child can be fully integrated in school before libido has
been transferred from the parents to the community (phase 6).
Where the passing of the oedipus complex is delayed and phase 5 is
protracted as the result of an infantile neurosis, disturbances in

[1] If, by "mourning" we understand not the various manifestations of anxiety, distress, and malfunction which accompany object loss in the earliest phases but the
painful, gradual process of detaching libido from an internal image, this, of course,
cannot be expected to occur before object constancy (phase 3) has been established.

adaptation to the group, lack of interest, school phobias (in day
school), extreme homesickness (in boarding school) will be the order
of the day;

that reactions to adoption are most severe in the later part of
the latency period (phase 6) when, according to the normal disillusionment with the parents, all children feel as if adopted and the
feelings about the reality of adoption merge with the occurrence of
the "family romance";

that sublimations, foreshadowed on the oedipal level (phase 5)
and developed during latency (phase 6), may be lost during preadolescence (phase 7), not through any developmental or educational
failure, but owing to the phase-adequate regression to early levels
(phases 2, 3, and 4);

that it is as unrealistic on the part of the parents to oppose the
loosening of the tie to the family or the young person's battle against
pregenital impulses in adolescence (phase 8) as it is to break the
biological tie in phase 1, or oppose pregenital autoerotism in the
phases 1, 2, 3, 4, and 7.

SOME DEVELOPMENTAL LINES TOWARD BODY INDEPENDENCE

That the ego of an individual begins first and foremost as a
body ego does not imply that bodily independence of the parents is
reached earlier than emotional or moral self-reliance. On the contrary: the mother's narcissistic possessiveness of her infant's body is
matched from the child's side by his archaic wishes to merge with
the mother and by the confusion concerning body limits which arises
from the fact that in early life the distinctions between the internal
and external world are based not on objective reality but on the
subjective experiences of pleasure and unpleasure. Thus, while the
mother's breast, or face, hands or hair, may be treated (or maltreated) by the infant as parts of his own organization, his hunger,
his tiredness, his discomforts are her concern as much as they are
his own. Although for the whole of early childhood, the child's life
will be dominated by body needs, body impulses, and their derivatives, the quantities and qualities of satisfactions and dissatisfactions
are determined not by himself but by environmental influence. The
only exceptions to this rule are the autoerotic gratifications which

from the beginning are under the child's own management and, therefore, provide for him a certain circumscribed measure of independence of the object world. In contrast to these, the processes of feeding, sleeping, evacuation, body hygiene, and prevention of injury and illness have to undergo complex and lengthy developments before they become the growing individual's own concern.

From Suckling to Rational Eating

A long line has to be passed through before a child arrives at the point where, for example, he can regulate his own food intake actively and rationally, quantitatively and qualitatively, on the basis of his own needs and appetites and irrespective of his relations to the provider of food, and of conscious and unconscious fantasies. The steps on the way are approximately as follows:

(1) Being nursed at the breast or bottle, by the clock or on demand, with the common difficulties about intake caused partly by the infant's normal fluctuations of appetite and intestinal upsets, partly by the mother's attitudes and anxieties regarding feeding; interference with need-satisfaction caused by hunger periods, undue waiting for meals, rationing or forced feeding set up the first—and often lasting—disturbances in the positive relationship to food. Pleasure sucking appears as a forerunner, by-product of, substitute for, or interference with feeding;

(2) weaning from breast or bottle, initiated either by the infant himself or according to the mother's wishes. In the latter instance, and especially if carried out abruptly, the infant's protest against oral deprivation has adverse results for the normal pleasure in food. Difficulties over the introduction of solids, new tastes, and consistencies being either welcomed or rejected;

(3) the transition from being fed to self-feeding, with or without implements, "food" and "mother" still being identified with each other;

(4) self-feeding with the use of spoon, fork, etc., the disagreements with the mother about the quantity of intake being shifted often to the form of intake, i.e., table manners; meals as a general battleground on which the difficulties of the mother-child relationship can be fought out; craving for sweets as a phase-ade-

quate substitute for oral sucking pleasures; food fads as a result
of anal training, i.e., of the newly acquired reaction formation of
disgust;

(5) gradual fading out of the equation food-mother in the oedipal
period. Irrational attitudes toward eating are now determined
by infantile sexual theories, i.e., fantasies of impregnation
through the mouth (fear of poison), pregnancy (fear of getting
fat), anal birth (fear of intake and output), as well as by reaction
formations against cannibalism and sadism;

(6) gradual fading out of the sexualization of eating in the latency
period, with pleasure in eating retained or even increased.
Increase in the rational attitudes to food and self-determination
in eating, the earlier experiences on this line being decisive in
shaping the individual's food habits in adult life, his tastes,
preferences, as well as eventual addictions or aversions with
regard to food and drink.

The infant's reactions to the changes in phase 2 (i.e., to weaning
and to the introduction of new tastes and consistencies) reflect for
the first time his leaning toward either progression and adventurousness (when new experiences are welcomed) or a tenacious clinging to
existing pleasures (when every change is experienced as threat and
deprivation). It is to be expected that whichever attitude dominates
the feeding process will also become important in other developmental areas.

The equation food-mother, which persists through phases 1-4,
provides the rational background for the mother's subjective conviction that every food refusal of the child is aimed at her personally,
i.e., expresses the child's rejection of her maternal care and attention,
a conviction which causes much oversensitiveness in handling the
feeding process and underlies the battle about food on the mother's
side. It explains also why in these phases food refusal and extreme
food fads can be circumvented by temporarily substituting a stranger,
i.e., a noncathected or differently cathected person, for the maternal
figure in the feeding situation. Children will then eat, in hospital,
in nursery school, or as visitors, but this will not cure their eating
difficulties at home, in the presence of the mother. It explains also
why traumatic separations from the mother are often followed by

refusal of food (rejection of the mother substitute), or by greed and overeating (treating food as a substitute for mother love).

The eating disturbances of phase 5, which are not related to an external object but are caused by internal, structural conflicts, are not affected by either the material presence or the material absence of the mother, a fact which can be utilized for differential diagnosis.

After phase 6, when the arrangements for food intake have become the mature individual's personal concern, the former food battle with the mother may be replaced by internal disagreements between the manifest wish to eat and an unconsciously determined inability to tolerate certain foods, i.e., the various neurotic food fads and digestive upsets.

From Wetting and Soiling to Bladder and Bowel Control

Since the desired aim on this line is not the comparatively intact survival of drive derivatives but the control, modification, and transformation of the urethral and anal trends, the conflicts between id, ego, superego, and environmental forces become particularly obvious.

(1) The duration of the first phase, during which the infant has complete freedom to wet and soil, is determined not maturationally but environmentally, i.e., by the mother's timing of her interference, in which she in her turn is under the influence of personal needs, familial, social, or medical conventions. Under present conditions this phase may last from a few days (training from birth based on reflex action) to two or three years (training based on object relatedness and ego control).

(2) In contrast to phase one, the second phase is initiated by a step in maturation. The dominant role in drive activity passes from the oral to the anal zone, and due to this transition the child stiffens his opposition to any interference with concerns which have become emotionally vital to him. Since in this phase the body products are highly cathected with libido, they are precious to the child and are treated as "gifts" which are surrendered to the mother as a sign of love; since they are cathected also with aggression, they are weapons by means of which rage, anger, disappointment can be discharged within the object relationship. In correspondence to this double cathexis of the body products, the toddler's entire attitude toward the object world is dominated by ambivalence, i.e., by violent swings

between love and hate (libido and aggression not fused with each other). This again is matched on the ego side by curiosity directed toward the inside of the body, pleasure in messing, molding, play with retaining, emptying, hoarding, as well as dominating, possessing, destroying, etc. While the trends shown by the children in this phase are fairly uniform, the actual events vary with the differences in the mother's attitude. If she succeeds in remaining sensitive to the child's needs and as identified with them as she is usually with regard to feeding, she will mediate sympathetically between the environmental demand for cleanliness and the child's opposite anal and urethral tendencies; in that case toilet training will proceed gradually, uneventfully, and without upheavals. On the other hand, such empathy with the child in the anal stage may be impossible for the mother due to her own training, her own reaction formations of disgust, orderliness, and punctiliousness, or other obsessional elements in her personality. If she is dominated by these, she will represent the demand for urethral and anal control in a harsh and uncompromising manner and a major battle will ensue, with the child as intent to defend his right over unrestricted evacuation as the mother is on achieving cleanliness and regularity and with them the rudiments and *sine qua non* of socialization.

(3) In a third phase the child accepts and takes over the mother's and the environment's attitudes to cleanliness and, through identification, makes them an integral part of his ego and superego demands; from then onward, the striving for cleanliness is an internal, not an external, precept, and inner barriers against urethral and anal wishes are set up through the defense activity of the ego, in the well-known form of repression and reaction formation. Disgust, orderliness, tidiness, dislike of dirty hands guard against the return of the repressed; punctuality, conscientiousness, and reliability appear as by-products of anal regularity; inclinations to save, to collect, give evidence of high anal evaluation displaced to other matters. In short, what takes place in this period is the far-reaching modification and transformation of the pregenital anal drive derivatives which—if kept within normal limits—supply the individual personality with a backbone of highly valuable qualities.

It is important to remember in respect to these achievements that they are based on identifications and internalizations and, as such, are not fully secure before the passing of the oedipus complex. Pre-oedipal anal control remains vulnerable and, especially in the beginning of the third phase, remains dependent on the objects and the stability of positive relations to them. For example, a child who is trained to use the chamberpot or toilet in his home does not exchange them automatically for unfamiliar ones, away from the mother. A child who is severely disappointed in his mother, or separated from her, or suffering from object loss in any form, may not only lose the internalized urge to be clean but also reactivate the aggressive use of elimination. Both together will result in incidents of wetting and soiling which appear as "accidents."

(4) It is only in a fourth phase that bladder and bowel control become wholly secure. This is brought about when the concern for cleanliness is disconnected from object ties and attains the status of a fully neutralized, autonomous ego and superego concern.[2]

From Irresponsibility to Responsibility in Body Management

That the satisfaction of such essential physical needs as feeding and evacuation[3] remains for years under external control and emerges from it in such slow steps corresponds well with the equally slow and gradual manner in which children assume responsibility for the care of their own body and its protection against harm. As described at length elsewhere (A. Freud, 1952), the well-mothered child leaves these concerns largely to the mother, while he allows himself attitudes of indifference and unconcern, or, as a weapon in a battle with her, downright recklessness. It is only the badly mothered or the motherless who adopt the mother's role in health matters and play "mother and child" with their own bodies as the hypochondriacs do.

On the positive progressive line, here too, there are several consecutive phases to be distinguished from each other, though our present knowledge of them is more sketchy than in other areas.

(1) What comes first, as a maturational step in the first few months of life, is an alteration in the direction of aggression from being lived out on the body to being turned toward the external

2 See H. Hartmann (1950) on "secondary autonomy of the ego."
3 Also sleep.

world. This vital step sets limits to self-injury from biting, scratching, etc., although indications of such tendencies can be seen in many children as genuine remnants also at later ages.[4] The normal forward move happens partly due to the setting up of the pain barrier, partly due to the child's answering to the mother's libidinal cathexis of his body with a narcissistic cathexis of his own (according to Hoffer, 1950).

(2) What makes itself felt next are the advances in ego functioning such as orientation in the external world, understanding of cause and effect, control of dangerous wishes in the service of the reality principle. Together with the pain barrier and the narcissistic cathexis of the body, these newly acquired functions protect the child against such external dangers as water, fire, heights, etc. But there are many instances of children where—owing to a deficiency in any one of these ego functions—this advance is retarded so that they remain unusually vulnerable and exposed if not protected by the adult world.

(3) What comes last normally is the child's voluntary endorsement of the rules of hygiene and of medical necessities. So far as the avoidance of unwholesome food, overeating, and keeping the body clean are concerned, this is inconclusive here since the relevant attitudes belong to the vicissitudes of the oral and anal component instinct rather than to the present line. It is different with the avoidance of ill-health or the compliance with doctor's orders concerning the intake of medicines, and motor or dietary restrictions. Fear, guilt, castration anxiety, of course, may motivate any child to be careful (i.e., fearful) for the safety of his body. But when not under the influence of these, normal children will be remarkably uncompromising and obstructive in health matters. According to their mothers' frequent complaints, they behave as if they claimed it as their right to endanger their health while they left it to the mother to protect and restore it, an attitude which lasts often until the end of adolescence and may represent the last residue of the original symbiosis between child and mother.

---

[4] Such remnants should not be confused with the later "turning of aggression against the self" which is not a defect in maturation but a defense mechanism used by the ego under the impact of conflict.

FURTHER EXAMPLES OF DEVELOPMENTAL LINES

There are many other examples of developmental lines, such as the two given below, where every step is known to the analyst, and which can be traced without difficulty, either through working backward by reconstruction from the adult picture, or through working forward by means of longitudinal analytic exploration and observation of the child.

The Line from Egocentricity to Companionship

When describing a child's growth in this particular respect, a sequence can be traced which runs as follows:

(1) a selfish, narcissistically orientated outlook on the object world, in which other children either do not figure at all or are perceived only in their role as disturbers of the mother-child relationship and rivals for the parents' love;

(2) other children related to as lifeless objects, i.e., toys which can be handled, pushed around, sought out, and discarded as the mood demands, with no positive or negative response expected from them;

(3) other children related to as helpmates in carrying out a desired task such as playing, building, destroying, causing mischief of some kind, etc., the duration of the partnership being determined by the task, and secondary to it;

(4) other children as partners and objects in their own right, whom the child can admire, fear, or compete with, whom he loves or hates, with whose feelings he identifies, whose wishes he acknowledges and often respects, and with whom he can share possessions on a basis of equality.

In the first two phases, even if cherished and tolerated as the baby by older siblings, the toddler is by necessity asocial, whatever efforts to the contrary the mother may make; community life at this stage may be endured but will not be profitable. The third stage represents the minimum requirement for socialization in the form of acceptance into a home community of older siblings or entry into a nursery group of contemporaries. But it is only the fourth stage which equips the child for companionship, enmities and friendships of any type and duration.

The Line from the Body to the Toy and from Play to Work

(1) Play begins with the infant as an activity yielding erotic pleasure, involving the mouth, the fingers, vision, the whole surface of the skin. It is carried out on the child's own body (autoerotic play) or on the mother's body (usually in connection with feeding) with no clear distinction between the two, and with no obvious order or precedence in this respect.

(2) The properties of the mother's and the child's body are transferred to some soft substance, such as a nappy, a pillow, a rug, a teddy, which serves as the infant's first plaything, the "transitional object" (according to Winnicott, 1953) which is cathected both with narcissistic and with object libido.

(3) Clinging to one specific transitional object develops further into a more indiscriminate liking for soft toys of various kinds which, as symbolic objects, are cuddled and maltreated alternately (cathected with libido and aggression). That they are inanimate objects, and therefore do not retaliate, enables the toddler to express the full range of his ambivalence toward them.

(4) Cuddly toys fade out gradually, except at bedtime, when— in their capacity as transitional objects—they continue to facilitate the child's passing from active participation in the external world to the narcissistic withdrawal necessary for sleep.

In daytime their place is taken increasingly by play material which does not itself possess object status but which serves ego activities and the fantasies underlying them. Such activities either directly gratify a component instinct or are invested with displaced and sublimated drive energies, their chronological sequence being approximately the following:

(a) toys offering opportunities for ego activities such as filling-emptying, opening-shutting, fitting in, messing, etc., interest in them being displaced from the body openings and their functions;

(b) movable toys providing pleasure in motility;

(c) building material offering equal opportunities for construction and destruction (in correspondence with the ambivalent trends of the anal-sadistic phase);

(d) toys serving the expression of masculine and feminine trends and attitudes, to be used

    (i) in solitary role play,

    (ii) for display to the oedipal object (serving phallic exhibitionism),

    (iii) for staging the various situations of the oedipus complex in group play (provided that stage 3 on the developmental line toward companionship has been reached).

Expression of masculinity can be taken over also by the ego activities of gymnastics and acrobatics, in which the child's entire body and its skillful manipulation represent, display, and provide symbolic enjoyment from phallic activities and phallic mastery.

(5) Direct or displaced satisfaction from the play activity itself gives way increasingly to the pleasure in the finished product of the activity, a pleasure which has been described in academic psychology as pleasure in task completion, in problem solving, etc. By some authors it is taken as the indispensable prerequisite for the child's successful performance in school (Bühler, 1935).

The exact manner in which this pleasure in achievement is linked with the child's instinctual life is an open question still in our theoretical thinking, although various operative factors seem unmistakable such as imitation and identification in the early mother-child relationship, the influence of the ego ideal, the turning of passive into active as a mechanism of defense and adaptation, and the inner urge toward maturation, i.e., toward progressive development.

That pleasure in achievement, linked only secondarily with object relations, is present in very young children as a latent capacity is demonstrated in a practical manner by the successes of the Montessori method. In this nursery-school method the play material is selected so as to afford the child the maximum increase in self-esteem and gratification by means of task completion and independent problem solving, and children can be observed to respond positively to such opportunities almost from the toddler stage onward.

Where this source of gratification is not tapped to the same degree with the help of external arrangements, the pleasure derived from achievement in play remains more directly connected with praise and approval given by the object world, and satisfaction from the finished product takes first place at a later date only, probably as the result of internalization of external sources of self-esteem.

(6) Ability to play changes into ability to *work*[5] when a number of additional faculties are acquired, such as the following:

(a)   to control, inhibit, or modify the impulses to use given material aggressively and destructively (not to throw, to take apart, to mess, to hoard), and to use them positively and constructively instead (to build, to plan, to learn, and—in communal life—to share);

(b)   to carry out preconceived plans with a minimum regard for the lack of immediate pleasure yield, intervening frustrations, etc., and the maximum regard for the pleasure in the ultimate outcome;

(c)   to achieve thereby not only the transition from primitive instinctual to sublimated pleasure, together with a high grade of neutralization of the energy employed, but equally the transition from the pleasure principle to the reality principle, a development which is essential for success in work during latency, adolescence, and in maturity.

Derived from the line from the body to the toy and from play to work and based predominantly on its later stages are a number of allied activities which are significant for personality development such as daydreaming, games, and hobbies.

Daydreaming

When toys and the activities connected with them fade into the background, the wishes formerly put into action with the help of material objects, i.e., fulfilled in play, can be spun out imaginatively

5 What is attempted here is not a definition of work with all its social as well as psychological implications, but merely a description of the advances in ego development and drive control which seem to be the necessary forerunners of any individual's acquisition of the capacity to work.

in the form of conscious daydreams, a fantasy activity which may persist until adolescence, and far beyond it.

Games

Games derive their origin from the imaginative group activities of the oedipal period (see stage 4, d, iii) from which they develop into the symbolic and highly formalized expression of trends toward aggressive attack, defense, competition, etc. Since they are governed by inflexible rules to which the individual participant has to submit, they cannot be entered successfully by any child before some adaptation to reality and some frustration tolerance have been acquired and, naturally, not before stage 3 on the developmental line toward companionship has been reached.

Games may require equipment (as distinct from toys). Since this is in many instances of symbolic phallic, i.e., masculine-aggressive, significance, it is highly valued by the child.

In many competitive games the child's own body and the body skills in themselves play the role of indispensable tools.

Proficiency and pleasure in games are, thus, a complex achievement, dependent on contributions from many areas of the child's personality such as the endowment and intactness of the motor apparatus; a positive cathexis of the body and its skills; acceptance of companionship and group life; positive employment of controlled aggression in the service of ambition, etc. Correspondingly, functioning in this area is open to an equally large number of disturbances which may result from developmental difficulties and inadequacies in any of these areas, as well as from the phase-determined inhibitions of anal aggression and phallic-oedipal masculinity.

Hobbies

Halfway between play and work is the place of the hobbies, which have certain aspects in common with both activities. With play they share a number of characteristics:

(a) of being undertaken for purposes of pleasure with comparative disregard for external pressures and necessities;

(b) of pursuing displaced, i.e., sublimated, aims, but aims which are not too far removed from the gratification of either erotic or aggressive drives;

(c) of pursuing these aims with a combination of unmodified
     drive energies plus energies in various states and degrees of
     neutralization.

With working attitudes as described above, the hobbies share
the important feature of a preconceived plan being undertaken in
a reality-adapted way and carried on over a considerable period of
time if necessary in the face of external difficulties and frustrations.

Hobbies appear for the first time at the beginning of the latency
period (collecting, spotting, specializing of interests), undergo any
number of changes of content, but may persist as this specific form
of activity throughout life.

Correspondence between Developmental Lines

If we examine our notions of average normality in detail, we
find that we expect a fairly close correspondence between growth
on the individual developmental lines. In clinical terms this means
that, to be a harmonious personality, a child who has reached a specific stage in the sequence toward emotional maturity (for example,
object constancy), should have attained also corresponding levels
in his growth toward bodily independence (such as bladder and
bowel control, loosening of the tie between food and mother), in the
lines toward companionship, constructive play, etc. We maintain
this expectation of a norm even though reality presents us with many
examples to the contrary. There are numerous children, undoubtedly, who show a very irregular pattern in their growth. They may
stand high on some levels (such as maturity of emotional relations,
bodily independence, etc.) while lagging behind in others (such as
play where they continue to cling to transitional objects, cuddly
toys, or development of companionship where they persist in treating contemporaries as disturbances or inanimate objects). Some
children are well developed toward secondary thought, speech, play,
work, community life while remaining in a state of dependency with
regard to the management of their own bodily processes, etc.

Such imbalance between developmental lines causes sufficient
friction in childhood to justify a closer inquiry into the circum-

stances which give rise to it, especially into the question how far it is determined by innate and how far by environmental reasons.

As in all similar instances, our task is not to isolate the two factors and to ascribe to each a separate field of influence but to trace their interactions, which may be described as follows in the present case:

We assume that with all normally endowed, organically undamaged children the lines of development indicated above are included in their constitution as inherent possibilities. What endowment lays down for them on the side of the id are, obviously, the maturational sequences in the development of libido and aggression; on the side of the ego, less obviously and less well studied, certain innate tendencies toward organization, defense, and structuralization; perhaps also, though we know less still about this, some given quantitative differences of emphasis on progress in one direction or another. For the rest, that is, for what singles out individual lines for special promotion in development, we have to look to accidental environmental influences. In the analysis of older children and the reconstructions from adult analysis we have found these forces embodied in the parents' personalities, their actions and ideals, the family atmosphere, the impact of the cultural setting as a whole. In the analytic observation of young infants it has been demonstrated that it is the individual mother's interest and predilection which act as stimulants. In the beginning of life, at least, the infant seems to concentrate on development along those lines which call forth most ostensibly the mother's love and approval, i.e., her spontaneous pleasure in the child's achievement and, in comparison, to neglect others where such approval is not given. This implies that activities which are acclaimed by the mother are repeated more frequently, become libidinized, and thereby stimulated into further growth.

For example, it seems to make a difference to the timing of speech development and the quality of early verbalization if a mother, for reasons of her own personality structure, makes contact with her infant not through bodily channels but through talking. Some mothers find no pleasure in the growing infant's adventurousness and bodily unruliness and have their happiest and most intimate moments when the infant smiles. We have seen at least one such mother whose infant made constant and inordinate use of smiling in his approaches to the whole environment. It is not unknown that early contact with the mother through her singing has consequences for the later attitudes to music and may promote special musical aptitudes. On the other hand, marked disinterest of the mother in the infant's body and his developing motility may result in clumsiness, lack of grace in movement, etc.

It has been known in psychoanalysis long before such infant observations that depressive moods of the mother during the first two years after birth create in the child a tendency to depression (although this may not manifest itself until many years later). What happens is that such infants achieve their sense of unity and harmony with the depressed mother not by means of their developmental achievements but by producing the mother's mood in themselves.

All this means no more than that tendencies, inclinations, predilections (including the tendency to depression, to masochistic attitudes, etc.) which are present in all human beings can be eroticized and stimulated toward growth through forming emotional links between the child and his first object.

The disequilibrium between developmental lines which is created in this manner is not pathological as such, though it becomes a pathogenic agent where the imbalance is excessive. Moderate disharmony does no more than produce the many *variations of normality* with which we have to count.

BIBLIOGRAPHY

Alpert, A. (1959), Reversibility of Pathological Fixations Associated with Maternal Deprivation in Infancy. *This Annual*, XIV.

Bowlby, J. (1960), Separation Anxiety. *Int. J. Psa.*, XLI.

Bühler, C. (1953), *From Birth to Maturity*. London: Routledge & Kegan Paul.

Freud, A. (1949), Aggression in Relation to Emotional Development: Normal and Pathological. *This Annual*, III/IV.

—— (1952), The Role of Bodily Illness in the Mental Life of Children. *This Annual*, VII.

—— (1962), Assessment of Childhood Disturbances. *This Annual*, XVII.

Hartmann, H. (1950), Comments on the Psychoanalytic Theory of the Ego. *This Annual*, V.

Hoffer, W. (1950), Development of the Body Ego. *This Annual*, V.

—— (1952), The Mutual Influences in the Development of Ego and Id: Earliest Stages. *This Annual*, VII.

James, M. (1952), Premature Ego Development: Some Observations upon Disturbances in the First Three Years of Life. *Int. J. Psa.*, XLI.

Mahler, M. S. (1952), On Child Psychosis and Schizophrenia: Autistic and Symbiotic Infantile Psychoses. *This Annual*, VII.

Spitz, R. A. (1946), Anaclitic Depression. *This Annual*, II.

Winnicott, D. W. (1953), Transitional Objects and Transitional Phenomena. *Int. J. Psa.*, XXXIV.

—— (1954), Metapsychological and Clinical Aspects of Regression within the Psycho-Analytical Set-Up. In *Collected Papers*. New York: Basic Books, 1958.

THE PROBLEM OF MOTIVATION IN THE EDUCATOR'S VOCATIONAL CHOICE

ELIEZER ILAN, M.A. (Jerusalem)

In *Civilization and Its Discontents* (1930) Freud added some remarks on professional work to the paragraph in which he dealt with the method of fending off suffering by displacement of libido. In a footnote, he wrote: "The possibility it offers of displacing a large amount of libidinal components, whether narcissistic, aggressive or even erotic, on to professional work and on to the human relations connected with it lends it a value by no means second to what it enjoys as something indispensable to the preservation and justification of existence in society" (p. 80). In this context Freud spoke of the sublimation of drives, but he stressed that the psychic processes that play a part here are not yet fully elucidated. The concept of sublimation has, in fact, not been defined uniformly in psychoanalytic literature, although it has been made use of to explain a considerable number of diverse phenomena. Hartmann (1955) emphasized the double meaning of the concept of sublimation: first, it is a deflection of the sexual drive from instinctual aims; second, it involves a transformation of drive energy, a desexualization of libido or neutralization of aggression corresponding to a qualitative change of cathectic energy. Kris (1955) suggested that the term sublimation should be confined to the mechanism of displacement of an instinctual aim, while the process of desexualization or transformation of aggressive-drive energy should be referred to as neutralization. It is indeed difficult to see the justification for including under the collective term of "sublimation of anal drives" such diverse mental processes which are, for instance, at work in the toddler who smears thick brown paint onto a piece of paper with great pleasure,

---

Presented to the Israel Psychoanalytic Society, Tel-Aviv, January, 1961, and to the Hampstead Child-Therapy Clinic, London, November, 1962.

or the schoolboy who derives gratification from calligraphy, or in the pawnbroker who gets satisfaction from the accumulation of all sorts of objects. It would be essential in these cases to understand and consider the qualitative differences within the instinctual transformation.

However, before discussing the problem of sublimation further, I would like to introduce Szondi's (1948) conceptual scheme of operotropism, which concerns itself with the mental processes that manifest themselves in the choice and practice of professional work. The thesis of operotropism postulates that apart from other factors, the choice and practice of a professional work are determined by the instinctual constellation of the person who makes the choice. Szondi views operotropism only as a special case of a general tropism, i.e., a particular affinity for certain stimuli which, according to him, has genetic biological roots and determines to a certain extent the choice of a love object, the professional choice, the choice of disease, and mode of death.

In his comprehensive work *On the Psychology of Occupational Choice and Occupational Disturbances* (1953), the Swiss psychoanalyst Ulrich Moser attempts a further elaboration of Szondi's concept of operotropism. Moser does not concern himself with Szondi's conception of the genetic roots of the drives. Without touching upon this problem he uses the concept of operotropism only on the psychological level as instinctual tropism; that is, he investigates the effects of certain instinctual constellations as unconscious determinants on the choice and practice of specific professions. The drive-energic cathexis of a profession differs from person to person and also changes within the same person in the course of his development. Particularly those instinctual needs which cannot be discharged directly or sufficiently in the libido-tropic choice of a partner become effective in the operotropic choice of profession. Moser distinguishes between three different forms of operotropism: primary operotropism, defense operotropism, and safety-valve operotropism. Primary operotopism designates the socialization through specific professional work of instinctual strivings overemphasized by hypertrophy or by damming up due to frustration. Thus, for instance, a person with strong aggressive tendencies will become an executioner, a woodcutter, or an assistant in dissection in an anatomical institute. Moser talks of defense operotropism if a person chooses a profession that suits his defense mechanisms, which have been established against instinctual needs threatening his ego. This occurs particularly in character structures in which reaction formations are of importance, and where the need for punctuality and strict ritual are made socially useful through the profession. Particularly suited for a choice along these lines are occupations such as a statistician, taxation expert, proofreader, and many others. Moser speaks of safety-valve operotropism when a neurotic conflict forces a person into libidinal regression to specific pregenital fixation points in his libido development, so that these regressive needs are gratified within the chosen occupation. This would be the case if a failure to solve the oedipal situation led to a regression to the oral level, allowing for corresponding gratifications in occupations such as a cook or innkeeper, for example. Here it is not the strength of the drive in question or the impossibility of its direct discharge but rather the neurotic conflict which regressively reinforces the drive and thus leads to the necessity of a safety valve in form of the chosen professions. According to Moser, a person's choice of his occupation is frequently not determined by a single form of operotropism. Analysis of the unconscious motivation which led to the choice may reveal the operation of all three forms. Moreover, a particular profession may offer opportunities for different forms of operotropism through variations in the mode of its practice. Moser's conceptual scheme seems useful because it permits a differentiation between processes which show dynamic similarities without being identical. However, it is not very helpful in solving the problem mentioned earlier, namely, that of clarifying the processes of sublimation. In the primary as well as in the safety-valve type of operotropism, instinctual strivings become socialized through the occupation. In the defense operotropism, reaction formations become reinforced and socially useful. Moser believes that one is justified to speak of sublimation if, in the vocational choice, primary and defense operotropism coincide, i.e., if in the chosen vocation the original instinctual needs and the defenses against them emanating from ego and superego are satisfied simultaneously. However, his conceptualization of sublimation remains insufficiently clarified.

According to Freud's terminology, we would have to use the term sublimation for every successful socialization, that is, for every displacement of an instinctual aim which transforms it into a socially acceptable one. However, in all drives which are capable of having an "operotropic" effect, libido and aggression are not completely neutralized. Here a distinction introduced by Ernst Kris (1952, 1955) seems important. Proceeding from analytic observations of the creative process in artists he became convinced of a difference in the psychological processes effective in artistic routine work and those prevalent during great creative effort. In the latter he could always find the exacerbation of instinctual conflicts and the pressure of scarcely neutralized libidinal and aggressive strivings. Accordingly, he differentiates on the one hand between the energies which are permanently at the disposal of the ego and which he calls "reservoir," after Hartmann, and on the other hand, those drives which are neutralized to a small degree only and become effective in extraordinary performances; these he calls "flux." In the creative activity, flux and reservoir are both present in varying proportions. For the purpose of investigating the operotropic factors which influence the choice of education as a profession and its practice, it is relevant to focus particular attention on Kris's concept of "flux," that is, on the instinctual conflicts and nonneutralized drive energies which lead to exceptional performances in this vocation.

I

The vocation as an educator makes certain demands on the person who is to perform it successfully. It encompasses a broad field of various activities and aims. In this presentation I shall investigate only the specific field of personality or character education. Even this field includes manifold activities such as that of the teacher in a class, the educator in a home or club setting, the social caseworker whose educational activity either concerns individual children or groups of children. Each of these activities involves particular demands of training and technical knowledge. Here I am concerned only with the common denominator of these activities, namely, the formation of the child's personality through educational attitudes and measures. My object is the investigation of the personality structure of those who are capable of dedicating themselves successfully to this task. The literature concerned with this problem is not voluminous. Based on his analysis of the educational practice, S. R. Slavson (1948), in his book *Creative Group Education,* enumerates fourteen virtues that ought to be among the qualities of an educator. These are: (1) insight; (2) adaptability; (3) readiness to let others share in one's own intellectual experiences; (4) respect for the personality of fellow men and their views; (5) broad social interests and a social view of life; (6) the ability to let others develop intellectually according to their own rhythm; (7) emotional maturity; (8) readiness to cooperate; (9) resourcefulness; (10) creative powers and respect for other people's creativity; (11) love for others; (12) equanimity and cheerfulness; (13) knowledge; (14) a sense of humor. An educator possessing such a wealth of noble qualities will probably be more suited to become the leader of a future ideal state of the world than to concern himself with the education of a group of children or juveniles. One has the impression that such high ideals and lofty demands represent the reverse, that is the overcompensation for the contempt of the poor village teacher in the nineteenth-century society. Three other authors, approaching the problem from very different philosophical and psychological angles, attempt to throw a more realistic light on the process of education and on the personality structure of the educator. Georg Kerschensteiner (1921), a philosophical and idealistic educator, treats the question from the point of view of Spranger's psychology; Siegfried Bernfeld (1925) approaches the structure of the educator from a psychoanalytic-marxistic point of view; and A. S. Neill, a radical English educator, influenced by Wilhelm Reich, analyzes the educator's personality and problems in his book *The Problem Teacher* (1944).

The conclusions arrived at by these three authors will be briefly outlined here. For Kerschensteiner, the essence of educational activity lies in the fact that the educator refrains from exploiting the inherent character attributes of his pupils for his own aims, but rather takes them fully into account on their own. For this, empathy and love are needed. In conformity with Spranger's typology, he assigns the educator to the social type who is determined by his love for his fellow men as the all-embracing law of his life. More particularly, the educator is characterized by his love for the child, which is due to an inner affinity of values and views between educator and child. This educational love which is "always hopeful and never despairs" arises from the similarity between the educator's and the child's mind. This enables the educator to understand the child intuitively and to relate to him with educative tactfulness. Humor is stressed as an important quality of the educator. The author also points to certain liability in the educator's personality: he believes that the educator will have to reassess his own values continuously in the process of reliving his own past through the child.

Bernfeld analyzes the processes that take place between educator and pupil. These two form a paired group determined by the adult's affects of love and hate for the child. These two affects are constant variables in the adult's relationship to the child, and they are determined by unconscious sources, namely, by the death wish of the primal father against the son and by the primal love of the woman for the child who represents a part of her own body. Both affects are effective in individually differing proportions in the case of male and female educators and determine the degree of their strictness or leniency toward the child. In the educator, for whom his occupation is a real vocation, a great measure of only apparently sublimated instinctual wishes is effective besides sublimated ones, because other objects for instinctual discharge are either inaccessible or forbidden. According to Bernfeld, the educator is subject to the unconscious repetition compulsion of attempting to master his own unsolved oedipal situation. In the paired group of the professional educator and the child, the educator appears in a double role: he is both educator and child. As an educator he repeats his own parent-child problems, even when his own attitude differs from that of his parents.

For Neill, the professional educator is a person who has remained a child and who is afraid to act in the realm of grown-up people in real life. Neill distinguishes two types of educators: the one who loves to be and to remain a child, and the other who hates his incapacity to be an adult. In Neill's view, the first type is the ideal educator who identifies with and affirms the instinctual wishes of the child; the second is the problematic, negative educator, who punishes himself in the image of the child or who identifies the child with hostile objects from his own past, thus taking this revenge on them. He has to be authoritative in order to suppress his own infantile drives. The female educator who plays with the children like a little girl does with her dolls, is less problematic because such women may

gratify a strong motherly instinct. Neill also describes another type
of female educator who attracts young girls in particular, and in
whom homosexual elements play an outstanding part. He calls it
"the higher-life type."

These authors, though starting from different points of view,
arrive at views that are not too far apart. All of them regard the
process of education as a field of activity particularly attractive to
specific drive constellations. It shows an affinity for people who have
a particular love or hate for the child, people who have not completely grown up yet, who have not mastered certain conflictual situations, and who are therefore driven to repeat them in one form or
another within the process of education. This formula is also valid
for Kerschensteiner's "ideal educator" who relives his own childhood
in the child and who is forced repeatedly to reassess himself and his
own values. We are dealing here mainly with socialization of instinctual drives which were reinforced by regression. The educator
who fails at a certain point of his progress toward maturity turns
regressively toward an infantile level of his development and attempts to find gratification at that level through his vocation. Bernfeld mentions sublimated and apparently sublimated instinctual
wishes which are active in the educator with respect to the child.
This probably refers to the extent of desexualization, but he does
not discuss the problem.

In her paper "Adult Empathy with Children" (1953) Christine
Olden attempts to analyze the faculty of empathy with children and
she too points out that "people who can adjust to the child's world,
who can not only work but live with children are those who have
preserved some infantile traits." Olden demands that these infantile
traits should not dominate their personality, or interfere with their
sense of reality, their responsibility, or their efficiency when working with children. She does not deal explicitly with the dynamic
problems of a mature personality who had to preserve infantile traits
strong enough to decide his professional choice.

An unexpected confirmation of the assumed psychoinfantilism
in the educator comes from the Rorschach test. Besides responses of
particular content that characterized subjects with specific pedagogic
gifts as, for instance, an inclination to fabulation and fairy-tale
motives, Bohm (1951) found a characteristic response otherwise

prevalent only in children and in senile dementia. These are responses of inversive interpretation which appear only in normal adults with a particular pedagogic talent.

The views presented by these authors are results stemming from theoretical formulations and from personal experience. They offer valuable material for the further investigation of our problem.

II

Another approach in tackling the problem of motivation in the educator's profession was attempted by myself in an unpublished more extensive paper (1954) in which I investigated the motivation of well-known and successful educators. It takes its point of departure from an analysis of their educational aims and methods and relies on biographical and autobiographical material. I should like to describe briefly the results in respect of the personality of three educators, namely: A. S. Neill, already mentioned, Director of Summerhill, an English progressive educational institution (1950); Gustav Wyneken, the famous German educator and founder of the Landschulheim Wickersdorf (1922); and the Russian, A. S. Makarenko, Director of the Gorki Colony, an educational home for wayward youth, described in his book *The Road to Life* (1951).

Some traits of Neill's personality are worth mentioning. He is "one of the gang" in his educational institution, and his educational idea is one of maximal instinctual freedom for children and juveniles. In his book he describes himself as one who loves to tell the children stories, to play with them, and to do handicraft work. The habits are those of a child in prepuberty. His style is confused and aphoristic, aimed more at shocking or amusing the reader than convincing him with facts. His book on Summerhill is entitled *That Dreadful School* (1950). Neill openly admits that he identifies with the child. He sees a great advantage for the educator in the educational activity of a progressive school, in that his work takes place in an atmosphere which insures that he himself can be free of any fear of authority. In this, we can see an essential motive for Neill's professional choice and the specific quality which he gives his profession as an educator. In his books he rages against the "father principle," and would have the world run on matriarchical lines. He attacks Freud's theories since they overstress the father's importance in the oedipus complex and in the formation of the infantile mind. He writes that he himself experienced learning difficulties and lack of concentration as a child. He argues bitterly with the Freudians who accuse him of perpetuating his struggle against the father in his educational system and of finding a way to enjoy instinctual freedom through identification with the child and thus to break paternal prohibitions and, more than that, to throw out the father and his authority, tolerating only the all-forgiving and all-permitting mother love. "What of it," he asks, "if my school derives from the fear of my father fifty years ago? This fear does not exist any more, but Summerhill stands as an example for what a school can be" (1944). The irate and grotesque fight against the father and his authority apparent in everything created and written by Neill as a pedagogue leaves us in no doubt that the fear of the father persists. Nevertheless, it is correct that this endopsychic conflict with the father enabled him to achieve pedagogic results. His educational activity offered him a specific means of discharge which secured him an apparently happy and relatively conflict-free life.

Gustav Wyneken and Anton Makarenko fulfilled their tasks as educators in very different social settings and had extremely dissimilar educational aims and educational methods. Nevertheless, E. Simon in his paper "Pedagogy of Struggle" (1942) points to common traits in both personalities. Both of them highly valued the principle of the leader (*Führerprinzip*) in education, both stressed the quality and power of their personalities as the most essential agent in their work. In both of them this high self-esteem bordered on the pathological. Thus, Wyneken (1921) writes of himself as a conquerer who struggles not for himself but for the spirit who sent him, or as a creator destined to rule by divine grace and decree. In Makarenko (1951), we find sentences like: "The struggle that Napoleon had to fight was incomparably easier than my task." Together with this narcissistic-megalomaniacal ego expansion, a very severe superego, making highest moral demands on them and their pupils, was a characteristic of both educators. For Wyneken, it was the devotion to the spirit; for Makarenko, the devotion to the task that held them completely in bondage. Wyneken openly confesses his love for the boys as the essential driving force of his educational activity. He

talks of the "demon Eros" and found it difficult to keep his relationship to the juveniles within the boundaries of the purely sublime.
"A hug and a kiss as conclusion of a serious and cordial talk with one
of my young friends were for us a simple confirmation of our close
relation" (1921). In Makarenko we also found this homoerotic attitude toward the pupils, although in a slightly different form, with
greater accentuation of aggressive aspects. In his paper "On Some
Neurotic Mechanisms in Jealousy, Paranoia and Homosexuality"
(1922) Freud described the mechanisms of homosexual object choice
as the result of solving a rivalry conflict. Jealousy of a particularly
strong intensity, mostly in regard to older brothers, leads to an emotional transformation, so that the earlier rivals against whom the
person harbored feelings of impotent rage later become his homosexual love objects. Freud could find this specific mechanism only
in cases of a homosexual disposition but not in manifest homosexuality. It is interesting to recall in this connection the following
episode from some autobiographical notes by Wyneken (1924),
decisive, as he himself thought, for his vocational choice. When
Wyneken was thirteen and a half years old his father, a Protestant
parson, with strict moral views, sent him to be educated at the Royal
Boarding School of Ilfield Monastery. A third of the boarders were
sons of the German nobility who completely dominated the other
pupils. These were sons of impoverished landowners, of officials and
clergymen. The young Wyneken tried to stage a revolution against
the aristocratic minority but failed in this and was boycotted for
years by the great majority of the pupils. He writes: "I suppose that
the experience of four and a half years in that boarding school left
me with an unconscious need to take something like a positive and
perfect revenge and that it was the sublimation of this need for
revenge which drove me to found a boarding school for juveniles, a
boarding school with true self-education and a beautiful, noble youth
life" (1924). "A beautiful, noble youth, pleasing the eye as a noble
race" (1922): this was the object of Wyneken's educational devotion.
Makarenko educated proletarian wayward youth. He himself came
from a poor working-class family. His strict father sent him to a gym-
nasium in town at the age of twelve and, like Wyneken, he spent his
adolescence in an environment of socially higher strata. His father
sent him to school with the following password: "Such schools are

not for people like us, but you will show them! Only the best marks, do you understand?!" (1951). Both pedagogues were involved in sharp struggles with their environment during their pubertal years and compensated for their feelings of inferiority by an excessive, narcissistic ego expansion. In Makarenko, the narcissistic, aggressive powers prevail; in Wyneken, libidinal ones. Thus Wyneken talks of "demon Eros," while Makarenko refers in almost identical words to the "seducing demon of unfettered hate," who interfered at times violently and disruptively with his educational efforts. At the same time this became a source of empathy with the wayward juveniles. Both educators succeeded particularly with youngsters of pubertal age and describe their gladness in their self-realizations, in Wyneken's words, "as the recognized leader of a youth gang." Neill, for his part, took care of children especially in their latency period.

These educators show unsolved psychological conflicts which furnished a fundamental motive for their occupational choice and activity. These conflicts drove them toward specific educational attitudes and to successful work with specific age groups from particularly chosen social strata. In their cases we can certainly not speak of sublimation in the sense of desexualization and desaggressivization. Yet their successful educational efforts are not simply due to repetition of their own realm of conflict but to the experience which Wyneken called a "positive and perfect revenge." In other words, a traumatic situation from the past is repeated within the educational process, thus finding a solution which is acceptable to both ego and superego. It seems that a definite admixture of neutralized drive energy and sublimated but unneutralized energy is a precondition for such a positive outcome. The neutralized energy determines the level at which the personality can utilize his natural giftedness while the regressive instinctual needs revived by unsolved conflict endow the educational activity of these pedagogues with its particular impetus and specific orientation. At the same time they set the conditions for the special dangers of simple regressive behavior. In certain situations of tension these educators are unable to bring their regressive instinctual needs to a positive fulfillment; and through the defusion of neutralized and nonneutralized energy, the demon, that is, the instinctual drive, appears in his undisguised form. These are the moments of failure in their educational attitude, manifested in the case of Wyneken, for instance, in the direct instinctual gratification of embracing naked boys, which brought him into conflict with the law, or in the case of Makarenko, in his uncontrolled outbursts of rage against pupils and himself.

III

A third approach to the problem of motivation in professional educators is possible by direct psychoanalysis of successful pedagogues. Steff Bornstein (1933) describes a particular mental constellation which she found in a number of cases she analyzed. These pedagogues identified in their work not with a parent but rather with an educational figure, from whom they received love in childhood or youth. In contrast to their conflicting relationship with their parents, their relation to this teacher was ideally positive. Occupational choice and activity were determined here in no small degree by the identification with educators who give their love to children other than their own. Their successful pedagogic activity was, at the same time, a positive revenge against their parents: "Look, one has to behave toward children like this pedagogue and like myself." A classical example of this relationship (not mentioned by Steff Bornstein) is that between Pestalozzi and Baebele, the old maid servant in his mother's home. The point of view expounded by Bornstein is particularly relevant if we think of the close relation between sublimation in the sense of neutralization and positive, early identification with loved objects. A source of energy within the personality of the pedagogue is given here which allows for regressive needs to be channellized in a positive way.

In her *Introduction to Psychoanalysis for Teachers* (1930), Anna Freud describes a particularly successful educational action carried out by a woman pedagogue with a boy who had been neglected by his parents. The analysis revealed that this teacher could identify with the specific situation of the child through her own feelings toward her own parents. Her exceptional educational effort was in a way an appeal and a reproach addressed to her parents: "This is how you should have acted towards me in order to make my happy development possible."

In what follows I shall present material from the analysis of a very successful nursery school teacher. She worked in a day nursery, succeeded in establishing an excellent educational contact with normal and particularly with disturbed children, and found satisfaction and general recognition in her work. She started analysis at the age of thirty-three, expecting to deepen and enrich her educational activity, but mainly in the hope of finding therapeutic help for her problems. She suffered from intense feelings of insufficiency in relation to any form of authority and felt like a small child unable to bear anybody becoming angry with her, responding with tears and unhappiness to the slightest attack of criticism. She also felt an overly strong childish dependency toward her husband. She was childless, having had several abortions and a stillborn child. Already before coming to analysis she had decided to adopt a child and entered her name on the waiting list. However, she doubted whether she and her husband could be such parents as a child needs for his development. This was also a problem which she wanted to clarify in analysis. Without entering into the details of analysis, I should like to give some relevant psychodynamic factors for a better understanding: from childhood until the death of her mother about five years before the beginning of treatment, she had been in violent conflict with the mother. This was a sadomasochistic union wherein she felt dependent on the mother, and yet constantly compelled to pick arguments with her. Oral dependency and oral sadism played a role in this relationship. In contrast to three younger brothers who were less concerned, she always pulled herself together and tried to be a good child. Jealousy and envy of the brothers were more or less conscious, like her preference in childhood to be a boy, and she remembered her tomboyish behavior in her youth. Her relationship to her father, who had died in a Nazi concentration camp when she was ten years old, was shrouded by amnesia. He had been an art dealer frequently away from home. She was seven years old when her father lost his savings and his business suffered bankruptcy. Although few direct memories were recalled, the analysis of the transference and dreams revealed that oedipal wishes and masturbation had been suppressed and repressed as a consequence of severe prohibitions by the mother. The disappointment caused by her weak father played an important role. Subsequently, regression and vivid homosexual fantasies as well as identifications with the father and the brothers took place. These homosexual wishes generated anxiety and were incompatible with the demands made by her superego. As a defense, further regression to the oral-passive and oral-sadistic levels ensued. Due to fixations and the special support from the mother this regressive move was less in opposition to the demands of her superego. Her mother, who was an excellent cook and an efficient housewife, continuously tried to win her daughter back by offering her titbits. The patient, however, occasionally staged hunger strikes in order to hurt her mother, but at the same time felt utterly dependent on the food-providing mother. The patient considered her childlessness as a punishment for her sexual transgressions and felt that it was a result of having been cursed by her mother. In this psychological constellation various determinants for her educational work presented themselves. Her extremely patient, loving, but not pampering, attitude toward children was the exact opposite to the treatment meted out to her by her mother. She stressed that her mother could do so many things better than herself, but she was more successful in educating children. Mother ust did not know how to go about with children. This was her positive revenge against her mother and a triumph. In spite of her mother's curse, who had prohibited sexual gratification and had condemned her to childlessness, she now had many children and could treat them better. Identifying with these children she permitted them, and thus permitted herself, aggressive and libidinal expressions formerly forbidden to her. On the other hand, an identification with the dominating mother, who always placed herself in the center of things, played a part. She found a powerful narcissistic gain by being recognized and esteemed by the children and by being the center of things. She recalled that she had loved to play school with smaller children when she was eight to nine years old, and had controlled them in her role as teacher. In contrast to her fear of grownups, she did not fear children and their expressions of affect. Her attitude toward children was determined, among other things, by identifications with good permissive house-maids and particularly by her identification with her father. She remembered how at the age of six she had torn out all the flowers in the front garden of their house, out of spiteful revenge, how she had expected a terrible thrashing from her father, and how surprised and shaken she had been when he only admonished her kindly.

Material emerging in a phase of treatment shortly before the adoption of a child revealed the strong sexual significance which from
time to time appeared in her work with children. A slight delay in
the procedure of adoption had given rise to strong anxiety and hate
against mother figures who wanted to deprive her of a child and of
her husband, but suddenly these affects disappeared completely and
with them the wish to have a child. These affects and wishes were
replaced by descriptions of her happy feelings in her work with
children, and by emotion which she compared with sexual excitement as if somebody had stroked her breasts. She was a benign,
nourishing mother and enjoyed the intimate union of mother and
suckling baby actively and in the identification with the children,
passively. It was exactly at that time that she succeeded in establishing a meaningful relationship with the most difficult children of her
group.

It seems that ego-building identifications with real persons of her
own past may be distinguished here from defensive attitudes of the
ego. While she identifies with the dominating mother who is the
center of things, with the loving, permissive housemaid, and with
the understanding, forgiving, and kind-hearted father, she wards off
instinctual needs and conflicts by putting into play such defenses as
the "positive revenge" and triumph over her mother, the withdrawal
from contact with adult authority figures, and the regression to the
level of dual union between mother and child. With reference to the
distinction between reservoir and flux (Kris, 1955), one could see a
permanent source of energy for the reservoir in the ego identifications, whereas poorly neutralized unbound energies, that is, flux, are
seen to be mobilized by the respective instinctual conflicts and defensive attitudes. The reservoir predestines her professional choice
and educational activity by stimulating her gifts and putting at her
disposal sublimated, neutralized energy for permanent psychic structures. The free, hardly neutralized energies exert pressure in a
specific direction of vocational activity and provide the source of
power for extraordinary pedagogical performances. These performances, necessary, for instance, in the education of difficult children,
would then be mainly dependent on unsolved conflicts which are put
to good use in the profession.

IV

In his paper "Regression in the Service of the Ego" (1958), Roy Schafer defines this concept as a partial, controlled lowering of the level of psychic functioning in the service of furthering adaptation. This regressive lowering of the psychic level makes a number of essential functions possible, such as creative fantasy, orgastic gratification, motherliness, empathy, and therapeutic activity. As a precondition for these regressions in the service of the ego, Schafer enumerates conditions such as well-developed, reliable affective signals; a secure feeling for one's own self, i.e., ego identity; relative solution of early traumata; a mild rather than an archaic severe superego; a past of confidence and mutuality in interpersonal relationships; and finally the circumstance that this process be valued and seen as important by society. It is clear that Schafer sketches here a psychological structure tantamount to the ideal image of the mature human being enjoying maximal mental health. However, he hastens to add that the thesis of regression in the service of the ego taking place in the favorable circumstances mentioned does not get conclusive support from case material of creative artists and scientists. In the fourteen qualities Slavson assigns to the ideal educator, we have already met the stipulation that the educator should be an ideally healthy person mentally. Such an ideal psychic structure leaves little room for an understanding of the pressing necessity to regress. More specifically, for the problem of vocational activity in education it leaves little room for the understanding of the instinctual pressure toward the education of children. Actually, in one form or another, I did find some of the conditions enumerated by Schafer in some cases of successful teachers: ego-building identifications which guarantee the feeling of identity in the educator and also a certain mildness of the superego. In cases where a strict superego shows itself, we find certain lacunae which make tolerance for the child's weaknesses possible, gaps that probably represent the roots of the sense of humor which always prevails in the successful educator. An additional support for the superego of the pedagogue is the fact that his educational activities are highly valued by society. However, we hardly find a relative solution of early traumata or a past of confidence and mutuality in interpersonal relations in the

educator. Quite the contrary: we have seen that extraordinary performances in the profession subserve partial mastery of early traumata, and it is precisely these unsolved conflicts which form the soil
on which these performances grow. I referred to the danger contained in this situation for education and educator alike. In Anna
Freud's previously mentioned example from the analysis of a teacher
who had an outstanding success in the education of a boy neglected
by his parents, the failure of that same educator is also described.
She had to break all contact with her pupil after having helped him
to the point of his becoming the pride of his family. Feelings of
jealousy in regard to her successful pupil made an educational attitude toward him impossible. In this connection, Anna Freud postulates the neccessity of analysis for the educator. She takes those to
task who might point to the likelihood that this teacher would
probably not have had such a blatant educational success after having
been analyzed. She does not question that this might be true, but
expresses her opinion that such successes are too dearly paid for,
that their counterparts are failures with those children whose constellation does not allow the pedagogue to make a positive identification with them. She is generally against a situation in which the
children are used as an opportunity to abreact the unsolved difficulties of their educators. And indeed, the problem areas of those
personalities discussed here showed us the limitations in their efficiency which stemmed from their unsolved difficulties. However, in
her discussion at that time, Anna Freud did not consider a point of
view which sees precisely the endopsychic conflict situation as a
source of highest performances in the vocation of a pedagogue. I
would like here to point out the tendency of a number of educators
who went through the psychoanalytic experience to change from
education to psychotherapy, a tendency which is certainly not only
due to the wish for a better social and economic position. By helping
the teacher to resolve early traumata and to achieve maturation of
his ego structure, successful analysis possibly robs him of the inner
urge to share his life with the child. It could be assumed that the
capacity for empathy and the inclination to be concerned with the
child, founded as they are on permanent ego identifications, would
be but little changed by the psychoanalytic working through. On
the other hand, the analytic dissolution of conflicts might well lower

the inner need for intensive educational tie to the child and for extraordinary educational performances as they are particularly needed in the education of difficult children. We face here the dilemma that after analysis the pedagogue possibly loses an essential motive power for his educational activity, while without analysis he is restricted in his range of efficiency and exposed to the danger to react inadequately to certain situations or to certain children. It would be interesting to investigate the results of analysis of teachers from this point of view. Possibly a more suitable form of help for the mentally more or less healthy educator might be worked out on the basis of the model of supervision as it was developed in individual social casework. It might protect him from involvement in specific pedagogical difficulties without interfering with the deeper motivations of his vocational activity by analytic working through.

SUMMARY

Starting from an examination of Freud's concept of sublimation, I found Hartmann's views and Kris's distinction of reservoir and flux, that is, of neutralized and little neutralized sublimation fruitful for my subject. Moser's concept of safety-valve operotropism also proved valuable for this investigation. It describes the socialization of instinctual currents which had been forced to regress by unsolved conflicts. A review of relevant literature showed that several authors arrived at similar conclusions in spite of their greatly varying points of view. They found that the vocation of an educator attracts those people who have a particular relation to the child on the basis of their psychoinfantilism and who repeat unsolved conflict situations within the educational process. Investigating the motivation of three well-known educators, I could confirm that unsolved conflicts represent an essential motive in their professional choice and activity. However, the specific constellation found was not a mere repetition of conflict, within the educational process, but rather a positive outcome of a traumatic situation, an outcome equally acceptable to ego and superego. The degree of participation of free energy deriving from unsolved instinctual conflicts endows the educational activity with its particular impetus and specific coloring; at the same time, however, it restricts the activity and entails the danger of pedagogical transgressions. The psychoanalytic treatment of a number of successful educators elucidated the distinction between these teachers' ego-building identifications on the one hand and their unsolved conflicts with their own parents, which exert a regressive pull on the other hand. The former put neutralized energy at the pedagogue's disposal and are part of the permanent reservoir out of which energy is channeled into educationally useful activity. The unsolved conflicts, on the other hand, urge him on in a specific direction toward extraordinary performances and find solution, respectively discharge, in a life shared with the child. Finally, I examined the question of help for the educator whose motivation for his professional activity always carries dangers of regressive attitudes. In my view, a comprehensive psychoanalytic help contains a certain problematic aspect which merits basic investigation because it might lead to the elimination of the conflict factor in motivation. Supervision offers a possible solution, because it could take up problems and involvements of the educator without interfering too much with his deeper motivations.

BIBLIOGRAPHY

Bernfeld, S. (1925), *Sisyphus oder die Grenzen der Erziehung*. Wien: Internationaler psychoanalytischer Verlag.

Bohm, E. (1951), *Lehrbuch der Rorschach Psychodiagnostik*. Bern: Hans Huber.

Bornstein, S. (1933), Ein Beitrag zur Psychoanalyse des Pädagogen. *Z. psa. Pädagog.*, VIII.

Freud, A. (1930), *Introduction to Psycho-Analysis for Teachers and Parents*. London: Allen & Unwin, 1931.

Freud, S. (1922), Some Neurotic Mechanisms in Jealousy, Paranoia and Homosexuality. *Standard Edition*, XVIII. London: Hogarth Press, 1955.

—— (1930), Civilization and Its Discontents. *Standard Edition*, XXI. London: Hogarth Press, 1961.

Hartmann, H. (1955), Notes on the Theory of Sublimation. *This Annual*, X.

Ilan, E. (1954), Educational Attitudes and Their Motivations. Unpublished Master Thesis at the School of Education (with Prof. E. Simon), Hebrew University, Jerusalem.

Kerschensteiner, J. (1921), *Die Seele des Erziehers und das Problem der Lehrerbildung*. Berlin-Leipzig: Teubner.

Kris, E. (1952), *Psychoanalytic Explorations in Art*. New York: International Universities Press.

—— (1955), Neutralization and Sublimation. *This Annual*, X.

Makarenko, A. S. (1951), *The Road to Life* (An Epic of Education). Moscow: Foreign Language Publishing House.

Moser, U. (1953), *Psychologie der Arbeitswahl und der Arbeitsstörungen*. Bern: Hans Huber.

Neill, A. S. (1939), *The Problem Teacher*. London: Herbert Jenkins.

—— (1944), *Hearts Not Heads in the School*. London: Herbert Jenkins.

—— (1950), *Selbstverwaltung in der Schule*. Zurich: Pan-Verlag.
Olden, C. (1953), On Adult Empathy with Children. *This Annual,* VIII.
Schafer, R. (1958), Regression in the Service of the Ego. In: *Assessment of Human Motives,* ed. G. Lindzey. New York: Rinehart.
Simon, E. (1942), *Pedagogy of Struggle*. Tel-Aviv: Haaretz.
Slavson, S. R. (1937), *Creative Group Education*. New York: Association Press.
Szondi, L. (1948), *Schicksalsanalyse*. Basel: Benno Schwabe.
Wyneken, G. (1921), *Eros*. Lauenburg: Adolf Saal.
—— (1922), *Wickersdorf*. Lauenburg: Adolf Saal.
—— (1924), Schülererinnerungen. *Die Grüne Fahne,* I. Leipzig: Ernst Oldenburg.

THE CONCEPT OF CUMULATIVE TRAUMA

M. MASUD R. KHAN (London)

Every phase of theory-making in psychoanalysis has influenced the current concept of trauma and its clinical evaluation (Fenichel, 1937). I shall, somewhat arbitrarily, divide the total span of analytic researches into five stages. This is an artificial division to show what new ideas emerge at which stage. One stage does not cancel out the other. They run parallel, reinforcing and partially correcting each other, and each time a new strand is added to the growing complexity of psychoanalytic metapsychology.

In the first phase, 1885 to 1905, while Freud was postulating the basic concepts for the understanding of the unconscious—dream work, primary and secondary processes, the psychic apparatus, symptom formation, and the etiology of hysteria and obsessional neurosis —the concept of trauma played a very vital and significant role (Freud, 1893, 1895). Trauma was conceived of essentially as (a) an environmental factor that intrudes upon the ego and which the ego cannot deal with through abreaction or associative elaboration: "hysterical patients suffer from incompletely abreacted psychical trauma" (Freud, 1893); and (b) as a state of strangulated libidinal energy which the ego cannot discharge. The paradigm of this traumatic situation is sexual seduction. We have a vivid account by Freud himself (1887-1902, letter 69; also 1914b) and by Jones describing (1953) how frustrated and demoralized Freud felt when he discovered that these traumatic events of seduction had never actually happened. During this phase the corresponding theory of anxiety is: "Neurotic anxiety is transformed sexual libido" (Freud, 1897). The chief defense mechanism discussed is repression.

Different versions of this paper were read at the Hampstead Child-Therapy Clinic, London, January 16, 1963, the Institute of Psycho-Analysis, London, February 6, 1963, and the Topeka Psychoanalytic Society, April 12, 1963.

The second phase, 1905 to 1917, is characterized by systematic attempts at working out infantile sexual development (Freud, 1905) and psychoanalytic metapsychology (Freud, 1914a, 1915a, 1915b, 1915c, 1917). In terms of infantile sexual development and libido theory the paradigmatic traumatic situations are (a) castration anxiety, (b) separation anxiety, (c) primal scene, and (d) oedipus complex. Trauma pertains to the strength and urgency of sexual instincts and the ego's fight against them. It is in terms of unconscious fantasy and inner psychic reality that all conflicts and hence traumatic situations are envisaged. During the latter half of this phase Freud worked out his first systematic statement of metapsychology, and we have the concept of ego libido, primary narcissism, and ego ideal on the one hand, and a detailed examination of the mechanisms of introjection, identification, and projection on the other. The paper on "Mourning and Melancholia" (1917) marks the end of this phase, and by opening up the discussion of aggression and guilt starts the next.

The period of 1917 to 1926, the third phase, gives us the "final phase" of Freud's metapsychological thinking. In *Beyond the Pleasure Principle* we have the first statement of the repetition compulsion as a principle of psychic functioning and its relation to the death instinct (principle of inertia in organic life). Here, Freud arrived at his dualistic theory of instincts, and from his earlier distinction between sexual instincts and ego instincts moved on to the duality of life versus death instincts. With the hypotheses of instincts and repetition compulsion, and the definition of psychic structures in terms of ego, id, and superego (Freud, 1923), the concept of trauma took on an exclusively intersystemic and instinctual frame of reference. The vast literature on guilt, masochism, melancholia, depression, and internal anxiety situations documents at great length such traumata and the ego's mode of handling them. The extreme and most detailed discussion of such intersystemic and instinctual traumata is perhaps by Melanie Klein (1932) in her description of paranoid and depressive positions. This phase in Freud's own researches achieves its culmination in his revision of the concept of anxiety in *Inhibitions, Symptoms and Anxiety* (1926).

The fourth phase, 1926 to 1939, is launched by the revision of the concept of anxiety and inaugurates the beginnings of ego psychology proper. Strachey (1959, pp. 77-86) has given us a masterly summary of the evolution of Freud's concept of anxiety. I shall single out for comment only the fact that in *Inhibitions, Symptoms and Anxiety* Freud clearly distinguished between traumatic situations and situations of danger, corresponding to which are the two types of anxiety: automatic anxiety and anxiety as a signal of the approach of such a trauma. "The fundamental determinant of automatic anxiety is the occurrence of a traumatic situation; and the essence of this is an experience of helplessness on the part of the ego in the face of an accumulation of excitation . . . the various specific dangers which are liable to precipitate a traumatic situation at different times of life. These are briefly: birth, loss of the mother as an object, loss of the penis, loss of the object's love, loss of the super-ego's love" (Strachey, 1959, pp. 81-82).

With the revised concept of anxiety and traumatic situations the role of environment (mother) and the need for "extraneous help" in situations of helplessness comes into the very center of the concept of trauma. Thus the intrapsychic, intersystemic, and environmental sources of trauma are integrated into a unitary frame of reference. Toward the end of this phase in his two papers "Analysis Terminable and Interminable" (1937) and "Splitting of the Ego in the Defensive Process" (1938) Freud focused his attention on the ego in terms of the modifications acquired during the defensive conflicts of early childhood, as well as through primary congenital variations and the disturbances of the synthetic function of the ego. This is why I have characterized this phase as inaugurating ego psychology proper. These new formulations have far-reaching implications for the evaluation of the source and function of trauma.

The last phase is from 1939 to today. In this the developments of ego psychology through the researches of Anna Freud (1936 onwards), Hartmann (1939, 1950, 1952) and others, and the whole new emphasis on infant-mother relationship, have changed our very frame of reference for the discussion of the nature and role of trauma.

FUNCTION OF MOTHER AS PROTECTIVE SHIELD

In *Beyond the Pleasure Principle* (1920) Freud set up a conceptual model to discuss the fate of a living organism in an open environment. "Let us picture [he said] a living organism in its most simplified possible form as an undifferentiated vesicle of a substance that is susceptible to stimulation." Freud next proceeds to point out that the two sources of stimuli possible are the external and the internal ones. He continues: "Then the surface turned towards the external world will from its very situation be differentiated and will serve as an organ for receiving stimuli" (p. 26). This gradually develops into a "crust" and eventually into a "protective shield." Freud postulated that *"Protection against* stimuli is an almost more important function for the living organism than *reception* of stimuli. The protective shield is supplied with its own store of energy and must above all endeavour to preserve the special modes of transformation of energy operating in it against the effects threated by the enormous energies at work in the external world" (p. 27). Continuing his argument Freud postulated that this sensitive cortex, which later becomes the system *Cs.,* also receives excitations from within. It is, however, less effective against inner stimuli, and one way the organism protects itself against the unpleasure from inner stimuli is to project them to the outer environment and treat them as "though they were acting, not from the inside, but from the outside, so that it may be possible to bring the shield against stimuli into operation as a means of defence against them." In this context Freud described as "traumatic" any

... excitations from outside which are powerful enough to break through the protective shield. It seems to me that the concept of trauma necessarily implies a connection of this kind with a breach in an otherwise efficacious barrier against stimuli. Such an event as an external trauma is bound to provoke a disturbance on a large scale in the functioning of the organism's energy and to set in motion every possible defensive measure. At the same time, the pleasure principle is for the moment put out of action. There is no longer any possibility of preventing the mental apparatus from being flooded with large amounts of stimulus, and another problem arises instead—the problem of mastering the amounts of stimulus which have broken in and of binding them, in the psychical sense, so that they can then be disposed of [p. 29f.]. [Developing his argument further, Freud concluded:] what *we* seek to understand are the effects produced on the organ of the mind by the breach in the shield against stimuli and by the problems that follow in its train. And we still attribute importance to the element of fright. It is caused by lack of any preparedness for anxiety, including lack of hypercathexis of the systems that would be the first to receive the stimulus. Owing to their low cathexis those systems are not in a good position for binding the inflowing amounts of excitation and the consequences of the breach in the protective shield follow all the more easily. It will be seen, then, that preparedness for anxiety and the hypercathexis of the receptive systems constitute the last line of defence of the shield against stimuli. In the case of quite a number of traumas, the difference between systems that are unprepared and systems that are well prepared through being hypercathected may be a decisive factor in determining the outcome; though where the strength of a trauma exceeds a certain limit this factor will no doubt cease to carry weight [p. 31f.].

The total context of Freud's discussion is the observation of an infant's play with a reel that related to "disappearance and return" (of the mother) and the traumatic dreams in general. If we replace in Freud's model "the undifferentiated vesicle of a substance that is susceptible to stimulation" by a live human infant, then we get what Winnicott (1962) has described as "an infant in care." The infant in care has for his protective shield the caretaking mother. This is the uniquely human situation, in so far as this dependency in the infant lasts much longer than in any other species that we know of (Hartmann, 1939); and from this prolonged period of dependency the human infant emerges as a more highly differentiated and independent organism vis-à-vis his environment.

My aim here is to discuss the function of the mother in her role as a protective shield. This role as a protective shield constitutes "the average expectable environment" (Hartmann, 1939) for the anaclitic needs of the infant. My argument is that cumulative trauma is the result of the breaches in the mother's role as a protective shield over the whole course of the child's development, from infancy to adolescence—that is to say, in all those areas of experience where the child continues to need the mother as an auxiliary ego to support his immature and unstable ego functions. It is important to distinguish this ego dependency of the child on the mother from his cathexis of her as an object. (Ramzy and Wallerstein [1958] have discussed this aspect in terms of *environmental reinforcement*.) Cumulative trauma thus derives from the strains and stresses that an infant-child experiences in the context of his ego dependence on the mother as his protective shield and auxiliary ego (cf. Khan, 1963a, 1963b, 1963c).

I want to stress the point that what I am describing as breaches in the mother's role as protective shield are qualitatively and quantitatively different from those gross intrusions by the mother's acute psychopathology which have been often discussed in our literature in relation to schizophrenic children or overtly hostile and destructive patterns of behavior in delinquent children (e.g., Beres, 1956; Lidz and Fleck, 1959; Mahler, 1952; Searles, 1959, 1962; Shields, 1962; etc.). The breaches I have in mind are in the nature of maladaptation to the infant's anaclitic needs (Winnicott, 1956a).

The mother's role as a protective shield is a theoretical construct. It should include the mother's personal role vis-à-vis the infant as well as her management of the nonhuman environment (the nursery, the cot, etc.) on which the infant is dependent for his total well-being (cf. Searles, 1960). I should emphasize also that the breaches in this protective-shield role, as I envisage them, are not traumatic singly. To borrow the apt phrase from Kris (1956b), they have the quality of a "strain," and do not so much distort ego development or psychosexual evolution as *bias* it. In this context it would be more accurate to say that these breaches over the course of time and through the developmental process cumulate silently and invisibly. Hence the difficulty in detecting them clinically in childhood. They gradually get embedded in the specific traits of a given character structure (cf. Greenacre, 1958). I would like to restrict myself merely to stating that the use of the word trauma in the concept of cumulative trauma should not mislead us into considering such breaches in the mother's role as protective shield as traumatic at the time or in the context in which they happen. They achieve the value of trauma only cumulatively and in retrospect. If the concept of cumulative trauma has value and validity, then it should help us to identify more accurately what sort of ego distortion and disturbance of psychosexual development can be related to what type of failure of environmental provisions, in relation to anaclitic needs in the infant and the child. It should help in replacing such incriminating reconstructions as bad, rejecting, or seducing mothers, as well as such anthropomorphic part-object constructs as "good" and

"bad" breast. Its place could be taken by a more meaningful examination of the pathogenic interplay of specific variables in the total
relationship of an infant-child's psychic and physical equipment and
how the environment meets it. This in turn would sponsor the
clinical search for effective therapeutic measures rather than merely
prescriptive ones. I have given a detailed account elsewhere, from
the treatment of a female patient, to show how an early disturbed
relation between mother and daughter led to homosexual episodes
in her adult life (Khan, 1963a).

In the past two decades, research in ego psychology and infant-
care techniques have gained in complexity and depth.[1] From these
researches it is possible to distinguish theoretically between four
aspects of a human infant's total experience:

(1) the role of the caretaking environment and its contribution
toward the release and stabilization of the intrapsychic potentialities
and functions (cf. Freud, 1911, p. 220);

(2) the special sensitivity of an infant making demands on the
primary environment, which I am designating here as a mother's
role of protective shield (cf. Escalona, 1953);

(3) the unfolding of the maturational processes, autonomous ego
functions, and libido development; and

(4) the gradual emergence of the inner world and psychic reality, with all the complexity of instinctual needs and tensions, and
their interplay with inner psychic structures and object relationships.

In our literature, perhaps, one of the most sensitive and elaborate
descriptions of the caretaking role of the mother is in Winnicott's
writings. According to Winnicott (1956b), what motivates the mother
for her role as a protective shield for the infant is her "primary
maternal preoccupation." The incentive for the mother's role is her
libidinal investment in the infant and the infant's dependence on
it for survival (cf. Benedek, 1952). From the infant's subjective point

[1] It is not possible to review this work here. Brody (1956) has surveyed this literature exhaustively. I shall point out a few of these contributions which have been
especially valuable to me in arriving at my concept of cumulative trauma. These are
by: Benedek (1952), Beres (1956), Bowlby (1958, 1960), Erikson (1950, 1956), Escalona
(1953), Anna Freud (1951, 1958), Fries (1946), Greenacre (1954, 1958, 1959, 1960c),
Hartmann (1939, 1952), Hoffer (1945, 1950, 1955), Kris (1950, 1951, 1956b, 1962),
Lichtenstein (1961), Mahler (1952, 1961), Ramzy and Wallerstein (1958), Spitz (1945,
1959, 1962). Winnicott (1945a, 1948b, 1949a, 1956b, 1960, 1962).

of view there is at the beginning little perception of this dependence or of the need for survival.

What the mother's caretaking role achieves in optimal circumstances is:

1. Through making herself available as a protective shield the mother enables the growth of the maturational processes—both of autonomous ego functions and instinctual processes. The mother's role as a protective shield defends the infant against the mother's subjective and unconscious love and hate, and thus allows her empathy to be maximally receptive to the infant's needs (cf. Spitz, 1959).

2. If her adaptation is good enough, then the infant does not become precociously aware of his dependence on the mother—hence does not have to exploit whatever mental functions are emergent and available toward self-defense (cf. Freud, 1920).

3. The protective-shield role of the mother enables the infant to project all the unpleasurable inner stimuli onto her, so that she can deal with them and thus sustain the illusion of omnipotence of well-being in the infant. Erikson (1950) has defined this sense of well-being as "trust," Benedek (1952) as "confidence," and Kris (1962) as "comfort" (see also Searles, 1962).

4. Through functioning as a protective shield, and so providing a model, the mother enables the infant's psyche to integrate what J. Sandler (1960) has called a "qualitative organizing component." In later ego development and functioning we can identify this as guiding the synthetic function of the ego in its discriminating role, both in relation to inner instinctual reality and to the demands of the external environment.

5. By providing the right dosage of life experience (Fries, 1946) and need satisfactions through her body care, she enables the infant's inner world to differentiate into id and ego as well as gradually to demarcate inner from outer reality (cf. Hoffer, 1952; Ramzy and Wallerstein, 1958).

6. By lending her own ego functions as well as her libidinal and aggressive cathexes (through her role as a protective shield) she helps the infant to build up supplies of primary narcissism, neutralized energy, and the beginnings of the capacity and wish for object cathexes (cf. Hoffer, 1952; Kris, 1951). Both what she provides

and what emerges through the infant's maturation interact and supplement each other (Erikson, 1946; Freud, 1911; Hoffer, 1949; Winnicott, 1953).

7. If these tasks are accomplished successfully, then the shift from primary dependence to relative dependence can take place (Winnicott, 1960). In this stage the function of her role as a protective shield becomes more complex; it takes on an essentially psychological aspect. She has now to help the infant with his first experiences of inner instinctual conflicts on the one hand, and yet sustain for him that flux from primary identification to realization of separateness which is the essence of disillusionment (Winnicott, 1948b) and a precondition for a true capacity for object cathexes (cf. Milner, 1952; Anna Freud, 1958).

8. If she is successful in these achievements, then the infant gradually becomes aware of the mother as a love object and of his need for her love. This is now an object cathexis which employs instinctual (id) cathexes that have become available in the meantime (Anna Freud, 1951).

9. By providing phase-adequate frustrations she sponsors the capacity for toleration of tension and unpleasure, thus promoting structural development (cf. Kris, 1962). Rubinfine (1962) in his valuable discussion of this aspect of maternal care concludes:

> . . . where need satisfaction is always and immediately available (i.e., deanimated), there should be a relative absence of tension. Without appropriately timed experiences of frustration and delay, there may result retardation in the development of various ego functions, among them the capacity to distinguish between self and nonself. Such failure of differentiation of self from object, and the consequent failure of defusion of self- and object-representations, leads to interference with the development of the capacity to discharge aggressive drives toward an external object, and results in the turning of aggression against the self.

Winnicott (1952) has stressed the point that a mother should and indeed must fail the id, but never the ego of the infant.

The vehicle of all these transactions between mother and infant is dependency. This dependency is to a large extent not sensed by the infant. Similarly, it is important to keep in mind that the mother's role as a protective shield is a limited function in her total life experience. In the beginning it is an all-engrossing one for her. Still, theoretically it is significant for us to be able to see it as a special instance of her personality and emotional functioning. Spitz's (1962) distinction between the totality of the infant's anaclitic needs and the implementation of the mother's diatrophic attitude in response to these needs is pertinent to remember in this context. Unless we can do this we cannot identify how this role as a protective shield can be and does become invaded by her personal needs and conflicts. It is the intrusion of her personal needs and conflicts that I characterize as her failure in respect of her role as a protective shield. The mother's role as protective shield is not a passive one but an alert, adaptive, and organizing one. The protective-shield role is the result of conflict-free autonomous ego functions in the mother. If personal conflicts intrude here, the result is a shift from the protective-shield role to that of symbiosis or rejective withdrawal. How an infant will react to these failures depends upon the nature, intensity, duration, and repetitiveness of the trauma.

In our literature three typical instances of this type of failure of the mother as a protective shield have been thoroughly discussed:

1. The most extreme and pathogenic is through the excessive intrusion of the mother's psychopathology. Winnicott (1949a, 1952) has discussed it as failure of the good-enough holding environment leading to psychosis or mental defect. Mahler (1952, 1961) has coined the phrase of symbiotic relationship between mother and child that leads to schizophrenic illnesses. In this context I would like also to mention, among others, the researches of Beres (1956), Geleerd (1956, 1958), Lidz and Fleck (1959), and Searles (1959).

2. The breakdown of mother's role of protective shield has also been discussed in terms of loss of or separation from her. Here again the pioneer researches of Anna Freud and Burlingham (1942, 1944) and Winnicott (1940, 1945b), and the later exhaustive investigations of Bowlby (1960), Spitz (1945, 1951), and Provence and Lipton (1962) stand out as particularly important (also cf. Hellman, 1962).

3. The third instance of breakdown of mother's role as protective shield occurs when either some constitutional sensitivity (Escalona, 1953) or physical handicap (Burlingham, 1961; Anne Marie Sandler, 1963) impose an impossible task on the mother, or when a severe

physical illness in the infant or child creates a special demand which
no human adult could possibly meet (cf. Anna Freud, 1952; Frankl,
1961).

ETIOLOGY OF CUMULATIVE TRAUMA

I am here tentatively trying to conceptualize a fourth type of
partial breakdown of the mother's role as a protective shield, which
becomes visible only in retrospect as a disturbance and can be designated as cumulative trauma. I have been specifically guided and
helped in arriving at this hypothesis through the researches of
Winnicott, Kris, and Greenacre.

Over the past twenty years Winnicott has been persistently
drawing our attention to the importance of the mother's caretaking
function, the vital role of dependence for the infant's emergence
into self-status, etc. James (1962) has recently given us a valuable
critique of Winnicott's researches. What is pertinent for my purposes in Winnicott's hypotheses is his elucidation of the role of
regression to dependency needs in the therapeutic process (1949b),
his researches into the antisocial tendency (1956a), and his careful
delineation of the early psychic and affective processes of integration
in the child (1945a).

It is Winnicott's basic hypothesis (1952) that all relative failures
in infancy of the good-enough holding environment (mother's role
as a protective shield) set up a compulsion in the relatively matured
child and the grown adult to correct the imbalances and dissocia-
tions in ego integration. This is achieved through regression to
dependency needs. In Winnicott's idiom, establishment of "the false
self" is one result of such caretaking environment's failure to adapt
through good-enough holding (1949a). What Winnicott calls "the
false self" is a characterological consequence of the disruption and
distortion of ego autonomy. What Winnicott calls "impingements"
are the failure of the mother in infancy to dose and regulate stimuli
—both external and internal. Winnicott believes that these impingements are disruptive of true ego integration, and lead to premature
defensive organization and functioning (1948b). What Kris (1962)
has described as "a specific kind of provocative overstimulation
which was bound to produce mounting tension in the child without

offering appropriate avenues of discharge," and also as "tantalizing," Winnicott designates as "impingements." I am here considering these as some of the most pathogenic genetic elements in cumulative trauma (cf. Erikson, 1950).

Kris in his paper "The Recovery of Childhood Memories in Psychoanalysis" (1956b) has distinguished between "shock trauma" and "the strain trauma." The latter he has defined as the "effect of long-lasting situations, which may cause traumatic effects by accumulation of frustrating tensions." The clinical examples that Kris offers here and in his contemporary paper on "The Personal Myth" (1956a) leave me in no doubt that "the strain trauma" and the screen memories or precocious early memories that the patients recount are derivatives of the partial breakdown of the protective-shield function of the mother and an attempt to symbolize its effects (cf. Anna Freud, 1958). Kris's sensitive and consummate account of the predicament of the infant Anne in his paper "Decline and Recovery in a Three-Year-Old" (1962) is the most apposite material in relation to my concept of cumulative trauma. It is interesting to note in Kris's account that even though the mother and infant were observed from the start, it was only later, i.e., in relative retrospect at thirty-four weeks, that the fact of disturbed maternal handling constituting a "tantalizing" situation for the infant Anne could be definitely established.

Greenacre's studies (1954, 1960a, 1960c) have been largely concerned with the vicissitudes of the maturational factor in infancy and its effect on ego and instinctual development. In 1959 she introduced the concept of *focal symbiosis* to identify a specific variant of what Mahler has described as symbiotic relationships. Greenacre defines focal symbiosis as "an intensely strong interdependence (usually between mother and child, but sometimes, as in my cases, with people other than the mother) which is limited to a special and rather circumscribed relationship rather than a nearly total enveloping one. . . . In limited or focal symbiotic relationships, there is often a peculiar union of the child's special need with the parent's special sensitivity, and . . . the total personality of either parent or child may not be as much involved as in the severe case of symbiotic psychoses described by Mahler" (pp. 244, 245). Greenacre (1959, 1960a, 1960b) furthermore relates a great deal of the psychopathology of perversions, borderline cases, and body-ego development to focal symbiosis. In her concept of focal symbiosis she has fruitfully extended the range in time and developmental process through which the child and his human environment can involve each other in terms of the archaic dependency relationship.

In the context of these formulations I shall now examine the nature and function of the cumulative trauma. Cumulative trauma has its beginnings in the period of development when the infant needs and uses the mother as his protective shield. The inevitable temporary failures of the mother as protective shield are corrected and recovered from the evolving complexity and rhythm of the maturational processes. Where these failures of the mother in her role as protective shield are significantly frequent and lead to impingement on the infant's psyche-soma, impingements which he has no means of eliminating, they set up a nucleus of pathogenic reaction. These in turn start a process of interplay with the mother which is distinct from her adaptation to the infant's needs. This interplay between mother and infant can have any or all of the effects described below.

1. It leads to premature and selective ego development. Some of the emergent autonomous functions are accelerated in growth and used in defensive action to deal with the impingements that are unpleasurable (James, 1960; Winnicott, 1949b).

2. It can begin to organize a special responsiveness to the mother's mood that creates an imbalance in the integration of aggressive drives (cf. Winnicott, 1948a; Sperling, 1950).

3. The involvement of precocious functions with the mother's collusive response militates against developmentally arriving at a differentiated separate "coherent ego" (Freud, 1920) and self. This in turn leads to a dissociation through which an archaic dependency bond is exploited on the one hand and a precipitate independence is asserted on the other. A specific result is that what should have been a silent, unregistered dependency state now becomes an engineered exploitation of instinctual and ego dependence, with a precocious narcissistic cathexis of the mother.

4. As a further consequence the disillusionment that belongs to maturational separating off from mother is sidetracked and a false identificatory oneness is manipulated (cf. Searles, 1962). This way,

instead of disillusionment and mourning, an ego attitude of concern for the mother and excessive craving for concern from the mother become established. This concern is quite different from the concern that belongs to sadistic instinctual attack on the mother and the ensuing feelings of guilt (cf. Klein, 1932). This concern is an ego interest that substitutes for a true object cathexis (cf. Winnicott, 1948a).

5. Through the impingements that derive from failure of mother's role as protective shield, a precocious cathexis of external and internal reality takes place. This organization of inner and outer reality leaves out a very important function of the ego's subjective awareness and experience of itself as a coherent entity. Its synthetic function is also disrupted (cf. James, 1960).

6. The strain and impingements from the failure of mother's role as protective shield, which I am designating here as cumulative trauma, have their most specific effect on the vicissitudes of body-ego development in the infant and the child. The researches of Coleman, Kris, and Provence (1953), Greenacre (1958, 1960b), Hoffer (1950, 1952), Kris (1951), Milner (1952), Spitz (1951, 1962), and Winnicott (1949a, 1949b, 1953) have stressed the importance of the maternal caretaking procedures (protective-shield role) for the development of the body ego in the context of the earliest stages of the ego-id differentiation and the gradual integration of a sense of self. Here I want to refer, only very briefly, to my inference from clinical material that the breaches in the mother's role as protective shield leave their precipitates most sentiently and effectively in the body-ego development of the child. These residues over the course of maturation and development gather into a specific type of body-ego organization and form the substratum of the psychological personality. Pertinent here are the observational data offered by Coleman, Kris, and Provence (1953), Kris (1951), and Ritvo and Solnit (1958). In the adult patient it is through the clinical observation of the idiosyncrasies of the body-ego behavior in the transference neurosis and the total analytic setting that we can hope to reconstruct what are the particular genetic patterns of the cumulative trauma in a given case (Khan, 1963a). The concept of cumulative trauma tentatively offers, in terms of early ego development and in the context of infant-mother relationship, a complementary hypothesis to the con-

cept of fixation points in libido development. In this sense it tries
to map out what were the significant points of stress and strain in
the evolving mother-infant (child) relationship that gradually gather
into a dynamic substratum in the morphology of a particular character or personality.

Once this interplay between infant and mother starts, it brings
into its sphere of action all new developmental experiences and object
relations. In many significant aspects this later pathogenic interplay
between mother and child aims to correct the earlier distortions
through impingements. This is what I think Greenacre (1959) refers
to as the drive behind "the union of the child's special need with the
parent's special sensitivity." That these attempts at recovery only
complicate the pathology is an irony of human experience. This is
perhaps at the root of many attempts at cure through love and passionate involvement in our adult patients. I have tried to discuss this
aspect in my paper (1962) "The Role of Polymorph-Perverse Body-
Experiences and Object-Relations in Ego-Integration" (see also
Alpert, 1959; Khan, 1963; Lichtenstein, 1961).

I have so far stressed only the pathogenic effects on infant development from breaches in the mother's role as protective shield.
It would, however, be a gross misrepresentation of the total complexity of the interplay between mother and infant if we fail to state
that although the infant ego is weak, vulnerable, and extremely
dependent on the mother's role as protective shield, the infant has
also a great inherent resilience and potentiality (strength). It not
only can and does recover from breaches in the protective shield,
but it can use such impingements and strains as "nutriment" (Rapaport, 1958) toward further growth and structuration (cf. Rubinfine,
1962; Kris, 1951). It is important to remember that though the ego
can survive and overcome such strains, exploit them to good purpose, manage to mute the cumulative trauma into abeyance, and
arrive at a fairly healthy and effective normal functioning, it nevertheless can in later life break down as a result of acute stress and
crisis. When it does so—and this is of great clinical importance—
we cannot diagnostically evaluate the genetics and economics of the
total processes involved if we do not have a concept like cumulative
trauma to guide our attention and expectancy. It has often been
remarked in our literature during the past three decades that the

character disorders of a schizoid type, which have become the more frequent type of patient in our practice, present a clinical picture whose etiology needs constructs that include disturbances of infant-mother relationship that were at the time neither gross nor acute (Kris, 1951; Khan, 1960). I am suggesting that the concept of cumulative trauma can help us a great deal here. The human infant is well endowed to struggle with the vicissitudes of his internal and environmental stresses. What is important for us is to be able to identify in the clinical process what effects this struggle has left and how it has shaped the adult character (cf. Greenacre, 1954, 1960b; Lichtenstein, 1961; Khan, 1963b).

One treacherous aspect of cumulative trauma is that it operates and builds up silently throughout childhood right up to adolescence. It is only in recent years that we have learned to evaluate as pathogenic a certain precocious development in children. Such precocity had previously been celebrated as giftedness or strong ego emergence or a happy independence in the child. We are also inclined to view with much more caution and reserve, if not suspicion, a mother's boasts of a specially close rapport and understanding between herself and her child.

Clinical experience shows that the phases of maturational development where these impingements from mother's failure in her role as protective shield tend to get organized into an active collusive relationship between mother and child are the late oral, early anal, and phallic phases—the phases where the emergent instinctual process and the maturational ego process test the mother with their full need and demand. It is also these stages where the stimulus hunger asks for maximal psychological adaptation, response, and restraint from the mother in her role as protective shield. The chief psychic process involved in such collusive relationships is identification, as Kris (1951) and Ritvo and Solnit (1958) have stressed. This identification remains essentially of an incorporative and projective type, interfering with internalization and assimilation of new object representations, and thus confuses a proper differentiation and growth of internal psychic structures. This holds true also of the distortion of the libidinal strivings and object relations of the oedipal phase (cf. Schmale, 1962).

The phase at which the child himself acutely becomes aware of the distorting and disruptive effects of this collusive bond with the mother is at adolescence. Then the reaction is dramatically rejective of the mother and all the past cathexes of her (Khan, 1963c). This, of course, makes the adolescent process of integration at once tortuous and impossible. At this point attempts at integration which willfully negate past libidinal investments, ego interests, and object ties are instituted. This leads either to collapse of personality development into inertia and futility, or a short, magical recovery into omnipotent isolation, or a passionate craving for new ideals, new objects, and new ego interests (Beres and Obers, 1950; Erikson, 1956; Geleerd, 1958; Khan, 1963b; Spiegel, 1951).

CONCLUSION

The concept of cumulative trauma takes into consideration psychophysical events that happen at the preverbal stage of relationship between mother and infant. It correlates their effects on what later becomes operative as a disturbed relationship between mother and child or as a *bias* in ego and psychosexual development (Khan, 1962, 1963a). Once an infant emerges out of the preverbal stage we can never see directly the first impingements and failures in the mother's role as the protective shield. What we see in direct observation or clinically are derivatives of these mental processes and capacities. What I am conceptualizing here as cumulative trauma has been described by Anna Freud (1958) in another context. She states "that subtle harm is being inflicted on this child, and that the consequences of it will become manifest at some future date."

Even though we have now available many sensitive accounts of direct observations of the feeding situations and the total relationship between infant and mother (J. Robertson, 1962), there is still doubt as to whether we can identify at the point of its actuality the breakdown of the mother's role as protective shield in relation to the infant's anaclitic needs. As Kris's (1962) account of the infant Anne makes abundantly clear, even though an infant was observed by a team of highly skilled professionals, it was only in retrospect that the effects of such breakdown of a good-enough provision of maternal care began to be visible. In the case of Anne we see how the impingements from the mother's handling already began to gather into the structure and function of the cumulative trauma. It is important for us to be able to chart out clearly the earliest nature and role of these failures, because only thus can we organize our clinical expectancy and arrive at true diagnosis. As Anna Freud (1962) expressed it:

> . . . if our present direction of interest is no more than a turning of our glance from the effects of dependence on to the contents and processes in the period of dependence, it is still a turning-point of decisive importance. By taking this line we change the direction of our interest from the illnesses themselves—neurotic or psychotic—to their pre-conditions, to the matrix from which they arise, i.e. to the era where such important matters are decided as the selection of neurosis and the selection of the types of defence [p. 240].

BIBLIOGRAPHY

Alpert, A. (1959), Reversibility of Pathological Fixations Associated with Maternal Deprivation in Infancy. *This Annual*, XIV.
Benedek, T. (1952), The Psychosomatic Implications of the Primary Unit: Mother-Child. In: *Psychosomatic Functions in Women*. New York: Ronald Press.
Beres, D. (1956), Ego Deviation and the Concept of Schizophrenia. *This Annual*, XI.
—— & Obers, S. J. (1950), The Effects of Extreme Deprivation in Infancy on Psychic Structure in Adolescence. *This Annual*, V.
Bowlby, J. (1958), The Nature of the Child's Tie to His Mother. *Int. J. Psa.*, XXXIX.
—— (1960), Separation Anxiety. *Int. J. Psa.*, XLI.
Brody, S. (1956), *Patterns of Mothering*. New York: International Universities Press.
Burlingham, D. (1961), Some Notes on the Development of the Blind. *This Annual*, XVI.
Coleman, R. W., Kris, E., & Provence, S. (1953), The Study of Variations of Early Parental Attitudes. *This Annual*, VIII.
Erikson, E. H. (1946), Ego Development and Historical Change. *This Annual*, II.
—— (1950), Growth and Crises of the Healthy Personality. In: *Identity and the Life Cycle* [*Psychological Issues*, Monog. 1]. New York: International Universities Press.
—— (1956), The Problem of Ego Identity. *J. Amer. Psa. Assn.*, IV.
Escalona, S. (1953), Emotional Development in the First Year of Life. In: *Problems of Infancy and Childhood*, ed. M. J. E. Senn. New York: Josiah Macy, Jr. Foundation.
Fenichel, O. (1937), The Concept of Trauma in Contemporary Psychoanalytic Theory. In: *Collected Papers of Otto Fenichel*, 2nd Series. New York: Norton, 1954.
Frankl, L. (1961), Some Observations on the Development and Disturbances of Integration in Childhood. *This Annual*, XVI.
Freud, A. (1936), *The Ego and the Mechanisms of Defense*. New York: International Universities Press, 1946.
—— (1951), Observations on Child Development. *This Annual*, VI.
—— (1952), The Role of Bodily Illness in the Mental Life of Children. *This Annual*, VII.
—— (1958), Child Observation and Prediction of Development. *This Annual*, XIII.

—— (1962), The Theory of the Parent-Infant Relationship: Contributions to Discussion. *Int. J. Psa.*, XLIII.

—— & Burlingham, D. (1942), *War and Children*. New York: International Universities Press, 1943.

—— —— (1944), *Infants Without Families*. New York: International Universities Press.

Freud, S. (1887-1902), *The Origins of Psychoanalysis*. New York: Basic Books, 1954.

—— (1893), On the Psychical Mechanism of Hysterical Phenomena. *Standard Edition*, III. London: Hogarth Press, 1962.

—— (1895), On the Grounds for Detaching a Particular Syndrome from Neurasthenia under the Description "Anxiety Neurosis." *Standard Edition*, III. London: Hogarth Press, 1962.

—— (1897), Abstracts of the Scientific Writings of Dr. Sigm. Freud 1877-1897. *Standard Edition*, III. London: Hogarth Press, 1962.

—— (1905), Three Essays on the Theory of Sexuality. *Standard Edition*, VII. London: Hogarth Press, 1953.

—— (1911), Formulations on the Two Principles of Mental Functioning. *Standard Edition*, XII. London: Hogarth Press, 1958.

—— (1914a), On Narcissism. *Standard Edition*, XIV. London: Hogarth Press, 1957.

—— (1914b), On the History of the Psycho-Analytic Movement. *Standard Edition*, XIV. London: Hogarth Press, 1957.

—— (1915a), Instincts and Their Vicissitudes. *Standard Edition*, XIV. London: Hogarth, 1957.

—— (1915b), Repression. *Standard Edition*, XIV. London: Hogarth Press, 1957.

—— (1915c), The Unconscious. *Standard Edition*, XIV. London: Hogarth Press, 1957.

—— (1917), Mourning and Melancholia. *Standard Edition*, XIV. London: Hogarth Press, 1957.

—— (1920), Beyond the Pleasure Principle. *Standard Edition*, XVIII. London: Hogarth Press, 1950.

—— (1923), The Ego and the Id. *Standard Edition*, XIX. London: Hogarth Press, 1961.

—— (1926), Inhibitions, Symptoms and Anxiety. *Standard Edition*, XX. London: Hogarth Press, 1959.

—— (1937), Analysis Terminable and Interminable. *Collected Papers*, V. London: Hogarth Press, 1950.

—— (1938), Splitting of the Ego in the Defensive Process. *Collected Papers*, V. London: Hogarth Press, 1950.

Fries, M. E. (1946), The Child's Ego Development and the Training of Adults in His Environment. *This Annual*, II.

Geleerd, E. R. (1956), Clinical Contribution to the Problem of the Early Mother-Child Relationship. *This Annual*, XI.

—— (1958), Borderline States in Childhood and Adolescence. *This Annual*, XIII.

Greenacre, P. (1954), In: Problems of Infantile Neurosis: A Discussion. *This Annual*, IX.

—— (1958), Towards the Understanding of the Physical Nucleus of Some Defence Reactions. *Int. J. Psa.*, XXXIX.

—— (1959), On Focal Symbiosis. In: *Dynamic Psychopathology in Childhood*, ed. L. Jessner & E. Pavenstedt. New York: Grune & Stratton.

—— (1960a), Regression and Fixation. *J. Amer. Psa. Assn.*, VIII.

—— (1960b), Further Notes on Fetishism. *This Annual*, XV.

—— (1960c), Considerations Regarding the Parent-Infant Relationship. *Int. J. Psa.*, XLI.

Hartmann, H. (1939), *Ego Psychology and the Problem of Adaptation*. New York: International Universities Press, 1958.

—— (1950), Psychoanalysis and Developmental Psychology. *This Annual*, V.

—— (1952), The Mutual Influences in the Development of Ego and the Id. *This Annual*, VII.

Hellman, I. (1962), Hampstead Nursery Follow-up Studies: 1. Sudden Separation and Its Effect Followed Over Twenty Years. *This Annual*, XVII.

Hoffer, W. (1949), Mouth, Hand and Ego Integration. *This Annual*, III/IV.

—— (1950), Development of the Body Ego. *This Annual*, V.

—— (1952), The Mutual Influences in the Development of Ego and Id. *This Annual*, VII.

—— (1955), *Psychoanalysis*. Baltimore: Williams & Wilkins.

James, M. (1960), Premature Ego Development. *Int. J. Psa.*, XLI.

—— (1962), Infantile Narcissistic Trauma. *Int. J. Psa.*, XLIII.

Jones, E. (1953), *Sigmund Freud: Life and Work*, Vol. I. London: Hogarth Press.

Khan, M. M. R. (1960), Clinical Aspects of Schizoid Personality: Affects and Technique. *Int. J. Psa.*, XLI.

—— (1962), The Role of Polymorph-Perverse Body-Experiences and Object-Relations in Ego-Integration. *Brit. J. Med. Psychol.*, XXXV.

—— (1963a), The Role of Infantile Sexuality and Early Object Relations in Female Homosexuality. In: *The Pathology and Treatment of Sexual Deviation*, ed. I. Rosen. London: Oxford University Press.

—— (1963b), Ego Ideal, Excitement and the Threat of Annihilation. *Journal of the Hillside Hospital*, XII.

—— (1963c), Silence as Communication: Clinical Notes on an Adolescent Patient. *Bull. Menninger Clin.*, XXVII.

Klein, M. (1932), *The Psycho-Analysis of Children*. London: Hogarth Press, 3rd ed., 1949.

Kris, E. (1950), Notes on the Development and on Some Current Problems of Psychoanalytic Child Psychology. *This Annual*, V.

—— (1951), Some Comments and Observations on Early Autoerotic Activities. *This Annual*, VI.

—— (1956a), The Personal Myth. *J. Amer. Psa. Assn.*, IV.

—— (1956b), The Recoveries of Childhood Memories in Psychoanalysis. *This Annual*, XI.

—— (1962), Decline and Recovery in the Life of a Three-Year-Old; or: Data in Psychoanalytic Perspective on the Mother-Child Relationship. *This Annual*, XVII.

Lidz, T. & Fleck, S. (1959), Schizophrenia, Human Integration and the Role of the Family. In: *Etiology of Schizophrenia*, ed. D. Jackson. New York: Basic Books.

Lichtenstein, H. (1961), Identity and Sexuality: A Study of Their Interrelationship in Man. *J. Amer. Psa. Assn.*, IX.

Mahler, M. S. (1952), On Child Psychosis and Schizophrenia. *This Annual*, VII.

—— (1961), On Sadness and Grief in Infancy and Childhood. *This Annual*, XVI.

Milner, M. (1952), Aspects of Symbolism in Comprehension of the Not-Self. *Int. J. Psa.*, XXXIII.

Provence, S. & Lipton, R. C. (1962), *Infants in Institutions*. New York: International Universities Press.

Ramzy, I. & Wallerstein, R. S. (1958), Pain, Fear and Anxiety. *This Annual*, XIII.

Rapaport, D. (1958), The Theory of Ego Autonomy: A Generalization. *Bull. Menninger Clin.*, XXII.

Ritvo, S. & Solnit, A. J. (1958), Influences of Early Mother-Child Interaction on Identification Processes. *This Annual*, XIII.

Robertson, J. (1962), Mothering As an Influence on Early Development: A Study of Well-Baby Clinic Records. *This Annual*, XVII.

Rubinfine, D. L. (1962), Maternal Stimulation, Psychic Structure, and Early Object Relations; with Special Reference to Aggression and Denial. *This Annual*, XVII.

Sandler, A. M. (1963), Aspects of Passivity and Ego Development in the Blind Child. *This Annual*, XVIII.

Sandler, J. (1960), The Background of Safety. *Int. J. Psa.*, XLI.

Schmale, Jr., A. H. (1962), Needs, Gratifications and the Vicissitudes of the Self-Representation. *The Psychoanalytic Study of Society*, II. New York: International Universities Press.

Searles, H. F. (1959), The Effort to Drive the Other Person Crazy: An Element in the Aetiology and Psychotherapy of Schizophrenia. *Brit. J. Med. Psychol.*, XXXII.

—— (1960), *The Nonhuman Environment*. New York: International Universities Press.

—— (1962), Scorn, Disillusionment and Adoration in the Psychotherapy of Schizophrenia. *Psychoanal. Rev.*, XLIX.

Shields, R. S. (1962), *A Cure of Delinquents*. London: Heinemann.

Sperling, M. (1950), Children's Interpretation and Reaction to the Unconscious of Their Mothers. *Int. J. Psa.*, XXXI.

Spiegel, L. A. (1951), A Review of Contributions to the Psychoanalytic Theory of Adolescence. *This Annual*, VI.

Spitz, R. A. (1945), Hospitalism. *This Annual*, I.

—— (1951), The Psychogenic Diseases in Infancy. *This Annual*, VI.

—— (1959), *A Genetic Field Theory of Ego Formation*. New York: International Universities Press.

—— (1962), Autoerotism Re-examined. *This Annual*, XVII.

Strachey, J. (1959), Editorial Introduction to Freud's *Inhibitions, Symptoms and Anxiety*. In: *The Standard Edition*, XX. London: Hogarth Press.

Winnicott, D. W. (1940), Children in War. In: *The Child and the Outside World*. London: Tavistock Publications, 1957.

—— (1945a), Primitive Emotional Development. *Collected Papers*. New York: Basic Books, 1958.

—— (1945b), The Evacuated Child. The Return of the Evacuated Child. In: *The Child and the Outside World*. London: Tavistock Publications, 1957.

—— (1948a), Reparation in Respect of Mother's Organised Defence against Depression. *Collected Papers*. New York: Basic Books, 1958.

—— (1948b), Paediatrics and Psychiatry. *Collected Papers*. New York: Basic Books, 1958.

—— (1949a), Mind and Its Relation to Psyche-Soma. *Collected Papers*. New York: Basic Books, 1958.

—— (1949b), Birth Memories, Birth Trauma and Anxiety. *Collected Papers*. New York: Basic Books, 1958.

—— (1952), Psychoses and Child Care. *Collected Papers*. New York: Basic Books, 1958.

—— (1953), Transitional Objects and Transitional Phenomena. *Collected Papers*. New York: Basic Books, 1958.

—— (1956a), The Anti-Social Tendency. *Collected Papers*. New York: Basic Books, 1958.

—— (1956b), Primary Maternal Preoccupation. *Collected Papers*. New York: Basic Books, 1958.

—— (1960), The Theory of the Parent-Infant Relationship. *Int. J. Psa.*, XLI.

—— (1962), The Theory of the Parent-Infant Relationship: Further Remarks. *Int. J. Psa.*, XLIII.

THOUGHTS ABOUT DEVELOPMENT
AND INDIVIDUATION

MARGARET S. MAHLER, M.D. (New York)

At an advanced stage in their lifework, some psychoanalysts seek to come closer to the actual fountainhead of their reconstructive efforts. Some, like myself, seek verbal and preverbal observational data—*statu nascendi*—such as will confirm, refute, modify, or elaborate psychoanalytic hypotheses. Through a study of normal infants and their mothers, I have been trying, not only to complement my psychoanalytic work with neurotic adults and children, but also to gain additional perspective and to validate previous studies in the area of infantile psychosis.

I have maintained a rather personal interest in one specific aspect of the rich heritage that Freud bestowed upon us, namely, his emphasis on the fact that a lifelong, albeit diminishing, emotional dependence on the mother is a universal truth of human existence. The biological unpreparedness of the human infant to maintain his life separately conditions that species-specific prolonged phase which has been designated "the mother-infant symbiosis." I believe it is from the symbiotic phase of the mother-infant dual unity that those experiential precursors of individual beginnings are derived which, together with inborn constitutional factors, determine every human individual's unique somatic and psychological make-up.

The Abraham A. Brill Memorial Lecture, given to the New York Psychoanalytic Society on November 27, 1962.

This paper is partly based on a research project which was originally sponsored by the Field Foundation, and is presently sponsored by the National Association for Mental Health, Inc.; the Psychoanalytic Research and Development Fund, Inc.; and the Taconic Foundation.

Clinical Professor of Psychiatry, Albert Einstein College of Medicine.

From the Masters Children's Center, 75 Horatio Street, New York 14; with the collaboration of Manuel Furer, M.D., and Mrs. Anni Bergman; with the assistance of Mrs. Edith Atkin, Ann Haeberle, Ph.D., Mrs. Emmagene Kamaiko, David L. Mayer, M.D., Fred Pine, Ph.D., and Herman Roiphe, M.D.

307

But translation of the observable phenomena of the symbiotic phase into psychological terms is exceedingly difficult. Extrapolations drawn from preverbal behavioral data are even more precarious than the use of hypotheses deduced from observational data of later phases of childhood. To understand preverbal phenomena, we are compelled to seek out their connotations through their continuance into later stages, or through appraisal of regressive manifestations (Bonnard, 1958). Thus, the understanding and conceptualization of symbiotic phenomena seemed to me to require following them into a later phase of the mother-infant relationship, namely, the "separation-individuation" phase (Mahler et al., 1959). In order to study the symbiotic phase, I organized a research project, and we are still struggling with its methodology, designed to investigate the phenomena of the infant's emergence from the symbiotic relationship.

Our research into the separation-individuation phase consists of a systematic study of average mothers with their normal babies from six months through the second and third year of life. Numerous papers dealing with the sequelae of separation from the mother have greatly enhanced our knowledge of the traumatic effect of the child's physical separation from the mother, and its pathogenic influence on personality development. In contradistinction to those studies, the design of our research project emphasizes the normal individuation-separation process of the infant in the actual presence of his mother (Mahler and Furer, 1963). Although in our setting, the individuation process also confronts the child with those minimal threats of object loss which the maturationally predetermined ascendance of autonomous functioning by necessity entails, nevertheless, because of the libidinal presence of the mother, the developmental process is characterized by the predominance of the child's pleasure in independent functioning. During this phase, the infant develops into a toddler, and his hitherto symbiotic relationship at the level of need satisfaction is gradually transformed into object relationship. I repeat, this is normal individuation-separation, in contrast to situations of traumatic separation, and it takes place in the presence of the mother.

In this separation-individuation study the mothers with their babies may avail themselves of our indoor, playgroundlike setting for two and a half hours, four mornings a week. I shall not in this paper embark on a discussion of our complex methodology, which has been described in a separate paper by Pine and Furer (1963). But since the present study is derived from my previous work, I shall briefly summarize two of my cardinal hypotheses which formed the backbone of this research.

1. In the symbiotic psychotic child the maturation of ego apparatuses, which is biologically predetermined, takes place alongside of a lag in development toward emotional separation-individuation and is therefore experienced as a catastrophic threat. The panic reactions which ensue when such a child is confronted with the possibility and the necessity of separate functioning trigger the psychotic defense mechanisms and create restitutive pictures described in the literature.

2. The second hypothesis, developed in several of my papers from 1957 on, stated that normal separation-individuation is the first crucial prerequisite for the development and maintenance of the "sense of identity." My concern with the problem of identity arose from observation of the puzzling clinical phenomenon that the psychotic child never attains a feeling of wholeness, of individual entity, let alone "a sense of human identity." I had discussed (1958) autistic and symbiotic infantile psychosis as the two extreme disturbances of "identity." I could not help noting that something had gone basically astray at the root of these extreme disturbances, that is, in the very earliest interreactions within the mother-infant unit. Briefly, one could summarize my hypothesis as follows: whereas in primary autism there is a deanimated frozen wall between the subject and the human object, in symbiotic psychosis, on the other hand, there is fusion, melting, and lack of differentiation between the self and the nonself.

I have suggested that the feeling of identity may be defined as the cohesive cathexis of our securely individuated and differentiated self-image, and that its beginnings may be traced back to the first two years of life, at which time the child gradually emerges, that is to say, "hatches" from the symbiotic common membrane. I likened this subphase of individuation to a second birth experience.

In conceptualizing the genesis of the eventual "sense of identity," I tend to regard demarcation of the body image from the image of the object, the mother, as the core of the process. Greenacre (1958) and Jacobson (1961) have stressed the fact that the sense of identity, or awareness of identity, is maintained by comparison and contrast. The matrix of the first experiences of comparison and contrast is in the realm of sensorimotor sensations during the symbiotic phase. We know that for the formation of structure, predictable rhythmic alternations of gratification-frustration experiences are necessary. The predictability of this rhythm associated with the availability of the love object lays the foundation for the development of object constancy in Hartmann's sense (1952, 1953).

Striking a balance between mothering without undue frustration on the one hand, and without intrusion or stifling of the infant's individual, inborn rhythm of needs on the other hand, is a task not easily achieved by the average mother in our culture. The perplexities, anxieties, and conflicts, the unconscious fantasies of mothers, have been the subject of scrutiny in the psychoanalytic situation. We have all had the opportunity to analyze maternal behavior, which ranges from normal, through neurotic patterns of conflict, to severely narcissistic reactions; from a more or less easy adaptation to motherhood, to severe reactive and defensive struggles. In the present separation-individuation study, we do not have material gained through psychoanalysis. Nonetheless, we believe that from the wealth of samples of behavior obtained from our bifocal, multiobservational and interview material, in the course of our long acquaintance with the mother-baby pairs, the mother's unconscious conflicts may be deduced with fair accuracy. The Leitmotifs of their maternal vicissitudes are reflected in their children's individuation. For professional reasons, I shall refer to the maternal role in the individuation process only to the extent that it is absolutely relevant to an understanding of those aspects of the individuation process which I wish to discuss.

We believe that our study bears out the assumption that the optimal evolution of the infant's partial ego functions—whose maturation follows a timetable, and which we, along with Hartmann (1939), attribute to the conflict-free sphere of the ego—is either facilitated or hindered by the conscious and, more particularly, the unconscious attitudes of the mother.

We begin by studying elements of the genesis and dynamics of the highly unique and distinctive patterns of interaction of the baby-mother pairs at the height of the symbiotic phase at six to eight months of age. We study changes in the variables of each pair's interaction, as well as in certain variables of the child's individuation patterns over time. We compare clusters of data culled from participant and nonparticipant observations, from weekly interviews with the mother, and from other more formal procedures: such as tests, and controlled ratings of independent variables in certain areas. Certain variables were found to be particularly pertinent for the assessment of the individuation process.

Since we have had the repeated opportunity to observe younger siblings of previously studied toddlers, we seem to be able to determine the very first signs of individuation by the end of the third, or the beginning of the fourth month. We have tried to devise methods by which certain changes and differences in postural behavior, molding or its opposite, stiffening of the body, can be determined, the mother holding the infant as compared with somebody else holding him. We have observed changes in the same infant, and differences among the infants with regard to visual focusing, visual following, scanning, and smiling (Spitz and Wolf, 1946; Spitz, 1950, 1957).

Certain action and ministration schemes of the mother, which are evident in the symbiotic phase, seem to be assimilated by the infant. This is an imitation without mental content, a complex individual patterning acquired within the symbiotic community. These patterns are too complex to be regarded as inborn, yet they seem to be irreversibly established at an age at which they could not have been the outcome of ego identifications.

In the second half of the first year, certain sensorimotor patterns and autonomous developmental profiles unfold rapidly and in rich variation. They seem to reflect the basic general and leading individual themes of the mother's fantasies, unconscious and conscious expectations, predilections, anxieties, and idiosyncrasies. These seem to have acted upon the infant's equipmental endowments, and they influence both its inborn and its symbiotically acquired reaction patterns.

Marjie and Mathew, born just one week apart, are set on the mattress in the baby corner of our nursery; they are six months old. Both are delightfully alert, each in individually quite characteristic and different ways. Marjie, plump, rosy-cheeked, and a tiny bit flabby, with a frequent and easy smile, takes in the world with her big dark eyes. If something or somebody is in her proximity, she uses her hands to explore; and only once in a great while is she seen to put the object of exploration to her mouth. Mathew, wiry and a bit pale, seldom remains in a sedentary, prone, or supine position; instead he explores large segments of reality with his whole body, his mouth wide open, using a rapid crawling motion. He mouthes everything within his reach.

Marjie is a little girl, to be sure, and Mathew a typically motor-minded baby boy. Yet, from our long acquaintance with Mathew's mother, Mrs. A—Mathew is the third of Mrs. A's children to be in our research—we know that all her children preferred motor and oral modalities of exploration and contact. Her only daughter Genie, who was in the first group in our study, was the most conspicuously motor-minded of Mrs. A's children. This motor-mindedness had multiple determination. There was undoubtedly an inborn motor proclivity, or a very early hypercathexis of the motor apparatus, but to this constitutional basis was added a powerful secondary impetus: the mother's predilection for her children's independence, her insistence that they learn to "shift for themselves" as soon as possible. In Genie's case, the preference for locomotion, her incessant climbing, balancing herself on the seesaw, and other kinesthetic and muscular activities seemed, first of all, to serve a pleasurable autonomous pursuit. Secondly, these skills were exercised persistently in spite of bumps and falls, because she sensed her mother's approval. Thirdly, however, her agility and hyperactivity served a defensive purpose as well: it seemed to make up for the unfulfilled need that ensued from her mother's tendency to ward off physical closeness and cuddling. Danny, Mrs. A's middle child, had also used motility and mouthing quite extensively when he was an infant. In other words, what we saw in Mathew, as early as at six months, had been characteristic of Mrs. A's daughter as well as of both her sons. It was not primarily determined by the male child's greater motor-mindedness.

When we observed Mrs. A with Genie, the mother's peculiar defensive attitude concerning bodily closeness and cuddling was very conspicuous; she even protested against any of the observers picking Genie up. Reconstruction of the motives underlying Mrs. A's unconscious conflict, from which this attitude derived, became possible by our bifocal, multiobservational and interview method, during our observation of Genie and of her two later infants.

So much for the "A family."

To return to the little girl Marjie: her older sibling, Tommy, has also been a member of our separation-individuation study. By contrast with Mrs. A's children, both of Mrs. B's children—Tommy and Marjie—seemed to reflect *their* mother's predilection for quiet passivity. When Mrs. B joined our project, Tommy was one year old. Tommy's most conspicuous feature was then, and has been ever since, his soulful, often melancholy brown eyes, with what Ernst Kris has described as the "searching look." He appeared solemn, passive, and somewhat suspicious.

Tommy's individuation process reflected the vicissitudes of his mother's conflict about maternity and her perplexities in child rearing which acted upon this oversensitive infant's inborn endowment and influenced his early experiential patterning. That Tommy must have felt his mother's tension can be deduced from the fact that, from a very early age on, he had been particularly fretful at wakening, which in turn had distressed his mother. Reconstructive data about Tommy's earliest somatopsychic patterning in the symbiotic phase led us to conclude that Tommy's sleeping-waking pattern was evidence of ego precocity since, at so very early an age, the transition from sleep to wakefulness had become difficult for him. Furthermore, intolerance of any change in routine as well as stranger anxiety manifested itself particularly early. From four to five months on, it was impossible to leave Tommy with any substitute for his mother. At four months, he is said to have become terrified when he saw his mother with a shower cap on. He seemed to have developed a premature perceptual awareness, a capacity for Gestalt perceptions such as is not commonly encountered at the age of four months. Tommy's symbiotic history is slightly reminiscent of that of the oversensitive infants described by Bergman and Escalona (1949).

We may assume that, because Tommy's rudimentary ego was far advanced in its sensory-perceptive faculties, the balance between his sensory-perceptive intake (which was added to the enteroceptive-proprioceptive stimuli), and his motor discharge, seemed to be out of kilter. This imposed a heavier than ordinary organizational task upon his primitive ego (Escalona and Heider, 1959).

Tommy's mother, Mrs. B, was undoubtedly confronted with a very difficult task in her efforts to be "a good-enough mothering partner," in Winnicott's sense (1957), to her oversensitive infant. But now that we have the opportunity to observe Mrs. B with her smiling and placid second infant, Marjie, we recognize that her difficulties with that task did not arise only from Tommy's oversensitivity as an infant.[1] Mrs. B is particularly happy and comfortable with Marjie, a fact which she herself explains in this way: "Marjie does not express anger when I go out, and is always happy and joyous to see me come back; but Tommy, ever since I can remember, was angry and desperate whenever I left him, and never showed any joy upon my return." Yet, even with Marjie, Mrs. B is clearly unable to respond specifically enough to the infant's specific cues.[2]

The average toddler, whose symbiotic phase is more satisfactory than Tommy's was, seems from the end of the first year on to become so preoccupied with practicing the emerging autonomous functions of the ego, that he does not seem to mind his mother's casual short departures from the familiar playroom.[3] Some infants behave as though they were drunk with their newly discovered ability to toddle in space and to widen their acquaintance with large segments of reality. The average infant, following the inception of toddling, does not clamor for his mother's attention and bodily closeness during this practicing period. He toddles up to his mother once in a while, for what Dr. Furer aptly calls "libidinal refueling," but his behavior seems to indicate that for the most part he takes his mother's emotional presence for granted.

However, as soon as free locomotion is mastered, the normal toddler seems to need to return to the mother to seek proximal communication with her in a quite directed way. The phenomenology of this behavior leaves no doubt that the representations of his self and that of the love object are now well on their way to differentiation.

[1] The differences in innate factors have been variously conceptualized as "congenital activity type" (Fries and Woolf, 1953), "variations in drive endowment" (Alpert, Neubauer, Weil, 1956), "differences in sensory thresholds" (Bergman and Escalona, 1949), etc.

[2] Compare a similar case reported by M. Kris (1957), where observation of the mother with her second child helped to elucidate her conflict with her first child.

[3] Compare Mahler (1963) and the film presented at the workshop on "Ongoing Research" at the Annual Meetings of the American Psychoanalytic Association, St. Louis, 1963.

After an interlude of greatly varying length, ranging from a few weeks to a period of months, and with various degrees of insistence and impetuousness, the toddler's active approach behavior toward his mother gains prominence. It is interesting to note how, in general, by the time the toddler has mastered the ability to move from and to the mother, the balance dramatically shifts within the bipolar mother-toddler interaction from activity on the part of the mother to activity on the part of the child. Once the toddler has mastered locomotion and begins to learn manipulation, these important partial functions and every new skill become elements of a language weighted with a steady accretion of secondary and largely unconscious meaning—a wordless appeal for love and praise from the mother, an expression of longing, a search for meanings, a wish for sharing and for expansion. The mother, as the catalyst of the individuation process, must be able to read the toddler's primary-process language. Modulated vocalizations, which vary widely among infants, appear at first as mere accompaniments of the toddler's ventures. Gradually the infant begins to express, and thus to communicate, a wide range of affects: fear, pleasure, annoyance, affection, jubilation, distress, astonishment, and the rest. This expressive jargon is the essential raw material out of which his representative symbolic language develops.

With the average mother-toddler pair, the hatching from the symbiotic orbit takes place smoothly. But in a number of presumably normal mother-toddler relationships, rapprochement occurs with conspicuous drama and may even constitute a crisis in the mother-toddler relationship.

As soon as Tommy started to walk, his separation anxiety manifested itself with even greater urgency: he followed his mother relentlessly, like a shadow. He was one of those toddlers in whom locomotion had already brought about an awareness of the self as separate from the mother, before he was emotionally ready to cope with this awareness of individuation. The danger signals in such cases are ever so often temper tantrums lasting not, as in normal cases, a few minutes but much longer.

The period of growing awareness of separateness is ushered in by a behavior which we observe rather frequently in our setting and which I would like to call "shadowing the mother." In Tommy's case, the outstanding feature of his individuation process was this phenomenon of "shadowing": his refusal to let his mother out of his sight. He would follow her every move from out of the corner of his eye. He would dash in her direction as soon as she walked toward the door. His widely ranging vocal communications were directed exclusively to his mother and gradually developed into predominantly petulant and not clearly enunciated verbal communications to her.

The mother too has to adjust to the anticipated crucial event of that inescapable separation which the maturation of apparatuses dictates. She must face the fact that her formerly completely dependent lap-baby can and does actively move to and from her. We know from the psychoanalysis of mothers that, in their unconscious, the infant's body during the presymbiotic and symbiotic phase is part of the representation of her "self." In the same way, through psychoanalysis of mothers, we have learned that the phallic meaning of the baby's body is often, if not always, discernible.

In our study we have also gathered evidence that her infant generally represents a part of the mother's body, and we sometimes see, in the way some of the mothers talk about the baby's body, how they hold and handle it, that the infant has the meaning of an illusory phallus for the mother (Mahler and Furer, 1963). Furthermore, as is also to be expected, each individual child has a certain specific meaning for the mother, according to the general and the specific fantasy connected with each child by that mother. This Leitmotif with its elaborations changes with the maturation of the infant, and is dependent in turn upon the development and adaptation of the mother to the emotional and actual task of motherhood (Coleman, Kris, Provence, 1953; Bibring et al., 1961). We have seen veritable mourning reactions to the anticipated event of active locomotor separation. We have also seen a rationalized unconcern about the event. Frequently we hear a mother saying about her child who has just taken his first unaided steps into the world, "Now he is grown up." Depending on her own adjustment, the mother may react, in the period of rapprochement following the child's mastery of locomotion, either by continued emotional availability and playful participation or by a gamut of less desirable attitudes. From the data we have accumulated so far, we would hypothesize that the mother's emotional availability is essential if the child's autonomous ego is to attain optimal functional capacity. If the mother is "quietly available" with a ready supply of object libido, if she shares the toddling adventurer's exploits, playfully reciprocates and thus helps his attempts at imitation and identification, the relationship between mother and toddler progresses to the point where verbal communication takes over, even though vivid gestural behavior, that is, affecto-motility, still predominates. The predictable emotional participation of the mother seems to facilitate the rich unfolding of the toddler's thought processes, reality testing and coping by the end of the second or the beginning of the third year. The toddler's "shadowing" at fifteen to twenty months of age seems obligatory to an extent, except in the cases of those mothers who, by their protracted doting and intrusiveness due to their own symbiotic-parasitic needs, become themselves the "shadowers" of the child. In normal cases, a slight shadowing by the toddler after the hatching process gives way to object constancy toward the end of the third year. However, the less emotionally available the mother has become at the time of the above-described rapprochement, the more insistently and even desperately does the toddler attempt to woo her. In some cases, this process drains so much of the available developmental energy that, as a result, not enough neutralized energy may be left for the evolution of the many ascending functions of the ego.

In Peter's case his mother's second pregnancy as well as his weaning occurred at the height of the symbiotic phase. His mother, Mrs. C, joined our project when Peter was a little over nine months old. He crawled to his mother frequently and clamored to be taken on her lap; he seemed to need contact and steady "refueling" by his mother. This occurred before he began gracefully practicing the preliminaries of upright locomotion, short of walking, a period in which he, like the other infant toddlers, seemed completely happy and self-sufficient. Peter's earlier approach behavior, occurring prematurely before the upright locomotor practicing period, had been due to his mother's conspicuous emotional aloofness, At eleven to thirteen months, Peter was carrying out motor feats which surpassed those of the other children in his age group and which were admired by everyone, but were only taken for granted by his mother. After he had finally mastered active locomotion, his mother did not respond to his renewed active wooing. Thereupon Peter proceeded to adopt more and more exaggerated voiceless devices to appeal to her. Even during the hot summer months, he would perspiringly carry heavy toys in both arms up to his mother as quasi-"offerings," but to no avail. The exaggerated character and the repetitiveness of this approach over a period of weeks was obviously symptomatic and overdetermined. In it were incorporated elements of the mother's practice from the very beginning of substituting toys instead of herself. It contained somatopsychic elements of identification with the mother's far-advanced gravidity as Mrs. C. smilingly interpreted herself. Peter's symptomatic behavior also contained elements of compliance with his mother's conscious and unconscious wish that her son be big and strong (he was rather puny). Finally, it also contained elements of primitive defense.

If an appeal for comfort or reaching out for contact goes unheeded, the child seeks substitutions. In our study, we observed that the substitution used most frequently was eating, rather than autoerotic sucking activities. In the home setting, the bottle retains a similar emotional meaning. But, of course, oral gratification is not an adequate substitute for emotional supplies. Wherever there is a greater than average conflict, the normal phenomenon of active wooing of the mother and pleasure in sharing with her turns into repetitive, coercive, aggressive patterns of wooing. Shadowing of the mother becomes a desperate appeal to, and pursual of, her. The toddler aggressively excludes any other goal-directed activity, or substitute comforting by any person other than the mother. In such cases, the social adaptive functions of the ego, particularly the modulated and object-related language development and synthesis of partial functions, may show a developmental lag, a disharmony or an unevenness. Somewhat stereotyped behavior such as throwing things, hitting, etc., soon follows. If this unpatterned, diffuse and aggressive behavior is not counteracted by object love, it may lead at a very early age to the toddler's turning his aggression against his own body. Under such libido-economic conditions, socially adaptive as well as autonomous ego development is less than optimal. This may mean that the child's primarily autonomous functions have become enmeshed in intrapsychic conflict.

As one would expect of a research team made up of psychoanalysts and other psychoanalytically trained workers, we are trying to understand the phenomena of the autonomous unfolding of the ego in the context of psychosexual development. In progressing from symbiosis to separate functioning, the toddler seems to show a bipolar mode of self-orientation: his own body and its functions, along with the erogenic zones, representing the landmarks of one pole; the mother representing the other pole. We have seen how the oral phase enters into the process of separation-individuation. But we get only glimpses of the anal phase, even though we know that it must contribute substantially to individuation in terms of the distinctions between inside and outside, animate and inanimate, I and non-I. In some children we are able to reconstruct with impressive accuracy the details of their very early discovery of the anatomical sexual difference.

The overlapping of oral, anal, and phallic strivings and conflicts, as well as the steps of her separation-individuation process, could be reconstructed with particular clarity in Cathy's case, because she is so eminently verbal.

On one occasion, while waiting for her mother to come for her, Cathy, then aged twenty-six months, caught sight of one of our workers seated on a low stool. In response to Cathy's question, "Why don't you go home?" the worker playfully replied that she was about to, and left the room. A few minutes later, after playfully searching for the worker, and inquiring as to her whereabouts, Cathy went toward the bathroom, saying, "Oh, she is sitting on the potty." The fact that this reasoning had its roots in the matrix of bodily functions can be inferred from the merging of the idea of the worker's disappearance with the disappearance of the cyballum; and further, from her playful transformation of a previous dramatic acting out of the idea of castration. At Cathy's age, the belief in the magic power of words and wishes is paramount. It is implied in the sequence of first her provocative question: "Why don't you go home," and then the worker's disappearance which her words had brought about and which she now playfully wished to undo.

Very early in her life Cathy and her mother had to cope with separation when her father left for the services at the beginning of Cathy's second year of life.

In Cathy's utterances and behavior we observed a striking succession of stages as she attempted to cope with the separation-individuation problem. When she was only a little more than one year old, Cathy would woo every adult who happened to enter the nursery. This was a pattern of behavior which, we now feel in retrospect, may have served her well to prevent the development of prolonged and too exclusive symbiosis with her mother, during the absence of her father. The earlier indiscriminate, and seemingly quite shallow, object relationship took on a deeper and more modulated character, and became more specific toward the mother, and toward Cathy's father, upon his return when she was just two years old. At the Center, Cathy graduated at this time to the room in which the mothers of the two-year-olds take turns going out of the room and, later, out of the building. In this period, when Cathy arrived at the Center, she would invariably cling to her mother, although she did not fail at the same time to smile back at whoever happened to look at her. When Mrs. D announced for the first time that she was going to leave the building, Cathy looked momentarily distressed, but then quickly took to reassuring herself by repeating her mother's parting words, while she started to play. During this same period, she would playfully admonish her mother, at home, that she may go into the next room at the Center, but may not leave the building to go shopping. Only a short time later, Cathy dealt with her mother's temporary absences from the Center in a more actively playful fashion, hugging her and making a kind of exchange of snacks with her as she made ready to leave and, upon her return, greeting her with "Hi, mommy!" and smiling coyly at her (see Bowlby et al., 1952).

In a still later stage of Cathy's coping with the separation problem, the picture with regard to the mother's return became somewhat reminiscent of a reaction which we have come to know so well as a first behavioral sequelae in such a traumatic experience as, for example, a young child's temporary hospitalization. In such situations, as we know, when the mother comes to take the child back home, the child will often refuse even to acknowledge her presence as a way of punishing her for the previous act of separation. In Cathy's case, on this occasion, she rather pointedly asked, upon her arrival, about a toddler-mate who had not yet arrived; when he did, Cathy busied herself with him and did not respond to her mother's parting words. After her mother left, Cathy immediately made an aggressive attempt to wrest their jointly used toy from her toddler-mate. As this was unsuccessful, she withdrew to help herself to a large amount of pretzels and raisins, eating them all by herself. When her mother returned, Cathy paid no attention to her greeting, even though it was repeated, pretending to be too engrossed with a playmate even to hear it. It was only after several such unanswered greetings by her mother that Cathy gave up looking at her out of the corner of her eye and turned to smile squarely at her.

By contrast with Cathy, Tommy underwent great and prolonged separation anxiety. Imperceptibly but gradually, and along with a spurt in speech development, he came to accept his mother's leaving the room for increasingly extended periods and played contentedly. On such an occasion, Tommy spontaneously set up a kind of talking session with a baby group leader whom he, by then, accepted as a substitute. He earnestly related the story of "the event," for him undoubtedly symbolic of all separations: "Mommy, go away— Mommy come back—Marjie come back," and, with a sort of pride, "Tommy not cry, mommy come back."

It is amazing to observe to how great an extent, and with what resiliency, the child's autonomy unfolds from within his own ego, if only he feels a fair degree of emotional acceptance and a fair degree, of what I, for brevity's sake, would call *communicative matching* on his mother's part (see Pine and Furer, 1963). One can recognize in the toddler's increasingly concentrated, less motor-minded, and less diffuse play, in which manipulation and fantasy have become an integral part, the consolidation and organization of what shortly before were unintegrated islands of ego.

Though we have observed seeming contamination of the conflict-free sphere of the ego in Peter's case as early as in the second half of the second year, and though it was observed that this hindered the optimal unfolding of his communicative language, his capacity for substitute satisfactions, and play, it was nevertheless amazing how readily he could cope with structured situations when the mother held him quietly on her lap. We believe that a fairly satisfactory period of symbiosis saved Peter from irreversible damage, in spite of the described traumata during individuation.

In conclusion, a few words of explanation for my having chosen to share with you tonight, thoughts which are derived in part from observations made and impressions gained in a still ongoing study. I felt that we psychoanalysts are so very much habituated to seeing the results, and reconstructing the genesis, of pathological conflict solutions, that these examples of the powerful and rich adaptive faculties of the human infant, of those which are innate as well as of those acquired symbiotically, would be interesting to contemplate.

I feel that our study has already proven clinically, clearly enough, that the libidinal availability of the mother, because of the emotional dependence of the child, facilitates the optimal unfolding of innate potentialities. I have tried to demonstrate by specific instances how this factor contributes to, or subtracts from, harmonious synthesis of the autonomous functions in the service of the ego, the neutralization of drives, and sublimation, by activating or temporarily hindering the flux of developmental energy, a process, which Ernst Kris (1955) has so beautifully described. The rich abundance of developmental energy at the period of individuation accounts for the demonstrated regeneration of developmental potentialities to an extent never seen in any other period of life, except perhaps in adolescence. It illustrates the sturdiness and potential adaptive capacity of the human species and demonstrates the importance of the catalyzing influence of the love object. I hope I have succeeded in conveying what I wished to indicate in particular, the extent to which the normal infant-toddler is intent upon, and usually is also able to extract contact supplies and participation from the mother, sometimes against considerable odds; how he tries to incorporate every bit of these supplies into libidinal channels for progressive personality organization. On the other hand, I also want to point out in what predicament mothers in our culture find themselves: in spite of their own unconscious conflicts about their maternal role, and while struggling with their fantasies about the growing infant, they must nevertheless respond to the rapidly changing primary-process-dominated cues of their infant's hatching from the symbiotic membrane to become an individuated toddler.

BIBLIOGRAPHY

Alpert, A., Neubauer, P. B., & Weil, A. P. (1956), Unusual Variations in Drive Endowment. *This Annual*, XI.

Bergman, P. & Escalona, S. K. (1949), Unusual Sensitivities in Very Young Children. *This Annual*, III/IV.

Bibring, G. L., et al. (1961), A Study of the Psychological Processes in Pregnancy and of the Earliest Mother-Child Relationship. *This Annual*, XVI.

Bonnard, A. (1958), Pre-Body-Ego Types of Mental Functioning. *J. Amer. Psa. Assn.*, VI.

Bowlby, J., Robertson, J., & Rosenbluth, S. (1952), A Two-Year-Old Goes to Hospital. *This Annual*, VII.

Brody, S. (1956), *Patterns of Mothering.* New York: International Universities Press.

Coleman, R. W., Kris, E., & Provence, S. (1953), The Study of Variations of Early Parental Attitudes. *This Annual*, VIII.

Escalona, S. K. & Heider, G. M. (1959), *Prediction and Outcome. A Study in Child Development.* New York: Basic Books.

Freud, A. (1951), Observations on Child Development. *This Annual*, VI.

Freud, S. (1923), The Ego and the Id. *Standard Edition*, XIX. London: Hogarth Press, 1961.

—— (1926), Inhibitions, Symptoms and Anxiety. *Standard Edition*, XX. London: Hogarth Press, 1959.

Fries, M. E. & Woolf, P. J. (1953), Some Hypotheses on the Role of the Congenital Activity Type in Personality Development. *This Annual*, VIII.

Greenacre, P. (1958), Early Physical Determinants in the Development of the Sense of Identity. *J. Amer. Psa. Assn.*, VI.

—— (1960), Considerations Regarding the Parent-Infant Relationship. *Int. J. Psa.*, XLI.

—— (1962), The Theory of the Parent-Infant Relationship: Further Remarks. *Int. J. Psa.*, XLIII.

Hartmann, H. (1939), *Ego Psychology and the Problem of Adaptation.* New York: International Universities Press, 1958.

—— (1952), The Mutual Influences in the Development of Ego and Id. *This Annual*, VII.

—— (1953), Contribution to the Metapsychology of Schizophrenia. *This Annual*, VIII.

Hoffer, W. (1950), Development of the Body Ego. *This Annual*, V.

Jacobson, E. (1961), Adolescent Moods and the Remodeling of Psychic Structures in Adolescence. *This Annual*, XVI.

Kris, E. (1955), Neutralization and Sublimation: Observations on Young Children. *This Annual*, X.

Kris, M. (1957), The Use of Prediction in a Longitudinal Study. *This Annual*, XII.

Mahler, M. S. (1952), On Child Psychosis and Schizophrenia: Autistic and Symbiotic Infantile Psychoses. *This Annual*, VII.

—— (1957), On Two Crucial Phases of Integration Concerning Problems of Identity: Separation-Individuation and Bisexual Identity. Abstracted in Panel on Problems of Identity, rep. D. Rubinfine. *J. Amer. Psa. Assn.*, VI, 1958.

—— (1958), Autism and Symbiosis, Two Extreme Disturbances of Identity. *Int. J. Psa.*, XXXIX.

—— (1961), On Sadness and Grief in Infancy and Childhood: Loss and Restoration of the Symbiotic Love Object. *This Annual*, XVI.

—— (1963), Subphases of the Separation-Individuation Process. Paper and film presented at the Annual Meetings of the American Psychoanalytic Association, St. Louis.

—— & Furer, M. (1963), Certain Aspects of the Separation-Individuation Phase. *Psa. Quart.*, XXXII.

—— —— & Settlage, C. F. (1959), Severe Emotional Disturbances in Childhood: Psychosis. In: *American Handbook of Psychiatry*, ed. S. Arieti. New York: Basic Books.

Pine, F. & Furer, M. (1963), Studies of the Separation-Individuation Phase: A Methodological Overview. *This Annual*, XVIII.

Ritvo, S. & Solnit, A. J. (1958), Influences of Early Mother-Child Interaction on Identification Processes. *This Annual*, XIII.

Spitz, R. A. (1950), Relevancy of Direct Infant Observation. *This Annual*, V.

—— (1957), *No and Yes: On the Genesis of Human Communication*. New York: International Universities Press.

—— & Wolf, K. M. (1946), The Smiling Response: A Contribution to the Ontogenesis of Social Relations. *Genet. Psychol. Monogr.*, XXXIV.

Winnicott, D. W. (1957), *The Child and the Outside World*. New York: Basic Books.

—— (1960), The Theory of the Parent-Infant Relationship. *Int. J. Psa.*, XLI.

—— (1962), The Theory of the Parent-Infant Relationship: Further Remarks. *Int. J. Psa.*, XLIII.

STUDIES OF THE SEPARATION-INDIVIDUATION PHASE

A Methodological Overview

FRED PINE, Ph.D. and MANUEL FURER, M.D. (New York)

Some time ago, Mahler (1952) advanced the hypothesis that in certain predisposed children the maturational spurt of locomotion and other autonomous ego functions, with a concomitant lag in emotional readiness for functioning separately from the mother, causes organismic panic. This panic is followed by arrest in ego development and fragmentation of the ego and eventuates in the clinical picture of symbiotic child psychosis. In later writings, Mahler (1957, 1958; Mahler, Furer, and Settlage, 1959) has suggested that there is a *normal* and *universal* separation-individuation phase in childhood that confronts every child with certain potential crises. But, in contrast to the symbiotic psychotic child, the normal toddler has an amazing capacity "to extract contact supplies and participation from mother" (Mahler, 1963) while growing away from the symbiosis with her, and thus usually to deal with these crises effectively.

Earlier studies of separation of infant from mother (e.g., Spitz, 1945, 1946a, 1946b) had indicated the traumatic force of certain separation experiences and their disturbing effects on personality

This work is being conducted at the Masters Children's Center, 75 Horatio Street, New York 14, N.Y. The work with the symbiotic psychotic children has been supported by a grant from the National Institute of Mental Health, USPHS (Project M-3353, Margaret S. Mahler, M.D. and Manuel Furer, M.D., Principal Investigators). Funds making possible the study of normal children, and their comparison with the psychotic children, were generously provided by the Psychoanalytic Research and Development Fund, the Taconic Foundation, the National Association for Mental Health, and, earlier, by the Field Foundation.

Dr. Pine is, since September 1962, at the Psychology Laboratory, Department of Psychiatry, State University of New York, Downstate Medical Center, Brooklyn, N.Y. Dr. Furer is Medical Director, Masters Children's Center.

development. This work had focused primarily on a particular kind of separation experience: the infant was physically separated from the mother, often for long periods, for reasons beyond the infant's control. The child was passive in relation to the separation. The present study, in contrast, attempts to define a separation process in which the child plays a more active role, a process that is a prerequisite for normal development. The normal separation-individuation process involves *the child's achievement* of separate functioning *in the presence of the mother* while the child is continually confronted with *minimal* threats of object loss. In contrast to situations of traumatic separation, this normal separation-individuation process takes place in the setting of a developmental readiness for and pleasure in independent functioning made possible by the continual libidinal availability of the mother (Mahler, 1963). Separation and individuation are conceived of as two complementary developments —the one consisting of the child's emergence from a symbiotic fusion with the mother (cf. Mahler, 1952) and the other consisting of those achievements marking the child's assumption of his own individual characteristics.

We currently have two interrelated research projects in process at the Masters Children's Center in New York City, each bearing on the separation-individuation phase. The first is a study of the natural history of symbiotic child psychosis. Mahler has attempted to illustrate the failure of these children to meet the developmental crises of the separation-individuation phase (e.g., 1952, 1961). The second project is a study of normal toddlers from six months of age through the third year, the general age period of the separation-individuation phase. Thus, the over-all research is set up so that we can study two groups of children: (1) toddlers who are presumably going through the separation-individuation phase normally, and (2) symbiotic psychotic children (from three to five years of age) in whom something presumably went awry during this same phase. The present paper will describe the general methodology of the study in relation to the issues under investigation.

Historically, the work began with studies of symbiotic psychotic children and led to hypotheses about events presumed to have taken place during the separation-individuation phase. It then seemed wise to take a firsthand look at these events as they occur normally. This led into the study of the normal toddlers. One of the broad issues that we were interested in investigating was the relation between the separation-individuation process, the development of ego functions in the setting of particular mother-child relationships, and the psychosexual stages of early development.

While, historically, the psychotic children were studied first, at present the work with the two groups of children shows a good deal of interchange back and forth. For example, at an earlier period we became interested in the preferred modalities of communication between the individuating child and his mother. In the study of symbiotic psychosis, gaps in the communication process wherein mother and child could not respond to each other's signals and cues —a "communicative mismatching"—were a recurrent phenomenon. This led us to turn to intensive observation of the process of signaling and cueing between mother and child in the normal toddlers. The richly varied material that we gathered in that study brought into focus the crucial importance of mother-child intercommunication for the *successful achievement* of normal individuation. This in turn highlighted the possible importance of communication failures in the development of the psychosis as well as in the symptom picture.

As we conceive of it now, the cues and signals between mother and child are particularly important for the resolution of the normal crises of the separation-individuation phase. The very young child can sustain some degree of separation from his mother only if he is able to come into contact and communication with her when he needs it. This requires an increasingly complex and finely differentiated set of interactions between mother and child so that they can keep in close communication with each other even while the child becomes more and more of a separate individual.

We are now in a position to observe the normal limits of the misperception of cues in our normal mother-toddler group and the more extreme distortions in the psychotic group. It is certainly true that the normal mothers can more readily "read" their children than can the mothers of the symbiotic psychotic children, and that the normal children are easier to read. But there are similarities, some perhaps even more important, between the psychotic children and normal toddlers as well—for example, prior to speech development in the normal toddlers, communication in both is of course nonverbal. And it is also true that there is some communicative mismatching even in these normal mother-child pairs, though it does not reach such proportions or such rigidity that mother and child cannot adapt to each other's mode of signaling and responding. The limits of the normal range of such communication failures requires a good deal of further study.

SETTING AND GENERAL METHOD

At present, in our therapeutic work with the symbiotic psychotic children, each child is seen together with his mother by a therapist, the three together in the same room. Each child-mother pair is seen from three to five days a week in sessions that range from one and a half to two hours. The purpose of our seeing mother and child together was indicated in a general way by Mahler and Furer in an earlier paper (1960). While the overwhelming symbiotic needs of these children make it necessary for them to have an intimate and personal tie with a single adult, this tie must ultimately be to the mother with whom, in contrast to the therapist, they must sustain a lifelong relationship. But the tie to the mother is often best effected through the therapist. There are phases in the treatment when the child's symbiotic demands are heightened to a degree not readily accepted by most mothers, especially from these children who are no longer infants, and the therapist must absorb some of these demands, help the child to relive (and to develop beyond) the symbiotic phase, and to form an attachment to the mother to which she can respond. While the children are, as noted, typically seen together with mother and therapist in a single room, this is not always the case. Certain clinical considerations supervene from time to time so that we must see the child without the mother. These include the emotional readiness of the mother to receive and respond to emerging demands for contact from the child and her capacity to understand and integrate interpretations that have to be given to the child.

Our material on the symbiotic psychotic children derives from the following sources: (a) daily reports of the therapists; (b) reports of the supervising psychiatrists (including reports of weekly interviews with the mother, observations of the child, and weekly conferences with the therapist); (c) reports of the social worker about her weekly or twice weekly interviews with the mother, and with the father in special instances when changing intrafamilial dynamics requires that he be seen; (d) monthly summaries concerning the therapeutic progress of the mother-child pair as well as the parents' progress; (e) minutes of the weekly clinical conferences. In addition, we have nonparticipant observations and psychological test reports of the children and their mothers. At weekly research meetings this material is evaluated and areas for further investigation are sorted out.

The work with the normal toddlers takes place in a playroom setting where a group of babies and their mothers are free to talk, play, and interact as they please. We want, and have apparently succeeded in creating, a situation where the spontaneous day-to-day relationship of mother to child can be observed in a natural setting. The playroom has a smaller area reserved as a sitting room for the mothers, in which they chat, sip coffee or read—and from which they have a full view of and free access to the children. There is another large area that has many attractive and colorful toys, and the children tend to move back and forth freely between the toy area, the section where the mothers generally sit, and all other parts of the room. The mother-child separation is by no means complete in the physical arrangements of the room; it is quite unlike the school situation, e.g., where the mother gives over charge of her child to the teacher for a period. It is more like an outdoor playground setting where the children play where they please while the mothers sit on benches and talk—with their children in full view and with the opportunity to attend to whatever mothering is required of them.

While there is no doubt that these mothers, who are aware that they are part of a research project, must to some extent be influenced in their behavior by such awareness, nonetheless we have been impressed by the great variety of seemingly quite natural behaviors that we have been able to observe. Indeed, with mothers and children seen for four mornings a week over a period of years and often with second (and even third) children, it would be hard to maintain that they show only a pose and an unrepresentative sample of their behavior with their children in the periods during which we observe them.

Our task in setting up the study of the normal toddlers was to obtain material comparable to that already obtained from the therapeutic action research program with the psychotic group. We therefore have psychoanalytically trained workers (each of whom participates now or has participated in the past in the therapy project) interview the mother of a normal toddler each week and observe the mother-toddler interaction. We have found that this procedure gives us valuable material even from these normal mothers who are not explicitly motivated by a need for treatment. As the material from these interviews has been studied in our research conferences, we have been able to focus our investigation on areas that are most comparable to the material from the treatment group.

We have material available from the notes of participant observers (the two toddler-group leaders) and from nonparticipant observers, from the interviews described above and from repeated testing of the children. This material, too, is discussed and assessed at our weekly research conferences and set in relationship to the material from the psychotic group.

SOME RESEARCH STRATEGIES

How to deal with the mass of data available? We have employed a variety of research strategies, attempting to explore in whatever way possible the issues under study. We have neither committed ourselves to the (soon apparent) impossibility of systematically treating all of the clinical data, nor have we limited ourselves to any too-discrete single mode of study that might blind us too much to that which may be of interest. We have used clinical approaches where seemingly appropriate—quantifiable approaches where workable—in each case varying and modifying our strategies where the phenomena or methodological difficulties required it.

Clinical Work. By far our greatest expenditure of time and effort has been in the observation of both the normal and the symbiotic psychotic children and their mothers, in attempts to formulate the dynamics of the mother's and the child's functioning and of their relationship to each other, and in minute and regular observations of developmental and therapeutic changes. The clinical observations, and the clinical research conferences based upon them, have been our major source thus far of new formulations. Through them we have come to learn of a pathological equilibrium of the symbiotic psychotic child and his mother (abandonment by the mother of her maternal commitment to the symbiotic demands of the child complemented by secondary autistic withdrawal by the child who then makes only minimal demands); and we have come to see, as described earlier, the communicative mismatching between the symbiotic psychotic child and his mother with each unable to respond to the other's cues, and the parallel misperception of cues within normal limits in the normal mother-toddler pairs; and we have come to see the significance for the normal mother of the increasing individuation of her child, an event requiring a developmental step in motherhood wherein the mother must prepare herself for the coming separation of the child from his symbiotic tie to her (cf. Mahler, 1963; Mahler and Furer, 1963).

The clinical explorations have thus far been highly productive of new, though untested hypotheses. Many of our formulations stem from observations that we did not anticipate in advance and that impressed themselves on us with particular clarity and force. We have tried to balance our approach to the data with more focused research strategies (see below), and the early clinical observations and discussions have provided a basis for developing some trial attempts at this in both the clinical and the quantitative work.

The clinical work confronts us with so many data on each child and each child-mother pair that we can barely cover the material in conferences, pin it down, and work with it, before new ideas are thrust forward by new clinical observations. And yet, at the same time, there are constant gaps in our information that prevent our following through more fully on specific hunches, and that require us continually to seek new modes of access to new information. One reason for the gaps in our information about the children is clear: we work in a research setting and not an analytic situation. While we are doing a good deal more than straightforward observation of natural life events, we do not get the kind of data in depth that are produced in psychoanalysis.

Our research setting offers us certain distinct advantages, however. It permits us to see phenomena that are not ordinarily observable during analysis. We do not here get unconscious fantasies of the mother, but we do have a chance to see the mother-child relationship in actual process. This special situation of clinical observation leads us to special kinds of data and hypotheses. In addition, the fact that at least our normal mother-baby pairs are not in any formal treatment at the research project has the advantage that we do not essentially change the phenomena we are studying in the very act of studying them—at least not to the same extent that observation through psychoanalysis does this. These mothers are certainly a special group, but, so far as we can determine, their patterns of mothering do not basically change through their contact with us during the period that we study them, although certain developments and changes in their attitudes during the subphases of their infant-toddler's progress in the course of separation-individuation must be taken into account (Mahler, 1963; Coleman, Kris, and Provence, 1953).

Because of the potential bias in the more open and impressionistic kinds of clinical work, and because of the presence both of floods of data and of gaps in what we do have, we are currently attempting more systematic modes of data collection within the general setting of the clinical work. We drew from our clinical notes and impressions a set of areas that seemed to us important to pursue further. Each interviewer and observer was then asked to amass data in these areas for each child and mother seen in both the normal and psychotic groups. Our hope is that the collection of these data in specified areas will simultaneously limit the clinical data at hand and give more complete coverage in these few areas.

The areas cover certain general points: (1) significant family events; (2) conspicuous aspects of the mother's behavior; (3) the child's relationship to his father—something that we do not ordinarily have the opportunity to see in process at the research center; (4) typical and exaggerated behavior of the child; and (5) differences between the child's behavior at home and at the research center. They also cover specific central aspects of the very young child's life: (6) feeding behavior; (7) toilet training; (8) discovery of the anatomical sexual difference; (9) separation anxiety and stranger anxiety; (10) imitative behavior; (11) speech development; and (12) the sleep pattern. Lastly, two additional areas of particular interest have emerged from our present and past work: (13) the child's and the mother's reaction to significant locomotor advances in the child; and (14) the mother's self-preparation for her child's separation from her as he grows older.

Our aim was to arrive from these data at formulations concerning the role in the separation-individuation process of certain commonly observed phenomena in very young children. Mahler's (1952) work on the role of locomotor advance in precipitating crises at this phase, and our comments earlier in this paper on the function of cueing and communication in maintaining mother-child contact while separation increases, are examples of this approach.

In the treatment of the symbiotic psychotic children some of our important advances in understanding have come where difficulties arose in the communication process between the child and his mother on the one hand and the research group on the other. Thus, it was a difficulty in making interpretations to certain of the psychotic children in the presence of their mothers that led us to see the need to keep the mother out of the therapy room at critical points in spite of our general conviction that her presence is necessary. And again, it was the withdrawal of certain children from treatment by the mothers that led us to see the pathological equilibrium of the mother-child relationship described above; as the therapy freed the child to some extent from his secondary autistic withdrawal, and as he subsequently made renewed symbiotic demands upon the mother, the mother terminated the treatment.[1]

The problems which arise in the work with the normal mother-toddler pairs are somewhat different from those arising in the research with the symbiotic psychotic group. Here we have to tread a cautious line between having the mothers withdraw from the project in disinterest or fear (since they are volunteers, not coming for therapy, with no explicitly sought therapeutic gain in coming) and having them get too involved with the group leaders or with their interviewers, making demands that cannot be met in the nontherapy

[1] We can well understand the mother's plight when a child, now perhaps four or five years of age, makes the symbiotic demands for intimate physical contact and all-absorbing attention more characteristic of infants, and ordinarily characteristic of only *brief* periods in the infant's day at that. It becomes imperative for the therapist to absorb some of this symbiotic claim so that the mother will not be overwhelmed by it.

research setting. In actual fact, recently we have found the mothers to be quite committed to the group, deriving certain satisfactions from it (in terms of social contact in pleasant surroundings), and yet quite reticent and at times reluctant to give information in certain sensitive areas—a reticence that, in these persons who are not coming for treatment, we must learn to live with.

Behavior Ratings. As noted, the clinical observations and discussions provided a basis for some initial attempts at quantifiable approaches to the data. In our initial broad approach, all of the normal toddlers and their mothers as well as all of the symbiotic children and their mothers were at first observed and rated on a set of fifty-eight variables by nonparticipant observers working together in pairs. The variables were culled from earlier clinical notes. A series of three half-hour observations was made by a pair of raters on each child before they made a final rating of the child on each variable. The series of three observations was repeated at a later point when the child was several months older to make possible the assessment of developmental changes. Preliminary scanning of these ratings has shown excellent interrater reliability, and the preliminary analyses of the data suggest that the ratings pick up significant aspects of the individual mother-child interaction. Similar observations and ratings were initially being carried out with both groups of children so that comparisons would be possible, though this has since changed (see below).

What are the variables? One set has bearing on the development of object relationship: the child's reaction to his mother, to other adults, to other children, and to inanimate objects. This includes time spent with the mother, spatial position in relation to her, and preferred sensory modalities of communication between mother and child. We also study the amount and the quality of the mother's comforting and the child's receptiveness to it; the range of comforting behaviors available to the mother in her contacts with the child, and the degree of manipulativeness of her comforting. We study also the nature of the child's appeal to the mother for comforting, and the degree to which he can sustain this appeal in the face of delay by mother in providing it. In general, we are studying a variety of modes of approach and contact between mother and child for their bearing on the separation-individuation process.

A second set of variables culled from our participant and non-participant observational notes and impressions relates to the development of ego functions which have for us some indicator value about the course of the separation-individuation process. This includes signaling-communication and motor functions. The first of these bears on the communication processes necessary for maintaining contact between mother and child even as the child becomes increasingly separate from the mother. Our interest in the second (motor development) stems initially from Mahler's hypothesis about the rapid development of locomotion which, outpacing the child's emotional readiness for separation, may be the trigger that sets off the symbiotic psychotic fragmentation of the ego. Variables related to communicative activity include the development from autoerotic to communicative use of the mouth, and some developments in language. In the latter, we examine, for example, the specificity of the child's communications and the ways in which such communication is used to appeal to the mother. Motor behavior, too, is under study; and patterns of motility (in relation to separation from the mother, to mastery of the environment, to motor grace) are assessed.

All of these issues—in mother-child interaction and in the child's development—have been translated into specific descriptive categories that are currently being rated. For example, one item is entitled "focus in motor behavior." The rater is asked to decide whether a child's motor behavior is (1) typically wandering and rarely goal-directed, (2) slightly more wandering than goal-directed, (3) slightly more goal-directed than wandering, or (4) typically goal-directed and rarely wandering. Or, in another category, entitled "success in evoking maternal response," when the child wants or needs some response or satisfactory substitute from the mother, and when the mother does not seem instantly aware of the need, the rater is asked to decide whether the child (1) ably evokes a response every time, (2) can generally though not always evoke a response, (3) can rarely evoke a response, or (4) is unable to evoke a response and seems at a loss. The general plan in the analyses of these data is to assess individual patterns of mother-child relationships and to correlate these with particular patterns of the emergence of ego functions and of their integration in the child.

To *illustrate* the nature of these data:[2] in preliminary analyses of the data for the normal mother-child pairs we find that those mothers who typically get no pleasure out of comforting their child tend, not surprisingly, to be manipulative in their efforts with the child; they also tend to respond only to the child's more explicit demands for comforting, ignoring the more subtle appeals that the child sends out. A second set of relationships in the rated variables suggests the following pattern: mothers who comfort in many different ways tend to use these diverse modes of comforting in ways that are related to *specific* needs of the child and when *the child* seems to need comforting. On the other side of the coin is a pattern where the mothers who have fewer kinds of comforting in their repertoire (*only* picking up, or *only* feeding, or *only* speaking, etc.) seem to comfort when *they* (not the child) feel the need for it, and in ways unrelated to the child's needs. A next step in the analysis of the data would be to study the relations of such patterns of mothering to the ego development of the child in the language, motor, and other rated areas. This will be done when all the data have been collected.

While this plan of study is being followed in general, a variety of complications have developed which bear consideration. This research strategy suffers from providing both too much and too little of the very specification and concreteness that the rating categories were designed to provide.

When we were initially faced with the problem of deciding how to collect comparable observations and descriptions on all of the children, we considered recording descriptions of certain kinds of behavior as they occurred, and then quantifying them in some way for comparative purposes. But it quickly became apparent that we needed more concrete specification of the "certain kinds" of behavior to be observed. And we ran into the problem of defining what were the units of a behavior sequence—when did it begin and end? Practically, collecting extensive descriptions that would later have to be codified and rated would have run us into time and financial demands not easily met. Hence we decided on the system described

---

[2] It should be emphasized that the relationships described here are illustrative only. They were suggested by analyses of data for the first few normal babies and mothers, but we do not yet know if they hold up for the total group.

above—with *a priori* descriptions of behavior possibilities (drawn from our past observations and clinical experiences) and with direct rating of a child by a rater (by having the rater simply check off one of the *a priori* descriptions rather than record observed behavior in detail). We planned that the more descriptive material, lacking here, would come from the clinical work. But such *a priori* descriptions as were used in the categories at times did not quite fit any one child in the groups studied later. Raters would then force their ratings, often into the more innocuous categories, with the result that the categories did not always differentiate adequately among the children. In addition, some ratings within categories were simply too broad and included all of the cases, allowing no ratings of the other three positions in the scales.

On the other hand, the category descriptions were often not specific enough so that each rater would consider slightly different behaviors in making his ratings of a particular child. It has certainly become clear that, the more the rating categories are spelled out in terms of observable behaviors, the more rater consensus will there be. Thus, we found it considerably easier to work with descriptions of motor patterns than with inferences about the child's reaction to internal body processes or with the development of body image. Other more subtle and more tentative research approaches have to be developed for the study of the latter.

Midway through the collection of data we eliminated those categories which did not permit the raters to differentiate among the children and in which interrater reliability was low (i.e., when raters could not agree on what a child was like). Eliminating the poorest categories on these counts meant dropping out about one fourth of the original fifty-eight categories. We are currently working with the remainder.

The elimination of the poorer categories by no means solved all of our problems. The rapid developmental changes taking place in the normal toddlers created other problems for the behavior ratings with that group. We cannot take a picture of a child if he won't hold still. And hold still he won't. New developments are constantly taking place, and the variations from moment to moment even within the course of a day (say, with fatigue or hunger) are great. Moving pictures, yes; but a photograph, no. And yet the rating procedure is relatively static. It cannot show all of these moment-to-moment variations or the dynamics of change. We initiated more frequent observations and ratings (bimonthly, within the limits of our staff facilities), but even these give no more than a series of relatively static descriptions of the child, and we replaced them with continuing observations of specific behavior of interest to us.

If, in the clinical work, the processes of information-gathering and of discovery are temporally closely linked for the researcher, in these behavior ratings and subsequent correlational analyses the two are far apart. When ratings are collected for even a dozen children over a year or two, there is a long delay between any specific rating and the final correlational analyses carried out when all of the data are in. While, in some research settings, this delay need not be a problem, we have found it to be a major problem here because it makes it difficult to compare the quantitative findings with the clinical events at any specific moment. Our research, based, we had hoped, on a cross-fertilization between more clinical and more quantitative procedures, has not always had such cross-fertilization because of the delay required to carry through the formal research design. It is true that the clinical and quantitative data may mutually enrich each other at a later date, when all analyses are completed; but for the present we have been trying to bring the clinical and quantitative work closer together—through use of ratings in conjunction with clinical case studies, and currently through written descriptions of the observed phenomena on which ratings are based —with greater degrees of success.

Once again, as in the clinical work, some of our early findings with the behavior ratings were made where there was a break in the information-gathering process. Take, for example, the ratings of the several categories having to do with the child's appeals to his mother for aid and the mother's comforting of her child; the raters often found themselves unable to rate these categories as the babies in the normal group grew older because the relevant behaviors just were not observed—an indication of the not-surprising fact that at least the child's gross appeals to the mother (in a playgroup setting) and her comforting of him became less frequent as the child grows from late in the first year of life to late in the second year.

A considerably more problematic rating difficulty arose with the symbiotic psychotic children. Here, the rater (like the mothers in many instances) could not tell when (and if) the child was appealing to the mother or the therapist. How to interpret some of the stereotyped behavior patterns of the psychotic children? When as appeals? When as discharge phenomena? When as magical restitutive behavior? Or what? We have gradually come to see more clearly the need to decode specific behaviors in the psychotic children before relying on specific rating procedures for them. Problems such as these have made it necessary for us to go back to the clinical phenomena to refine the rating categories for these psychotic children, making them more fitting to the observed behaviors. We are no longer rating the psychotic children on the variables described above, but are instead attempting to discover just what variables can be rated.

Comparative Observations of the Children in the Mothers' Presence and Absence. Another avenue of study involved an experimental and observational procedure. The level of functioning of children in both groups was observed and evaluated when their mothers were present and when they were absent. We were interested in the extent to which certain achievements are maintained by the child in the mother's absence. In which children is ego functioning not impaired in the mother's absence, and in which areas? Here, with brief separations of the child from the mother, we hoped to study the dependence of the child's functioning on the physical presence of the mother.

We assessed six areas: play, attention span, understanding and use of language, and gross and fine motor skills. Raters were asked to judge whether the level of functioning in each of these areas is higher or lower in the mother's presence than in her absence, according to criteria that were spelled out in a rating manual. If such changes in functioning are found in the mother's absence, it still remains for us to draw on our clinical material to explain them. Developmental tests of the children in the toddler group were matched with these six areas so that we could explore the question whether those functions which the child has developed to a higher level are retained better in the mother's absence than are less fully mastered ego functions.

This work was initially set up in an attempt to create a relatively compact, and yet meaningful, experimental situation—varying only the presence of the mother and gauging changes in the child's reaction (presumably referable to the mother's presence or absence). The problem with young toddlers, however, is that no sooner is the mother out of the room than the mothers of other children and the two toddler-group leaders markedly change in their handling of the child. They become more watchful and nurturant; in short, they assume the maternal function. In the symbiotic psychotic children, when the mother is absent, the relationship of the therapist to the child also changes markedly at times—the therapist becoming more closely engaged with the child. Thus, more than the mother's presence varies, and it is difficult to refer specific changes in the child solely to the presence or absence of the mother. But in spite of this, the method gives some interesting observations which are relatively comparable for all of the children.

In the normal toddlers, for example, the children not only worsen but also improve in certain kinds of functioning in the mother's absence, and also change in the quality of their functioning. In any of these cases there is a suggestion that the child's functioning is not yet autonomous but draws in some way upon the mother for its enhancement or impairment. Thus, one child—a child whose gross motor (locomotor) behavior is highly developed for his age, and whose mother has always nurtured and valued that behavior— falls off in the level of his gross motor behavior when the mother is absent. This child has always obliged the mother by performing well, in the way that she wanted, but such performance still seems dependent on the mother's presence to some extent. At what point will motor excellence become autonomous (Hartmann, 1939) in the sense that it is maintained even in the mother's absence?[3]

Another child, in sharp contrast, had a motor pattern that was typically aimless and wandering; he fell often, and hard, without a whimper. His mother had a hand's-off policy in many aspects of her son's care, refusing to frustrate him, neglecting to support bowel and bladder control, ignoring his many hard falls. His aimless motor

[3] The motor apparatus has a certain primary autonomy, yet can be, to some extent, drawn into conflict and into motive patterns. The final achievement of secondary autonomy seems to be to some degree dependent upon the mother-child relationship and the child's endowment (Hartmann, 1939).

behavior seemed to lack in internal direction what he lacked in direction from his mother. But this behavior, too, seemed to be associated with the physical presence of his mother; in her absence he improved in his gross motor behavior—falling less, for example, and becoming somewhat more goal-directed. This close link between his motor functioning and his relationship to his mother perhaps foreshadowed the later improvement in motor functioning that came when the mother-child relationship changed. When verbalization developed in the child, and the mother was able to use this medium of communication to provide a more focused and organizing care, the child showed a developmental gain not only in the verbal area but also in the motor area.

In the symbiotic psychotic children, other phenomena were observed. As has been pointed out previously (Mahler, Furer, Settlage, 1959), these children often show a secondary regression to autistic mechanisms. In our observations, a psychotic child in whom autistic mechanisms currently predominated showed almost no reaction to the mother's absence. It was extremely difficult for observers to make differential descriptions of the child's level of functioning when mother was present or absent; she behaved at both times according to certain stereotyped autistic patterns. Another psychotic child by contrast, one in whom symbiotic mechanisms were currently strong, showed a marked reaction to the mother's absence—his behavior in the two situations (mother present, mother absent) being markedly different. Thus, in the psychotic children, the reaction to the experimental variation of the mother's presence may itself be an indicator of the degree to which autistic or symbiotic mechanisms predominate. (Similar phenomena are seen in the normal babies. At certain subphases of the separation-individuation phase there is normally a quite intense reaction to the mother's absence, whereas in other subphases the pleasure in exercising the function then ascendant seems to render the child relatively oblivious to the mother's temporary absence.)

SUMMARY

We have described an interconnected group of studies bearing upon the separation-individuation process. The settings that we have evolved for observing children—a specially planned playroom for

normal toddlers and a therapeutic situation for psychotic children—
were described. While we are convinced that these observational
settings offer rich possibilities for research, our experience is that a
changing array of research strategies best allows us to take advantage
of these possibilities. We have presented here some of our research
strategies, some problems that they presented, some incidental findings that grew out of these very problems, and some illustrative
findings.

BIBLIOGRAPHY

Coleman, R. W., Kris, E., & Provence, S. (1953), The Study of Variations of Early
Parental Attitudes. *This Annual,* VIII.
Hartmann, H. (1939), *Ego Psychology and the Problem of Adaptation.* New York:
International Universities Press, 1958.
Mahler, M. S. (1952), On Child Psychosis and Schizophrenia: Autistic and Symbiotic
Infantile Psychoses. *This Annual,* VII.
—— (1957), On Two Crucial Phases of Integration Concerning Problems of Identity:
Separation-Individuation and Bisexual Identification. Paper read at American
Psychoanalytic Association.
—— (1958), Autism and Symbiosis, Two Extreme Disturbances of Identity. *Int. J. Psa.,*
XXXIX.
—— (1961), On Sadness and Grief in Infancy and Childhood: Loss and Restoration of
the Symbiotic Love Object. *This Annual,* XVI.
—— (1963), Thoughts about Development and Individuation. *This Annual,* XVIII.
—— & Furer, M. (1960), Observations on Research Regarding the "Symbiotic Syndrome" of Infantile Psychosis. *Psa. Quart.,* XXIX.
—— —— (1963), Certain Aspects of the Separation-Individuation Phase. *Psa. Quart.,*
XXXII.
—— —— & Settlage, C. F. (1959), Severe Emotional Disturbances in Childhood: Psychosis. In: *American Handbook of Psychiatry,* ed. S. Arieti. New York: Basic Books.
Spitz, R. A. (1945), Hospitalism. *This Annual,* I.
—— (1946a), Hospitalism: A Follow-up Report. *This Annual,* II.
—— (1946b), Anaclitic Depression. *This Annual,* II.

ASPECTS OF PASSIVITY AND EGO DEVELOPMENT IN THE BLIND INFANT

ANNE-MARIE SANDLER (London)

Work with blind children (who have been born blind or have gone blind soon after birth) has been going on for a number of years at the Hampstead Clinic, and has resulted in the accumulation of a number of observations on their behavior and development. The children observed have been members of a blind nursery group, together with a small number of cases in analytic treatment. An additional few children (mostly of prenursery school age) have been seen in their own homes. Some of the observations made have been reported by Dorothy Burlingham (1961), who has discussed various aspects of the personality development of blind children as compared with sighted. Burlingham's paper describes the broad framework within which this present study is set.

The ideas reported here have been prompted by direct observations made by the author in the Hampstead Blind Nursery, and by the discussion and classification of indexed observations recorded by the members of the Blind Study Group. A direct stimulus was the difficulty which was encountered in the recording of appropriate and meaningful observations on very young blind children. Although psychoanalytic theory provides us with a basic frame of reference for making and assessing our observations, we lack a specific theory which would account for the peculiarities of the blind child's development. This paper attempts to provide a tentative theoretical

Acknowledgments are due to the staff of the Nursery Group for the Blind at the Hampstead Child-Therapy Clinic, and to the members of the Study Group for Problems of the Blind led by Mrs. Dorothy Burlingham. In particular a debt is owed to Miss Doris Wills who has contributed much to the discussions which finally led to this paper.

The Nursery Group for the Blind is maintained by the Grant Foundation, New York. Analyses of several blind children are financed by the Psychoanalytic Research and Development Fund, Inc., New York.

model relating to an aspect of the behavior of the child who is born blind, or who has gone blind soon after birth. The conclusions reached here are based on the observation of a very small number of children, as well as on case reports in the literature. Without some sort of theory, observation will of necessity tend to be rather random and not systematically directed toward the crucial data. After a certain point observation cannot be rewarding without theoretical formulations which will focus these observations and lead to a progressive modification and refinement of our hypotheses.

It is very understandable that there is a tendency for workers in this field, and the parents of blind children, to attempt to minimize, quite unconsciously, the differences between the blind and sighted. This process is fostered by the fact that blind children will use the vocabulary of the sighted, and their education is directed toward making them as much like sighted children as possible. The blind child, in his effort to comply, will often eagerly assimilate the words and phrases of the sighted world, in complete ignorance of their deeper meaning. There is a sort of unconscious collusion between sighted adult and blind child. As Burlingham has pointed out (1961): "The children evidently fear to display the inadequacy of their functioning of which they are aware dimly and therefore make every effort to conform. The mother's wishes certainly go in the same direction."

The hypothesis which will be elaborated here is that practically from the very beginning, because of the absence of a major sensory modality, the ego development of the blind child will tend to proceed along different lines from that of the sighted. The present study is based on the premise that the ego development of the blind child is hindered or distorted by his sensory handicap. To understand the blind child at any age necessitates taking into account the whole history of his development. Thus the peculiarities and limitations of the blind have to be assessed in terms of (a) their present sensory defect, and (b) the effect on their progressive development of their having been blind from birth.

On entering the Hampstead Blind Nursery (this has also been reported by observers at many other institutions for the blind) one is soon struck by a phenomenon which seems to be characteristic of most blind children as compared with sighted children of the same age. This phenomenon is the tendency of these children, no matter how much they are stimulated by their teachers, to lack any sort of real creative drive toward, or interest in, the progressive mastery of the outside world.

Winifred, aged six, had asked me to bring my handbag to the nursery with some special surprises in it. When I did this, she showed delight and eagerly emptied the bag. Although she did this deftly and skillfully, once the bag had been explored she appeared to withdraw attention from it and its contents, and simply sat silently, tapping her face and the table in a repetitive way. No amount of suggestion that she play further with the contents of the bag had any effect.

Georgina, aged five and a half, had developed a game in which she played the role of a mother who went shopping with her baby in a pram. She played this game on several occasions, with little variation, but would abandon this activity whenever she came into contact with anything which remotely resembled a bottle. She would then sit in the pram on her own, sucking the bottle and rocking slightly. At times she would rub her eyes, and was perfectly contented to be pushed around in the pram until she had to leave. It appeared that, given the chance, she would be content to be pushed around in the pram indefinitely.

Percy, aged four, showed some interest in a guitar the teacher had brought to the nursery. He explored it and twanged the strings. When the teacher slackened her own attention, he immediately stopped exploring the guitar, put his head on his knees, and began rocking.

It appears that many of these children are abnormally content to be left alone, and to indulge in repetitive self-stimulating movements or stereotyped nonadaptive activities. Strenuous efforts on the part of the teacher may often elicit the cooperation of these children, and they may even appear to enjoy such activities as group games, but this enjoyment is rather shallow, and the moment the teacher's efforts slacken, they appear to sink back into a state of lethargy. In playing "Ring-a-ring-o'-roses," a substantial effort may be required on the part of the teachers to persuade the children to rise again once they have fallen down. Their progression as a response to the teacher's pressure is a temporary one, and what we see in most of these children is a constant and powerful pull back to self-centeredness, a limiting of their interest in the outside world, and a turning toward the experiencing of bodily sensations of one sort or another.[1] Gesell (1953) speaks of the blind infant as being wrapped up in his subjective self, and this is indeed an appropriate description. Burlingham (1961) also refers to "a passive attitude which seems as natural to the blind child as it is his greatest danger."

It seems that it is not only the simple lack of sight which operates to bring about this sort of absence of creative drive or interest in the outside world. The peculiar "pulling back" which so many blind children show has to be accounted for in terms of the aftereffects of their special developmental vicissitudes. The view taken here is that the self-centeredness and passivity of the blind child are rooted in a specific ego deformation which occurs as a consequence of a divergent development commencing at about the end of the first quarter of the first year of life. Briefly, the thesis to be advanced is that the development of blind and sighted children follows roughly parallel courses for about twelve to sixteen weeks after birth, but that at the time of transition from the first (predominantly passive) oral phase to the second (predominantly active) phase, the ego development of the blind child pursues a course which results in his passive self-centeredness and lack of striving toward mastery at later ages.

The discussion which follows is presented from the point of view of the child's intrapsychic development. The behavior of the child's real objects naturally affects his ego development considerably, and it is true, for example, that the common depressive reaction of the mother who discovers that her baby is blind can lead to an emotional withdrawal from her child, and that this withdrawal can have far-reaching consequences. Nevertheless, the present hypothesis is that the ego deformation resulting from the blindness occurs in its own right, and is linked with a path of development which basically cannot be reversed by the environment, although its outcome can be modified to a large extent by suitable mothering.

---

[1] It is worth noting at this point that a very few of our children appear to have developed the capacity for sustained active behavior. These exceptions to the general rule are of extreme interest, and two such children, Matthew and Daniel, will be discussed later in this paper.

The First Phase

At birth the infant responds to stimulation with relatively fixed reflex patterns. As the weeks pass he gradually learns to modify these reflex responses, and his primitive affective sensations of pleasure and pain become linked with other sensory experiences. The blind child will, as a consequence of his sensory defect, experience a narrower range of stimulation than his sighted cousin. He will have a smaller set of cues upon which to build the progressive modification of his inborn reflex responses, to increase his sensorimotor differentiation and his recognition and control of his body and the outside world. It is, of course, possible that he will cathect his smaller range of sensory cues with greater intensity. We can assume that the early memories associated with pleasure and pain will not differ grossly from those of the sighted, except that they will be limited to kinesthetic, auditory, tactile, and perhaps gustatory and olfactory spheres.

The Dominance of the Oral Zone

Although the experiences of pain and pleasure associated with tension and its relief are obviously not restricted to the oral zone, sensations arising therefrom dominate the infant in the first weeks of life. The child has a need to relieve oral tension and to gain erotic pleasure through sucking, a need which exists over and above his physiological need for food. As Fenichel (1945) remarks: "the pleasure gained from breast or bottle is based not alone on the gratification of hunger but on the stimulation of the erogenous mucous membrane as well." There is evidence (e.g., Jensen, 1932) that when the infant has stopped sucking, but is still in contact with the breast, other stimuli (such as pulling the hair or pinching a toe) will again initiate sucking. It would appear that any form of discomfort experienced by the child will, to a greater or lesser degree, increase oral tension.

The Role of Mouth, Hand, and Eye

The infant is endowed with a number of inbuilt reflex responses to facial contact which enable him to find the nipple with his mouth successfully. Since the observation of Samuel Pepys (1667) that the touching of an infant's cheek causes a turning of the head and an opening of the mouth to grasp the finger, a great many observers have described head-mouth orientation movements, occurring particularly when the infant is due for a feeding. The so-called "search reflex" or "rooting reflex" even exists prenatally (Minkowski, 1928). Thus sucking will be evoked by facial contact with breast, bottle, or the infant's own hand.

The hand is frequently brought to the face (either reflexly or accidentally), and the search reflex enables the infant to orientate his mouth to it and to suck on it successfully, i.e., with pleasure. Gradually he learns to associate pleasurable relief of oral tension with the act of bringing the hand to the mouth. By about the age of twelve weeks, as Hoffer (1949) has shown, we find the infant capable of *purposively* bringing the hand to the mouth for the gaining of oral gratification.

The child also possesses inborn reflex responses to visual stimulation. Many authors have described orientating reflex responses to visual stimuli in very young infants. Peiper (1926) demonstrated an oculo-neck reflex which is dependent upon the intensity of the visual stimulus. Chase (1937) has shown that infants as young as fifteen days followed colored moving spots. The convergence of the two eyes to produce fixation on a bright light occurs soon after birth (Gutmann, 1924). These reflexes combine to provide visual pursuit movements, termed by Tilney and Casamajor (1924) the "oculo-cephalogyric" response. In discussing this type of reflex response, Pratt (1946) points out: "The visual pursuit movements...constitute further evidence that the newborn infant possesses responses which enable it to orient to some aspects of its environment. These orientations, unlike mouth orientation, have increasing importance among the activities of the organism. Indeed here is an early manifestation of what has been termed attention."

The sight of the hand, so often brought close to the eyes, thus plays an increasingly important (though not crucial) role in the progressive refinement of the infant's coordination, particularly that of hand and mouth. Gesell and Ilg (1937) and Hoffer (1949) have commented that the infant gradually begins to suck when he sees the breast or bottle. To this must be added the stimulus value of the sight of the infant's own hand as a potential and actual source of oral gratification.

In spite of the major role played by sight in mouth-hand coordination, through the development of the capacity for visual recognition, it does not seem to be essential for the development of purposive finger and hand sucking.

Marjorie, seen first at six months of age, was said to have used her hands and fingers for comforting herself for some time past. At six months, she was observed to put her left index finger and thumb into her mouth and to suck contentedly.[2]

Kinesthetic and tactile sensations appear to be adequate at this early age to replace the sighted child's visual-kinesthetic-tactile basis for hand-mouth coordination, although visual recognition plays an increasingly dominant part in the modification of the innate reflex responses to his environment. As the infant begins to be aware of the difference between that which is always available and that which is not, he will learn that his hand can be recalled at will, while breast and bottle cannot.

The Role of Hearing

Hearing does not play a part comparable to vision at this early stage. There is evidence (e.g., Stubbs, 1934) that at birth the infant can react to sound, but there does not appear to be any innate reflex orientation to sound as there is to visual stimulation. Although after some time the child may learn to turn toward the sources of auditory stimulation, this orientation appears to be auxiliary to his visual search for the stimulus. Head movements cannot modify auditory sensations to the same degree as head and eye movements affect visual impressions. Consequently, we do not get auditory "searching" to the same degree as searching with the eyes.

THE SECOND PHASE

Until the beginning of the fourth month both the blind and sighted child are in a roughly comparable situation. In the early weeks they had been in a self-centered, undifferentiated, primary

2 All the observations on Marjorie were made by Miss C. Legg.

narcissistic state in which they felt no distinction between self and mother, simply experiencing pleasure when needs were satisfied and unpleasure when they were not. After a while the pleasurable and unpleasurable sensations were attached to excitations arising from the outside world, and primitive part-object representations began to be organized and cathected. With biological maturation and increased channeling of the drives, and as instinctual aims become less passive, the child experiences increasing frustration which constitutes a threat to his original narcissistic-omnipotent state. Frustration now acts as a spur to ego development. As Freud (1914) points out: "The development of the ego consists in a departure from primary narcissism and gives rise to a vigorous attempt to recover that state."

From this point the paths of development of the sighted and the blind child diverge more radically than before. The child enters a critical phase in his development.

The Sighted Child

At birth the mouth is the dominant grasping and searching organ. As Halverson (1938) remarks: "At birth the mouth is superior to the hand in what might be called directed activity and definiteness of function. Upon proper stimulation the mouth can both open and close and with the aid of head and neck institute a strenuous search for the stimulating object." With the beginnings of the second phase the parts played by hand and eye become increasingly important. The child gradually begins to use his hand in a more aim-directed way, for example, by placing it on breast or bottle, attempting to manipulate it actively as part of the act of feeding. He explores and grasps his mother's face, pulling it to his mouth. From being an extension of the breast *the hand now becomes an extension of the mouth, an apparatus which grasps and explores, as originally the mouth grasped and explored the breast.*

In the first phase the hand had become libidinized as a satisfying part object. Now it is further libidinized and aggressivized in its capacity as a mouth extension. Just as the mouth sought the nipple, so the hand searches for sources of stimulation. Everything that can be grasped is brought to the mouth by its servant, the hand.

Vision plays a corresponding and complementary role in this move forward. As with the hand, the eye becomes a searching and grasping organ in the service of the mouth. Even before the infant has any facility in grasping with his hand, he grasps, as Gesell, Ilg, and Bullis (1949) put it, "with eyes alone." This intrinsic property of vision is of paramount importance in initiating progressive ego development of the sighted child and his turning to the outside world.

Eye and hand begin to work in close cooperation in the second phase. As Gesell and his associates remark (1949): "in normal child development, vision early assumes and retains a directive role. Vision also serves to integrate the total action system in its multitudinous activities. To a considerable extent, the forces of integration radiate to and from the central citadel of vision." Hoffer (1949) succinctly describes the development of hand and eye function in this context. He says: "The range of activities widens rapidly during the second and third quarters of the first year, and no longer shows an exclusive preference for the oral zone . . . . the hands, after being libidinized during the intensive sucking period, now function more independently of the oral zone and are more under the influence of the eyes, playing the part of an intermediary between eyes and mouth. They have at this stage become a most active extension of the growing ego."

One might say that as the hands and eyes slowly become independent of the mouth, they become masters in their own right, whereas they had previously functioned as servants. The hands and eyes have now taken over both the libidinal and aggressive attributes of the oral drive, although the energies involved gradually become neutralized as hand and eye functions attain a relative autonomy as part of the growing ego. Exploration and mastery of the world partially replace and become independent of sucking and biting, and yield, as any observer can testify, a pleasure of its own.

The outside world gradually becomes organized and differentiated in the representational world[3] of the child, and receives increasing cathexis. *The child's center of interest becomes partially removed from his own body and his aims no longer consist exclusively of direct zonal stimulation.*

Robert, a sighted child aged eight months, manipulated his hand for long periods, keenly watching the shadow thrown by his moving hand on his bed clothes.

[3] For a discussion of the representational world, see J. Sandler and Rosenblatt (1962).

William, a sighted child of five months, accidentally struck a string of beads hanging from the side of his cot. This immediately captured his interest, and he repeated the striking action, looking with interest at the swinging beads.

All of this occurs under the pressure of the child's maturational development and the inevitable frustrations he experiences. It represents his first steps on the long journey he has to make in the attempt to recapture his original narcissistic union with his mother.

By the end of the first year the child has developed a most active attitude toward his environment and its objects, seeking to control and master through a variety of activities. His interests lie much more outside himself than before, and he exhibits a high degree of curiosity and a strong drive toward exploration of the world in which he lives. A substantial degree of differentiation between self and not-self will have occurred, and although his needs may not be immediately gratified, he will be able to retain much of his primitive narcissistic omnipotence through successful manipulation of his environment in a most active and purposeful fashion. A great deal of his skill in doing this will have been gained through his beginning capacity for imitating the important persons in his world, a capacity which is intimately bound up with knowledge gained through sight.

The Blind Child

It can be assumed that the blind child experiences the same biological changes as the sighted at about three or four months of age (making any necessary allowance for premature birth). Like the sighted child, he shows increasing sensorimotor coordination and a move from a passive to an active orientation. However, whereas in the sighted child the changes which occur are usually reflected in a turning toward the external world, in the blind this turning outward is hindered and retarded.

The retardation which occurs can be attributed to a number of factors related to the absence of sight. The blind child receives a grossly diminished quantity and variety of stimulation from the outside world. Many authors have pointed out that the fundamental activity of the sighted infant at this age is the visual exploration of his environment, his eyes moving frequently and freely, fixating on one object after another. Before the infant has any facility in reaching toward and grasping any sort of object with his hands, he is picking up objects in his physical environment with his eyes. This is denied the blind child who will as a result be without the continuity with his environment afforded by visual contact. Further, he will be deprived of the continual visual feedback of emotional response from his mother, a response which rewards and stimulates his efforts.

Unfortunately sound can only replace vision to a limited extent in the life of the blind child. As Burlingham (1961) points out, "Hearing does not seem to give the same impetus to turn toward the source of sound as sight does." The blind child will experience frustration in his attempts to follow and to make sense of auditory stimulation.

Marjorie, aged six months, was observed to react to the sound of the clock chiming, and to the noise of the curtains being drawn, by turning her head in the approximate direction of the sound, and stopping her activities. Some months later she showed no reaction at all to these sounds.

It would appear that sounds may cease to attract attention because they do not lead to meaningful action, to some sort of integration with the child's activity so that he can affect and control the stimulation. Sound will, of course, play an important role in the blind child's relationship to his mother. Because the mother responds to her child, and shows this in her handling of him, he will learn to recognize the different meanings attached to the noises made by his mother, and will learn to react to these sounds with an increasingly wide range of behavioral and vocal responses of his own.

Sound will, however, be involved in the blind baby's investigations of his immediate world, and will be part of his pleasurable activities and of primitive attempts at mastery.

Marjorie, aged seven months, was observed to be alternately scratching and rubbing her pillow, appearing to pay attention to the different sounds generated by these two activities.

Daniel, aged two and a half years, a very retarded child, was seen to shake a tinkling ball, clearly paying attention to the sound. After a while he threw the ball ahead of him and edged toward it, guided by the noise it made. This maneuver was repeated many times.

Thus it seems that the blind baby is able to make use of sounds where he can directly control them. But sounds which can (because of their relatedness to his activities) acquire meaning for the blind child will nevertheless lack the sensory continuity afforded by visual stimulation. This lack of continuity must inevitably hinder the integration of the child's sensorimotor experiences. It follows that although auditory cues help the blind baby in attaining a degree of spatial orientation (in conjunction with tactile and kinesthetic experience), and some satisfaction in mastery and exploration, their inconstancy must make the process exceedingly difficult, when compared with the sighted child who has constant visual information at his disposal. Smell and taste help the child little in attaining mastery of his environment, and will principally serve as aids to recognition.

From all that has been said, it is clear that the blind baby meets with great difficulties in regard to the thrust outward at the end of the first quarter year of life. He will experience frustration in regard to reaching, grasping, localizing, and in general to mastery of his surroundings. From the information available about blind babies studied at Hampstead, there is evidence of marked retardation. Activities such as the picking up of rattles or toys, putting the hand to the bottle in an attempt to manipulate it, and attempting to recover objects, seem to take longer to be established than in the sighted child. In his effort to make sense of the world around him the blind baby will be forced to stay close to bodily cues. He will, for example, tend to bring everything he can grasp to his mouth for a much longer period than his sighted counterpart. For the blind baby, sucking, biting, and sniffing will supplement his tactile and kinesthetic experiences, and all his activities will therefore be wedded to immediate somatic sensations.

Matthew, aged four and a half years, showed a book to a visitor. (This was a book specially made for the children with a toothbrush, sponge, etc., stuck on the pages.) He touched his mouth to each article stuck in the book, as well as fingering it. Matthew was very familiar with this book, so that touching his mouth to each article was not necessary for recognition.

Unfortunately these very bodily experiences, so important in enabling the blind child to make sense of his world, bring with them the kernel of pathology, in that they lead attention back to somatic experience. The blind child's lack of sight makes the transition from mouth grasping to hand grasping more difficult, and because of this the development of hand autonomy, with neutralization of the drives involved, will proceed to a lesser degree than in the sighted child. The hand is forced to remain subservient to direct body gratification, to remain linked with modes of satisfaction characteristic of the first phase. Thus the most meaningful avenue of exploration for the blind child remains dangerously close to direct bodily gratification and discharge. The absence of vision, which is the prime neutralizing agent in that it interposes a distance between the perception of the object and zonal stimulation, has hindered the hand in becoming an autonomous agent of the growing ego, and the pleasure of the blind child remains far more directly sensual than that of the sighted child.

As a direct consequence of the difficulties in mastery encountered by the blind child he will tend to concentrate his attention and interest on his own bodily experiences rather than on sources of external stimulation. The blind child will not be able to develop the same reservoir of neutralized energies, and thus of free and mobile attention cathexis, as the sighted child. Whatever attention cathexis he may have will be in danger of being contaminated by crudely instinctual aims, and his subsequent ego development will be accordingly distorted. The blind infant experiences a constant self-seduction.

We can conclude that the blind child may be limited as a consequence of these processes, not only by his immediate sensory handicap, but by the lack of satisfaction he can achieve from the outside world. When he does relate to the things and people around him, his relationship seems colored by his drive to direct bodily gratification. In the face of frustration he will often tend to resort to repetitive self-stimulating behavior, or to lapses into passivity, and he will have the greatest difficulty in sustaining activities which do not lead to immediate somatic stimulation and discharge.

IMPLICATIONS AND CONCLUSIONS

By the end of the first year we can see substantial individual differences in blind babies. They will have had their development influenced by limitations in their endowment (and by any superimposed brain damage), and also to a considerable degree by the maternal care they have received. But however excellent the mother's handling of her child may have been, the regressive pull toward self-centeredness and the basic retardation in ego development will always be present. On the side of drive development there will be some degree of fixation to passive instinctual aims, and on the side of the ego there will be a relative lack of neutralized energy (necessary to sustain interest in the outside world). We will generally observe a much lesser drive to mastery and to progressive adaptation than we have learned to expect in normal sighted children. It is inevitable that this must have a profound effect on later stages of development, but a discussion of later development lies outside the scope of this paper.

The commonly observed retreat into passivity—or more appropriately, the retreat from the external world—appears to differ in an important respect from the neurotic withdrawal into fantasy which, on the surface, it resembles. In the neurotic withdrawal overt activity is replaced by a proliferation of the child's fantasy life in which the child continues his forbidden activities in secret, so to speak. This fantasy life is rich in ideational content, and the objects of the child retain their full cathexis, although they are now manipulated in fantasy. It seems that in most of our blind children, on the contrary, there is a turning rather to the evocation of sensory experiences which are rich in erotic or aggressive sensations, but poor in ideational content. The mental life of these blind children will thus be much more directly related to the sensations arising from the instinctual zones, and will be connected with need satisfaction of a primitive type.

It has often been stressed that the blind baby, who ought to receive an extra amount of stimulation to make up for his lack of vision, usually receives less than he otherwise might, because of his mother's reaction to his deformity and the difficulty she experiences in making contact with him. She may lack much of the intense pride and pleasure a mother would have in a normal baby; but, in addition, whatever positive response she may have to her baby's progress, it will be generally difficult for her to communicate it successfully to him. He will not see her facial expression, her look of pleasurable expectancy, her smile or encouraging glance, and this lack of feedback will seriously affect the blind baby's achievements and pleasure in outward-directed activity.

Two children, Matthew and Daniel, observed at the Hampstead Clinic, show features which appear on the surface to contradict the formulations given above. Both Daniel (observed regularly from the age of two years eight months), and Matthew (who came to the Clinic at two years ten months, subsequently entering the blind nursery) presented the picture of very active children.

Daniel, a very backward child, could always be drawn easily into active play, and would explore his environment on his own for very long periods, making a variety of noises, or following toys which he had thrown ahead of him. However, he did show at times a marked liking for autoerotic gratification (he would, for instance, bump rhythmically against pieces of furniture). Matthew was described in his diagnostic interview as being very active, alert and interested in everything. He is reported to have always touched things spontaneously, and would touch his own body as well as his mother's with interest. He is also said to be particularly attached to his hobby horse, and will listen quietly to music for very long periods.

Unfortunately little firsthand information regarding the first year of life of these children is available. It is known, however, that the quality of the maternal care they received from very early on was extremely high. Daniel's mother is exceptionally devoted to her child, and seems to be able to tolerate a remarkable degree of body contact and play, without seducing him. He has certainly had a high degree of stimulation within a warm mother-child relationship. Matthew's mother is equally ready to do the best for her child, and is intent on making him into a normal boy. She has ceaselessly encouraged and stimulated him, and has systematically tried to offer him the means for activity whenever she observed a tendency on his part to withdraw. For example, when she noticed, toward the end of the first year, that Matthew was beginning to rub his eyes, she would place objects in both his hands so that they would be occupied.

The active behavior which could later be observed in these two children is undoubtedly related to the measures taken by their mothers. Nevertheless, careful observation of these two children at later ages has shown that they do in fact have many of the characteristics of the children who remain passive. They both show a paucity of activities which would normally come about as a result of progressive neutralization. Their activities appear to be predominantly based on their capacity to turn passive into active; and the link with direct bodily gratification, of a libidinal and aggressive nature, is usually wholly or partially retained.

Daniel, at the age of three years, would pat his tummy in the same way as his mother patted him, and has gone on to pat the walls, furniture, floor, etc. This activity is very repetitive, and does not appear to have developed further.

Matthew, aged six years, came into the nursery prancing about in imitation of the pony he had ridden on the previous day. He told us about the pony and wanted to act its movements.

A month later, another child was playing with a spinning top which Matthew very much wanted. He asked her if he could have a turn at it, but she refused. Matthew began to pout, and then got up and whirled himself round like a spinning top. (He had done this previously at "music time.")

At the age of four, Matthew wanted to play at "making tea," and said to the teacher, "You sit down and be grandma." He fetched cups and saucers, and poured water from a jug into a cup, passing it over and making polite conversation. "Do you like sugar, Grandma?" "Would you like another cup of tea?" etc. He did not seem to expect any answer, and allocated the teacher a very passive role.

Much of Matthew's activities involve a direct re-creation of pleasurable memories, nearly always in the context of his relationship to his mother.

When he was three and a half years old, Matthew swished water around noisily, spilling it all around himself and on the floor. He accompanied this with comments: "I'm doing the washing . . . handkerchiefs, pants." Without any alteration in his activities he went on to say, "I'm baking a cream cake . . . a honey cake . . . a chocolate cake."

At approximately the same age Matthew played with water and poured some into a jug. He commanded the teacher "say to him" (meaning himself) "come and show me if it has water in it." When the teacher did as instructed, he walked over to the teacher, who told him that there was still water in the jug. He then returned to the water tank and poured the water out, saying to the teacher, "Say to him—is any left, come and show me?" The teacher has noted, in reference to this episode, that Matthew showed no response when she asked him to feel in the jug to see if it contained water. It was concluded that Matthew was intent on re-creating an experience at home with his mother.

The ability of both Daniel and Matthew to be active is a great asset in their striving to maintain omnipotent control of their experiences, but the behavior of the sort described above is much more connected with maintaining their object relationships than with indicating a move in the direction of displacement from a close object tie toward normal autonomous ego achievement. The skills which they do achieve are very closely linked in their mental life to their relationship with their gratifying objects.[4] Their activity does not appear to lead to the same creativity as in the sighted child. They show impoverishment of their inner life, which leads to the relative "emptiness" of the blind, so often described in the literature.

In conclusion, there appears to be evidence that all children blind from birth shows a degree of fixation to the very earliest phase of development, in which the passive experiencing of bodily gratification is dominant. The degree to which progress toward mastery of the external environment can be made will be a function of the degree of skill shown in the material care which they receive, but it seems highly probable that the basic pull toward self-centeredness and the modes of gratification characteristic of the first phase of life will always be present.

BIBLIOGRAPHY

Burlingham, D. (1961), Some Notes on the Development of the Blind. *This Annual*, XVI.

Chase, W. P. (1937), Color Vision in Infants. *J. Exp. Psychol.*, XX.

Fenichel, O. (1945), *The Psychoanalytic Theory of Neurosis*. New York: Norton.

Freud S. (1914), On Narcissism: An Introduction. *Standard Edition*, XIV. London: Hogarth Press, 1957.

Gesell, A. (1953), Development of the Infant with Retrolental Fibroplastic Blindness. *Field of Vision*, IX.

[4] A study of the development of object relationships in blind children is in progress.

360   ANNE-MARIE SANDLER

—— & Ilg, F. L. (1937), *Feeding Behavior of Infants*. Philadelphia: Lippincott.
—— —— & Bullis, G. E. (1949), *Vision. Its Development in Infant and Child*. New York: Hoeber.
Gutmann, M. I. (1924), Über Augenbewegungen der Neugeborenen und ihre theoretische Bedeutung. *Arch. ges. Psychol.*, XLVII.
Halverson, H. M. (1938), Infant Sucking and Tensional Behavior. *J. Genet. Psychol.*, LI.
Hoffer, W. (1949), Hand, Mouth and Ego Integration. *This Annual*, III/IV.
Jensen, K. (1932), Differential Reactions to Taste and Temperature Stimuli in Newborn Infants. *Genet. Psychol. Monogr.*, XII.
Minkowski, M. (1928), Neurobiologische Studien am menschlichen Foetus. *Handb. biol. Arbeitsmethoden*, VB.
Peiper, A. (1926), Über einen Augenreflex auf den Hals in frühem Säuglingsalter. *Jb. Kinderheilk.*, CXIII.
Pepys, S. (1667), *The Diary of Samuel Pepys*. London: G. Bell, 1920.
Pratt, K. C. (1946), The Neonate. In: *Manual of Child Psychology*, ed. L. Carmichael. New York: Wiley.
Sandler, J. & Rosenblatt, B. (1962), The Concept of the Representational World. *This Annual*, XVII.
Stubbs, E. M. (1934), The Effect of the Factors of Duration, Intensity, and Pitch of Sound Stimuli on the Responses of Newborn Infants. *Univ. Iowa Stud. Child Welfare*, IX, No. 4.
Tilney, F. & Casamajor, L. (1924), Myelinogeny as Applied to the Study of Behavior. *Arch. Neurol. Psychiat.*, XII.

THE STRIVING FOR AUTONOMY AND REGRESSIVE OBJECT RELATIONSHIPS

BENJAMIN SPOCK, M.D. (Cleveland)

I was never able to explain why almost all breast-fed babies can be weaned easily to the cup between six and nine months of age, whereas so many bottle-fed babies at the same age become increasingly devoted to the bottle and suspicious of the cup.

Most breast-feeding mothers will report spontaneously, when the baby is about six months old, that his interest in the breast is decreasing markedly. Instead of nursing eagerly for a quarter to a half hour, he now releases the nipple after a very few minutes, smiles and coos at his mother, has to be reminded to resume nursing several times during each feeding. (If the mother wishes the breast feeding to continue for a number of months longer, she can persuade the baby to keep at it.)

Some bottle-fed babies at this age will show the same decreasing interest in the bottle, and will take increasing amounts of milk from the cup. Others, particularly those who are allowed to hold and drink their own bottles in bed, become more and more enamored of the bottle at seven, eight, and nine months of age, watching it all the while they are taking their solid food, reaching for it eagerly when it is offered, fondling it and murmuring to it as they drain it to the last drop. These babies, even though they were formerly willing to take sips of milk from the cup at five or six months, are now apt to turn against it with suspicion. They clamp their mouths shut when the cup is offered and knock it away. A few of them permit the mother to pour the milk into their open mouths but, grinning, let it all run onto their bibs. Yet, interestingly enough,

From the Child Rearing Study at Western Reserve University Medical School, supported by the William T. Grant Foundation, New York.

they remain quite willing to take water and fruit juices from the cup. It is only milk-in-cup which they will not tolerate.

There are other phenomena which mothers begin to describe at the age of six or seven months, when most infants learn to sit and to handle objects deliberately. Diapering becomes increasingly difficult because a baby who has learned to sit will indignantly refuse to lie down, even for a minute. Though he formerly took his solid food cuddled in his mother's arm, he may now elbow his way out of this dependent position and demand to be fed sitting up. He may also want to take his bottle sitting up, though this involves craning his neck in a position that looks uncomfortable. Most babies now want to hold onto their own bottles, and some of them will impatiently jerk the bottle sideways while drinking, to get the mother's hand off it. These all seem evidences of the baby's drive to outgrow the symbiotic enveloped relationship at this age.

A mother who responds to her infant's cues, seeing that he no longer wants her to cuddle him or hold his bottle, may form the habit of laying him in his crib, where he drinks his bottle and puts himself to sleep in one convenient process. Once this pattern has been established, it usually becomes obligatory until the child is between eighteen months and two years; he cannot possibly fall asleep unless he has his bottle.

In our current Child Rearing Study the dozen babies who were breast fed for six months all showed the usual early readiness for weaning. They were weaned easily to the cup as soon as their mothers were able to take the cue. Some of the mothers needed prompting from their counselors, however. As for the mothers who were bottle feeding, they were advised not to give the bottle in bed and they followed this advice. The only babies who remained on bottles into the second year were those whose mothers were unwilling to wean—most often for fear that not enough milk would be consumed from the cup alone.

As a result of observations of weaning behavior I came to the hypothesis many years ago that perhaps the most influential factor in readiness for weaning is not the lessening of the baby's need to suck but his urge to outgrow the totally dependent and closely cuddled relationship with his mother. That is to say, he gives up the breast—or the bottle which his mother holds—because he cannot use it apart from her. When he takes a bottle to bed, he can have his sucking pleasure and his autonomy too. This hypothesis, however, did not explain the *increasing* infatuation with the independently held bottle after six months. When our staff was discussing the attachment of a majority of the children in our study to such soft objects as a favorite blanket, diaper, woolly toy, to fondle at regressive times of day (half of these children sucked their thumbs at the same time) our attention was called to the papers of Winnicott (1953) and Stevenson (1954) on transitional objects. Winnicott used the word "transitional" to signify an object that lies, developmentally speaking, between the autoerotically sucked thumb and the ordinary toy which has its own reality to start with and is presented as a gift. Stevenson chose not to include the nursing bottle or the pacifier (dummy) among the variety of objects she discussed, on the basis that their use is comparatively brief.

But the reading of those two articles stimulated another train of thought in my mind: the nursing bottle to which many a baby becomes increasingly attached after six months is similar in several respects to the soft transitional object. The child's greatest need for either is at bedtime, when he is both regressed and separated from his mother. His dependence on either may be almost desperate. He is suspicious of any substitution. The bottle continues to provide the oral component of the earlier symbiotic feeding situation. The soft transitional object continues to provide the tactile pleasure which the baby used to gain, between three and six months, by gently stroking his mother's skin or clothing, or the blanket in which he was wrapped, while he was being fed in her arms. (This may be a vestige of the instinct, seen for instance in puppies and kittens, to massage the mother's udders during nursing, presumably to aid the release of milk.)

This analogy suggested to me that the soft transitional object and the bottle in bed each acquires its very special cathexis because the child's developing nature is now obliging him to detach himself from his mother. Soft object or bottle allows him to have within his own control, at times of regression, an object which affords some of the autoerotic pleasure and the reassurance that he formerly secured through the symbiotic relationship, without his having to relinquish his newly won autonomy.

This concept would explain the increasing attachment to bottle and suspicion of cup after six months which causes so many weaning problems. It would substantiate my belief that weaning from bottle as well as from breast, when properly conducted, is not a deprivation imposed on babies but a step in maturation which they ask to take. It would give a rational basis for the impression I have always had that the sucking of thumb or pacifier satisfies the sucking need up to about six months of age but thereafter satisfies the need for a comforter at times of regression. (Thus the thumb sucking itself acquires a transitional as well as an autoerotic meaning.) And finally this concept suggests that the precious soft object, or the precious bottle after six months, could be called transitional in more than one sense: its appeal is both autoerotic and as an object. It is cathected at the time of sharpest transition from symbiosis to early autonomy. It is reminiscent of pleasurable aspects of mother, it is a substitute for mother, but it is also a defense against re-envelopment by mother. It invites regression but also limits it.

Incidentally, the suspiciousness with which a child rejects any substitute for the favorite soft object and rejects milk-in-cup as a substitute for milk-in-bottle is reminiscent of the specificity of the process of "imprinting": very young animals, such as newly hatched ducklings, become exclusively attached to the mother (or whatever other creature is present at the crucial period) and fearful of strange members of the species as well as of other species (Scott, 1962). The analogy with imprinting suggests the original biological importance of the exclusivity of all such attachments. It suggests the reason why in the human infant the phenomena of stranger anxiety, separation anxiety, depression as a result of maternal deprivation, all appear in the middle of the first year.

BIBLIOGRAPHY

Scott, J. P. (1962), Critical Periods in Behavioral Development (a review). *Science,* CXXXVIII.
Stevenson, O. (1954), First Treasured Possession. *This Annual,* IX.
Winnicott, D. W. (1953), Transitional Objects and Transitional Phenomena. *Int. J. Psa.,* XXXIV.

CLINICAL CONTRIBUTIONS

A STUDY OF IDENTICAL TWINS

Their Analytic Material Compared with Existing Observation Data of Their Early Childhood

DOROTHY BURLINGHAM

In cooperation with ARTHUR T. BARRON

(London)

Bert and Bill

The development story of a pair of male identical twins which follows here is based on five different pieces of evidence and their comparison with each other:

1. The detailed direct observation made in The Hampstead Nursery between their fourth month and their fourth year (Bert: 1942 to April, 1945; Bill: 1942 to September, 1945) and published in my book on *Twins* (1952) under the names of Bert and Bill.

2. An inquiry in 1953 by Mr. Shields with special regard to the twins' identical births. Mr. Shields also traced the course of their external lives from the time of their departure from the Hampstead Nursery to their appearance in the Home for Maladjusted Children

This paper forms part of a research project, entitled "Study Comparing Analytic Material with Existing Observation Data." This project has been financed by the Ford Foundation, New York, and carried out in the Hampstead Child-Therapy Clinic, an institution maintained at present ·by The Field Foundation, Inc., New York; The Anna Freud Foundation, New York; The Grant Foundation, Inc., New York; The Estate of Flora Haas, New York; The National Institute of Mental Health, Bethesda, Md.; The Old Dominion Foundation, New York; The Psychoanalytic Research and Development Fund, Inc., New York; The Taconic Foundation, Inc., New York.

Thanks for active help in this study are due to Mr. James Shields, Lecturer, Institute of Psychiatry, for providing for testing as to identity and intelligence, and for collecting and collating the information concerning the years from November 22, 1945 to 1953; to Miss Hanni Koehler, now Mrs. Benkendorf, Child Therapist in Western Reserve University, Cleveland, Department of Psychiatry, for keeping past and present contact with the twins; to Miss Nancy Proctor-Gregg for help in summarizing and organizing the available documents.

run by Mr. Arthur Barron, a qualified therapist of the Hampstead
Child-Therapy Course and Clinic.

3. Direct observation of their behavior in the Home for Maladjusted Children undertaken by Mr. Barron and covering the
period from age twelve to thirteen and a half (1953-1955).

4. Material from their psychoanalytic treatments, with Bert from
thirteen to sixteen years (1955-1958) with Bill from thirteen to fifteen
years (1955-1957).

5. Some follow-up data.

Evidence gathered from these four periods in the twins' lives will
be used for a number of purposes:

(a) To check predictions on their developments which were made
at the time of their dismissal from the Hampstead Nurseries.

(b) To establish links between their behavior and the conscious
and unconscious motivations of it, as revealed in their analyses.

(c) To compare the analytic material during adolescence with
the observational data gathered during their first years of life.

Detailed Observation from Four Months to Fourth Year (1941-1945)

What follows here are partly direct quotations from, or summaries of such quotations distributed through, the whole of the book
on *Twins* (1952),[1] or material from development charts, or observational cards beyond those actually published in the book for reasons
of abbreviation. On no point does the material given here go beyond
what was collected between the years 1941-1945.

SUMMARY OF FIRST FOUR YEARS

Bert and Bill were illegitimate children, "their mother a young
office worker of 21. From the maternity hospital, where they were
born, they were sent to an evacuated baby hostel where they stayed
for their first four months with their mother. When the mother had
to return to work they were admitted to the Hampstead Nurseries"
(p. 17).

Bert was the first born weighing 4 lbs. 13 oz.; and Bill, the second
born, was the heavier, weighing 5 lbs. 13 oz. (Chart 11). Bert by
degrees made up some of this weight.

1 Throughout this paper, all page references and charts refer to this book.

Identical Looks

Their identical looks made it impossible to tell them apart, they were therefore continually mistaken one for the other, not only by the nurses who cared for them but by their mother who visited them, at first daily and then once or twice weekly (Charts 11, 12, 16). To weigh them was often the only way to straighten out the confusion. "The twins were not only alike in appearance, took the same positions, and copied each other, but from the moment they arrived in the Nursery at 4 months, they were the mirror picture of each other. When they lay in their baskets, Bill on his right side, Bert on his left, Bill sucked his right hand and right thumb and Bert his left hand and left thumb; at 17 months they still sucked these same thumbs and when they masturbated they usually did so with the opposite hand from the one they used for sucking.

"As they got older they were often found asleep in exactly the same position on their stomachs, Bert's head turned to the right, Bill's to the left, or lying on their backs, eyes covered with one arm. They would sit on the floor opposite each other with one leg tucked under their bodies; they would both stand in their cots in exactly the same position, one arm hanging over the edge of the cot. At 14 months, they would move absolutely alike when they crawled. At 15 months, they would rock in the same rhythm holding on to the bars of the cots at the same height, head bent in the same way, their mouths usually open. At 15 months, they pushed their cars at the same time, with absolutely the same movement and with the same expression. At 17 and 19 months they would start rocking at the same moment and in the same rhythm.

"They also had the same physical marks, birthmarks over forehead and eyes, more distinct in Bill than in Bert; these disappeared in both at about 7 months. They often had the same infectious diseases at the same time, which was not surprising since they were always together, Bert generally more severely than Bill. But at 8 months, they also had a blister on their chins developing one day apart, and both developed hydrocele at 14 months, Bill's on the right side much more pronounced than Bert's which was on the left side and of a more bluish colour. These disappeared about the same time and reappeared again several times, always together; Bert's always less distinct than Bill's, disappearing completely a few weeks before Bill's when they were 20 months" (p. 24).

Relationship to Each Other

It was Bert who first took notice of Bill at 7 months, smiling at him. Soon Bill as the stronger of the two was the one who was making overtures to Bert and disturbing him so much that Bert had often to be protected (p. 19). At 8 months he was already taking away whatever Bert was holding, and at 12 months Bill was throwing him over and sitting on him. Bill was not only stronger but the more active as well. He was the first to crawl and stand. Bert noticed these achievements of his brother and was cross and unhappy until he could do the same (p. 21, Chart 14).

Copying Games

"It appeared that it was Bert who started copying-games with Bill. At 14 months he clapped his hands and Bill did the same; he banged bricks on the table; Bill followed suit. These actions were always accompanied by laughter from both children. Soon it was impossible to tell who copied whom. At 13 months both twins were lying in their cots on their backs. One would start to shout and kick and the other would watch him and laugh; then the other would take his turn to shout and kick and the first one would watch and laugh.

"At 15 months the twins provoked each other to join in these games. One would kneel suddenly and laugh; the other would then do the same and laugh too. Or from a sitting position, one would throw himself on to his back looking at the other twin, and immediately the other would copy him. Laughter was an essential element in these games. Both twins tried to find new ways of entertaining the other. It was Bill who started grimacing, making sudden jerky clownish movements, jumping from one foot to the other, standing up and throwing himself down, making funny noises and laughing uproariously. Bert would imitate him. Bill would get himself and Bert more and more excited until the game was like an orgy" (pp. 24-25). Bert with his quieter ways often used these games with a purpose in mind, i.e., if Bill was unhappy to distract him, while Bill was carried away by his inner excitement. These games became more and more complicated but never stopped so long as they were in the Nursery (p. 25).

The twins were so carried away by these games that they were quite oblivious of the other children, they ignored them, completely wrapped up in each other. It was also impossible for their mother, nurses, or anyone else to get their attention at such a time. They were beyond control (pp. 25-26). "Wild movements about the room, aggressive actions against adults, children and each other were generally the result of these games. Bill was more aggressive, more uncontrollable and less able to be influenced than Bert. Bert was not able to cope with Bill's aggressive actions, he became afraid of him and in the last months at the Nursery it was felt best to separate them" (p. 26).

These copying games did not further the twins' development. Bert, carried away by Bill's dominant, domineering, and erratic nature, could not develop normally. Bill got sensations of pleasure and excitement by watching Bert's responding reactions which excited him still further (p. 26).

Aggression

Aggression toward each other started at a very early age. As babies they naturally wanted to get hold of whatever the other was holding. They grabbed, hit, and screamed until one let go crying with temper and frustration. Pulling the twin down who was standing, then hitting and rolling on him was a frequent occurrence. As already mentioned, the copying games usually ended by Bill's becoming aggressive as a result of his excessive excitement. But their rivalry was the main cause for their aggression. This rivalry started as soon as they became aware of each other. In the feeding situation when one twin was fed first, the other wanted to be fed too (p. 20). This was soon followed by the wish to have whatever the twin possessed, ranging from material objects to development achievements. This caused a great impetus to their learning processes and seemed to contribute to both twins becoming able to do the same thing at almost the same time (pp. 21-23). In the relationship to the visiting mother the rivalry was at its height, both demanding impatiently and passionately to be picked up and loved at the same moment. They would hit and push away the rival so as to get to the mother and hit and bite the mother because she was not able to respond to both. As a result both twins would end up on the floor frustrated, screaming, and in a temper tantrum (Charts 17, 21).

Love Relationship

It would be a mistake to assume from the description of the twins' jealousy and rivalry of each other and the resulting aggressive acts against each other that they did not have a positive relationship as well.

From the time around their first year when the twins began to take notice of each other they showed signs of affection and at times could even be gentle with each other. They tried to touch each other's faces, hold each other's arms and legs (Chart 15). Bert would bite Bill very gently and repeat this affectionately, and he would rub up against him. Bill at 13 months rubbed himself against Bert biting him affectionately everywhere, head, arms, and legs (Chart 16). Bert would often try to comfort Bill when he cried and would try to distract him (16 months) (Chart 19). Bill would pick up toys for Bert (23 months) (Chart 24) and get a chair ready for Bert at the table when he was absent (2 years) (Chart 24). When put to bed in the shelter, their bunks separated by a partition, they would talk to each other excluding all the other children (Chart 24). And when separated at 2 years 5 months and living in different houses Bert insisted on going to see Bill before going to sleep (Chart 24).

Reaction to Separation

It was quite evident that both twins missed each other when separated. At 14 months they both showed that they were aware that the other was missing and showed pleasure when reunited. At 16 months they ignored each other when together again, much in the way a child reacts when reunited with a mother after separation (pp. 39-40). At 17 months they learned the word "gone" at a time of separation and used it not only in connection with each other but also for disappearing objects. With Bill the reaction to the separation was so great that he repeated the words "all gone" continually when put to bed from 10 P.M. to 3:30 A.M. At this time balls were their favorite toys and they tried to master the situation of separation by throwing and fetching the ball accompanying this activity with the words "ball all gone" (pp. 40-41).

When separated they mistook their mirror image for the twin. Bert at 17 months enjoyed eating, watching his reflection in the mirror, and again, when separated at 2 years 3½ months, he called out "Billy" when he saw his own reflection in the mirror (p. 44).

Twins as a Team

Bert and Bill did not only enjoy their uproarious copying games together, they also turned to each other in activities where one found it impossible to do them alone. At 17 months, they were able together to move another child's cot and showed tremendous pleasure over their success (Chart 20). They also protected each other. When one twin was threatened by another child, the other twin came to his rescue. And when one twin attacked another child, the other twin would attack him as well. At 20 months when Bert hit a boy who cried and crawled away Bill followed the boy and hit him on the head (Chart 23).

Autoerotic Activities

Both boys sucked their hands at 4 months and continued this for some time. Bert seemed to prefer sucking his left thumb and Bill his right one (Chart 11). At 11 months both played with their genitals (Chart 14); they both masturbated from then on, Bert more than Bill. They used to rock when left in their cots (Chart 17).

Bert at 13 months was crawling on the floor when he bumped

his head on a table leg. This interested him and he deliberately bumped his head again and again until he finally cried (Chart 16). Both twins then starting banging their heads, Bert when cross, Bill not only when cross, but for no obvious reason (Chart 20). Bill at 18 months was banging his head so hard that it was bruised. He accompanied this head banging with shrill screams, and kept it up until exhausted (Chart 21). At 21 months he was resorting to head banging when emotionally upset (Chart 24). At 22 months he would say "again" each time he banged his head. He hardly cried, he seemed indifferent to pain. At 2 years 5 months he seemed still insensitive to pain whether he hurt himself or was hurt by other children. Both boys when frustrated would bite their own hands (Chart 24).

Ego Development

At 12 months their habit training was started (Chart 15) and at 2 years 4 months they were showing signs of becoming clean. At 3 years they were sometimes clean; Bill was without nappies but Bert still had his (Chart 24). Bill crawled at 11 months, Bert a few weeks later (Charts 14, 15). Bill walked at 18 months, Bert a few days later (Chart 21). Bill's first word was "ball" at 16 months, taken up immediately by Bert (Chart 19). Bert seemd to be more imaginative and more purposeful in the copying games (p. 25). Both boys were always considered intelligent after the second year, although from their intelligence tests they were shown to be backward from their infancy. They were tested (Buehler Tests) at 8 months and were considered 2 to 3 months retarded. Bill was slightly more advanced than Bert (Chart 12). They were tested again at 9 months and showed hardly any progress (Chart 12) and again at 2 years 4 months when they still showed three-months retardation (Chart 24).

Superego

There was practically no superego formation in either boy. There were quite often hopeful signs which were quickly destroyed by the twins' greater involvement in each other (Chart 24). They did not wish to copy adults, only each other. Bill enjoyed the qualities in Bert which caused him excitement and no adult could fulfill this role for him (p. 26). There were rare occasions when they showed a wish to make up for having hurt one of their nurses (Chart 24). It would be too much to say that they ever showed guilt for what they had done.

Mother

The mother of the twins was a gentle woman and very much in love with a married man, who made her pregnant. She stopped work before they were born and resumed work when the twins were 5 months old (p. 17). She had planned to name a baby boy Bert (Chart 13). Thus, she gave the name Bert to her first-born twin. Both boys' middle names were her own father's name.

Although most of the time she could not tell her babies apart (Charts 11, 16, 21), she said that Bert looked like his father and gave him attributes of his father, while she thought Bill was like her (Chart 14). She used to say that she loved Bert best, but in the handling of the twins it appeared that she preferred Bill. Soon after the twins had entered the Nursery, a differentiation was noted in the way the mother handled them. She paid more attention to Bill, held him more often and longer, she fed him first (Charts 12, 13). It is true that he was the stronger, and therefore made his demands imperative. But she showed her preference in many ways, giving him the larger piece of cake, having Bill immediately changed when both were caught out in the rain (Chart 13). When Bert was in the sickroom she hurried to Bill although Bert was crying for her. She seemed more attracted to Bill because he was the stronger, the more active and aggressive of the twins. She remarked that he was more mischievous, more like herself (Charts 13, 14).

Around the nineteenth month Bert's aggressive ways intensified and he often hurt Bill. The mother noticed this and now turned her attention to Bert, stayed longer with him when he was ill, and said that he was more a boy now (Chart 22).

It was also at this time that the mother's relationship to the father ceased. When the twins were 2 years 2 months old the mother married another man. Her visits to the Nursery became less frequent, she became pregnant, and one month before her new baby was born, her visits ceased entirely.

Since at this date the children were moved to the country with the whole Nursery because of the increase of bombing, it was six months before their mother visited them again; by then, the aggressiveness of the twins had increased, especially Bill's, and she felt helpless when faced with both of them (foster parents' letter).

In 1945, at the end of the War, when the Nursery closed down gradually, it was decided that Bert should go home first to mother, stepfather, and baby sister, since he was the more manageable of the twins and there was the hope that the mother might be able to deal with him (foster parents' letter).

From now on, whenever the mother visited Bill who remained in the Nursery, she had to bring along not only the baby but Bert as well. These visits were a catastrophe. Bill was overwhelmed with jealousy not only of the baby but of Bert. Bill attacked Bert viciously, and there was not a moment during these visits that the twins were not fighting. In consequence the mother decided that she could not take Bill to live at home. She tried to place him in a residential institution when the Nursery closed, but was unable to do so. Bill therefore joined the family five months after Bert had gone home, very much against her wishes. Several months later she placed both in a residential nursery. At this date Bert had been home eight months and Bill three months.

Father

There was little known about the twins' real father, except that the mother talked about him in a loving way. He was a soldier and on duty abroad (the mother's father had also been a soldier and been torpedoed in the First World War) (Chart 14).

The father kept in contact with the mother by letters, and she was very upset when an expected cable was lost in the post and did not arrive for the twins' first birthday. He visited the twins twice, the first time when they were 3 weeks old, before they were in the Hampstead Nurseries and the second time when on leave and in uniform when they were 17 months old. At this time the father remarked that Bert looked like his family (Chart 20).

In the charts only one observation is noted concerning the twins' reaction to a father figure: "Bert imitates his stepfather" after a visit home at age 3 years 4 months (Observation Card).

Relationship to Nurses

While the twins were in the Nursery, great effort was made to give them nurses (mother substitutes) who were as permanent as possible. The twins shared the same nurse (Eva) from 4 months to 19 months. When she had to leave it was thought advisable to have them with two different nurses to avoid rivalry. Consequently Bill was assigned to nurse Hanni, with whom he remained from 19 months to his departure at 4 years 11 months. Bert unfortunately had two more changes, even returning to nurse Eva at one time.

Both boys proved that they were able to form object relationships. They formed them to these mother substitutes; they reacted to the nurses' day off by sometimes showing pleasure when they returned, at other times anger at having been left. Both were sensitive to disapproval, Bert far more so than Bill (Charts 23, 24).

At times when the twins were separated from each other owing to illness, the nurses were hopeful that they had gained an influence over them, but they were invariably disappointed when the twins were reunited, and when their former behavior was resumed and all improvement given up (Chart 24).

Events between Hampstead Nurseries and Mr. Barron's Hostel for Maladjusted Children

There was no direct contact with the twins, from the time they left their mother, Bill four years one month (11.22.45), Bert one month later, until at the age of twelve years they turned up at Mr. Barron's Home for Maladjusted Children.

However, Mr. James Shields of the Institute of Psychiatry was able to collect information about them from the various agencies and institutions which had to deal with them during this period. The information comes from two sources—contemporary reports and retrospective ones—the first carry a note of bewilderment, almost of despair, the latter a note of amusement over the difficulties the twins created.

A summary of the salient facts pertaining to this period runs as follows:

When the mother realized she could not cope with the twins at home, she tried repeatedly to place them in an institution. They were first admitted to a residential nursery, which specialized for difficult children (11.22.45).

In April, 1946, when the twins were four and a half, a visiting welfare officer noted that they were "difficult," had violent outbursts against each other, but were improving rapidly. Need careful handling in quiet surroundings. Hopes their future will receive careful consideration and above all that they will not be separated. "They are so closely tied I think it would be psychologically dangerous to separate them."

In October, 1946, the twins, now five years old, were removed to a large children's home where they remained two and a half years (May, 1949).

In a contemporary report from the headmaster (3.24.49), twins aged seven and a half years, reference is made to previous requests to have the twins removed from the Homes. ". . . both very difficult on admission, little if any improvement."

Bill has made some progress in school under pressure and is beginning to read. Can add units and tens. A constant upsetting influence in the school, needs whole of teacher's attention, conduct often unbearable, disobedient, spiteful, antisocial. In the cottage a constant source of trouble.

Bert even worse than his brother. Very backward and lazy. Left-handed, awkward, careless in writing. His numbers show fair progress. Conduct in school and in the cottage very unsatisfactory and most unreliable. Disobedient, spiteful, foul-mouthed, constant source of quarrels and trouble.

Retrospective impression of some staff members:

Two teachers who remembered the twins reported to a welfare officer (5.14.54) that they were regarded as most difficult children, had to be separated early on, when Bill was moved into a higher class and later on the twins were put in separate cottages. They were always doing things to themselves, accidentally cutting knees, etc. Still just as troublesome separated, it was not a case of one influencing the other. In personality, no difference remembered, but it is claimed that they had no difficulty in knowing who was who.

The Matron of the Homes (5.14.54) said she remembers the twins well. "They were really handfuls but very lovable and friendly little people." When in mischief the teacher never knew which one to punish with the result that they both got off with a caution rather too often. Neither regarded more difficult than the other, but it is easier for the staff to deal with them separately than together.

Early in 1948 (aged six and a half) Bill moved into a different cottage, while Bert remained with the same housemother. When separated they continued to play together, they either had their arms around one another or were fighting violently. No nervous habits recollected, except occasional bed wetting, Bill more often than Bert. Neither regarded as dominating the other.

While in this home the twins had the minimum contact with their parents.

In May, 1949, at the age of seven years seven months, the twins went to a special boarding school. This is a small establishment for forty-five children, who are in three separate houses. The school is a separate unit and a fair proportion of the children attend outside schools in the area.

During their first term the twins were in the same "house." A retrospective report from the headmaster (11.25.53) says: "They were extremely aggressive toward each other and had outbursts of very violent behavior. Their general behavior was irresponsible, very noisy, and their language was appalling . . . this behavior persisted. It was noticed that Bill, although the larger of the two, was less sure of himself and usually had the worst of it in their fights."

The housemother in a contemporary report comments: "Bert: fights with his brother but is the quicker thinker and generally outwits Bill. An objectionable child.
"Bill: resents his twin and causes fights. Filthy mind and bad influence on other boys."

The schoolteacher who had them both in his class is not so distressed, he comments:
"Bert: a nuisance, but improving, a busybody, persistently monopolizing, aggressive, disobedient, daring, talkative. Making progress.
"Bill: a general nuisance, but improving, aggressive, disobedient, very daring, persistently talkative and mischievous. Could do much better work. Schoolwork generally a little ahead of Bert."

The psychotherapist notes (8.26.49) that there was much tension between them.
"Bert: more sure of himself, better adjusted and happier, stronger and better liked than his brother.
"Bill: probably higher I.Q. but feels crushed by his brother. To be moved up to next cottage to encourage him and so that he will no longer be constantly compared with his twin."

Christmas term 1949 (aged eight years two months):

Bert: with same housemother who comments that the relationship to her is unchanged. His behavior "naughty," spiteful toward other boys, very highly strung. The schoolteacher describes him as noisy, daring, no team spirit.
Bill: the new housemother comments that he was rather out of hand after a visit to his home. His relationship with other boys is "fair"; he needs constant supervision.

Christmas 1949:

Bill: the same teacher refers to him as "overdependent, aggressive, fools about."
Both: Individual psychotherapy ceased. "Very fair" at games.

Easter term 1950:

The housemothers report that the twins are generally unchanged; Bill was unruly and troublesome after visiting his home at Christmas. Anxious to get on at school, always talking about his lessons.
Bert is described again as highly strung, always in trouble.

The schoolteacher's report indicates considerable progress. Their conduct is described in the same terms, but their educational progress is marked thus:

Reading: Bert reading book 4.
                      Bill reading book 5.

Spelling: Bert very good.
                      Bill good.

Arithmetic: Bert worked half of second book of sums.
                      Bill worked three quarters of second book.

Art: Bert fertile imagination but color and execution crude.
                      Bill more decorative and fastidious than last term, has delightful and delicate color sense.

Writing: Bert fair.
                      Bill very fair.

Practical work: Bert on the whole an excellent worker. Steady progress.
                      Bill fair ability. Behavior during this lesson quite good.

Sport: Bert?
                      Bill good. Steady improvement, better cooperation. Has made progress, works better in absence of his brother.

Summer term 1950 (aged eight years nine months):

Again the housemothers record no change in the boys' conduct in the houses, but Bert's housemother adds to the usual description: "but has sunny disposition, will invariably laugh his way out of his difficulties."

The schoolteachers' reports indicate that each day is maintaining his improvement level of working, but each tends to do rather badly in the other's better subjects. Thus:

Reading: Bert inclined to be careless.
                      Bill very good, tries hard.

Spelling: Bert good.
                      Bill below average but not too bad.

Art: Bert not nearly so good as last term.
                      Bill some extremely sensitive work, takes great pains.

Writing: Bert very fair.
                      Bill not bad.

Practical work: Bert poor, interfering, and quarrelsome.
                   Bill tries, has quick good tool sense.
Sport: Bert very good indeed. Alert, active, noisy.
                   Bill not too good, very noisy.
Conduct: Bert fairly good, disobedient at times.
                   Bill talkative, has quite a temper, tearful
                       when not having his own way, yet
                       works well, tries to be helpful.

During this term the boys were in different classes.

Reports for the period Christmas, 1951 until December, 1952 indicate that the twins maintained good but not outstanding progress in their lessons first at the special school and then in separate schools in the area from January, 1952.

In the houses their behavior showed no marked change but decreased in intensity. They both were able to get on "well" or sometimes "very well" with other boys. Their relationship with the housemothers shows the least improvement, such terms as "very little improved," "not greatly improved," "same" appearing in the housemothers' report to the end. The relationship between the twins is reported to be "more friendly," "not quite so violent," as well as the more usual "much ill feeling." They are sometimes described as "very lovable nature," Bert "lovable" boy, "quick-tempered" Bill.

The special schools' achievement can be summarized in the reports that they prepared when the twins were about to be discharged:

Psychiatrist's report (10.29.52): "On admission Bert dominated and overwhelmed Bill, but now Bert is less aggressive and Bill is quietly confident and making better progress than his brother. Both are still occasional enuretics. . . . Bill is quieter and more considerate than Bert.
"Bert seems to care very little about others . . . they are now friendly and seem to have lost their hostility for each other."

The headmaster (11.28.53): "both boys have been very good; both play in their school soccer team. Bill has made considerable measurable improvement in vocabulary from 27 to 67 on Burt's tests in two years, but in numbers when he is very impetuous the figures are 26 to 54. His I.Q. on the latest testing was 95.
"Bert's improvement in vocabulary is from 22 to 77 and in numbers from 29 to 48. His I.Q. is 98."

The school authorities urged that the children should go home 1952 (eleven years): "It is thought that if the boys do not get back home now, they will never get back. It is realized that the situation at home may break down, particularly in the case of Bert . . . but it is a case of now or never." They were at home from December, 1952 to October, 1953.

The mother complained three months after the twins had returned home that she could not control the boys. They would not do anything she asked them. If she forced them or sent one up to bed as a punishment, they crashed and stamped around up there.

They refused to go to bed, fought over washing. They continually fought between themselves. If they asked to sit to listen to the radio, one kept poking the other and there was no peace for the rest of the family. Their swore a great deal, their language was filthy, other children ceased to play with them. "When they came home there was a constant uproar."

Things deteriorated further during the eight months it took to get the twins placed at the Hostel. They threw cups at one another; on one occasion one took up a knife to strike the other but the mother intervened.

At the school they attended from their home no abnormality of behavior was noted, although the level of their work appeared to be below that which they produced previously and it was noted that they spent the best part of their time outside classwork in scragging one another. They were not allowed to sit next to one another in class.

At age twelve years five months, Mr. Shields saw the twins at the Genetic Unit of the Institute of Psychiatry where their status of being identical twins was investigated. Mr. Shields's report runs as follows:

Establishment on Monozygosity, or Being Genetically Identical Twins

The twins turned out to be alike in eight different blood groups. Their fingerprints were taken, and they were given phenylthio-carbamide to taste, which neither of them tasted as bitter. If one knew nothing at all about them except their blood groups and fingerprints, one would predict that there was only a 1.3 per cent chance of their *not* being genetically identical twins. Needless to say, I confirmed their striking likeness in build, eye and hair color, and appearance generally, down to a pimple on the nose. Indeed, the feature by which I found it easiest to distinguish them was the fact that Bert wore two badges in his lapel, while Bill wore none. Bill was still a trifle bigger. Taken along with this likeness in appearance monozygosity was regarded as firmly established. Incidentally both boys showed me with pride the scars they had on their legs from various accidents. Bill had had two lots of stitches on his left leg and two years ago he broke both wrists.

Other Findings (aged twelve and a half)

Besides collecting reports from people who knew them between the ages of four and twelve, I also took the opportunity of giving them some intelligence tests we had recently given to a group of normal twins of their age, and of having EEGs done. Their EEGs were closely similar. Dr. Pond thought both records showed poorly organized rhythmic activity and should be regarded as mildly abnormal for their age. On Thurstone's Primary Mental Abilities Test, Bert scored higher than Bill, but they scored just as well as twins attending the ordinary schools and the difference between them was no greater than the average for identical twins. They both did relatively well on tests of spatial perception. Previous tests on the Binet Scale at ten and a half years and at eleven and a quarter years centered round I.Q. 100, sometimes one twin, sometimes the other, doing a little better on the day of the test.

These results brought out further similarities between the twins in maturational level. From the evidence of the EEG there is the possibility that constitutional factors play a role here in addition to psychodynamic ones. However, with identical twins it is the differences that are of particular interest. I shall comment briefly on the personality differences as they struck me at the time.

In the first place, there seemed to have been a change-over in some aspects of the relationship between the twins. In the Nurseries Bill had been the more aggressive in their mutual relationship and was thought possibly to be retarding Bert's development. At the special boarding school, the psychiatrist referred to Bert as "overwhelming" Bill. Around the time I saw the twins, Bert was still reported as being the more aggressive, Bill the quieter. Bert was also the more anxious, for instance, over the intelligence test I gave them and over the Rorschach given in the Hampstead Clinic. Bert's nails were more badly bitten, and he had a more neurotic score on a questionnaire. Bill on the other hand was doing better at school; he could sometimes settle down to read a book. He was a little ahead in physical adolescent development (information from Mr. Barron). He could perhaps have been regarded at that time as being neater and more fastidious—witness his art reports; another psychologist had recently commented that Bill was fussy about neatness and straight lines; after the fingerprinting Bill wanted to wash his hands straightaway, while Bert did not mind so much having his hands covered in black ink. The difference is relative only and must be seen in the setting of essential similarity—on the one hand, aggressive, uncontrollable, accident prone, antisocial, and with serious problems in relation to each other; on the other hand, friendly, enthusiastic, "lovable" (as they were so often described), good at sport, and now of adequate intelligence.

THE TWINS AT MR. BARRON'S HOME FOR MALADJUSTED CHILDREN

The following material was taken from Mr. Barron's notes and reports concerning the twins during the first eighteen months of their stay in his Hostel, that is, before the start of their analytic treatment. The twins turned up at the Home for Maladjusted Children at the age of twelve years (1953) brought by their mother. Mr. Barron writes:

> The mother made a poor impression on me, she said she and her husband had decided to get rid of the twins; and added, "I wish you joy with them, I don't wish to see them again." She could give no intelligible description of their behavior, and they themselves acted as if they did not hear what I said. I took them . . . to the gardener; when I later went to find them, the gardener came running toward me: "Come quickly, quickly, they are murdering one another." The boys had attacked each other with choppers and were still fighting, rolling on the ground, punching and kicking each other. . . . The boys took no notice of me. I had literally to pull one off the other and hold them apart. As I stood holding them apart, they continued the quarrel as if I were not there. . . . Each boy's eyes, his whole attention was completely absorbed in the other twin. In an effort to make some contact, I demanded to know which was which. Two voices replied simultaneously and identically: "I'm Bert, he's Bill." They were jeering at me in unison. Rather desperately, I demanded to know which was Charlie and which Sydney; Bert admitted to his second name of Charlie and I said they would be known accordingly, whereat Bill said, "Eh, it's not fair, why should he be a Charlie and not me." I thought this was a joke, but Bill was serious.
>
> I have recounted this opening scene because it is a keynote for much that follows. They had no object relationships except in attacking each other, or together, as a gang, attacking the group.
>
> The twins were introduced to the group at teatime on their first day, a short time after their fight. From the moment of entering the room, they began to shout disparaging remarks to each other about the other children, to giggle together about a child's peculiarities, to push and misuse any child who was near them. . . . They disregarded the staff member conducting the meal and

turned what was normally an orderly social occasion into complete disorder.

Unlike rebellious children they followed the routine but reduced everyone about them to incoherence, and turned the Hostel mealtimes, playtimes, and bedtimes into chaos.

The twins were deliriously happy in the chaotic conditions to which they reduced every activity. Their excitement would mount as the whole group was drawn into their aggressive abuse. When the twins were finally frightened, they lost their confidence and would whine, accusing the other children and adults of being against them. They would leave the room and sulk separately in odd corners, later complaining that no one liked them.

The very existence of the Hostel as a social group was, after a few weeks of the twins, threatened. Separation seemed the only practical way out. Throughout this period it seemed to us that it was Bert who was the most unmanageable and aggressive, the mother and stepfather sharing this opinion. Therefore tentative plans were made to have Bill go home to his parents, Bert to remain in the Hostel. But since separating the twins had already often been tried with no success and physical separation could possibly hinder their psychological separation, the plan was given up.

Instead it was decided to isolate the twins to some extent, for their own protection as well as that of the Hostel life. In order to reduce the daytime hours spent with the group they were sent to a distant day school. I acted as their close keeper at all other times. I hoped in vain to develop a relationship to them. But it was impossible to make emotional contact with the boys, and their disruptive behavior continued whenever our police system failed. I could not for four months even tell them apart; if some distinction appeared, such as Bert's red nose or Bill's boil, the other boy speedily developed the same.

On the point of abandoning the twins, I tried an "Aichhorn technique": to show myself to each boy the sort of person he showed by his behavior that he admired. Their behavior shocked others into submission—so I shocked them. To give two examples: I challenged them to a swearing match (they retreated); and I drove them wildly and fast in my car, frightening them after their initial defiant jeerings. This worked like magic, in the sense of procuring a dependent relationship at last. They competed for my attention, they sought my company. I no longer had to be keeper to them: they were my keepers. I was literally followed about by one, or more usually both boys. No moment of my life was private. They walked into my bedroom, they would wait outside the toilet for me. I was not permitted to have a conversation with my children, my wife, or even with emotionally unimportant people such as county officials. They would butt into every conversation. They would demand my attention. They would ignore everybody. The most intense emotion on the part of anyone else would be completely ignored; but toward me every nuance of feeling, every nuance of voice was noted, recorded, and responded to.

Eventually we managed to distinguish them, which helped toward separate relationships, but the boys themselves began to let distinguishing signs of dress, hair, etc., appear.

Although they had a relationship to me, it was only on the basis of including me into their gang. They expected me to gang up with them against the other Hostel children, who in turn became jealous of the attention I paid the twins and attacked them, and I had to try and protect them. However, Bert was attacked one time and he struck his assailant with a dinner plate cutting him in the ear severely. (It is interesting that in his other hand, the right one, he was holding a knife, which he did not use, thereby showing some control.) The boy fainted in a pool of blood and Bert thought that he was dead and showed anxiety. This show of fear enabled the group of boys to identify with him, comfort him, and accept him. Bill was furious that Bert was accepted into the group and accused his brother of being a murderer.

My relationship with Bill was now strong enough to make him stop attacking Bert, and he too was accepted into the group.

Both boys had made exceptional educational progress at this time.

The mother was pregnant during this period. But although the boys went home for week ends, they consistently refused to believe this fact. Instead they made excuses to avoid going home. When the baby was born, Bert was nauseated in the presence of his mother. He was excited by the baby but unable to touch the little girl. Bill was affectionate toward her, kissed her, and was proud of her, pushing her out in the pram.

The dependent relationship that had been fostered in the boys had now to be given an aim. Analytic therapy became the aim. The preparation for treatment consisted in telling the boys that in their present state, in spite of their improvement, they would never be able to live outside an institution or be able to live independent lives. They themselves now began to wish for treatment and finally demanded it repeatedly and urgently.

Decisions for and Events during Therapy

For the boys to have the head of the Hostel as their therapist, the person who had personally provoked and furthered their dependency to him, was inevitably adding a serious complication to their treatment. Besides, that the twins should have the same therapist was bound to cause still further difficulties.

The only reason for accepting such a situation was that there was no alternative. To remove the boys from the Hostel to London was an impossibility. There was no other therapist in the neighborhood —therefore this attempt of therapy within the Hostel and with Mr. Barron, the head of the Hostel, seemed the only possible way to help. Mr. Barron himself was fully aware of the difficulties inherent in the situation.

Both boys started their therapy on the same day, June 13, 1955, when they were thirteen years eight months old. Bert was willing to start, Bill reluctant and bargaining; when he saw that Bert would be taken in any case Bill said: "Well, if he is going to, I might as well." The boys then found it difficult to decide which should have the first session. Bert came first.

The material in the first weeks concerned Bert's acquisition of a bicycle (Bill already had one). Bert was proud and pleased with his bike; determined to look after it as well as Bill did; he feared that it might not work properly and that he might not be able to control it, especially downhill.

Each boy feared to formulate or verbalize his thoughts and feelings because to do so seemed equivalent to revealing himself to his twin. Further, it appeared that each boy feared that the other would murder him. Each identified with the other and assumed that his thoughts were identical with those of the twin and thus feared an attack.

The competition between the boys proved to be the main spur to all their efforts. Bert was a fraction shorter than Bill and because of this felt inferior to him. Bert had many fantasies and fears related to his twinship: was he only half a boy, was he defective, why did his mother have to have a baby twenty minutes after him? He was extremely resentful of his mother for not leaving him his birthright of being the first-born. He denied feeling aggressive toward Bill, and maintained that it was Bill who tormented him. He recounted an accident to his own leg and brought the memory of damaging Bill's leg with a red-hot poker; finally, with marked affect he said, "I feel I would like to murder him sometimes."

Bert had a screen memory of a lady telling him he had not put his knife and fork correctly on his plate and that he must copy Bill and he tried all the ways he could to copy him, but however hard he tried he was unable to get it right.

One recurrent dream of Bert's of being chased and locked in a cupboard led to the memory of an event important in both boys' material. Bill, in the Children's Home, had been naughty and was shut in a cupboard, screamed that he was hurt, but jeered when he came out. Bert was then naughty and being mistaken for Bill was put in the cupboard again, where his finger was jammed in the door, but his screams ignored. When he was let out, his finger was found to be broken.

It was clear that the twins had murderous intentions toward each other, and that Bert only by exercising rigid control over himself or by getting Bill to join with him in attacking others had in fact avoided murdering Bill. The twins also entertained a sadistic love play. Bert, after a ritual of chase provoked by Bill, would rhythmically punch the arm, leg, or trunk of his twin.

Bill in his turn was jealous of Bert's new bike. He, like Bert, thought his twin could read his thoughts. He was indignant when it was suggested that he might be frightened that Bert could hurt him, but then recalled incidents such as the poker throwing. It was clear that Bill's method of avoiding awareness of his impulse was to provoke behavior in others which he could then adopt in turn. He could masturbate only in a group; also he incited a group to delinquent acts in which he then joined, such as stoning a passing car.

Bill also felt abused that he was a twin. He felt he had come late into the world, at the wrong time; he should have been the only one, he had no right to be there at all, since his mother had had her baby already when he arrived. He wondered whether, being a twin, he was not incomplete. He was overwhelmed by conflict in his feeling toward his twin. He had many accidents, connected with fears of identification with the twin. If Bert had an injury, Bill acted as if he were responsible, and damaged himself. When Bert cut his leg severely in a fall, Bill fell from a tree and broke his leg.

Bill's whole outlook depended on competition with his twin; if he seemed likely to succeed in a situation which unconsciously meant disposing of his twin, he failed. In a football match, where at his own request he was allowed to play goal over the head of a rival, he let sixteen goals through, even scored one against his own side; after this he had an accident to his leg; and then could not play because he was unable to get his football boots repaired.

Choice of New School

The boys had done remarkably well in the school they had been attending the last two years. They took second and third place and were recommended by the headmaster for a technical school when his school closed at the end of 1955. They therefore had the choice to go either to another secondary school or to the technical school. Neither boy was able to make a choice.

Bert wanted to go to the technical school, but was afraid of not doing well. Yet if he did not go, and Bill went, it would be unfair. He was the eldest, he ought not to be faced with an equal choice but with the first choice. (He asked if they could go to different schools, but this was impossible to arrange.) In his sessions he abused Bill and his mother, and told how he enjoyed tormenting boys he disliked. He showed how he wanted to avoid being excited by Bill, but also showed his fear of desiring a separate school: "I never want anything until I see Bill with it." When he saw Bill in a fight, he had to join in to fight the other boy and then fight Bill, "I was jealous of him hitting Bill, I wanted to do that myself." He showed his demand that Bill should have no life apart from him, in effect, that he should be part of his body.

He met interpretation of his homosexual element with silent resistance. He acted out his fantasies with another boy; when the boy had a tonsillectomy Bert became silent identifying with his suffering. He wanted to visit the boy in the hospital, but fear prevented him. These fears concerned his inability to achieve anything he desired; the mere act of wishing denied it to him. He told how he dressed and made up like a girl to make the other boys laugh. When it was interpreted that perhaps he wanted to be loved like a girl, he told

of a girl who was obviously attracted to him without his being aware
of it. The analysis showed that he had fantasies of being the girl in
a pair of twins.

He at this time was flooded with material that he could not bring
under control. Outside the sessions he acted the fool.

Bill, too, was overwhelmed by the choice of school. It was clear
in the analysis that he wished desperately to go to the technical
school, but he was inhibited from knowing this, because if he knew
it, Bert would know, and would want to go too. He said, "I only
get what I want by not wanting it."

Bill's main affect was anger against all the authorities, past and
present, who had deprived and bamboozled him, and against the twin,
competition with whom was all that mattered. He wallowed in bitterness, said he had never been allowed to take the educational opportunities, which, in contrast to Bert, he had deserved, and claimed
that the present choice was really beneath him, because he should
have had a better one.

His wish to go to the technical school was affected also by the
fear of losing influence over Bert and the stimulating comparison
with him if the latter went elsewhere. And, in that event, he would
be near fulfillment of the forbidden wish—to get rid of Bert.

He was very resistant to interpretation of this ambivalence, pro-
claiming loudly his negative feelings toward Bert. At this time he
incited the outbreak of sadistic love play, but was infuriated by the
suggestion that he provoked Bert to punch him; according to his
feeling, it was Bert who tormented him.

In the end the authorities decided for them by sending both to
the technical school.

Breakdown of School and Hostel

Although Bert had wanted to go to the technical school, he was
afraid to meet aggressive boys there. This was a projection of his own
aggression toward Bill.

The material in therapy showed that his removal from his former
school to the technical school reactivated memories of past separations.

He felt it was Bill's fault that he had been thrown out of his
home in his infancy. He claimed that he had to make more moves

than Bill, that Bill was always allowed to remain. He brought a screen memory of the parting from his mother when the boys went from home to their first residential institution. He remembered that the mother left with them a joint parting gift, and that he had clung to this toy, refusing to part from it and not allowing Bill to have it. In telling this memory, it became confused with other partings, or reunions, and separations from Bill. A state of mourning set in for the old school, displaced from Bill. He blamed Bill for taking his mother from him and in the past causing him to be moved from one place to the other. In the Hostel he ill-treated especially the younger children (Bill was of course considered the younger by him); these children represented Bill as well as his younger siblings. He was blaming them as well as Bill for pushing him out of his home.

In an effort to solve the ambivalence toward Bill, he became a twin to himself. He was in reality gratified that Bill was sent to the same school but angry that this was so. The disappointment was the unfulfilled wish to manage without him. He mourned the old school, but he believed that he suffered loneliness and loss because he was a twin. If he could be a twin to himself, he would not suffer this loss.

Bert told of a game he played with himself: he would pair off two words and see which he could longest retain in consciousness; this went on to material about hurting and being hurt, which leg was last hurt, and then to looking for something, but he did not know what.

At school he was failing miserably. He could not cope. He spoke with great admiration of Bill, envied the quantity and quality of work he could produce. It was useless for him to try and compete in learning or in sport. The only way he could compete was by being a nuisance.

In the Hostel he began to learn American social history. This connected with Hanni, the nurse they had formerly had, Bill in particular, in the Hampstead Nursery. She had continued to write to them on their birthday and at Christmas over the years. It seems as if Bert was trying to win her back from Bill.

His damaging and disruptive behavior in school was intolerable, and complaints also poured in from railway, bus companies and his own home. He was finally expelled from school.

Bert made a twin relationship with another boy (Peter) who

replaced the real twin. Through this relationship, it was possible to learn of the erotic nature of the fights between the twins. He was unable to take part in boxing because it meant covering his hands with gloves, which upset the balance of his hands for him. He could fight only if he fought with his bare fists and feel the impact between his skin and the skin of his opponent. He and his friends resorted to delinquent acts, raiding the larder and roving around the country-side at night, reactivating in this way what he used to do together with Bill.

He had acute fantasies of being too small for his age. His failure everywhere only increased his acting out. It was decided to stop the sessions of which he did not make proper use. He was disturbed by Mrs. Barron's pregnancy. It seemed probable that Mr. Barron would be able to help him more by resuming the solely educational role than by also being his therapist in this crisis.

He was expelled from the technical school and found a place in a modern secondary school, where his ability placed him in the top of his class. In the Hostel his feelings of inadequacy and of being too small were allowed compensatory expression; he formed a gang, playing at rebels, and became leader of the younger boys and of the football team.

Bill in his turn in the technical school was surprised to find the new buildings familiar, not realizing that what was in reality familiar was Bert at the desk next to his. He did not mention Bert's failure in school but instead was behaving badly himself. Complaints from home and the bus company were reported about him also. He hoped to provoke his removal from a situation with which he was unable to cope.

At this time the twins had formed an antisocial gang in school; that no one could distinguish them roused Bill's anxiety and loss of identity. He began to panic at his learning difficulties, cheating and copying Bert's exercises. All that mattered was that he should not fall behind Bert, although Bert was doing so badly. The rivalry was expressed in an incident where Bill, with his bare hands, took a hot iron bar from tongs which Bert was holding. He said, "When I saw him with it, I just had to have it."

In reaction to the attention which Bert was getting by means of his impossible behavior, Bill brought thoughts about his unknown father, with complaints that a boy is no good unless he knows about his father. He hoped that each time he moved to a new place he would meet his father. But he also feared intensely what would happen when they met. He fantasied of having a devoted father who faced death and torture to reach his own son.

He had the fantasy that his position of being the younger but larger twin could be tolerable only for a girl, not for a boy.

After a week end at home, and at the time when Bert had formed his football team, Bill collected a rival group and began to make a cricket pitch next to and overlapping Bert's football field. The two teams fought until the two leaders faced each other. They were on the point of striking each other, when Bert suddenly rushed screaming from the field, got Bill's bicycle and smashed it. This reduced Bill to raging sobs. He acted as though the attack on his bike had been an attack upon his body; he did not repair the bike, but retained it as a reproach against Bert and as proof that he ought to be separated from his murderous twin.

There came a time when he retired to bed with a swollen ankle, after keeping secret that he had infected his foot. The injured place oozed and he compulsively sucked it. This revolted him, but he was driven to do it by the fear of "losing something good from my body." He also fantasied that he was two persons, the good right half and the bad left half, the good half always getting damaged, and the bad half angry at being left out. As he was in the fantasy a twin to himself, he needed only to damage one half and preserve the other. He identified not only with Bert but at times with Mr. Barron's pregnant wife.

He was accident prone; one accident clearly occurred because he was in danger of realizing an ambition. When success was in his grasp, the successful activity became linked with the desire to be the only one, to dispose of the twin. On such occasions he actively damaged himself; for example, he ran full force into a wall, severely damaging his knee.

One determinant of the need to hurt himself was the fear that if he did not do so, the twin would. Thus he cheated the twin of the pleasure of hurting him. Another determinant was that, when he saw his twin hurt, he felt he was responsible for the damage and therefore he damaged himself, to prevent the twin from taking revenge upon him. Once when he saw his twin in pain, his death wishes came so near to consciousness that he assumed the twin would become aware of them and damage him in revenge. At this point the therapist unfortunately fell ill. The Hostel had to close for two months, and the twins were sent home.

Reaction to Hostel Closing and Return Home

Forced to return home abruptly and without preparation both boys acted out their feelings in a violent manner.

Bert stayed out at night, spent his time in pubs and with gangs of Teddy boys,[2] and had a fight with a soldier whose jaw he broke; finally he attacked his mother at the midday meal. His stepsister had dropped bread in his soup plate, to which he had retorted by calling her a bastard. The mother intervened, saying it was he himself who was the bastard. He attacked the mother violently, was pulled off by Bill with whom he then fought, and ran finally from the house. When the police, called by the father, looked for him he came forward and gave himself up, saying he was the culprit. He found it difficult to convince them, as it was now Bill who had hid himself, afraid that he would be mistaken for Bert. It was clear that Bert did all he could after Bill had pulled him off the mother to avoid further provocation.

Bill had great difficulties at home as well, covering an intense conflict over his twin. He had, in fact, acted out the wish to be rid of Bert. Bill himself had hit the mother some weeks previously, but she had not charged him in court as she did with Bert. He was able to repeat the pattern according to which he did something first with the effect that when Bert followed suit, the latter was considered to be the real offender. This is a reminder of the incident of the cupboard and the broken finger.

When the Hostel reopened, in September, 1956, Bert was in a Remand Home awaiting trial before a juvenile court because of his murderous attack on the mother, while the parents had requested that Bill be permanently discharged from the Hostel and live at home.

---

2 Teddy boys are adolescents or postadolescent young men who affect an Edwardian style of dress and haircut and who often travel about in gangs provoking fights, much as zoot suiters used to do in America.

Bert, from the Remand Home, repeatedly asked for Mr. Barron. The latter had faith that he could get Bert back into his Hostel. With difficulty this was accomplished. On his return, Bert was withdrawn and inhibited and then began to attack other children, usually the smallest, with alarming violence. Treatment was resumed because of the real concern that he might harm someone. In his sessions it was put to him that he might end up by killing somebody. It became clear that he attacked the little ones in the Hostel because he blamed his stepsiblings for his banishment from home, not only now, but from his infancy onward. He also complained that they had a father while he had none.

With the re-establishment of the transference, Bert demanded to be sent back to the Remand Home. When surprise was shown at the nature of such a wish, Bert himself was astonished. It showed how terrified he was of the impulses which he could not control. He was jealous of Bill at home with his mother and feared what he might do to him. The specific event leading up to this material was that the mother had sent him birthday greetings via Bill with a promise that she would knit him a pullover "like the one I made for Bill."

Regarding Bill it was agreed that he should be discharged from the Hostel and return home as the parents had requested, on condition that he should continue daily sessions. At this he was very disappointed. He denied that he had difficulties at home, concealed and lied about his twin's crime as though it was his own. He had a fantasy, contrasting his own unhappy lot, beset by family cares, having to do a morning round to get money for clothes, with Bert's happy lot in a group with all the company, food, and clothes he wanted. He thought Bert might escape and he be taken in his stead. The policemen became father figures, and Bert was imagined to be with the missing father. The guilt was reversed, to deny that it was he, Bill, who had deprived Bert of the mother.

Bill's sessions at this point had to be used to check his acting out, to prevent him from following Bert into the Remand Home. He came near to it, after an incident when he caused a bus to crash by inciting some "silly girls" to throw apple cores at the driver and then joining in. His difficulties at home were exemplified by an incident when his mother was ill and he attempted to give a helping hand like the others. He dug up the whole garden, destroying the plants and obliterating the paths. In reality, he secretly resented doing work for others and thought that such a situation did not occur in an institution.

The End of School Life and Choice of Jobs

At this time the twins went to different schools. Bert seemed to have cut himself off from Bill after his release from the Remand Home, when at a first meeting they had resumed their puppy play. At school, he spoiled the last few weeks of his attendance, provoking his headmaster by trying to belittle him, by smoking in class, etc. If the headmaster had not been very sympathetic, he would have been severely punished. As it was, he was removed from attendance some weeks before the end of term to avoid expulsion.

The problem that now arose was to find a job for him. He had two ideas about work, to do hostel work like the head of the Hostel, his therapist, or to join the army. As a first step toward learning a skill for community life, he chose gardening. This was determined by a wish to make his body stronger than Bill's; hence the need of a healthy outdoor life. Both of his choices were based on homosexual inclinations. He was set to work in the Hostel garden, but this proved a failure. He was unable to work because of longing for his twin when alone, so that he left to seek companionship, but when working with somebody else ruthless competitiveness was aroused.

The army for him was the abode of killers but also the protective institution where men were permitted homosexual contacts in the form of "puppy play."

Material relating to the father now occupied the sessions. Bert demanded to know about his father. His therapist informed him that the father was a market porter now, married with children, and that when the mother had the twins, she had expected to marry him but had refused to break up the father's marriage. His mother wrote answering Bert's request for his father's name, but he lost the letter, then spent days going through the telephone book hoping in this way to recall his father's name. He wished to find his father but was afraid of him as well. He told of a childhood fantasy that soldiers like his father get more money for every person they kill. His daddy had killed hundreds of people. One day he would come back to kill

Bill, but he might mistake him for Bill, and kill him, Bert. In bringing this fantasy, Bert told how he had felt compelled to fight the
young soldier. He was so sure that the soldier would kill him, that he
fought with all his strength and with his second punch broke the
soldier's jaw.

Surprisingly, regarding jobs, he acted on his own. With another
boy he went to the Forestry Commission, inquired about the conditions for work and both signed up.

Bill's school life was very stormy too. His desire to be rid of his
twin, and guilt at having succeeded in this were uppermost. An
example of his acting out was a football match. He could not face
the position of goal, as this was the position where Bert had played.
When changed to another position, he could not play then, as it
meant to mark another man. Everything associated with his twinship
became intolerable, even the voice of one person talking to another
on the bus. In the transference, the therapist was accused of being
cruel; Bill felt helpless, so helpless that boys at school knocked off
his cap and he did not know what to do about it. He showed clearly
at this time how dependent he was on his twin for dissipating his
aggression. He was so terrified that his own aggression would lead
him to kill the other boys that he could not defend himself at all.
He begged for boxing gloves (in contrast to Bert who could only
fight bare-fisted). His fear of his own aggression was reinforced by
Bert's absence in two ways; the sight of Bert was a reassurance that
he had not destroyed him, and their horseplay acted as a safety valve.
He began to hang about the Hostel before and after his sessions,
hoping unconsciously to find Bert. Consciously he was aware of his
wish to be back at the Hostel. He started a course of acting out in
which, unknown to his therapist, he brought something of Bert's
possessions with him on each visit, until all trace of Bert was removed from the home; the stepfather as well forbade the mention
of Bert in the house.

It became necessary in the sessions to concentrate on restraining
his acting out. He fought his teacher, and gave his headmaster cause
for frequent beatings. He would come to the sessions in suppressed
excitement, very voluble but almost unintelligible. One determinant
of this was that all correction or misunderstanding of his speech
linked back to the time when the twins could understand each other

without words. In the treatment it appeared that his behavior turned on the lack of a father. How could he be expected to manage if neither the headmaster who beat him nor the analyst who failed to protect him and did not arrange for him (as he did for Bert) would put things right. He half craved to get back to an institution. His provocation at school passed all bounds, and finally, before the end of term, he was withdrawn from school, as Bert had been. It was an achievement that he was not formally expelled or brought before the courts.

Choice of work came up in the last weeks of his school life. He said that he wished to become a teacher; this was in identification with the punishing headmaster and the disappointing therapist. The headmaster was cast in the role of the hated father, but was also the father whom he wished to follow.

He complained that his mother had decided that he would have to join the army immediately on leaving school. This was interpreted as his own wish in identification with his own father, a wish which he characteristically projected onto the mother. He made her force him to do what he really wanted, namely, to return to an institution and under the control of authority.

On leaving school his stepfather found him an apprenticeship with a patternmaker, a job which could eventually lead him to work with his stepfather. With the beginning of his working life Bill failed to keep to his sessions and broke off treatment. Fifteen months later it was learned that he had changed jobs and was working on the railroad, while still living at home.

Bert at Work

As soon as Bert started work with the Forestry Commission, his behavior in the Hostel became much more mature, he got himself up early, made his own breakfast, and washed up before leaving. He also came eagerly to his sessions and used them to gain insight into his disturbed working relationships.

He had chosen this job because it started out with a twin relationship, although the boy who signed up with him soon withdrew. Bert first worked with a very disturbed and unpopular man, but admired his skill and knowledge and tolerated his faultfinding and highhanded manner and competed with him. He also hoped to gain the

great physical strength which some of the men displayed. He earned
ten to fifteen shillings more than his wages because of good work.
His next fellow worker was an older man, a slow and thorough
worker, whose ways he found intolerable and with whom he coped
in a kind of hare-and-tortoise race. He would let the man get ahead
of him and then race to overtake him, thus introducing the element
of competition which was necessary to his functioning. When he had
to be absent at one time because of illness, another boy took his
place. This created a three-cornered situation, which was beyond
him. His therapist had to use all his skill to prevent him from giving
vent to his aggression against this boy and from killing him. His
work deteriorated, he earned considerably less. He spent much time
sleeping and playing cards, an identification with his stepfather.
When women were given the job that he had neglected, he was
angered. He asked to be given another chance, was able to work
again, and was soon being taught the most coveted job of felling
trees. He was given a big axe which became his most treasured possession, but at the same time he was unable to use it properly, fearing
he would cut himself down instead of the tree. His stance when
wielding the axe was that of a sprinter, ready to run as if the axe
were the aggressor. Turning his own aggression against himself was
the only way in which he could keep control over his murderous
impulses.

Foster Family

Bert now had to leave the Hostel and a foster home had to be
found for him. Some time was spent searching, and he had to visit
various members of a Rotary Club who were trying to help him.
Here he gained much pleasure from the fact that he was known by
his own name now, not as Billybert or Bertbilly as had been his fate
repeatedly.

The foster family that took him in were a young couple with
two children, a boy and a girl, both under five. He became fond of
the foster mother, appreciated her care, but kept away from the house
except for eating and sleeping. He fantasied that his own mother
would become jealous of this woman and would take him back into
his own home. He could not decide whether to write to his mother
giving her his address, or to leave it to her to search for him. His

indecision was based on his longing for his twin and his fear that Bill might come and destroy his foster home. This fear sprang from an unconscious fantasy of making an exchange with Bill—Bill to have the foster home and Bert the mother. He coped well with the foster father, achieved the position of eldest son, became a hero for the little boy, and successfully managed the little girl through a feeding difficulty. Instead of bullying her as the parents did, he would take her on his lap and get her to eat in identification with himself. He perceived and understood that her difficulty arose from his entry into her home and her jealousy of her older brother.

Longing for His Twin

Bert had now an hour's journey to his sessions and was often late, losing his way. This made sense when it was discovered that he was traveling toward his own home. Then he began to arrive an hour early, in reaction to a fantasy that his therapist was seeing his twin and he would thus meet him. He obtained much information about his twin on these journeys, for he was often mistaken for him. On discovering that Bill earned more than he did, he began to earn more himself. One day, he "accidentally" saw Bill on a bicycle in his work clothes. He remarked that one could see that this was no ordinary kid for he "held himself like a king." On an impulse, he wrote to his mother that he would visit her. He took all his money from the savings bank and in new clothes started for home. Before going into the house he found Bill playing football and watched him, noting minute details of his appearance and behavior. Then he invited him and the boys into a pub and stood drinks lavishly. Bill responded by producing from his pocket a giant packet of expensive cigarettes.

On this occasion Bert's visit home went off well. His mother drew him aside and spoke tenderly to him. Yet on a subsequent visit she told him to get out. Bert reacted first by taking his stepfather's chair and reading his paper, then he said, "Well, good-by Mum," and walked out.

On both occasions Bert had taken all his money to give his mother. He was wondering secretly whether his mother had been a prostitute (they were bastards), and in this way he acted out the wish to buy her from his stepfather.

Bert Fighting and Being Beaten

During the last six months of Bert's treatment there was a mounting crescendo of fights. He severely injured a paper boy who was cheeky to him, so that he had to be in a hospital for many days. He blamed the therapist for his belonging nowhere, neither to the ordinary youths of the town because he was under the court and had been brought up in an institution, nor to the "club" of criminal youths who had graduated through the approved schools and Borstals.

He picked fights in the dark of a cinema with a gang of Teddy boys. They threatened to beat him up, he took up the challenge and withdrew to the lavatory. There he disclosed his powerful body and challenged the leader of the gang. On seeing his murderous intention and powerful physique, the leader of the Teddy boys refused to fight. This made him afraid that he must be mad if he could frighten a gang of Teddy boys; he also feared that they would waylay him and kill him.

After this he became involved in fights with gangs in which he was severely battered. He came to his sessions covered with blood, his suit ruined, and told how he complied with the rules of boxing and never defended himself as the others did. He further described how happy he felt when booted by the gang. "I was so happy, I was so happy," he reiterated. The fantasy underlying this was that if he suffered intensely enough, his twin would come to him and together they would fight and destroy the gang, then would fight each other. Another version was that they would compete to see which one could overcome the greatest number in the gang. The winner to be acknowledged by the unknown father.

Fights on a lesser scale continued until he joined in with the gang. He wished to break off treatment, fearing the dark on his journeys to the sessions. Finally he did so.

COORDINATION AND COMPARISON OF MATERIAL

When Bill and Bert left the Hampstead Nurseries at the age of approximately four years, the predictions as to their future development were not optimistic ones. There were too many factors which they had against them. So far as environmental circumstances were concerned, there was illegitimacy, residential upbringing, insecurity in the relationship to the mother, a stepfather who did not welcome their appearance. Developmentally, they were found not to be up to age in intellect and almost totally lacking in educational response. Emotionally, their strongest tie was to each other, and this twinship was a factor of overriding importance in disturbing other contacts. Their aggression was out of control, and any adaptation to group life almost nonexistent.

It was not easy under these conditions to make provision for their future upbringing. So far, in the Hampstead Nurseries, separation from each other had proved the only method which brought favorable results. Although, in the face of their close and exclusive attachment, this was not an easy step to take, it was considered in their case. There seemed to be a chance that Bert, less aggressive and more lovable and intelligent than his brother, might win the mother's affection. He was her first-born son whom she professed to love best. On the strength of this she might be able to cope with him, and it was thought therefore that he should go home. This, of course, would leave Bill in the worse position, separated from his twin, unloved and rejected by the mother, with a very slender chance of finding somewhere in an institution a fatherly authority able to control and guide him. What was also considered was the possible guilt aroused by such arrangements in the favored twin.

However that might be, this was the first solution tried, with full awareness that in the case of these boy twins only the formation of new object ties could prove to be a beneficial factor of their eventual socialization. It was considered also as a possibility that all efforts might be in vain and that it was too late to undo the consequences of their failure in educational response in their first four years of life.

When investigating, on the basis of the material collected, the factors which are responsible for the difficulties of development, it is natural to give first place to the twinship of the boys, since this seemed the cause of their withdrawal from other human contacts. In the comparison between past and present, accordingly, the material is arranged in the following order of importance: identity of appearance; mirror image; struggle for their own identity; excitability; antisocial development; differences in the personality of the twins.

Identity of Appearance

As identical twins, Bert and Bill were the mirror image of each other, at first with no distinguishable marks. The complications in their lives caused by this fact hardly altered over the years, although in time the effect of it on their own feelings began to have increasing repercussions.

So far as the environment was concerned, their identical appearance led to confusion and to consternation in those who had their care. As reported in the material, the mother herself was put out by her uncertainty in distinguishing between the twins, never knew for certain whether she was handling one or the other, made statements concerning one which, in reality, referred to the other child, and in her preference for Bert or Bill was guided by single traits such as activity, aggression, mischievousness (p. 16) rather than by an attraction emanating from the whole personality of the child. There was no doubt that under such circumstances her object cathexis of the children was uncertain, weak, shifting, and lacking efficiency and warmth.

The difficulties which arose with their nurses were not dissimilar. Here it was above all the doubt whether affection or dislike, praise or blame were attached to the right or wrong child, a difficulty which persisted far beyond the Nurseries into their latency periods and adolescence. At times it led to their being treated with unjust severity (see the incident of Bert, being mistaken for Bill and shut in a cupboard); at other times it led to their being let off too lightly to avoid injustice (see the matron's report, 1954). In either case a correction applied with such uncertainty cannot but have had a negative effect. Even in adolescence, Mr. Barron paid tribute to the effect on him and the whole Hostel by their identity of appearance by reporting that he could make no contact with them until he knew "which was which," and that "no separate relationship" started until it was discovered that Bert's and Bill's "jaws were slightly different."

In so far as their personal problems with identity of appearance were concerned, there was a definite difference between past and present. As infants or young children they were first oblivious and then enjoyed being like each other (see Mirror Image), and there is no doubt that in latency they made use of it in the service of delinquent behavior. It was only toward and in adolescence that this impinged on their problems of identity and aroused resentment and anxiety, as revealed in the treatment situation. It showed manifestly in Bill's fear that the police might mistake him for Bert when arresting the attacker of the mother, or catch him instead of Bert as a fugitive from the Remand Home. In both cases identity of appearance had become a symbol for identity of crime, or guilt. It showed also, less overtly, in both boys in their inability to tolerate the physical presence or nearness of the twin (see Choice of New School).

But even in adolescence, after the twins had parted company, their identical appearance was still used in the service of their positive attachment, for example, on the occasion when Bert used the confusion between their looks to glean information about Bill.

Mirror Image

The relationship of infants to their own mirror image has been studied at length,[3] and descriptions have been given how children not only enjoy meeting their own reflection but pet and stroke the image, etc. Confusion between their own mirror image and sight of the twin was noted with Bert and Bill at seventeen months and again at two and a quarter years. There is little doubt that living in the presence of the twin was for them synonymous with living in the presence of their own reflection. There were indications also (see Chart 20) that the intensity of their reaction to being separated from each other contained narcissistic elements, loss of the twin representing in this sense the loss of a portion of their own person.

In infancy, the twins' relationship to each other was compounded, therefore, of a mixture in which it was impossible to assess the relative importance of narcissistic trends on the one hand and of object-directed strivings on the other. Teaming up together in mischief, doing exactly the same thing at the same moment without giving a visible signal to each other, moving about the room in the same position and with identical gestures (p. 38) point to narcissistic unity and identification rather than any known form of close early object relationship. So does the understanding without words, the deliberate

3 See Lacan (1949), and also *Twins* (1952), Chart 24.

copying games (pp. 24-25), calling each other by the same name, displaying the same needs and wishes at the same moment (p. 20). Doubtless this identification based on narcissism was broken up only gradually by the dawning realization that the twin was not merely a duplication of the self, whose identical reactions heightened the wishes, needs, impulses of their own person, but also a rival to the self, capable of monopolizing wanted objects and means of satisfaction. This realization reached a climax in the later feelings of rivalry and the conviction that pleasure gained by one twin automatically implied the failure of the other twin to attain a coveted object or desire.

On the other hand, the unconscious material elicited in the treatment of the boys in adolescence emphasized the elements of object cathexis even in their earliest relationship. It is well known nowadays that in adolescence, the individual institutes a struggle against his early object ties partly to remove these persons from being drawn into his regressive incestuous fantasies, partly to prepare himself for forming new ties to strangers outside the circle of the family. This struggle against the early objects, normally the parents, can take various forms from bodily removal and avoidance of their presence to emotional indifference toward them, or of passionate hate and denigration.

That Bert and Bill reacted toward each other in adolescence in all these manners, overtly and unconsciously (i.e., removed themselves from each other, avoided each other, abused and hated each other, etc.) seems to prove that they were, indeed, each other's earliest love objects, not only each other's narcissistically cathected mirror images. In this case, it is the later analytic explanation which makes a decisive pronouncement on an instance of uncertainty in direct observation.

On the other hand, narcissistic elements did not cease to play their part also at this late stage. When at sixteen, Bert saw Bill from the distance on his bicycle and reported in his session that he "held himself like a king," there was no doubt about his narcissistic enjoyment of this "mirror image," in the middle of all the negative, derogative, hostile feelings toward the twin which belonged to the rejection and reversal of the object relation.

Struggle for Their Own Identity

All adolescents have to go through a phase when they struggle to establish themselves as a person in their own right vis-à-vis themselves, their families, their contemporaries and the wider community. What they come up against during this process are the preoedipal and oedipal identifications which have become part of their own superego. To grow truly into himself, the adolescent finds himself therefore at war not only with the objects but also with the moral and aesthetic demands, aims, and ideals of his past.

In Bert and Bill, with their abortive relationships to adults and the defects in their superego formation, little or nothing of these normal conflicts became visible in the adolescent material. For them, to "be a person in their own right" had one meaning only: to be without the twin. If, in their case, adolescent treatment had not been preceded by a detailed observation of their infancy, the therapist might have gained the impression that here were children in whom hostility for an ever-present rival and competition had played a decisive role from earliest beginnings. This would have been an error. It is true that the twins were in rivalry from infancy: in the relationship to their mother when both cried for her, wanted to be picked up by her first, fed first (Charts 17, 21); in the Nursery when both wanted to be loved and cared for exclusively (pp. 21-23); when they wanted to grasp and possess the same toy at the same moment. But this rivalry, although present, was not the element which shaped their childhood. The factor responsible for this was the opposite one of extreme closeness and possessive intimacy with the twin, the copying games, the understanding without words, the constant companionship, the increase in personal power and efficiency through ganging up with the twin (Chart 20), the complete absence of loneliness. The intensity in their rejection of the twin in adolescence has to be understood therefore, not as commensurate with infantile rivalry, but as being in reverse ratio to the earlier closeness.

To get rid not only of the external presence but also of the internal image of the twin was the aim for which both boys struggled in adolescence and for the accomplishment of which they were willing to accept the therapist's help. Their efforts were given expression in treatment in various ways. There were manifest complaints about the twin birth, memories and cover memories which confirmed the harmfulness of the twinship; direct threats expressed against the twin. Less directly expressed, there were also the hostilities against other children as displacements from the twin, as well as displacements onto inanimate objects such as the bicycle. Finally, there was the full impact of the murderous wishes which both boys harbored against each other and which determined much of their behavior. It is significant in this respect that both were fully aware of the other's enmity against themselves and were afraid of it; but that both, before treatment, were equally unconscious of their own wish to kill, and of its projection onto their partner.

In spite of this, the advantages of twinship were not given up easily, and made themselves felt by means of regressive pulls back to the infantile enjoyment of them. This becomes very evident in Bert's treatment, at the time when he tried in fantasy to become "a twin to himself," substituting for the rejected brother a play either with words, or with the right and left part of his own body.

"Togetherness" in infancy persisted also in another form, namely, in the constant thought preoccupation with the absent twin, the ongoing comparison of earnings and possessions, the fear (and underlying wish) for his reappearance and its consequences, etc.

Excitability

In normal development a child's involvement in autoerotic activities limits the influence which the objects in the environment can exert on him. His ability to provide pleasurable sensations and excitement for himself renders him independent to some degree of the objects, of their approval and disapproval and of their pleasure- and comfort-providing actions.

With Bert and Bill, to excite the twin and to be excited by him took the place of autoerotic stimulation, as shown in the first four years by their touching and biting games, their puppy play (pp. 21-26). Since the twin and the games with him were ever present, the effect of this on withdrawal from environmental influences was considerable.

There was also the added factor that "autoerotism in partnership" produced a higher degree of stimulation than is seen usually when similar activities are carried out in isolation, the excitement of each partner acting as a further seduction and incitement for increased abandonment on the other. With Bert and Bill this came under observation from their crawling days onward and destroyed completely any atmosphere of internal or external peacefulness in their lives. Whatever was initially merely interesting to them was turned by such interaction into intense agitation which intensified and increased until they were both overwhelmed by it (especially Bill, see p. 25). Nothing else mattered at such times (pp. 24-25). Touching each other's bodies started often in a gentle way but turned invariably into rough handling (pp. 24-25, 34; Charts 15 and 16); what started with rubbing ended with biting, etc. It was also notable that this tension was heightened, not diminished, when both their attentions were directed toward an ulterior aim (such as the mother's attention) and when they were in rivalry. In these instances they were deaf to any interference and completely unaware of any approach to them (p. 34; Chart 19). Tension was accompanied by screaming (especially shrill and intense in Bill).

Excitement of this kind was not only generated in partnership, as shown by Bert's banging his head against a table leg on his own, and developing head banging as an "autoaggressive" activity (Chart 16) which was taken over only subsequently by Bill (Charts 21, 25, 26). But even this became a common activity since at two years five months the twins, reunited after a separation, greeted each other by banging their heads against each other. To such exciting pleasures, pain was no barrier. They inflicted it on themselves, on each other (as well as on other people), for example, by biting (especially Bill).

There is the possibility that the twins' mother fostered rather than discouraged these attitudes by enjoying activity, aggressiveness, and mischievousness, first in Bill and later in Bert. But this was not really the impression recorded in the observations. It was rather that the twins, through constant interaction, had a highly developed erotic response to every kind of tension and influx of stimulation and used every opportunity offered to extract the highest pleasure yield from the events.

When comparing the infantile shared autoerotism of Bert and Bill with the equivalent features as they appeared in their later treatment, the outstanding impression is one of sameness, of an intact survival of the infantile trends without adaptation, modification, and certainly without sublimation. There was the same uncontrollable excitement which they engendered in each other, and which did not allow them to have a moment's peace. There was the same heightening of tension in rivalry, as expressed by Bert: "I never want anything until I see Bill with it," or by Bill when he seized a red-hot poker because Bert was holding it: "When I saw him with it, I had to have it," an excitement which did not allow for any consideration of consequences and urged them as blindly toward wish fulfillment as it had done at the toddler stage.

What had not changed either, in spite of adolescence, was that the mother (probably by virtue of her absence and imaginary, rather than real, role) was continually in the center of their thoughts as the coveted prize to be won away from the other, especially so in states of tension and excitement. When Bill was claimed by the parents in adolescence, and Bert rejected, the former could not do enough to erase every trace of the brother from the home surroundings. This, very effectively, revived and reversed the infantile situation, when Bert was home and Bill relegated to the Nursery.

It was not only the bodily presence of the brother which influenced the other twin, any reminder of a relationship between two people was enough to cause tension. In Bill's words: "Even the voice of one person talking to another is unbearable." At the same time the competitive element which had meant companionship in their past was too precious to be missed (see Bert and his "hare-and-tortoise race" in the Forestry job).

Unchanged continuance of the past was most noticeable in the openly homosexual elements in the adolescent twins' relationship. Here, bodily nearness to each other was sufficient to cause touching, whether this was of friendly or of hostile kind. The early "puppy play" was still there, even if developed into a sadistic rolling on the ground, punching rhythmically the arm or body of the twin. As in the past, such games served skin erotism. If Bert was unable to fight with boxing gloves (because he needed to feel the bare flesh), and Bill could fight only when gloved, this showed both boys' fixation to skin erotism, even if in this case Bill had gone further than his brother in rejecting it.

Homosexual possessiveness of the other's body showed also when Bert, after seeing Bill fighting with a stranger, reported to his therapist: "I was jealous of the other boy hitting Bill. I wanted to do it myself."

Secondarily, their own body fights were also displaced onto the world at large, with distorting consequences for their conception of reality. The army, for example, was seen by both boys as an assortment of people who fight—as in their puppy play—and fighting as an exciting fantasy could be increased to murdering, turn into an orgy of killing, as in the imaginary picture of their soldier father who was thought to have killed hundreds of people, and would finally destroy the twin.

Another feature which remained unchanged from infancy to adolescence was their masochism. Just as painful head bangings had been pleasurable in the Nursery, beatings provoked by Bill in school, by Bert from the gangs, were welcome. When Bert came to his session in a pitiable state, kicked and maltreated by the gang members, all he could describe was an overwhelming feeling of excitement and pleasure: "I was so happy, I was so happy."

The same feelings could be aroused in them also by self-inflicted damage, i.e., by their accident proneness (Bill more than Bert). Significant in this respect for both of them was engineering situations which subsequently they could not control; Bill taking off his bicycle brakes, or running in front of an oncoming car; or as shown in the follow-up, Bill possessing a motor cycle which Bert envied as a "death machine," and on which he had had already six accidents, etc.

This is not too unlike the accidents which the twins inflicted on themselves in the Nursery, such as Bert falling out of his cot at fifteen months, hurting his finger on a tin at eighteen months, falling, cutting eyelid, having to be stitched at two years four months; or Bill "being insensitive against pain, whether he has hurt himself or is hurt by other children" at two years five months (Chart 24). Also Mr. Shields reports from the examination of the boys: "Both twins showed me, with some pride, the scars they had on their legs from various accidents. Bill has had to have two lots of stitches on his left leg and two years ago he broke both wrists," at twelve years five months.

There is only one difference emerging here between past and present. Perhaps already as a result of treatment, Bert especially became aware of the dangers in which he placed himself, to the degree that he pleaded even to be returned to the Remand Home where he would be controlled by external authority.

Antisocial Development

It is obviously out of order to apply the term dissocial or anti-social to infants and toddlers since no understanding for social necessities and little compliance with them can be expected of them. In spite of this, many of the observers who saw Bert and Bill in the Hampstead Nurseries were tempted to regard them as belonging to this category. They stood out among the other population of the Nurseries as being wild, passionate, overexcited, aggressive, out of control. They were the despair of their nurses and they created pandemonium (pp. 25-26). As they grew from infants into toddlers and from toddlers into nursery-school children, they did not quieten down in their behavior, and they did not become more constructive in their actions.

There were several features in their early development which gave rise to grave concern regarding the possibility of future social adaptation.

There were, for one, those inherent in the fact of twinship, namely, the absence of a symbiotic relationship with mother or mother substitute which could lead to useful identifications; and instead the symbiotic relationship with the twin which served merely to intensify existing behavior patterns by reciprocal infection and cross-stimulation.

There was an overdevelopment of narcissism (owing to the narcis-sistic tie to the twin) and an underdevelopment of object libido, caused by the insecurity of the mother relationship and institutional life with consequent withdrawal from the adults and disregard for their wishes.

There was imperfect differentiation between self and twin, their own identity at the toddler stage tending to become lost and identi-fication with the twin exaggerated. There are many observed ex-amples of this with Bert and Bill, especially in rivalry when a rapid change of identity took place. In wishing for what the rival had at the moment, the child experienced his own self as frustrated, but identification with the twin served to give him a share of the latter's enjoyment—a process tending to interfere with the development of a clear concept of the self.

Their age-adequate advances in speech and muscular control were placed at the service of pleasurable interaction with each other and used for the expression of passion and excitement in shouting, screaming, joking, "puppy play." There was no constructive use of toys and no beginning neutralization of drive energies.

There was little use of mother or nurse as comfort giver. On the contrary, due to the existing rivalry, turning to a shared adult (mother or nurse) merely served to heighten tension and increase excitement.

There were few advances toward other children who were treated in the main as disturbers, or as if they were the furniture. Only occasionally a child was used as substitute for the twin, usually in the twin's absence.

Lastly, and perhaps most ominously, adult objects, even if cathected, were not used for purpose of imitation, identification, and ideal formation. Bert and Bill were not unattached in the Nursery, in the sense in which autistic children are withdrawn. They had a special relationship to nurse Eva, for example, who took care of both of them from the age of four to nineteen months. As toddlers, they expressed their positive feelings about being in her presence by increasing excitement, flinging themselves about, throwing toys and plates, laughing and screaming alternatively. When she left the room, they would scream with despair; when she reappeared, scream with pleasure. They expressed their competition for her attention by biting and hitting her and each other. But the relationship went no further than this. The nurse had no influence over them and no power to control them, which distressed her greatly.

By the time Bert and Bill arrived at their treatment in Mr. Barron's Hostel (age twelve), there was no doubt that they could be classified legitimately as antisocial. They were unruly, boisterous, intolerant of authority exercised over them, in constant difficulties with housemothers, matrons, teachers, headmasters, always on the verge of being excluded or expelled from school. They were in conflict with the police, and Bert was brought before the Court. They either fought gangs or became themselves members of a gang of Teddy boys with whom they shared the characteristics of indifference for the feelings of other people, enjoyment of terrorizing, of hurtful and cruel acts, and a continuous dissatisfaction that went with the desire to oppose law and order.

Every analytically trained therapist who treats an antisocial boy is faced in the patient's material on the one hand by the delinquent's mood of bitterness and rage against parents, family, community, and on the other hand by the "delinquent character," i.e., by the patient's inability to control himself or be controlled; the urgency of his desires; the impulsiveness of his actions; his irritability and, at the same time, the repetitiveness of his behavior. All of these were present in the case of Bert and Bill. The questions which every therapist poses to himself invariably are whether and how far the patient's resentments are justified, i.e., whether he had been rejected and discriminated against in reality or merely in his imagination; which was the point at which his antisocial development deviated first from the norm; and, above all, is the patient's irresponsive, infantile way of pleasure-seeking equivalent to a breakdown, a regression from a more advanced level of socially adapted functioning, or is it representative of an arrest at the normal toddler stage, i.e., at the level of irresponsibility and primary-process functioning?

In the case of Bert and Bill, we were in the advantageous position of being able to check the answers suggested by the treatment material against the childhood records of the boys. Both boys filled their sessions with bitter accusations against the mother who, according to them, had "cheated them of their birthright" (Bert), against the unknown father who had deserted them (Bill), against the siblings who had displaced them in the home (both), and against the stepfather who had thrown them out. A fantasy image of the unknown father appeared (Bill) in which the latter was a cruel and victorious killer of men, but also a hero who braved every danger to find his son. In these family romances of both boys, realistic and imaginary elements were blended in the usual manner: it was real that the mother had ceased her regular visits to the Nursery shortly before the birth of the next baby; also that they were unwelcome in the family (above all due to their being unmanageable) and that they had never had a proper chance of home life. What the material at this stage did not reveal was the fact that there were chances given in the Nursery to form attachments to mother substitutes (nurses Eva, Hanni), of which they were unable to make appropriate use. The image of the nurses did not appear until after adolescence and after the relationship to the twin had ceased to be an active force. There was no reality behind the father fantasy, except the detail of the soldier's uniform worn in the war, seen at seventeen months. The actual father was a kindly, inoffensive, modest married man onto whom the heroic killer attitudes were projected from the twins' own wishes.

The other question, whether Bert's and Bill's delinquency represented an arrest in development or a regression, was answered fully by the comparison of the boys' behavior in and outside treatment with the Nursery records and the follow-up of behavior during latency. Treatment material showed that they were at the mercy of their instincts with regard to rivalry, competition, the expression of hate displaced from the twin onto other children: all this an exact repetition of their inner state of mind described in the Nursery records (pp. 25-26); that they were impervious to influence by adult authority as they had been as infants (Chart 24); that they expressed their possessiveness of adults by hurting and attacking (compare Bert's attacks on the mother with the boys' behavior to nurse Eva; Charts 23, 24); that they used other persons to reproduce the twin relationship; that they had pleasure in creating chaos in their surroundings (compare Mr. Barron's report on their influence on the Hostel with the "pandemonium" created in the Nursery; p. 25); that there was fear of each other, of aggressive boys at school (Bert), of the army (Bill), but no evidence of guilt for any of their actions (compare the lack of the precursors of guilt in infancy such as the rarity of the occasions when they felt sorry for having hurt a nurse; Chart 24). Above all, the quality of their relationships remained the same: they formed attachments narcissistically, on the basis of feeling that the other person resembled themselves, or possessed qualities admired by them, rather than relationships based on cathexis with true object libido (compare here the infantile relationship to the twin with their fascination with Mr. Barron after he had impressed them by being "reckless," their friendship with Teddy boys, etc.).

On the basis of these items it may be justified to draw the conclusion that the twins' delinquency did not represent a regressive process, similar in structure to a neurosis, but an arrest and defect in personality development, i.e., in defense organization, ego control over the impulses, and in superego and ideal formation. It may also be justified to conclude that these defects are due to imperfectly developed early object relationships and undue autoerotism and narcissism developed in the twinship.

Differences in the Personality of the Twins

So far, for the purposes of this study, Bert and Bill were treated as if they were indeed "identical," not only in looks but in personalities as well. Actually, this was not the case; although they had many important characteristics in common, there were at the same time differences in their personalities significant for their fate, their treatment, and their future development. So far as could be ascertained none of these personal differences were the direct result of being either first- or second-born since Bert was, in his treatment, seen to be as resentful of having a brother born in immediate succession to himself as Bill resented having been immediately preceded by one.

As shown by the Nursery records and further by the result of Mr. Shields's inquiries, there was a gradual change-over (from Bill to Bert) in regard to physical strength and aggression toward the twin. An opposite change-over was felt to happen in Nursery times in regard to cleverness, since first Bert, then Bill were observed to have the best ideas and to initiate games. In one of the residential homes (at seven years nine months) Bert was regarded to be the "quicker thinker"; at the same time another opinion considered "Bill's schoolwork generally a little ahead of Bert." Actually, it was the psychologist's opinion that the twins were both of average intelligence, sometimes one, sometimes the other doing a little better on a formal test.[4]

[4] Age	Bert	Bill	Test
10½ yrs.	98	95	Binet (I.Q.)
11¾ yrs.	99	106	Binet (I.Q.)
12 5/12 yrs.	104	88	Thurstone's Primary Mental Abilities (Total weighted score)

There is no doubt that, so far as the use of intelligence was concerned, rivalry, competition, and the general wish to outdo the twin acted as a source of stimulation for them and proved beneficial for their school successes.

What proved to be the most portentous difference between them was Bert's greater sensitiveness and responsiveness in infancy. Probably, initially this was no more than his answer to Bill's greater size and strength which threatened him. However this may have been, it was Bert who cuddled into the arms of nurse or mother while Bill appeared indifferent to attention (Charts 16, 18), and it was this greater gentleness which prompted the mother to take him home at four and a half years while Bill was left in the Nursery. This meant that Bert experienced, for a few months at least, the sensation of being the unrivaled eldest son in the home, preferred to his twin, and that he had a chance to develop the rudiments of normal family relations. That he had a possessive oedipal relationship to his mother at this time is suggested by two later reactions, both turned into the negative, it is true: by his murderous attacks on the mother when she taunted him with his illegitimate birth; and by his reaction of avoidance and disgust to her pregnancy. More important still: it may have been this boost to his object libido which came to the help of his treatment by cementing the treatment alliance with Mr. Barron and lessening the narcissistic versus the object-related elements in the transference to him.

In contrast to this, Bill, as the rejected twin, showed through his later childhood more of the characteristics of the unloved "institutional" child ready to revenge himself on others, more eager to inflict pain on people or animals, found to push a boy in front of an oncoming car, inciting other children to unlawful acts, causing a bus to crash, etc. He turned the tables on his twin when he finally succeeded in inducing the parents to allow him home and keep him there for good, but at the age of almost fifteen, this was too late to make up for the missed oedipal relationship.

In contrast to Bert, Bill did not resent the mother's renewed pregnancy. Also in contrast to Bert, he could not maintain the treatment alliance with Mr. Barron and broke off his therapy abruptly, as many children or young people with institutional backgrounds are apt to do.

FOLLOW-UP

Contrary to the more pessimistic predictions which were expressed several times during the boys' treatment, their antisocial outbursts ceased after adolescence. Since the material concerning this consists exclusively of external data (in conversations, letters, etc.), it does not allow for valid conclusions as to the reasons for the change. We can speculate only what played a part in it and concerning the significance that should be allocated to the various factors.

There are external and internal circumstances to be considered in this respect. Among the former we list with regard to Bill his reacceptance by the family at the age of fourteen years eleven months, with regard to both boys their bodily separation from each other which marked at the same time the breaking up of the antisocial twin gang. To the internal factors belong, above all, the effect of treatment in which the interpretation of the unconscious hostility to each other played the leading part. Since both boys were inexorably tied to each other by this unconscious hostility, the analysis of this element may have been decisive in enabling them to grow apart and to form new and positive relationships.

Information on Bill

There is only meager information about Bill after he left his treatment at the age of fifteen years. As reported before, he had two jobs until he settled down as a bus conductor. He continued to live at home and no further complaints from the parents reached the authorities. One source of information were letters written by Bert containing the following facts about Bill: At age thirteen years four months (like Bert) he was collecting books as a hobby. At fifteen years two months "he has grown much stronger and heavier than Bert." At sixteen years nine months he "has just bought a death machine with the help of his dad—a 350 B.S.A. motor bike." At seventeen years eight months he had an accident on his motor bike, also he "has had five accidents since last November but this one is the worst . . . he has had some stitches" in his face.

At nineteen years, Bill "is quite happy in his work. Bill is courting still and is still saving like mad to get married."

At nineteen years two months, he is reported to be engaged to his girl friend Julia.

At twenty years nine months, Bert writes, "Bill got married to a girl called Julia. I don't know her well except that she was at school with me."[5]

At twenty-one years, "Bill seems to like being married; he does not talk of anything else."

A second source of information was Mr. Barron himself who wrote to Bill after hearing of his engagement and received the following answer:

> I have just recently got married and was very lucky to get a house, it was offered to us so we took it, it's much better than living with in-laws.
>
> Bert has been in the Air Force for three years now and he is enjoying himself. He has been abroad quite a lot, and is in Singapore now.
>
> My mother has been a different woman this last year or two, we have got on quite well together. She is very pleased that I have got married and a house of my own, and gets on well with Julia (my wife). They have got on well together from the first time I took Julia home.
>
> My mother is very pleased to have heard from you. Give my regard to Mrs. Barron and the little ones who have grown up now.

Bill also visited Mr. Barron with his wife to introduce her, which Mr. Barron describes as follows:

> Bill makes a very good impression. He has a quiet manner and was well dressed in very good taste. He is obviously extremely pleased to have a home of his own, and his conversation was mainly about the things he had grown in his garden and the plans he has for cultivating it next. He spoke of the difficulty he had at home after his stepfather's death, and was able to give a vivid description of his mother's depression and said that although he sometimes found himself arguing with her, by and large he was able to "coax her along."
>
> He showed considerable enterprise to find a house before he married. His wife impressed me as a very nice person.

[5] According to Mr. Barron's impression, Julia was in love with Bert at that time, a fact of which he was oblivious.

Information on Bert

In marked contrast to his brother, Bert was not offered new opportunities to establish a real family relationship after his treatment.
On the other hand, he showed the same ability to make new contacts. He selected for this partly the actual foster family where he
was placed after leaving the Hostel and for the other part began to
form an elaborate and constant tie to a figure in the distance whom
he treated as an imaginary mother substitute.

As mentioned before, in their prehistory in the Hampstead Nurseries a young nurse in training, Hanni Koehler, had been assigned
as mother substitute to the twins when they were twenty-one months
old. She took care of both for a short time and then was chosen for
Bill exclusively at the age of two years eight months to three years
ten months. After the closing of the Hampstead Nurseries she had
tried to keep in contact with them by sending them cards or presents
for Christmas and their birthdays. She received no replies until the
twins were thirteen years and three months when Bill thanked her
for a Christmas present. Her correspondence with Bill ended with
this. But Bert surprisingly enough took over from here and from
then onward communicated with her with increasing frequency and
intimacy, treating her quite clearly as an important person in his
life. His letters which began at thirteen years four months, i.e., when
still in the Hostel, were written in the beginning mostly at times
of stress and loneliness, for example, when Mr. Barron fell ill, later
when Mr. Barron left the Hostel, when he himself started work and
had not found a place to live, etc. The letters ranged over many
topics such as work, foster family, his own family, and included a
real concern about Hanni's doings and family members. The following are some quotations:

> [At age fifteen years two months:] When I leave school and
> live in digs I may never see Bill or the family again because I
> am in the care of the County Council.
> [At sixteen years five months, he writes about a new job as
> mate on a delivery van.] I have changed my job of working on
> the Forestry Commission . . . because I wanted to have my
> thoughts to myself looking at the scenery of the Surrey downs and
> the country sides of Kent, and also because I wanted to travel
> a bit. . . .

I would not say I was handsome, if you are judging me by that photo, I would say it was the summer air because I was on holiday.

I do get very lonely even when I am around with the other boys, I feel as if I am not one of them. I sort of doze off and when someone speaks to me I just don't know what he is talking about, I try to keep myself to myself, sometimes I go for long walks by myself in the eve until about 10 o'clock. Sometimes I go into the café and get a drink and sit in a corner table by myself and think about all sorts of things and I don't speak to anybody. I don't really want to bother you with my loneliness. . . . P.S. I enjoy every minute of reading your letters and writing to you, but when I write I am in a sort of dream so you must excuse the spelling and writing and the mistakes.

[At sixteen years nine months, when he reports on Bill's motor bike he says:] All the boys and girls I know asked me how long and where I got my bike, but I had to tell them it was not mine but my brother's, they said they could swear it was mine. I hope to get a motor bike soon, a much bigger one than Bill's.

At eighteen years he wrote to Hanni as well as to Mr. Barron, that by the time he heard from them he would be in the R.A.F. and had joined up for five years, that he had been thinking a long time about it before deciding to enlist. He did not know yet what trade he would want to take up, but would try for a physical training instructor. "When I come home on leave my mother and father say I can come home to stay." He had been visiting them regularly and was getting on well with them.

At seventeen years, "I went home to see my mother and family, they seemed very glad to see me."

Further letters to both reported from his R.A.F. address that he had finished his training and was off to Malta, that his stepfather had died of lung cancer but that his family had not been able to reach him as he had not given them his address, "My mother did not like that much."

There was an interruption in letters since Bert omitted to send his Malta address to Hanni; but they were taken up again at twenty years when he was back in England on the point of leaving for "another 2½-years tour of duty in Malaya or Singapore."

At twenty years two months, "I spent Christmas at home and really enjoyed myself. Mum was very pleased because we all could come home and Teddy got a few weeks from R.A.F. training camp. Bill has got engaged to a girl from N."

Quotations from the letters that follow contain a surprising amount of interest in his family without any reference to the fact that he had been the one rejected by them, nor do they show any hate or rivalry for his siblings. Apart from the flow of information about Bill quoted above, he reports the following about his younger brother:

> Teddy, my younger brother, has just left school and will be entering the R.A.F. as a boy entrant. [About his little sister:] I took my small sister out for a walk. She is very sensible when crossing the road, and in her talk is very grown up. [About his mother:] Mum is not the same as she was when Dad was alive, she seems to be drawn into herself and won't get out anywhere any more, she gets very moody at times, it is very difficult to know what to do for her.
>
> [At twenty-one years:] I always visioned my birthday at home, but it looks like I was robbed of it. . . . [He goes on to say that] everyone at home is just fine. . . . Mum has decided that she may get married again now that her children are gradually leaving her to go out and fend for themselves, Mary[6] has got herself engaged to a London policeman.
>
> [About Hanni's child, Judy, and her home he writes at sixteen years four months:] Has she any playmates of her own age to play with?
>
> [At sixteen years five months:] It is rather a funny thing you should have mentioned the way Judy pronounced my name the way she does because my landlady's little boy calls me "Bertrey." . . . It is a very kind thought of Judy's to be thinking of me that way, it had me quite taken back.
>
> [At sixteen years nine months:] . . . so glad that Judy can talk and recite nursery rhymes, it is surprising what kids of two or three come out with. My landlord's little girl of three says the most awkward things at times that you don't know how to answer them.
>
> [At seventeen years:] Judging by the photos of your new home it looks very comfortable and warm, as you say it looks very English. . . . I hope Judy will get used to living in her new home.
>
> The best way to get the tree down is to get some experienced

6 His younger stepsister.

men, who will chop the top branches down and work it down-
wards until there is nothing left.

[At eighteen years:] Is Judy at school yet and does she like
it? My landlady's daughter has started school this summer and she
is thrilled with it . . . give Judy a big kiss for me.

[At twenty years three months:] I hope you enjoyed your
Christmas as much as I enjoyed mine, and Judy too, all my best,
give Judy a big kiss from me.

[At twenty years four months, on receiving a photo of her
daughter:] Judy does look very well, doesn't she? I never expected
her to be so big. I have always imagined her as a very small girl.

You never told me you were going to have another baby. You
must be very happy to have a little boy and Judy will have someone to look after and spoil.

Bert also describes some events which give some clue to his reactions to his surroundings and his attitude to life in general.

[At twenty years three months:] Singapore is not quite what I
expected it to be, in fact it is totally different except for the
people. For a start it is very smelly and full of diseases of every
description . . . for some places are notorious for fleas, flies and
violent Chinamen.

[And in another letter:] Now I find it very nice, it [Singapore]
compares with London any time, the people here are very different from what I expected, they are very polite and ready to help
us, but they are also ready to rob us whenever they can, it does
not seem possible that these things go together, it is very educating to see them. . . . I have tried some of the Chinese foods and
like them. My favorite is Masi Gorang; if you go out to a Chinese
restaurant, you will have to try some, it's delicious.

[In this same letter he also refers to] Jane, my girl friend.
[In another letter:] I have been on a two month detachment at
Gan. Gan is an island 600 miles South West of Ceylon among
the Maldive Islands, it is 1½ long by ¾ wide and is used by the
R.A.F. as a stepping stone for transport Command; it is spaced
evenly between Singapore and Aden exactly 200 miles from each,
we had a fabulous time there. The sea is nice and clear like the
Med. and lots of fishing, boating, swimming and sunbathing. But
there is one snag and that is, that there are no Females, to see
or talk to, except one Nurse and a W.V.S. woman. I expect I will
be there for Christmas as well, apart from the Female situation,
it is about the best posting that the R.A.F. offer.

[And in another letter:] I have decided that I should take up
a hobby, out here you have to do something or you go nuts, the

hobby I have taken up is aeroplane modeling. I have already
made a good start on a stunt model, have flown it twice and
wrecked it twice, I flew it today and it went straight into a post
and broke the left wing into bits, it's great fun making them and
mending them when they crash.

It looks like everyone has decided on some fighting, what with
the Cuba situation and India with China. It's about time we were
put on active service again like at Cyprus, it would relieve the
monotony of training for it like we are always doing. I know it
sounds a bit macabre and gruesome but that is how I feel, even to
spend a few weeks on Jungle patrol in Malaya or Borneo would
help a bit.

[Then the allusions to marrying become more frequent.] Bill
writes to me ever so often, he likes married life and has managed
to get a house which is very lucky for him, it is next door to his
in-laws. I went to school with his wife, she is a nice person, although I do not think she has forgiven me for pulling her pig-
tails. I write a lot to Jane my girl friend and I have no trouble
in that direction. We have an understanding together that restricts neither of us while we are split up, it works, because for
4 years we have been courting and for 2½ years of that time I
have been overseas. She is a wonderful girl and I hope to marry
her when I get home in 1964.

[And the last letter:] I have only another 9 months to do in
Singapore and Jane is very pleased. She says that I am not going
overseas again without her, so it looks like I have been given
direct order. You asked me what I am going to do when I leave
the Forces. Well, I really don't know, I first have not given it
enough thought. I may even decide to stay in the RAF. I like the
life and the travelling but I do not like the moving every two
years or so, especially if I marry, it just is not fair on the woman
and she won't like it when we go away for months at a time,
which we do too often for the married men in the SQD. Their
whole attention is not on the job half the time and that can cost
someone his life. Jane would have to put up with quite a lot. So
I will have to make my mind up as to whether I want to get
married and settle down in civy street or stay in the forces and
enjoy myself while I can, it's a difficult thing to decide as I don't
think I am responsible enough yet for married life, even though
Jane thinks I am.

Concluding Remarks

Quotations from Bert's letters have been given at length because
of the striking contrast which emerges between the unruly, incon-

siderate, antisocial boy in the Hostel and the thoughtful, sensitive, and attached postadolescent who he turned out to be. What is stressed in the letters repeatedly is on the one hand his sympathy with mother figures and their concerns (his own mother, Hanni) and on the other hand his understanding of small children and their needs, i.e., feelings which were manifestly lacking in his past (compare his attack on his mother, his hate for his younger siblings).

Another new feature in his personality is the withdrawal into himself and the enjoyment of solitude, both feelings probably possible only after separation from the twin.

It is a further interesting point to view the intense hostility of the twins to each other, as revealed in their treatment, in the light of a remark made by Bill to Mr. Barron during the follow-up visit with his wife at age twenty-one. When asked if it had been wise to separate him and Bert when it happened, he answered that he did not think so as he missed him so very much.

It is also interesting to note that, after all, the fates of Bert and Bill remained intertwined: Bill chose for his wife a girl formerly in love with Bert, while Bert chose as his "pen-mother" a woman who had been Bill's nurse much longer than his own.

BIBLIOGRAPHY

Burlingham, D. (1952), *Twins: A Study of Three Pairs of Identical Twins.* New York: International Universities Press.
Lacan, J. M. (1949), The Mirror-stage. Abstract in *Int. J. Psa.,* XXX.

NOTES ON THE PSYCHOANALYTIC
CONCEPT OF CURE

K. R. EISSLER, M.D. (New York)

A twenty-seven-year-old unmarried woman was in psychoanalysis because of a severe neurosis, the leading symptom of which was erythrophobia. Because of her fears, she was seriously incapacitated in her social relationships as well as in her sexual life, and the prospect of having to remain unmarried, as the result of her symptom, greatly depressed her. The patient left treatment after three years, deeply disheartened, and without having made any progress either in the enlargement of her insight into her psychopathology or in the alleviation of her symptoms.

Eight years later, however, when I inquired into her condition, I received a letter from her that sounded exceedingly happy. Not only had she married; she had had three children, and had been equally successful in other respects that had seemed altogether outside her reach at the time of treatment.

It is rather exceptional for a patient to leave psychoanalytic treatment after three years without having obtained some kind of profit. But it is equally exceptional for even a successful analysis to be followed by a patient's obtaining the fulfillment of practically all her wishes—at least in so far as they can be fulfilled by external events. In this case, it was all the more remarkable in the light of the fact that it apparently came to pass in spite of the persistence of the patient's leading symptom.

A concatenation of events, any one of which occurs only infrequently, makes it worth while to consider in detail the implications of this clinical situation.

The patient was a white, American-born, Protestant woman of New England descent, who sought treatment for shyness, lack of confidence, and severe erythrophobia. The psychological tests that had been made at the request of the referring physician revealed the following diagnostic impression: anxiety hysteria with significant obsessive-compulsive features. The young woman was described as a person of superior intelligence, whose intellectual efficiency had not suffered because of her illness, but whose general cultural interests had become restricted, because of extensive repression, such as is encountered in hysteria. A projective trend and an aversion to introspection and free fantasy were also noted.

The patient was a good-looking woman, well-mannered and desirous of being freed of her leading symptom. She was the third child of a prosperous upper-middle-class family. The father, who had died in his early forties, when the patient was thirteen, had been a successful professional man. Her mother, a housewife, was an active person who had always been in good health.

The patient was the third among five siblings, two sisters being respectively five and three years older, one sister five years younger and a brother three years younger. None of her siblings showed any outstanding sign of permanent neuroticism; all of them could rightly be called well adjusted in the conventional sense, the two older sisters being happily married and with children. This made the patient feel all the more bitter about the necessity of having to go into psychoanalysis, which she evidently regarded as a bad mark or an injustice against her, or as a sign of personal ill-fatedness.

She had been timid from early childhood on, never daring to express her thoughts, out of fear that something might be found out about her. She suffered from various manifestations of anxiety, such as palpitation, sweating of the palms, and a fluttery feeling in the stomach. Yet the center of her apprehensions was the fear lest she blush.

It was difficult for her to determine how often this actually came to pass. Someone told her that she had done so, when she had not been aware of it; on the other hand, when she did feel a sensation of heat in her face, she was not certain that she had actually blushed, for once she had had the sensation while looking into a mirror, and she did not then observe any change of color (cf. Bien 1930, p. 71). Her most frequent complaint had to do with the feeling of approaching blushing.[1]

---

[1] Cf. Bien (1930) who reports that in his patients the fear of blushing was more troublesome than the blushing itself.

Thus, the unpleasantness seemed centered in the alleged pre-blushing phase, about which she never knew whether or not it would lead to an actual blush.[2] New situations, the necessity of making a decision or of talking to a group made her feel uncomfortable, and the approach of such situations easily aroused symptoms. The fear of blushing was of varying intensity; occasionally, when she would have expected it, she was free of it. At times it occurred, as far as she could judge, without provocation by external circumstances. The symptom was less likely to occur with strangers than in her contact with people whom she knew well or liked. It was almost certain to happen when anything occurred, or was spoken about, that could be even remotely connected with a sexual theme.

She was free of the fear when alone. Also when the room was dark, and she was certain that others would not notice it, she was not afraid of blushing.[3] Thus, it would be more correct to say that she was afraid of *being observed while blushing,* since the occurrence of blushing per se was not experienced as a danger. From her report, I got the impression that her actual blushing had occurred, if anything, less frequently than can be expected in the average person.[4] It is also noteworthy that the patient had never been exposed—as far as she could recall—to any humiliating remark or traumatic experience as a result of blushing.

The patient was free of the symptom before she went to college. When she was nineteen, it happened that she blushed two days after she had kissed a boy for the first time. She was not perturbed by this, however. Initially, she blushed only in relation to the boy who had kissed her; soon, however, the blushing spread, or at least she feared that it would, and the anticipation of it became the bane

[2] Feldman (1922, p. 27) appropriately calls this phase an "aura." It is not, however, an indispensable part of the symptom. Some patients do know which events will elicit blushing, in which case their fears are directed primarily toward the possibility of encountering such events (von Bechterew, 1897a; Weiss, 1933). This clinical sign seems to me to be important with regard to the prognosis.

[3] According to Feldman (1962), this would be exceptional: "In his fantasy, the blusher is always seen" (p. 370). Von Bechterew's case was symptom-free when alone (1897a).

[4] It seems that the question of the frequency of actual blushing has been in general neglected, and most reporters have accepted the patient's claims as valid, even though patients only rarely have the opportunity to verify whether the sensation is accompanied by the somatic event. Donath (1912) reports cases of erythrophobia without blushing (p. 354).

of her life. This fear threatened to drive her into isolation; it made her rigid and fearful of company; social circumstances permitting, she occasionally had to leave the room out of fear that the hated symptom would occur.

She watched herself more or less constantly, and had the feeling of acting a role. It seemed that the depersonalization occurred in the wake of the phobia, a kind of desperate grasp for relief, which in turn became a source of discomfort.

Her fear of blushing was a secret.[5] Only during the course of treatment did she dare to confide it to her mother. Once, when she started a new job and her superior, a woman, told her casually about her own tendency to blush, she could hardly believe her ears, feeling dumbfounded that anybody could be so frank and unconcerned about such a terrible symptom. Yet she could not state what was the danger in blushing.

The patient dated men and permitted herself to be kissed, although often with the fear of suffocation. She even indulged in sex play, and occasionally had an orgasm when fondled genitally. But intercourse was out of the question, and she felt puzzled as to why she should feel such an intense objection to sex, when her siblings seemed not to mind it. She was intensely desirous of matrimony and motherhood. Having planned her whole future around marriage, she felt desperate, in the light of what were turning out to be insuperable hurdles.

The obstacles to choice of object alone were formidable. Most men she would have liked as husbands were married, and those men who pursued her were not to her liking. When she was in love with a man, her paramount aim was that nobody should notice her affection. Furthermore, she behaved in a way that was likely to repel a

---

[5] The necessity of guarding the symptom as a secret was described early (see Breton, 1896, p. 1183). It does not occur in all patients suffering from this disease, but it does seem to be more frequent with erythrophobia than with other phobias. Feldman (1922, p. 16) reported a patient who was in the habit of warning others that he would blush. In childhood phobias, this may become a distinctive prognostic sign. There are children who do not dare to let their parents know about their phobias. There seems to be general agreement that the diagnosis of phobia should be made only where the patient develops measures to protect himself against the occurrence of anxiety. In the children whom I have in mind, such measures, while latently present, do not emerge because of the excessive fears attached, in turn, to them. As is well known, the limitations enforced by a phobia are transgressed as soon as adherence to them would endanger the patient's life.

man, if she was in the company of one whom she found likable, whereas she behaved quite adequately when she was with men she was not seriously interested in. At times, when she wanted a man to like her, she did not want him any longer as soon as she had reached her goal.

It was not quite clear to what extent such behavior was compulsive. At any rate, doubts of an obsessive-compulsive nature aggravated her condition.[6] She could not make up her mind in what she should believe. She even thought that her decision to be analyzed had been determined less by her symptom than by the desire to find out what her real beliefs were.

She joined a church after her sister had done so, but felt like a hypocrite while attending it. She did not know what people feel when they take communion. About her first communion, she said: "Mother cried. Nobody ever explained it to me." She wished that Christ had prevented His Crucifixion, because then He could have told her what to believe in. When she asked her father why she should do something, his answer was: "Because you were told to do it."

Shortly after she had confided to her mother her doubts about Christ, she expressed belief in the possibility that God had given her the idea of going into treatment, in order for her to clarify her mind. The doubt regarding convictions and beliefs extended also to the emotions, so that she often felt undecided about what emotions she was actually feeling. Once she started the session as follows: "I feel like mad. I would like to get mad. Do I really feel like that or do I think I feel mad? Perhaps I try to show an emotion."

The patient was correct, in view of the seriousness of her neurosis, in fearing that she would never get married. This prospect not only frustrated her object-related wishes, but also loomed as a defeat of her ambitions, since her two older sisters were married and, to her despair, her younger sister became engaged a few months after she started her treatment. Her rivalry with women was in general intense. To accept female authority was even harder for her than to cooperate with a man in a superior position. She was hypercritical

6 Bien (1930) very ably discussed the interrelation between phobia and obsessive neurosis in erythrophobia.

of women, quick to discover their weaknesses or deficiencies, and merciless in her evaluation of them.

As is obvious, her critical attitude toward women was related to her feelings about her mother. She loved and adored her mother, and praised her for her being ever ready to help not only her children but anyone who needed her help. Despite the mistakes she reproached her mother with having made in her upbringing, the patient was aware that the mother had devotedly loved her children and had put herself fully into their service.

Nevertheless, she felt annoyed during most of the time that she spent with her, and responded strongly to any difference of opinion, always being convinced that she was right and her mother was wrong. She also felt annoyed upon noticing the unavoidable dysfunctions that began to become apparent in her aging mother. She could stand it least when her mother showed signs of timidity.

A few times during her adult years, the patient lost her temper and indulged in violent quarrels with her mother. The causes of these tantrumlike outbreaks were, however, forgotten. Whenever she succeeded in spending time with her mother in a relaxed and pleasurable manner, she happily made a special note of that fact.[7]

Her ambivalence to women could be well observed in her relationship to her sisters. After a period of rivalry and envy, she loved her oldest sister dearly. This love extended also to her sister's husband, to whom she had made a positive father transference. The sister nearest her in age, with whom she had never gotten along well, was the object of her contempt. She described her as an empty conformist; in the same way, she looked down on that sister's husband, about whom she had only the worst to report. Thus, the two components of ambivalence were separately directed toward each of her two older sisters. In her relationship with her younger sister, she had acted like a bossy mother. The latter's engagement aroused much bitterness; and she described her sister as no longer being in need of her—thus rationalizing the evanescence of her own interest.

The patient felt that she was pitied by her family for being

---

[7] I believe that the reason why the patient asked for treatment at the particular time she did was that she was approaching the age at which her mother had been married. Apparently, it was extremely annoying for her that she should still be unmarried at an age when her mother had not been.

unmarried and unhappy. She may have been right that she was on the verge of being regarded as the traditional unmarried aunt, who can always be called upon for help when it is needed, but is a subject of constant worry as to where she will spend Thanksgiving and Christmas. Thus, on such occasions as her being invited to go with her mother to the theater, because another member of the family was prevented from doing so, she felt more pain or annoyance than pleasure.

She seemed to be right in regarding her family as snobbish, since her parents had fully integrated New England standards, and looked with disdain upon "outgroup" values. In protest—as the result of her own rebellious inclinations—she dropped her snobbishness after she left college; she often took the side of the underdog, and defended him against his opponents. But it became clear that behind her critical attitude toward snobbishness she was, if anything, more snobbish than her milieu. She felt pained that her family did not belong to the highest stratum of the community, and any indication that anyone thought of her as not being close to the peak of the social pyramid was encountered with anxiety and anger.

There were signs of fear on her part that I might be Jewish; she preferred to remain ignorant about it, "since it would offend you if I asked you about it." She once dreamed that she was being analyzed by a woman who told her she would recover only after she had become "anti-anti-Semitic." In conformity with New England standards, cleanliness ranged high in her value system; much time and energy were spent in keeping everything meticulously clean and well ordered, her reaction formations staying well within the boundaries of a compulsive personality in this respect.

As the psychological test had so rightly stressed, while her intelligence had not suffered as a result of her illness, her cultural interests had become narrowed down. There were no cultural pursuits that she was engrossed in. Evidently her disorder had infringed upon her sublimations. The total picture suggested that her conflicts had begun to settle into an (irreparably?) rigid character; resentfulness, envy, disappointment, and aggressiveness would complement the customary picture of the hypersensitive and disgruntled old spinster (cf. Bien 1930, p. 17).

Her psychopathology had set in early. While she was a charming baby, her temper tantrums soon made her a difficult infant. It is likely that these were her response to her mother's pregnancy. Since the father had been disappointed by her being a girl, it is probable that the parental interest was drawn more than customarily, and perhaps unavoidably, toward the prospect of a new baby. Be that as it may, her tantrums must have been excessive, since many a nurse could not stand being with her for any length of time, and the turnover was considerable.

Her reaction must have been all the sharper because the new rival was in fact a boy. Her dreams revealed undisguisedly an excessive penis envy.

The patient's psychopathology with regard to aggression was not too puzzling. When she said that it would have been so nice if there had been three older children in her family and two younger ones, but that, unfortunately, there were two older children and three younger ones, she graphically described one particular aspect of the strain prevailing in her childhood. She occupied the exactly middle position among the children; although she felt entitled to be counted as a member of the higher stratum, she was considered in social reality as belonging to the minor class—surely an important factor in her later siding with the underdog.

This also explains her preoccupation with questions of status. Her uneasy middle position in the line of children was aggravated by the feeling of distance that she had to either parent. The patient recalled that, at the age of eight, she concluded that her mother did not care for her. She had cut a finger with a pair of long scissors. When she ran to her mother, the latter showed no concern, but simply asked, "Why did you use those scissors?" and told her to go to the father to be taken care of.

Compulsive features in the parental technique of bringing up children had an unfortunate effect on her character development. When she was in a rage, she was locked into a closet for five minutes; if, upon being released, she continued to misbehave, she was locked in again, for a longer period of time. Food that was not eaten at lunch had to be eaten at dinner; regularity in bowel movements was enforced by the mother's insistence on daily inspection. The father's spanking her on her bare buttocks was not infrequent.

Around the age of nine, she was sent to bed daily shortly after her return from school, ostensibly because she was nervous, although she knew that it was really meant as a punitive measure, in order to break her stubbornness. For her father was afraid that she might turn out to be like one of her aunts, a severe neurotic, who had been sporadically institutionalized and was a constant source of irritation to the family. The father thought that she was spoiled, and sternness was the countermeasure he believed in.

No wonder that it became necessary for the parents to take her one day (the patient believes she was nine years old at the time) to a child psychiatrist. As far as the patient could remember, this was done because she had developed a tic. She thinks it was a single visit: she remembered the elevator and the house entrance, but the rest of the visit was covered by amnesia.

After the father's death, the mother felt depressed by their surroundings, which constantly reminded her of the deceased; and the family therefore spent one and a half years abroad, where the patient was sent to a private school in which the country's language was spoken. She felt discriminated against, not without justification, since the brother attended an American school, while her three sisters stayed with the mother. They had all the fun, whereas the time she spent at boarding school was the most miserable she could remember. From a diary she kept during that period, she found out that she had hated everybody and had thought that the world was against her.

Upon their return to this country, the family settled in the mother's home town, where the patient missed the relative prominence that had been associated with the father's position in the city in which she had spent most of the previous years.

Around the age of ten, the patient suffered from an unusual phobia. She was afraid that the rosebushes in front of her window might start to burn at night. She did not dare to look at them, for fear she might see them burning. The fantasy went on: the house would catch fire, and the family would not rescue her (cf. Freud 1905, pp. 72-76). When the family moved to another place, this latter part of the phobic fear was replaced by the more hopeful prospect of being rescued.

It was behind those bushes that the patient had carried on her earliest sexual experiences, with a cousin of her own age. Thus the fire that threatened to start in the bushes was a symbol of the fire she herself had felt when she was hiding behind them. It is highly probable that the fear of seeing burning rosebushes was in the service of defense against masturbatory impulses. It apparently meant: "When I see the rosebushes burn, my sexual desires will be aroused and my parents will not stand by to protect me against damaging myself by masturbation." Both roses and fire share an important quality with the sensation of facial heat, the dreaded signal of blushing.[8]

At the age of six, she started masturbation, after an orgasm elicited by climbing a rope. She discontinued masturbation two years prior to commencement of treatment, because she took it to be a sign of malady. Between fifteen and twenty-five, masturbation had occurred infrequently, once every two or three months, and without fantasies. As a child, she had had the fantasy that she was a patient, and that masturbation was a treatment she was supposed to get, something forced upon her.

Masturbation was a secret, about which no one was supposed to know;[9] but later a far more dangerous secret was added, when she entertained a sexual relationship with a dog, at a time when she was between eleven and twelve. She also denied the responsibility for this, insisting that she had been taken by surprise when the dog started to lick her genitals, after she stepped out of the bath. While she was aware of masturbatory guilt feelings, she denied feeling guilty or ashamed of her sexual dealings with the dog, for in this case it was "purely physical," and had nothing to do with anything human.

Apparently, this patient's drives were particularly unruly. Despite a strongly developed superego, she was again and again overpowered by instinctual demands. In this context, it is noteworthy that, as a child, she had evolved techniques for cheating her mother. She evaded measures that the mother habitually took when a child had not had a bowel movement, by flushing the toilet and making her

[8] The connection between fire and erythrophobia has been observed by many (see Bien, 1930, p. 54; Kratter, 1932, p. 198).

[9] Von Bechterew (1897b) seems to have been the first one to set forth masturbation as a source of shame in erythrophobia. However, Freud seems to have spoken of "sexual guilt" in connection with erythrophobia as early as 1895(b). The role played in erythrophobia by secrets, as well as the fear of their betrayal, has been stressed by many (Freud, 1895b; Breton, 1896; von Bechterew, 1897b; Stekel, 1912, p. 250; Bien, 1930, p. 79).

mother believe she had had one; hypocritically, she would apologize for having forgotten to call her mother for the daily inspection. She would also fake having taken a bath, and would change those parts of her attire in school that she did not like, but which her mother wanted her to wear. All this may serve as evidence that, as a child, she did not accept parental demands as valid (to be sure, they were excessive in many instances) or inherently binding; she accepted only the necessity of giving the appearance of obedience.

As a little child, upon entering the porch for breakfast, where her father and mother were waiting for her, she once suddenly put out her tongue at them—whereupon she was immediately sent back to her room. She was certain that she had not chosen to act the way she did, and that the derisive gesture was involuntary. Here her aggression against her environment was carried out openly; yet the self repudiated its responsibility. The next step led to the child's sneakiness, which at least helped her to preserve social decorum.

Yet one cannot look at the patient as a delinquent, even though some of her actions may at times seem to suggest such a classification. The self was sufficiently aware of societal demands and the consequences of their transgression, to preserve—at least externally— a well-ordered status in the community. In view of the intensity of the instinctual demands, however, the patient might well have developed later into a delinquent. I believe that it was the father's death that caused so much guilt and regret about her past misdemeanors that the neurotic solution of her conflicts prevailed.

The image of her father was tinged with sadness. When she was told that he had died, she thought that now he would never know that she was not a naughty child, but a good one; the distressing feeling emerged that the image of a naughty girl that the father had formed of her was henceforth irreparable. When the tragedy occurred, she was stunned; what followed was a dreamlike state, in which she was incapable of feeling any emotion. No doubt she had felt much affection for her father. But he had been a busy man, with little time for his children, who could spend only Sunday playing with them.

She had observed that her father's behavior toward his children was quite different from that which he displayed toward others. With the former, he was rigid and strict; with the latter, he was flexible, friendly, and helpful. Justifiably, she suffered from the feeling that she had never received adequate affection from her father; and in her relationship with her oldest sister's husband, whose personality served well as the realization of an ideal, she successfully sought a belated substitute for what had been so severely lacking in her childhood. Curiously enough, she was only aware of her negative feelings toward her father, and thought that she did not like him; yet this might very well have been the obverse of her having observed a deficit in the father's affection, of which she had, after all, so little.

Although she did not talk much about her father, one often felt his presence. Her actions may have been habitually evaluated in terms of his presumed approval or disapproval. A not inconsiderable hindrance to the progress of her treatment was her probably quite correct feeling that her father would not have approved of her undertaking analytic treatment at all.

An aggressive action she had committed against her second older sister five years prior to the father's death must have increased the feelings of guilt that inevitably set in following a father's death, particularly with a character such as that of the patient. In a fit of rage, she had thrust a pencil against her sister; the point had broken off and become stuck in a finger. She was told that the sister would get blood poisoning from the foreign body, and she became terrified. When the patient was told that the father had died from blood poisoning brought about by a boil, the association with the previous incident could hardly be avoided.

The patient's puberty stood under the shadow of delayed menstruation. At thirteen, she kept a diary along with four other girls. They read each other's entries. She felt frightened writing it, but could not stop, because the others would have wondered about it. She wrote down everything religiously, because she felt they would find out about her anyway. Yet she developed a code that would fix events that she did not want others to know about: she made an ink blot, whenever she was successful or enjoyed something. "I did not want anybody to know I enjoyed something." The ink blot seems to have stood for the menstruation that she was so eagerly waiting for.

"Physically I didn't develop at all," and therefore she was pre-occupied with menstruation; she tried to find out about it, but never dared to ask. She felt guilty about her curiosity and her investigations concerning the sisters' sanitary napkins. She felt once again defeated, an underdog and discriminated against.

The effects of both premature and delayed maturation upon personality development have been studied. It is believed that delay in puberty has a greater impact on girls than on boys, although it is not quite clear why this should be so. In this instance, it had a lasting detrimental effect. The impatient waiting for the event, combined with the feeling of hopelessness that it would never occur, and the ensuing shame and embarrassment, revived infantile conflicts and certainly contributed to the periodic pessimistic outlook upon herself that was so significant of her character. Since she was greatly worried that masturbation might have destroyed her childbearing capacity, it is easy to guess the nature of the conflict involved in waiting for the menarche.

The relief was great when menarche at last occurred at fifteen. Yet her pleasure was spoiled by the fact that her mother did not want to take it in a "natural" way, but forbade her to go on a hike and ordered her to bed. Her problem, she claimed, was not a wish to be an adult, but simply to be older. She hated her younger sister for being dressed the same way as she was. In the year when blushing began to plague her, she noticed (on the occasion of a wedding) when going to the ladies' room that menstruation had made a spot on her white dress. She was not perturbed at all, but hid the spot with her coat.

It was my opinion that this was the trauma that finally led to the erythrophobia, but the patient was adamant: menstruation had never been a worry and its betrayal by leakage was not among her fears. Although she complained about many past events, she denied that the delay in menarche had any meaning to her at the present time. She now understood well that she was just slower than others, and that was all there was to it. This denial was significant of her total dismissal of the menstrual problem, in which a principal fear and worry of hers apparently were focused.[10]

According to her presentation, her principal problem was how to behave in such a way that no suspicion would be aroused in others that she knew about sex. As a child, she was very modest, and did

[10] The connection between erythrophobia and menstruation was noted early (see Breton, 1896, p. 1184; also Bien, 1930, p. 67).

not want to take a shower at school. While she felt averse to exposing herself, she also felt uneasy lest her modesty become noticeable: blushing would betray her knowledge. In this respect, the patient was definitely right. The image of the blushing virgin has been praised by poets, because it assures us of the presence of virtue plus excitability. The nonblushing woman is either shameless and hardened—or else she is just stupid. Thus, from the viewpoint of social reality, the patient could have been proud that she was capable of blushing.

In the German language, I think, no poet has expressed this more beautifully than Friedrich von Logau (1604-1655) with the following verse:

> Wie willst du weisse Lilien/ Zu roten Rosen machen?
> Küss eine weisse Galatee:/ Sie wird errötend lachen.
> [How do you want to make white lilies into red roses?
> Kiss a white Galatea and she will blushingly laugh.]

The patient, however, would never have agreed with this poetic view. Sexual ignorance was to her the prime moral value. When she anticipated that a man she dated but did not like might seek to kiss her, she faced an unsolvable problem: if she was on guard and withdrew on time, she would betray her anticipation and thus her knowledge about kissing; if she behaved in a casual and ignorant sort of way, she had to risk the unpleasantness of a repulsive kiss.

The genetic line went from the rosebushes that had concealed her earliest sexual games to the fear that the bushes might burn; from the menstrual spot on the white dress to the fear that blushing might betray something that should remain concealed. As can be easily imagined, this "something" covered a wide area. I have mentioned the loss of innocence, the many sexual transgressions of which she had been guilty, without ever having told anybody. But it also referred to the "dirtiness" of the female genital.

In her opinion, only the genitals of children were attractive; those of adults were ugly. In view of her unusually strong penis envy, the female genital was for her a contemptible organ. Menstruation was, of course, a function of which she felt ashamed, and which had to be concealed. Yet it seemed to me that what really had to be concealed, not only from others but primarily from herself, was an imagery unrelated to the aforementioned conflicts, all so well known from the study of erythrophobia.

From some of the patient's dreams and food rituals, I received the definite impression that she was warding off the impulse to eat feces—an impulse which served the purpose of acquiring the father's penis. The impulse was rather complex. It contained aggression, in so far as it was a castrative wish, and debased the father's organ to something dirty, worthless, and contemptible; it expressed an endless and insatiable longing for closeness to him and at the same time it was expressive of self-debasement and humiliation. This inseparable confluence of orality and anality, of love and hatred, of activity and passivity, of instincual gratification and punishment, of sadism and masochism into one repressed impulse, imposed on the defensive apparatus a particularly difficult task.[11]

Yet still worse, she recalled that when as a child, after her father's death, she stood in the bedroom and looked at him, he did not appear dead to her at all. She wanted to go downstairs and tell people that her father was alive. The patient formed the idea that he had not really died but that the mother had buried him alive, a fantasy that was quite alive in her and was indicative of the intensity of the preoedipal cruel image of the mother. I would rather tentatively suggest that it was her character that was genetically related with that early phase.

Her superego was cruel, not only to her but also to others.[12] She was merciless in her moral castigations of her fellow men, and was aware of her wish that she had lived in the times of the Inquisition, when people could be subjected to physical torture for moral reasons.[13]

The defensive function of her disease was patent, but one dream, I thought, brought forth material suggestive of the great part which wish fulfillment played. One day, when she woke up late, she won-

[11] Orality and anality in erythrophobia have been separately noted by von Luzenberger (1911), Feldman (1922), Stekel (1931), Bien (1933a, b). Benedek (1925) described, in a case of erythrophobia, the repressed wish to incorporate the father.

[12] The patient oscillated between feelings of inferiority and superiority, which Stekel asserted to be true of cases of erythrophobia generally (1931, p. 74).

[13] It remained unclear to what extent the paternal grandmother—a rigid, extremely moralistic, Presbyterian lady, who stayed for long periods with the family, and who died before the patient reached her twelfth birthday—enhanced and fortified the patient's archaic, sadomasochistic superego.

dered that she had had no dream. Suddenly at lunch she recalled a graphic dream of intercourse with a man whom she did not know, or knew only casually. It was a very realistic dream: "I went to bed with an individual. I had the sensation of something entering the vagina. I did not respond to it. I thought that was good, because it meant I wouldn't become pregnant. The only thing I worried about was that the man noticed I didn't respond. He told me to hold thumbs and we would see whose thumb would first become red." The patient added that the man was married, but that she had no sense of guilt, because his wife knew that she was going to bed with him and did not mind. In a way, she was worried that someone would find out about her intercourse; yet this could happen only by an ensuing pregnancy.

She thought it was wrong to dream about such things: "The fact that sex bothers me, bothers me. I'm not adjusted. The American reaction to sex can be compared to that of the child: it is obscene, and can be expressed only by indirection." The dream was like a lesson in how it should be done. She was lying on her side and the man was behind her. The thumb test concerned timing. He had a stop watch to check how long it would take the thumb to get red.

The manifest content of this dream points in various directions. Intercourse is appraised in a way comparable to that in which masturbation had been: it was imposed upon her for didactic purposes. Actions are evaluated, not by their intrinsic value, but in terms of appearances. Everything is permitted, so long as it does not arouse public condemnation. If the partner is married, that still does not matter since his wife does not object. The position, aside from its anal implications, reflects the problem of seeing and being looked at. She is out of danger so long as the man cannot observe her facial expression. Orgasm was equated with pregnancy, an important theme that did not occur in her analysis.

From previous remarks we know that the patient was tormented by qualms about how to behave in direct sexual situations. The man must be kept ignorant of her own sexual knowledge and past sexual experience. If she did not respond, aside from protecting her against pregnancy, this would also indicate sexual ignorance. Yet such a lack of response to intercourse would arouse doubts as to her womanhood. Could she respond to intercourse at all? Since masturbation had deprived her of her capacity to bear a child, it had probably also deprived her of her capacity to respond orgastically.

The test works, finally, to her advantage. Although there was a delay in her thumb's becoming red, still she possessed a sexual potency equal to that of the man. Redness appears here as the saving grace. The underlying idea seems to be that male genitality is preferable to female, since the erection is a visible sign of excitement, whereas the woman has no means of visible proof. All she can contribute is her feeling or sensation. In this context, redness very definitely implies a reference to her observations of dogs, which after all had been of importance in her sexual development. Yet, in first intercourse, redness is also important as a sign of virginity, and had masturbation not destroyed her virginity? We may recall that the accident with the red spot on the white dress occurred when she was attending a wedding; and if this is accepted as more than mere coincidence, then we may regard it as an acting out of a hysterical identification with the bride.

Thus a woman, in order to prove her femininity, needs redness in two important respects: she must bleed at first intercourse, and she must have her monthly period (which had been so long delayed in her puberty, and for whose occurrence she had had to wait much longer than for the thumb's becoming red in the dream). However, if a woman has a penis, like a man (or a dog when sexually excited), then she has no reason for worry. It is the reverse of the fantasy that so many men have, who envy women for having passed through castration, and for being able to enjoy sexual genitality at any time, independently of erectile capacities, and therefore fearlessly.

If we consider redness as the central element of the dream, then blushing is discernible as the fulfillment of a fourfold wish whose fulfillment, in terms of the unconscious, has been destroyed by masturbation: she is a virgin, and will bleed in intercourse; she is capable of menstruating; she will have an orgasm; and she has a penis like a man or a dog.

It was the function of wish fulfillment in blushing that initially struck the psychoanalytic investigators. The symptom was suggestive of the well-known displacement from the lower to the upper part of the body (cf. Freud 1905, pp. 30, 82, n. 2). Feldman (1922) made the genitalization of the face and the castration complex the center of his explanation.

It is for purposes of more than historical interest that I refer to a passage that can be found in a review of a lecture Freud held on October 21, 1895. There the following is reported:

The following example shows how, through the repression of a recollection, the consciousness of guilt is accentuated and as a result a hysterical obsession comes into existence: A girl, burdened with sexual guilt, is seized by fear lest she betray herself to others by blushing. She represses the recollection—and the accent falls upon the blushing. Along with the seemingly unmotivated compulsive blushing [Zwangserröthen], the weird feeling emerges that something is known about her. If she succeeds altogether in breaking herself [of the habit] of blushing, the feeling increases that others regard her as guilt-laden. In this way, at each repression, she burdens the succeeding link of the hysterical chain with a hysterical obsession.

[Wie durch Verdrängung der Erinnerung das Schuldbewusstsein accentuiert wird, und daraus der hysterische Zwang entsteht, lehrt folgendes Beispiel: ein Mädchen, mit einer sexuellen Schuld beladen, wird von Furcht befallen, sich durch Erröthen den Andern zu verraten. Sie verdrängt ihre Erinnerung—und der Accent fällt auf das Erröthen. Zugleich mit dem scheinbar unmotivierten Zwangserröthen taucht das unheimliche Gefühl auf, man wisse etwas über sie. Gelingt es ihr vollends, sich das Erröthen abzugewöhnen, so erstärkt die Empfindung, die Anderen hielten sie schuldbeladen. So belastet sie bei jeder Verdrängung das folgende Glied der hysterischen Kette mit dem hysterischen Zwang.] [1895b, p. 680].

Four years later Freud had the following to say about erythrophobia in a letter to Fliess, February 19, 1899:

Do you know why our old friend E. turns red and sweats whenever he sees a certain class of acquaintance, particularly at the play [in the theater]? He is ashamed, no doubt; but of what? Of a phantasy in which he figures as the "deflowerer" of every person he comes across. He sweats as he deflowers, because it is hard work. Whenever he feels ashamed in someone's presence, an echo of the meaning of his symptom finds voice in him like a growl of defeat! "Now the silly idiot thinks she has made me feel ashamed. If I had her in bed she'd soon see whether I felt em-

barrassed in front of her!" [1950, p. 278].[14] [It is of interest to
note how many observations Freud made at the beginning of his
psychoanalytic research that only many years later were to find
their proper place and valuation in psychoanalytic theory.]

Here it may be worth while to mention a peculiarity of the patient's dreams. It was rather exceptional when the dreams of any
given night did not contain some unpleasant elements. This unpleasantness was often quite marked and dominated the whole content of the dream, as in the patient's being assaulted, humiliated or
deathly sick, or having lost something, or doing things the wrong
way. At other times, the element of unpleasantness was reduced to
a mere detail. When she reported having beheld in a dream the
image of an appetizing potato, one could be sure that one would
hear next that the skin of the potato was too thick. Whether this
disturbance should be appraised as being related to masochistic impulses, or whether the high frequency of unpleasant contents is
indicative of a disturbed operation of the dream function per se
related to an ego defect, must remain undecided here, although the
prevalence of the masochistic component in the patient cannot be
doubted.

The patient's transference seemed initially to move in a positive
direction. At least, I took her question as to what I would say if she
told me that she was in love with me as such a harbinger. However,
she added that she was always acting in such a way that the boy she
liked would not be able to think that she was in love with him. If
she did like me, she certainly stuck to her principle throughout the
treatment. She felt disappointed and discouraged now even more
than before, since, according to her, she had found out in her treatment what a bad person she was. Yet, to her younger sister, she
maintained how wonderful the treatment was.

Despite the disappointment, for a while she was ready to stick
to a decision she had made when she started the treatment—namely,
that she would like psychoanalysis. But soon an avalanche of re-
proaches, criticisms, and expressions of annoyance set in and persisted throughout the rest of the treatment. She resented the fact

14 Stekel (1931) attributed to this mechanism of depreciating the object that causes
embarrassment a leading function in erythrophobia.

that everything she said must have a meaning; that when I was late I saw her longer, but when she was late I closed the session at the regular time; that I insisted that I was always right and she was always wrong. She had always heard that psychiatrists are "nutty" themselves; she found me obtuse and callous, and felt quite angered when I spoke with a calm voice about things that generally are considered horrible or tragic.

Here she was in rivalry with me, for her ideal of adjustment was to be able to talk about all sorts of things without feeling any emotion. It turned out that she had now made up her mind that psychoanalysis would not help.[15] She had reported initially that she did not feel embarrassed in my presence, although she almost regularly felt that emotion in the presence of men. Nevertheless, the verbalization of positive feelings in the transference situation was apparently beyond her tolerance.

Yet her fears went far deeper. She once brought up the possibility of suicide, and raised the question of a diagnosis of schizophrenia in her.[16] Such apprehensions were, of course, potent blocks to a show of emotions.

It sometimes happened that she was in good spirits and laughed; yet with the progress of the treatment, the rigidity spread; finally, she spoke most of the time without the slightest betrayal of affects. I discovered an almost imperceptible high-speed, tremorlike rubbing of the medial sides of her feet against each other. I assumed that this ticlike habit was a channel for emotional discharges. It disappeared abruptly—and did not return—after I called it to her attention.

The analytic treatment also served as her revenge upon her family. Not only was it the fault of others that she needed treatment, the treatment itself proving her innocence and the guilt of her parents; but the fact that she was in treatment was a disgrace to the

[15] Eisler (1919) was the first one to emphasize the particular transference difficulties one encounters in the psychoanalysis of erythrophobia.

[16] Suicidal tendencies have been noted in erythrophobia by many observers. It is of interest that an early reported case of erythrophobia ended in suicide (Caspar, 1846). The case history published by Caspar is also noteworthy in so far as this seems—as Hoche (1897) claimed in his discussion with von Bechterew—to be the earliest report on a patient the center of whose symptomatology was fear of blushing. There seems to be national rivalry as to the discoverer of this syndrome. In the French literature, Boucher is usually cited for that purpose. London (1945) unjustly put in the same claim for Bow (1836).

whole family, and all the more so, since it proved ineffective in her case.

Yet to describe this patient's severe psychopathology without emphasizing her social assets would be to give a one-sided picture. Her professional work was impeccable, and she was highly valued because of her reliability, conscientiousness, efficiency, and ambition. Her tendency to argue was easily forgiven in view of her many virtues. On the social level, the patient was well organized; the social image that she cast outside her narrow family circle, her phenotype, was not at all that of a neurotic.

There were many reasons for this, not the least of which, by any means, was the way in which she had learned to master her passive wishes. When she was eight, her older sister had dressed her as a baby and put her into a baby carriage; even as a grownup, whenever she felt the first sign of oncoming sickness, she still wished that she could return to her mother and be taken care of by her. But passive gratifications were for her forbidden pleasures, and this fight against passivity made her active—and quite successfully, at that—on the social level.

During the summer of the third year of her analysis, the patient expressed some doubt as to whether or not she would go on with her treatment. She said that her mother's suggestion to discontinue had "put a bug into her ear." She informed me that, upon her return from her vacation, she would let me know what her decision was. I told her that I was in no position to promise to hold the hour free for her, but that in case her hour had not been taken by another patient in the meantime, I would be glad to continue her treatment upon her return, if she should then desire to do so. The patient was apparently not satisfied with my reply, for I did not hear from her any further after she left for her vacation.

The degree of permissiveness compatible with the psychoanalytic technique has never been clearly stated. I recall a patient who was suffering from an unusually severe psychopathology, which was not amenable to a strictly classical technique, but might be dealt with successfully if the technique were slightly adapted to his extreme immaturity.

When his mother felt the first signs of his dawning independence, she induced the family physician to advise him to seek the counsel of a psychiatrist who claimed he could cure this patient within two months. The patient asked whether I would mind a consultation; I agreed. After a few interviews, the consulting psychiatrist suggested a sodium amytal interview. This, I thought, was a demand that was unacceptable, and I told the patient that he would have to choose between psychoanalysis and the consultant's therapy.

There are many psychoanalysts who would have issued such an ultimatum earlier, at the time when the patient requested the consultation, in order to enforce the discipline indispensable for the psychoanalytic technique. Yet at that stage the patient had not formed a dependable, positive transference, and he was without insight into his severe psychopathology: an interpretation of resistance and acting out would have been ineffectual and senseless. Furthermore, he was not ready to face his mother's determination to hold him under her sway.

If I wanted to analyze him at all, I had to give in at that point. But was I right in regarding the sodium amytal interview as out of the question? I admit that I cannot state in precise terms just why I think such permission to be incompatible with any kind of even modified analytic technique. Yet I am aware that continuation of treatment, even under such aggravating conditions, might have led to the formation of adequate transference; for, as I found out later, the psychiatrist after a few weeks of treatment had to admit—somewhat like the "faith healer" who had claimed he could revive the dead—that "such a neurotic he had never seen before."

I am not certain that my refusal to wait through the vacation for the young woman patient's decision was altogether wise. The probability that the patient would decide against continuation was great, in any case, for she was disappointed by the treatment and greatly dissatisfied with the course that it had taken. Also, it is to be considered that, had I consented to her request, I would have probably lost the last shred of my authority and created the occasion for transference fantasies, which the patient in all probability would never have been able either to admit or to verbalize.

Be that as it may, the patient did not return. When she left, I was quite pessimistic with regard to her future. I saw no way in which she would be able to step out of, or to overcome, the rigid psychic shell in which she lived. The erythrophobia seemed excessive enough to establish an actual impossibility of intercourse.

I do not know whether or not the reader will agree with me when I say that I got a fair—although far from complete—insight into the structure of this patient's disorder. Be that as it may, the insight that I gained did not, apparently, lead to such interpretations as might have had an effect upon her symptoms. Whenever I ventured to give her an interpretation, she either cut me off altogether, or told me, after listening to it, that it was wrong, unfriendly, or humiliating. In general, interpretations elicited nothing but negative reactions. Only once did she express agreement, and that had to do with an instance in which some remark that I had made about another person was confirmed by later events.

I should like to stress here the fact that the patient's rejecting attitude was directed toward *any* kind of interpretation, whether it referred to the ego or the id or to the very attitude itself with which she met any of my suggestions. Thus I was stymied, and had to agree with the patient when she pointed out, before leaving, that the analysis had had not the slightest effect upon her disorder, that it had not provided her with any sort of benefit, such as an increase of insight or at least an intellectual clarification of one or the other of her problems—a rather distressing state of affairs after a comparatively long analysis.

For a patient to leave treatment without having derived the maximum benefit from analysis, or even without substantial change of symptomatology, is not especially rare; but that a patient should be able rightly to claim that she has not derived any kind of advantage from her treatment, and is leaving the treatment in the same state as she entered it, I consider to be quite exceptional. And, as is perhaps inevitable under such conditions, the patient left with the further claim that she was now even worse off than she had been three years earlier; for at that time she had at least had the hope that there was something that might alleviate her distress, whereas now she knew that she was hopeless.

From the structure of the patient's defenses, I am compelled to draw the conclusion that, for this patient, even the tentative acceptance of an interpretation would not have meant possible enrichment or growth of insight, but rather defeat, castration, and an increase of power for an adversary who would surely abuse the advantage thus gained. Thus, the possibility that the analyst might be correct and any admission on her part to that effect were dangers that had to be averted at all cost; and since acceptance of the interpretation of such a resistance also fell within the scope of this same danger, we were facing here the situation of the snake that bites its own tail.

However, I do not want to state that the patient was actually unanalyzable; I only want to state that I myself do not know how this kind of defensive pattern can be overcome by interpretation. In my experience, it occurs almost solely in women, and I surmise that the process of interpretation has in these instances the unconscious meaning of a rape—at least, the patient unconsciously experiences the acceptance of an interpretation as if she were forced to submit to rape.

If further speculation is admissible, I would also assume the existence in such patients of a considerable erotization of the analytic situation, leading to a forceful defense against a deeply repressed masochistic wish to be raped. The feeling that masturbation was imposed upon her may have been the genetic nucleus of that fantasy. Yet, with all this, I still do not want to imply in any way that this patient was objectively unanalyzable, for I am aware that another analyst might have freed the patient of her erythrophobia.

When I reported earlier that the patient was in psychoanalytic treatment for almost three years, that statement per se did not contain too much factual information, and it may therefore be appropriate to interpolate two general remarks here. First, the term "psychoanalysis" covers today such a broad spectrum of techniques that, when one reads that a patient has been "in analysis," such a statement is no more precise than if a surgeon were to record that he has "operated on" a patient.

The situation is somewhat improved when it is further made clear that the classical technique has been used. But the factual information that can then be derived is little more than that the patient was probably given daily the opportunity to express for an hour in the supine his free associations. We would not yet know how much use the patient actually made of this opportunity; furthermore, what is more important, we would not know what areas were covered by interpretation, not to speak of what interpretations were integrated by the patient.

Therefore, I do not agree with those analysts, typified above all by Franz Alexander (1956), who deal with the classical psychoanalytic technique as if it were something invariable, so that, if it did not lead in any particular instance to success, it would be spoken of the way we do when we say that a given disease does not respond to penicillin, and therefore should be treated with another antibiotic. The classical technique is a subtle instrument; in almost all instances of psychoanalytic writings not enough details are published to make it clear whether it was actually used properly.

The classical technique is, after all, a procedure that is determined by a number of variables. In each instance of interpretation, the analyst faces a huge number of choices regarding the content and the timing of the interpretations. We may be able to set forth a formal rule which will contain the specifications that an interpretation should live up to, in order to comply with psychoanalytic standards. But anybody who has ever attended technical seminars must know that agreement on what is correct technique is rare among psychoanalysts, even when they adhere to the principles of the classical school.

Secondly, from this situation some erroneous conclusions are sometimes drawn—namely, that any divergence of opinion about the structure of a patient's disorder, and consequently about the most reliable or suitable technique, proves that psychoanalysis is no science. Here one has to state that other sciences have also gone through phases in which research did not lead to wholly unambiguous advice as to how to proceed in practice. The subtlety of the problem encountered in psychoanalysis, the number of variables, and the impossibility of using experimental methods—all these create a situation unlike that in any other science.

The fact that, in specific instances, the decision is limited to a choice of one among a few alternatives of interpretation is itself a sign of major progress, even if it cannot be determined at present which choice does contain the best solution. This lack of certainty regarding the most suitable and the most effective interpretation, in fact, makes psychoanalysis as a technical procedure an exciting adventure. The resulting difficulty is a challenge to scientific ingenuity, rather than a disproof of scientific standing.

Even when the psychoanalysis of a patient has led to success, one often has the feeling, in reviewing the path taken, that he would proceed differently if the analysis could be started all over again. Yet this very impression is the result of having learned something in the particular instance, and one rarely learns from experience without gaining insight into improved ways of dealing with the subject of one's learning. In reality, there is no reason to deny, or to be ashamed of, the fact that psychoanalysis is an art to a larger extent than is true of other techniques that are based on scientific insight.[17]

To return to my patient, I wish to repeat that I have not presented this report with any intention of proving that the unsatisfactory outcome was unavoidable, although the voices are not infrequent of those who believe erythrophobia to be a disorder that should not be regarded as a pure neurosis. Fenichel (1931, pp. 100, 187) and Nunberg (1932, p. 156) regard it as closely related to paranoid states. (See also Yamamura [1940, p. 200], Hitschmann [1943, p. 445].) Bergler (1944), however, considers the stress on the paranoid factor "an excuse for the lack of therapeutic success" (p. 45). Indeed, writers such as Weiss (1933), Bien (1930), Stekel (1931), Heyer (1949) report impressive therapeutic successes, often after relatively short periods of treatment.[18]

In the evaluation of the psychoanalytic technique one faces a particular difficulty, in so far as almost every symptom—or better, syndrome—may appear in one of three different forms, or at one

[17] I am aware that this view may be countered by the following argument: To be sure, the psychoanalytic procedure has not yet reached that degree of precision that can be observed in surgery. When the surgeon speaks about an appendectomy, he is referring to a well-defined event; in so far as he has stuck to the rules, one can predict the condition of the area affected by the operation. Even though such a degree of precision is as yet unobtainable in psychoanalysis, nevertheless the state of the analyzed patient can be determined approximately, if it is made certain that the requirements Freud has specified have been fulfilled. These are: reconstruction of the infantile and childhood period, and insight into transference reactions and ego defenses. I can safely leave out additional requirements, since they will have been necessarily fulfilled if these two goals have been realized.

[18] It may be noteworthy that, particularly in the older psychiatric literature, cases are reported that may create the impression that erythrophobia is a state close to psychosis (Caspar, 1846; Breton, 1896; Pitres and Régis, 1897).

of three different levels. One has to refer here to Freud's classification (1922) of the clinical forms in which the analyst encounters jealousy (competitive or normal, projected, and delusional), recognizing that Freud, with regard to a particular emotion, has described a generally valid aspect of psychopathology.

It has occurred to me that, in the study of patients suffering from anorexia nervosa, there are three groups of symptomatically identical patients. One is plainly neurotic, belonging probably to the group of hysteria. Frequently such a patient will suffer from the disease for about nine months, and will then recover. Plainly, the anorexia is here based on a neurotic identification with pregnancy.

A patient belonging to the second group was described by Schur and Medvei (1937). Her anorexia lasted for sixteen years, during which time her weight temporarily went down to 58 pounds. No medical treatment was of any avail; later she sought treatment by a "homeopath," who applied vaginal massage. After three years of this treatment, the patient had gained 19 pounds, and the menstrual period had become normal in spite of the previous sixteen years of amenorrhea. She became active in sports, and had to be regarded as cured.

Then there are those patients who are incurable—unless the new tranquilizers or energizers should also prove beneficial in these instances. Years ago, I had the opportunity of following up such a case. No psychotherapy of any kind, or organic treatment, had any appreciable effect. The disease broke out in the form of vomiting on the occasion of her first intercourse on her wedding night, and relentlessly took a downhill course, until she died from a probably unintentional overdose of hypnagogue.

We may discover in these three levels the well-known classifications of neurosis, borderline case, and psychosis. However, it should not be forgotten that a group of functional psychoses, which is nowadays covered by the single term "schizophrenia," may also appear in three different forms, as can be shown in the differentiation of "hysterical psychosis," a concept that is regrettably almost regularly disregarded in modern psychiatry; the "emergency psychosis" of the schizoid personality,[19] which is usually misdiagnosed as schizo-

19 Berze's (1935) excellent concept of schizoid psychosis has unfortunately not found acceptance in psychiatry.

phrenia, and to which so many psychiatrists owe their reputation for having "cured schizophrenia by psychotherapy"; and the true "process schizophrenia."

I suggest tentatively that erythrophobia may also appear in these three forms.[20] The psychological testing which I have reported earlier suggested strongly that this patient's disorder fell into the neurotic group; if this was so, then my technique must have been deficient (although this also requires a reservation that I shall discuss later). Yet, reviewing the patient's material, I am compelled to express a doubt whether, behind what appeared like a *bona fide* neurosis, even though it was characterized by unusually strong resistances, there was not lurking a far more malignant disorder.

We speak of the wisdom of the body; there is also a wisdom of the psychic organism. When a patient shows such intense resistance —leaving aside the question of whether the proper technique was employed—that may be nothing but an all-too-well-justified measure, protecting an ego whose fabric would not be strong or solid enough to withstand the power of id derivatives, once they were given access to the preconscious or conscious systems.

The psychological report contains a reference to the patient's aversion to introspection. She was not a person whose general personality make-up would justify a lag in introspection, such as can regularly be found in delinquents, and more often than not in narcissistic types, especially endowed to deal with reality in a superior and successful way. Both groups persistently claim that there is not much to report about their inner lives. This patient, in my opinion, had a genuine capacity for excellent introspection, and she reported a wealth of material; but she did not use all this for the purpose of increasing knowledge of self. This must have happened for good reasons, which may be sought for in latent pathology of a more serious order than met the eye.

There is one feature in erythrophobia that warrants particular attention. The great benefit afforded by a phobia consists of the conversion of an inner danger into an external one, against which the patient can defend himself by flight, or other measures. In erythrophobia, curiously enough, the phobic mechanism does not

---

[20] Pitres and Régis (1897) distinguished three degrees of the disease: (1) *ereuthose simple;* (2) *ereuthose émotive;* (3) *ereuthose obsédante (ereuthophobie).*

provide this advantage. Although there are attempts at externalization of danger, in so far as blushing is experienced as ego dystonic—
so to speak, intruding (according to the subjective experience) from
outside the psychological self—the patient experiences the proximate
cause of danger as being within the confines of the psychobiological
unit, and flight is impossible. Thus, the erythrophobic is cheated of
a principal advantage that the disorder should provide.

There are, of course, other forms of phobia in which the externalization of danger is similarly not carried very far. Patients who fear
that they may be overcome on the street by an indomitable urge to
defecate, or may collapse of a heart attack, can at least resort to
protective measures. But the erythrophobic patient may be exposed
at any time to an attack of anxiety. It seems that phobias such as
agoraphobia whose occurrence is limited to certain, well-defined
situations provide insufficient protections for personality types that
later develop a phobia of the kind I am discussing here. It looks as
if the erythrophobic patient were overaware of the fact that the
instinctual danger may arise at any time, and that he therefore was
in need of a guardian whose effective protection could be instituted
at any time, irrespective of the paraphernalia of the external situation. It is the internalization of the source of the alleged danger that
gives erythrophobia its particular coloring.

In this context, it is also to be noted that erythrophobia is one
of the few phobias which the patient's self cannot rationalize at all.
The agoraphobic patient, after all, may say in his defense that the
street occasionally proves to be a dangerous locale, and almost every
other type of phobia contains a seed of possible reality danger, no
matter how preposterous and bizarre it may be; but erythrophobia
is devoid of any such possible rationalizations. It implies an im-
moderate amount of masochism for a life to be spent in fear of events
that under no circumstances contain any actual danger, yet against
which no measure of protection is possible, and it also has to be
considered that this neurosis is structured in such a way as to leave
practically no area of daily life except solitude—if even that—untouched.

The desire to torment herself was also visible in the patient's
inclination to set up situations that contained no possibility of solution: when she did not receive privileges, she felt unloved and irate,

but when she did receive them, she felt guilty and worried about how others would feel; when the family praised her for preparing a very good meal, she felt annoyed, but when the meal she cooked was taken for granted, she felt neglected and exploited; she made no acquaintances, because she was afraid of being considered maladjusted, and yet she worried because, by avoiding acquaintances, she might appear even more maladjusted.

I have to report here a technical mistake of which I was guilty in the early phase of the patient's treatment, for it may shed some light on the patient's final social recovery.

Some patients are in the habit of asking questions after the treatment session has ended and they are on their way to the door. I have made it an iron rule not to answer such a question—unless it betrays that the patient is in an emergency situation; instead I suggest that we discuss the subject at the next session. The necessity for such a rule can hardly be doubted. Questions which are asked in the process of leaving have usually been held back by the patient; they refer to emotionally quite important issues; when they are asked, the patient is not aware that he is in effect trying to inveigle the analyst by surprise into a trap.

Once this patient, just before walking through the door, pointed to a painting on a wall of my office and asked whether it was painted by Cézanne. I answered in the negative—and regrettably added: "It is painted, however, by a person who, I hope, will be one day equally famous." I have often thought about the possible reasons for this mistake; I believe that it did not occur out of a countertransference, but out of the feelings I harbored for the artist who had created the painting. The patient had apparently taken me by surprise, so that the analyst's unconscious, poorly disguised, entered the operational field as the result of one of those tricky combinations of circumstances, the necessity for guarding against which makes the analyst's own analysis so important.

As can be imagined, I carefully scanned the field for any sign that would indicate what consequences my mistake might have had for the patient. But nothing was noticeable and when, on the proper occasions, I tried to air the question, I was regularly told that the patient did not know what else my remark should have meant to her, beyond what it contained.

In view of all the circumstances involved, one can easily imagine my surprise when, eight years after the treatment had been terminated, I received the following reply to a letter in which I had inquired into the patient's condition:

> Since we last met much water has gone under many bridges. I was married seven years ago today (my husband is out of town, hence letter-writing rather than celebrating) and have subsequently produced three children, a boy aged 6, and two girls, almost 5, and 21 mos., respectively.
>
> We lived four and a half years in X and have been out here for almost three.
>
> I am reasonably happily married, adore being a mother, am active in the League of Women Voters, school activities, have recently served on a committee studying the local juvenile courts for the Mental Health Association, lead an average social life, ski, swim, play tennis during the appropriate seasons.
>
> Still have most of the old emotional problems, but manage to cope with them. I assume analysis did some good, or I wouldn't be where I am—but don't feel I would ever take it up again. I am more than satisfied with the job ahead, and feel I can do at least an adequate job—I refer of course to my children. My son has many personality traits similar to mine—the girls have all the social graces of Perle Mesta.
>
> Forgive me for not writing sooner, but letter-writing is one of the many things I keep putting off, due to lack of both time and inclination!

A truly amazing problem is here encountered. A patient who had not accepted one single interpretation, whose treatment was therefore, if viewed analytically, a failure, nevertheless had become capable of carrying out all the actions of which she had felt totally incapable, and thus obtained the fulfillment of all her wishes, so far as they could be fulfilled by external events. Matrimony and motherhood had been the ardent wishes of this patient, and she had given up any hope of obtaining them, at the time when she discontinued treatment. Furthermore, a social role of importance and high prestige, which was not missing from her list of ambitions, and which had appeared particularly distant in the light of her symptom, had been realized.

The letter sounded as though it had been written by a person who was living a rich life—the narrowness and the compulsive masochism, the stubborn self-denial having apparently disappeared, at least on the surface. It really created confusion in my mind when, furthermore, the patient intimated that the leading symptom had not appreciably changed. When the patient wrote, "I assume analysis did some good," she was right; but the analyst cannot add much more. Her social recovery and her psychoanalytic treatment were, of course, related; but what kind of relationship actually existed between them remains even now shrouded in darkness.

The matter becomes even more puzzling when one considers that if this patient's treatment and posttreatment course were typical of psychoanalytic therapy, or if equivalent sequences could be guaranteed to every patient, the analyst's office would be overrun by patients. What patient would not be ready to bear the pain inherent in his neurosis if his most cherished ambitions and wishes regarding external reality were nevertheless fulfilled? Of course, this state of affairs mainly concerns predominantly narcissistic wishes. The price to be paid would, with few exceptions, not be considered too high.[21]

Strangely enough, it must be admitted that if the patient had answered that her symptom had subsided, that she felt fairly free and uninhibited in intercourse, but that she had preferred not to marry or had had no opportunity to marry, I would have felt entitled to record her as cured; whereas, under the present conditions, despite the stupendous clinical success, the patient cannot, from the psychoanalytic point of view, be regarded as having been successfully treated.

Notwithstanding the necessity of renewed analysis, if one is truly to assess the patient's present capacity for well-functioning, some speculation is in order. Her surprising functional recovery might become understandable if we knew the intervening events in her immediate environment. It may be worth while to report here two instances that may shed some light on the problem. One had occurred in the life of a patient who had hesitated to start sexual relations for many years, although there had been ample opportunity. As soon as he had heard that a girl to whom he had been

[21] One is reminded here of Baranyi, who became a Nobel Prize laureate, after Freud had refused to accept him as an analyst because "he was too abnormal" (Jones, Vol. 2, p. 189f.).

strongly attached as a child had married, he initiated intercourse for the first time.

The other incident was quite similar. A male patient, extremely inhibited sexually, was almost always rebuffed by the girls whom he propositioned. While I was on vacation, a much older girl, who had been taken into his family when he was a little boy, became engaged. He became quite depressed and had the feeling that he just had to get a mistress. That same evening, he made advances to a young woman whom he had known for quite a while, and with whom he had several times tried in vain to start a sexual relation. That evening she gave in, and later they became married.

It is rather obvious what must have occurred in both instances. The unfaithfulness of an incestuously loved person left them free to be unfaithful now in their turn. A rearrangement in the diagram of unconscious forces, precipitated by events in external reality, made it possible for them to go ahead and to do what unconsciously they had considered to be impossible, and which they had been afraid to have happen.

There are reality events of a different order that sometimes facilitate a patient's progress. A relative improvement in the condition of schizophrenic patients has been observed after the loss of a parent (Stärcke, 1921). I am certain that many other examples of the sort have been observed; the possibility cannot be excluded that an equivalent event or events had occurred in this patient's environment such as were likely to remove an inhibition, or to provoke increased activity. If I had to guess, I would surmise that the triggering event might have been her brother's engagement, in case that did actually take place.

It must also be considered that the patient had had the opportunity, during the course of her treatment, to verbalize a huge amount of fantasies, recollections, guilt feelings, and what not. Although she apparently felt dissatisfied with what she called my lack of participation, the fact that she had not been rebuffed or castigated may have had a soothing effect on her guilt feelings.

Furthermore—and I hesitate to bring up this point—I cannot avoid the impression that my uncalled-for remark regarding the personal hopes I had about the artist whose painting had aroused the patient's curiosity may have been related to her recovery. I hesitate to attribute to an indeniable mistake in technique a socially wholesome effect, at a time when the psychopathology of the analyst is almost being recommended as a tool of *bona fide* technique. At least some papers on countertransference (cf. Tower, 1956) seem to justify the characterization of the present phase of psychoanalytic technique in just such words.

It all apparently started with Clara Thompson (1938, p. 307), who reported the wholesome effects upon the patient's recovery of her having forgotten a childhood memory which the patient had told her at least once, if not three times, before.[22] One, therefore, has to add a warning, when pointing to a clinical coincidence of the analyst's acting out and the possibility of a patient's clinical improvement. At a time when some analysts like to base their technique on purely pragmatic principles, such as "Nothing succeeds like success" (Alexander and French, 1946, p. 40), extreme caution is indicated in the discussion of the beneficial effects that an undeniable technical mistake may have had on a patient's later vicissitudes.

Be that as it may, my remark must have whetted my patient's rivalrous appetites and, indeed, she outdid the artist in whom I had put so much hope. The latter has not acquired Cezanne's fame, after all; but the patient did accomplish her heart's most cherished ambitions, thus surpassing the highest expectations I could possibly have harbored with regard to her clinical recovery, and simultaneously "showing me up."

Indeed, this patient is also unique in other respects. I do not recall a patient ever reporting that all of his wishes were so splendidly fulfilled, as seems to have happened with this patient. There is something almost uncanny about the cornucopia of blessings that fate showered her with. When we remember Freud's early statement that the cathartic treatment has the function of "transforming . . . hysterical misery into common unhappiness" (1895a, p. 305), we must say that this patient was not ready to do that at all, but rather

[22] Countertransference was clearly defined by Freud as a psychic process in the analyst that is detrimental to the psychoanalytic process. It amounts to no less than a perversion of theory and practice when it is heralded as highly effective in bringing about the patient's cure. Jokingly, I might say that we seem to be not far from the point when candidates will be advised to resume their training analyses, because they do not form countertransferences to their patients.

seems to have held on to her neurotic suffering, in order to achieve everyday bliss.

From her short note, no reliable conclusion can be drawn as to the present structure of her personality. One may surmise that the symptom she is retaining is different from the one for which she sought treatment; or else one may speculate that the self has acquired the capacity to deal with that same symptom in a more constructive way. Of course, the two probabilities do not exclude each other, and either may be present to a certain extent. However, I would feel inclined to assume the existence of processes closer to psychopathology than either of the two just mentioned.

I believe, in fact, that the patient's admirable achievement was attained, not in spite of her neurotic symptom, but, paradoxically, because of it. It probably cost her a great inner effort to carry out the realization of her wishes, but the pain inherent in the symptom may have been the price she continued to pay to her inordinate feelings of guilt. I can well imagine that, had the inner qualm inherent in her symptom subsided, she might have been thereby rendered, ironically enough, incapable of carrying her activities to the level of success that she actually reached. Thus, we may surmise that she now isolates the guilt reaction from the prohibited gratification.

I would like to compare the difference between the old and the supposed new state with the difference between sepsis and local infection. When germs pervade the organism, its total capacity is reduced; when pathology affects a circumscribed area, a single limb may be paralyzed. Quite generally, there is a group of patients whose psychopathology is structured exactly in this way. I once observed a woman who suffered from an extreme degree of ophidiophobia, but claimed to live a most satisfactory sexual life, with no inhibition regarding the penis and full orgastic response. I was also once told of a prostitute who suffered from hypsophobia, and as a result actually could not attend to her profession if a client lived in a room above the fourth floor.

Such patients are of interest, because in them the symptom apparently does not serve the function of preventing prohibited activities. It is questionable whether such phobias should be regarded as truly neurotic symptoms. We may attribute such "atypical" neuroses to the primitivity of the ego, whose demands can be bought off at a comparatively low cost. By decomposing entities into part aspects, and then keeping the latter constantly separated from each other, the self may pin-point the defense and thus safeguard most of its functional potential.

Thus sexual relations with men may be made possible when the feared, preoedipal, maternal aspect of the penis is displaced upon snakes; or promiscuity may be made possible when the feared orgasm is displaced upon the perception of heights. The ability to dismember so effectively that which belongs together presupposes a degree of archaism in the ego which may take this group of patients altogether out of the neuroses.[23]

The patient under consideration, I believe, does not fall into this group. Her phobia had had its full effect upon the structure of the self; her good performance was not the *terminus a quo* but the *terminus ad quem*. If anything, she may be closer to that group of patients who deny the existence of a symptom rather than acknowledge its meaning. The fact that she objected to practically every interpretation I gave does not exclude the possibility that these interpretations had an effect on her. From the analytic process, however, not only an effect upon the symptom is expected, but also an accumulation of true insight. This she was incapable of achieving. Here was a definite limitation of the functional potential of the patient's self.

It is not known to what extent her self-knowledge had increased at least on the preconscious level during the treatment, and whether she was prevented only from taking that final step of self-assessment which probably would have infringed painfully on her narcissistic pride. If that were the case, it would greatly surprise me. There are patients of whose improvement one has evidence in terms of vastly improved functioning, and yet, in listening to their verbalizations in the psychoanalytic situation, one may think that nothing has changed. In this patient's instance, however, there was no evidence of change in any area, so that when she left, it was my impression that she was the same as she was when I met her for the first time.

Nevertheless, interpretations, even though rejected by the self,

---

23 The psychopathology of this group of patients cannot be explained by a mechanism that Alexander described as the bribe of the superego.

may have an effect on the repressed. I feel inclined to compare this with the effect that the anxiety signal has upon the id. The self does not know what the cause of the anxiety is. Anxiety is mobilized to curb an impending thrust of the repressed. The ego responds to the danger of that thrust with a shot in the dark, so to speak; yet more frequently than not it hits its target.

Comparably, the interpretation, although rejected, may have the effect of a warning, which may be understood by the patient as if it meant: If you behave or feel the way you do, or if you have this or that symptom, then people may think that this or that is going on in you. In earlier days, Freud (1912, p. 149) thought that if the meaning of symptoms came to be generally known, the neurotic might feel inhibited about showing them, just as ladies would no longer say at a garden party that they were going to pick flowers, once it was generally known that this was a subterfuge to hide the necessity of going to the bathroom.

When through the analytic process the repressed obtains greater buoyancy, and the accustomed defenses are no longer strong enough to keep the unruly repressed in its place, the subject has, in the most general terms, two choices at his disposal—namely, to recall, that is to say, to verbalize the contents of the repressed, or to act them out. Blos recently (1963) called to our attention the fact that certain types of acting out are constructive, or at least introduce a phase of constructive action. Similarly, rather than being confronted with the recall of highly unpleasant and humiliating recollections, a patient may prefer to resort to what appears on the social level to be healthy action.[24]

I could observe this in a patient whose disorder was not a minor one. He responded to my interpretation with rejection or skepticism; yet, strangely enough, he started—very slowly but consistently—to behave in a way distinctly different from the way he had previously. A comparison of the initial state with the end result showed an enormous difference, in terms of the many things he could do now, that he had been inhibited from doing before.

Yet all this took place—as could be clearly observed in the analytic

[24] There is no objection to calling such behavior "acting out," so long as one is aware that the pathology of such actions is not reduced by the mere fact of their fitting into a social reality.

situation—against a background that showed the persistence of his old personality. One could not help seeing that the old conflicts had retained their cathexis; all that had been achieved was a new façade glued to an old and dilapidated structure. The two were rather isolated from each other, which might have been the reason why he was able to build up a new life in the present, which was strictly disconnected from the past.

It was also quite clear how the new façade protected him against having taken cognizance in his analysis of the secrets with which the history of his childhood and adolescence was replete. The underlying principle was: "I would rather act sanely than face the truth about myself."

The information I received from the patient eight years after she left me is extraordinarily important, in so far as it disproves some of the new principles a few analysts have tried to introduce, in order to "improve upon" the technique on which Freud's work was based. A principle such as "Nothing succeeds like success" has no place in a psychoanalytic approach. If anything, the patient's success prevented her from ever taking a further step on that road of: know thyself.

This is also true of the second patient I have just mentioned. If his first step toward adjustment, which he made without the corresponding insight, had been frustrated, he might, to be sure, have lost hope and turned away from attempts at an increase of self-knowledge, as well as from further thrusts toward reality. But he might just as well have found out that adjustment without insight is futile, and his resistance might then have crumbled.

Be that as it may, it must be acknowledged that there are patients who cannot do better than to adjust or to be successful, whose self is not strong enough to bear truth. The analyst must never become an evangelist: insight into psychological processes, to the analyst an end in itself, is usually aspired to by patients for purely therapeutic reasons. It is one of the many apparent paradoxes I have encountered in the science of man's mind that just those patients who are less interested in their therapy, but become absorbed in the delight of increasing their knowledge of self have, in my experience, a better chance of recovering from their psychopathology than those who adhere to what psychoanalysis offers at the social level—a therapy.

It is important to re-emphasize that, in matters of the mind, the pragmatic, utilitarian viewpoint is doomed to failure. Only those ignorant of the real goals of analysis would list the patient whose vicissitudes I have presented under "cured" in the statistics of psychoanalytic successes and failures—and do so although it is evident that no structural change of personality had been brought about.

BIBLIOGRAPHY

Alexander, F. (1956), *Psychoanalysis and Psychotherapy*. New York: Norton.
—— & French, T. M. (1946), *Psychoanalytic Therapy*. New York: Ronald Press.
Benedek, T. (1925), Notes from the Analysis of a Case of Ereuthophobia. *Int. J. Psa.*, VI:430-439.
Bergler, E. (1944), A New Approach to the Therapy of Erythrophobia. *Psa. Quart.*, XIII:43-59.
Berze, J. (1935), Vom Schizoid. *Z. ges. Neurol. & Psychiat.*, CVIII:600-621.
Bien, E. (1930), *Die Angst vor dem Erröten*. Stuttgart: Enke.
—— (1933a), Zwei Defäkationsträume einer Ereuthophobin. *Psa. Praxis*, III:173-175.
—— (1933b), Tagebuchblätter einer Zwölfjährigen. *Psa. Praxis*, III:59-68.
Blos, P. (1963), The Concept of Acting Out in Relation to the Adolescent Process. *J. Amer. Acad. Child. Psychiat.*, II:118-143.
Boucher,— (1890), Une forme particulière d'obsession chez deux héréditaires (l'érythrophobie). Paper read at the first psychiatric convention in Rouen, quoted after Bien (1930).
Bow, W. F. (1836), On the Existence of Nervous Induction in Functional Processes. *Lancet*, I:927-932.
Breton, A. (1896), Un cas d'Éreutrophobie obsédante. *Gazette des Hopitaux*, XCVI:1182-1184.
Caspar, J. L. (1846), Biographie eines fixen Wahnes. In: *Denkwürdigkeiten zur medicinischen Statistik*. Berlin: Duncker & Humblot, pp. 163-191.
Donath, J. (1912), Über Ereuthophobie (Errötungsfurcht). *Z. Neurol. & Psychiat.*, VIII:352-360.
Eisler, M. J. (1919), Ein Fall von krankhafter Schamsucht. *Int. Z. ärzt. Psa.*, V:193-199.
Feldman, S. S. (1922), Über Erröten. *Int. J. Psa.*, VIII:14-34.
—— (1962), Blushing, Fear of Blushing and Shame. *J. Amer. Psa. Assn.*, X:368-385.
Fenichel, O. (1931), *Perversionen, Psychosen, Charakterstörungen*. Vienna: Internationaler Psychoanalytischer Verlag.
Freud, S. (1895a), The Psychotherapy of Hysteria. In: Studies on Hysteria, by J. Breuer & S. Freud. *Standard Edition*, II:255-305. London: Hogarth Press, 1955.
—— (1895b), Review by A—r of Freud's lecture, "Über Hysterie," held October 21, 1895 in the Wiener medizinisches Doctorencollegium. *Wien. klin. Rundschau*, IX:679-680.
—— (1905), Fragment of an Analysis of a Case of Hysteria. *Standard Edition*, VII:15-122. London: Hogarth Press, 1953.
—— (1912), The Future Prospects of Psycho-Analytic Therapy. *Standard Edition*, XI:141-151. London: Hogarth Press, 1958.
—— (1922), Some Neurotic Mechanisms in Jealousy, Paranoia and Homosexuality. *Standard Edition*, XVIII:223-232. London: Hogarth Press, 1955.

—— (1950), *The Origins of Psychoanalysis. Letters to Wilhelm Fliess, Drafts and Notes: 1887-1902.* New York: Basic Books.

Heyer, S. R. (1949), Erythrophobie. *Hippokrates,* V:184-186.

Hitschmann, E. (1943), Neurotic Bashfulness and Erythrophobia. *Psa. Rev.,* XXX:438-446.

Hoche, A. (1897), Mittheilung an den Herausgeber. *Neurol. Cbl.,* XVI:528.

Jones, E. (1953-1957), *The Life and Work of Sigmund Freud,* 3 Vols. New York: Basic Books.

Kratter, O. (1932), Das Erröten in den Träumen eines Ereuthrophoben. *Psa. Praxis,* II:195-199.

London, L. S. (1945), Psychopathology of Ereuthrophobia (Blushing). *J. South. Med. & Surg.,* CVII:293-296.

Nunberg. H. (1932), *Principles of Psychoanalysis. Their Application to the Neuroses.* New York: International Universities Press, 1955.

Pitres, A. & Régis, E. (1897), L'obsession de la Rougeur (Éreuthophobie). *Arch. Neurol.,* III:1-26.

Schur, M. & Medvei, C. V. (1937), Über Hypophysenvorderlappeninsuffizienz. *Wien. Arch. innere Med.,* XXXVII:67-98.

Stärcke, A. (1921), Psycho-Analysis and Psychiatry. *Int. J. Psa.,* II:361-415.

Stekel, W. (1912), *Nervöse Angstzustände und ihre Behandlung.* Berlin-Vienna: Urban & Schwarzenberg.

—— (1931), Zur Psychologie der Ereuthophobie. *Psa. Praxis,* I:73-79.

Thompson, C. (1938), Development of Awareness of Transference in a Markedly Detached Personality. *Int. J. Psa.,* XIX:299-309.

Tower, L. E. (1956), Countertransference. *J. Amer. Psa. Assn.,* IV:224-255.

von Bechterew, W. (1897a), Die Erröthungsangst als eine besondere Form von krankhafter Störung. *Neurol. Cbl.,* XVI:386-391.

—— (1897b), Neue Beobachtungen über die "Erröthungsangst." *Neurol. Cbl.,* XVI:985-989.

von Luzenberger, A. (1911), Psychoanalyse in einem Falle von Errötungsangst als Beitrag zur Psychologie des Schamgefühls. *Zbl. Psa.,* I:304-307.

Weiss, E. (1933), A Recovery from the Fear of Blushing. *Psa. Quart.,* II:309-314.

Yamamura, M. (1940), Über Menschenscheu. II. Mitteilung. *Arbeiten aus der Psychiatrischen Klinik der Kaiserlichen Tohoku Universität (Beiträge zur Psychoanalyse und Psychopathologie),* VII:197-200.

SELF-PRESERVATION AND THE DEVELOPMENT OF ACCIDENT PRONENESS IN CHILDREN AND ADOLESCENTS

LISELOTTE FRANKL, M.B., B.S., Ph.D. (London)

When following the child's development from irresponsibility to responsibility in body management, the diagnostician tries to trace the slow and gradual manner in which a child assumes responsibility for the care of his own body and its protection against harm. The successes and failures of progress in this developmental line are of vital importance for the child's self-preservation and the development of accident proneness.

Among the children and adolescents in analytic treatment at the Hampstead Clinic are some who either themselves had been involved in accidents or brought material relating to accidents their friends had caused or suffered. Since almost nobody consciously wants to be involved in an accident, the psychoanalytic exploration of these cases should contribute something to the understanding of the development of those personalities, who in adult life are described as accident prone; and possibly provide pointers to the prevention of accident proneness.

When studying the development of accident proneness many factors—psychopathology, education, the failures of the educational approach as well as practical conditions of life—have to be taken

This investigation was supported in part by Public Health Service Grant No. M-5683, MH (1), from the National Institute of Mental Health, Washington.

The material used has been collected at the Hampstead Child-Therapy Clinic, a therapeutic and research center maintained at present by The Field Foundation, Inc., New York; The Anna Freud Foundation, New York; The Grant Foundation, Inc., New York; The Estate of Flora Haas, New York; The Old Dominion Foundation, New York; The Psychoanalytic Research and Development Fund, Inc., New York; The Taconic Foundation, Inc., New York.

I am grateful to Anna Freud, Sidney Axelrad, and John Benjamin whose constructive suggestions and cogent criticisms helped me in the writing of this paper.

into account. Whichever aspect is selected for study, it is important to remain fully aware of all the other aspects as well. There is ample statistical evidence available concerning accidents and accident proneness. Hypotheses which adequately explain the facts and consequently contribute to their prevention are needed.

An accident may be regarded as a symptom which, like many other symptoms expressing childhood disturbances, is not specific for any one underlying conflict, but may represent a compromise solution of a variety of conflicts or the final outcome of a series of conflicts in the past and present. It may be a response to a temporary stress situation leading to transitory regression or symptom formation, or it may be the expression of a permanent character trait. In order to investigate the occurrence of accidents and the development of accident proneness, the development of the function of self-preservation and the factors influencing it have to be reviewed.

This study has been undertaken following the tradition of Kris and Hartmann who in 1952 wrote: "The integration of reconstructive data with data gathered through direct observation of early childhood represents one of the more pressing demands on our analytic thinking." To reconstructive data from adult analysis and direct observation of children is added another source of material as a result of psychoanalytic treatment of children at the critical period of their development when they are passing through the preoedipal, oedipal, latency, or adolescent phase.

When studying self-preservation and accidents an activity can be observed by the method of direct observation. The factors involved in and leading to those actions which result in what is described as an accident require, however, careful study by the use of the psychoanalytic method as a tool of investigation, and the psychoanalytic theory as a frame of reference. Moreover, I hope to show that psychoanalytic treatment, preferably undertaken prior to the onset of maturity, can influence fundamentally the pathological formations to be described.

SELF-PRESERVATION

The Concept of Self-Preservation

In the early period of Freud's writing, according to Strachey (1957), "The 'self-preservative' instincts had scarcely ever been referred to, except indirectly in connection with the theory that the libido had attached itself to them in the earlier phases of its development."

In 1910 in the paper "The Psycho-Analytic View of Psychogenic Disturbance of Vision," Freud discusses the opposition of instincts which subserve sexuality and "those other instincts, which have as their aim the self-preservation of the individual—the ego instincts." "Aggressive trends were ascribed to the ego instincts as being among their essential constituents" (Bibring, 1941). This was, however, not considered a fundamental assumption, merely a working hypothesis. In 1920 Freud speaks of narcissistic libido which had "to be identified with the 'self-preservative instincts' whose existence had been recognized from the first." And he adds: "now . . . we describe the opposition as being, not between ego instincts and sexual instincts but between life instincts and death instincts." And in *Civilization and Its Discontents* (1930), he says: "This aggressive instinct is the derivative and the main representative of the death instinct which we have found alongside of Eros." Following the development of Freud's later, structural view of the mind, he wrote (1940): "The ego has set itself the task of self-preservation, which the id appears to neglect."

Hartmann (1952) has developed these ideas further, especially from the developmental point of view. "In the ego's relationship with the body, we can now describe three aspects: the postulated physiological processes underlying activities of the ego; the apparatus that gradually come under the control of the ego and which in turn influence the timing, intensity, and direction of ego development; and, third, but not necessarily independent of the two others, those special structures that underlie what we call the body ego." Hartmann refers to the "close tie between the ego and aggression since this organization normally controls motility."

The Development of Self-Preservation

In earliest infancy the problem of self-preservation does not arise for the human infant; it is the mother who retains this function even after the child's birth. The problem of self-preservation arises when the toddler gradually "delimits his own individual entity" (Mahler, 1952). During the "individuation phase" (Mahler) attempts at self-preservation are clearly observable and individual variations can be noticed.

According to Anna Freud's (1963) lines of development, the main advances in ego functioning pertaining to self-preservation are: increasing orientation in the external world, understanding of cause and effect, and control of dangerous wishes in the service of the reality principle.

Examples of Developmental Stages Observed in Normal Children in the Nursery Group[1]

Norman, 3:4   Oliver, 3:6

Oliver is doing somersaults on the bar in his usual fearless and competent manner. Norman, a great admirer of Oliver, rushes on to the bar, and without much contemplation wants to copy Oliver; not yet having Oliver's skill, however, he falls to the floor. Norman is quite bewildered by this different outcome of his action.

Norman, 3:6   Oliver, 3:7

Several children are engaged in running up and down the stairs; coming down they jump first from the first step, then the second step, and Oliver, who is the most daring, manages to jump down from the fourth step. He is admired by the other children. Norman, who is impressed by Oliver's achievement, goes up to the fourth step, considers the situation for a while, then says: "This is too high for me." He goes one step lower, again considers for a moment, then proceeds to the second safe step and says: "I'll jump from here." The game is not spoiled for him, and he continues jumping from the second step several times with great pleasure.

Cecily, 4:6   Clara, 3:6

Cecily has been teaching Clara to do somersaults on the bar, which is fixed on one step before the highest one. Cecily asks me to move the bar up to the highest level and succeeds in doing the somersault in this position. Clara follows suit, climbs up to the bar, contemplates the action for a moment, and climbs down again saying: "That's too high for me; when I am bigger I can do that."

The next important step refers to the development of object relations, the development of emotional ties to the parents or parent

---

[1] I am indebted to Mrs. M. Friedmann, head teacher of the nursery, for making available these data.

substitutes, etc. In the paper "Ocular Psychoneuroses of Childhood," Winnicott (1944) writes: "Children quite naturally feel that they are custodians of their eyes, or of any part of their body, and if they do not keep their eyes healthy, they feel they have failed in a trust." Winnicott indicates how this function is related to the infant's experiences in early life and how satisfactory development depends on the "good enough environment," as he calls it, in the first months of life. He shows that already in infancy the baby needs a human being who has to bring the world to the baby in understandable form, and in a limited way, suitable to the baby's needs. He speaks of the importance of the mother supplying this active adaptation, but says that it is also a "characteristic maternal function to provide graduated failure of adaptation, according to the growing ability of the individual infant, to allow for relative failure by mental activity, or by understanding. Thus there appears in the infant a tolerance in respect of both ego need and instinctual tension."

Anna Freud (1949) has repeatedly drawn attention to the role of the mother in enabling the child "to model himself on the pattern of the adult world which surrounds him." In a verbal communication she emphasized how the function of self-preservation is very gradually taken over by the child from the mother who fulfills this function in the child's early life.

Examples

Ralph, aged nineteen months, paused at the top of the stairs, and said "Careful" in a questioning voice. His mother now repeated after him, "Yes, careful," as she had said to him many times before, and Ralph proceeded to negotiate the stairs.

A three-year-old boy with a proud expression showing his pleasure in mastery, and using his mother's oven mittens, carried a hot baking sheet carefully to the table.

Anna Freud stresses that it is normal for children to be reckless; one cannot expect them to take care of their body as long as the mother is present. Children will take over the care of their own body if the mother does not do so, or if she is absent. She quotes the example of children who will climb dangerously high up a tree in the presence of an adult, and will look after their own safety only when the adult goes away.

THE DEVELOPMENT OF ACCIDENT PRONENESS

Considering the pathology—failures in the function of self-preservation—leading to accidents, more detailed investigation of the factors influencing different stages of the development of the self-preservative function becomes necessary. To these will have to be added forms of pathology which arise after this function has become established as a result of regression, symptom formation, etc.

Hartmann, Kris, and Loewenstein (1949) write: "Freud was used to comparing the relation between narcissism and object love to that between self-destruction and destruction of the object. This analogy which might have contributed to his assumption of self-destruction as of the primary form of aggression, to be compared to primary narcissism. . . ." Applying this assumption to hypotheses in connection with the development of accident proneness, it would imply that some individuals who tend to have accidents momentarily regress as a result of cumulative or temporary stress to this earliest phase of development.

The earliest stage when truly accidental, i.e., not purposive, self-injury can be observed is very early indeed in a child's life, even in the first few weeks of his existence when some children scratch their faces as a result of the movements of their hands while lying in their cot. Hartmann, Kris, and Loewenstein (1949) discuss the significance of this phenomenon at the stage of incomplete differentiation in the psychic apparatus.

> The motor discharges we observe and which we are used to considering as aggressive discharges are during this phase of infant development not directed against an organized world. At the present stage of our knowledge we are unable to decide whether, during this phase, acts of actual or "true" self-destruction occur, or whether the observed destructive actions of the infant—such as self-infliction of damage, i.e., by scratching—can be explained by assuming that the distinction between self and external world is not yet possible; and that unpleasure or pain are not yet recognized as signals warning of danger, because of the incomplete awareness of the bodily self as represented in the image of the body [p. 26].

Hoffer's work (1950) on the pain barrier and the development of the body ego has to be considered here. Hoffer's observation on a highly abnormal infant girl who severely injured her arms and hands by biting, in spite of attempts by the nursing staff to protect her, indicates that it is primarily the pain barrier which protects the infant against the destructive instinct attacking his own body in line with the process of libidinization of the body. As Hoffer aptly formulates it, "The infant does not hurt himself because he likes himself so much." Hoffer refers only to the failure of steps toward deflection of self-destructiveness such as "damage to oneself by biting, refusal of food and starvation which opens up the subject of pathology of the body ego." In the context of our considerations I would focus on the failure of steps toward deflection of self-destruction leading to damage to the body as may be found in some accidents later on in life.

Anna Freud (1949) also considers that "in the very early phases aggressive energy may find outlets on the child's own body, just as sexual energy may find outlets in autoerotic activities." She refers to the head knocking of infants as a self-destructive equivalent of the autoerotic rhythmical activity of rocking. She also draws attention to what appears, at least descriptively, similar to hypochondriacal tendencies in very young children who prematurely take over the concern with their bodily health, illness or safety, i.e., at a time when this should still be lodged in the mother. Excessive concern over safety in young children is a sign of neurotic development rather than a welcome, healthy achievement.

Among the factors contributing to the later failure of self-preservation, the effect of complex forms of relative deprivation of object love, lack of adequate cathexis of the child's body, can be studied in observing the children in the Well-Baby Clinic. An example illustrating this is Amy, a first-born child of middle-class parents. Mrs. Model, the Assistant of Dr. Stross, the pediatrician, reports:

> We have seen the child regularly since she was three weeks old. In the early contacts we note the mother showed little pleasure in her baby. She did not nurse her and cuddle her. At three and a half weeks mother told us of her fear that the child might choke, and she has brought up such fears subsequently.
>
> Our comment at ten weeks is: The baby was extremely alert but unrelaxed . . . a lack of babyishness about her brightness.
>
> At eight and a half months: Some of Mrs. O.'s remarks linger

in one's mind as they typify her strange relationship with her baby. Having wrapped the child up prior to leaving, Mrs. O. laughs and refers to her child as "a strange-hooded figure." She forgot to bring a dry napkin with her, but was not bothered. She bent to pick up a toy and in so doing banged the baby's head on the table. Amy is still dressed in a nightgown which looks unironed and grubby.

At one year: We think Amy is an infant who with more maternal care could be considerably more advanced (apparent awareness of the reality situation; appropriate reaction to the pediatrician). Amy will not have experienced the steady smiling encouragement and stimulation that makes for the picture of a well-developed, alert, responsive child.

At fifteen months: Amy is now a small fair-haired toddler with an uncertain smile and watchful eyes. It took some time today before we could get a smile from her; she sat quietly on her mother's knee watching carefully. She is rather tense, and on reading through our notes made just after the consultation it seems relevant that Mrs. O. mentioned that Amy (1) eats soap, edges of match boxes, cigarette ends; (2) is always falling; on one occasion banged her head quite severely when her mother was speaking on the telephone to her husband who was abroad.

These two aspects of toddler behavior concern most mothers, and most mothers take steps to protect their child as far as possible. With Mrs. O. the element of concern and wish to protect her baby is not to the forefront; she has a casual exhibitionistic manner when she relates these events; it is almost as though she says to Amy: "This is life and you must learn about it the hard way."

At eighteen months: (Mother complains of a sleep disturbance.) Amy looked like a forlorn little waif today. Her mother, looking at her with a mixture of amusement and contempt, observed, "Heavens, she looks like something from an institution," and the description was apt. We have never seen Amy in a mood of serene contentment. We thought today that while there is a close bond between the mother and child, the mother is too unpredictable for the child to be able to experience security.

A lowering of libidinal cathexis of the self results from complex forms of relative deprivation of object love, and leads to an increased tendency to accidents as described in the case of Amy. The effect of one of the factors contributing to this state can be observed in children brought up in some institutions and in children in whose life continuity in the relationship to an early love object has been lacking. From our limited experience, it seems possible that the frequency of accidental injuries, other than age-specific ones, occurring in children brought up in residential care might represent an index of "early mothering" resulting in adequate or inadequate libidinal cathexis of the body.

For example, the superintendent of a residential nursery where the children felt greatly valued and appreciated by the staff, maintained that she could not remember any accidents apart from those which are characteristic for children struggling with certain age-specific conflicts.

On the other hand, in reports about the past and present life of children referred to the Clinic after unsatisfactory residential care, accidents were frequently mentioned. For example, Robert, aged eight, was referred by the superintendent of a children's home without the parents giving information about his past, since neither of them had been consistently looking after Robert and his siblings. Robert was described as willful to the point of "self-destruction." He had hurt himself three times, once necessitating hospital treatment, through persistence in dangerous activities in spite of warnings.

In tracing different forms of pathology of the function of self-preservation, we must take into consideration the manifestations indicating the result of delay or impairment in the fusion of aggressive and libidinal drives together with disturbances of functions controlling drive activity, i.e., the persistence of impulsive behavior beyond the age when it normally occurs in children "and to a degree in excess of the normal." Persistence of expression by action rather than by fantasying or thinking, for whatever cause, is a major element which contributes to the development of accident proneness. Were it not that these children and adolescents in situations of potential danger continue to use "irrational action" (Hartmann, 1947), together with certain defense mechanisms, rather than action in the service of the ego, they might not have accidents.

The defense mechanism of turning aggression against the self is considered by Anna Freud (1936) to be chronologically among the very earliest defense mechanisms employed by the ego against the drive impulse. For the purposes of presentation, the motivations, mechanisms, and processes leading to accidents had to be singled out from their complex matrix. Those chosen as illustrations were considered the most important from the genetic point of view.[2]

Owing to the ease with which regressive processes are set in motion in very young children, a tendency to self-injury due to conflict may still be expressed on their body. Among the children in psychoanalytic treatment during the preoedipal phase was Timothy, aged two years ten months. The analyst reports:

> During a session in which his fear of being bitten was expressed in a verbal fantasy, an interpretation about the child's fear of being hurt as springing from his wish to hurt made the child angry, and he threw toys all around the room. At the end of the session he ran into a wall, bumped his head, and started to cry. This was interpreted as his having hurt himself because he would rather do that than hurt the analyst—but another factor was understood in this, namely, that he wished to call on the analyst's pity and to be comforted by him. This self-injury was not only defensive, but was also an expression of his wish that the analyst should see him as not responsible for aggressive impulses, but only as a little boy who was in need of love and comfort.

This and other examples from this child who later on would throw himself on the floor and lift his arms to be picked up, after injuring himself, raises the whole problem of secondary gain in these cases. The term "appeal function," which Stengel (1960) has introduced in connection with suicidal attempts in adults, has to be considered here.

The tendency to accident proneness as related to the dominant phase-specific conflict can be observed in the manifest behavior of children at the anal-sadistic and phallic-oedipal phases. In the cases in treatment at the Clinic, the overlapping of preoedipal and oedipal tendencies can be studied. In the following case, the sadomasochistic relationship was confined to the mother. I quote from the report:

> Alice, aged five, provoked her mother before and after the sessions had finished. She would threaten and sometimes begin her attempts at climbing onto window ledges with the intention

[2] I am grateful to Dr. J. Bolland, Mrs. P. Cohen, Miss E. Daunton, Mr. E. Freud, Mrs. E. M. Mason, Mrs. E. E. Model, Mr. B. Rosenblatt, and Miss V. J. Thompson for permission to use examples from the cases they have treated. I am also greatly indebted to Mrs. L. Neurath for her kind assistance.

of climbing out of the window, or she would climb over the bannister onto the heater. Her mother was panic-stricken and with a look of horror on her face she would shout, grab at Alice's hand, and sometimes smack her. After a visit to her doctor who "lectured" her, the mother said she was trying not to react to Alice's behavior, in order to avoid scenes, but described her fantasies as she sat on the tube station platform, as Alice jumped about: "I can see her whole body all broken up on the lines."

Alice commented one day after father had told her not to climb the bannisters and she had given in to his wishes, "My daddy never lets me climb, he does not want me to be hurt. Mummy doesn't care." She must have sensed the mother's unconscious hostility in her controlling, while the father's similar efforts were interpreted as a protection.

The development of the age-specific fighting relationship with the mother, expressed in the form of self-destruction on the child's own body, followed by self-injury as a result of castration anxiety, could be traced particularly clearly in a case of simultaneous analysis of mother and child reported by Burlingham, Goldberger, and Lussier (1955).

[Bobby had been referred to the Clinic at the age of four and a half because he was extremely provocative.] His provocations included dangerous actions by which he frightened his mother, e.g., he would jump down from great heights. This behavior reached its climax in the symptom which led to his referral: namely his tearing himself from her in the street when he would run in front of cars and buses.

Much of Bobby's behavior could be traced to his castration fears. In his behavior toward his own body he identified with the sadistic, castrating mother image, and developed tendencies of self-injury: he would bang his head when thwarted, pick the skin of his lips, bite his nails until he drew blood. This also served as punishment for his sadistic wishes toward the mother. . . .

There is a definite link between Mrs. N.'s [the mother's] sexualization of the traffic and the symptom of running into the traffic which had led to Bobby's referral to analysis. For mother and child, the buses were phallic symbols. What appeared as a phobic attitude in the mother appeared in the child as an almost compulsive play with the toy buses which he held in front of him when dashing himself against the walls of the room and further in the irresistible attraction which the traffic held for him. Mother and child acted, although in a different manner, under the domination of an identical fantasy.

The following is an example of aggression turned against the self in the service of the superego, the mechanism being in this case prompted by a strong unconscious guilt feeling[3] in a boy at the beginning of the latency phase; there seems to have been marked lack of fusion between libido and aggression and the oedipal conflict was unresolved.

[Report on Tommy, aged six:] Combined with Tommy's overwhelming aggressive impulses, we find a very severe superego. This leads to both his multiple fears (through guilt) and to his tendency to turn his aggression against himself. This in turn reinforces the ferocity of his superego.

Tommy will inflict an injury on himself at times when he has almost succumbed to behaving aggressively toward another person. The first time this pattern showed itself very clearly already in the third week of treatment, when he was reacting with aggression to the week-end breaks. He tried to poke a stick in the therapist's eye, but retracted it quickly and hurt his own eye with it. Similar incidents have occurred at other times, and always his desire to hurt himself, when faced with the unacceptable wish to hurt someone else, has been interpreted.

He found it very difficult to express his angry feeling directly, and instead became passive and helpless, complaining of being ill and needing to be looked after. At the same time he became markedly accident prone, banging his head on a lamppost, falling down and grazing his knees and bumping into things. Thus he gratified two impulses simultaneously—the need for self-punishment and the need to be looked after. At other times during the same period, Tommy appeared to be "unhappy" as his mother called it. In treatment these moods were seen to be depressive in character. He sat in a chair listlessly, unable to move or show interest in anything. These moods came particularly when intense aggression was unexpressed and turned against the self.

[3] See Freud (1901): "It is well known that in the severer cases of psychoneurosis instances of self-injury are occasionally found as symptoms and that in such cases suicide can never be ruled out as a possible outcome of the psychical conflict. . . . Many apparently accidental injuries that happen to such patients are really instances of self-injury. What happens is that an impulse to self-punishment, which is constantly on the watch and which normally finds expression in self-reproach or contributes to the formation of a symptom, takes ingenious advantage of an external situation that chance happens to offer, or lends assistance to that situation until the desired injurious effect is brought about. . . . They betray the part which the unconscious intention plays by a number of special features—e.g. by the striking composure that the patients retain in what is supposed to be an accident."

From the Road Accident Statistics (1961), it is apparent that in adolescence a new peak of road accidents occurs. This might have been expected on the basis of psychoanalytic knowledge of the main characteristics of adolescence (A. Freud, 1958; Eissler, 1958; Spiegel, 1958). Speeding and many other forms of reckless behavior on the roads can be observed which are liable to lead to accidents. Fighting relationships and playing with danger, seen in the fights in the school playground, become dangerous and a cause of accidents when they occur between cyclists and drivers on the road. The ability to maintain adequate reality adaptation in spite of the adolescent turmoil is of crucial importance in the avoidance of accidents as can be seen from the following example:

Some years ago, a seventeen-year-old adolescent patient had had a slight cycling accident with his friend Jack, when going down a hill. The other boy ran into him, and Denis fell off his bike, but did not get hurt. He reported that he had just heard that this boy, Jack, who previously caused him to fall down, had now been involved in a serious accident with a motor bike while driving a sports car. Denis had been thinking a great deal about this accident and how it could have happened. He thought that his friend Jack and his girl friend must have gone at great speed for their sports car to overturn. Denis imagined that the accident might have happened north of the school. There are gangs of boys on motor bikes north of his school, sometimes forcing drivers of vehicles into the kerb. A driver would then have to brake very hard to avoid overturning his car should it hit the kerb. Denis thought that the feeling of being driven into the kerb would have aroused great anxiety in his friend; he linked falling with the fear of being feminine, being passive. As a result of intense anxiety, and in order to ward off this passive fantasy, Jack might have become angry and aggressive, and gone straight ahead without regard to anything, and gone into the back of one of the motor bikes ahead. If he did this with great speed, the car might have turned over when it hit the motor bike.

The conflict between masculine and feminine tendencies was a central problem for the patient who reported the accident.

The part played by masturbation fantasies in his riding a bicycle at an earlier age was vividly described by him; it was not a bicycle he was riding, he had a big head and was flying an aeroplane; he would flash by, passing the other cyclists on the road. Cars did not count, they were too big; they were rockets and meteors, there could not be men in them. The sexualization of the danger situation when cycling was experienced in either just getting to school in time or just being too late; time being represented not by the clock, but by the presence of a prefect at the school gate. Since, as he only realized much later, the prefect too would often arrive late, he allowed less and less time in order to get to school, and cycling to school had the significance of a race. This could be traced back to the lack of control and the struggle over gaining control, the fight with his nanny, the regression to omnipotent fantasies in the course of his early toilet training.

Denis stressed that he was more reasonable and better adjusted to reality than his friend. He recalled that he had always been more reasonable. When he was two years old they had a pond in the garden. He was all by himself and walked toward the pond. His nurse ran down in great excitement, afraid that he might fall in, but his mother said that she should let him look after himself. In fact, he was lying down near the edge of the pond and carefully put his arm over the edge into the water.

Acting out rather than verbalization of his conflicts was, however, one of Denis's main problems in treatment. Not long ago he had again been knocked down in the road at a stage in his analysis when he was fighting against gaining insight into his own prostitution fantasies and passive wishes. Having no light on his bicycle, he pushed it across a crossroad and got knocked down by a driver who offered him ten shillings for the repair of his bicycle which was bent as a result of the accident; Denis was not hurt apart from an abrasion on his leg.

Mood swings from elation to deep depression, and the alternation of infantile clinging with attempts at loosening of the infantile object ties, led to the causation of an accident which really represented a suicidal attempt.

Eric was referred to the Clinic at the age of fourteen on the advice of the school for persistent school failure, and also because he was becoming increasingly withdrawn and moody. The boy himself complained that he could not concentrate. The headmaster suggested that the boy's disturbance might be related to the fact that he had never been told that Mr. T., whom the mother married when Eric was five, was his adoptive father. The psychiatric examination, however, suggested that this was a severely disturbed boy.

When Eric began to question in his own mind his parentage he became very depressed and tried constantly to provoke the adoptive father to show some sign of affection, finally crying and saying, "What would you do if I committed suicide?" The adoptive father then told him the story of his own brother's suicide, adding that if Eric was so cowardly as to kill himself, he could not care less. At this period Eric had many outbursts of rage with his mother, and on these occasions tended to damage his own possessions rather than hers; for instance, he smashed some of his own records.

In the following month the parents reported that "Eric had put his eye out with a dart." The facts were that the boy was in bed with flu, and alone in the flat. He started playing darts, tying the string to the dart in order to pull it back after throwing it. As he jerked it back, it pierced the lens of his right eye. He did not tell the parents for some time, and they did not take any action, even when told. Finally, after some hours, he was seen by the family doctor, and admitted at once to a hospital. He was described as being extremely cooperative, very cheerful, and brave.

He said constantly, "I threw the dart at something else, and it turned round and hit me," and was able to see how frequently he turned his aggression toward others against himself. He also at this time became quite aware that he turned his aggression against himself in order to attack the parents, saying that he had disappointed them always and now he had hurt them badly by having this accident which would result in his being even less successful at school.

Accidental injuries suffered early in life may influence later development and accident proneness. Among the cases at the Clinic are some who suffered accidents in early childhood, before the function of self-preservation was fully developed.

At the age of thirteen, George developed a compulsive fear that he might fall out of the train on his journey to and from school. At the age of two and a half he had actually opened the door of a car in which he was having a ride, fell out of the car, and hurt himself badly.

At the time of referral he showed intense passivity and inhibition of his aggression, which played an important role in his learning problem and school failure. In the course of treatment he became gradually aware of the motivation which had led to this inhibition, as can be seen from the following example.

He asked, "Why do I play war?" referring here to a game called "Attack" which he played by himself for long hours at a time. "Is it my killer instinct?" he asked. My interpretation [writes the therapist] was that what he called a killer instinct probably meant being very angry at someone. He then recalled that he did sometimes get mad at Tim, his brother. It was easy to damage people, he thought, especially oneself, and he recalled his fear that he would commit suicide by jumping off the train. The next day it took him almost the whole hour to remember what we had discussed the day before.

All those who work with children, or treat them, would be able to collect case material which would throw light on the different ways children are influenced later on by accidents in their early life. It would be interesting to study how far this is determined by the understanding and help that is given at the time after the first accident occurred, and other preventive measures that can be taken.

Accident Proneness Untreated and Treated

Extreme examples of increased tendency to self-destruction in the form of accidents due to early disturbance in object love, in particular deprivation of object love with consequent insufficient fusion of libido and aggression and greater tendency to aggressive cathexis of the body and the self whenever the object world proved disappointing, or whenever other situations of stress occurred, could be seen in some of the children who spent their early life in concentration camps or in hiding, separated from their parents.

One of these cases was referred for treatment at the age of fifteen but broke off treatment after a very short time. His parents and two older siblings were killed by the Nazis. Although the data on these children are often inaccurate, it was assumed that he was sent to complete strangers at the age of two, who took him only because of the money paid for him. He could not communicate verbally when he left home; a grandmother, who two years later came to stay near the place where he was, reported that he had been cruelly treated.

Among accidental self-injuries the following were mentioned: Daniel was reported at one time to have always fallen and bruised himself. During treatment he had the tip of his right forefinger cut off while "mucking about" at work. He injured himself with an axe while cutting wood. He often raced on his bicycle, even on wet days, with the idea that this might end in disaster. He constantly seemed to have minor mishaps, like breaking his spectacles, damaging his watch, having something wrong with his bike.

This boy emigrated and finally committed suicide[4] while he was in the army by shooting himself.

[4] Freud (1901) wrote: "Anyone who believes in the occurrence of half-intentional self-*injury*—if I may use a clumsy expression—will be prepared also to assume that in addition to consciously intentional suicide there is such a thing as half-intentional self-*destruction* (self-destruction with an unconscious intention), capable of making skilful use of a threat to life and of disguising it as a chance mishap."

In the following case of a two-year-old child turning of aggression against the self was an outstanding feature, together with some impairment of object love in infancy, due to the mother's state of withdrawal. The successful therapeutic result of psychoanalysis could be seen already in the later course of the child's treatment:

One of the mother's initial complaints was that Nella had no fear, giving as example that Nella would wander away from the parents in a shop, would scream, and lie in the road if they tried to hold her hand when crossing the road. She was a child who in treatment quickly showed her preoccupation with frightening and violent fantasies. These fantasies were a fairly constant preoccupation and resulted in periods of withdrawal during which she was inaccessible to influence from the outside, for instance, in the nursery school.

One of the first themes that came into the treatment was of loneliness and the feeling that she was of no value. She constantly played at being a sick baby and an ill baby and would say, "Leave me alone, I dead." She expressed the feeling that she had been "thrown away" when admitted to the hospital for one night for a tooth extraction.

In her fantasy world she was surrounded by witches and crocodiles. In the treatment, her inability to accept an adult's warning about physical danger was seen when she would try to climb out of the window. She would deliberately and provokingly lean through the bars and begin to climb out. Interpretation of her wish to get the therapist to protect her or to express her concern, or of her wish to throw herself away, made little difference. When she was lifted down from the window with the verbalization of why this was done, she would first turn her fury on the therapist, scratch, kick, and scream, and then dart round the room or out of the room, and invariably at this point she would hurt herself in some way—catch her fingers in the door, bang into a cupboard, or turn quickly and fall. She seemed to want to say, "It's all your fault" but would sob stormily and remain isolated.

This particular behavior was at its height at the beginning of the oedipal phase when the realization that she had no penis reinforced her conviction that she was no good, "My tummy is silly." During the oedipal phase the mother was pregnant for the third time, and analytic work connected with this event strengthened Nella's awareness of reality though it brought the element of jealousy to the foreground. Her fantasy play contained a marked masochistic element in which damage and hospitalization, with herself as the victim, were recurrent themes. In her treatment she dramatized fairy stories and myths in which the heroine, with whom she was identified, was badly treated and misunderstood. There was, however, no parallel in her life situation: she did not hurt herself or become ill. In fact, the absence of damage to her body was quite striking, though after trouble at home she would say sadly: "Sometimes I feel as if I had fallen on rocks and other rocks had fallen on top of me."

Only when Nella was at the beginning of the latency period was she able to cathect her own body in a positive way. She began to show pride in her appearance, to be able to anticipate events, and care for her own possessions.

The changes in this patient are of particular interest because it has been possible to see how she can bring her problems with the help of her strikingly rich fantasy life, and the analysis of these fantasies has had the result that the underlying feelings are no longer acted out in a self-destructive manner.

SUMMARY

The function of self-preservation develops gradually in the pre-oedipal and oedipal phase as functioning according to the pleasure principle is gradually replaced by the reality principle and the child takes over the self-protective function from his parents.

I gave examples which highlight age-characteristic factors leading to accidents. Among the factors resulting in accidents are: the tendency to express mental conflict in bodily terms may still be found in the early preoedipal phase of development; anal-sadistic conflicts, age-specific castration anxiety, in combination with the defense mechanism of turning aggression against the self, the mode of expression in action rather than in fantasy or thought, may result in accidents. In adolescents, the same result may come about through the dramatization of sexual fantasies, for instance, together with exhibitionism and sudden, often deep regression.

On the basis of our knowledge of factors leading to the occurrence of age-characteristic accidents as distinct from those accidents which are expressions of a more permanent character disturbance, criteria for the early diagnosis of accident proneness can be worked out in connection with Anna Freud's scheme (1962) for the "Assessment of Childhood Disturbances."

Though many aspects of this complex problem could not be dealt with, one of the conclusions reached on the basis of psycho-

analytic treatment of children and adolescents at the Hampstead
Clinic would point to the importance of treatment being undertaken
as soon as accident proneness has been spotted and before maturity
has been reached. By treating children and adolescents and, for
instance, freeing some of the aggression which had been turned
against the self and expressed in the symptom of accidents, a more
adequate object choice and form of work may be facilitated, as a
rule before final decisions in this respect have been made. Thus treatment of accident proneness at an early stage of the illness might also
lessen the incidence of fate neurosis in adults.

BIBLIOGRAPHY

Bibring, E. (1941), The Development and Problems of the Theory of Instincts. *Int. J. Psa.*, XXII.
Burlingham, D., Goldberger, A., & Lussier, A. (1955), Simultaneous Analysis of Mother and Child. *This Annual*, X.
Eissler, K. R. (1958), Notes on Problems of Technique in the Psychoanalytic Treatment of Adolescents. *This Annual*, XIII.
Freud, A. (1936), *The Ego and the Mechanisms of Defence.* New York: International Universities Press, 1946.
—— (1949), Aggression in Relation to Emotional Development: Normal and Patho-logical. *This Annual*, III/IV.
—— (1958), Adolescence. *This Annual*, XIII.
—— (1962), Assessment of Childhood Disturbances. *This Annual*, XVII.
—— (1963), The Concept of Developmental Lines. *This Annual*, XVIII.
Freud, S. (1901), The Psychopathology of Everyday Life. *Standard Edition*, VI. London: Hogarth Press, 1960.
—— (1910), The Psycho-Analytic View of Psychogenic Disturbance of Vision. *Standard Edition*, XI. London: Hogarth Press, 1957.
—— (1920), Beyond the Pleasure Principle. *Standard Edition*, XVIII. London: Hogarth Press, 1955.
—— (1930), Civilization and Its Discontents. *Standard Edition*, XXI. London: Hogarth Press, 1961.
—— (1940), *An Outline of Psychoanalysis.* New York: Norton, 1949.
Hartmann, H. (1947), On Rational and Irrational Action. In: *Psychoanalysis and the Social Sciences*, I. New York: International Universities Press.
—— (1952), The Mutual Influences in the Development of Ego and Id. *This Annual*, VII.
—— Kris, E., & Loewenstein, R. M. (1949), Notes on the Theory of Aggression. *This Annual*, III/IV.
Hoffer, W. (1950), Development of the Body Ego. *This Annual*, V.
Mahler, M. (1952), On Child Psychosis and Schizophrenia: Autistic and Symbiotic Infantile Psychoses. *This Annual*, VII.
Road Accident Statistics 1961. London: RoSPA Publication (Royal Society for the Pre-vention of Accidents).
Spiegel, L. A. (1958), Comments on the Psychoanalytic Psychology of Adolescence. *This Annual*, XIII.

Stengel, E. (1960), Old and New Trends in Suicide Research. *Brit. J. Med. Psychol.*, XXXIII.

Strachey, J. (1957), Editor's Note to Freud, S. (1915): Instincts and Their Vicissitudes. *Standard Edition*, XIV. London: Hogarth Press, 1957.

Winnicott, D. W. (1944): Ocular Psychoneuroses of Childhood. In: *Collected Papers*. London: Tavistock Publications, 1958.

THE ANALYSIS OF A YOUNG CONCENTRATION CAMP VICTIM

EDITH LUDOWYK GYOMROI, Ph.D. (London)

In her comments on "Grief and Mourning" by John Bowlby, Anna Freud (1960) refers to analyses of young concentration-camp victims who have undergone repeated traumatic separations from birth and infancy onward, and to the expectation that these cases will supply more detailed information concerning the links between early separation and later pathology. The paper which follows is based on the analysis of one of these children and represents an attempt to trace the difficulties of personality development as they occur under the impact of such fateful constellations.

Elizabeth's Prehistory before Arrival in England

Elizabeth's early known history consists of a small number of isolated data pieced together gradually from some information obtained from children in her group or their relatives. She herself had no memory whatsoever of the time before she came to England, with the exception of very few unconnected images. She and her elder sister, Helen, are presumed to have been born in Czechoslovakia and to have been taken to the Auschwitz concentration camp without parents. At least the names of both children were entered in the books of the camp without those of mother, father, or other relatives. The children had no camp documents, except for numbers tattooed on their arms.

In Auschwitz they formed part of a group of eight children kept alive for unknown purposes. The eldest among them, Charlie, played

This paper forms part of a research project entitled "Inquiry into the Development of Motherless Children" which is being financed by a grant from the Psychoanalytic Research and Development Fund, Inc., New York, to the Hampstead Child-Therapy Clinic.

It was presented at a meeting of the British Psycho-Analytic Society on June 5, 1963.

the role of protective big brother and—as told by adult survivors—was instrumental in saving their lives. As part of a constant war waged against the hated guards he had taught the children not to answer at roll call in the morning but to hide under their bunks instead. On the day when the Nazis in the face of the liberating armies swept through the barracks shooting the inmates, the children happened to carry out these instructions and were spared.

On liberation Elizabeth's age was established by medical examination as approximately four years, that of her sister as approximately five. They were fed and nursed somewhere for some subsequent months, but all attempts to trace where they spent the time between liberation and their arrival in England were unsuccessful.

Elizabeth's Early History in England

From her arrival in England until one year before the beginning of treatment Elizabeth and her sister lived in a children's home specially organized for concentration-camp survivors under the devoted and skilled care of Miss Alice Goldberger, who did her utmost to provide these children with natural, homelike surroundings as well as to give them every opportunity for growth, development, and adaptation. Miss Goldberger describes the sisters on arrival as looking like pale little women with puffy old faces, bad skin trouble such as scabies, and short-cropped hair. Their behavior was noisy and exaggeratedly cheerful; new experiences were greeted with delighted shrieks; dancing and singing were their favorite occupations.

While all children of the group showed intense loyalty to each other, Elizabeth and her sister were especially inseparable. Every evening they came to each other's beds, kissed and cuddled, and whispered words in a special baby language reserved for this intimate relationship. Even years after they could often be found in each other's arms, playing mother and child, with Elizabeth in the role of baby, imitating baby talk and behavior. Their excited behavior was noticeable also in the presence of visitors, especially men on whom they wanted to climb, to be taken on their lap and cuddled.

Elizabeth as a Latency Child

According to Miss Goldberger's reports, Elizabeth had little difficulty in settling down in her new surroundings. She responded well in her physical development, became proud of her beautiful curly hair, showed a lively facial expression appropriate to her age. If anything she appeared too good, as if being good were considered by her the most potent weapon in an incessant fight for special recognition in the group and for being singled out for special attention by the adults, to whom she became deeply and dependently attached. One of her first school reports approximately a year after arrival describes her as "very keen and interested in her work," having made "good progress this term." Although there still were difficulties in some subjects, the teacher had "no doubts that next term will find all problems solved. She shows great promise for the future. Her friendly manner and pleasing personality make her an addition to any class."

However, as Elizabeth grew further into latency, not all of this promise of good development was kept. It soon became apparent that her application to schoolwork was dependent on the relationship to the teacher rather than on a genuine interest in the subject matter and her wish to learn. From one term to the next her school reports were apt to change to the opposite extreme whenever there was a change of teacher. Whenever she could not be the ablest and favorite pupil, she was apt to become naughty, disturbing to the class and unable to learn. In the home too she changed from being overgood, gentle, an eager participant in occupations and in theatrical performances, to noisy, cheeky, overindulgent behavior whenever she felt not appreciated.

As far as could be ascertained at this period from her behavior and from her confidences, there were various ways for Elizabeth to deal with her missing mother relationship. One was the manifest and constant expectation that the mother might return, a wish kept alive especially by the sudden reappearance of another mother who had been thought dead. She refused to believe that her mother could be dead since "she was much too young." Opposed to this wishful thinking which was kept alive for years in spite of the disappointing reality, there was also denial of the need for the mother expressed through her deep attachment to Miss Goldberger. She reiterated repeatedly that no one could have been as kind, helpful, and good to her as Miss Goldberger, and praised her luck in living with the latter instead of with her own mother. It was only Miss Goldberger's own efforts which helped her to recognize her dreams and fantasies about the real mother covered by this defense.

That the figures of Miss Goldberger and the absent mother had fused in Elizabeth's mind was borne out by her reaction to the former's hospitalization when Elizabeth was approximately eleven years old. She visited Miss Goldberger in the hospital and wrote her charming, considerate, and loving letters. But simultaneously her appearance and behavior changed in a manner frightening to the observer. She looked unkempt and neglected, with her hair—which always reflected her moods—bushy, unattractive, and standing like straw round her head. There were complaints from the school that she had behaved rudely to the teachers and had refused to work. The headmistress herself recognized that it was the separation from Miss Goldberger which had brought about the change. How deeply Elizabeth was shaken was proved by one of her letters to Miss Goldberger in which she debated whether she could allow her to go on convalescence and finally found that she could do so, "because you will not go away for good like other people have done, but will come back like my mother would have done if she had been alive."

There was another, for Elizabeth fateful, way in which her dependent mother relationship found expression. Apart from the attachment to her own sister, she singled out for devotion one after another member of the staff or one of the older girls in the home and offered her friendship to them. Since she especially selected girls with considerable difficulties of their own, she laid herself open in this way to much unhappiness, suffering, and hurt. But instead of giving up she kept clinging to them, made her advances over and over again, did not tire of trying, of performing services unasked, of offering generously all her possessions and her help, only crying bitterly when she was rejected.

When Elizabeth was eight years old a family made advances to her and her sister, eager to adopt them. In this instance Elizabeth became the rejecting partner, rebuffing all overtures, harshly criticizing the generous couple for being "too rich," and refusing altogether to return to their place, her critical attitude evidently hiding the fear of separation.

Adolescent Changes

With entry into adolescence Elizabeth increasingly became aware of her inability to be a person in her own right, to believe in her own capacities, and to pursue her own wishes. The dependency which in latency could remain hidden behind a façade of a good, conforming, little girl began to assume frightening proportions when measured against the new developmental need for independence. It became obvious to everybody, including herself, how slavishly she had to copy whomever she had singled out for idealization at a given time. Whether this was a simple helper in the kitchen or an ambitious student working for exams, Elizabeth felt forced to copy their movements, behavior, attitudes, irrespective of her own likes, dislikes, or abilities. She was equally unsure of herself with regard to boys; with them she alternated unexpectedly between excited provocation, shyness, and withdrawal.

At the age of seventeen it was Elizabeth herself who expressed the wish for help through analysis, a move which was in part due to her own insight, in part based again on her imitation of and identification with some of the others in the home who had entered analysis before her.

Entry into Analysis

At the first interview I asked her what help she expected from me. She replied: "I am not a person, I am always somebody else." And this was the very thing which formed the core of her pathological behavior. Every day her hair was done differently; she moved in a different manner; it was impossible to see a real person behind the various roles she played. No movement of hers was spontaneous and natural, each was deliberately produced. Every step she took was made with the awareness that she was such and such a person walking in such and such a way.

Soon it was possible to link up the changes in her appearance and behavior with the short-lived friendships she entered into which never lasted more than a day or two. Those which did, on account of the partner's persistence, existed for her only during the hours when she was in the company of the friend in question.

She was a heavily built girl with a podgy face and short fat legs.

She wore such tight trousers that one wondered how she managed to put herself into them, heavy sweaters; then suddenly some flashy jewelery, or a ribbon in her hair. She insisted on lying on the couch like other adults, but she stepped on it with both feet and threw herself down as a toddler might. Her intelligence seemed to be very low, and it was doubtful whether she could understand what the analyst expected from her. Since it was not possible for her to verbalize any of her feelings, I had to put her problems into words step by step when they appeared to come within reach of her understanding. Great skill had to be applied in order to combat the danger of her sinking into absolute and empty silence on the couch.

Instead of reporting this analysis as it proceeded, it seems to be more useful to group the material in a way which will facilitate the understanding of the development of her personality before treatment and during its course. To start with, a special feature of her behavior during the sessions has to be described. This provided insight into the basic problems of her personality and opened up the possibility of handling her difficulties. This was the storytelling which followed the long initial period of silence.

Her stories were of two different kinds. Those which she told the boys she met were relatively easy to understand. She was unable to tell the truth about herself and invented a family living sometimes in Italy, sometimes in another part of the world. The purpose of this was clear. She felt deeply ashamed of being Jewish, of having been in a concentration camp. When she was eight, she and some other children insisted on the number tattooed on their arms being removed surgically. She said once: "It is impossible that so many people were locked in if they did not deserve it." There was a deep conviction of some shameful thing she had to hide, the thing which made her different from the other children at school and which made her mother abandon her because she was not worth caring for. These stories were intended to hide her shame.

The stories told on the couch were of a very different nature and very confusing. Complete silence alternated with elaborate reports of some experience or other. They all sounded unreal, because they did not fit together; they contradicted each other, not only in character but also with regard to details of time and place; if one was true, the other could scarcely have been so. They related most often to some theft, or some other kind of "bad thing" done.

The first explanation of these stories which suggested itself was that she felt she had nothing to offer which would make her interesting and worth while for her analyst. Therefore she had to invent experiences to keep my attention. In addition, it seemed as if she told "bad things" about herself to test me, whether I would give her up if I found out that she did something wrong. This explanation, as it was not sufficiently substantiated, was not advanced, and had in fact to be given up very soon.

It was more on the grounds of factual observation and outside information than as a consequence of the possibility of interpreting analytic material that I discovered that the stories she kept telling were not invented. They related to things which really happened, not to her, but to one of the other children. At this point I ventured the interpretation that she borrowed the experiences of others, in order to keep me interested, because she thought she was not good enough for me to bother about her. In the light of material gained later it became clear that this interpretation was wrong. In spite of this it had a positive result. The storytelling was given up, and for the first time she was able to form a friendship with a girl without trying to be like her. What caused a wrong interpretation to produce this effect will be examined later.

In the third year of her analysis she was able to bring memories. These concerned the first years she spent in England. They were confused, but threw definite light on the storytelling. It was now understood that it was based on a confusion of herself with the other children. It was as if for her there did not exist a well-defined "I," but instead there was help derived from the consciousness of "We" —the group of children who shared fate, love of persons, everything. The stories were now recognized as experiences belonging to this "We," which had to take the place of the not-existing "I." In the memories of the first few years in England this confusion of identities was sometimes so impressive that it left the feeling that there was no differentiation at all between self and not-self.

One of the most striking of these was the story of her lovely doll, given to her in Czechoslovakia by a person called Agnes, which she was not allowed to bring to England because it was too dirty. In fact,

Agnes is the name of a woman whose memory is cherished by the other children who came from Thereszin, and not from Auschwitz. It is unlikely that she too could have had an Agnes. Similarly she remembered having always wetted the bed as a biggish girl, which, according to Miss Goldberger, is untrue, though some of the other children, notably two boys, did.

I feel that this is the point at which some speculation about Elizabeth's early development is justified.

Object Relations

From the beginning the very primitive nature of her object relations made a strong impression on me. The friendships which lasted only while the partner was present, the imitation of the object, were in some way reminiscent of Helene Deutsch's (1934) "as if" patients. The difference is that the latter went through the motions of emotional reactions without feeling them, displaying feelings and thoughts they believed they ought to have, modeling them on those of the object of identification; but Elizabeth's imitation concerned only features of the object which were within the range of the most primitive perception like modes of dressing, movements, etc. It was fleeting and haphazard, and disclosed more the fantasy of merging with the object than the wish to be like the object (Jacobson, 1954a, 1954b; Reich, 1954). What she longed for in these relationships was not so much the need-satisfying object as need satisfaction itself. So far as the object existed at all it was in the external world, no mental representation of it was established, and it ceased to exist when it was not present. There was no realistic concept of the self "which mirrors correctly the limits of the bodily and mental ego" (Jacobson, 1954a), the boundaries of the self were not firmly outlined, the other children were not separate entities either but were included in it, and separateness itself seemed to be a danger.

Miss Goldberger and Elizabeth's friend Anne (one of the children from Thereszin) belonged to her world from the time she came to England; her sister throughout her life. The characteristic feature of these relationships was a tenacious clinging. This clinging seemed to aim at preventing the threatening separation. Separation anxiety does not seem to be a term exact enough for her state of mind in this respect. It was more a constant expectation of separation, to which when it occurred even for a short period she reacted with a dull and abject resignation. When the first summer holiday brought the first separation from me, I gave her an address where mail would be forwarded, in order to maintain the continuity of a relationship in danger of being severed. Elizabeth, who still at the end of her latency was able to keep contact through letters with Miss Goldberger, now did write several letters which she did not post because she could not imagine that letters would reach a person who was not present and therefore nonexistent. For the same reason making a telephone call was a very difficult task for her.

At times when Miss Goldberger and the other children were experienced as being separate from her, she endeavored to be a good girl to please them. She allowed herself to be exploited by her sister and Anne in every way. Her obedience and compliance, however, were directed not toward any internal agency but toward external objects as a bribe, because if they appeared to be divorced from herself they were potentially lost.

Aggression

Her aggression, so far as aggression occurred, appeared to be objectless too. It was the aggression of an infant, anxious to get rid of, or to destroy, something which is unpleasurable; in fact, it aimed at eliminating the "unpleasurableness" and not the object which caused unpleasure. Time and again she was rude, but the rudeness was directed not against persons but against unpleasant situations. "Hatred" was expected from persons who did not supply satisfaction of her emotional needs and therefore had to remain strangers. This expectation of hatred is reminiscent of cases described by Annemarie P. Weil (1953), where "projection of lack of relationship may lead to paranoid trends: 'they don't like me' and then 'they hate me.' "

The differentiation of self and not-self, and the development of self- and object representations, leading to the establishing of the boundaries of the self, are very slow processes indeed. Sandler and Rosenblatt (1962) differentiate between images and representations, the latter gradually developing out of a multitude of images, and they quote Piaget according to whom enduring representation cannot be said to be well established before about the sixteenth month of life. As they put it, self-representation is that organization which represents the person as he consciously or unconsciously perceives himself.

The sum total of self-representations is the foundation of what is usually called identity, which begins to take a final shape in adolescence (Erikson, 1956).

If we try to reconstruct the history of Elizabeth's first years, we may assume that she was separated from her mother very early, probably in her second year, at a time when identification may already have begun to move from *being one with* to being *like* the object. The first separation must have reactivated the need of merging with it again. According to Anna Freud (1952), between "five to twenty-four months, separation from the object causes extreme distress, but the infant is so exclusively dominated by his needs that he cannot maintain his attachment to a nonsatisfying object for more than a given period (varying from several hours to several days). After this interval, which is most upsetting for the child, need satisfaction is accepted from and attachment (cathexis) is transferred to a substitute." If in Elizabeth's case separation from the mother had been followed by the possibility of turning to a substitute, her development in respect of establishing object relations proper would have continued. We have to assume that Elizabeth's surroundings and the persons looking after her must have changed constantly so that libido could not have been invested in one and the same person for any length of time.

The concept of the self which gradually develops includes not only self-representations derived from the own experiences centered round need and satisfaction and all that follows the differentiation of inside and outside, but also the ideas the persons in the environment have of the child and which they convey to him. But a child which is moved from one place to another, handed on from one set of relatives living in the greatest insecurity to another, probably transported from camp to camp, does not experience the constantly repeated reaction of a mother or a mother substitute to him, a reaction which usually reflects the image this mother figure has about the growing infant.

When a wrong interpretation provoked a positive development in Elizabeth's analysis, what took place in fact was the following: granted that secondarily the interpretation had some justification, and the stories aimed at holding the attention of the analyst and testing me, this alone would not have made the storytelling unnecessary. What really happened was that the interpretation conveyed to Elizabeth the analyst's idea that she, Elizabeth, was a separate person who had her own experiences, different from those of others. Elizabeth, identifying with the analyst, accepted the analyst's idea of her as a separate person, added this to her scanty self-representations, and started to act upon it. This is similar to what happens in the normal development of children: the mother, for instance, regards the infant as being one who can already put food into his own mouth without help, and the infant now includes this in the concept he forms of his own self and acts upon it.

The wrong interpretation produced the first step in Elizabeth's maturation which had to be completed through her analysis.

The Development of Transference

It took a long time before the first transference reactions could be detected and understood. In the beginning I was for Elizabeth predominantly a real person, the first in her life who existed only for her, whom she did not have to share with anyone. I existed for her only in her sessions, not before and not after. She repeatedly expressed the wish to have sessions which would last eight or nine hours—an attempt at clinging. When after a few months it was inevitable for her to realize the existence of other patients, her reluctance to end the session was a mixture of an attempt at warding off separation and at maintaining the situation in which she had the undivided attention of a person, in which she possessed a person without having to share her. The remarkable thing was that Elizabeth did not show, either at that stage of her analysis or later, any jealousy. A careful interpretation was attempted in telling her that she wanted to prolong a pleasure which she did not enjoy before, namely, the feeling that she had a person for herself alone. After this suddenly she was able to verbalize a fear which, as she said, overcame her now very frequently, that I might die. Her long silences now signified a merging with the dead mother, simultaneously they re-established the mother-infant situation in which the mother understands the baby without his having to talk.

After the interpretation of the storytelling, when she started to think of herself as a separate person, I became the fantasy mother who possessed supernatural powers. But I was that mother too who would abandon her at any minute. The silences were interrupted with the repeated: "I am a rotten patient," indicating that a shameful shortcoming of hers was the reason why I would abandon her.

The silences formed a special feature of this analysis, and it was possible to observe subtle changes in them. The first type of silence seemed to be a regression to the preverbal stage as described above. It sometimes alternated with a sulky silence, usually after she had had some unpleasant experience. These silences were repeatedly interrupted by me, because there was a danger of her drifting further and further away.

At a much more advanced stage of her treatment there was a third type of silence. It occurred usually after some disappointment, or something which provoked anxiety in her. She behaved like a person in pain who uses all his available libido to cathect the painful organ. This silence was not interfered with. I permitted the feeling of safety in being able to withdraw, to comfort herself, and find peace again. This wordlessness was very different from the other two, and that she was allowed to remain silent gave her the feeling of security and confidence. She gave the impression of an infant who feels protected on her mother's lap. The danger of severing the tenuous contact between patient and analyst had by this time gone.

She now repeatedly remarked on my silence, "You could be dead behind me." This showed how the ideas "mother" and "dead" belonged together. She had no memory of a living mother—she knew only about a dead one.

After this a further step was made and expressed in the transference. Somebody told her that I too had experienced losses and had had a son who died. Now she was not only silent but lay on the couch completely motionless. This dead rigidity helped me to recognize that in order to re-create the mother-child relationship she now reversed the roles: now she was dead and so she became my child. When I interpreted her transference at this point (this was at a time when direct interpretation was already possible and accepted), she replied in a sulky way: "You have your own children to love." This did not express any jealousy. She used what she thought to be reality to disprove with it my transference interpretation; what she proved in this way was her total hopelessness about ever having a mother for herself.

Until the very end her transference showed various aspects of her need for re-creating her mother.

Problems Concerning Her Amnesia

The establishing of a transference relationship and the possibility of interpretation did not introduce the process of lifting the amnesia covering her first five years of life. Even now, after an analysis which justifiably can be called successful, there is no recovery of memory for this period. This raises the question how her particular way of blotting out the past differs from the usual type of infantile amnesia.

We are accustomed to regard an individual's forgetting of his early years as the result of repression set up against retaining in consciousness the primitive infantile drive experiences against which the child has turned. What sets the defense in motion is not only the repudiation of infantile sexuality, aggression, death wishes, etc., but equally the unpleasure, namely, the frustrations, disappoint-ments, and humiliations connected with the events.

But it is also true that the preoedipal and oedipal experiences of an individual do not fall victim to the infantile amnesia without leaving traces in the form of cover memories. While for the purpose of consciousness these phenomena obscure, hide, falsify, and distort the past, for the purpose of analysis they serve as potential entrance doors to the id, i.e., as focal points from which transference mani-festations, interpretation of the unconscious, and recovery of past experience can proceed. Such cover memories, and the repressed memories which lie behind them, are organized invariably around the important adult figures in the child's early life and set securely within the framework of his physical environment. Likewise, our analytic interpretations take the path toward re-establishing consecu-tive stages of past object relationships and use as their clues with regard to time and age whatever changes in the physical surround-ings have occurred in an otherwise stable environment due to mov-ing house, traveling, etc.

There seems to be no question that on both counts—quantity

of unpleasure and stability of external surroundings—Elizabeth deviates from the norm. The frustrations of her infantile needs and wishes were undoubtedly massive; and while normally the animate and inanimate objects in a child's life are predictable and more or less stable, in her case there must have been a bewildering kaleidoscope of figures, short-lived relationships, passing images, experiences, and even languages. There is no certainty how often the children were passed from one place to another, with complete change of regime, before as well as after Auschwitz. Adult figures must have changed due to extermination. Nationalities were mixed. The guards and camp staff were German; camp inmates came from a variety of countries; the children's first language and that after liberation may have been Czech, their actual language on arrival was a mixture of Czech and Yiddish. It is no wonder that under such circumstances, memory was clouded and the focal points for its recovery were scarce.

On the other hand, it is of interest to note that even under these adverse conditions Elizabeth was not without a cover memory. This consisted of an image that she had once slept on a table and that she slept together with Charlie (the elder brother figure, himself a child, who had protected the younger ones, stolen bread for them braving punishment, and who, as other sources report, had finally saved their lives). This cover image formed the core of a few fantasies, allowing the conclusion that the wooden bunks without bedding (usual in camps such as Auschwitz) had been her "home" for a significantly longer period than any other place, and that—in the absence of stable adult objects—her fantasies had probably organized themselves around the one available figure of the "elder brother."[1]

[1] The Thereszin children reported on by Anna Freud and Sophie Dann (1951) spent two to three years in the same children's ward there. Though the persons looking after them changed frequently, and being themselves prisoners were anxious and insecure, they were a few who continued there. In addition, the quarters though poor and restricted, the bare yard, remained the same too. This may account for it that though the store of their memories was very poor indeed, they did remember considerably more than Elizabeth. Anna Freud and Sophie Dann mention these in connection with the fears of the children—of dogs, of a van, etc. They mention, too, memories of a little boy, of things he overheard the adults speaking about. It must be that however insecure life in Thereszin was, the fact that the children remained in the same place for years meant a relative, though deficient, stability, as compared with the constant change in Elizabeth's life.

Relation to Reality

If we are correct in assuming that, maybe after a very short gratifying period of infancy in which she may have achieved a primitive identification with her mother, separations from mother substitutes and constantly changing environment followed, we may borrow Spitz's (1951) term "emotional deficiency" for Elizabeth's apparent pathology. He used it for psychogenic diseases in infancy caused by the restriction of the mother-child relationship. I take the liberty of extending it to include purely psychic consequences arising from the same cause.

However terrible the objective reality of the concentration camp was, the child was affected not by this but by the fact that her innate needs remained unsatisfied and that there were no lasting objects the relation to which would have made normal ego development possible. The small child was not in a position to compare life in the camp with what we call normal living conditions. We connect the idea of Auschwitz with all we know about its atrocities, and we have to remind ourselves that the interpretation a child puts upon an event may be different from that of an adult.

My impression is that the Thereszin children who lived in cruel conditions, yet conditions less "denaturalized" than those in Auschwitz, were more exposed to traumata than the children in the extermination camps, though living conditions there and the constant danger of torture, humiliation, and extermination were much more extreme. A trauma is an isolated instance in which too much excitation enters the mental apparatus and far too suddenly to be mastered. Even series of traumatic events are isolated occurrences. The traumatic conditions in which Elizabeth grew up were, however, her established and persisting reality.

In working with Elizabeth I was often reminded of the little girl whose case was reported by Mary E. Bergen (1958), the girl whose mother was murdered by her father in the child's presence. In the course of the analysis it was established that the outstanding traumatic feature of the event from the point of view of the child was not the murder but that her mother, wishing to save the child the frightening experience, shouted at her: "You get out of here." In Elizabeth's case, too, the pathogenic factor seems to have been not the horror of the camp but the loss of the object before object constancy was achieved; in addition, life among adults who were either hostile or who lived in constant fear and insecurity.

That in spite of this, analysis was able to achieve integration of her personality has to be ascribed to a specially good ego endowment. Freud (1937) states, "We think it credible that even before the ego exists its subsequent lines of development, tendencies and reactions are already determined." We are justified in assuming that a process of maturation does take place even though hindered by events obstructing libido development and that of object relations. Hartmann (1939) distinguishes between three kinds of developmental processes: "those which occur without any essential and specific influence of the external world; those which are co-ordinated to typical experiences (that is, which are triggered off by average expectable environmental situations . . .); and finally, those which depend upon atypical experiences." In the case of Elizabeth the following problem arose: her ego development did achieve a capacity for reality testing to a fair degree. Yet the reality she had to learn to anticipate and to recognize was based on such extreme and atypical experiences as are scarcely met with in analytic practice.

If in London or New York a person were worried that going to the toilet, he might meet a leopard, we would think he had no sense of reality at all. But if someone in a remote jungle outpost thinks of this possibility we do not doubt his judgment. If a child after experiencing shorter and longer separation is incapable of learning that after separation the beloved object may reappear, that somebody who is absent still exists, then we have to think that at this point his judgment of reality is impaired. But that Elizabeth, who lived in a world where persons who disappeared were gassed, did not learn that a summer holiday does not mean death, does not signify in any way that she did not achieve a degree of reality testing and judgment. In her case it means that she learned to know a special kind of reality and what she failed to achieve was the adaptation to another.

Her ignorance of the significance of money, for instance, and of the fact that it has to be earned by work, was not different from that usual in institutionalized children. This, too, cannot be regarded as a failure in reality testing. It is closely related to the circumstances of her life which was very different from that of an average family, where the children soon learn that the parents have to work in order to earn money for the family's needs.

Libidinal Development

Elizabeth's past is known to us only from the time she was five years old. The clinging, the primitive mode of identification hint at oral fixation, but I could not detect strong pregenital orientation of her libido. The libidinal drives appeared to be without great dynamism, in some way her pregenital urges were underdeveloped. Experience of gratification increases the wish for its repetition, its absence also strengthens the need. I asked myself whether a continuous and extraordinary lack of gratification would not result in the stunting of the drive. Anna Freud and Sophie Dann observed that the Thereszin children who were fed on dull and starchy food there were uninterested in food and unwilling to try new tastes and dishes.

We know little about the development of Elizabeth's anal drive. Though there was preoccupation with the question of dirtiness (to which I shall have to return later), it is not known what kind of toilet training resulted in the fact that she behaved in an age-adequate way in this respect at the time of her arrival. Toilet training *par excellence* depends on the relation to the love objects, and we have to ask ourselves what made it possible for Elizabeth to be clean. We remember that the Thereszin children lived in children's wards and were looked after by fellow prisoners who took the trouble to take some of them up two or three times every night. This is unthinkable of Auschwitz. The reports all mention the incontinence of the generally sick adult population and the suffering inflicted on everybody by the dirt and the stench. Lack of anal control is no doubt gratifying to infants, but if the child is not cleaned, drying fecal matter and urine may cause great distress indeed. It is not impossible that what could be extreme gratification in normal circumstances turned into a painful experience which made bowel control preferable.

There is little information about her phallic phase either. Miss Goldberger remembers her passionate riding on a rocking horse, which was no doubt an autoerotic activity on the phallic level. Memories which emerged in a later stage of her analysis showed a preoccupation at that time with the difference between the sexes and penis envy and castration fear which persisted and were greatly reduced in analysis through interpretation and ensuing insight.

With regard to the relationship to persons in her environment, Elizabeth at the time of her arrival was not very different from the Thereszin children. The attachment to the other children was very strong; jealousy and envy were absent; and though she clung very much to some of the adults, the feeling toward the group was very much more positive than to the latter. But in Elizabeth's case even the relationship to the group had the character of clinging, and especially her sister and she were bodily inseparable.

There were no attempts even at substituting oedipal objects or experiencing oedipal relations in fantasy, as it is observed most often in institutionalized children (Anna Freud, 1951). Of her mother she spoke only on rare occasions, but she did have some fantasy image of her. (She had long blonde hair—hair, as will be described later, was the attribute of those who possessed power and importance.) But once when she brought one of the memories shared with the other children, concerning their dolls which were father, mother, and baby dolls, I asked her to describe the father doll to me. At this she volunteered the information with surprise that she never thought of ever having had a father. Later she did remember male persons, partly real, partly imaginary, who were important to her and who seemed to be father substitutes, but at a preoedipal level. Her fantasies about Charlie belong here, but though Charlie was for her a protective male, he was not a figure in an oedipal setting. Throughout her whole analysis no memory of any rivalry of an oedipal nature, either in reality or in fantasy, emerged. Miss Goldberger, to whom she was very attached, was not used either as a figure in any oedipal fantasy.

The Ego Ideal

Though elements which are regarded as the precursors of the superego must have been present in her earliest identifications, neither her libido development nor that of her object relations made the establishing of a superego in the sense in which we use the term possible. She was a good little girl, yet not in obedience to an internal authority, but in order to please and bribe the persons in her environment so that they would not abandon her. As mentioned before, analytic material revealed that she felt she was abandoned because she could not be liked, the reason for this lying in some anal misdeeds. The "memory" of the doll she was given by Agnes, which was taken up in the course of her analysis on various levels, threw light on the connection between these two things. In her memory she had to leave the doll behind because it was dirty. But the doll had long fair plaits, like her fantasy mother, and it was understood that this memory was a reversal of the idea that she was abandoned because she did something bad, something that made her unlovable. This was her dirtiness (the annexation of the bed wetting of the boys must have been connected with this anal—or urethral—anxiety which merged with her later penis envy).

She appears to have felt much more shame than guilt. Piers and Singer (1953) suggest that guilt is the result of tension between ego and superego, and shame between ego and ego ideal. Elizabeth did not develop a superego, but she very early built up an ego ideal to which more features were added in the course of her later identifications.

This ego ideal was based on the image of a woman with beautiful hair, wonderfully dressed, in every way good-looking, who had, in addition, the power to do as she liked. Where could this ego ideal have originated? If we recall what we know about the concentration camps, the answer to this question is immediately at hand. The prisoners were emaciated, their hair was cropped close, they were dirty, stinking, verminous. (Every drop of water was a treasure and cleanliness was impossible.) In contrast, there were the guards—well dressed, well groomed, and with carefully set hair. In addition, they had power, and they treated the mass of prisoners with contempt and disgust. Elizabeth's preoccupation with her hair, her dejection about her looks, her shame about belonging to the dirty ones is the consequence of her impossibility to live up to her ego ideal. This is the cause of her shame and her lack of self-esteem.

Edith Jacobson (1954a) holds that the degree of self-esteem is rooted in discrepancy or harmony between self-representation and the wishful concept of the self. Elizabeth could never be in harmony with the wishful concept of her self. Even in analysis she had to see herself as a "rotten patient." To the dirtiness of those to whom she belonged, who had no hair and could never be like the one with the beautiful hair-do whom she wanted to imitate, another characteristic was added. The dirty ones were bodily degraded and sick, decrepit—castrated. When she complained about her appearance she always followed this up with the fantasy of plastic surgery. Plastic surgery unconsciously meant the undoing of her castration. Dirtiness and castration were closely linked with each other.

(It is necessary to point out that her equation of dirtiness with castration, her dejection about the impossibility of ever being good-looking, with lovely hair, a person of power and importance, were gone into very thoroughly. But as no memory emerged concerning the history and the origin of these feelings, the reconstruction made above was never suggested by the analyst. Her feeling of shame alone could be connected productively with her conviction that having been in a concentration camp was proof of merited disgrace, since this was verbalized by her.)

Anxiety

Yet castration fear was less prominent than penis envy. In fact, Elizabeth did not display strong anxieties (with a single exception—when my foot was bandaged she refused to enter the room). Anna Freud and Sophie Dann (1951) observed the same in connection with Thereszin children and thought that "the fact that they have never known peaceful surroundings rendered them more indifferent to the horrors happening around them." Probably the same indifference protected Elizabeth from great anxieties later too.

Catching Up with Missed Development in Analysis

Elizabeth's analysis had to achieve not so much the solution of unconscious neurotic conflicts as to make it possible for her to reach an age-adequate maturity and to achieve the necessary readaptation to a different reality. It also had the task of helping her to develop an internal authority which regulates gratification not only on the basis of what is "possible" or "dangerous" but on the basis of some criteria of "good" or "bad." I doubt that we are justified in calling this authority the superego which Freud defines as the heir of the oedipus complex, the development of which, though it has its beginnings in preoedipal identifications, is brought to its conclusions through the dissolution of the oedipus complex.

Elizabeth's analysis had to help her to make the step from imitation of external objects to identification proper and to forming internalized object representations. She had to achieve, too, an internal guidance. The fact that she developed into a young woman who can regulate drive satisfaction according to her own views of right and wrong poses the question whether this capacity can be attained without experiencing the drama evolving out of the oedipal relationships. It would be worth while to examine the difference in the behavior of the superego which is a representation of the oedipal parents and that faculty which, as in this case, develops in direct line from the preoedipal identifications up to maturity.

Our material suggests that the agency which now provides Elizabeth with internal guidance is more protective than punitive. This is caused by the fact that due to the difference in the etiology of the two, the quantity of aggression invested in it is negligible as compared with the amount which goes into the formation of the superego.

Elizabeth's analysis offered her the possibility of going through the development she missed. I remained to a great extent a real person for her for a long time. I mattered only as a supplier of the comfort of belonging to her alone. She attempted to imitate me, to be the analyst in order to avoid separation, but there was too little material to enable this to be achieved as she had only a minimal possibility for observation. She tried to enact my way of speaking and my intonations; she wanted to arrange her room like mine. When I became in transference the fantasy mother ("You must have had blonde hair when you were young"), this mother figure was really a fusion of the one who abandoned her and the other with the beautiful hair and power—the female guard. In addition, she attributed to this figure all that was demanded of her by Miss Goldberger, teachers, all that the heroes of the many novels she read represented, the whole ideology accepted as proper by the world she lived in now, ultimately achieving an identification with it. This was not imitation any more, it became identification on a higher level. The object was internalized, and slowly she started to behave in the way she thought was demanded of her even when she was unobserved.

Sandler (1960) concludes that when the formation of the superego is achieved "what is introjected is neither the personality nor the behavior of the parents, but their authority." Though the agency responsible for internal guidance in Elizabeth is different in its genesis and its character from that of the superego, yet what went into its formation was, as in the superego, the authority of the object which the analyst became in transference. Needless to say, it took years to achieve this.

Gradually she managed to form new and lasting friendships. Her intelligence became quite keen (though not remarkable), and she was able to train for a craft which now provides her with a living and makes her independent of help and charity. She learned to reassess reality, and with this her fear of separation left her. Her friend Anne went abroad, most of the children are scattered in various countries and she maintains the contact with them. To reinforce this attainment she made an important decision—turning passive into active—and on her own initiative made arrangements to go for six months to Israel. She made sure that the analyst would be ready to continue her treatment on her return—demonstrating her new knowledge that separation can be undone.

Relation to the Other Sex

Her relationship to the other sex underwent very definite changes. When she started her analysis she was anxious to have boy friends, but this was a purely narcissistic need. Other girls had them; if she could not attract anyone, it was proof of her shortcoming. There was no real contact between herself and the boys, she told them lies about herself (the stories), and she did not know anything about them either. There was some passionate sex play without intercourse, of which she was afraid. Fear of penetration played a great part in her reluctance to have intercourse with the boys who demanded it, and this was brought into analysis. She also emphasized always that she was not in love (love was a very great thing), and she would like to sleep only with someone she was really in love with.

After repeated attempts at friendships with boys which brought a great deal of material into her analysis, she met a young man who became slowly a real person to her. She was not "in love," but very attached to him. This was a friendship based on identification with the analyst. The boy was very disturbed, a stammerer, and Elizabeth wanted to help him to overcome his difficulties. At this time she sometimes spoke, though very reluctantly, about masturbation and fantasies of sexual intercourse.

In Israel the narcissistic need to be found attractive was reactivated and she fell back into storytelling—probably because the fight to bear up with separation resulted in a partial regression. Very soon she understood on her own what had happened to her; she was even able to tell a friend that all she had said to him was lies; and though the hurt of being unable to find a boy to love her was very acute, she felt much better and much more secure. The Israel experience left her somewhat disappointed. She understood in her analysis that she attached to it the unconscious hope of returning a completely changed person, someone who was not castrated, and the wish for plastic surgery which reappeared was now ultimately understood and given up. With this her appearance changed, she dressed with taste and carried herself well, her movements were natural, she was well groomed, and she discovered that with care one can make oneself look quite attractive. The ideal of the woman with the beautiful hair-do lost its phallic character and was not unattainable any more.

That she achieved firm opinions of her own became manifest in connection with a relationship to a young man which ended in a painful disappointment. He was very charming, and it was flattering to her that he showed her persistent attention. She stressed that she was not in love, though she was able to tell him the complete truth about herself. It was at this time that she first uttered the word "Auschwitz" in her analysis. If ever she referred to the time before she came to England she spoke of Czechoslovakia (it is noteworthy that Thereszin is in Czechoslovakia, Auschwitz in Poland). The shame of being Jewish, having been in a concentration camp, left her completely; she started to think about the events responsible for her early experiences and she joined the Yellow Star movement.

The tie between her and the young man became closer, and she started to wonder whether it was not love after all, had fantasies about giving in to his demands and having intercourse with him. She then discovered that he lied and was unreliable. That she found out that he was having a sexual relationship with another girl was not the upsetting factor. It did not make her jealous, she found the girl very nice. Here too it was impressive how different her behavior was from that usually observed. Her relation to this young man did not follow an oedipal pattern, and this may explain the complete lack of feelings of rivalry. What she resented was his untruth, a thing she had managed to give up and judged now very adversely. In spite of all this she continued to be very attracted by him. The break came when on one occasion they had a conversation in which he expressed strong approval of Apartheid and the suppression of the African. Elizabeth was very shocked and immediately gave up meeting him. What cannot be overlooked in this event is that she, the Jewess (who never wanted to admit being one), identified with the Africans on the ground that they were the downtrodden ones, accepting herself in this way as belonging to the dirty prisoners, and this, too, without the slightest feeling of shame.

Another event reflects the stage she reached at the end of her analysis. For the first time in her life she lived in a flat with a normal family consisting of father, mother, and child, renting a room there. She felt terribly lonely without knowing why. Then one day it was the child's birthday and she bought a present for him. Returning home after work with her present she found the flat empty, the family having gone out to celebrate. She felt deeply dejected at having been left out. The birthday cake was on the table and she had a strong impulse to steal a piece of it. She had to put up a determined fight against it, but she was able to restrain herself and she felt greatly ashamed. The significance of this experience is manifold. She now was able to feel envy and sorrow at having been deprived of normal family relations; she was also capable of an aggressive impulse; but more than that, she had the strength to restrain herself from turning impulse into action. This experience was gone into thoroughly and it now made possible the discussion of an episode which took place quite early in her treatment. She was then living in the flat of Miss Goldberger and a young couple came to visit them with their few-weeks-old infant. Elizabeth looked forward to meeting them. But when they arrived and she saw the parents with the child, utter confusion seized her and she ran away. She felt very upset without knowing why, spent the evening in a cinema, and returned home late at night in order to avoid meeting the visitors. It was impossible to help her to understand what made her take flight. Now she herself verbalized the feeling of despair at not belonging to any family, at having been "left out" ever since she existed. She decided that living with a family was too distressing for her, and in order to avoid painful experiences she made up her mind to move into a hostel and share the life of working girls who had to forego the pleasure of a regular home. "I am not running away, but I don't want to be reminded of things that hurt," she said. This shows that her assessment of reality is normal, she is able to anticipate the effects of certain conditions on her emotions, and she can find rational solutions for herself. In the hostel she soon became very popular and the helper and adviser of the girls.

If I may be permitted to make a prediction, I suggest that she will master her dejection about not having had a family in the same way as that over separations: by turning passive into active (as when she went to Israel), creating a family for her future children.

Elizabeth is now twenty-two years old, a pleasant, cheerful working girl. She finds ample opportunity for sublimation in her work which puts her in contact with sick, suffering people. She is especially good in dealing with children. She has a good relation with the people she works with. She does not see Miss Goldberger very often, but when she does she enjoys her company and thinks of her with affection. She is attached to her sister, but is critical of her shortcomings. She keeps in touch with the other children, but regards only a few of them as close friends. Of one girl of the group she said: "She is so different; because we grew up together I need not like her."

And now she confessed to being in love. The object of this feeling is a boy who belonged to the group and who met her after a long absence in another part of the world and was impressed by the change in her. This is a very normal, very romantic, late adolescent love with all the pangs of being unsure of the response to her secret longing. It provokes a very relevant question. We find that this relationship, too, lacks the typical oedipal features normally recognizable in adult sexual relationships. She turns to the sibling and develops heterosexual genital fantasies connected with him and not with a father substitute. Are we justified in assuming that just as there is a constitutionally determined ego potential which does achieve maturation under adverse circumstances too, so a favorable constitution may allow libido development in spite of serious obstructions to proceed from pregenital aims to heterosexual genital ones, even under conditions which do not provide the child with the typical experiences in its relations to objects? Could the relation to male siblings, especially Charlie, have paved the way for this? Of course, whether she will be capable of normal genital gratification will have to be seen. It is likely that the idea she will form of her heterosexual partner will include the image of her pregenital female objects.

The boy returned to the country he came from and Elizabeth, who once could not understand that letters could be read by someone absent, has an intense correspondence with him. That he knows everything about her and shared a lot of her experiences gives her a feeling of security.

The disoriented little girl who started her analysis with "I am not a person," ended it saying: "You know, I like being myself."

Conclusion

The problems brought into focus by Elizabeth's analysis, which were examined in order to attempt a closer understanding of the pathology of motherless children, are as follows: can one reconstruct a person's ego development and libidinal development only through dissecting her present personality and observing its changes in the analytic process, without the emergence of specific early memories; in what way is it possible to adapt the analytic technique to the task of treating a person whose object relations did not proceed beyond the identifications of earliest infancy; and, is it possible to help to build a new concept of reality instead of the first conditioned by artificially cruel circumstances?

The work done with Elizabeth was used to throw light on these problems. I have tried to describe the very atypical evolution of transference and the way she used her analysis to remodel her ego, which was distorted by a normal attempt at adaptation to an abnormal environment and thwarted by the severe blocking of her libidinal development. The agency which now, after concluded treatment, provides her with internal guidance was compared with the superego as defined in analytic theory. It was found that such an agency can be established without being built up on the basis of identification with the oedipal objects and that, on account of the difference in its etiology, this agency is not invested with so much aggressive energy as the superego normally is, and appears therefore to be more protective than punitive.

BIBLIOGRAPHY

Bergen, M. E. (1958), The Effect of Severe Trauma on a Four-Year-Old Child. *This Annual*, XIII.
Deutsch, H. (1934), Über einen Typus der Pseudoaffektivität (Als Ob). *Int. Z. Psychoanal.*, XX.
Freud, A. (1951), Observations on Child Development. *This Annual*, VI.
—— (1952), The Mutual Influences of Ego and Id: Earliest Stages. *This Annual*, VII.
—— (1960), Discussion of John Bowlby's Paper. *This Annual*, XV.
—— & Dann, S. (1951), An Experiment in Group Upbringing. *This Annual*, VI.
Freud, S. (1937), Analysis Terminable and Interminable. *Collected Papers*, V. London: Hogarth Press, 1950.
Hartmann, H. (1939), *Ego Psychology and the Problem of Adaptation*. New York: International Universities Press, 1958.
Erikson, E. H. (1956), The Problem of Ego Identity. *J. Amer. Psa. Assn.*, IV.
Jacobson, E. (1954a), The Self and the Object World. *This Annual*, IX.
—— (1954b), Psychotic Identification. *J. Amer. Psa. Assn.*, II.
Piers, G. & Singer, M. B. (1953), *Shame and Guilt*. Springfield: Thomas.
Reich, A. (1954), Early Identifications as Archaic Elements in the Superego. *J. Amer. Psa. Assn.*, II.
Sandler, J. (1960), On the Concept of the Superego. *This Annual*, XV.
—— & Rosenblatt, B. (1962), The Concept of the Representational World. *This Annual*, XVII.
Spitz, R. A. (1951), Psychogenic Diseases in Infancy. *This Annual*, VI.
Weil, A. P. (1953), Certain Severe Disturbances of Ego Development in Childhood. *This Annual*, VIII.

THE DEVELOPMENTAL PROFILE

Notes on Some Practical Considerations Regarding Its Use

HUMBERTO NAGERA, M.D. (London)

The following pages describe some aspects of the work of the Diagnostic Research Group at the Hampstead Clinic.[1] In general our aims were to conduct an inquiry into the difficulties of diagnosing infantile disturbances, and to re-evaluate initial diagnostic impressions and predictions which were recorded after the initial interviews and in the Diagnostic Conference. This initial material was compared with that gained from the same children after psychoanalytic treatment. It was hoped that as a result of this research, errors in assessment would be reduced and a more satisfactory and systematic technique for evaluating the initial findings would be evolved.

Several different approaches to the problem have been followed, but this paper is concerned with only one of these: the Developmental Profile as outlined by Anna Freud (1962). The Profile is not yet a finished product, and has undergone numerous modifications and adaptations in the course of our work.[2]

[1] The Diagnostic Research Group has been engaged in research for some years and has been headed by Dr. L. Frankl (Physician-in-charge at the Hampstead Child-Therapy Clinic).

During the course of the work of the Research Group, Anna Freud proposed a diagnostic scheme or, as she has called it, a *Developmental Profile*. This Profile was subsequently systematically applied to the cases being studied in the Diagnostic Research Group. Anna Freud made these suggestions after she had delivered her lectures "Four Contributions to the Psychoanalytic Study of the Child" (1960) in New York, lectures which contained the basic elements for the Developmental Profile.

[2] A three-year research program has recently been started in order to attempt to improve and develop further the Developmental Profile through the constant application of it to our clinical material.

This paper forms part of a Research Project entitled "Assessment of Pathology in Childhood" which is conducted at the Hampstead Child-Therapy Clinic, London. It has been financed by the National Institute of Mental Health, Washington.

The Profile can be considered to be a way of thinking; more precisely, a metapsychological way of thinking and of organizing clinical material within the psychoanalytic frame of reference. It collects from the mass of information available, clinical or otherwise, that which is relevant and necessary to gain a proper picture, as complete as possible, of a given personality at a given moment of development. It tends to discard the irrelevant, and at the same time highlights the areas in which the available information is incomplete though essential for the proper understanding of a child's whole personality and conflicts.

This very point is one of the assets of the Profile. It largely solves the difficult question of how much and what kind of information is needed for a proper diagnostic evaluation of any specific case. By its very nature, the Profile is a metapsychological cross-section of a personality structure at a given moment.

Attention should be paid to the fact that, in the Profile, *pathology is seen against the background of normal development and its possible variations.* This is, of course, of particular importance in child diagnosis, because the child, unlike the adult, is not yet a finished product.

The picture we may gain of a normal child and of his reactions will be different at different ages and stages of development. His capacity to react is different as he develops. Many phenomena seen in children represent aspects of development and are normal or nearly so at certain ages. Thus, for example, sleeping disturbances appear quite commonly in the second year of life. Similarly the child may deal with frustration or aggression by temper tantrums before more appropriate ways have been achieved developmentally. At a particular age, however, both symptoms lack the ominous quality they would have at a later age.

The developmental orientation of the Profile has a further advantage: by constantly forcing us to examine what is normal or pathological at different ages, it makes possible a clearer understanding and conceptualization of normal development.

As a concrete illustration of the Profile, I shall present the material of the diagnostic study of Arthur Z., eleven and a half years old. The information will be described and discussed under the main headings of the Profile.[3] Examples will be given to illustrate some of the arguments and the many possibilities opened up by this approach. In addition, I hope to show the correlation existing among the various headings and I will attempt to convey something of our present experience in the use of the Profile.

Developmental Picture and Guide to Diagnosis[4] (Profile at the Diagnostic Stage)

Material Used:

Social History, June 11, 1954—Mrs. Mason
Psychiatric Interview, June 15, 1954—Dr. L. Frankl
Intelligence Test Report, June 25, 1954—Miss D. Wills

I. REASONS FOR REFERRAL

The mother felt that the child was retarded on account of persistent thumb sucking (which occurs only when he is at home and not when he is out). He has difficulties in school where he does not cooperate and is not progressing properly. He is frequently absent from school due to slight rise in temperature, stomach pains, sickness, etc. His health has been checked several times and is fine.

II. DESCRIPTION OF THE CHILD

Arthur has a slight negroid appearance because of his crinkly hair and thick lips. He is a nice-looking lad, wears glasses, and is the size of a thirteen- or fourteen-year-old boy.

---

[3] The first four sections of the Profile are self-explanatory. Section III, Family Background and Personal History, is related to the subsection, External Conflicts, which occurs in Section VII. These initial four sections are intended to give a full picture of the child and his background.

[4] At Hampstead the diagnostic procedure varies according to the nature of the case involved. Broadly speaking, however, it consists of a social history, a psychiatric interview with the child, and psychological tests where indicated (but always, where possible, an intelligence test). Additional psychiatric interviews with parents and other relatives may be carried out as necessary.

A word needs to be said about our use of psychological test results. At the very beginning of the application of the Developmental Profile to our cases, we utilized mainly descriptions of the child's behavior in the test situation. The I.Q. was stated, but no special attention was paid to the content of the child's responses except where it gave information about the status of certain ego functions (relevant for this heading in the Profile). This procedure was followed because initially we wanted to base our assumptions as much as possible on purely clinical grounds. A much wider use of the test results (content) is of course perfectly valid and useful, and we are presently organizing a pilot study on this very aspect.

He can be quite independent (in spite of difficulties over separation) and will go anywhere alone. He will go skating or bicycling with his friends, though he is described as not making friends easily and being rather reserved.

Arthur tends to copy his little brother who is said to play with imagination. He likes his mother to read to him and prefers little-girl stories.

III. FAMILY BACKGROUND AND PERSONAL HISTORY

Arthur comes from a Jewish nonorthodox background.

Mother: She has been in analytic treatment with Dr. W. She became increasingly depressed when the husband was away during the War. At that time, when Arthur was about two years, she started working to cope with her misery. When she was pregnant with her second child, Arthur was three years nine months to four years six months old. She found him so irritating that she could not stand him. Arthur was then sent to a kindergarten.

It seems as if a certain amount of seduction goes on between Arthur and his mother. There are references to his making jokes about girls and laughing about nude pictures with his mother. He giggles saying "ooh" whenever he sees his mother not fully dressed.

Father: He is now established in business. He was away during the War when Arthur was between one year eight months to two years six months. At that time Mr. Z. is said to have returned home after two months of convalescence following a nervous breakdown.

He was himself a difficult child, separating from his mother with difficulty. The father likes bathing the children on week ends (Arthur is now eleven and a half years) and has always cooperated a great deal in the care of Arthur.

Siblings: There is a seven-year-old brother. Arthur tends to copy this younger brother who is said to be imaginative. Arthur is now very jealous of him and constantly hits and teases him.

Friends: He is said not to make friends easily. While he did not refer to any special friend, he mentioned that he went out on his bike with a school friend and that he played with others in the street.

Personal History: The mother was well during the pregnancy. Arthur was born three weeks premature, but the birth is said to have been easy. The mother described him as a beautiful and happy baby. He was breast fed for six months; was fed to the hour; and was weaned to the bottle at six months, refusing it at first.

He walked at a year; talked between two to two and a half years with slight setbacks when he went to the nursery. He has sucked his thumb since birth.

His toilet training is described as having been difficult. Arthur used to retain his bowel movements and still does so. He had bowel movements only at home. Frequently his pants were slightly soiled and still are nowadays. He achieved urinary control at the age of two years, though there were occasional accidents later.

IV. POSSIBLY SIGNIFICANT ENVIRONMENTAL INFLUENCES

1. Mother's and father's seductive attitude toward the children.
2. There have been a number of enforced early and later separations (and withdrawal on the mother's side due to her depression) that may have played a role in Arthur's difficulties. He tended to react to these experiences with extreme distress and regression.

For example, when during the War Arthur's mother became depressed due to the absence of her husband, Arthur (then aged two and a half) was sent to a nursery. There he never settled in, stood in a corner, sucked his thumb, bit and scratched the other children. There was a setback in talking as well. He was kept at this place for three months.

At the end of this third year he was sent to kindergarten. The mother, who was then pregnant again, referred to her not being able to stand the child at the time. He had always to be dragged screaming to the kindergarten.

At the age of five he went to a progressive school, where he was again not able to settle. He started soiling, wetting, and developed a tic in one eye.

V. ASSESSMENT OF DEVELOPMENT

GENERAL COMMENTS

This section has three main subsections: the development of drives (libido and aggression); of ego and superego; and of the total personality.

In regard to libido development, the essential point is the determination of whether a child has ever reached the phallic (oedipal) phase, at about the age of three or four. The type of object relationship is included here; attention should be paid to the way in which libido and aggression are used in relation to the objects and the self, and how objects are used in general.

In a similar way, we can ask at a later age whether the child has ever entered latency or puberty; whether this is a normal latency or puberty or one disturbed by neurotic conflicts or in some other way.

It is important in this context to distinguish the phallic phase from isolated phallic manifestations which may occur even though the bulk of the libido is still at an earlier stage. For example, we

may have penis envy for purely narcissistic reasons in a two-year-old
girl. We speak here of phallic dominance as a phase, and not as
isolated phallic manifestations while another phase is dominant.

Has regression from the phallic phase taken place and, if so, to
where? Of course, a relationship exists between this heading and
that of Section VI, Regression and Fixation Points, since one of the
prerequisites for regression is the existence of previous developmental points at which the libido has remained fixated.

It is not always easy to determine clearly how much of the libido
one sees at a particular pregenital fixation point is present there as
the result of regression and how much has always remained fixated
at that point and has never moved forward. In brief, how much can
be attributed to regression and how much to fixation? We have
gained the impression that in many cases it is possible to have a
relative, quantitative, idea of how much of the libido seen at a
particular point may be attributed to fixation and how much to
regression as a consequence of conflicts at later stages. A thorough
developmental history of the child is necessary here.

In this connection, several possibilities may exist. Take, for
instance, a child who was able to pass through the pregenital phases
without too many difficulties and who shows what may be called the
usual and normal fixation points at the oral and anal level. Further,
let us suppose that as a result of the conflicts of the oedipal situation
and because of castration fear the child regresses from the phallic
level to the anal and oral levels.

The developmental history may show the picture of a child with
no more than slight signs, if any, of fixations at the earlier levels.
These may not be very outstanding, but at a certain point in development, for example, at the age of five years, as a consequence of the
regression mentioned above, we can begin to observe the appearance
of libidinal manifestations appropriate to the oral and anal phases,
either as symptoms or as pieces of behavior which were previously
absent.

If one pays proper attention to the details of the social history
and in particular the developmental history, it will be seen that this
picture differs markedly from that of another child in whom thumb
sucking (or some other oral manifestation, e.g., excessive clinging

and demandingness) had been present throughout his development, far beyond the age at which such behavior corresponds to a specific stage of development and is therefore accepted as normal. The picture also differs from that of a child who shows in some way that his character bears the imprint of difficulties in one particular phase of development. The latter child may have moved through to the phallic phase, but the manifest signs of fixation to the early levels will at no point have disappeared from his developmental picture. If at a later stage conflict induces a regression of libido from the phallic phase, reinforcing the libido already present at earlier levels, one may be able to assess how much is attributable to this reinforcement through regression and how much to the ever-present fixations (though only in relative terms).

The outcome of further regression is an intensification of such manifestations as thumb sucking, clinging, and demandingness, or indeed of whatever signs of the anal or oral phases are present. What we observe is a reinforcement and intensification of the manifestation previously present.

Such a distinction is naturally of prognostic importance. It is no doubt easier to help the forward movement of libido which has regressed than of libido which has always been arrested at earlier stages. In assessing the total personality it is of value to have a relative estimate of how much of the libido was able to move forward to the phallic phase, even though it may at present be seen in a regressed state. It is important to know that at some time most or part of the libido has moved forward and had made its contribution at the proper time to the development of the ego and to the personality as a whole. This is in contrast to those cases in whom, through excessive fixation, large amounts of libido have remained arrested and were unable to contribute to normal development at the time when that contribution was required.

We believe that through collecting the material of a sufficient number of cases, light will be thrown on how, when, where, and why the libido makes its contribution to proper development. The same argument applies to the aggressive drive which will be dealt with below.

Finally, an examination of the libido is required in regard to its distribution in the self, objects, etc. Similarly, whenever relevant and possible, the statements as to the mechanisms and self-esteem regulation and well-being can be included.

I return now to the assessment of development in the case of Arthur Z.

CASE ILLUSTRATION

A. *Drive Development*

1. *Libido*

(a) *With regard to phase development*

Arthur has reached the phallic-oedipal phase. (He giggles and says "ooh" whenever he sees his mother not fully dressed; he makes jokes about girls and laughs about nude pictures with his mother; used to write "like love letters" to mother when away from her at nine years, etc.) There is evidence that he has very strong fixation points at the oral and anal levels to which large amounts of his libido are now regressed.

The latency period is being interfered with by the lack of a proper solution of the oedipal conflict and the regression that has followed. It can be said that latency is further complicated by a certain amount of seduction and stimulation exerted particularly, though not exclusively, by the mother. This factor makes it all the more difficult for him to renounce the pleasure he experiences when he succeeds in inducing his mother to care for him and look after him physically as if he were a younger child (being dressed, bathed, etc.).

(b) *With regard to libido distribution*

(i) *Cathexis of self:* The cathexis of the self in Arthur's case seems to be interfered with in certain circumstances (like in the test situation where he showed an unusual degree of diffidence and self-criticism). He would present perfectly correct solutions, saying he was sure they were wrong: "I am not very good at this. . . ."

Similarly, the excessive use of turning aggression against the self may point either to a low narcissistic cathexis of the self (in relative terms) that allows and accounts for the choice and excessive use of this mechanism of defense or at least to a secondary interference with that cathexis when pressure on the side of the aggressive drive rises and defense has to be enforced.

(ii) *Cathexis of objects:* Arthur has, of course, reached the stage of object constancy, but that stage is constantly interfered with due to very strong and early fixations at the oral level.

2. *Aggression*

Here we look for the presence or absence of aggression on the surface, since we still know little about the vicissitudes of the different phases.

Quantitative, qualitative, and directional considerations are appropriate here.

The types of defense utilized to deal with aggressive drives should be noted and included here if relevant, or under the heading Ego, Defenses.

We hope that in time the systematic collection of information under this heading, and the correlation of that information with other aspects covered by the Profile, coming as it does from children of all ages and from all sorts of pathology, will ultimately make a contribution to our knowledge of the vicissitudes and development of the aggressive drive.

In Arthur's case the following material is recorded under the subheading of aggression.

Arthur has not achieved adequate control of his aggressive impulses. Arthur's aggression breaks through frequently, particularly in the relationship with his mother. Whenever he is frustrated by her in any way, he attacks her and screams and yells with temper. On the other hand, at school he finds it difficult to read in a loud voice.

There is constant teasing and hitting of the brother.

He deals with aggression partly by turning it against himself (hurting himself frequently) and by means of his passivity.

B. *Ego and Superego Development*

This is the second main subheading in Section V, Assessment of Development. Under this heading are four main subdivisions: (1) ego apparatuses; (2) ego functions; (3) defenses; and (4) secondary interference of defenses with ego functions.

Ego development, like drive development, must be viewed against the background of normal development. One must constantly make allowances for the fact there are many variations or deviations in the normal development of ego function, and that, developmentally speaking, the child is not yet a finished product. Because of this, temporary regressions in ego functions or in libidinal development must under certain conditions be considered as normal.

Further allowance must be made for the processes of interaction between the child's endowment or innate capacity and the function of the environment as the releasing agent for the development of these innate capacities and as the stimulating agent for further ego development. For every infant and every environment (mainly represented by the mother at this early stage), the types of interaction will vary greatly.

The releasing and stimulating role of the mother depends of course on her interests and the possibilities for cathexis she provides. This factor plays a large role in the many variations of development which occur within normal limits.

It has previously been mentioned that there exists a link between the stage of libidinal development and the contribution made by it to further ego development.

(1) Under the subheading Ego Apparatuses, the intactness or defects of the ego apparatus are examined.

(2) Under the subheading Ego Functions, we look for the intactness of the various functions, always bearing it mind the age and stage of development of the particular child. We assess these functions against the background of our picture of normal development.

Particular attention should be paid to the existence of primary or developmental deficiencies.

When this point in the Profile has been reached we are able to categorize a very large number of cases diagnostically, i.e., those with an arrested libidinal or ego development. The value of the information recorded under this subheading for differential diagnosis and for prognosis cannot be overemphasized.

A good developmental history allows us to follow when certain functions appear, what their character is, and how they have developed since early in life. This is most useful for clarifying whether there is a "primary disturbance" based on an ego defect (organic damage being the possible substrate in many cases), or whether there is a "developmental disturbance" of the particular function or functions under consideration. In the latter case the cause might well be the lack of proper and adequate mothering. In this case the environment has failed in its releasing and stimulating function necessary for the proper development of the ego functions and apparatus (the extreme cases being those described by Spitz [1945] as "hospitalism").

The final picture presented by both types of cases may be similar, particularly if in the brain-damaged or deficient cases the neurological examination happens to be negative. Yet in one case there is an organic substrate, while in the other case there is a more functional defect (which nevertheless might be as irreversible as the first).

Both types of cases have a poor prognosis. The outcome depends not only on the extent of the damage but also on the particular functions affected and the degree to which this has occurred. In these cases analytic treatment will be limited since we cannot undo the organic defect, nor can we provide at a later date the stimulation and care which was required earlier.

A careful developmental history within the social history will help us here, and will at times allow us to make a differential diagnosis. For this purpose we should at the same time consider heading E in Section VII, Dynamic and Structural Assessment (Conflicts): External Conflicts, as well as the heading Background in Section III. There we will find descriptions of the sort of mothering the child has had in early life. Such details as normal siblings, coupled with the absence of information which might make us suspect the early mother-child relationship, and so on, will assist us. In other cases, the typical picture of the institutionalized child will complete our diagnosis.

On the other hand, in many cases of arrested ego development (of whatever nature), it is not possible to show or to point to conflicts of an internalized character (conflicts between superego, ego, and id), but only to conflicts of an internal nature (between opposites in the id) and to those of an external character. At a given age the absence of or incomplete picture of internalized conflicts can be a strong indicator of this type of problem, as shown by the lack of development in the structural sense. Furthermore, some of our cases used and needed their objects as auxiliary egos, to deal with fear and anxiety. They showed "an obsessionallike" organization. Any small change in the daily routine aroused extreme distress and anxiety. These cases are not obsessionals in the true meaning of the word but resemble them due to the incapacity of their egos to deal with any new situation or any change. These children were not withdrawn or autistic, but were quite able to cathect objects as long as they were approached at the level to which they had been able to develop. This latter point is important for the differential diagnosis of withdrawn or autistic children.

Some of these children showed phallic manifestations and reactions, but the ego development that should go with it and the rich fantasy life (oedipal) that should accompany these phallic reactions in normal children were never present. This is of great significance for the purpose of differential diagnosis. These cases represent the more or less extreme end of a scale which comprises all sorts of grades. The diagnostic procedure, and especially the prognostic evaluation, becomes more difficult as we approach the other end of the scale.

(3) Our third subheading under Ego and Superego Development deals with defenses, which we scrutinize in terms of their age adequacy.

Denial, identification, and projection are primitive defenses. Complete denial is adequate for a two-year-old but very abnormal later on. By the time of latency most of the primitive defenses should be in the background; one would then expect to see repression, reaction, formation, sublimation, identification with the aggressor, turning passivity into activity, etc.

In adolescence all the primitive defenses seem to reappear for a time. Personal problems are now looked at impersonally, expressed in racial, social struggles, etc. (externalization). Attention should be paid to the excessive and untimely use of specific defenses, the availability of a variety of defenses, and the ego's effectiveness to deal with the drives in an adequate form. We should examine the type of defense not only in relation to its age adequacy but also in regard to the economic factor involved; whether, for example, the types of defense used require permanent and large expenditure of energy in the form of countercathexis. It should be borne in mind that the ego can use functions and mechanisms not normally meant for the purpose in a defensive fashion at a given time.

(4) Secondary Interference of Defenses with Ego Functions is the

fourth subheading in the section Ego and Superego Development. Here we try to describe how the type of defense used by the ego interfere with these ego functions can be removed during the course were intact and properly developed. As soon as the defenses which interfere with these ego functions can be removed during the course of treatment the functions will reappear intact, in contrast with the primary defective functions.

It is easy to see, for example, that excessive use of withdrawal into fantasy will to a greater or lesser degree affect such functions as attention, perception, apperception, concentration, memory, thought processes. At a given age this implies a severe interference with schooling and the process of learning. Other defenses will affect different functions. Excessive use of projection interferes with reality testing and thought processes. Aggression turned against the self may temporarily interfere with motility and result in accident proneness. Regressive processes, particularly on the side of the ego, can imply a serious disturbance of very many ego functions.

If in a given case there is no particular conflict or type of defense that would explain the existing state of affairs, it is of great value when the Profile discloses a marked inhibition or lack of proper functioning of the ego as a whole. This suggests some sort of arrest in development; by looking to the other headings in the Profile, it becomes possible to find pointers to the real causes of disturbance.

We may ask: how will the faulty functioning of one function affect the development of the others? How does the ego attempt to compensate for this, and what is the result in terms of the final structure? This developmental approach which traces the lines of development of specific ego functions is bound to provide answers to these questions. The same approach is also valid in relation to the secondary interference of defenses with ego functions at different ages and stages of development, and to the manner in which this interference affects further development.

CASE ILLUSTRATION

1. *Ego Apparatuses*

Arthur's ego apparatuses seem to be intact. There are no symptoms or signs of primary defects there.

2. Ego Functions

There are no signs either of primary deficiencies in his ego functions. Arthur is a highly intelligent boy, who cannot at present make full use of his very good potentialities. He has an I.Q. of 137. Nevertheless his schoolwork is poor and his learning capacity seems to be impoverished in spite of his high I.Q. There is no doubt that there is an important secondary interference of his defensive system with many of his ego functions.

3. Defenses

Arthur's defense organization consists mainly of repression, regression (to anal and oral levels), reaction formations, very marked passivity, clinging and dependence, turning of the aggression against the self, and withdrawal into illness. This group of defenses is mainly directed against his phallic oedipal wishes for both parents as well as against his aggressive drives. This defense organization is in any case far from effective at present, resulting in anxiety and symptom formation.

4. Secondary Interference of Defenses with Ego Functions

It is not difficult to see how such a vast and excessive use of these types of defenses have led to an interference with his schooling and learning processes. His marked passivity plays a specially important role here.

Arthur's tendency to control his aggression, partly by means of turning it against himself, seems to interfere with his motility leading frequently to falls and accidents, where he hurts himself. The function of speech is interfered with by his oral aggression and the defenses against it, particularly in a given set of circumstances, i.e., when he has to read in a loud voice at school.

C. Development of the Total Personality (Lines of Development and Mastery of Tasks)[5] or Age-Adequate Responses

GENERAL COMMENTS

For didactic and methodological purposes we have artificially isolated the drive development from the ego development and have assessed each independently. Under this heading we now aim to see the whole personality, reacting to what Anna Freud has called *life*

[5] At present, one of the aspects of our research program on the Developmental Profile consists of the application of a number of *developmental lines* to our cases. This has been suggested by Anna Freud (1963) who points out: "Far from being theoretical abstractions, developmental lines, in the sense here used, are historical realities which, when assembled, convey a convincing picture of an individual's personal achievements, respectively of his failures in personality development."

task. This reaction is partly dependent on the stage of development reached at any given moment. Life tasks are situations with which the child is confronted at different stages of his development. Many of these are common to every one, but some may not be so usual or apply so generally.

Examples of life tasks that will confront children at different times are: going to nursery school at three and a half years; the birth of a sibling; the death of a close relative; hospitalizations (of the child himself, the mother, etc.); separations from the parents; moving house, etc.

We expect that the child's reaction differs at different ages, according to the means the child has acquired through the course of development to deal with such situations.[6] In these situations the personality as a whole reacts to the particular life task under consideration. The child as a whole adapts himself to the new situation and during this process makes use of all the resources at his disposal.

We can learn a great deal about each individual child. We can obtain information about his ego development and his capabilities, the sorts of defense he can mobilize, his capacity to tolerate frustration, his possibilities of sublimation, of toleration for anxiety and his ways of dealing with it, his ability to accept substitute or neutralized gratification with enjoyment, the progressive forces present in him as contrasted with the regressive ones and so on.

CASE ILLUSTRATION

In Arthur, the age-adequate achievements are lacking in the main. He has remained closely attached to the family (one positive element here is his ability to go biking with a friend). He prefers the family (both father and mother) to look after him and his body as if he were a small child.

The relationship to the parents, particularly to the mother, has remained highly sexualized. His interests in literature are sexualized.

VI. REGRESSION AND FIXATION POINTS

GENERAL COMMENTS

As previously described, we look here for signs that reveal fixation points in pieces of significant behavior, fantasies, and in certain symptoms.

[6] An excellent example of what is meant here is given by Gauthier (1960).

In some cases the fixation points will show themselves as precipitates in the character structure. Observation of the different imprints which the various libidinal phases left on the character structure can be very relevant. They may manifest themselves either directly as the characteristic traits of any given phase or through corresponding reaction formations, for example, excessive cleanliness instead of dirtiness.

The relevant material is classified under the subheadings: Oral, Anal, and Phallic.

As has been mentioned, there is a link between this heading and drive development. It is obvious that the various aspects of the Profile are intimately connected. Therefore there is a constant need to correlate the material recorded under each heading and to consider how each completes and qualifies the other. This process of correlation helps us to think in an organized fashion. In addition and even more important, each section provides checks of the material in the other sections, and the sections pose questions to one another, questions that are relevant to the consideration of the case. This brings out apparent or real contradictions in the material. It constantly forces our minds to translate clinical observations into our conceptual frame of reference and vice versa.

In working with the Profile, the following questions and thoughts occurred to me in relation to the heading Regression and Fixation Points: what, if any, will be the difference between fixation points coming about as a result of deprivation and frustration (extreme cases being institutionalized children) and those which are a consequence of excessive gratification (those overwhelmed by stimulation or intense seduction)? Is there any difference in diagnostic or prognostic significance between these two possibilities?

Deprivation or frustration experienced early in life will under certain circumstances severely damage the child's possibilities for development, and these damages may not be reversible. What will be the counterpart of intense deprivation if we are dealing instead with excessive gratification or stimulation? Will the outcome be similar or even comparable?

Deprivation (intense frustration) or excessive gratification, when it occurs later in life and development, does not seem to have the same significance once a certain stage of development has been reached. After this point it looks as if, in some cases, intense stimulation (excessive gratification) is a more dangerous element than frustration as far as further development is concerned.

A further observation of interest in regard to fixation points is that these points may be almost all that remains of later levels and stages of development, once massive regressive processes have taken place (both on the ego and libidinal sides). Generally, the existence of strong fixation points is a potentially dangerous situation, because when faced with obstacles during later stages of development the libido that has remained behind pulls back the forward-moving libido.

In one of our cases we could observe that this whole process had been reversed. In view of this experience it might be justified to assume that fixation points also exert a forward pull (in this case, toward development) on the libido which, due to regression, has gone back to the very earliest stages. If further observations and clinical material were to confirm these speculative thoughts, we would be forced to add a new dimension to the function of fixation points. Side by side with their potentially pathogenic role in cases of neurosis, in other cases of more severe regressions and disorganization of the whole personality we would have to view fixation points as anchorage points in stages of higher development that had to be abandoned. They would not only be indicators of the stages reached, but would favor (by their "pulling" attraction in the descriptive sense) the forces of recovery. If this is the case, the presence of the fixation points in severe cases of regression would have prognostic value.

CASE ILLUSTRATION

As already pointed out, Arthur has very important fixation points at the oral and anal levels to which part of his libido has regressed.

Oral Level: According to the mother, Arthur slings his food down, eats at an abnormal rate, and is always hungry. He still sucks his thumb when he is at home. He is supposed to have bitten the side of his wooden cot so that the wood was chewed away. At three he used to bite other children at the nursery. Now he screams and yells and has an inhibition to read in a loud voice at the school.

Anal Level: The mother described the toilet training as difficult. Arthur retained, and still does, his bowel movements. He has bowel movements only at home, and he constantly comes home with his

pants soiled. He is said to be obstinate and to have a violent temper
that may well be the imprint of this phase of development on his
character. The relationship with the mother has a sadomasochistic
character.

Phallic Level: The relationship with the mother is still highly
sexualized. He giggles and says "ooh" when he sees his mother not
fully dressed. He is always making jokes about girls and laughs about
nude pictures with his mother. Arthur's battle at the oedipal stage
is still going on; as a result of this, part of his libido has regressed
to the previous phases. It is also noticeable in the intensity of his
positive attachment to the father, which has defensive aspects but
which is undoubtedly linked with the intensity of his bisexual conflicts and therefore primary in character. The father himself plays an
important role in this connection: he bathes Arthur on week ends.

VII. DYNAMIC AND STRUCTURAL ASSESSMENT (CONFLICTS)

GENERAL COMMENTS

This heading is subdivided into (a) External, (b) Internalized,
and (c) Internal Conflicts.

(a) Much of the material that one feels tempted to include under
External Conflicts belongs in fact in Section III, Family Background
and Personal History, and in Section IV, Possibly Significant
Environmental Influences. Entries under this subheading are prominent in the profiles of those cases in which a final structure of the
personality has not been achieved (superego). The conflicts are
between id-ego agencies and external authority figures. This may be
due to the child's age who is still too young to have completed his
structural development, but it applies equally to those cases in which
an arrested ego development makes final structure impossible, figures
in the outside being used both as ego and superego auxiliaries. A
similar situation is present in certain cases of defective superego
development, in which the conflict takes place with external figures
or with society (certain types of delinquent, etc.).

(b) The subheading, Internalized Conflicts (between id, ego, and
superego), is of great significance. In itself it indicates that a final
development in the structural sense has been reached. Fear of external authority has been internalized and has become fear of superego.

Guilt feelings appear and become the measure and expression
of tension between the ego and superego. The presence of guilt in

the material is a pointer to the existence of the superego as a functioning mental agency.

The internalized conflicts must be described in metapsychological
terms, and a dynamic, economic, and structural analysis must be
made of the conflict or conflicts involved (either of a libidinal or
aggressive character). For this purpose it is necessary to refer back
to the information examined and collected under the other headings,
mainly those under defenses and fixation points, describing which
drives are defended against and so on.

(c) The subheading Internal Conflicts is meant to cover conflicts
between opposite drives—masculinity and femininity, activity and
passivity, etc.

The assessment of this is not always an easy task. The older the
child the more difficult it can be to sort out how much belongs to
the initial bisexual conflict, how much to environmental influence,
and how much to a defensive attitude developed at the time of the
oedipal relationship and a consequence of castration anxiety. Nevertheless, in many cases it has been possible to complete the sorting
out successfully.

One is reminded here of Freud who said: "in both sexes the
relative strength of the masculine and feminine sexual dispositions
is what determines whether the outcome of the Oedipus situation
shall be an identification with the father or with the mother. This is
one of the ways in which bisexuality takes a hand in the subsequent
vicissitudes of the Oedipus complex" (1923, p. 33).

In view of Freud's statement, it is clear that the outcome of the
oedipus situation will itself be a pointer to what the original bisexual
constitution was like. This can be shown with clinical material and
observation. Moreover, in the area of the drives the child is not as
open to environmental and external influence as he may be in other
areas (ego development).

The process of sorting out thus becomes more feasible. When
we are confronted with an apparently passive-feminine identification
in a boy we can always ask whether what we observe is the result
of the original bisexual constitution or rather the outcome of external influences, or perhaps the result of defensive measures brought
about by castration anxiety, or of an early feminine identification.
Freud gives us an answer in the passage I have quoted. The passive-

feminine identification was possible and is the outcome of the
oedipal situation in a particular child, precisely on account of the
strong feminine element in his constitution. If this had been otherwise, in spite of everything this possibility would not have been
open for him. Similarly, an early feminine identification (implying
a true modification of the ego on the basis of the identification) is
only open to those children who have an original bisexual constitution which facilitates such an outcome.

On the other hand, one must realize that in relation to this
problem, as anywhere else in the Profile, the interaction between
endowment and environment cannot be overlooked or underrated.
The concept of complemental series" is as valid in regard to bisexual
constitution as anywhere else. The influence of the environment
is more prominent precisely in those cases which have a weaker
endowment (e.g., a boy not strongly endowed with masculinity, and
consequently with a relatively strong feminine element in his bisexual constitution).

In working with the Profile we found that, in order to evaluate
the problems belonging to this particular subheading, a good developmental history is a great asset. In it we will look for pointers to
the nature of the bisexual constitution, particularly (if it is possible)
to its character before defensive measures against castration anxiety
had the chance to exploit the basic bisexuality conflict and to form
a final picture in which it may be more difficult to discern how much
is the outcome of defense and how much is primary.

The possibility of an early identification of a passive-feminine
character (with the mother, for example, before the phallic phase),
as a consequence of, let us say, compliance with the wishes of the
mother for a girl, will not be open if a strong masculine element is
present. If it does occur and is an identification (with subsequent
ego modification), this fact again constitutes a pointer to the
marked bisexual conflict of the particular case. One has to distinguish
certain types of "as if" identification, which are the result of compliance, from true identification. In the former, the child's drive,
strivings, and fantasies remain masculine.

In the developmental history data about all aspects of the child's
behavior since early life, his physique, his voice and speech manner-
isms, the way he walks, his body language in movements, facial

expressions, the way he runs, climbs, the way he asks for things, the way he reacts in different situations, his games, and so on, may be possible pointers to his original bisexual constitution.

(a) *External Conflicts:* While Arthur's conflicts are mostly internalized, there are some conflicts with the external world that play an active role in his actual pathology and stage of development. This is due to the amount of seduction and external interference with his development (factors already referred to at different points).

(b) *Internalized Conflicts:* These are libidinal and aggressive in character and mainly centered around the oedipal situation (both mother and father aspects playing an important role), as a result of which part of his libido is now back at oral and anal levels. As mentioned previously, not only the positive oedipal attachment to the mother but the strong oedipal attachment to the father must be noted here. Part of it is defensive, but part is no doubt linked with the intensity of his bisexual conflicts and primary in character. Arthur's conflicts at the oedipal level are frequently expressed in anal and oral terms.

(c) *Internal Conflicts:* There are numerous hints of conflicts between opposite drives (male, female; passive, active). In both cases these conflicts seem to be partly of a primary character and partly a defense against anxiety provoked by one of the elements of the pair of opposites.

VIII. Assessment of Some General Characteristics

GENERAL COMMENTS

This heading has four subsections: (a) Frustration Tolerance; (b) Sublimation Potential (Capacity to Accept and Enjoy Substitute or Neutralized Gratification); (c) Over-all Attitude to Anxiety; (d) Progressive Forces versus Regressive Tendencies. It will be noted that these are mainly, though not exclusively, of great prognostic value. For this reason, they have been singled out from other areas and headings where they might belong. The prognostic value of these subsections relates to the possibilities of further normal development, to treatability by the psychoanalytic method, and to long-term prognosis.

(a) Frustration Tolerance is not always easy to assess. (This heading overlaps to some extent with the two following ones, which are

in some ways related.) The lower the capacity of any child to tolerate
frustration, the worse he is equipped for life. Frustration tolerance
refers to the immediate reaction that follows the postponement or
total lack of fulfillment of an instinctual wish. When trying to assess
a child's frustration tolerance we cover three points: tolerance in
regard to the frustration (i) of libidinal drives, (ii) of aggressive
drives, and (iii) of failure when engaged in neutralized activities.
It should be kept in mind that frustration tolerance varies at various
times in life, from practically none at birth and in the child's early
life, to different levels at some later stage. When, for example, regression to the oral phase occurs, the level of frustration tolerance will
be very diminished. It must be taken into account that the tolerance
of frustration may be different in relation to different component
instincts.

(b) Sublimation Potential—The Capacity to Accept and Enjoy
Substitute or Neutralized Gratification—is a measure of an important safety valve for mental health. Those who have a good capacity
in this area are safer in life.

In most cases the material available for diagnostic purposes
gives one some impression of what the child looks like in this area.
Accounts of the child's behavior, usually given by the mother, generally suffice for this purpose. In addition, descriptions of work and
behavior at school may be useful. The presence of sublimation is
another pointer.

(c) Under the heading Over-all Attitude to Anxiety, as far as
possible a metapsychological description of the facts should be given.
In one sense this heading is the other side of the picture described
under Internalized Conflicts. There a metapsychological account of
the conflict situation was asked for. Here, we want to know about
the rearrangements that have taken place, precisely as a result of
that conflict, in the structure of personality and in character formation, viewed in dynamic, economic, and structural terms. In short,
what is required here is the rearrangement brought about as a result
of the conflicts and defenses used in the structure of personality and
in character formation, as well as an estimate of the child's basic
attitude toward anxiety.

There are great variations in the amount of anxiety which different children can tolerate without resorting to symptoms and defenses.

If the child can meet anxiety in an active way, this is a positive factor and he is in contrast to those who will either regress or develop phobic symptoms.

(d) Looking at the Progressive Forces versus Regressive Tendencies, we make an attempt to obtain a feeling of the underlying general tendencies in the child. There may be a tendency to progress and develop in spite of external difficulties and stresses, or the contrary may be the case. Many pathological manifestations can be absorbed by a strong impulse to development.

CASE ILLUSTRATION

(a) *Frustration Tolerance:* Arthur has a relatively low capacity for the toleration of frustration.

(b) *Sublimation Potential:* So far there is no evidence of his having a high sublimation potential, though the real picture here may be somewhat blurred and interfered with by the undue stimulation and seduction on the side of the parents.

(c) *Over-all Attitude to Anxiety:* Arthur tends to withdraw from situations where toleration and mastery of anxiety are required. This can be observed in the reading inhibition he developed when having to read in a loud voice at school (at home his oral aggression breaks through in shouting and yelling) or in his regression to earlier levels of drive discharge and gratification, resulting from castration anxiety and intolerable oedipal strivings.

His ego over-all attitude to this type and amount of anxiety is inefficient; the result has been symptom formation and a tendency to restrict the ego, in spite of very high potentialities.

(d) *Progressive Forces versus Regressive Tendencies:* There is a pull back, a tendency to regress to more primitive levels of libidinal development and more primitive sources of libidinal gratification. This has involved, on occasions, the temporary regression of certain controls and ego functions already achieved when the frustration period sets in (i.e., speech).

IX. Diagnosis

GENERAL COMMENTS

In this section we are only concerned with a broad formulation of the type of disturbance. Broadly speaking, we can distinguish between normal development and its variations, neurotic (i.e., regressive processes in development), atypical (i.e., arrested processes in development), and psychotic and borderline (i.e., malignant processes).

Arthur belongs in group (3) of our provisional classification (A. Freud, 1962), showing neurotic conflicts with regression to the anal and oral levels, symptom formation and marked ego restrictions.

DISCUSSION

This section of my paper is devoted to some general considerations and comments concerning the Developmental Profile and the subject of diagnosis.

After using the Developmental Profile for a period of about a year, the diagnostic discussions of a number of cases revealed that it meets the requirements for these procedures. Diagnostic discussions are of necessity limited in time, as far as any one case is concerned, after which a diagnostic decision is attempted. However, this time limitation, so necessary for obvious reasons, has certain dangers.

The Profile meets some of the shortcomings of ordinary diagnostic evaluations in a more appropriate way. It forces us, from the very beginning, to pay attention to and cover each and every area of the personality. A case must be seen as a whole, due attention being paid to every aspect. In this way we avoid some of the dangers implicit in the ordinary procedure, particularly the tendency to focus on a particular symptom or striking piece of behavior. Important as this symptom or piece of behavior may be for the assessment of a child, they should not be considered in isolation, in which case they might acquire quite a different diagnostic meaning and significance. They must be viewed in the context of the whole personality, as part of a total structure, because they can be properly assessed and qualified only in this context.

As far as the time invested in elaborating a Profile is concerned, it can be said to be negligible. Since the Profile is truly a way of thinking and of organizing clinical observations and material, metapsychologically and within the conceptual frame of psychoanalysis, it can be built up as soon as one has finished reading the material available (i.e., social history, psychiatric interview, etc.). I have already commented on the fact that the classification of material under different headings is done for didactic and methodological reasons. The analysis of specific areas, for the time being artificially isolated from other areas with which they are closely interconnected, is only the initial step. This must be followed by the synthesis that the Profile represents.

The Profile is meant to be an extremely dynamic and alive picture of a given person. This requires the selection of relevant clinical material, which will convey meaning and imbue the Profile with liveliness. For those who want to achieve this, an important warning must be given: this is not to work from the headings to the material, a procedure which will never make a Profile, but rather the other way round, from the clinical material to the headings. Working in this way the clinical material will tend to classify itself whenever it is a relevant piece of information under a given section. Frequently, the same piece of material will "place itself" under several headings, making a different and valuable contribution to each and throwing light on the particular personality being examined. This makes the Profile meaningful, dynamic, and alive.

If, on the other hand, one "feeds" the headings simply because they exist, if one goes from the heading to the clinical material, one may be able to collect much information under each heading. But this is static and at times meaningless information. The Profile will lack that integrating thought process that is necessary for the construction of a meaningful picture of a person. It will also lack that which enriches the Profile and ourselves by teaching us to correlate our theoretical model, our conceptual frame, with clinical observations and vice versa. In short, the metapsychological approach is missing, and the process of trying out every possible angle in our own mind is lost. The finished Profile constitutes, after all, nothing more than a summary of our mental activities while reading the material, a sort of summary of our mental exercises in correlation, in assessment, in the translation of clinical observations into theoretical concepts and vice versa.

It may have been noticed that the headings belong to different levels of concept formation. They are hierarchically different and collect and organize the material at different levels of conceptualization. I have mentioned several times that a close relation exists among the different headings, and consequently of course among the clinical data that are classified under these various headings.

Furthermore, some headings are built up mainly on the information which has already been analyzed in several of the others. For this reason the information which is given in and analyzed by the different headings is not all at the same level or in the same conceptual category. Some headings collect the material in a rather simple way, others organize it at a more complex level of concept formation; and finally when we arrive at the summit of the Profile, we have the metapsychological formulations.

The Profile highlights the various areas of conflict, at times giving a very clear picture of the intensity and magnitudes of the forces involved. It permits us to make some quantitative assessment (in relative terms) of the magnitude of the drives, present as the result of a person's endowment, and to make comparisons with other cases. In this way a clearer understanding of the economic aspects is possible.

A good developmental history not only helps us to achieve all the purposes mentioned, it also allows us to understand the vicissitudes of the drives at various developmental stages; vicissitudes which are the result of the interplay with forces and figures of the environment, and later the interplay with the inner representatives and heirs of these external figures and conflicts.

With the information available at any time during the course of treatment, or after completion of treatment, a Profile can be constructed which may be compared with that obtained at the diagnostic stage on the basis of the information then available. This enables us to check on how far our diagnostic assumptions, our understanding of the case, and our predictions were correct, and how much of what later emerged in treatment was visible at the diagnostic stage, and so on. It allows us to check whether our metapsychological assessment of the material at the diagnostic stage was correct and whether it coincides with the assessment we could make after several years of analytic treatment.

The results obtained by the application of the Profile in this way have been satisfactory and instructive. The comparisons of Profiles obtained at the diagnostic stage and after the completion of treatment have shown us that the Profile pin-points at the very beginning the child's basic personality structure and main conflicts.

We then examined a number of cases in which we knew our

initial diagnostic assessment to be incorrect or incomplete. The Profile was applied by a worker familiar with its use but who had no knowledge of the particular case. Again, we were impressed by the results and regretted that no Profile had been available at the diagnostic stage of these cases. The analysis of causes of failure in the diagnostic procedures, in the light of knowledge gained after the analytic treatment of these cases, will lead to improvements.

The Profile constantly feeds back information that can, in its turn, improve our diagnostic techniques and our evaluations of the material. The very nature of the Developmental Profile provides checks on the reliability of our different sources of information (mother, father, etc.). We do not rely as much as we did in the past on a particular account given about a patient and on the accuracy of that account. Rather we rely on the internal picture we construct with all the information about the conflicts and the structure of a given personality. This picture must fit with the one familiar to us from our experience with neurotic, atypical, borderline, or psychotic pictures. Our ideal is to achieve a positive diagnosis. As in general medicine, we attempt to construct a syndrome in which all the symptoms and signs must correspond to and fit with what we know about neurotic conflict or atypical cases. For this purpose we follow the role played by the drives, by the different structures of the mind, the mechanism of symptom formation, defenses, the degree of maturity of the systems involved, etc. (the medical equivalent being anatomical, anatomopathological, physiological, and physiopathological considerations, etc.). The whole clinical picture thus arrived at must be properly delimited from others and must be internally consistent. If it is not, the Profile highlights contradictions and inaccuracies and permits us to trace them back to their sources.

Furthermore, the Profile poses questions which must be answered in order to resolve such inaccuracies and contradictions; it asks for more information on specific points, before a correct judgment can be arrived at. In this way the Profile checks itself or rather leads us to do the checking. If we obtain an incomplete picture of the structure of a neurotic conflict we will be warned to look more closely and to be prepared for a diagnostic surprise of one sort or another. For example, we may have a child with neurotic conflicts similar to those which any other child might have. But in addition, this child has, within certain limits, a faulty or defective ego. We will see the usual picture of neurotic conflict, but also that the child is not able to deal with the anxiety and the conflict situation in quite the same way as other children with normal egos do. This child will be in greater distress, more overwhelmed by his anxiety, and more helpless. The problem here may be a quantitative one, the ego not being able to cope beyond a certain point.

I have mentioned before that the Profile can be applied at any given point during the course of treatment, yielding a cross-section of the personality at that particular moment. It follows that the Profile is thus a useful tool for the assessment of the progress of analytic treatment. Applied at the end of treatment it provides an assessment of changes brought about by treatment.[7] The Profile evaluates the results of treatment by scrutinizing the inner changes and the structural rearrangements brought about by the analytic treatment rather than by assessing certain particular external manifestations. This method examines closely the changes in the defensive systems, the disappearance or diminution of the original conflicts in terms of the relative magnitude of the forces involved, the processes of sublimation that have been favored by the treatment situation, and the like. It also takes into account the ego's new capacities and techniques for dealing with anxiety. In short, it tries to highlight the structural, dynamic, economic, and adaptive rearrangements that may have taken place as the result of analysis.

In a number of cases we have repeated the Profile at the end of treatment (psychoanalytic treatment five times a week for a period of two, three, four, or more years).[8] It cannot be overemphasized that the inner picture may be very different from the one based on an assessment of external manifestations, which can be very mis-

[7] At the panel on the Curative Factors in Psycho-Analysis (1961), the question of how to improve our assessment of the results of treatment was posed to the members of the panel. Anna Freud, in her answer, referred to the use and potentialities of the Profile in this connection.

[8] The material utilized here consists of the reports made by the therapists on the treatment. At Hampstead we make written reports on every child in analysis at weekly and bimonthly intervals; in addition, each case is presented at least once a year to the general staff meeting. After completion of the analysis a summary of the treatment is prepared by the child's therapist. This material is available for research purposes.

leading. This is well brought out by the case of Arthur whose Profile has been presented here.

Arthur was eleven and a half years old at the beginning of his treatment. A Profile was made with the material recorded after three years of analytic treatment and subsequent follow-up. A superficial assessment might give the impression of a very much improved child, with no apparent trace of the conflicts and anxieties that had brought him into treatment. However, a closer examination, making use of the Profile, showed that most of the main conflicts and anxieties remained even though they were no longer as apparent as at the diagnostic stage.

He is now nineteen years old. His passivity and his tendency to revert to it as a consequence of castration anxiety or disappointment were seen at the diagnostic stage and are still present though they are less transparent. The diagnostic Profile also revealed a disturbed mother-child relationship. At present his relationship to his mother is still a highly sexualized one. His school problems and his learning inhibitions (in spite of his high capacities) are no longer present in their original form, but he has renounced his ambition of becoming an engineer and is at present undertaking a training well below his capacities. His difficulties centering around his aggression are still present.

Arthur's neurotic conflicts and symptoms are no longer as apparent as they were at the diagnostic stage. It seems that he has achieved a more stable equilibrium. However, he has paid the price of having to maintain a number of ego restrictions and limitations. He has also developed a number of rather undesirable character traits. He has not solved his conflicts by inner change but rather avoids them. Thus his interest in girls tends to lead to failure, to fear of competing, and to retreat into passivity. When another boy appears he simply withdraws. Similarly the decision that Arthur has made to enter his father's business is apparently not based on a healthy identification with the father but rather seems to be the outcome of a passive submission to the father's wishes.

We believe that time will confirm the expectations we have concerning the use of the Profile as a research tool. It has already proved its usefulness in many ways. The collection and comparison of large amounts of material obtained from specific cases and many different ones may prove valuable as a means of validating many theoretical assumptions and propositions.

In the experience of those who have worked with it, the Profile has stimulated, improved, and trained our thought processes in the field of psychoanalysis. We consider it to be of value in the training of candidates. It helps the student to learn the metapsychological approach. It sharpens the capacity for translating clinical observations and material into concepts, and helps us to use our theoretical formulations in the scrutiny and evaluation of clinical observations.

It may prove to be the basis on which an analytic classification of childhood (and adult) disturbances can later be built. It brings to such a classification not only a balanced view of the interaction of heredity, endowment, and environment; it also includes the developmental aspects, and the point of view of normality. All of these are basic considerations in any attempt at classifying or evaluating childhood manifestations, either normal or pathological.

Moreover, the genetic point of view has been given its proper place within the Profile. We can thus avoid the frequent mistakes that can occur when the genetic approach is taken further than it can really go, particularly at the diagnostic stage. When treatment has given us a much deeper understanding of the case and the forces and influences operative, it becomes possible to fill the gaps that may exist in this area.

BIBLIOGRAPHY

Freud, A. (1960), Four Contributions to the Psychoanalytic Study of the Child. Lectures presented at New York.
—— (1961), In Panel: The Curative Factors of Psycho-Analysis. International Psycho-Analytical Congress, Edinburgh.
—— (1962), Assessment of Childhood Disturbances. *This Annual*, XVII.
—— (1963), The Concept of Developmental Lines. *This Annual*, XVIII.
Freud, S. (1923), The Ego and the Id. *Standard Edition*, XIX. London: Hogarth Press, 1961.
Gauthier, Y. (1960), Observations on Ego Development: The Birth of a Sibling. *Bull. Phila. Assn. Psychoanal.*, X.
Spitz, R. A. (1945), Hospitalism. *This Annual*, I.

TREATMENT OF A DYING PATIENT

JANICE NORTON, M.D. (Denver)

Case reports of dying patients are rare. In 1915 in "Thoughts for the Times on War and Death" Freud discussed our attitude toward death as being "far from straightforward. To anyone who listened to us we were of course prepared to maintain that death was the necessary outcome of life, that everyone owes nature a death and must expect to pay the debt—in short, that death was natural, undeniable and unavoidable. In reality, however, we were accustomed to behave as if it were otherwise. We showed an unmistakable tendency to put death on one side, to eliminate it from life. We tried to hush it up" (p. 289). Considering the universality of the experience of dying, the relative rarity of case material dealing with dying patients would suggest a continued reluctance to deal with dying. Nearly all authors writing of dying patients remark on this (Aronson, 1959; Brodsky, 1959; Eissler, 1955; Feifel, 1959; L. and E. LeShan, 1951; Sandford, 1957; Saul, 1959; Weisman and Hackett, 1961). At the same time they also make a plea for more thorough study of the psychology of dying and insist that the psychiatrist may have a psychotherapeutic role with the dying. Freud (1915, 1916) and Eissler (1955) deal most adequately with both conscious and unconscious reasons for avoiding the dying, and I do not propose to repeat their discussions here.

What follows is a detailed case summary of the last three and a half months of life of a gallant and articulate woman. The case report owes its existence to the fact that all those on whom we usually rely to spare us the necessity of listening to dying patients, family, clergy, friends, other physicians, had already relinquished

Assistant Professor, Department of Psychiatry, University of Colorado School of Medicine.

I would like to express my indebtedness to René Spitz whose ideas and encouragement were invaluable in this case.

their roles and could not be induced to resume them. I was faced with the choice of allowing this patient to die a miserable and lonely death, possibly by suicide, or of trying to relieve her suffering in so far as I could.

CASE REPORT

Mrs. B., the thirty-two-year-old married mother of two sons, five and three, reluctantly came to see me at the urging of her sister, a social worker from a distant city. Her sister had been visiting and had become alarmed at Mrs. B.'s increasing depression and her hints at suicidal thoughts. While the patient frankly told me both were present, she herself felt no need to see a psychiatrist as both depression and a wish to commit suicide seemed to her to be entirely reasonable under the circumstances. She had substantial pain, cough, hemorrhagic tendencies, anemia, and increasing fatigue from metastatic breast cancer; she was losing weight and strength rapidly, had little appetite, slept poorly, and it was apparent to her that X-ray therapy, hormones, and repeated transfusions were having increasingly little effect in controlling the relentless progression of the disease toward her death. She was using very small doses of morphine, mostly at night, in a partial attempt to control the pain and in order to sleep, but had been told to use narcotics very sparingly because of the possibility of addiction. She felt it quite reasonable to wish to stop her suffering by suicide and also felt her suicide would considerably lessen the burden she was imposing on her parents, her sons, and her husband. She told me all this in a quite matter-of-fact way, underscoring the idea that she felt no need to see a psychiatrist and was only coming in once in order to please her sister. She felt she had the right to die as she pleased, had drugs readily available to her, and that her suicide could be made to look like death due to the disease if she took an overdose of morphine at some time when she was unusually sick. She had not confided this plan to anyone, although her statements about her wish to die without a prolonged terminal phase of pain and increasing incapacitation had alarmed her sister; the rest of the family had taken these to mean that she was sick and in pain but "just talking" at times when she felt most uncomfortable.

The breast cancer had been diagnosed very late in the pregnancy with the younger son and a radical mastectomy was performed immediately; following delivery she had bilateral oophorectomy and irradiation to the breast area. She was initially worried about recurrence or spread of the disease, but as several months passed without symptoms she felt encouraged, and except for occasional feelings of regret about the imposed limitation on the size of her family, she was pleased with her life: her husband was enthusiastically beginning his career; her sons were doing well and gave her much pleasure; and she herself was engrossed with her life. Eight months before she came to see me, she had begun to suffer with chest pain and X-ray immediately demonstrated metastases to the ribs, spine, and pelvis. Both her husband and surgeon had frankly discussed this with her at her request, and although for about two months she tried to convince herself that X-ray and hormones might either cure her or give her "years" yet to live, the steady accumulation of symptoms was more than she could deny. She became very conscious of the fact that death was imminent in the immediately foreseeable future.

She did not become depressed at this point, but instead turned to religion. Her father had been a minister until his recent retirement, and she had been brought up in a religious home. In college she had gradually become more and more intellectually doubting of her faith and had finally lost interest in religion. With the knowledge of her impending death, however, she attempted to return to religion through a Protestant minister whom she engaged in lengthy philosophic discussions, particularly on the subject of immortality. Unfortunately, he took her intellectual arguments at face value, agreed there was no scientific proof of an afterlife and that her doubts were well founded. He offered her faith as a substitute for logic, but this patient, although deeply religious, remained quite skeptical of standard religious doctrine. For several months, however, she continued to find talking with him comforting. Gradually their conversations became more personal and less religious, although occasionally when she was feeling unusually ill he would read to her from the Bible. She became increasingly involved with him and about two months before she came to see me, she had confided to him that she felt she might be falling in love with him. He responded by telling her that this was unrealistic, that she was sick, and by sharply curtailing their time together. In fact, he very shortly stopped seeing her entirely except in a superficial and perfunctory way. Her depression and suicidal preoccupation began at this time. She also became increasingly anxious and had several acute attacks of anxiety, which she attributed to bouts of increased pain and weakness.

Concurrent with this experience were other mounting difficulties in her relationships with important people. She presented everyone with a picture of a young woman visibly dying an early death who had a great need to come to terms with her feelings about this. As subsequent therapy with me bore out, listening had its problems as the entire situation was tragic. She was an appealing, attractive woman, warm, intelligent, well read, interested in many things, and capable of very intense feeling. One result of this was that all who loved her most and might have been expected to help her with her feelings about dying were intensely and understandably involved in grieving. Talking to others of her feelings about dying was virtually precluded by the intensity of the feelings she provoked in them. Her parents, both chronically ill and in their seventies, lived nearby and periodically cared for the children, but they could not bring themselves to see her because they "hated to cry" in her presence. Her husband, increasingly miserable at her impending death, busied himself with his work. Her doctors, increasingly frustrated at her lack of medical response to their various forms of treatment, became hearty and hollow; and her sister, frightened by the patient's obvious loneliness and despair, lived a great distance away and referred her to me. At the time I first saw her, her relationships with the two boys were about all that remained even relatively intact. She had not yet spent any protracted time in the hospital and was using what strength she had to continue to care for them as she always had, although this was becoming an increasing problem for her.

That this patient had remarkable ego strengths was immediately evident. She had faced surgery, pain, sickness, and the knowledge of her impending early death with impressive insistence on reality, and was doing her utmost to adapt to very adverse circumstances. She had continued her life as usual within the limits of her physical condition, did not resort to the drugs readily available to her, and the only demands she had made on those around her were that they allow her to share her experience with them. It was only when she became aware of their increasing withdrawal from her that she became suicidal. Her attitude toward her parents, her husband, and her doctors was essentially maternal, that she was protecting them from pain by not insisting that they listen and help her with her ever-increasing distress. At the same time she was well aware of her need for help and had done her utmost to find it.

Treatment: Early Phase

All of this became apparent in my initial interviews with the patient and despite her superficial objections to psychiatric treatment, it was possible to get her to continue to see me on a regular basis by agreeing that she had no serious, long-standing psychiatric problems, that she was facing an extraordinarily painful reality situation with admirable courage, but that it might be of some help to her if we were to talk over her feelings about this. In addition, with the relieved consent of her surgeon, I took over the management of her narcotics and sedation so that very soon she became relatively free of pain and began to sleep at night. I explained this to her as essential both for her comfort and for her ability to care for the children as she wished to. She never did agree very whole-heartedly to the idea of seeing a psychiatrist and even in the last week of her life teased me about what an "unpsychiatric psychiatrist" I had been in that I had never lived up to her stereotype of what a psychiatrist should be, a silent, remote interpreter of dreams and of the oedipal situation. The implication was that she had not really had psychiatric treatment but had found someone with whom she could talk, who fortunately happened to be a physician and was, almost by unhappy accident, a psychiatrist as well. My initial treatment plan was to help her with her depression, prevent her suicide if at all possible, and to see if I could help the family to deal with the situation somewhat more effectively. By this time, however, both her husband and her parents had so decathected their relationship with the patient that it proved impossible for them to help; to them, in many respects she was already dead or had in any event delayed her dying too long. Her sister lived too far away to be of any immediate help although she did come to stay with the patient and care for her during the last three weeks of her life. As a result of this, my treatment goal was very rapidly changed to that of trying to make this patient's death less lonely and frightening. To this end, I saw her daily in my office, the hospital, or at her home, depending on her physical condition, for the last three and a half months of her life. I made it explicit that I would be available to her at any time, and would be for as long as she needed me (see Eissler, 1955, pp. 126, 197).

She was the older of two girls. Her sister had had training as a social worker, but was happily married and no longer working. Her parents were hardworking, well meaning, somewhat simple people with very clear-cut Fundamentalist ideas of right and wrong. Although the patient had rebelled considerably against her parents' religious beliefs during adolescence, she and her family had remained on good terms and quite close. She had been her father's favorite, had felt closer to him than to her mother, and they had shared many intellectual interests. She had repeated many aspects of her relationship with her father in the relationship with the minister, and subsequently repeated these early in treatment with me. She felt that she and her mother had never had very much in common and described her mother as timid, overanxious, and not much interested in anything outside of the home. This was in contrast to the patient who, although very interested in her husband and children, read a great deal and was active in local politics. The patient felt that her mother had been much less helpful than she might have been during her growing up. This particularly referred to adolescence when the patient had been quite rebellious and argumentative in her attempts to free herself from this somewhat close and restrictive family. The patient's mother had handled her rebellion by silent but visible worry and by impatiently telling the patient that she had to learn to think for herself. The patient felt let down by her mother's refusal to help. These were, of course, current complaints as well. This problem recurred in treatment in that she was very anxious about allowing herself any regression with me at first and felt that I, too, placed a high premium on her acting like an adult no matter how she felt.

Her childhood had been relatively unproblematic. She had done well in school, had had a series of best friends, been popular in high school, had begun to date then and had been "in love" with two different men before she met and married her husband. In late high school and college she had vague career plans of teaching English literature and of writing. She did teach for a while early in her marriage while her husband was still in school, and she had continued to write poetry for her own pleasure until the birth of their first child. She began again to write poetry in the months following the appearance of the metastases.

Her husband was a warm, sensitive, intelligent, ambitious young man who shared his life with her to her very great pleasure. Except for occasional arguments about his somewhat problematic and widowed mother who periodically decided she wanted to come to live with them, the marriage had presented no problems. Mrs. B. was basically a cheerful, optimistic, highly intelligent woman who had derived much pleasure from her marriage and her children. Her sexual life had been deeply satisfying to her and another contributing factor to her presenting depression was that pain and fatigue, combined with some reluctance on her husband's part, had sharply decreased the frequency of sexual intercourse in the months preceding my seeing her. She attributed falling in love with the minister to this. She was very worried that her husband no longer found her attractive now that she was ill.

The patient's relationships to her two sons were complex. Both were happy, spontaneous boys whom she enjoyed. It early became apparent that she at times identified with the older boy. As she became less and less well and more concerned about dying, she became fearful about his starting school without her and about how lonely she expected he might feel. A major goal for her became that she stay alive until he was safely started in school and not "by himself." In fact, she did accomplish this, became totally bed-ridden shortly after he started school, and died within three weeks. She had much less to say about her younger son. It was apparent that this relationship had been considerably more ambivalent from the start because the malignancy had been part of the pregnancy and the early months of his life. She struggled to fight off the irrational feeling that she might never have had cancer had it not been for this pregnancy. It felt to her increasingly that he was living at her expense and she was much troubled by her impatience with him. Talking about this helped substantially, but their relationship was never free from problems. It was this son about whom she most worried during a brief period in which she wondered if cancer might be either hereditary or contagious.

Treatment can perhaps most easily be summarized in terms of her relationship to me. The very fact of her prospective death had seriously disturbed her relationships with those who meant most to her but had in no way impaired her need for people, had in fact increased it. She very quickly became intensely involved with me. My statement that she was entitled to help and comfort and my intervention regarding the drugs undoubtedly facilitated this. In the second hour she questioned me about my training and my professional life and made it clear that she was worried that I might feel as defeated about her dying as her other doctors seemed to. I assured her that I was willing to help her in any way that I could and that this certainly included helping her with her feelings about dying. When she asked if this might not make me uncomfortable, I replied that I would try to help her in any event. She then began to discuss religion and philosophy with me, in large part I think to see whether I was really willing to help her with her feelings or would, like her parents and the minister, succumb to religious platitudes or withdraw out of my own discomfort. I did neither, and out of these discussions emerged several problems. She was afraid of dying alone, of becoming less and less attractive, "sick," and having people lose interest in her, a fear which was partially substantiated by the way her family had turned away from her. She also feared the gradually increasing sense of helplessness that her physical incapacitation was giving rise to and was in part using her intelligence to help to master this difficult situation. She was also using the philosophic discussions in an attempt to gain my approval of how "adult" she was being. Discussion of these problems gradually led to a diminution of her depression, complete absence of any talk of suicide, impressive absence of anxiety, and an increased sense of well-being and of hope which was quite at odds with her deteriorating physical condition. She was physically more comfortable during this period because of adequate medication. At this same time she asked to borrow some books of mine, which I loaned her, and she began to bring me poetry which she had written earlier. I quote one poem to illustrate her preoccupation with separation.

> To die is such a lonely thing,
> We cannot take one friend along.
> To hold a hand would make it
> Far less a frightening song.

With this she began to share with me her grief over dying, which to her essentially meant leaving those she loved best. Despite occasional interruptions by her worsening physical condition, mourning continued in one form or another until her final coma. She began by talking about the relationship to the minister and how hurt and angry she had been at his misunderstanding her need for him and his present avoidance of her. She told me in detail how they had met, the discussions they had had about her illness, and what they discussed during the times she was discouraged. She wept over his leaving her when she needed him most. She was very scornful of this kind of "religion," but also felt that he was to be pitied as he apparently did not have the strength to remain with her to help.

This led to her feelings about her husband's withdrawing from her. She understood that he was grieving himself, was hurt by his inability to help her with her feelings, but for the most part was protective about his feelings. Except for occasionally talking of feeling irritated by the lengthy hours he worked, she expressed little anger about him. She gradually told me about her marriage and relationship to her husband, of their courtship, honeymoon, the earlier happy times that they had had, his hopes and aspirations about his profession, and how she shared these. She was deeply grieved by the fact that she would not be around to continue to share his life with him; she hoped he would marry again, but preferred not to think about this. She discussed both pregnancies and her relationships with both sons in equal detail, again with emphasis on how sorely she would miss future participation in their lives. She allowed herself some daydreaming as to what she hoped their futures would be like. All of this seemed very much like working through in mourning, was accompanied by appropriate crying and by occasional denial, although the denial was almost always in the form of giving herself an extra year or so of life, not of being cured. Her ego never permitted her any convincing fantasies of a hereafter in which she might continue to be aware of the lives of those she loved. Death to her meant the end of these relationships and a separation from those she loved best. She was angry at the unfairness of her early death and talked with intense feeling of the impending loss of those she loved most and the experiences she would never have with them. She tried to console herself by reminding herself of the things she had already had, but until she was much sicker physically, she found little comfort in this.

She was both angry about and defeated by her parents' current minimal participation in her life. For the most part, however, she viewed her parents protectively and felt she was saving them pain by not insisting they spend time with her. This seemed to repeat aspects of her adolescent emancipation from her parents. Memories of earlier aspects of her relationship to them never appeared directly except for the nostalgia for the intellectual relationship she had shared with her father, which was now precluded by his age and illness as well as by his feelings about her death.

Her pain and insomnia during this six-week period were well controlled by drugs, but her weakness and weight loss were increasing, and she had had several hemorrhages from minor bruises. Her surgeon decided to hospitalize her for another course of X-ray and for transfusions. By this time she was beginning to look grotesque because of skull metastases, and shortly after hospitalization she became comatose, presumably from increased intracranial pressure. She was promptly treated and regained consciousness gradually over a period of three days.

First Regression: Externalization of Superego and Identification

However, this sudden severe clinical change brought about a striking change in our relationship, the first obvious regression, and from this point on there was no question that she was repeating with me aspects of her earlier relationship with her mother. She herself perceived the regression and was briefly apologetic "for being such a baby," but as I explained this as an expected part of her illness, she became less ashamed. My manifest response to her underwent a change at this time, too, in that she was obviously much sicker, and communication was no longer on an exclusively verbal level. She frequently needed physical care during the time I spent with her, and I made her bed comfortable, fed her at times, and at other times simply sat quietly with her. She often asked me to stay with her while she fell asleep. Essentially I responded to her regression by assuming certain necessary kinds of ego functions for her, in effect began to function as an external ego in much the same sense that the mother's ego functions as an external ego for that of the developing child. Clinically, the patient's affective response made it easily possible to judge the amount of this that was necessary: too little help made her ashamed about the regression, whereas too much made her impatient and angry with me.

As she became more alert, she reported the only dreams she told me during therapy. These were a series of dream fragments having to do with physical activity: she was a child again and running happily; she was swimming at the country club to which she belonged; she was jumping rope as a young girl; she was playing tennis as she had done the previous summer. All of these dreams seemed essentially to represent the wish to be well and active; they also illustrate regression to the simple wish-fulfillment dreams of childhood. They were reported with sadness, but, as she associated to them, she began to be irritated with me. Discussion of the irritation brought into focus her intense envy of me which had been present but unverbalized from the beginning. She envied my relative youth, my health, my activity, the fact that I was not sick and helpless as she was. She also was jealous of me, said she had recently become very troubled by a recurring idea that I might marry her husband and care for her children after her death. She also reported that she was even more worried that her mother-in-law would replace her with her children and had made her husband promise that he would not permit his mother to move in with him after her death. Her jealousy and envy of the minister's wife had also been intense, but she had been too ashamed of this to tell me earlier. As she spoke of these feelings about me she first apologized but gradually became very angry and demanded that I stop seeing her because the comparison between our relative states of health and attractiveness was more than she could bear. I told her that these feelings were certainly understandable in these circumstances, that I understood how angry she was at me, but that I did not feel that this precluded our continuing to work together, that I really wanted to help her. I also made the only transference interpretation I ever made to her, vague and incomplete though it was: that part of what troubled her was that because she was sick, she was refeeling with me some of the feelings she had had as a child about being a child and not able to do what her mother did. She seemed relieved by this, smiled, and said she had changed her mind about firing me. Both of these issues came up several times again but never with the same intensity, and were more often apparent in attempts to identify with me. She knew my schedule of teaching activities, for instance, and would imagine herself in my role at various times of the day, spent considerable time imagining what I was doing and where I was. The oedipal transference was readily apparent and the ambivalence apparently solved by her childlike identification with the positive side of the ambivalence. In essence I allowed her to externalize her punitive superego and gave her an ego ideal she could live up to when I accepted the jealousy and envy as part of her illness.

Her strength partially returned and she again went home and resumed some care of the children. The older boy's starting school increasingly became a focus of worry and, for her, a compelling reason to husband her energies. She made repeated references to the hope he would not have to do this without her as she was sure this would be terrifying for him. Initially this was a puzzling preoccupation, especially so in that her own first days at school had not been in any way disturbing, a fact confirmed by the patient's mother as well as by the patient. Continued discussion of this, however, indicated that she was equating his starting school with her own approaching death and that she was quite troubled by the idea that she "knew no one there," would in effect be a stranger among strangers as she expected her son to feel in his early days at school. That this patient had had no deaths in those closest to her may have contributed to this preoccupation as she had no one to "join in death" in fantasy (Brodsky, 1954; Jones, 1911).

After a brief period at home she again became so weak that hospitalization was necessary for rest and for transfusions. She had been complaining of periodic visual difficulties for several weeks and feared she was losing her sight, although she had hopefully attributed this to bouts of weakness. While in the hospital she gradually became intermittently blind. She showed more severe anxiety about this than she had about any previous symptom. It was a concrete sign of the nearness of her death, of course, but to her this meant that she was about to be completely cut off from the people around her, by this time especially from me, and she was terrified of what she envisioned as a life in which she was mentally alert but remote from contact with people.

Second Regression: Externalization of Ego

During the first few days of her blindness I spent extra time with her and at her request visually described and identified for her hospital personnel and the details of her room; she was particularly interested in knowing what clothing I was wearing and was pleased when it was something familiar to her. I also did my utmost to demonstrate that while visual communication was seriously interfered with, we retained the equally important avenues of communication of talking and of touch. She likened these to the way a baby must feel, that feeling physical closeness and hearing the sound of mother's voice might be of as basic importance as seeing. I read to her—she particularly liked the 23rd and 121st Psalms—and I sat close enough that she could touch me or I her at any time. She often drowsed or fell asleep during these hours, and I had the impression that my physical presence and the tone of my voice were almost more important than the verbal content of what I said.

This outbreak of acute anxiety, in fact the only such outbreak during treatment, at a time when her relationship to me was threatened by blindness is an impressive illustration of the level of ego regression. By this time I had assumed for her many aspects of ego functioning. Her anxiety signaled the danger of ego disruption at the threatened loss of my supporting ego. This is, of course, an infantile form of separation anxiety. I responded to her anxiety with a marked increase in my availability to her and by "loaning" her my sight as well as by reassuring her that her loss of sight did not mean a disruption of our relationship. Her anxiety diminished with this.

Third Regression: Introjection

Further ego regression assured continuation of the relationship, for soon thereafter she began to talk of an all-pervasive sense of peace and contentment which was quite at odds with the clinical picture but was related to what she described as her "silly illogical imagination." Instead of imagining me in the various aspects of my life, she now felt I was with her twenty-four hours a day and she began to carry on imaginary conversations with me. Most of these that she reported at this time dealt with discussions of her feelings, but increasingly she felt as if I were always there comforting her, assuaging pain or physical discomfort and telling her she need not be afraid, that she was not alone.

She felt that her death was quickly approaching, asked that she be allowed to die at home, and I encouraged her sister to come and care for her there. At home she rallied briefly to get her older son started in school and then became partially bedridden. Her sister cared for her physical needs, and we both continued to talk with her, read to her, and to keep her as comfortable as we could. She drowsed frequently but remained very much alert and interested in the lives of her family when she was awake. The blindness was intermittent during these weeks. She began occasionally to call her sister by my first name and at the same time to me made several uncorrected slips of calling me "mother" (Saul, 1959). She questioned me closely about the time of my last visit and the length of my current visit (I was seeing her twice a day at this point) and always expressed surprise at my answers as she now "almost" had the conviction that I was always there. Occasionally she would wake in pain and be surprised to find me absent.

Eissler, in *The Psychiatrist and the Dying Patient,* says, "It is conceivable that through the establishment of transference, through an approach which mobilizes the archaic trust in the world and reawakens the primordial feelings of being protected by a mother, the suffering of the dying can be reduced to a minimum even in case of extreme physical pain" (1955, p. 119). Freud also mentions this as a possibility (1926, p. 171). The psychological suffering of the patient is also reduced to a minimum; in fact, this sense of peace and contentment seemed massively to protect against all affects of unpleasure. It was only at times of severe physical pain that the protection of this "hallucination" failed and then only briefly and without anxiety; the expectation was that I would "soon" arrive and provide relief. Here the regressive level is to that developmental stage in which the object is clearly perceived as an object, felt as continuously present, and the borders between external and internal are at times hazy. This not only had the effect of minimizing physical pain and psychological suffering but also seemed to prevent the narcissistic, hypochondriacal preoccupation that is so frequently a part of serious illness. That this level of regression in object relations coexisted with nonregressed ego functioning in other areas indicates only the complexity of the concept of regression.

She remained troubled by the conflict between this feeling of my continuous presence and the reality of the situation, however, and began to talk of her unhappiness that I would not be with her when she died. I at first thought she was referring to my physical presence and tried to reassure her, but it turned out that she had long since taken my presence during her death as an established fact. What she meant was that I would not be dying with her, that this we could not share.

Three days before her death and a few hours before she became terminally comatose, we had a long conversation about her dying. She told me her only remaining fear was that dying was strange and unknown to her, that she had never done it before. Like birth, it was something that only happened once to any individual, and that similarly one might not remember what it was really like, only know that it had once happened. She no longer worried about what was to happen to her after death any more than an infant being born could worry about what his future life might be; she felt that she might be unnecessarily concerned with the actual process of death itself. She then asked me if I had been with other patients when they died and seemed relieved by my affirmative answer. One very comforting recurring thought to her was that throughout the centuries many people had died before her; more importantly, it had occurred to her that I would share this experience with her, although not at this time. I agreed that this was certainly so and added that I hoped I might equal her courage. She was pleased by this, and she then reminisced about our relationship. She recalled our first meeting and smiled in retrospect at her needless reluctance at seeing a psychiatrist. She thanked me for having helped her, particularly not to commit suicide, which she now felt would have been most difficult for her family, especially her sons. I was obviously moved by the finality of all this, and she chided me about being much more involved with her than doctors should be with their patients, and abruptly cried. Her regret was that we had known each other so briefly, that she was dying without ever knowing me really well. I said she had known me rather better than she might think, that I felt it a great privilege that she had shared this experience with me and that I, too, wished we had had more time together. She asked me if after her death I would wear for her a red dress she had bought just before she became too sick to have any fun—she wanted "the dress to have some fun." I agreed, thanked her, asked whether there was anything else I might do for her, and she asked that I again read the 23rd Psalm. In the midst of this she interrupted me by crying. She said she would miss me terribly but somehow knew I was "always there" and asked that I hold her hand while she fell asleep. I did, and this was the last time the patient was conscious except for very brief periods that afternoon. She became comatose later on in the day and died three days later without regaining consciousness.

Eissler feels that mourning would ease the plight of the dying patient by accomplishing a decathexis of objects prior to death and that therefore death could be accepted as a "natural consequence of an energic constellation in that moment." But he feels that this is not likely while "perception conveys the fact of the existence of the love objects" (1955, p. 181). Mourning was a very prominent feature of this patient's last few months of life; although part of this seemed to have resulted from the emotional withdrawal of those around her, part was also related to her knowledge of her death, its meaning to her of separation, and to the physical changes in herself. It is worth noting that the order in which she grieved was chronologically significant. She began with the most recent relationship, the minister, and followed this by mourning the loss of her husband, and her parents. The grief about her two sons was a relatively continuous process in that mourning them was very intimately related to mourning the loss of her health, her productivity, and her own future. What seemed to happen was that libido detached from objects through mourning gradually found a transference substitute in me. However, at the end she was presented with the impending conclusion of our relationship by her death. During the last hour she mourned this but also solved the problem by extending her own life through me through the gift of the red dress, and by taking me with her in death "although not at this time."

DISCUSSION

This case has been presented in considerable detail because of the relative rarity of such cases in the literature and because of its theoretical and therapeutic implications. The patient's presenting despair and grief about dying are far from unusual; that family, friends, physicians, and clergy often turn from the dying in one way or another need not surprise us. As Eissler points out, many factors have tended to exclude the psychiatrist or the analyst from the bedside of the dying patient, not the least of which are the unusual demands on time (1955, pp. 240-253).

Eissler says that the technique of the treatment of the dying patient must center around what he calls "the gift situation" in which the psychiatrist must create the proper time to make the right gift. The gift is experienced by the patient as "an unusual . . . favor of destiny" (p. 126). This case would suggest that the really crucial gift the therapist can give is that of himself as an available object. The treatment of this patient can be simply summarized as a process in which I helped the patient to defend herself against object loss by facilitating the development of a regressive relationship to me which precluded object loss.

The patient came into treatment with me anxious, depressed, and contemplating suicide in her despair over the failure of those around her to respond to her need for them. Once she established my willingness to be with her and to try to help she quickly agreed to psychiatric treatment. She initially tested my willingness to help her by engaging me in religious and philosophic discussions of the meaning of death, as if to make certain that I would not be driven away by the mention of death as an abstraction. In retrospect I think she was also exploring my own attitudes about death. Satisfied that

I could listen and remain with her, she then allowed herself to grieve with me the actual and potential losses she was facing—her husband, children, family, her health, and her future.

While the mourning was still in progress, she became temporarily physically very ill, briefly comatose, and from this point on she was consciously very preoccupied with her relationship to me. One of her first worries on regaining consciousness and perceiving her regression was that she might have become "too much of a baby" for me to continue to help. When I reassured her about this, she for the first time began to express the envious, hostile competitiveness of the oedipal transference, which was also a threat to the relationship. My interpretation of this combined with her intense need for a relatively unambivalent relationship with me allowed her to re-externalize her superego and to identify with the positive side of the oedipal ambivalence.

Later on, when blindness intervened, the anxiety was again that this seriously threatened her relationship to me. She solved this by a further regression to a level of object relationship in which she hallucinated my presence and the boundaries of external and internal were at times blurred. The tenacity with which she clung to this object relationship despite all vicissitudes was extremely impressive. In the last hour she solved the problem of threatened loss of me by feeling that I would be with her in death, "although not at this time." In the course of dying this patient's ego permitted massive regression in many areas, all of which was apparently in the service of maintaining an intensely cathected object relationship with me.

The protection this relationship provided her against anxiety and depression was extremely impressive. Although she grieved throughout treatment, depression was never a serious problem, and the only massive anxiety occurred briefly at the time of her blindness. In addition, despite both pulmonary and bone metastases, she was relatively free from pain on comparatively small amounts of morphine. Freud remarks in *Inhibitions, Symptoms and Anxiety* that "when there is a psychical diversion brought about by some other interest, even the most intense physical pains fail to arise" (1926, p. 171). This case amply bears this out. Interestingly enough, the intensity of the relationship also precluded the increased narcissism and bodily preoccupation that are so frequently associated with severe illness. It would certainly suggest that such symptoms, often assumed to be an inevitable part of the chronic or fatal illness, can be obviated by a therapeutic approach such as the one presented here. It is tempting to speculate that at least in certain patients many problems frequently met with in dying patients, i.e., denial, anxiety, depression, increased narcissism and apathy, may be a result of actual or anticipated object loss and are by no means intrinsic to the psychological response to death. Certainly there is no question that a therapeutic approach such as I have outlined could be expected substantially to ease the suffering of many dying patients and add greatly to our knowledge of the metapsychology of dying.

In summary, the essential therapeutic tools in the treatment of the dying patient are the therapist's constant availability as an object, his reliability, his empathy, and his ability to respond appropriately to the patient's needs. Once Mrs. B. was truly convinced I meant it when I said I would be with her until her death, she made few demands for extra time; I did, however, offer this unasked at crucial times for her, such as during the early days of her blindness.

An essential prerequisite of therapy with the dying is consciously accepted countertransference. The dying patient specifically confronts the analyst with guilt and with an injury to his narcissism; that the patient is actually dying inevitably mobilizes the analyst's childhood death wishes and at the same time serves as a painful reminder of his own mortality. Defenses against either or both countertransferences in large part explain why dying patients are so often left to die alone. The analyst's defenses against these will distance him from the patient in one way or another and inevitably seriously interfere with his ability to respond appropriately to the patient's needs. The last hour illustrates this well. Both the patient and I knew she was very close to death; she solved the problem of our separation by taking me with her in death. She generously provided me with a partial defense by adding "although not at this time." She also relinquished to me the oedipal struggle by bequeathing me her favorite dress, the one she had bought "for fun." I was aware of grief, guilt, anxiety, and anger during this hour, but I am sure it is apparent that defenses against any of these countertransference responses, whether denial, reassurance, repression, overprotectiveness, false optimism, or intellectualization, would have markedly interfered with my usefulness to the patient as the object she needed. My conscious awareness of the sources of these responses was what made it possible for me to respond appropriately in terms of her needs. In essence, the dying patient inevitably provokes countertransference responses in the analyst, but acceptance and utilization of these can be most therapeutic for the patient.

Summary

A case report of the treatment of a patient during the last three and a half months of her life has been presented. The case suggests that a major psychological problem of the dying patient is that of both actual and threatened object loss. A method of treatment has been described which provides massive protection against both physical pain and psychological unpleasure, and certain theoretical conclusions about the psychological problems of the dying have been drawn.

BIBLIOGRAPHY

Aronson, G. J. (1959), Treatment of the Dying Person. In: *The Meaning of Death,* ed. H. Feifel. New York: McGraw-Hill, pp. 251-258.
Brodsky, B. (1959), Liebestod Fantasies in a Patient Faced with a Fatal Illness. *Int. J. Psa.,* XL.
Eissler, K. R. (1955), *The Psychiatrist and the Dying Patient.* New York: International Universities Press.
Feifel, H. (1959), Attitudes Toward Death in Some Normal and Mentally Ill Populations. In: *The Meaning of Death,* ed. H. Feifel. New York: McGraw-Hill, pp. 114-130.
Freud, S. (1915), Thoughts for the Times on War and Death. *Standard Edition,* XIV. London: Hogarth Press, 1957.
—— (1916), On Transience. *Standard Edition,* XIV. London: Hogarth Press, 1957.
—— (1926), Inhibitions, Symptoms and Anxiety. *Standard Edition,* XX. London: Hogarth Press, 1959.
Jones, E. (1911), Dying Together. *Essays in Applied Psychoanalysis,* I. London: Hogarth Press, 1951.
LeShan, L. & LeShan, E. (1951), Psychotherapy in the Patient With a Limited Life Span. *Psychiatry,* XXIV.
Sandford, B. (1957), Some Notes on a Dying Patient. *Int. J. Psa.,* XXXVIII.
Saul, L. (1959), Reactions of a Man to Natural Death. *Psa. Quart.,* XXVIII.
Weisman, A. B. & Hackett, T. P. (1961), Predilection to Death. *Psychosom. Med.,* XXIII.

A SEVERE NEUROSIS IN AN ADOLESCENT BOY

BERNARD ROSENBLATT, Ph.D. (London—Worcester)

This paper describes the analytic treatment of a boy, Harold, who was suffering from a disabling neurosis when he came for treatment at the age of thirteen years and eight months. The special value of the case derives from the fact that the patient had not yet entered adolescence when he began treatment, so that it was possible to follow his progressive development into this maturational phase in the closest possible way. In addition, other features of the case gave it more than usual interest; these features include: an unusual symptomatology; Harold's extraordinary ability to verbalize his thoughts and feelings; the fact that little modification of psychoanalytic technique was needed to carry out the treatment; and, finally, the material gathered in the analysis throws light on two areas of special interest in the study of adolescent patients, namely, the formation of the therapeutic alliance and the loosening of the libidinal ties to the parents.

In this paper I will report not only the communication of the patient in detail, but will also give more attention than is perhaps usual to verbatim accounts of the interpretations I gave. I do this partly because it is a habit acquired during training in the Hampstead Child-Therapy Course (especially from work on the Hampstead Index), but mainly out of the conviction that increased understand-

This paper forms part of a Research Project entitled "Inquiry into the Analysis of Adolescents" which is being financed by a grant from the Psychoanalytic Research and Development Fund, Inc., New York, to the Hampstead Child-Therapy Clinic, London.

The case described in the paper was treated by the author at the Hampstead Child-Therapy Clinic, and grateful acknowledgment is given to Dr. Ilse Hellman for her supervision of the treatment. In addition, the author's participation in the research project on analysis of adolescents, led by Dr. Hellman and Dr. Liselotte Frankl, served as an invaluable source of stimulation.

Now Director of Research at the Worcester Youth Guidance Center, Worcester, Massachusetts.

ing of technique can come only from detailed reporting and from debate about details. As Eissler (1958) has pointed out: "Comparative technique is a fruitful area, but neglected in the literature of psychoanalysis."

Background Information

The First Referral

Three years before treatment began, Harold's brother, Sidney, referred Harold to the Clinic. Sidney, who is four years older, had had several years of analysis by that time and was close to termination.

Harold was described by his mother at that time as an abnormally small boy with a gentle, sensitive, and artistic temperament. He was very keen on dancing and his mother felt he was more like a girl than a boy. His intelligence was tested with the Stanford-Binet and his I.Q. was 142. Among numerous disturbing symptoms were fears that his mother would die, bad dreams in which mother was run over by a car, and very poor schoolwork in spite of his good intelligence. Although there were many indications of Harold's great need of analysis, his mother did not accept the offer of treatment because she wanted him to enter a certain desirable school and she feared that the school would reject Harold if they discovered he was in treatment.

The Second Referral

After three years had gone by Harold's mother returned to the Clinic with an urgent request for treatment. He had developed a very disturbing symptom: he poked his feces out of his anus with his finger, and he had great anxiety that the feces would not come out. He spent almost an hour in the toilet each morning and evening. A number of doctors were consulted, but no physical basis for the trouble could be found. A few months before treatment was started his mother began to give him enemas; Harold learned to take the enemas himself, but soon stopped the practice. Significantly enough, it was the family physician who impressed the mother with the seriousness of the symptom; she, apparently, did not recognize it as a sign of emotional disturbance.

Harold had been preoccupied with cleanliness in lavatories for a long time, and the school lavatories were usually too dirty to meet his exacting standards. On holiday, when going to a hotel, his first task was to inspect the toilets, and in making arrangements for their holidays Harold and his father had to plan very carefully, using the appropriate touring guides, to make certain that their journey would not take them out of range of good, clean toilets.

In addition to the zonal regression[1] which this symptom represented, there were other manifestations of serious disturbance. Harold had withdrawn from his former friends and now spent most of his time alone. His favorite amusement was playing games which involved moving pieces on a board, e.g., Monopoly. In these games he would take both sides himself, substituting an imaginary opponent for a real one. When he occasionally played with other children they were usually younger than himself and he permitted them to dominate the situation. He had developed new fears, an important one being the fear that he would fall out of the train on his trips to and from school. Finally, his jealousy of his older brother, Sidney, had become very intense, and he resented any attention Sidney got from mother. For example, when Sidney prepared to go on a trip by himself Harold became furious with his mother because she went to the cleaners to get his brother's clothes.

The Diagnostic Interviews

In his diagnostic interviews Harold expressed a great deal of dissatisfaction with himself. The dissatisfaction did not reach the level of morbid self-recrimination, however, and his affect was not depressive. He felt that he was too childish and described how he took a number of stuffed animals to bed with him. At times he struggled to give up this habit and tried to put the animals in the cupboard, but then he would fear that the animals would be too lonely, he would give up his resolve and take the animals to bed. He very clearly wanted treatment, and this was mainly because of his anal symptom,

[1] Anna Freud has called our attention to an important distinction in the forms which regression may take, namely, between regression which is confined to the ideational or fantasy level and regression which involves the actual stimulation of an erogenous zone.

which he called his "trouble." It was noteworthy that he spoke of his symptom with complete candor and apparently without the shame and embarrassment one might especially expect to find in an adolescent patient. He said that he often spoke of the symptom with his mother, but not with his father. He explained that doctors used a procedure similar to the one he used himself, except that they used a rubber glove, and he mentioned that he used vaseline to facilitate the "poking."

Another feature of the diagnostic interviews was that in a number of ways Harold compared his own situation with that of his brother. If he were to have treatment he wondered whether his sessions would take place at the same hour as his brother's, and he wanted a male therapist just as Sidney had had. In this connection he mentioned that he talked with his mother about his troubles, but he felt this was a special case because she was his mother; it did not mean that he would be very satisfied with a female therapist.

The over-all assessment was that Harold's disturbance could best be classified as a severe neurosis. There were some misgivings, however, because of the severity of the illness, and one felt that the depth of the anal regression gave a possibly ominous touch to the picture.

Harold's Family

The family was Jewish and middle class; they attended no religious ceremonies, however, and made no religious observances. The father was a successful professional person. Sidney, who was eighteen years old when Harold entered treatment, had decided to prepare himself to enter his father's line of work. He had had many characteristics in common with Harold, including severe learning difficulties; he would probably have gone much further in his education had he been completely freed of his neurosis. The mother was known to us as an intelligent woman with a long-standing preoccupation with physical illnesses of many kinds. She was very interested in psychoanalysis, and she explained that she had had three months of analysis herself, purely out of intellectual interest. The material of Harold's analysis brings out many of the manifestations of her hypochondriacal attitude.

Harold's Infancy

The mother told us that his birth was normal and that there were no difficulties for the first three weeks. But then a circumcision was performed, and the mother felt that the "shock" of circumcision brought harmful changes. Harold began persistent vomiting and looked dreadful. When two months had gone by a diagnosis of pyloric stenosis was made and he was hospitalized for a week. Until he was six months old he was given diluted baby foods and atropin at all feeds. Although the vomiting ceased, he was always drowsy and did not gain weight. Finally, another doctor took him off atropin, changed him to a normal diet, so that by twelve months his weight was normal.

TREATMENT

Although the analytic material had its own uneven course of development, for the purpose of clearer exposition and to make this presentation easier to follow, I will describe it as though it fell naturally into distinct phases. First will be an account of the work done on the anal symptom which led to its rapid disappearance; next I will describe the work done on Harold's relationship with his mother; following this I will present the material on his inhibited competitiveness and ambition. The foregoing made up the first year of treatment. In the second year Harold recaptured his masculinity, and this brought to the fore much of his castration complex and many of the fears which his interest in heterosexuality stimulated. The concluding section will deal with the terminal phase of the analysis and some of the oral material which was revived at that time. It should be understood that in spite of the attention to detail, this paper is a highly condensed report of very rich material, gathered in hundreds of hours of work.

Throughout this account I have tried to describe the work in such a way as to cast light on the two main areas of interest which were studied by the Adolescent Research Group of the Hampstead Clinic, i.e., the factors which enhance the formation of the therapeutic alliance in adolescent patients and the process by which the adolescent loosens the libidinal ties to the parents. Anna Freud

(1958) has laid special stress on this last process in her paper on Adolescence.

The Work on the Anal Symptom

At the beginning of treatment Harold was a small, pale, thin boy with a very worried look. Although he was almost fourteen years old, he looked eleven. He was very anxious to please me and made himself agreeable in an obsequious way. He talked readily and in a constant stream so that it was sometimes hard to follow him in his first few hours. He quickly demonstrated his excellent intelligence and his capacity to express and understand subtle nuances of thought and feeling. As he had done in his diagnostic interviews, he talked easily and with little embarrassment of his "poking," holding up the index finger he used to accomplish the act. He brought photographs of members of his family so that I would know what the people he mentioned looked like, and when he used an expression I did not understand he humorously suggested that I would need to learn his family's "private language." In this and other ways he expressed his strong wish for help, so that the rapidity with which he exposed his pathology and the seemingly undefended and exhibitionistic manner in which he described his main symptom could be understood more optimistically as a positive sign of his determination to use the analysis for constructive purposes. He showed a highly developed sense of humor, which he often used for mockery of himself or authority figures.

During the first week he also brought out his fear of madness. He asked whether there really was such a thing, adding that his mother had said madness was not really madness. My reply to his question was that he wanted me to say there was no such thing; then he could dismiss it from his mind as nothing to worry about.

It was noteworthy that Harold decided in his first few sessions that he would not use play materials, but would sit in the chair and talk. He had a difficult struggle to decide this because he did not want to give up the pleasure of games and he was aware that talking would lead more directly to his conflicts. He was surprised when I did not decide the issue for him. I had said that he could bring toys or games to his sessions if he wanted to do so and that the main thing was whether bringing them was a help to the treatment; if it did not help, then we could change our minds.

By the fourth week a number of features of Harold's pathology had come into the analyis. These included his intense jealousy of his brother and his fear of his own destructive wishes. Most prominent was the pathologically close tie to the mother, especially in matters relating to body function and illness. This last factor played a part in the unusual way which Harold chose to give up the anal symptom, the "poking."

His mother went away to be with her own mother who was gravely ill. Harold promptly went to bed with an obscure illness. The main symptom of this illness was a temperature of 98.4 degrees, which Harold called a fever. (In England the normal body temperature is 98.4 degrees rather than the 98.6 degrees which is considered normal in America.) He told me on the phone that *for him and his mother* a normal temperature was 97 degrees. With such a baseline one can readily see that all Harold or his mother need do to establish themselves as ill was to take their temperatures. I also learned at a later date that Harold's whole concept of physical illness was bound up with the concept of temperature; that boils, for example, did not constitute an illness for him if there was no fever.

Harold was absent from treatment for two weeks. In the middle of the second week his mother returned and spoke with me on the telephone. Her own mother was near death and she felt there was little she could do for her, but she thought she might be able to help her son in his illness. She wondered whether his illness was in some way related to her absence, and I did not hesitate to admit this possibility. She hated to think that Harold could be so dependent on her and assured me that she very much wanted him to come to his analysis. She did not want to force him, but she would do everything in her power short of force to get him back to me. She intended to consult a certain physician who had "saved Harold's life" in infancy when all other doctors could not help. I said it was no wonder that she had such great confidence in this doctor, and I agreed that it was very sensible to consult with him to make sure whether Harold's illness had an organic basis. After this consultation, which showed no physical illness, Harold came every day to his sessions without fail for a month.

At the end of the second month of analysis I learned from Harold that he and his mother had been to a number of doctors to see if they could discover what was causing his stomach pains and fevers. He had X-rays for chest and appendix, and a diagnosis of "grumbling appendix" was made by a famous doctor. Evidently this referred to a chronic, mild condition. During this period his mother would suggest that he stay home from school if he did not feel well; his father took the opposite view and urged Harold to go to school.

When Harold told me about the consultation with the specialist who had presumably saved his life, I took this opportunity to say that he seemed to treat his body with great caution as though it were not to be trusted to do its work properly. Perhaps his overcautious attitude was in some way related to the idea he had told me about, namely, that he had been close to dying when he was a baby. Harold suddenly recalled that when his mother was away on her recent trip he had held a thermometer in his hand and had a momentary lapse in which he forgot that he held it. "Wasn't this an odd thing to have done?" he asked. Two items came to him in his associations to the incident: one was the word "baby" and the second was the thought of being put to bed. I said that he seemed to be treating himself as a mother should treat an ill baby. In response to this interpretation he told me for the first time about his custom of taking toy animals to bed with him so that they would not be lonely. He also brought in more of his difficulties: he feared growing up to be a menial worker like a street cleaner, he feared he might lose control and shout out about his symptom in school assemblies, and he hinted at masturbation.

When one of his doctors suggested an appendectomy Harold became afraid of a sudden attack of appendicitis. He expressed the notion that "something was growing in there" which had to come out. In a sarcastic tone he said that if he went into the hospital, it would be a waste of my "precious time," but this turned out to be a fear that I would replace him with another patient in his absence.

In the tenth week of his analysis Harold informed me about the detailed plan for the surgery: *he and his mother would be operated on at the same time in the same hospital.* He seemed pleased rather than disturbed at the prospect, and I called this to his attention. He explained that he was pleased because his mother would have recovered from her breast operation (for a cyst) first, and she could come to his room to turn on the TV set. Also the surgery proved that his father was wrong because it showed there was truly a physical rather than an imaginary basis for his complaints, and he had the word of a distinguished surgeon to prove it. I made an over-all interpretation at this point, saying that the operation gave him a victory on many fronts: it proved his father wrong, it kept him close to his mother geographically and psychologically, it would keep him out of school which he hated, and, finally, it would satisfy that part of him which wanted to hinder the analysis.

Harold laughed and said we would have to reject that part of himself which created hindrances, but I replied that, on the contrary, in treatment we had to accept that part and talk about it and understand it; if we did not, it would be even more resentful and make more trouble for us. For the first time he spoke of some of the ideational content which accompanied the act of poking. It made him very anxious and worried, he said. "I am trying to find something, there is something there; I'm afraid my bowels have lost their strength; I'm trying to discover something." I interpreted this last notion as a derivative of early childhood, that when he was little his backside was a mysterious place because it could not be seen and he had been curious about what was there.

The next day, for the first time, Harold wondered what would happen if he gave up the poking. He was very anxious as he said this, and I remarked that he feared he would lose both me and the treatment if he lost his trouble; I added that I was interested in all of him, all of his worries and troubles, not just this particular one. He added another fear to his long list. He was afraid that it would be too late, there would be no cars to drive, pathetically showing his anxiety that it would be too late to recapture his lost masculinity.

In the next week, which immediately preceded the appendectomy, his castration anxiety was intensified and came into the treatment in a meaningful way. The surgeon had promised that Harold would change after the operation, and Harold was afraid that he would change in the active, masculine direction; this was a danger because it meant leaving home. He feared that the surgeon might slip, he might cut up to the heart. (I said this would hardly be a slip.) He mentioned a number of internal organs which might be damaged, including his bowel. I called his attention to the fact that he had listed a number of organs inside the body which might be injured, but he had left out the organ which was on the exterior of the body and closest to the place where the incision would be made. Harold's next thought was about the broken television set at home. "I am deprived of my major entertainment," he said. It was at this point that I directly interpreted his castration anxiety, saying he was afraid the surgery might damage his penis.

Harold blushed profusely and expressed one aspect of the peculiar representation of the body which had been built up in his mind. He said: "That [the penis] is part of the bowels, isn't it? I'm all muddled up." He went on to explain how he had arrived at the notion that the penis and bowels were connected. His reasoning was that "there is water in diarrhea; and there is a white, sticky stuff, half way between milk and butter [semen]; they are both liquids and I thought they were all the same." I said the white, sticky stuff sounded to me like what was usually thought of as coming out of the penis. Harold blushed again and said he knew that, but it wasn't what he had meant. He could not elaborate further.

The next day he started to speak of his serious illness in infancy, supposedly caused by "circumcision shock." He had great difficulty in saying the word "circumcision," but after several minutes of struggle he could articulate the word. I asked him what he meant by circumcision, and in his reply he ran into even more trouble. Finally, with long pauses between words, he said: ". . . they take . . . they do . . . a bit of skin . . . off the penis." After a long silence he said he was experiencing a recurrent feeling that others were somewhat lifeless or unreal, a kind of reversal of depersonalization; to this I said that he probably got this feeling after some especially unpleasant thought. He said, "If you're unreal, it's because I don't trust you with my secrets yet," and I replied that if I were unreal, I could not be dangerous.

The following day was the last before he left to go to the hospital. He returned again to his fear of being changed by the surgery, against the fear of masculinity and activity. "If I give up poking, will I do something else?" he asked. What might this be? "Some action," he replied. In his associations he had difficulty once more, but he could say that a patch of skin might get sore or something might be broken as a result of his actions. At this point I interpreted his masturbation anxiety. I said he had given us a number of useful clues: circumcision meant removing a patch of skin from the penis; he had also spontaneously suggested that the poking was a substitute for some other action. From this I deduced that he was afraid the poking was a substitute for touching his penis and he feared if he touched his penis it might get sore or broken. He looked very relieved and said, "We are going deeper, aren't we? It's not so much around the edges." At the end of the hour we arranged to keep in contact by phone during his stay in the hospital and his convalescence at home.[2]

Harold was absent for three weeks. He came to see me for one hour just before the beginning of the Christmas holidays. He began the hour by saying that he had enjoyed his stay in the hospital, and next he told me he had stopped the poking. When I congratulated him on this achievement he said that he had only been able to stop it because the anesthetic had knocked him out and made him unable to poke. I replied that he left out his own role in the accomplishment and that he had good reason to feel proud of himself if he could stop something which had caused him so much trouble. (He had antici-pated giving up the symptom in the hour just preceding the surgery, specifically because of the anesthesia.) In subsequent associations he wondered whether he ought to start taking laxatives because he was "doing only half as much" since the surgery. It was like coming in fourth rather than third in a race. Since he had previously told me enviously about Sidney's enormous bowel movements, I verbal-ized his competitive wish, to outdo his brother with larger bowel movements.

One might partially reconstruct the genesis of the anal symptom in the following way: under the pressure of severe castration anxi-ety Harold gave up his pubertal, phallic masturbation when the increased instinctual tension that characterizes puberty had only

2 Although the link between the poking and the masturbation seems very obvious, the cautious exploration of such connections is especially necessary, it seems to me, in the treatment of adolescents. The transference of ideas of parental omnipotence to the person of the therapist is particularly dangerous to the formation of the therapeutic alliance when the theme of the analysis is masturbation. I was very careful to show the patient the reasoning on which I based my interpretation, trying thereby to reduce the danger of transferred omnipotence.

begun to exert its inexorable pressure. (We do not know whether this masturbation led to seminal emissions or not, but the reference to "white, sticky stuff" suggests that this was so.) The renunciation of phallic masturbation was accompanied by a zonal regression to the anal level, with stimulation through the anus as one of its manifestations. It is important to note, however, that there was no *conscious* pleasure in this source of stimulation, and the activity remained entirely ego alien. This last factor was probably the essential feature which distinguished Harold's neurosis from a perversion.[3]

An interesting possibility as to the locus of the regression arises, however, if we consider Harold's confusion about what was inside and outside the body. As mentioned, he thought the penis was part of the bowels and that the white, sticky stuff and diarrhea were all the same. It may be that he was able to gain a kind of unconscious pleasure which was not completely anal in its nature, but retained a connection with the phallic function. I refer here to what Fenichel (1945) calls "collicular sexuality." Fenichel writes:

> If passive men, in whom passive and urethral tendencies are predominant over active phallic ones, are questioned as to where they feel the most intense sensations, they answer with about equal frequency: at the root of the penis, at the perineum, or in the rectum. What they actually refer to is *a point that is not accessible from outside* and that is equidistant from the root of the penis, the perineum, and the rectum. This point lies in the prostatic part of the urethra and corresponds to the embryologically important seminal colliculus. Much of what is supposed to be anal and urethral sexuality in men is in reality collicular sexuality [pp. 82-83; my italics].

I stress this possibility in an effort to account for the unusual body image Harold had constructed, that is, it was a representation of the body which attempted to explain to himself how the poking produced not only anal sensations but sensations from an inner area which was not visible and could only be investigated through the formal study of anatomy. The conclusion he drew, that the bowels and genitals were part of the same system, was a logical inference from the sensory evidence available to him. I hope that the material and formulation I have presented may have some relevance for a

3 Suggested by Anna Freud when this case was presented at the Hampstead Clinic.

neglected problem, what Eissler (1958) calls "our ignorance about the psychology of orgasm."

The Work on the Pathological Tie to the Mother

In the next phase of the treatment Harold's relationship with his mother occupied the most prominent place.

Before the appendectomy I, of course, had strong suspicions about the mother's role in arranging it, especially since I knew that she had procured an unnecessary appendectomy for Sidney some years before. When I presented this portion of the analysis to the Adolescent Research Group of the Hampstead Clinic, several of my colleagues suggested that some kind of work with the mother might have forestalled the acting out. But my own feeling about this question was based on the assumption that contact with the mother might endanger the analysis and the long-range goals which analysis ought to have. With hindsight, I can say that I reasoned in the following way: First, no matter whether I was successful or unsuccessful in preventing the surgery, both Harold and his mother would hold my efforts against me for a long time. Secondly, any contact with his mother on this issue might reduce the feeling of independence and maturity which my concentration on Harold provided. Finally, an active move on my part might well be taken by Harold and his mother as an attempt to rupture the powerful tie between them rather than allow the son to loosen it gradually, and spontaneously, and at his own pace.

Before the operation I had discussed the plan for Harold's hospitalization with his mother on the telephone. She made a significant slip of the tongue: she meant to tell me that while the surgeon examined the boy he could really feel something; instead, she said, "He could really *feed* something." I thought this indicated the possibility that she had an active pregnancy fantasy which she had displaced to her son. Another instance of the displacement of her preoccupations was suggested when Harold told me that he was taking cold compresses for his stomach pains, at mother's suggestion. Her physician had prescribed the compresses for her own pains and, in her view, it was appropriate for Harold to have the same treatment. For a fuller account, derived from simultaneous analysis, of the methods by which a mother can communicate her anxious preoccupations and wishes to her child see Hellman, Friedmann, and Shepheard (1960).

After the operation I learned that the mother had gone to extraordinary lengths to bring about the surgical symbiosis, as it were. The doctor who had done her operation had been consulted five years before to do an appendectomy on Harold. He had refused on the grounds that the operation was not needed. This time she persuaded the specialist for whom she had great respect to refer Harold to another noted surgeon, one who was inclined to do appendectomies. When her own surgeon learned of this arrangement, as he was bound to do, he became very angry with the doctor who had referred Harold to another surgeon. The net result of these complicated negotiations and maneuvers was that all the parties involved no longer spoke to one another.

Throughout the analysis I was especially alerted to those aspects of Harold's relationship with his mother which interfered with his achievements, with going to school, with work at school and work in the treatment. On his fourteenth birthday his mother suggested that he miss his therapeutic hour in order to go to the opera. Harold arranged matters so that he could do both things, saying he had decided to come to his hour because otherwise "you would say I was trying to get out of things." With this expression of his positive attachment to me I felt he was safely established in analysis. He told me that he had not been able to do much schoolwork during his long absence, but he had done a little French with his mother. I remarked that he could work if he did it together with his mother, but work on his own seemed dangerous because it meant growing away from her.

A few weeks later when I suggested that he use his family doctor about some boils which were troubling him, he said that his doctor did not treat boils properly, he only lanced them. He and his mother had a private joke about the doctor: they called him "Sir Lance-a-Lot." "Wasn't it funny to think of this man as going about with a big pole?" he asked. At this point I made the interpretation that *he and his mother maintained their close intimacy through various illnesses and that he had taken over his mother's attitude toward his own body and made her attitude his own.* (I lay special stress on this interpretation and the response to it for in looking backward at the course of the treatment I thought it was the most crucial of the first year of analysis.)

"Don't I get anything nice from my parents?" Harold asked angrily. I said that I knew he got many nice things from them, but in the treatment room, naturally enough, the disturbing things came to the fore. He vigorously resisted my interpretation through most of the hour, but at the end he said, "My argument is really camouflage,[4] isn't it? You are always right and after I leave I agree with you." My reply was that his feeling that I was always right came from his attitude toward his mother. I reminded him that he felt she was always right and that she was an expert on psychotherapy as well as all things medical.

Next day he began with a long, drawn-out account of a military game he had invented. This made little sense to me until he asked whether an army driven out from its motherland could someday fight their way back. I then saw that he referred to my interpretations of the previous hour and I said that he felt my remarks drove him away from his closeness to his mother, that on this issue he felt like fighting me.

The Work on the Inhibited Ambition and Competitiveness

Throughout the treatment it was necessary to pay careful attention to the particular manner in which Harold had distributed his aggressiveness. Even a partial liberation of his aggression in the early days of the analysis showed that his passivity was an exaggerated character defense against a vaulting ambition and an intense, jealous competitiveness.

In the fourth week Harold noticed a small spot of plasticene on the floor and wondered what had gone on in the room. He recalled that his brother had once hit his therapist and had called him funny names at home. He had not called him names to his face, of course, said Harold. I interpreted this material as an expression of his fear that he might do something hostile or destructive to me. Soon afterward he began to come to his hour two or three minutes

---

[4] The use of the term "camouflage" was Harold's contribution. I had used other language in making interpretations of the defensive process. It was typical of his active intellect and the mental work he performed on my remarks, to give an idea his individual stamp, showing thereby how he made use of interpretations in his personal world.

late. The purpose was to avoid seeing the patient who preceded him, and he was very annoyed when the bell rang while he was still in the room upon the arrival of another patient. He could admit anger only with the Clinic, not with me, for making such faulty arrangements. "A therapist," he said, "should make the patient feel there is no one else he is interested in." It was very interesting that he could admit jealousy of his brother on the oral level, but phallic jealousy was explicitly negated. In his words: "If mother gives Sidney more chocolate, I am jealous; but I am not jealous because he can drive a car or because he is going on a trip to the Continent."

There were many instances of inhibited activity at school, repetitive failures to accomplish what should have been easy for him. For example, although he took great pride in his mathematical ability, he had an intense dislike of the teacher, and he would sabotage his efforts by deliberately doing his exercises in a different and shorter way than she had suggested. He would then make simple, arithmetic mistakes and be marked wrong for them. Finally, he would salvage his wounded pride with the idea that the teacher was anti-Semitic or had a prejudice against boys and favored the girls in his form.

His reasons for avoiding various school subjects were interesting and selective. He hated biology and stayed away from it because one had to cut things up. There were also sexual dangers in the study of biology because reproduction was discussed. Chemistry came too close to his anal preoccupations, and he complained bitterly about the stinks and anxiously about the danger of explosions. Homework was intolerable to him because he maintained a sharp split in his mind between home and school; the two areas of his life should have nothing to do with each other. He blamed much of his inactivity on laziness, and it came as a surprise to him when I interpreted his laziness as an inhibition stemming from anxiety. There were numerous opportunities to interpret his passivity as a defense against his destructive wishes. I had to say many times that in his mind activity of almost any kind was linked with destructiveness. It was only after months of work in this area that material directly related to his competitive feelings toward his brother and father emerged clearly, and in what follows I will try to give suitable illustrative examples of the process.

Harold mentioned one day the plan his brother had to join

father in his work. Harold feared there would be an explosion because Sidney was so openly critical of father and this generated heated arguments. Next day he started to tell me about his father's intention to buy a certain small car; he began to say it was a better car than a Morris Minor (which I owned at the time), but in the middle of the sentence he changed the content and said it was more expensive, rather than better. I pointed out that he knew I drove a Minor, and he had stopped himself from saying the other kind was better out of fear that I would take this as a critical remark. Even the suggestion of hostile criticism scared him. Harold laughed and said it was funny, but he did have to hide things sometimes in order to feel safe.

On another occasion he talked about his games at home. He played "Attack" and other military games. "Why do I play war?" he asked. "Is it my killer instinct?" I said that what he called a killer instinct probably meant being very angry with someone. He recalled that he did sometimes get very mad at Sidney, and he remembered that he had once tried Judo on a boy and had almost hurt him. It was easy to damage people, he thought, especially oneself, and he said that sometimes he feared he would commit suicide by throwing himself off the train. My interpretation was that first one was very angry; then one felt guilty and frightened; this in turn was followed by turning the anger on oneself in the form of suicidal thoughts. On the following day he could not remember what we had talked about, and he spent a good part of the hour trying to recall the content of our discussion. He could understand that whatever it was, it must have made him very anxious to have raised up such a powerful protective barrier. He finally recalled that he had been talking about his anger with Sidney and his so-called "killer instinct." After much work of this kind he told me that his mother thought he was more "explosive" and that he now shouted and argued sometimes the way his brother and father did. Several times I had to lean in the other direction and point out that there were other ways of defending one's rights besides shouting. I could point to his treatment sessions, for example, in which he was able to argue with me without shouting or exploding.

It is noteworthy that the suicidal thoughts did not come very strongly or for very long into the analysis despite the fact that on face value they represented a grim and possibly dangerous symptom. We did not know that Harold had suicidal thoughts during the diagnostic period; they were first reported by him in the first few months of analysis. The problem with aggression and the pervasiveness of the death wishes did play a prominant part in his material, however, and the continuing verbalization and interpretation of his destructive thoughts in the treatment no doubt reduced the necessity for turning aggression upon himself. Another factor of importance is that Harold's ego was so organized that the secondary process always remained dominant; the suicidal thoughts were truly thoughts, and the problem of impulse control was never a serious one. All of this was in line with his obsessional character formation, in which the delaying power of thought and the importance of thinking as an anticipatory and preparatory function were highly developed.

To defend against his disappointment in himself Harold was full of profuse denials about the impact of his failures on his self-esteem. Either he did not care about the failures or he glorified them because they satisfied his wish to frustrate his teachers. With persistent interpretation of this defense he was able to bring out his true feelings. To him, "learning equaled cheating"; the good marks which one student got meant that another was deprived. When this was interpreted as a derivative of his competitive feelings toward Sidney he responded very seriously that it was true. Sidney had only passed three GCE exams (these were examinations for the General Certificate of Education) and if Harold passed more exams than this, it would make his brother look stupid, it would make him "nothing." Both brothers knew their I.Q.s, and Harold derived much gloating satisfaction that his I.Q. was a few points higher. Harold also kept a jealous watch on the monetary value of gifts or services which he and his brother received. An accordion for Sidney was balanced by braces on Harold's teeth; a motorized bicycle had to be compensated in his mind with a gramophone of equal value; and so on.

He complained bitterly one day about showing off. Was it not terrible that people showed off so much? Perhaps, he wondered, he was too inhibited to show off. With the interpretation of an active wish to show off, he mentioned for the first time his wish to go to a university. But with this came his doubts and fears as well. Suddenly he complained that his school was terrible; the pace was too slow and the teaching was awful. How could a boy get anywhere if the school itself was so bad? And the next day he complained that in his marks for the past term he was twenty-third out of twenty-eight in the form. He was crushed. He had boasted about how good he was, yet when the marks came he was near the bottom. I pointed out that since he had only begun to do any work at all in the past few weeks, his teachers could hardly know yet that his attitude had changed. In addition, he had much catching up to do. Frankly, I said, I was glad he was so disappointed in his school standing for it meant that he could admit that he cared and could therefore do something about it.

He spoke of some good marks he had got and wondered why he told his father only the bad marks. When I interpreted his fear of father's jealousy, I added that his father had not gone to a university. Harold adopted a humorous, Cockney accent and said: "E'd get the shock of 'is life if I came top." We both laughed at this, but I added that this was another example of the link between his hostile wishes and the idea of achievement for he felt that coming top would give father a shock. He reflected a moment and said it was true, he did have the thought that his father might die of a heart attack if he shocked him with high marks. He said, "Imagine I'm a boat going at half speed; father is standing on deck; suddenly I speed up and father goes overboard." (It was interesting that the idea of competitive success had first been expressed in displaced form some months before, when he had thought his chief rivals in school might die of heart attacks.)

Harold's next thought was about a boy in school who was failing and would have to leave soon; this other boy did not work and always messed about. Strangely enough, now that Harold was exerting some effort to do well this boy encouraged him to work as though he gained something from Harold's success. "Was this not similar to the kind of pleasure which parents got from their children?" I asked. He admitted that his parents did encourage him. Suddenly he recalled that his father's mother had left father and an uncle in danger under a totalitarian government. They escaped through the lucky accident that grandpa had been a British subject. I related this recollection to his fear that mother would leave him stranded if he did well. Certainly, I added, as he grew up he would lose his mother in a certain sense, but he would get more from her in other ways. He thought about this for a few minutes and then replied: "I've been thinking about what you said about my fear of losing mother; maybe I poked to stay close to mother, hoping that if I stayed in the lavatory long enough father would get impatient and say, all right, stay home."

Next interview he said that he had mentioned getting some good marks to his father for the first time. He added, "You said I was afraid of losing mother and since then, for the first time,[5] I put my 'family' away in the cupboard. I didn't take the toy animals to bed with me last night." He had sat on the edge of his bed and argued with himself to put the animals away. He liked to imagine them as being alive, and he feared they would be lonely. I said this must have taken a lot of courage, and I congratulated him. Harold thought my praise was exaggerated, that I was "putting it on." I reminded him that he had felt the same way when his father praised him for getting good marks.

By the end of the first year of treatment, despite occasional oscillations in his moods and attitudes between grand fantasies of great achievement and hopeless feelings of worthlessness and disinterest, he had developed a positive attitude toward school and began to work. He had developed what he called "form spirit," that is, some identity of interest with the boys in his form. Monday morning and the return to school were no longer a torment to him. He was not so afraid of fights, and instead of staying in the library during lunch break he played football with his schoolmates. He began to do at least a little homework, whereas previously he had maintained a sharp split between home and school in this respect. He was less provocative with his teachers, and his worry about the teacher's anti-Semitism had disappeared from the scene.

There was also a corresponding shift in his attitude toward his mother's hypochondria. He now spoke of her "supposed" illnesses and no longer took her complaints at face value. I felt that his changed attitude represented an identification with his father's skep-

[5] The phrase "for the first time" appears often in this report. It is one of the special rewards of work with adolescents that so much in their lives is new and fresh to them, and change is so rapid.

ticism in these matters as well as a certain degree of libidinal detachment from his mother.

The Recapture of Masculinity

Toward the end of the first year of analysis Harold began to bring material about his sex life. The topic was ushered in with great anxiety and confusion about menstruation. When I interpreted his fear that the blood was proof of woman's castration, his thoughts shortly afterward turned to his fear that his genitals had been damaged by mutual masturbation with boys at school. With distressing anxiety and great resistance he persuaded himself to tell me that he masturbated himself. He greatly feared my disapproval when he confessed that he rubbed his penis while watching wrestling on television. And he brought numerous examples of his primitive, sadistic conception of intercourse and the confusion which derived from it. Intercourse was dirty and wicked and dangerous. "The sperm sticks its nut into the egg and the tail drops off." He thought that people have intercourse only to have children; that since his parents had had two children, it meant that they had had intercourse only twice. When I interpreted the defensive aspect of this notion, Harold said: "Blimey, if what you say is so, I have much more to look forward to in growing up than I thought."

It was noteworthy that throughout the treatment Harold had always been keenly aware of the action of his superego in producing resistances, guilt feelings, and anxiety. Interpretation of the strictness of his conscience often succeeded in eliminating resistances. It may be a significant factor for understanding the ease with which he joined forces with me and for the stability of what he regarded as our collaborative relationship that the superego was a highly structured and differentiated agency within his personality. Many of the special difficulties which arise in the analysis of adolescents may stem from the diffusion of guilt feeling in a form which does not allow interpretation to have a tension-reducing effect. In Harold, by contrast, there was unusual awareness of his feeling of guilt, the ability to express it in diverse ways, and he was usually able to recognize and speak of the particular impulse which generated it.

At the end of the first year of analysis, partly in reaction to the school examinations and partly because of the coming holiday separation from me, there was some revival of anal material in the analysis. The wish to outdo Sidney in the exams had an anal competitive aspect, for Sidney often boasted about his large bowel movements and often jokingly commanded members of his family to stand clear when he was about to enter the toilet. Harold recalled at this time that when he used to poke he would think the words, "Come out of there, you," as though his stools were alive. In the same week he spoke of Sidney's analysis and how it had not succeeded in helping his brother to do well in school. Later he expressed ideas of a kind of anal castration, e.g., doing well in school meant making a big bowel movement and that a big bowel movement might be too much; some of his insides might fall out. His grandmother had died, so he had been told, because of "tangled insides." But despite the profusion of this anal-sadistic ideation, the zonal regression which his poking had represented did not again take place.

The Progression to the Phallic Level

Returning from the long summer holiday Harold showed in unmistakable fashion that he had regained the phallic level of libidinal development and was struggling with the anxieties and impulses appropriate to it. He told me about some of his intense, loving feelings toward a girl tennis player whose face had been beautiful to him. He was careful specifically to exclude interest in her figure. He spoke of his temptation to dance after he had watched his brother dancing with a girl, volunteering spontaneously that he was afraid of dancing because it made him think of sexual intercourse. And he went into considerable detail about his new interest in astronomy which he had developed as a sublimation of his scoptophilia.

This astronomical interest also brought with it a great deal of knowledge about optics, the laws of light, and the function of lenses, as well as curiosity about the stars. He set about building his own telescope, and for several days I was able to fill in some of the gaps in my own knowledge of optics. But one day Harold came to treatment, sad and dejected, and sat silently brooding. At last he told me that he had broken a new and valuable lens which was to form a crucial part of the telescope. It had fallen out of his bicycle bag. When I suggested that perhaps there had been some unconscious reason for the accident he replied that he had thought of that, too. "Sexy looking," he said. With much resistance he went on to explain that when a person looked at the stars from a roof top it was not very hard to tilt the telescope downward and look into someone's window. Then there would be the possibility of seeing a pretty girl undressing. I said that it was not only the heavenly bodies he was interested in seeing, and we both laughed heartily at this.

Next day he began with a long discourse on space travel, on the question whether man could escape from the solar system, and on related scientific matters. For example, man had made amazing progress lately and might soon reach the stars. But how then would the space traveler maintain himself, how could he keep warm and fed? In response to this I said that such matters made fascinating subjects for speculation, but in the light of what we had been discussing the day before, his new-found interest in girls was worrying him because it took his interests outside his immediate family, that is, outside his personal solar system. He wondered, therefore, where this interest would carry him. Harold laughed and said, "*These* interests certainly have to be outside the family."

It was notable now that in leaving his therapeutic hours he often bounded down the stairs full of energy, whereas in earlier stages he had impressed me with his slow, burdened gait.

With the return to school in the autumn he was again exposed to the presence of girls and his castration anxiety intensified. When I interpreted his fear for his penis directly, saying that his established interest in girls made him realize how valuable his penis was to him, he said after a moment's reflection, "I just thought that if heaven is for rejoicing and people can do what they like, people must have intercourse there all the time."

He soon afterward began to talk about homosexual dangers, and there were numerous occasions when it was necessary to interpret his oscillations between homosexuality and heterosexuality for their defensive quality. Returning to the subject of girls, he told me about a new girl named Nancy who had entered his form. As he talked about her he suddenly licked his lips, explaining that he still tasted some chocolate he had been eating before his session. When I remarked that he felt Nancy was rather sweet, he laughed. But he returned to the subject in the next hour and very seriously thanked me for saying that he liked Nancy. "That was very helpful," he said.[6] In succeeding sessions he brought out a number of ideas and emotions which are enlightening for an understanding of adolescent development in general and adolescent patients in particular.

He told me one day that he had drawn a picture of Nancy in art class and had been astonished and delighted when the other girls had crowded around him to admire his work. As he told this his mood suddenly changed; he looked very embarrassed and uncomfortable and wished he was not so inhibited. He went to the couch behind my chair for the first time and sat on it. Hesitantly he told me how he had started what he called "penis rubbing" over a year before after a sexual escapade with another boy. He had much trouble telling me about an obscene joke involving fellatio which his brother had related to him and his father. His discomfort continued at our next meeting, and I suggested that he might use the couch to make talking easier. As he probably knew, I said, this was what adults did in analysis. He replied that he would not want that, he would rather sit it out and talk "man to man." He feared that once he lay down he would not get up. My reassurance that we could be flexible about the use of the couch failed to reassure. He mentioned people who did peculiar things, and this was associated with the couch. He feared that his refusal of the couch might have offended me. He compromised with the notion that there might be times when he would want to sit on the couch and he added that if he ever wanted analysis later he could lie down; "Now I'm a boy and I can enjoy sitting up."

He went on to speak of his feelings about love. Since I told him he liked Nancy his thinking had changed and he no longer thought of falling in love as a kind of dangerous madness. It used to be that he watched other boys flirting with girls and he had dismissed such behavior as silly, stupid, and foolish. "I used to think about women abstractly," he said. "I thought I would marry and have children and that would be that. Now it's more real and instead

6 It is noteworthy that on several occasions when Harold expressed gratitude for an interpretation, my remarks had to do with his defenses against forward moves of the libido. He had, for example, been very grateful when I was not taken in by his protestations of laziness and had introduced him, so to speak, to his own ambition and his wish to excel. In the struggle between the progressive and regressive forces in adolescence the ego gratefully welcomes a progressive ally.

of thinking about women in general I can think of a particular woman. It was too frightening before; now I'm up and coming." When I interpreted his last remark as a reference to his emissions which had been a source of anxiety to him in the past, he responded: "I'm really in adolescence now; it's frightening now that it is beginning. But you are my ally, aren't you?" I assured him that I was. Later in the week he packed up the toys which he had been keeping in his bedroom cupboard and put them in the loft. He felt very sad "saying good-by to childhood," as he put it. In the week which followed he decided to move out of the room which he shared with his brother into a room of his own. It took him many weeks, however, before he could implement the decision and complete the move.

A series of dreams, transference reactions, and fantasies, which made their appearance over a period of several months, showed the line of libidinal progress. This phase of the treatment was heralded by the recognition of his severe reading inhibition, an inhibition which was all the more incongruous because of his excellent vocabulary and his precise use of language for expressive purposes.

Harold dreamed that he was "in a room with a woman; I took off her clothes and had intercourse." He thought the dream was in some way linked with his reading problem. He began to say that in the dream the woman had a penis, but he could not say the word "penis" and went on struggling to say it for the better part of an hour. He moved to the couch where he continued the struggle and was finally able to utter what he called, half jokingly, "the sacred word." On the next day he reported that he felt less inhibited after this difficult session. He had allowed himself to use the word in his imagination and ask the woman of the dream whether she had a penis. He had been surprised when she said no.

Soon after this he admitted that he had never truly imagined sexual intercourse before with the penis going into the vagina. Since his next associations were about fighting and how silly it was to fight and get your head bashed in, I interpreted his fear of the vagina as a damaging organ and his notion of intercourse as a battle. A few days later he masturbated with the fantasy of possessing his brother's girl friend. While masturbating a third time he suddenly stopped himself out of fear that he would suffer a heart attack from too much masturbation. He also fantasied that his brother might stab

him in the back. I confined my interpretation to the guilt he felt
for imagining that he took his brother's girl away; he thought this
was a stab in the back and he feared retaliation in kind. Later he
returned to his fear of intercourse, saying the penis might go in, but
not come out. With partly conscious wit, he added, "I might come
to a sticky end."

At about this time it became necessary to move the place of
treatment from the flat we had been using to the main building of
the Hampstead Clinic, on Maresfield Gardens. He was shocked at
this news and tried hard to figure out what the move meant. He
speculated that Freud's money was running out and the Clinic was
contracting rather than expanding, on the assumption that the Clinic
was financed by a legacy from the founder of psychoanalysis. Most
of all he was angry and disappointed because he felt the move lowered our status. He felt that I treated him in a flat, in rooms separate
from the Clinic, because I was especially important, a more valuable
and powerful object than his brother's analyst had been, and therefore a greater potential source of good things. I interpreted his disappointment as a transference of feelings he had once had toward
his parents when he discovered that their omnipotence was tar-
nished.[7]

Midway in the second year of therapy Harold's marks at school
were higher than they had ever been. He set up two of his male
teachers as ideal figures. One was a young and easygoing history
teacher, the other a strict physics teacher who was a hard taskmaster.
Harold had great respect for this man and wanted his approval desperately, although he tried to hide his positive feelings by grumbling
about the difficulty of meeting the teacher's demands. When the
teacher assigned Harold an essay on Galileo he went through agonies
of anxiety about it and brought numerous rationalizations for not
doing the work. He thought, for example, that Galileo's life was a
warning to him, namely, that if one made discoveries it led to per-
secution. Since in the same hour he had also voiced some curiosity

[7] Anna Freud (1954) has published several instances in which the analysand's faith
in the power of the analyst was shattered by a rude blow from reality. In one case,
the fact that a bomb fell in the same street as the analyst's house was the instrument
which destroyed the illusion of omnipotence, for the patient had thought of the
analyst as invulnerable.

about myself and my family, and had spoken of the couch as a bed, I interpreted his fear of making discoveries and showing curiosity as a derivative of his earlier wishes to see and understand what his parents did in bed, now revived in the transference. After considerable material of this kind he finally settled down to work and completed an excellent essay on Galileo, the great discoverer and inventor of the telescope. He also admitted that he had allowed himself to look at the breasts of some of the school girls. "I started with the face," he said, "and I've got to the upper half of the body. I suppose the lower half comes next." It was typical of Harold that he reported his new-found freedom in looking on the same day on which it occurred, without the delay which adolescents often find necessary.

Parallel with these events his relationship with his parents underwent radical changes. He began to argue with them over everything. His mother's ideas he found particularly stupid, and although he had previously introjected her notions (and especially her hypochondria) *in toto,* he now rejected them absolutely. She had formerly put his stamps into his album for him; he now found this to be intolerable meddling. When I interviewed his parents some time later to discuss termination of treatment with them I explained to them, and to Harold when the occasion arose, that his rejection of them was a natural adolescent phenomenon, intensified because of his excessive dependency in the past and by the splitting of love and hate in the treatment which made me the totally good figure and his parents almost totally bad.

Harold had also overcome enough of his castration anxiety by this time to contemplate dancing lessons. His decision to learn dancing came immediately after he had related a fantasy in which a prehistoric monster devours a small animal, which I had interpreted as his vagina dentata fantasy. He became very frightened when he saw a television version of Ibsen's *Ghosts* in which a man inherits syphilis. When he had a nosebleed he thought it made him feminine because it was so much like menstruation. Finally it became clear that his concentration on girls' breasts derived from his need for reassurance about castration, i.e., they had something sticking out, too. "They even have more than men," Harold said.

Material on the Oral Fixation

I will here describe some of the analytic material which derived from Harold's oral fixation. The partial analysis of this resulted in a further freeing of libido which may stand him in good stead when the time for the choice of a love object is real rather than fantasied.

Harold began to grow pubic hair. He did not mention this change for some time, but he let me know about some of the customs in his family which had influenced his scoptophilia. It was customary, for example, for the males to go about the house naked, to bathe and shave with other males present, and never to close the bathroom door except to keep out cold. Mother had the right to enter at any time, but the door was closed when she used the bathroom. When Harold became unreasonably irritated with me for using the word "genital," it could be seen as a transference from his brother and father who exhibited big genitals to him and made him feel small—that is, when I used the big word for the genital it produced the same feeling in him. I learned only later that it had been customary for Harold to ask his father to shampoo his hair; with the growth of his own pubic hair he stopped this practice. In a frightened tone he said, "Dad might want to wash that hair, too."

The birth of my daughter disturbed the course of the analysis for a time because I had to cancel one and a half weeks of the analysis. Harold showed little reaction at first, but when I did not answer his questions about the name of the little girl he became progressively more annoyed. "What difference does it make?" he said. Jenny, Joan, Elizabeth—or Jupiter, the name did not matter and I ought to tell him. I interpreted the intensity of his curiosity about the name as a displacement of his curosity about what little girls were made of. His use of the name "Jupiter" suggested that he wanted to know if girl babies were truly born without a penis or whether it was later removed as he so greatly feared. He suggested that I needed analysis, not he, that I was "crackers." He said, "It's in your power to tell me, and you won't." He threatened not to tell me some important things if I continued to deny him the information he wanted. He tried to strike bargains with me and he threatened to use what he called "self-analysis." I interpreted the disproportionate extent of his anger and related it to old disappointments when he had felt excluded from his parents' secrets. He compared my withholding the name of the little girl with reading a thriller and coming to the last page to find it missing. What a frustration not to know the name of the criminal!

Several days later he recalled his anger with me and the tense situation which it had maintained. He said he had not forgotten his feelings, but had decided it was not worth it to be so angry because he needed treatment too much. He wondered whether I would have stubbornly continued to hold out on him if he had refused to talk, or would I have terminated the treatment. I said he had allowed himself to feel genuine anger toward me and was now afraid I would reject him in retaliation. He agreed that analysis without anger would stem from a false avoidance.

What seemed most interesting to me is that many adolescents develop similar transference feelings of jealousy and fears of retaliation, and this is often the basis for premature terminations of therapy and abortive beginnings. Spiegel (1958) has commented on "the preponderant role of action and acting out" in adolescence and on "the abruptness with which a shy, action-inhibited adolescent can turn to violent action." In Harold's case the significant difference was that he found the means to express the affect in words and to minimize the acting out.

It was shortly after this sequence of events that the oral fixation manifested itself in a form which was amenable to interpretation. He reported that he had been frightened when he looked at the bosom of his brother's girl friend. When I inquired further about the looking, he dramatized a kind of aggressive stare, with his mouth open. At the same time he made a biting motion with his teeth. When I remarked on the equation between biting and looking he saw a link between this aspect and his fear of reading. He began to bring a chocolate-covered biscuit to his sessions, and he spent the first few minutes of each hour quietly feeding himself. He had a dream in which the word "cream" appeared, and when I asked for his associations to this word he recalled that his father had once told him that sperm was carried in a milky fluid. He had had the idea then that the man sucked the woman's breast to get the necessary milk for his sperm. I reminded him that he also enjoyed the masturbation fantasy that the girl sucked his penis. He was able to accept my remarks at this point, although several weeks earlier when similar content had emerged he had strenuously rejected interpretation.

He arranged to go to dancing lessons during a school holiday, and this took a great effort of will for Harold. As the day for the first lesson approached he grew more and more anxious. What could one say to a girl? He did not know how to kiss a girl. It was senseless to begin dating anyway because one could only go to cinemas and coffee bars. There were gangsters in coffee bars and how could he defend himself against a gang of toughs? It was better to be a girl, he thought. Here I interpreted the projection of his own jealousy onto other boys and the consequent fear which made the feminine condition seem less dangerous. He had a dream before the first dancing lesson: "A girl had spots—a peculiar disease of the eyes." He associated germs and impregnation with disease and spots. He feared he would have an erection while dancing. And he thought his brother's advice—which was to walk aggressively across the dance floor and pick out a girl—was like being urged to be a bull charging across the floor and pinning the girl to the floor. I interpreted the disease in the dream as a punishment for aggressive looking and for the wish to impregnate a girl, a germ for a sperm, so to speak. I added that dancing was in fact very different from intercourse in spite of the unconscious equation between the two activities; and I said I hoped he would enjoy himself. After the dancing lesson he was delighted with himself because he had overcome a long-standing ego restriction. In his libidinal enthusiasm he went on to speak of his guilty wish to attend "A" films and strip-tease films where he could see even more. (In England an "A" film is restricted to adults because of the possibly harmful content for children.)

Shortly after this it was necessary to broach the subject of termination. My stay in London was soon to be over and the depth of Harold's relationship with me plus the gains he had made led us to believe that transfer to another therapist was contraindicated.

Soon afterward Harold almost decided not to "mess about with boys," i.e., not engage in mutual masturbation. But, since he had not put this resolve to the test of actual temptation, he was not sure he could make it stick. "You might *say* you won't eat an ice

cream cone," he said, "but you can't be sure until you see one."
He reflected on the dangers to his masculinity which stemmed from
his sexual interest in boys. He became very uncomfortable and after
some inner struggle he brought out his curiosity as to whether girls'
breasts were hard. He tried to press against them surreptitiously
in school, and there was one girl in particular whom he enjoyed
rubbing against. I said he wondered if breasts grew hard like a penis.
He recalled "an old childhood idea" (using a phrase I had often
chosen for making interpretations) that when he was three or four
years old he had thought there was a tube in the breast, surrounded
by fat. When I commented on the reassuring quality of imagining
that a woman had a penis at least somewhere on her body, he went
on to say that his mother had told him many times he had almost
died because he did not get milk from her; he had thought all babies
were born boys; they stored up milk and grew a penis; the ones who
were meant to be girls got less milk.

I said this complex of related ideas accounted for a large part of
his grudge against his mother. She had fed Sidney more milk and
made him bigger and more masculine. I could also understand
now why he was so angry that Sidney had had three years of analysis
while Harold got two; this meant to him that Sidney was fed more
once again, and I too was a bad mother to his way of thinking.
"Do you think I hated my mother?" Harold asked. If so, why had
he wanted to stay near her so much and clung to her? I answered
directly, saying that he had wanted to cover up his hatred and make
sure his death wishes did not come true.

Harold complained that Sidney was the bad one, while he himself had always been especially good. My interpretation was that
excessive goodness is the best concealment for hatred. He wondered
next whether he had ever hated his father, momentarily forgetting
that he had expressed his aggression toward his father on numerous
occasions. He remembered that he had always liked to have his
mother to himself. When this was followed by the recollection that
his father had told him about the milky stuff which carries the sperm
I made a general interpretation of his orally colored oedipus complex, saying that he had been jealous of both of his parents; that he
had imagined them feeding each other comfortably while he, the

little Harold, whose survival and masculinity depended on getting enough milk, was left out in the cold.

At the end of this hour Harold was philosophizing about the wonders of nature and the overwhelming mysteries of the universe. I thought it an interesting phenomenon, prominent especially in adolescents, that he mixed philosophical speculation and grand ideas with primitive notions of infantile sexuality.

On the following day he mentioned that he wanted to join the group of older and bigger boys at school who fooled about and playfully pushed the girls, making thereby a partly hidden exploration of the girls' bodies. And a few days later he said: "Since you told me about the milk and intercourse I'm not so afraid of girls."

The Termination of Treatment

In this last section I will describe Harold's reaction to termination, the problems which were aroused by it, and the way it was dealt with.

I had chosen to drop a hint about termination some weeks before making a definite statement about it. He had mentioned the organized games at school which his treatment kept him from joining. Although he had always been delighted because he missed games, he now speculated that he might like them. I said that his treatment was not as crucially important now as it had been when he started, that if he missed a session for sports now and then it would not matter so much. "So we will be stopping soon," he said. He said he had hoped to continue for another year until he took his GCE exams; he feared that if he stopped analysis, his ability to work would also stop. I was his "engine" and I made him go. He turned to other topics, but later in the week he began to recall his old symptoms and to review the gains he had made. For the first time in almost a year I heard material with anal content when he spoke of his dislike of strange toilets. With the coming holiday he would have to use strange toilets again. When I remarked that he thought of unfamiliar toilets as dangerous he suddenly recalled an incident on an airplane some years before. With severe tension and anxiety he told me that he had been suffering from diarrhea then and he had been traveling home from a holiday with his mother. He disliked the toilet on the plane and feared he would soil himself. His mother had given him a sanitary napkin to put in his pants in case he lost control of his bowels. He appeared terrified as he told me this, and I said he had feared his mother was turning him into a girl. In succeeding sessions he spoke a great deal about menstruation, the sight of blood in the toilet, and his unconscious idea that each time there was menstrual blood in the toilet it meant that mother was drowning a baby. This theme was unconsciously linked with Harold's fear of swimming, and it was interesting that after the connection was interpreted Harold resolved to take swimming lessons for the first time.

When there were ten weeks remaining I told Harold I would be leaving the country at the end of the school term. "All good things must come to an end," he said. He recalled instances of similar disappointments. For example, when he had become interested in popular music the disc jockey who ran his favorite radio show left the air a few months after Harold started listening to him. When I interpreted his anger with me, especially for leaving him no choice in the matter, he moved to the couch and was silent. He said he was fighting off tears. I stressed the positive aspect of ending treatment in his case, saying that in the not-too-distant future he would have begun to withdraw his interest from me and the analysis of his own accord. On numerous occasions I interpreted his over-evaluation of me in the transference, and I stressed the importance of investing more of his feelings in friends and activities which belonged to his age.

After several days he said he had three questions: How much could be accomplished in the remaining two months? Would he "slide back" after we stopped treatment? And would he have any contact with me afterward? I thought all of these questions were very relevant to the situation.

A few days later, on a Friday, he asked whether I had said that his homosexuality was a thing of the past. I was sadly mistaken if I had suggested this, he said, and he launched a long, detailed account of his current mutual masturbation with boys. Among other things, he wrestled with them and then this led to rubbing each other's penis through the trousers. One of his friends had called him a sex maniac because he did not stop the activity as soon as the friend wanted to. What Harold wanted me to say was whether these activities were right or wrong. He persistently demanded an answer. At the end of the hour he said, in an especially challenging tone, "Well, what do you say?" I replied that we had to know more. Returning on Monday Harold began his questioning again: Was it "right or wrong" to mess about with boys? I then made a general interpretation of his appeal to me to remain in London. I said that partly he was genuinely concerned about his homosexuality, but the most important thing he was saying at the moment, it seemed to me, was that he was a poor, little kid who did not know right from wrong or how to control himself, almost a sex maniac. I was to go home and tell my wife that I had made a serious mistake and we would have to change our plans; there was a boy here in London who needed me to stay on.

Harold laughed with pleasure at this interpretation, but his anger continued unabated for some time afterward. He told me that he had very seldom even felt unwilling to come to his sessions. His next, half-humorous, thought was that I was going to America to be sent up in a rocket. (John Glenn, the astronaut, had just completed his travels in space the day before.) I remarked that Harold felt particularly hurt and rejected by my leaving him because he had been so willing to come to analysis. For such ingratitude I deserved to be sent into permanent orbit.

It was at this stage that he brought the oral material described earlier.

Harold now began to report progress on many fronts. He had decided to ride full-fare on the buses instead of half-fare. With anxiety, but with great pride, he told me of the growth of his pubic hair. He bought clothes in considerable quantity, whereas previously he had paid no attention to them. White shirts were very important for him to have, partly, I believe, in identification with me. His voice broke and he delighted in the croaking sound it made. He had to go to the men's section of the clothing store for he was now too big for the boys' department.

He continued to work on his anxieties and the ego restrictions these forced upon him. He had always done poorly in French, for example, and he thought it was because the language frightened him in some way. (It should be noted here that in a much earlier part of the analysis, when he had complained that he disliked French because the word endings changed irregularly, I had interpreted this as a derivative of his castration anxiety; that is, the changed word endings reminded him of his fear that women were born with a penis and only later changed in their "ending." At that time my interpretation produced a powerful resistance and he had been convinced I was utterly mad.)

Now he recalled that when he was much younger he had been very good in French; he remembered a French class from his latency period in which a story was told about a little girl who had lost her puppet. I said that this recollection showed all the more convincingly how the changed word endings were linked in his mind with the notion that little girls lose something. He mentioned for the first time that he sat at the rear of the French class with a boy who distracted him from the work. He pretended astonishment when I said French would be easy and enjoyable for him if he were not too frightened to study it. But the next day he changed his seat in class, moved up front, and reported that he was finding the subject more interesting.

He devoted his attention to his fear of swimming. This had always been a problem and his summer holidays were partly spoiled every year by his fear of the water. Now he arranged to take swimming lessons. As the day for the first lesson approached he was very anxious; his sleep was troubled and he had disturbing dreams. His main fear was to have his head under water. But there were other aspects which roused his anxiety. He thought bathing trunks were symbolically like a contraceptive; in that case, I said, it meant he thought of his whole body as a penis. All his exhibitionistic fears and wishes were brought to the fore and he listed all the dangers to be found in and around the swimming pool. He might get an erection and be embarrassed. He might see too much of the girls. He might be too scared and not enter the pool at all; the others would be critical of such timidity. He found when he did go to the pool that he enjoyed the water and allowed himself some activity.

But his fear of putting the head under water remained. As we discussed this, the fear gradually narrowed down to a horror of having water in his nose; this was a vile and terrible feeling, he thought. A little later in the same hour he was preoccupied with his fear of what would happen to him after termination of treatment.

He wanted a photograph of me so that he could look at it when problems arose and imagine what I would say. I interpreted his wish for my picture as a product of his aggression: the picture would reassure him that I was not destroyed. He wondered if he would forget me. Sometimes, he said, his feelings welled up in him, inside himself, one after the other. He would get into a daze at such times. He gestured with his hands in front of his abdomen, indicating with successive movements of his hands, how the problems welled up and overwhelmed him.

I suddenly recalled his history of vomiting in infancy and I interpreted his horrified reaction to water in the nose as a derivative of the helpless and suffocating feelings he must have had as a child when the stomach contents rose up and overwhelmed him. Harold's response was to exclaim: "That's it, that's exactly it." He thought I should get the Nobel prize for this interpretation, expressing in this admiring way his pleasure in what he felt was a particularly clever or insightful interpretation. He could also see that his fear of forgetting me and of forgetting the things he learned at school was also partly derived from his early illness when he could not control what stayed inside and he persistently lost what his mother gave him.

As the end of the treatment approached the tension which built up around termination served to intensify his anxiety about the end-of-term school examinations, which coincided with the last weeks of treatment. We spent part of several hours going over his exam papers, and he used me to bolster his self-esteem and confidence. He felt that if he could take the exams without spoiling them, and without developing somatic symptoms such as diarrhea, it would prove that he could get along on his own. Much analytic work was devoted to going over and over his competitive feelings toward his father and brother which were displaced to his rivals at school. His rivalry with his brother was most intense and because of the powerful aggressive wishes which had been so long repressed he still feared that his guilt feelings would drive him toward failure rather than success.

In the physics exam he did very well, for the first time being top of his form, many percentage points ahead of his nearest competitor. He was delighted with this result, but typically had to pretend at first that he almost failed before springing his surprise on me. The fact that he had come first reminded him of his oedipal wish to be first with his mother and called forth all the fears of his brother's and father's jealousy which had kept him from work and study in the first place. Nevertheless, he was full of ingenious plans to present the results of the exams to his parents in such a way as to create the greatest possible astonishment. His results were: first in physics and history; second in English and mathematics; third in Latin; and eleventh and twelfth in geography and French, respectively.

Despite these fine marks he was very uncertain that he had the ability to go to a university. Although there was a severe scarcity of university places in England, I said I was absolutely sure he had the necessary ability; the only question in my mind was whether he could, or would, apply himself. He thought my remarks were very encouraging and a little later he said I was his "encouraging half." To this I replied that he felt he and I were one. He had felt the same way about his mother, who also encouraged him and from whom he had been inseparable. "Do you mean inseparable, or that I behaved as though we were?" he asked. When I said that an example of their closeness could be seen in their simultaneous hospitalization, Harold said: "That was pretty extreme—if I could have maneuvered that, there must have been many more examples." I said that this also had a bearing on the extreme rejection of mother which he was showing at the moment: he had been so close that now he compensated at the other extreme. I added that this also accounted, in part, for his overvaluation of me.

On another day in the same week he spoke of the confidences he had given to me. He thought that only in marriage could there be a comparable intimacy. He compared his feelings for me with that of a spouse. I added that perhaps he wished we were married, as he had wished to marry his mother. Then divorce and separation would be hard to arrange, we would be more likely to stay together.

The Last Week of Treatment

At the beginning of the last week of analysis Harold developed an intense resistance. He discussed his interest in attending a university in great detail, and it soon became clear that he used this genuine concern as an avoidance. What finally emerged as the source of this resistance was this question in his mind: how do girls mastur-

bate? Boys have a penis to rub, but what do the girls do? He struggled
for a good part of the hour before he could say that they put their
finger into their vagina.

The next day he sat silently in his chair for a few minutes. He
then began to strike one index finger against the other in a repetitive
way. I said that he probably meant by this behavior that he wanted
to continue with the topic he had brought up the day before and
Harold smiled and agreed. Since the finger he was demonstrating
with was the same index finger he had showed me in the first week
of therapy, the "poking" finger, I interpreted the long-disappeared
symptom as a product of his anxiety about his sexual wishes. The
finger in the anus stood for the finger in the vagina. By retreating to
the feminine position, by imagining himself as a girl penetrated in
intercourse, he had felt safer. Harold asked: "Did I wish Dad out of
the way?" I said that with the awakening of his adolescent sexuality
the old oedipal wishes that belonged to his childhood had been
rearoused as well. The wish to be rid of father was terribly frightening to him, and to be a woman or a girl in imagination seemed much
safer because it removed him from competition with, and death
wishes toward, his father.

The next day he discussed his masculine-feminine conflict at
length. He had thought of my idea about the poking as a representation of his feminine fantasies before I had uttered it. He wondered
if he would ever be able to settle his oscillations between masculinity
and femininity. I said this was a problem in growing up which everyone had to settle in his own way in time. I knew he had made a
start in this direction and now that he was fully aware of what the
problem was it would help him in his struggle. "The only thing
left now is termination," said Harold.

I thought it was fascinating that the material on the basic symptom appeared so clearly in the last week, almost two years after treatment began. It was as though the ego kept careful watch on the
course of analysis, reserving the last week for this last bit of material
in a calculated manner that seemed more like secondary-process
functioning than the primary-process of the unconscious.

Harold was very sad and tearful on the last day. When I compli-
mented him on his hard work in the analysis, I added that I was
glad to have had the chance to work with him in such a productive

way. He said my compliments only made him feel worse. "I suppose that's because I'm so angry about your leaving," he said. He finally decided that he wanted me to send him a photograph of myself and I agreed that I would.

DISCUSSION

Although I had originally planned to discuss a number of theoretical issues which are aroused by the material of this case, the length of the paper is already too great. Furthermore, the general psychoanalytic theory of adolescence which Anna Freud (1958) has put forward in recent years formed the theoretical framework in which the treatment was carried out and this paper is readily available.

On two issues, the special difficulties of forming the therapeutic alliance with adolescents and the problem of loosening the libidinal ties to the parent, Harold's case offers some useful information.

The manner in which Harold formed his positive relationship with me runs counter to numerous observations made by other therapists and analysts. Once he had established the tie to me he used the analytic method as a progressive rather than regressive opportunity. It is important to note that he did not leap precipitously into treatment, and it took almost three months before he allowed aspects of the crucial id contents of his neurotic symptom to appear in the analytic material. These emerged slowly over the whole course of the treatment with a logic and internal consistency one finds more readily only in adult analysis. It was a very mature and highly organized ego which functioned in this way, an ego with a highly developed self-observing function. The self-observing function also allowed Harold a great deal of pleasure in the discovery and observation of his defenses, what he aptly called the "detective work." The neutralization of what was clearly a strong scoptophilic drive probably played a role here, but whatever its source, this made analytic work a positive pleasure for the patient without leading to an oversexualization of the transference and all the difficulties such oversexualization brings. His attitude to my interpretations generally was such that I often said to myself and colleagues that Harold was "made" for analysis, as though his personality had been specially created to use the analytic method. If we follow the analogy made by Anna Freud in another context (the discussion of certain types of cases who make limited use of analysis), in which she compared analysis to a full-course dinner which is offered to the patient, we can think of Harold as a very hungry patient whose appetite could absorb even the most exotic and frequently indigestible psychoanalytic courses.

Although his readiness to cooperate in the treatment seemed at times too easily won, the notion that this feature derived only from his passive and homosexual attitude would be, I believe, mistaken. Such a view is based on the observation that adolescents often flee from treatment because of their fear of passivity. Harold, on the other hand, was afraid of activity rather than passivity, so that the necessary degree of acquiescence, acceptance, and surrender of autonomy was available to the treatment without producing panic reactions. Anna Freud (1951, 1958) speaks of the "fear of emotional surrender, with the accompanying fear of loss of identity" as a deep and troublesome anxiety in adolescence. Despite Harold's intense bisexual conflicts, the sense of identity was clearly established in him in the desexualized plane and the fear of loss of identity only manifested itself, in my opinion, at that point in the treatment when he prepared to give up his identification with his mother.

In the thirty-sixth week of treatment, after having clearly made the break with his mother's hypochondria and turned his critical attention upon her many odd ideas about body function, Harold reported a "strange and eerie experience." He had been walking across the street, had seen his shadow, and felt "I was looking at myself for the first time." At that time I said it seemed strange to him because few people ever spoke of this feeling; but I added that it was an important step in growing up because it meant he could now feel himself more separate from his mother and was not afraid of thinking of himself as a separate person. I thought this was a typical adolescent experience in which the new sense of identity paradoxically gives rise to a feeling of depersonalization and estrangement.

Another important factor which favored the establishment of the therapeutic alliance was the suffering that Harold experienced from his neurotic symptom. It caused him great discomfort and psychic pain, and it interfered with many areas of his life. He clearly wanted treatment and could express his wishes for cure verbally in his diagnostic interviews. As Ernest Jones (1953) has told us, there is probably no substitute for suffering as a motive for analysis.

The intense jealousy of and competition with his brother, Sidney, displaced from the oedipal rivalry with the father, also served as a spur to be a model patient and outdo his brother in this way. He also admired his brother and felt he gained a great deal from his own treatment. To invest himself in analysis, for Harold, was one more aspect of his efforts to model himself after his brother.

Finally, and this may have been the most important factor of all, Harold's mother, whom he loved and with whom he was so closely identified, always maintained a strong intellectual interest in and respect for psychoanalysis, her ambivalence notwithstanding. Harold had always had heart-to-heart talks with his mother and confided his worries to her. He brought out in treatment that he felt she was a kind of psychotherapist and in the beginning for a time he even compared her technique with mine. With her support, therefore, no conflict was created by Harold's devotion to analysis and his hard work pleased her, especially in the early phases.

One last issue: many analysts and therapists hesitate to subject adolescents to the demands and infringements which intensive treatment produces. What they are especially wary of is the regressive force that analysis unleashes, which for many patients in the adolescent phase is felt to be a weight on the wrong side of the balance between progression and regression. We might more carefully consider our assessment of adolescent patients with the idea that once a regressed state is clearly established by the young patient in an unsuccessful struggle, and he is openly and consciously aware of the regression, he is much more likely to welcome the therapist or analyst as an ally. (The therapist, of course, must come down firmly on the side of progress, but with tolerance of the regression.) Following Freud's (1916-17) famous simile, in which he compared the movement of libido in fixation and regression with the advances and retreats of military forces, we may say that it is in those conditions where the libidinal armies have not yet given up ground, when the terrain is obscured, and the battle situation is confused, that the young patient is likely to mistake the therapist as an enemy and the offer of help as an attack.

BIBLIOGRAPHY

Eissler, K. R. (1958), Notes on Problems of Technique in the Psychoanalytic Treatment of Adolescents. *This Annual,* XIII.
Fenichel, O. (1945), *The Psychoanalytic Theory of Neurosis.* New York: Norton.
Freud, A. (1951), A Connection between the States of Negativism and Emotional Surrender (*Hörigkeit*). Paper read at the International Psycho-Analytical Congress, Amsterdam, August 1951. Summary in *Int. J. Psa.,* XXXIII, p. 265, 1952.
—— (1954), The Widening Scope of Psychoanalysis: Discussion. *J. Am. Psa. Assoc.,* II.
—— (1958), Adolescence. *This Annual,* XIII.
Freud, S. (1916-17), *Introductory Lectures on Psycho-Analysis.* London: Allen & Unwin, 1922.
Hellman, I., Friedmann, O., & Shepheard, E. (1960), Simultaneous Analysis of Mother and Child. *This Annual,* XV.
Jones, E. (1953), *The Life and Work of Sigmund Freud,* I. New York: Basic Books.
Spiegel, L. A. (1958), Comments on the Psychoanalytic Psychology of Adolescence. *This Annual,* XIII.

AN ATTEMPT TO FORMULATE THE MEANING OF THE CONCEPT "BORDERLINE"

SARA KUT ROSENFELD and MARJORIE P. SPRINCE

(London)

While the material in this paper has been worked out and formulated by the two authors, the content is based on the studies undertaken by The Group for the Study of Borderline Cases, the members of which are Miss Agnes Bene, Dr. S. Fahmy, Miss S. Ini, Mrs. M. Kawenoka, Mrs. H. Kennedy, Miss A. Schnurmann, Mrs. M. B. Singer, and the authors.[1]

The Group has worked hard to develop a corporate form of thinking based upon exchange of experience and the actual thrashing out of individual thoughts about cases. This paper has been frequently presented to the Group and benefited from the stimulating and often controversial discussions. We intend that it should serve as an introduction to more detailed clinical studies undertaken by other members of our Group.

We have noticed a very wide divergence in the use of the concept "borderline" even among those of us with similar training and approach. We have been asked whether we use the term to represent a disease entity in itself, or whether we are referring to a group of children in whom the disturbance resides mainly in the ego and is characterized by disturbances of ego functions which for us indicate a specific condition that must be distinguished from the neurotic or psychotic illnesses.

The aim of this paper is to bring together our conclusions and recorded findings related to borderline features in the children we have studied. We hope that this will help us to indicate more precisely what we mean by the term "borderline."

[1] We would like to thank Mrs. A.-M. Sandler who has spent some considerable time clarifying Piaget's work for us.

Together with others writing about these children, we have found that the quality of ego disturbance and its variations are of greatest significance for each individual case, but these factors do not, in our opinion, adequately explain the etiology of the disturbances. Influenced by Anna Freud's unpublished papers on borderline states (1956, 1957), we began to direct our attention to a specific aspect, namely, the capacity for object relations, and especially the precarious maintenance of object cathexis.

We think that the development of the whole personality hinges on this capacity for maintaining object relations, and that further study along these lines may enable us to pin-point with greater accuracy some of the areas in which the borderline child can be recognized and differentiated from the psychotic.

The literature on childhood schizophrenia is voluminous and the reader is referred to Goldfarb (1961) for a comprehensive bibliography. We shall not mention again writers included in this bibliography unless their work has been of specific concern to our study.

Particularly pertinent to this paper have been contributions by Anna Freud, Elisabeth Geleerd, and Robert Knight. We shall refer frequently to A. Freud's unpublished papers on borderline states (1956, 1957). Geleerd's paper on borderline states (1958) aims at establishing certain categories of diagnosis, while Robert Knight (1946, 1953) has stimulated us to study more minutely those borderline characteristics which might distinguish our cases from psychotic patients.

Most other writers whose work has formed the background of our thinking concentrate on schizophrenic and borderline states as a whole. These authors include Ekstein and Wallerstein (1954, 1956), Freeman, Cameron, and McGhie (1958), Rank and MacNaughton (1950), Weil (1953, 1956). David Beres in "Ego Deviation and the Concept of Schizophrenia" (1956) examines his material specifically from the point of view of ego functions, their interdependence and interrelationships, and he suggests that this will enable the clinician to apply "to the child's clinical manifestations the measures of ego development and other aspects of dynamic psychopathology." He, like Geleerd, emphasizes the difference between child and adult patients in that the "ego deviation in the child is related to disturbance of the growth process."

Mahler and Gosliner (1955) draw attention to the unstable primacy of phallic development which gives way to either anal or oral features. According to these authors, this occurs when these children whose object representation is regressively fused with the self meet the problems and demands of the phallic and oedipal stage, namely, when the child is confronted with the ultimate need to separate from the love object. This paper further helps to distinguish between those children whose disturbance is due to arrest of development and those whose illness is determined by the degree of regression.

M. Katan (1950) maintains that regressive processes are responsible for the state of his patient. Specifically, the "loss" of the oedipus complex and the central role attributed to the bisexual conflict are emphasized. Katan concludes with the provisional statement that "schizophrenia results from the schizophrenic's incapacity to solve the problem of bisexuality in harmony with reality."

Papers by Frankl (1961), A. Freud (1945, 1952), S. Freud (1911, 1920, 1924), Hartmann (1939, 1952), Hartmann, Kris, and Loewenstein (1946), Kris (1939), Sharpe (1940), and J. Sandler (1959, 1960) will be referred to later.

It is clear that many of the cases we consider to be "borderline" would by others be considered to be frankly psychotic. It is also likely that children variously described as psychotic or otherwise deviant might be regarded by our group as "borderline." There probably is considerable support for the opinion that most of these children are already showing signs of a clearly diagnosable condition which might be said to fit into a definite category of mental illness. Elisabeth Geleerd (1958) differentiates between malignant, benign, and borderline psychosis, the latter presenting symptoms which might, however, never develop into manifest psychosis.

Over the past four years, we have tried to gather material to clarify our own thinking and this paper is a first attempt at formulation. We have studied a varied group of children, including some organic cases, autistic and symbiotic disturbances, and also some children whose disturbance appears to be on the border between obsessional and schizophrenic illness. The ages range from five to eighteen years. All these children show severe ego disturbances.

It is important to emphasize at the outset that while two of our cases showed features of very minimal brain damage and have been considered as possibly organic, there is no evidence of this in any of the other cases. In all our cases, however, there appears to be something akin to a predisposition which need not necessarily be inborn, although its very early appearance as a defect in the apparatus may lead one to assume that it is.

While it is always possible that future diagnostic tools will spot some physiological disturbance which we are overlooking, we must assume for the purpose of this investigation that we are dealing with psychological as distinct from physiological disturbances.

The selection of the children we have studied was based more upon a negative appraisal than a positive one. It is significant that the symptomatology of all these children could not be made to fit into any of our preconceived ideas of an infantile neurosis, nor are they psychotic in the accepted sense of the word. We became aware that quantitatively increased disturbance by itself is not indicative of a borderline state, since many children with extreme multiplicity of symptoms can fall into the framework of the neuroses. Our cases were brought together because we were forced to acknowledge that we had a group of children in whom the qualitative difference in their psychopathology distinguished them from the rest of our patients. We did not feel sure that illness was in all cases due to historical factors or to trauma. The history of these children does, however, give the impression that they often experience events as traumatic which other children would not experience as such.

We have approached our work with these children from the point of view that while development is still in process and symptomatology is fluid and changing, no firm or final diagnosis should or could be made.

We question whether even a "borderline" diagnosis can in fact be substantiated until after puberty. One might consider that such a diagnosis depends upon the possibility of movement away from the psychotic side of the border toward the neurotic side. It is not clear from Geleerd's paper whether she feels that a diagnosis of malignant, benign, or "borderline" can be reached before puberty.

Our first attempt was to gather material on the common features in the presenting symptoms. It was agreed that all our cases were characterized by a multiplicity of symptoms, anxiety bordering on panic, and poor control over impulses. These symptoms are so noticeable that they are apparent even to the outsider. In addition, some bizarre behavior was almost always reported. Often this was concerned with language characteristics which, normal at one age, would be bizarre at another. None of the children, with one possible exception, had hallucinations or delusions. In all the cases observed there appeared to be a serious disturbance in the interaction between mother and child, a disturbance which could often be spotted in the history. An interesting observation has been that parents of these children do not seem able to give reliable information about early stages and often give the impression of not remembering.

We feel it is significant that several of the children we have been working with have remained in the community, although often requiring special consideration. They have managed to attend schools, falling within the range of normal, or have taken on easy jobs. They come from a variety of homes and vary in their I.Q.s from 80 to 150.

CLINICAL EXAMPLES

Our examples are taken from a small number of cases which most effectively illustrate the relevant points. Our conclusions, however, have been reached as a result of studying approximately ten cases. The children fall roughly into two groups: those who were referred at the onset of puberty and those who were developmentally latency children.

Stanley,[2] aged seven and a half, was referred by the psychiatrist in charge of the High Wick Psychiatric Unit,[3] where Stanley had been sent because he was unmanageable at an ordinary school. He had withdrawn into a world of fantasy, was hyperactive, and spoke in unintelligible phrases confusing pronouns such as I and you. At times he showed uncontrollable behavior (e.g., biting) toward staff members.

Stanley's very strict and young parents considered his develop-

2 This case was treated by Marie Kawenoka.

3 Stanley and Brian (referred to later) are treated as part of a combined project between the Hampstead Child-Therapy Clinic and the High Wick Psychiatric Unit (psychiatrist-in-charge, Dr. George Stroh) for the investigation and treatment of borderline and psychotic children. We should like especially to acknowledge the work of Miss Ruth Thomas in coordinating and advising on this project.

ment normal until the birth of his brother when he was three. This baby, for whom he was not prepared, arrived unexpectedly early, and the father had to deliver it while Stanley was about the house. There are hints, however, that disturbances existed before this time; e.g., there are reports that he cried almost consistently during the night, until he was two years old, while he was unusually quiet during the day.

The main feature in this boy was the undue amount of anxiety with which he was unable to deal. Any new situation, however trivial, was apt to arouse it. Fear of death was pronounced. One of the ways of mastering his anxiety was by attempting to merge with the object, which he did in the treatment situation by checking whether he and the therapist had had identical experiences. Thus he asked whether she ate feces when little, whether she had been to a barber or washed her hair as he did, etc.

Derek,[4] aged nine and a half, came to treatment for bizarre conduct which took the form of behaving as if he were Mrs. Joe, a Dickensian character in *Great Expectations*. This identification was not confined to fantasy play since he wanted to wear women's clothes and dressed up to help his mother with the housework. Derek had had similar phases from the age of two when he was found eating flowers. Later he began playing at lorries and eventually became a lorry himself. In order to communicate with him at that time, or to get him to take food, the parents had to adopt an entire "lorry terminology" so that food had to be called "petrol" and so on.

What had appeared to be a united, balanced family emerged in treatment as a highly disturbed and seductive one, with parental discord and an impulsive, acting-out mother. The brother, three and a half years younger, was a bed wetter and had facial tics.

One of the most striking aspects of this case was the interrelationship between this boy and his mother, and it has been difficult to sort out whether Derek was presenting the therapist with his own or his mother's disturbance. This was closely related to the central theme of Derek's analytic material, which was the re-experiencing of observations of sadistic intercourse. These he had witnessed repeatedly throughout his early childhood, and had continually dis-

4 This case was treated by Agnes Bene.

torted. Moreover, the mother's impulsive behavior together with an intense hostility she felt and expressed toward Derek must be considered as additional traumatic factors.

Derek is an example of a boy whose potentially normal ego was disturbed in its development in the first year of life by these experiences. We have studied this case particularly from the point of view of the quality of the anxiety which characterizes so many of the borderline children and which in this case necessitated the living out of a fantasy until it intruded upon his daily life.

Brian,[5] aged ten years, is the eldest of three children of a mixed marriage which from the beginning had been marred by constant quarrels, violent scenes between his parents, numerous separations and reconciliations, and finally resulted in permanent separation when he was about seven. This necessitated placement in a residential children's home and in turn referral to High Wick Psychiatric Unit on account of hyperactivity coupled with lack of appreciation of danger, inability to relate to other children, and withdrawal into a fantasy world.

Throughout his early childhood there had been feeding difficulties which first appeared when solid foods were introduced. Although he began to talk at the usual time, language was not used for communication and was mainly echolalic. At a later age his confusions in thought and perception were reflected in his speech. His early environment had been chaotic, characterized by constant moves and changes, usually connected with parental quarrels and father's periodic refusal to give financial support. The culminating event was a desperate journey to Jamaica with his mother, just before her confinement with the third child, where Brian was left with relatives who were totally unknown to him, and who physically ill-treated and starved him.

Treatment was started when Brian was nine and a half years old. The main presenting symptoms were hyperactivity and outbursts of violent rages. His speech was stilted, most poignant at times but perseverative and bizarre at others. His voice was low, guttural, and monotonous, devoid of affect.

One of the most striking features of his psychopathology is the

[5] This case was treated by Hansi Kennedy.

undue amount of anxiety characterized by feelings of disintegration, depletion, and loss. In an attempt to deal with these anxieties he has built up a defensive structure geared toward getting a better hold of reality. This defensive structure, although not altogether effective, stands him in good stead, and on superficial acquaintance makes him appear less disturbed than he really is.

Kenneth[6] was referred to the Clinic when he was seven and a half years old after having been asked to leave three schools because of unmanageable, aggressive behavior. Although his I.Q. was 105, he appeared not to know either numbers or letters; his knowledge of the everyday world was almost nonexistent—he did not know his age, his home address, and had no idea about the value of money. He seemed unable to remember what had happened a day earlier. In contrast, Kenneth revealed a very precise knowledge of many things unrelated to present-day reality, such as the prehistoric world, the complicated happenings of the underwater world, and some of the laws of physics.

In treatment it gradually became clear that Kenneth was capable of normal, aim-directed ego activity, initially of a simple nursery-school nature, in which instinctual satisfactions were great and only thinly disguised. These occupations, however, could be maintained only with the help of the therapist's support. For many months Kenneth formed no real relationship with the therapist, except to use her as an extension or substitute for his own ego, as if she were an inner control against anxiety. The need for a supporting object was reflected even in his posture. Whenever he undertook a task requiring sustained effort, Kenneth found a way not only of getting close to the therapist but of literally leaning against her body. To the casual observer, he appeared to be a relatively normal boy. A breakthrough, however, could occur at any moment, often for no apparent reason, or as a result of a slightly upsetting event or failure to provide conditions of support.

At the beginning of treatment Kenneth discharged tension predominantly through the motor apparatus. When an activity was not immediately provided for him or when he was not immediately successful, his motor activity became chaotic; his whole body would

6 This case was treated by Agnes Bene.

become entangled in itself; he would hang upside down from chairs and tables, legs and arms muddled, his head popping up in some unexpected place. He could maintain such tangled postures for unusually long periods without apparent effort. He appeared to have little regard for pain or the possibility of danger. Wild fantasies of being chased and trapped, expressed in a high-pitched voice and slurred speech, accompanied these activities.

Later when the therapist was used no longer as a substitute ego but as an independent individual toward whom he had aggressive feelings, his movements were directed against her in wild, uncontrolled attacks.

The striking features in this boy's symptomatology were his need for support from an outside object, and the manner in which he would "unwind" himself into a primitive chaotic state when he did not get such support or was unable to use it. In dynamic terms, energies, bound with the support of an external object, would gradually "unbind" themselves and become instinctualized, resulting in an inner chaos, which was expressed in bodily form. (We shall refer to this case again in our discussion of the development of action into thought and its breakdown in our patients.)

Albert,[7] aged twelve, was brought into treatment because of an alarming symptom which had commenced at the age of seven after the birth of a younger brother. At that time he had begun to walk on railway lines and through tunnels with complete disregard for all personal danger.

Hints of an early disturbance could be traced back to the age of two and a half when Albert had first started to wander away from home, following the birth of his first brother. Albert's very close relationship to his mother had been interrupted by this birth which, because it and all subsequent births, had been Caesarian, entailed hospitalization for her and separation between herself and Albert. Shortly after the brother's arrival, Albert's father returned home from the army, so that the close union between the child and his mother could never be regained. Albert himself was hospitalized at the age of three, and further pregnancies all contributed to a very severe separation problem. There was marital discord between the

7 This case was treated by Marie B. Singer.

parents centered around the father's suspicions of mother's infidelity and his doubts about Albert's legitimacy. In addition, the father was jealous of mother's love for Albert. This circumstance, together with an admixture of guilt, caused her to deny the nature of Albert's disturbance, and to encourage both his hostility to the father and many of his symptoms.

In treatment it emerged that Albert's entire instinctual life and conflicts surrounding his relationship with his parents were condensed into a single womb fantasy which dominated his whole existence. He felt and acted as if he were a train because his whole body had become a symbol in the service of this fantasy in which he and his father entered the mother's body.

Trains had played an important part in Albert's early life— they were responsible for interfering with his union with his mother, for they brought father home for leaves; in addition, a maternal grandfather had lost a finger in a railway accident when Albert was four.

One characteristic of this boy's material was the regression to early defenses (mainly turning passive into active) to defend against the acute separation anxiety. These defenses covered an even more primitive terror—that he would separate from himself, that mind and body would fall to pieces. The many examples of Albert's terror of disintegration and his attempts to hold himself together through systems based upon fantasies of omnipotence are described by his analyst, Marie B. Singer (1960). For our study the case is significant for its material on that specific type of anxiety.

James[8] was taken into treatment at the age of thirteen when he underwent a change of personality marked by withdrawal from the environment, inability to cope with his schoolwork which had hitherto been reasonably successful, some confusion about his orientation in reality, and overwhelming fantasy activity. He was found to be entirely preoccupied with the world of insects, specifically bees and wasps which dominated his whole life. He read all the books he could obtain in an attempt to discover the composition and action of their stings. He obtained a tremendous amount of knowledge about the life and habits of bees and wasps, but one could observe

8 This case was treated by Sara Kut Rosenfeld.

his faulty reality testing when he maintained that his closest friend "actually claimed to own such a sting himself." This boy was diagnosed as belonging to the group of "borderline" cases, since the picture he presented did not fit into any of the established categories. He showed a multiplicity of symptoms, including obsessional features and phobias as well as severe anxiety attacks when disturbed in his rumination about the insects. Yet, he could also not be classified as psychotic, since his reality testing was disturbed only in this particular area. He was able to take care of his own person, manage his own affairs within certain limits, travel extensively without losing his way, and he continued to live in a community, that is, at boarding school, although concessions were made for his difficulties.

The analysis revealed two traumatic factors. The first was a highly disturbed older sister, believed to be frankly psychotic, who took up the mother's whole attention, and with whose disturbance he identified. The second factor of significance was the departure of a much-loved nurse who had had entire care of him until he was eighteen months.

Although these two factors were of immense importance in the development of his illness, they were not solely responsible for it. The analysis disclosed a symbiotic tie between mother and child which persisted into adulthood and in which both partners were fully involved. This tie has remained inaccessible to interpretation or management.

One can assume that James's ego, possibly already weakened by lack of mothering and the presence of a highly disturbed sister, could not deal with the loss of the nurse at a time when separation from the mother is the central developmental problem.

Arun[9] was an Indian boy of fifteen, with low-average intelligence; there was the possibility of minimal organic lesion which, however, was never medically diagnosed. He was the eldest of four children, was extremely backward, suffered from a congenital speech defect, and was referred because he had been expelled from three different schools on account of truanting, violence, and knife throwing. He was a firesetter.

At the beginning of treatment he was an impulsive, acting-out

[9] This case was treated by Marjorie P. Sprince.

boy, unable at times to exercise control over himself. He reacted with aggressive outbursts to every inner and outer provocation. He was a child who had to express every thought and instinctual impulse in action. In spite of this behavior, however, Arun's reality testing was not disturbed, except in one significant area, that is, where fantasies of his own omnipotence intervened.

During the course of treatment a number of factors emerged. As the eldest son of a distinguished father, Arun was a source of embarrassment to his parents, and shortly after the birth of a young brother he was sent to England under the care of various guardians. The need to deny the irreversibility of his shortcomings and their implications was one of the unconscious motives behind the omnipotent fantasies which disturbed his reality testing. In addition, there were a number of much earlier traumata. Until the birth of his brother, Arun had shared his parents' bed, often sleeping with his mother alone. At the age of three and a half to four, he had experienced a circumcision and a tonsillectomy, both with a minimum of anesthetic. None of the traumatic events in this boy's life could alone be considered to be responsible for his disturbance, but rather the accumulation of traumata upon an ego ill-equipped to deal with such extreme demands.

The attempts to battle with increased libidinal and aggressive urges could be seen in the massive and ineffective defensive system. Whether this boy suffered brain injury at or after birth is not significant for our purposes. His material is important because it indicates the significance of early ego damage in borderline cases.

METAPSYCHOLOGICAL DISCUSSION

Libidinal Development

The attempt to describe our thoughts in this area has caused a great deal of discussion in our Group and it has made us aware of gaps in our knowledge of the borderline child's libidinal state.

Anna Freud, in her paper "Indications for Child Analysis" (1945), discusses libidinal development in relation to the evaluation of infantile neurosis. Among other factors, she points out that "to ensure normality it is sufficient if the bulk of the libido reaches the organization which is appropriate to the age of the child."

The borderline child seemed to present a very different and unfamiliar picture, which was further complicated for us by the differing ages of the children we were studying. As we have said, these children fell roughly into two groups, those who had entered puberty, and those who according to their chronological age could be considered latency children. It was through this natural grouping that we came up against the fact that while biological development seems to influence the appearance of the material, the differences between these two groups of children appeared only to be superficial.

We came to their treatment from the analysis of neurotic children and we still tried to find some order in the material presented, or to discover some predominance of libido development which would be a guide to our understanding. Instead, we noted the presence of material belonging to all phases of libido development creating a confused and highly disturbed picture.

In discussing these findings with us, Anna Freud pointed out that this lack of phase dominance means that the interaction between drives and ego which brings the phallic trends into the service of the oedipus complex is interfered with. There seems to be a faulty relationship between the drives and the ego. At no stage does the ego give direction to the drives; neither does the ego supply the component drives with the special ego characteristics and coloring. It is as if the drives and ego develop independently and as if they belonged to two different people.

Some of the latency children treated and studied by members of our group have been in treatment for relatively short periods. Our impression is that there is little evidence of phallic or oedipal material. The bulk of these children's libido appears to be tied to the oral and anal phases, and object relationships are entirely on the need-satisfying level. These children appear to act immediately upon any instinctual demand. The inability to wait and postpone also belongs to the whole question of their inability to give up the pleasure principle, which we shall refer to again later.

Brian, aged ten, who at the beginning of treatment had lived in a psychiatric unit, gave the impression that his relationship to his mother was comparatively unimpaired and that his longing for his mother had an oedipal quality. It emerged, however, that he used her almost exclusively as a provider of sweets and toys. Just as he related to his mother on the basis of need satisfaction, so he related to the therapist.

His daily visits to the Clinic became important, and he reacted to interruptions just as he did to other changes in his daily routine. Changes aroused anxiety. He talked about his therapist both in and outside the Clinic and gave the impression that she had become an important object in his life. This was probably true in terms of his limited ability to establish relationships. It became strikingly clear that the person who gave him therapy was important, but not as an individual. He usually entered the Clinic, asking, "Where is my therapy?" Once when told about his therapist's forthcoming holiday, he immediately reacted with, "Who will be my therapist then?" Unlike other patients he has not brought any material indicating his interest or curiosity about his therapist's private life, made no comments about her appearance, her interests or activities. He does, however, expect his therapist to wait for him, and not keep him waiting at the beginning of his session, and to gratify his demands— at least on a verbal level.

The first adolescent cases treated were boys who had finally broken down at the onset of puberty. One could trace a history of disturbed development, but their families did not actively seek help until the time of breakdown. The analytic material of the adolescent boys was just as confused as that of the latency children and also presented us with features belonging to all phases of libidinal development. On first acquaintance it appeared as if this group, unlike the latency children, had made a jump to the phallic level. This was largely due to adolescent sexual changes and growing physical maturity which, giving rise to sexual fantasies and problems of adjustment, had their repercussions on the analytic material. In fact, we were mistaken in linking it with phallic development, since this apparently "phallic" material had an "as if" quality about it. We attribute this to the fact that there is at best an unstable primacy of phallic development which gives way to either anal or oral features; that is, phallic phase dominance was not achieved. According to Mahler and Gosliner (1955), this occurs when these children are confronted with the ultimate need to separate from the love object. If we assume that this inability to separate from the mother interferes with the full development of the oedipus complex, we may appear to be suggesting that these borderline children have "lost" the oedipal bond (M. Katan, 1950) before it was fully matured.

At one time we attributed the disturbance of these boys to bisexual conflicts and turned to Katan to help us in their understanding. The position with our children, who it must be remembered are not psychotic but borderline, seems, however, to be somewhat different from those described by Katan. It would be untrue to say that they do not show both negative and positive oedipal manifestations. But it appears that their weak cathexis is due to fixations at the oral level, and also that their oedipal manifestations remain within the realm of fantasy.

One of our cases has been studied in detail from the point of view of Katan's hypothesis. At the time of our examination James, an adolescent, had been in analysis for about two years. There was ample material to indicate both positive and negative oedipal fantasies and a struggle between his heterosexual and homosexual wishes, which at one time we considered to be at the center of his disturbance (as described by Katan). A closer look at this boy, however, revealed that although all the material seemed to be there, what was lacking was the counterpart of these fantasies in his object relationships. Although he formed a close attachment to a girl a little younger than himself, which we thought might develop predominantly heterosexual features, it transpired that this relationship was based on narcissistic identification: that is, identification based on narcissistic object choice (he wanted to be a girl to avoid the threat of castration as well as to become closer to his mother, who, he thought, would love him more if he had been a girl like his sister). When this was analyzed, it gave way to a need-satisfying type of relationship. This has remained the main feature of all his relationships to females as well as to males. Although he does not demand to be physically looked after by the man he is fond of, he does demand constant attention and intellectual "feeding."

We think that this lack of oedipal development—rather than the loss of an essential developmental step—may be one of the features characteristic of adolescent borderline cases, as distinct from the psychotic process observed by Katan. The borderline adolescent's attempt to maintain himself on the phallic and oedipal level as a defense against a strong regressive pull must therefore be differentiated not only from that of the neurotic patient who regresses *from* the phallic phase due to conflict, but also from that of the psychotic patient who loses the positive oedipus complex entirely. On the basis of this formulation it becomes understandable that the phallic and oedipal material of the borderline adolescent has an "as if" quality, and does not really seem to be truly cathected.

It also becomes clear that there is no contradiction between the material of the two age groups. The only difference that exists is due to physical maturation. Both latency and adolescent children have in common the fact that they are fixated to the oral phase and that their object relationships all show the characteristics of this stage of libido development; that is to say, none of them has developed beyond the stage of need satisfaction.

Aggression

Just as we have noted poor control of libidinal impulses, so we have noted poor control of aggressive impulses. All the children we observed had unusually marked problems around aggression. They either showed excessive and uncontrollable outbursts of aggression or the opposite. In either case the ego seemed to have insufficient means of dealing with these conflicts. It has struck us that this may partly have been due to the regressed nature of the aggressive drives as well as to other features such as unusually marked omnipotence of thought, characteristic of prephallic stages, a factor which readily blurs the border between fantasy and reality.

The excessive aggression characteristic of the prephallic stages and the loss of love that the child fantasies as a result of this aggression appear to reinforce the ambivalence which is a feature of the borderline child's object relationships. It also reflects the lack of fusion between sexual and aggressive drives, brought about through object cathexis. This lack of fusion may be significant in connection with the capacity to neutralize.

Object Relationship

Anna Freud, in an unpublished summary of typical features in schizophrenic borderline children, emphasizes a difficulty in maintaining object cathexis which has severe repercussions on the development of their object relationships. She suggests that these children are constantly on the border between object cathexis and identification, and describes how they revert to identification with the object and that this may lead to a merging with the object. She does not think that regression to the symbiotic phase of development alone explains this disturbance. She attributes it to the weakness of a particular function which she suggests remains throughout life. This particular weakness in the borderline child's capacity to maintain object cathexis threatens the intactness of the ego since it leads to a loss of personal characteristics which are merged with those of the love object (Anna Freud, 1952). This can go even further so that the child may fear that his body will change into that of the love object. Thus all his symptoms can finally be understood as a defense against this fear of merging.

We have recorded that this fault in object relations is crucial in the cases we have studied. There appears, however, to be a wide range of these disturbances, varying from those concerned with the concept of the body ego on the one hand, to those concerned with the distinction between self and object on the other hand.

We have chosen as an illustration the example of James because he himself verbalized the feeling at the age of eighteen and thereby confirmed the reliability of earlier evaluations.

The exclusive preoccupation with the sting of bees and wasps, for which James was referred, proved to be due to an identification with the queen bee. The choice of this fantasy was determined by the mother's actual wasp phobia. Thus by assuming the role of this powerful insect whom his mother feared in reality, he defended against his fear of merging with her, which was clearly illustrated at the only joint interview the therapist had with James and his mother. She was struck by the fact that they had to sit close together, touching bodies and holding hands throughout. James was completely passive, hanging onto his mother's words and repeating them as if they were his own. Later, during his session, when this interview was discussed, he said, "When I am with mummy I feel as if we are one."

Arun did not regress to body merging. Yet he had not established full self-boundaries and was still on an intermediate level in which part objects played a role. Objects for him were characterized by their functions and their attributes—and if he could imitate their functions, he hoped to acquire their attributes. He had no real relationship with the object, and he still saw his father entirely in relationship to himself and his own world. Thus he would sit behind the driver in a car, imagining himself to be an important dignitary like his father and waving to an imaginary crowd.

James heard by chance that the headmaster of his old school, a man to whom he was very attached and whom he still saw at regular intervals, was leaving the school and that an assistant master whom he knew would replace him. On this day he arrived for his session, with a wild appearance, looking very disheveled; and when he was able to speak about the forthcoming loss he demonstrated quite clearly that what seemed to matter most was not the loss of a friend but the fear that his needs would not be satisfied. In order to deal with the problem he had to regress temporarily to the stage of development when the function of the object was more important than the object itself. He expressed this by asking whether the new head would use the same room, the same chair and desk as the previous headmaster, and whether he would do the same things the old head had done. Moreover, he was concerned whether the new headmaster would also listen to him playing the piano, which had been a bond between the two, or would he, James, now have to do woodwork, which was the new man's hobby. Finally, he asked, "Will writing to him [the old head] mean he is still real? If I cannot see, touch and hear him, will he still be real? He seems to have merged into bits . . . he might just as well be dead. . . ."

Following the discussion of his anger and his death wishes toward the man who had disappointed him by leaving him in this way, James was able to express not only his angry feelings but also to talk about him again as a whole person whose presence he would miss. Thus, object cathexis was once more established, when he understood that he had to defend himself against sadness by regression.

Superego

We have already referred to the difficulties our children seem to encounter when they reach the phallic and oedipal phase, and we have drawn attention to the dilemma these children are faced with. Their self-boundaries are precariously established, and they easily regress to merging with the object. This wish to merge which at times of severe stress breaks through into the actual experience of merging is, however, also feared since it leads to obliteration of the child's individuality, and much of the child's behavior can be understood as a defense against this merging. In all our patients one can observe a reluctance, and even an inability, to separate successfully the self-from the object representation.

But the development of a healthy functioning superego depends upon the capacity to take just this step. These children sway between object cathexis and primary identification which leads to a merging with the object. If, therefore, we assume that there exists a disturbance in the distinction between self- and object representation, it follows that the capacity for internalization is impaired. This affects the mechanism of introjection which is essential to the building up of a healthy superego.

We are using the concept of introjection as it is defined in the Hampstead Index: "Introjection is regarded as a transfer of authority from the real object to its internal representation." Freud has shown that the development of the superego is linked with the resolution of the oedipus complex and that its formation is correlated with a partial and relative reduction of interest in and dependence on the real parents. J. Sandler (1960) has described the developmental stages of the superego in great detail. He says that

> The major source of self-esteem is no longer the real parents, but the superego. *Introjection* of the parents has taken place, and a structure has been formed which did not exist in this form before. . . . What distinguishes the introject from the internal schema is precisely the capacity of the introject to substitute, in whole or in part, for the real object as a source of narcissistic gratification. This implies that the introject must somehow be developed out of the schema, crystallized and structuralized within the ego, so that it can be given power to satisfy, and be felt by the ego to be a sufficient substitute for the objects. The construction of an introject is thus the sequel of a complete or partial dissolution of the relationship to the real object. Through introjection the *relationship* to the object is maintained and perpetuated, but the real object is no longer so vital to the relationship. It follows that what is introjected is neither the personality nor the behavior of the parents, but their *authority*.

Since the borderline children have not been able to reach the state of successful introjection and have not reached the oedipal conflict, we would expect their superego to be faulty. This does not mean that they do not have a superego, only that it is still to a greater or lesser degree dependent on the real objects. At times we may be led into believing that the child has achieved introjection as we understand it. He appears to have taken over the parents' standards and authority. A closer examination will, however, reveal that the child seems to be assuming the identity of the object and even temporarily to become the object on the basis of primary identification.

Just as the capacity to maintain object cathexis varies in our children, so they appear to be arrested at various stages in superego development.

Ego Development and Ego Functions

Ego deviations in borderline cases and cases of childhood schizophrenia have been widely described in the literature. We are therefore likely to repeat much of what is already known.

Hartmann, Kris, and Loewenstein (1946) describe the ego as a substructure of the personality which is defined by its functions. Freud has indicated that the ego does not develop altogether by modification from the id, but that there is a biological basis inherent in the potential development of the individual. This concept has been further developed by Hartmann (1939), who maintains that the ego develops partly out of conflict between the instinctual drives and the demands of reality, and partly out of autonomous, conflict-free growth.

Since the ego is defined by its functions, its development can be described only in terms of its separate functions. Our Group set out to look into some of the major ego functions and to study these in greater detail. We shall attempt to summarize briefly what we have found:

Perception. According to clinical usage, the definition of perception is the receiving and interpreting of stimuli. This immediately brings to mind Freud's comments (1920) on the importance of the protective barrier: "for the living organisms protection against stimuli is almost a more important task than the reception of stimuli." He points out how essential it is to be able to sample the outer world in small quantities, and that it is precisely this function of the sense organs which characterizes the highly developed organisms. Other authors, studying schizophrenic children, have pointed to a disturbance in this area, but we wondered whether this process could not be further broken down with the help of Piaget's studies. We do not want to go into the details of this study now, but one of the points which has emerged was that our children find it difficult to inhibit stimuli. They seem to get swamped by them, and are unselective in their choice of what is relevant and what is irrelevant. We think that the inability to inhibit and select stimuli, a circumstance leading to distractability as described by Piaget (1936) on an intellectual level, may extend to reactions to emotional stimuli. This would explain the emotional confusion which we have often observed in our children when they first come to treatment. They appear to be overwhelmed by stimuli from outside or inside and seem incapable of sorting them out, which hinders these children from following any one theme. It may be that this incapacity to select and inhibit interferes with the differentiation between self- and object representation. It probably goes back even further and influences the very first step in reality testing, namely, the distinction between what is inside the infant's own body and what is outside.

In so far as we could observe, the reality testing of our children was not unduly disturbed, except that one could at times observe a blurring of the distinction between fantasy and reality, since withdrawal into fantasy and being swamped by fantasy were characteristic features of these children. But when pressed, they would usually be able to recognize what was happening in the external world and what was a thought in their own mind. When discussing this particular aspect, we have wondered whether there may not be a connection between the blurring of the boundaries between fantasy and reality and the blurring of the boundaries beween self and object.

Defense mechanisms (denial, displacement, etc.) of course also interfere with perception. But this can be said of the neurotic as well as the healthy person. What seems to be specific for borderline cases is that projection plays such a great role and turns the world into a frightening place for our patients. It will be remembered that none of these children, with one possible exception, had hallucinations or delusions.

Motor Development. Like perception, motor development is normally an autonomous function of the ego. In our children it has become involved in the pathological process. Almost all of them showed disturbances in this sphere: a peculiar gait, unusual posture, rigidity, or hyperactivity. Lack of modulation in speech was also linked with motor disturbance. Motor actions often accompanied or supplemented psychic communication. We have tended to link this spilling over into the motor apparatus with the tendency overtly to act out fantasies and drive content, and it has sometimes been possible to understand motor peculiarities in that way. At the same time it has to be remembered that affect in the infant is expressed through the entire body. Kris (1939) has described how this process is gradually contained so that the bodily areas through which affect is expressed are limited, until finally only an appropriate signal is required to communicate with the environment. This stage overlaps with the development of speech as a means of making a more subtle contact with the environment.

Speech and Thought Processes. When we first set out to study our borderline children we concentrated on their speech peculiarities. We thought, rashly, that this was a simple matter, but we soon realized that speech was the end result of a developmental process which led back to the establishment of thought. We started to look into the development of thought in each of our children and found that all of them showed severe disturbances.

Unconscious processes are more easily accessible in children than they are in adults. Especially the young child will still have easy access to primary-process thinking, which we would accept as normal. The treatment of latency children has shown us, however, that unconscious material is already heavily defended, and much of the initial work of analysis has to be taken up with defense analysis. This is not the case with our borderline children. As have many other authors describing borderline and schizophrenic children, we have noted the existence of a faulty barrier between conscious and preconscious thinking. A defect in repression enables the patient to have undue access to his unconscious processes, and secondary-thought processes seem to slide over into primary-process thinking with relative ease. Indeed, mechanisms of primary-process thinking can be observed in all these children: the need for immediate discharge, ease of displacement and symbolization, relative disregard for reality, condensation and substitution of parts for wholes. Magical thought, i.e., "egocentric thought" (Piaget, 1924) is also much in evidence. Although some of our children are highly intelligent and capable of complicated thought processes and high-level intellectual work, this appears not to be stabilized but subject to breakdown as the result of tension or anxiety.

Another factor is the tendency toward direct translation from fantasy to action, or from drive impulse to action. It seemed to us that they are unable to contain particular drive manifestations within the realm of thought and immediately seek discharge via the motor apparatus. The Group spent much time on this particular mechanism, and we are in the process of sorting out our work on this subject. Indeed, we began to look at it from the point of view of normal thought development, taking the view that action precedes and is gradually converted into thinking and speaking. It was in connection with this study that we turned to Piaget (1936) for the detailed steps which take place during the first year of life and which he has described so vividly.

The close interrelation between thought and action was clearly demonstrated by Kenneth. His fear and wish to avoid reality are expressed in his defensive preoccupation with matters concerning happenings underground or in the air. These "mental displacements" are frequently accompanied by physical displacements. Thus, under stress, Kenneth often either climbed up onto the cupboard in his therapist's room and stayed there, or he could be found under the table or hanging from the climbing frame, but never on the same level as his therapist. Later on, when he was better able to face reality, he only hid his belongings on top of the cupboard; and eventually it was only the key of the cupboard in which he kept his belongings which was put up there.

Another example of the need to act was Albert, aged eighteen, who tried to convey to his therapist what he had been doing at work that day. While describing how he served tea at a meeting of executives he actually had to go out of the room, knock at the door, serve imaginary cups of tea, and finally collect the cups.

Another aspect to be considered has been described by Ella Sharpe (1940) who suggests that the acquisition of speech which aids the containment of action (as described by Kris, 1939) derives from the capacity to contain bodily products. She stresses that "the activity of speaking is substituted for the physical activity now restricted at other openings of the body, while words themselves become the very substitutes for the bodily substances."

We have been interested in the unusual reaction our children showed toward interpretation. It has been noticed repeatedly that verbalization of an impulse does not have the effect of an interpretation, but appears to be experienced as permissive. For instance, interpretation of masturbation anxiety was frequently found to relieve the anxiety while permitting the patient freedom to act out. When the acting out had been dealt with, another area would be subject to the identical process. We have linked this problem with the "acting" mentioned earlier and also with the possibility that this may be connected with the particular problem these children have around internalization and integration. Anna Freud (1957), in her summary, has pointed out two other aspects which have to be considered: first, the material does not follow as a result of interpretation—it is not produced as a result of analysis; second, in neurotic cases, interpretation of fantasy usually reduces fantasy production, but in the borderline cases, interpretations of fantasies are woven into the fantasy and do not seem to limit its production.

We have found in some of our cases that after a period of treatment the reaction to interpretation of fantasy becomes more like that of a neurotic.

Adaptation to Reality. None of the children were able to conform adequately to the reality principle. Postponement of gratification or indeed the relinquishing of an immediate need for the sake of a future gain were almost impossible for them to achieve.

Although some of our children recognized ego achievements as desirable and expressed a wish to achieve them, efforts in that direction tended to break down because of the domination of the pleasure principle. Thus, meeting the demands of reality caused considerable difficulty, and at least one of our children who is now a young adult has given up the struggle to do so. For him, to be an adult man—to be independent, to hold down a job and earn enough money to support himself, and to have heterosexual relations—is too frightening to contemplate. He wants to remain a "child," if not in age, at least in every other way. This boy, who in the course of treatment had shown his inability to deal successfully with the oedipal and phallic conflicts because of the inherent threat of separation, now broke down as an adult when reality made the demands which he had successfully avoided developmentally. This illustrates Mahler's view of separation as the cause of breakdown. Other adolescents seemed to have coped more successfully with the demands of reality.

Defense Mechanisms. In the course of his development, the normal child develops certain patterns of defense which become characteristic of himself and are resorted to in various situations to form the permanent character traits of the individual. Failure to achieve this results in severe pathology, for the infantile ego has only inadequate means of dealing with anxiety or other stimuli which ought to be warded off. The immature ego reacts to anxiety with a severe immediate response—often by discharge through the motor apparatus or into the soma. Because it has not yet acquired adequate defenses, the capacity for postponement of discharge or for containment of anxiety in thought has not yet developed.

In our borderline children we noted a multiplicity of defenses (one is tempted to relate this to the inability to select the relevant [see above under Perception]) with a predominance of projection, denial, displacement, introjection (all very early defenses), withdrawal into fantasy, and a strong tendency toward regression. Most striking of all is the particularly marked defect in repression—which will have become evident from our observations throughout this paper and particularly from our comments upon the unusual reaction toward interpretation. This was especially noticeable in the beginning of treatment, in almost all our cases. These children brought fantasy material, which is highly defended in the neurotic child, in a relatively undefended and easily accessible manner. This was so marked that we now regard it as a characteristic feature which merits a special technique whereby interpretation of content is avoided until it has become more defended. The handling of these cases aims at facilitating the development of the very defense mechanisms which in a neurotic child one would in fact attempt to undo.

An example of this was James who spoke without reservation of his envy of his father's large penis, but later was enabled to bring identical material in a displaced form when he envied his father's motor car and his capacity to drive it.

Some of our children have had quite pronounced obsessional defenses, such as reaction formation or isolation, which were treated as "normal" in the sense that we did not attempt to undo them since they seemed to serve a useful purpose.

The synthetic function of the ego cannot be studied in isolation, but must be assessed in relation to all the functions of the ego (Frankl, 1961). Its role is to mediate between the demands of the various psychic structures, different functions within the ego, and reality. Evidence of its presence can be found in every thought and action. It must be clear from the foregoing material that this particular function is extremely disturbed in our children. We have wondered whether the opportunity of observing a potential borderline case as a baby along the lines of Piaget would not disclose that this function is highly disturbed already then. Everything that follows—the uneven binding of instinctual energy which leads to the precariousness of neutralization, the sliding from secondary to primary process, the ineffective defense mechanisms, etc.—all these are probably effected by the faulty synthetic function.

Having described the faulty functioning of defense mechanisms and also of the synthetic function, it follows that these children have no adequate means of dealing with anxiety. We think it is generally agreed that even small amounts of tension and anxiety upset their equilibrium. Together with writers about these children, we come across an experience of anxiety which differs greatly from that which we meet in neurotic cases. Borderline children are flooded with a paniclike anxiety which we now think of in terms of sensations of self-annihilation.

Specific Quality of Borderline Anxiety

References have been made throughout this paper to the particular type and degree of anxiety which the borderline child seems to experience. In this section we shall bring together the points scattered in the body of this paper.

The anxiety reactions we observed in both our latency children and adolescents were intense, diffuse, paniclike, and seemed to involve an experience of disintegration and annihilation. It appeared as if the quality of anxiety differed from that of the neurotic child. Though the borderline child, like the neurotic, experiences anxiety as a signal danger, the ego of the borderline child, unlike that of the neurotic, cannot find appropriate measures to reduce the level of anxiety. Signal anxiety is therefore experienced as a threat which may lead to overwhelming feelings of disintegration (Sandler, 1959). Brian, a boy of ten, seems to illustrate this. His therapist, describing his ability to verbalize his feelings of disintegration, says:

At present Brian's main anxiety centers around his ideas of falling apart or breaking apart, and he has on several occasions expressed this most poignantly.

In the eleventh week of treatment he stated, "The trouble with me is that I get too excited. I am like electricity inside me. I have a safety valve and a fuse box." When I took up his wish for adequate controls because getting out of control and becoming too excited was so frightening for him, he replied: "It's like breaking in two—I'll draw it for you," and attempted to make a rough diagram indicating a triangular shape that had broken apart. In the seventeenth week of treatment when I had taken up his interest in washing tiles and exploring passages, holes, and drainpipes in terms of his thoughts about lavatory holes and body openings, he replied: "You are right. You never know what will happen when you sit on that hole—everything may fall out and you'd find yourself being a skeleton with nothing but this bit of skin holding you together."

Brian's fear of disintegration appears not to involve an object at all, but it is solely concerned with the breaking to pieces or falling apart of the child's own body.

We have examined the material in an attempt to understand why these children's egos, though they experience anxiety as signal anxiety, are unable to set in motion effective defensive measures. This has led us to consider the following possibilities:

1. In some of our children, the anxiety seems to represent a re-experiencing of an infantile traumatic situation which took place at a time when the ego was not sufficiently developed to deal with the overwhelming anxiety-provoking stimuli. This may in some way be connected with the observations we have described under Perception, in which we found that some of our children have difficulty in inhibiting and selecting stimuli.

Derek, aged eleven, repeatedly enacted scenes representing the sadistic primal scene which it is believed he observed as an infant. His rather striking facial immobility and his dead-still body when "he cast his mind back" might be the dramatization and reliving of the immobile panic-stricken state he found himself in when he observed his parents. His chaotic, sadistic states and movements might express his identification with what he, in his confusion, experienced as mad and sadistic adults.

2. All our children show defects in the maintenance of body ego and self-boundaries. As we have already described, they easily slip into primary identification which arouses their fear of loss of identity and might contribute to their feelings of annihilation. The "world catastrophe" anxieties so many of these children experience have thus been understood as an externalization of these internal feelings of being overwhelmed, coming apart, and being destroyed.

Derek easily slipped from one identity into another, and he thought that clothes and jewelry formed an integral part of his own body and that of other people. Any external change in his own or other people's appearance aroused great anxiety which seemed to us to indicate the degree to which his ego boundaries were faulty.

Under the impact of a small physical shock, Derek's fear of becoming his therapist broke through. When she had to restrain him from attacking her, she held his wrist firmly and inadvertently scratched him slightly. Derek broke into panicky sobs and feared that he would become, like the therapist, a dark-haired woman with a long nose.

The same mechanism was also shown with his mother. Derek stumbled on a step and sought physical comfort. He feared his leg would come off, felt a bone was sticking out of it, and wondered whether he was about to have a baby like his "mum." (This was a reference to a previous discussion about his younger brother's birth.)

Stanley, aged seven and a half, illustrates the ease with which ego boundaries break down with anxiety arising from events in the environment. When discussing whether insects, like a daddy-long-legs, can go down the drain, Stanley asked: "Am I an insect?" This seemed to the therapist to be a fleeting confusion of identity.

3. We have commented upon the defect in internalization observed in our borderline children, who cannot rely on stable

object representations and thus have increasingly to depend upon external objects. This lack of stable representations and the accompanying lack of security have repercussions on the development of action into thought, which is then precariously established and becomes another source of anxiety for these children (more so than for the neurotic) as aggressive thought easily becomes equated with aggressive act, additionally terrifying because it is coupled with faulty reality testing. While this tendency is linked with the undue amount of magical thinking prevalent in our children, one also has to consider that few of them have successfully made the step from concrete to abstract thought. One can observe these factors in the following examples.

After Brian's tenth birthday, Stanley, his friend, had objected to the "half" of his own age being mentioned. Stanley was intensely jealous of his friend, and his objection was interpreted in terms of his envy of Brian's penis. But the true significance of this objection became clear when, accompanied by a body gesture of cutting himself in half across the waist line, he said, "I wouldn't like it if somebody cut me in half."

Derek showed the absence of stable object representations mainly when he was overwhelmed with death wishes toward his mother. On one such occasion he asked his therapist not to tell the receptionist of his mother's death, because it might not be true, while he continued his burial games during the session.

We have many examples illustrating the relapse into concrete thinking. The best is of Derek, who, at the announcement that school would *break up* for the holidays, feared that some kind of terrible destruction would befall the school.

4. A defect in neutralization may be a further explanation for what appears to be a different experience of anxiety in borderline cases. Aggression and death wishes are often expressed directly in undisguised form, thus arousing intense fear of retaliation which may additionally explain fears of annihilation. The same applies to undisguised expression of sexual (and homosexual) impulses.

Derek, when angry with the therapist, wanted to be Eichmann who killed six million Jews. He asked his therapist to teach him a few German words so that he could be a better Eichmann and then caught a fly which he drowned in the sink. Following this, he became panic-stricken and wondered whether God would punish him by killing him.

Interests and Activities

One of the interesting points which emerged at a recent discussion was that the type of sublimation chosen by these children seems to be directly related to their disturbance. Many of them show particular gifts in the realm of the arts, painting and music and also literary capacity. While they are capable of quite high, although not always stable, performance in these fields, they are only able to pursue them alone. Their difficulties in relating to objects is thus circumvented. Intellectualization is a prevalent defense, and the capacity for abstract thought is evident. But this type of sublimation disintegrates very easily under any sort of stress, indicating that neutralization is highly precarious. Thus Arun's attempts to learn about the mechanisms of photography were terminated when he had to enter the dark room with his male instructor; at such times he experienced overwhelming sensations of fear which only later could be identified as anxiety about homosexuality.

James's tremendous interest in botany led to his learning so much about the subject that he was able to pass quite an advanced examination in it. His ability broke down when he had to join a class of young adults of both sexes to do laboratory work. He found himself overwhelmed by both heterosexual and homosexual urges which he could not control.

Summary

When we started to work as a group the term "borderline" was used roughly for those children who at the time of referral suffered from severe ego disturbances but whose behavior was not yet frankly psychotic—that is to say, they were not yet "over the border." We do not yet feel sure that successful treatment reversing the borderline process necessarily indicates that we may not have been handling a potentially psychotic person. It may well be that such a patient might without treatment have developed an overt psychosis, or he might have remained a borderline psychotic. Borderline psychotics living in a benign environment may be spared a breakdown, while external stress usually exacerbates their condition.

Our observations in general confirm the findings of those authors who believe the fact of ego deviation to be of vital significance. We nevertheless do not feel sure that assessment of the degree and multiplicity of ego deviation alone will help us to distinguish between the borderline and the schizophrenic.

It seems to us that the crucial area for assessment and prediction would be the assessment of the capacity for internalization and inner representation based upon object cathexis. We believe that the stages of development in this area could be studied in minute detail and pin-pointed more accurately. It could be that this capacity for object relations and inner representation determines the outcome of the disturbance and indicates treatment possibilities. The type of treatment chosen would depend upon the capacity for maintaining object cathexis for any length of time.

No single disturbance in any one area would indicate a borderline disturbance. It is the multiplicity of deviations in all the areas we have discussed, together with this failure in maintaining object cathexis, which we think may be decisive. The degree of borderline disturbance varies from case to case, and there seems to be a sliding scale into which we would like to be able to fit our cases. This hierarchy would apply to every aspect of the personality that we have described. It is possible, however, that a child may be on a different level in each area. Hartmann (1952), discussing the reversibility of ego functions due to conflicts and regressive tendencies in different individuals, points to the variations in the degree to which ego functions maintain their stability even in what we call healthy adults. He suggests that this partial reversibility is, in the normal person, not incisive enough to create serious trouble. We have tried to emphasize that the reversibility of ego functions in our borderline children is particularly labile.

Broadly speaking, we are all fairly clear about the border between neurotic and psychotic. However, we do not seem to be as clear about the border between psychotic and borderline.

The children we have used for this study have been diagnosed as belonging to the borderline group. Examining their analytic material, we have found indications of specific characteristics:

1. Although the bisexual conflict is always present, it does not seem to be at the center of their disturbance as has been postulated by Katan and others. Rather, the majority of our cases has not attained a phase of phallic dominance, and their oedipal material appears to have an "as if" quality.

2. In all our cases the ego apparatus appears to be faulty, which may be due to inherent or traumatic factors. Although the origin of the fault cannot be precisely pin-pointed, there is evidence that it exists already very early. Moreover, there seems to be some connection between this fault and an early disturbance in the capacity to select and inhibit stimuli. In spite of this, considerably high-level ego functioning is observed in all our children, but with characteristic instability.

3. We have found in our cases that anxiety is characterized by primitive feelings of disintegration and annihilation and that signal anxiety is itself experienced as an overwhelming threat rather than as a warning to the ego of impending danger.

4. Finally, we have taken as our main point Anna Freud's remarks on the precarious maintenance of object cathexis and the ease with which it slides over into identification. It may well be that the weak object cathexis is linked with the instability of the object representation. Many difficulties seem to stem from this, and many of the symptoms seem to represent a defense against this process. This together with the other points mentioned above, and the relatively correct reality testing, may point to a borderline rather than a psychotic state. Freud (1924) said, "A loss of reality must be an inherent element in psychosis."

BIBLIOGRAPHY

Beres, D. (1956), Ego Deviation and the Concept of Schizophrenia. *This Annual*, XI.
Ekstein, R. & Wallerstein, J. (1954), Observations on the Psychology of Borderline and Psychotic Children. *This Annual*, IX.
—— & —— (1956), Observations on the Psychotherapy of Borderline and Psychotic Children. *This Annual*, XI.
Frankl, L. (1961), Some Observations on the Development and Disturbances of Integration in Childhood. *This Annual*, XVI.
Freeman, T., Cameron, J. L., & McGhie, A. (1958), *Chronic Schizophrenia*. New York: International Universities Press.
Freud, A. (1945), Indications for Child Analysis. *This Annual*, I.

—— (1952), States of Negativism and Emotional Surrender. Abstract in: *Int. J. Psa.*, XXXIII.

—— (1956), Unpublished Papers on Borderline States.

—— (1957), Unpublished Papers on Borderline States.

Freud, S. (1911), Formulations on the Two Principles of Mental Functioning. *Standard Edition*, XII. London: Hogarth Press, 1958.

—— (1920), Beyond the Pleasure Principle. *Standard Edition*, XVIII. London: Hogarth Press, 1955.

—— (1924), The Loss of Reality in Neurosis and Psychosis. *Standard Edition,* XIX. London: Hogarth Press, 1961.

Geleerd, E. (1958), Borderline States. *This Annual*, XIII.

Goldfarb, W. (1961), *Childhood Schizophrenia*. Cambridge, Mass.: Harvard University Press.

Hartmann, H. (1939), *Ego Psychology and the Problem of Adaptation*. New York: International Universities Press, 1958.

—— (1952), The Mutual Influences in the Development of Ego and Id. *This Annual*, VII.

—— Kris, E., & Loewenstein, R. M. (1946), Comments on the Formation of Psychic Structure. *This Annual*, II.

Katan, M. (1950), Structural Aspects of a Case of Schizophrenia. *This Annual*, V.

Knight, R. P. (1946), Psychotherapy of an Adolescent Catatonic Schizophrenia with Mutism. *Psychiatry*, IX.

—— (1953), Borderline States. In: *Drives, Affects, Behavior,* ed. R. M. Loewenstein. New York: International Universities Press.

Kris, E. (1939), Laughter as an Expressive Process. In: *Psychoanalytic Explorations in Art*. New York: International Universities Press, 1952.

Mahler, M. S. & Gosliner, B. J. (1955), Symbiotic Child Psychosis: Genetic, Dynamic and Restitutive Aspects. *This Annual*, X.

Piaget, J. (1924), *Judgment and Reasoning in the Child*. New York: Harcourt, Brace, 1928.

—— (1936), *The Origins of Intelligence in the Child*. New York: International Universities Press, 1952.

—— (1945), *Play, Dreams and Imitation in Childhood*. New York: Norton, 1951.

Rank, B. & MacNaughton, D. (1950), A Clinical Contribution to Early Ego Development. *This Annual*, V.

Rapaport, D. (1951), *Organization and Pathology of Thought*. New York: Columbia University Press.

Sandler, J. (1959), The Background of Safety. Read before The 21st Congress of The International Psycho-Analytical Association, Copenhagen.

—— (1960), The Concept of the Superego. *This Annual*, XV.

Sharpe, E. (1940), Psycho-Physical Problems. Revealed in Language: An Examination of Metaphor. *Collected Papers on Psycho-Analysis*. London: Hogarth Press, 1950.

Singer, M. B. (1960), Fantasies of a Borderline Patient. *This Annual*, XV.

Weil, A. P. (1953), Certain Severe Disturbances of Ego Development in Childhood. *This Annual*, VIII.

—— (1953), Clinical Data and Dynamic Considerations in Certain Cases of Childhood Schizophrenia. *Amer. J. Orthopsychiat.*, XXIII.

—— (1956), Some Evidences of Deviational Development in Infancy and Early Childhood. *This Annual*, XI.

THE SEARCH FOR A SEXUAL IDENTITY IN A CASE OF CONSTITUTIONAL SEXUAL PRECOCITY

RUTH THOMAS, in collaboration with LYDIA FOLKART and ELIZABETH MODEL (London)

Sexual precocity is defined as the attainment of sexual maturity some years before the normal time of puberty. Novak (1944) states: "According to most authors, puberty should be considered abnormally early or precocious when it occurs below the age of nine, although some suggest a lower limit of eight." It is always due to hypersecretion of androgenic or estrogenic hormone.

The ovarian hyperactivity (which some authors state may be secondary to some hypothalamic-pituitary stimulus) is manifested by qualitatively normal sexual development, pubic hair, well-formed breasts, and even pregnancy, the last having been recorded as early as six years.

Novak postulates that the condition is dependent on abnormal genetic factors. Paschkis, Rakoff, and Cantarow (1958) on the other hand state: "The possibility that the initiating process affects the ovaries primarily rather than the pituitary, also deserves consideration, especially since gonadotropin excretion in these children is minimal. The ovaries may be unusually responsive to minimal amounts of gonadotropin; other factors not yet understood may have

This case was treated at the Hampstead Child-Therapy Clinic. Miss Lydia Folkart was the child's therapist and Mrs. Elizabeth Model interviewed the mother.

The Hampstead Child-Therapy Course and Clinic are maintained by grants given by the following Foundations: The Field Foundation, Inc., New York; The Ford Foundation, New York; The Foundations' Fund for Research in Psychiatry, New Haven, Connecticut; The Anna Freud Foundation, New York; The Grant Foundation, Inc., New York; The Estate of Flora Haas, New York; The Old Dominion Foundation, U.S.A.; The Psychoanalytic Research and Development Fund, Inc., New York.

The authors are indebted to Dr. Alfred Model, Dr. H. Nagera, and Dr. H. Rey for information contributory to the assessment of the medical situation.

initiated early maturation of the ovary, which in turn has 'awakened' the pituitary by back action. There seems to be little evidence that the condition is hereditary."

While in some forms of precocious puberty, the patients menstruate but do not ovulate, "in the constitutional group, the patients not only menstruate unusually early, but they also ovulate" (Novak, 1944). In the constitutional type the risk of pregnancy is therefore real.

In both sexes, precocity is associated with early union of the epiphysis. (Di George and Warkany, 1959). Although initial growth is well above average, ultimate height is below expectation. However, constitutional sexual precocity may proceed to a normal state.

Sexual precocity of early origin will necessarily generate considerable anxiety in parents and normal siblings. The nature of this anxiety will depend on and interact with the personal sexual orientation of each member of the family. Incest fears will be magnified in all possible heterosexual partnerships within the family constellation, for example, between father and daughter, or brother and sister. The relation between mother and daughter may generate novel competitive anxieties. These in turn will produce defensive measures in the family members in accordance with personal character patterns. The normal protective and educative attitudes of the parents will therefore be complicated in a special way by their own psychopathology.

Sexually precocious children have an abundance of physical energy and strength beyond their actual age, but they frequently appear clumsy. Their vigorous growth unfortunately gives rise to the expectation of behavior far in advance of their mental age and sometimes beyond their physical adaptiveness.

Not infrequently the diagnosis and treatment of this abnormality requires some degree of hospitalization and physical examination. Further traumatic factors are thus added to the normal vicissitudes of childhood.

To both child and parent, the age at which precocity makes itself manifest is important. An early precocity, say from birth, means to the parent a long waiting period before it is possible to accept the child as a normal being. Some part of this period is complicated by the recognition that the child is abnormally overgrown, and looks unusual among other children. To the child, manifest sexual abnormality appearing at or before the time when gender role is established may have a confusing impact on the body ego and the ability to establish gender role. Money et al. (1955a) place the age for the establishment of gender role at around eighteen months. If doubt about this matter is prolonged beyond this period, they believe it favors psychopathology. In the precociously sexual girl, the establishment of gender role includes not only the decision to think of herself as a boy or girl but also the decision as to whether she is a girl or a woman. Precocious breast development may complicate the resolution of her penis envy, and her unconscious choice of sexual role, and at the same time reinforce her fantasies of sexual identity with her mother.

To accept and understand this abnormal situation and to verbalize the problem it presents to the child at varying stages of growth constitutes a task which can of course be met, though parental readiness to deal with it is highly variable. We would therefore expect a qualitative element in child care which varies with the difficulties of the parents.

While our awareness of these factors has grown in the process of analytic work, as it will be reported, we had not expected them to be so outstanding in the analytic picture. Studies of these children are usually confined to their medical profiles. The single exception are studies by Hampson and Money, working at the Johns Hopkins Hospital, who examined sixteen children psychologically, eleven girls aged from fourteen months to fifteen years, and five boys aged two and a half to seven years. Information was gathered from detailed histories, test batteries, and interviews with both parents and children. The evidence on general psychological maturation seems to be more adequate than that on psychosexual maturation. The latter, based on interview and interrogation, is difficult to assess and far from conclusive. Hampson and Money (1955) assert that "Children with idiopathic sexual precocity do not automatically manifest psychosexual and general sexual precocity along with their somatic precocity. Psychologically their development resembles in manner and speed that of their somatically normal siblings and cousins. Like their dental development, it is not precocious."

It should be recorded that the present study was undertaken in the hope of clarifying the developmental picture of the drives in this one case. Physical maturation and menstrual functioning are not themselves evidence of psychosexual maturity at the level of drive development. Neurological maturation does not necessarily keep pace with endocrine development; and in sexual precocity, the somatic bases for drive development might therefore be at variance with the corresponding psychological development. For this reason it is of considerable interest to compare the libidinal phase development of precocious and normal children of comparable age. If an immaturely structured psyche has to deal with increased sexual drives of an intensity normally found in puberty, one might assume that this situation would highlight the use of primitive defense systems and could easily be compared with normal puberty. This approach proved oversimple and superficial in the face of the complex inner situation which the analysis disclosed.

In our case, the psychobiological effects of the abnormality (constitutional factors) and the effects of the abnormality on family and personal relationships (environmental effects stemming from the abnormality) had to be studied in a familial background dominated by the gross disturbances of both parents. The latter element could scarcely have failed to be pathogenic in the life of a physically normal child. The effects stemming from the abnormality were constantly overlaid by a cycle of environmental factors, originating for the most part from the personality and activities of a traumatogenic mother. Nevertheless, certain elements pertaining to the abnormality could ultimately be isolated in their effect on development.

Case Report

Susan, aged two years and nine months when brought to the Hampstead Clinic, was first noticed to have a white vaginal discharge at the age of six weeks. She was not seen by a consultant endocrinologist until the age of nineteen months. A vaginal smear at that time showed marked estrogenic stimulation. She was admitted for a rectal examination under anesthesia; no abnormal masses were found and cervix and uterus were both normal. At that time the mother stated that the child had a white vaginal discharge for three to four days every three to four weeks and during this time was sleepy, irritable, and emotional. She was seen again at the age of five. At that time her height was four feet (equal to a height age of seven years, eight months) and her weight was four stone, ten pounds (a weight age of about eight years, nine months). Other development was proportional. There was an increase in breast size. The 17-ketosteroids were found to be 5.5 mg. per 24 hours, well above the expected figure for a child of five, but approximately correct for a girl of thirteen or fourteen years. Her pregnanediol output was 0.2 mg. per 24 hours, a normal figure.

Although sexual precocity may be due to a variety of causes, the differential diagnosis in this case clearly established that the child was manifesting constitutional sexual precocity. No abnormality of the brain or endocrine glands was found. In this case no pathology could be postulated other than the abnormally early age at which hypothalamic-pituitary-ovarian activity commenced, and medical treatment was not available or indicated.

Reasons for Referral

At two years, nine months, Susan's main presenting symptom was an inability to allow her mother out of sight. Persistent clinging was said to begin after her hospitalization at twenty months. She became terrified at going into any building, and would drive away whoever attempted to speak to the mother in the street. She screamed when a stranger came to the door of her home, for fear they would take her into the hospital, would clutch her stomach and cry, "Susan's tummy all better now." Following this hospitalization Susan refused to return to the bedroom which up to this time she had shared with her brother John, four years older than herself. At the time of referral there were daily scenes with John. Susan waited for him on his return from school and attacked him with forks and cricket bats. On one occasion when a boy had broken his leg, she attempted to break John's leg and could be restrained only with difficulty.

She was capricious over food, refusing to eat food she had just asked for. There were numerous scenes at mealtimes, where she insisted on putting her feet on the table and upsetting dishes.

Her mother regarded the precocity as a separate problem, in no way related to the behavior difficulties, and did not adduce this as a reason for referral.

History and Family Background

Susan was the youngest of three children, born precipitately when her mother was forty-two years old. At the time of referral the eldest child, Gwen (aged fourteen), appeared the most stable member of the family. John (aged eight) was eventually taken into treatment and later sent to boarding school.

Susan's history was a disturbed one from birth. She weighed eight pounds and was fed by spoon, because for several months, as the mother stated, she continued to discharge quantities of nasal mucus, which interfered with breast or bottle feeding. She was taken into a hospital at six weeks—on the point of choking, the mother said—where she was bottle fed and where it is reported the nasal condition cleared up, though it recurred on return home. She walked at twelve months; her speech development is said to have been normal, and she could whistle at ten months! She was toilet trained at twenty months, though there was a breakdown of this achievement after her hospitalization. She was lifted at night till the age of four.

Mrs. S. first noticed the vaginal discharge on Susan's return from her first hospitalization at the age of six weeks. She also noticed that Susan's breasts were developing at this time. It was not till sixteen months that her persistent attempts to have these facts given consideration were successful. When finally at nineteen months Susan was seen by an endocrinologist, the child reacted with intense screaming to the hospital setting, the presence of a number of students, and the interference with her body for the vaginal smear. Hospitalization was arranged a month later to investigate the differential diagnosis between an undisclosed tumor and a constitutional abnormality, described to the mother as "just a strange development of nature." Susan again proved unmanageable.

Her hospital experiences may be summarized as follows: at six weeks a ten-day stay on account of nasal mucus; at nine weeks a month's stay on account of gastroenteritis; at nineteen months the taking of a vaginal smear; at twenty months a nine-day stay, with a rectal examination. At this time the diagnosis of constitutional sexual precocity was made, the presence of a tumor having been excluded.

It was stated that after the hospitalization at twenty months, a change in her object relations took place. Before this she easily attached herself to people. This event was said to mark the onset of her withdrawn states which lasted in an intense way till she was over seven. Before this and following the hospitalization, it was stated that she scarcely spoke to anyone outside the family and withdrew when any attempt was made to establish contact with her.

At three Susan was a well-made child with dark hair, cut in a sleek bob, and noticeable for beautiful dark eyes. She was attractively dressed and could have passed for a schoolgirl several years older. When first seen, she sat anxiously on her mother's lap with her face buried in her mother's shoulder. From time to time she sucked a piece of rag from which she was never separated. There was a strange contrast between her round babyish face and her mature little body, shapely hips and calves, and the noticeable development of her breasts, though she was dressed in a fashion which did not draw attention to these. Her expression could be eager and lively, though more often she lapsed into vacancy.

Susan showed herself at an early age very competent at household tasks; she could bathe herself and do her own hair at a normal age. She loved most to play with her dolls of which she had a great number. While her mother encouraged her household activities, other members of the family thought them a nuisance and tried to interfere. Susan would then become babyish and demand to be cuddled. She found it difficult to wait for a response to her wishes, and her mother tried to avoid scenes by as far as possible never directly refusing anything. Mrs. S. often pacified Susan by promises for the future.

At the time of referral, and for several years afterward, her general health was poor. She suffered from continual colds and minor ailments, was an excessive thumb sucker, and alternately masturbated compulsively. Her mother regarded the thumb sucking as an acceptable alternative to masturbation.

At three she was already attending nursery school, and was regarded as withdrawn and the kind of child it was easy to overlook. This continued to be the school picture for some years. She appeared not to learn, made no friends, and other children did not seek her company.

Susan was too withdrawn to have a mental test done before

treatment commenced, but a year afterward she achieved an I.Q. of 102 on the Stanford Binet Scale, though it was felt that 117 was a closer real estimate, allowing for her chaotic behavior and the domination of her response by fantasy.

Mrs. S. was a tense, excitable woman, intelligent, hyperactive and erratic. While she had a warm relation to her children and there was considerable latitude in the home, all her arrangements had an air of constant crisis in which she played a central and dramatic role. The unfortunate quality of her maternal care was accentuated by her need to subject Susan to overfrequent medical attention, the absolute necessity for which was often in doubt but proved difficult to gauge because of Susan's abnormality. The timing of the interventions and the mother's emotional approach to them were inevitably traumatogenic. Reference to the records of other clinics confirmed that Mrs. S.'s dramatizations on the theme of illness and the medical mismanagement of her children were as much in evidence in the early years of her marriage as later. When Gwen was six years old, she attended a London clinic because of excessive masturbation. Mrs. S.'s preoccupation at this time, brought as her husband's, was revealing: "My husband wonders if Gwen's genitals are deformed." John was then one and Susan not yet born. John was also taken to this clinic at the age of three, following his violent reaction to hospitalization for alleged constipation. The clinic clearly felt that it was Mrs. S.'s gross anxiety over her children's bodies that drove her to seek help.

It was a measure of Mrs. S.'s distress that with Susan, in whose case there was every justification, she did not present her child's body as the reason for seeking help, but used Susan's difficulties in separating from her. Superficially Susan's precocity may have been less devastating to her than to a more normal mother. Only at a late stage in Susan's analysis was Mrs. S. able to admit how distressed she had been to hear other mothers comment on her child when she towered over other children in a school play. There was no doubt that Susan's abnormality focused her mother's disturbance without being in any way the central feature of it.

A simultaneous analysis of both mother and child was indicated but not available. Instead Mrs. S. was supported in weekly interviews throughout Susan's treatment. It seemed at first that she would use the opportunity entirely as an abreactive therapy for her own pent-up needs. Her verbosity had the quality of the flight of ideas of the hypomanic: her paranoid ideas, especially against doctors, had an intractable and delusional quality, and her distortions on the theme of her own body states were clearly deluded. She constantly provoked crises which reverberated on her family, but equally and unpredictably had long active and constructive periods. In the handling of her children she was often surprisingly open to influence, and kept a humorous and benevolent relation to her therapist for seven years. Basically her personality remained untouched, though her acting out could be directed away from the children. In type, she approximated to the "chaotic mother," producing a state of "organized chaos" which distracted and bewildered her children (Winnicott, 1961).

Mrs. S. saw her husband as an ineffectual, wavering man, afraid of physical contact with her, whose acute anxieties about transport led him to leave home in the early hours, miserly and unpredictable about money, and with "uncanny" ways. Only in the later stages of Susan's analysis did he emerge as an acute obsessional character, who withdrew into a small workshop, relatively unrelated even in his business life to genuine adult interests, yet with surprising understanding of his children's sublimations and often a sensitive protagonist for them against the world outside the family. To his children he seemed often remote on account of his withdrawn states.

The Treatment

Susan's analysis extended from the age of three to the beginning of her tenth year, sessions being gradually reduced in the last two years. The first years of her analysis were marked by two outstanding features. It seemed as if all libidinal activity with considerable areas of ego functioning were forbidden, and that all areas of libidinal development were functioning simultaneously in an agglutinized fashion (Greenacre, 1954). For the first nine months of treatment Susan insisted that her mother remain in the treatment room, expressing fear that otherwise she would become excited and unmanageable. Babies were sent to the hospital for eating sweets, water play might lead to drinking something messy like urine, "and if you drink a lot of water, it has to come out." Susan was lifted at night around this time, but no restrictions were placed on her intake of liquids. Her hands had constantly to be washed after sand play, " 'cause Mummy be cross and Susan be cross." She restricted her urination for long periods and was afraid that to cuddle her Teddy would be too exciting. Susan feared that all these activities would find appropriate punishment in the hospital and in separation from her mother. She had above all a great wish to gobble people up and have them to herself, the punishment for this wish being nasty medicine and the extraction of teeth.

Susan's fantasy that she was a baby was fortified by the severe ego restrictions she imposed on herself in an endeavor to reduce excitement of any kind. When inevitably she could not always contain herself, she begged the therapist to join in her activity, to suck her own fingers, and suggested the therapist was disgusting and might have pooh-pooh in her pants. Both were forbidden to look, listen, or talk because they were dirty babies whose tongues could be cut out. But it was also clear that Susan was longing to talk about her problems with her unusual body and had great fears of doing so. Not only was talking itself exciting and liable to produce a situation in which she would feel overwhelmed, but Susan had a store of information about her body, secretly gathered from her mother's conversation and her own observation, which in part defied her ability to integrate and which on the other hand had implications too painful and frightening to allow of integration. Operations on her dolls indicated distorted fantasies of body functioning side by side with other play clearly based on a normal body image. Teddy's badness was extracted from his legs and poured into his eyes; he would scratch himself and infect his eyes, mouth, and hair with the badness of his legs. Covert references to hair, her genital discharge, and unusual height came only very slowly into the analysis. Her inability to control the discharge, conceived as an anal and urethral function, which could then through masturbation infect the whole of her body, accounted for some of the limitations she imposed on her activity. She felt she had infected her hands and, through them, her eyes and her tonsils; even her pubic hair was the result of her messy play. These features of her disability were confused with and ascribed to her lack of a penis. She felt that only a penis would remedy her defects. She was uncertain whether she or her mother was responsible for this great lack. "Once," she said, "I had a penis, but I put my finger through it and it bust." She then began to wash her doll's hair, saying it would look smashing, but added, "I used to cry when my mummy washed my hair and I fell down and it broke and it was a plastic and then I was another Susan."

Her anxiety about her abnormality was woven into all her object relations, dominating and further restricting her ego activities. Her brother John seemed to Susan the most fortunate one in the family. She drew him with a proper body and a gun in his belt, and represented herself beside him by vague lines and circles. He was clean, while she was messy. She often spoke of herself as John's twin, and drew them both with a seed bag in each hand, sowing seeds. She imagined she had a penis hidden in her pubic hair or that her height was a compensation for the lack of it. John was ashamed of Susan's appearance, and he and his friends tended to withdraw from her or tease her. Susan responded by roaming naked around the house and attempting to alleviate her own anxiety by frightening the boys. This behavior proved to be a repetition of exciting and frightening romping games with John when they shared a room in her infancy, the room from which she anxiously withdrew on her return from the hospital. Her later fury against him could be attributed to her feeling that he had remained normal and active in spite of these games, while she had been damaged. She constantly referred to these games in the analysis by means of current fantasies in which she and John were clambering about together on rocks.

While the normal girl's phallic wishes are entrenched in a firmly accepted body and a self, which she would like to exchange or enlarge by her phallic strivings, Susan saw herself at times as a nothingness—vague lines and a circle in her drawings. She seemed unable to differentiate herself from her clothes, and her sense of her body was related to whether she was dressed in a skirt or jeans. Her therapist once said, "You look nice in your skirt," and Susan replied with puzzlement, "*In* my skirt?" Having talked of herself as a boy or a baby, she would immediately ask anxiously, "But I am a little girl?" She often spoke of herself as a "big-little girl," and at other times she said, "I feel more like a lady than a big-little girl." On several occasions she suffered mild states of depersonalization. At these times she could not bear to play pretend games and would counter a make-believe remark with "But I am real." She seemed afraid she would disintegrate, and drew pictures of herself in pieces. Her intense anxiety over her body seemed to lead to a partial decathexis of her self-image, and her anxiety over what other people could or might do to her body led to a parallel inability to grasp their identities. Told that a lady might be coming to take some pictures of her, she asked anxiously if the lady could be telephoned to find out her name as if this would help her to maintain a grip on the situation. This lady was confused with the X-ray specialist who might undress her.

Susan was at times clearly unable to maintain the reality of herself and her objects in the face of intense fantasy, a phenomenon which at the outset of the analysis could have seemed not too unusual for her age. At a later stage, the bizarreness of her mother's outspoken fantasying had to be considered as a factor contributing to Susan's tenuous hold on reality in the area of her sexual life. Finally, the inherent weakness of her ego structure and its inability to handle her internal problems were brought into relief.

Susan spoke rarely about her father. In the first week of treatment she asked for a swing to be drawn with daddy on it, a reference to some pleasurable activity with her father which she resolutely refused to pursue. Instead she said that Dorothy, her teacher, used to swing her.

Susan longed to be able to break through her father's reticence. While he joked about her precocity, calling her Jayne Mansfield, an actress famed for her large breasts, his anxieties led him to be embarrassed about her in public and unresponsive to the point of appearing to shun her. After a wedding party when he had failed to take notice of her or to talk to her, she played that her doll's daddy was cross with her because she was a messy girl, and angrily tried to cut off pieces of her own hair and stuff them into her therapist's mouth. When her therapist tried to reassure Susan that their talking was different from her mother's and could help her to win over her father, Susan began excitedly to prepare a meal for them both, inviting the therapist to take the role of father. She was immediately overwhelmed with anxiety and tried too late to stop the game, saying she must not eat her mother's dinner. Then she lay on the floor twisting her legs and body in acute sexual excitement and asked to be spanked. This outbreak was much later repeated, very unfortunately before Gwen's boy friends.

Susan's states of disrupted identity and the confusion of her body image could now be seen to relate in part to recognition that her precocity made her in reality a sexual threat to her mother. In the case of her brother, Susan aggressively exploited her realization that her pubic hair created anxiety in males, but divested herself symbolically of it to appeal to her father. Reassurance that he could be brought to love her released the fantasy of an avenging mother, and precipitated an anxiety attack with a break-through of aggressive sexuality. Her mother's persistent and anxious interference with her body thus represented to Susan the danger of actual castration in constantly changing forms, an interdiction on assuming a feminine role, and a relegation to a sexual limbo. Susan once said that she thought of herself as a little girl who, having left her mother, was all alone out in space. Susan's precocity thus robbed her of a feminine role and of a normal child's measure of safety to indulge oedipal fantasy. In this respect her situation invited comparison with the sexually seduced child.

The fluctuations of Susan's self-images seemed to be caused by attempts at denying this dangerous uniqueness by establishing a different kind of common identity with each of her objects in turn. Susan drew a picture of her father as a house with a tall chimney extending over all the rooftops. Inside a witch was extracting some glass from his forehead. She represented herself outside as a flower that had grown too tall and was dying. Both father and Susan were thus castrated by the witch mother while simultaneously possessing male attributes.

While Susan's fantasies were not basically different from those of a more normal child, the quality of her anxiety and the extensive ego modifications stemmed from three areas in her personality where her resources were defective: the narcissistic, the object-related, and the more strictly oedipal. All the evidence indicated that Susan lacked the support of a normal relationship with her father and brother. The fact that they possessed a penis was, for her, of exaggerated and central significance, and left little room for normal interchange. The reality involved in her own sense of castration and their anxious rejection predated her oedipal phase and attenuated her resources for dealing with this problem. Instead the normal child's wish for a penis was in her case reinforced by her wish for a normal body conceived as male. Whatever assumptions one might have been tempted to make about the impact of Susan's precocity in producing an abnormal drive development had to be weighed against the poverty of inducement to an aim-inhibited relationship, a poverty which stemmed in part from Susan's defective personality and in part from the anxieties she aroused in her objects. In these circumstances, sexual acting out would have been an economic possibility in a child whose normal drive endowment was not in doubt. Only in the last stages of the analysis did a further important determinant of Susan's sexual exhibitionism emerge, namely, that Mr. S. frequently seduced Susan by undressing before her at bedtime. This could be directly related to the restriction of her visual activities and to the outbreak of anxiety before Gwen's boy friends in which she turned passive into active and repeated the exhibitionistic behavior she had manifested to her therapist earlier in the analysis.

Susan's relation with her mother was intimate, warm, and alternatively compliant and controlling. It manifested itself most positively in her play with a vast number of dolls and teddies, whom she tenderly cared for and protected; even more adaptive were her constant visits to a neighbor's twin babies with whom she played mother expertly. The dolls represented Susan herself, and her vigorous and sadistic control of them expressed her resentment that she was often prevented from doing much that she felt capable of.

Susan's compliance with her mother's fiction that she was too young to understand about her precocity was based on her taking over her mother's defenses which then enabled her to deny her satisfaction in listening intently to her mother's hypochondriacal ruminations on her own and her child's body. Susan would sing a little song called "Agony," equating her own medical experiences with her mother's sexual and feminine agonies. In one of her drawings they held hands, having placed a little mouse on each other's heads. Susan felt they were both subjected to frightening and magical experiences which made them uniquely different from other members of the family. When Susan spoke of herself as "a little girl with crates of milk in her bottom," her discharge featured to provide an organ identity with her mother's breasts. Her self-esteem was thus nurtured regressively, and her aggression defended against.

Mrs. S.'s projection of her hypochondriacal anxieties onto the child and her attempt to deal with them in relation to Susan's body (projective identification) were fundamental issues which emerged clearly even in the limited treatment it was possible to offer the mother. This situation made Susan's defense system and the defensive character of her fantasies of identity with her mother, based on their common wish to exhibit castration, the most intractable in the analysis.

Constant transference interpretations of her defenses against aggression had slowly enabled Susan to become more efficient at expressing her anger at her enforced passivity and more effective at equipping herself with useful knowledge about her own and her mother's medical procedures. At this point she developed a chaotic mode of speech and behavior (for the most part confined to the analysis) reminiscent of a borderline child. Her material for many months was expressed through primary-process functioning, over-condensed and symbolic at many levels, replete with cover memories and often unintelligible. Some more intelligible fragments, which focused interpretations at the end of this period, indicated that Susan attempted to explain her abnormality in terms that involved her mother and herself in mutual bodily damage. While the ambivalent nature of her fantasies was now more strikingly evident, they still expressed Susan's wish for an undifferentiated union; a constant pull toward symbiosis marked all her object relationships. The deep ego regression in which her fantasy life at this time involved her arose when the release of aggression through analytic work threatened this narcissistic maneuver.

Susan's birth was allegedly "six weeks overdue" and precipitate. One day she stuffed her doll under her dress and ran excitedly around the room. Her therapist was told to catch the doll because if she fell she would die. She must be X-rayed when she was pulled out, to see if she was still breathing, as now she was ripe. Her blood had to be extracted—it was red, blue, and green—and new blood injected. In this story Susan's mother was responsible for her condition because she let her "fall out." In another version, Susan was responsible for her mother's condition. Susan was in bed with mother and jumped about and kicked her in the tummy. Susan then had a bath and they went away on holiday. Everything happened in a hurry. Susan climbed about on rocks and when John came out, he said, "I am sorry you are so sad. Come inside." So Susan dived in head first. The substitution of "falling in" for "falling out" was the key to this anal birth fantasy which proved crucial in her diminished self-esteem. Susan was relieved to be told that her own intra-uterine kicks had not injured her mother, nor had her mother's delay in arriving at the hospital injured her in any way. While the rocks refer to her anxiety over her early games with John, to which she also attributed her abnormality, the meaning of "falling" was over-determined. It involved her fantasies of sexual experience with her father *in utero* (Leuba, 1950), and more deeply buried references to her experiences of anesthesia conceived as a sexual union. The latter were clarified only at a later stage of the analysis and disclosed her wish to be devoured in an ultimate union with both parents.

Shortly afterward, Susan enumerated the reasons for all the hospitalizations there had ever been in her family. When the subject of her own hospitalization at twenty months was broached, Susan asked for information. She was told that her mother had been worried because her body was growing so fast. The doctor said she was rather a special baby who would always be ahead of other children till they caught up with her at fourteen. Then they would all be the same again. Susan listened with rapt attention and asked for the story to be repeated. Soon thereafter Susan introduced the subject of menstruation, and the way was now open for a fuller discussion with her. The narcissistic distress she had suffered was greatly eased from this time with the reassurance that other girls would share this function with her. Her ability to integrate the information was evident in the direct ego advances she made almost at once (aged five years, ten months). Most importantly, she began to look forward to her future. Referring to the twins in a slightly later session, she said, "When I am grown up, I shall have a husband *instead*." This was the first occasion on which she gave evidence of imagining a normal future for herself.

The Emergence of a True Oedipal Phase

Susan's libidinal development closely approximates the phenomenon of "agglutination of phases" (Greenacre, 1954). Postulating that the overlap of phase development may be considerably greater than has been thought, "that in fact all lines of activity are present in some degree at birth or soon thereafter," Greenacre concludes, "it is the maturational peak and its relative prominence in the total activity of the individual organism that marks the phase; and the succession of maturational peaks which creates the appearance of a succession of phases." Severe prolonged stimulation or multiplicity of simultaneous stimulations may result in a flooding of the organism with excitement; and where all channels of discharge are utilized, there may be a generalized acceleration of all drives and a kind of basic amalgamation with sacrifice of special direction and appropriateness.

In Susan's case, the evidence is conclusive that though she received above-average care, her life from the outset was beset with maternal anxieties of a quite unusual type. At every stage of her development Susan was confused and disturbed by the impact of her mother's chaotic personality. It is likely that her early feeding problem resulted from Mrs. S.'s libidinal incapacity to deal with her nasal blockage. Frustration of her sucking needs from birth contributed to the persistence of gross oral features in her autoerotic activity and in her fantasy life as well as to the incorporative nature of her object relations. The sexualization of her perceptive activities also stemmed from this source.

There is every reason to suppose that Mrs. S. had handled Susan's toilet training not strictly but in an emotional way. Moreover, the hospitalization at twenty months and her mother's preoccupation with her genital discharge were influential factors in the persistence of her anal and urethral preoccupations. Little is known about the earlier hospitalization for gastroenteritis, which also must have played a significant role. Susan's strong reaction formations of disgust toward her own body may have derived initially from the frustration of her sucking and certainly from the handling of her discharge, the continuation of which served as a constant provocation of her anal impulses. Anal and oral anxieties were closely inter-woven in her poisoning fantasies.

While the wish for a penis appeared as an organizing element in her fantasy and the wish to share in her mother's bodily experiences was also a constant, undoubtedly oedipal element, a specific phallic response with true competitive strivings was barely apparent. The quality of her anxiety, her ego modifications, and the blurring of self- and object images gave the impression of being defensive against a loss even more fundamental than is involved in oedipal frustration. It was less that she was retreating from an oedipal posi-tion than that nascent oedipal wishes were threatening an already-precarious position where she felt unsure of her personal emotional existence.

In the early stages of analysis Susan's self-representation was similar in some respects to that of the fetishist. At one level she was well aware that she was a little girl and would be a woman. Equally she was aware of the sexual identity of her objects. At the level of her primitive fantasies, these distinctions were obliterated, and reality was replaced by a belief in the universality of the penis on the one hand, and the universality of castration on the other. The remarkable feats of integration which she attempted at both these levels were possible because there was no primary defect in her synthetic function. These endeavors were necessary because the in-soluble problem of her precocity reactivated basic narcissistic anxie-ties, which threatened to overwhelm her ego.

Susan's considerable adaptive capacities indicated a primary development in which ego integration had already taken place in large measure and was supported and developed by a very great degree of good mothering. Autoplastic modes of discharge (illness and prolonged autoerotic activity) were influential in limiting the degree of vulnerability of the ego (Anna Freud, 1954). But the failure of the synthetic function in the area of the "equilibrium of the instinctual drives" (Hartmann, 1939) interfered with processes of fusion in the drive systems, with consequent heightening of mo-mentum in each. Her early unrestrained attacks on John and later outbreaks of exhibitionism reflected this defusion and represented defensive attempts against a deeper ego regression.

Passive fantasies of incorporation by the idealized and degraded part objects marked the onset of this regression to primary-process functioning, releasing new aspects of both her self- and object images. Jacobson (1954) refers to the temporary weakening of the perceptive functions which accompany such fantasies of refusion of self- and object images. Susan's case is remarkable for the short spans of time in which each endured, often changing several times within the compass of one story. This situation reflected the fluid boundaries between self- and object images, the split in her ego organization, and the extent of her ambivalent conflict.

While the distinction between herself and her objects was so difficult to maintain and the cathexis of whole objects so inadequate, it is doubtful if it is right to speak of a true oedipal complex. With the ego's acceptance of the need for temporary frustration which followed on her enlightenment about her abnormality ("I shall have a husband, instead"), reaction formations in the form of pity, shyness, and consideration for the frustrations of others led Susan to a more real appraisal of her objects. An oedipal *conflict,* in contrast to what might be called her pregentital battle for phallic equivalents, could then develop.

At the age of five years eight months, Susan was hospitalized to undergo an operation for squint. When she returned from the hospital where she had been unusually happy and had participated in the school activities provided on the ward, she absolutely refused to speak or enter the treatment room and for three months had to be interviewed in the waiting room, where she was clearly the object of much curosity. She reproduced in this way the situation of her original hospitalization, silently soliciting interest in her new accomplishments while indicating in her drawings that bad analytic sexual talk was not in order. On occasions, however, she was sexually most provocative, sitting with her legs apart, or crawling round the floor, her face covered with a beret, and noisily and excitedly playing at being a cat licking milk from a saucer. One day she drew a forest with a little girl riding. Instantly she became frantic with anxiety, asked whether anyone had ever seen a tree with so many little twigs on it (pubic hair), and was that what a tree should look like? Was the little girl alright?

The pleasurable attention Susan was receiving as the focus of interest in the waiting room released memories of the original traumatic hospitalization at twenty months. She had been given anesthesia for a rectal examination (the beret on her face) when she became uncontrollable after being separated from her mother. It is not known in what form the anesthestic was administered. Susan also reacted with ego restriction to the excitement engendered by returning to her therapist with many new accomplishments. The splitting of the ego in the defensive process was thus seen to have originated in her attempted denial of the hospital experience with the overwhelming excitement and aggressive stimulation it involved.

At the age of six and a half years, Susan had her first period. Her second followed after an interval of six months, and thereafter she was regular. She was well prepared for the event and though it brought considerable excitement and anxiety, and a profusion of fantasy, this differed from the normal girl at the menarche only in that it was readily accessible and achieved a degree of belief (*Ichzugehörigkeit*) which is unusual. Her disappointment that she had not gained either a penis or a baby led to a pronounced reaction against the physical and verbal exhibitionism in her family and to the revelation that she identified her whole precocious little body with the penis which she and her mother so coveted. She felt that by maintaining her body and its precocity as an object of sexual interest, she fulfilled this need for her mother.

From this point on, Susan gradually developed her awareness of people. New phallic (oedipal) elements appeared in her relation with John and her father. Her envy of John was tinged with admiration, and a wish to catch up with him in school. She became aware of her mother's disturbance and the distress it caused to herself and the family, and was gradually able to be more detached. Her father's weakness and the impingement of his obsessions on the family were also admitted. A true oedipal conflict now emerged and could be analyzed as it manifested itself in the transference, in regard to her family, and via displacement outside the family. Her sexual deprivation was expressed in fantasies of starvation and her aggression in a tantalizing untidiness, directed against her father's obsessional rituals at mealtimes. In the untidiness, Susan was abetted by her mother, and identified with her mother's casual attitudes to her cleanliness training. Mrs. S.'s conflicts in this area of child care led her to project her distress onto her husband, while she maintained an overtolerant attitude herself. This pattern was carried over into her preoccupation with the discharge, and underlay Susan's complaint of her mother's part in alienating her from her father.

Susan now found constructive ways of coming to terms with her father's personality. Memories of early swinging games and of being carried half asleep in his arms were re-enacted in the transference. The memory of the swing brought in the first sessions now appeared as a cover memory for all these events. The idea of swinging away from the father's body contained both the denial of the penis as a male organ and a condensation showing the origin of the penis-body equation in excitements, disappointments, and anxiety, which primarily concerned her father. Fenichel (1936) stresses the importance of the prevalence of oral wishes in girls' fantasies of possessing and being a penis. "They identify themselves, i.e., their whole body, with a penis, via the pathway of oral introjection. The idea of having bitten off a penis or of having otherwise incorporated it is the continuation of the unconscious equation 'body = penis.' This equation, the aim of which is in fact that of a *totem* being taken into the body of the object, may therefore be regarded as a passive complement to the fantasy of swallowing a penis." Fenichel also stresses the heightened effect which the oral-sadistic tendencies have on the voyeuristic impulses.

With the emergence of Susan's fantasies of the primal scene in the final stage of the analysis, her fear of losing control was centered on ideas of becoming "hysterical," being hypnotized, and going "out into space" in a capsule. Susan linked the latter idea with a capsule given her against her will in the hospital and with a recent fainting fit of John's. These fantasies culminated in a panic attack on an escalator. Susan broke into a sweat and was "safe" only with her mother's arms around her. It was now clear that Susan equated the primal scene with her struggle to resist anesthesia at twenty months. The fear of "falling into space" was identical with her fear of being overwhelmed by sexual fantasy (Leuba, 1950), against which her internal resources in terms of maternal identification seemed too precarious a protection.

Susan's inability to establish a workable identification with her mother, a shift from "being one with" to "being like" (Jacobson, 1954), could now be seen from a developmental angle. Loewald

(1951) describes how the child's attitudes to reality, and his ability to build boundaries between his outer and inner world bears the imprint of the stages of his relation to his object. While the primary narcissistic identity with the mother constitutes a libidinal motive force for the ego's striving to progressive differentiation and unification of reality, it is also the source of a threat to perpetuate and re-establish this position and engulf the emerging ego into its original primary narcissistic unity, "an unstructured nothingness of identity of 'ego' and 'reality.' " Susan experienced castration in terms of a fantasied loss of identity both from the anticipated satisfaction of her phallic (oedipal) wishes and when she retreated from these to an "engulfing mother." Susan's fantasies of her own birth, where she was poisoned, overwhelmed, engulfed in the dangerous womb, and threatened with suffocation and extinction, represented an alternative castration threat. This fantasy seems to bear the imprint of memory traces of her feeding situation.

Susan's experience of body interference at twenty months and the reinforcement of her primary narcssistic fantasies by the administration of anesthesia provided a basis in reality for her essentially neurotic fears of loss of identity. This event occurred at a time when the boundaries between inner and outer reality were still fluid and her sexual identity was not yet fully established. Fantasies of oral impregnation arising in the current oedipal situation reactivated her wish for the mother's breast. Her fears of disintegration could now be seen as rooted in an ambivalent wish to be taken into her mother's arms. Fenichel comments: "The intention of disproving oral-sadistic tendencies against the penis by the fantasy of harmonious unity with it—'I am myself the penis'—seems in typical fashion a continuation of the intention of disproving oral-sadistic tendencies against the mother's body by means of the fantasy of harmonious unity with it." Fantasies of unity with the mother's body or the penis alternated in Susan's sexual identity.

Present Interests and Achievements

Susan at ten years of age is a normally adapted latency child. Although the tallest in her class, she is in no way conspicuous. Her mother finds Susan a competent and reliable help in the home. In her relationships with her parents, she is able to take a tolerant account of their difficulties and can discuss her problems sensibly. While she is entirely competent in managing her periods, before a recent visit with a school friend to Ireland, she had a serious discussion with her mother about the difficulties that might arise. Toward the end of her analysis Susan summed up the advantages she had gained from it as follows: "When Mummy wants me to change my clothes all the time, or wear something I don't want to, I just say, 'Oh Mummy don't fuss.' I never thought I would do that ever." Susan had no minor illness either neurotic or physical in the last year of her analysis.

In the seven years of treatment, Susan lost more than a third of her treatment sessions, and was simultaneously absent from school, on account of her own or her mother's indispositions. Ultimately, it became clear that the impact of Mrs. S.'s anxiety on her medical advisers provoked at least one long and unnecessary hospitalization (for a nonexistent heart condition). It could be surmised that many of Susan's absences for minor illness had been encouraged by Mrs. S. and had not been strictly necessary. Despite the long absence from school Susan is in the top group of her class, except in arithmetic where she is average. Her imaginative powers are now used for integrated story writing, which is ambitious and well organized. Her stories sometimes run into several chapters. At the end of treatment she expressed her pleasure in her own absorbed functioning as a writer, saying, "I never thought I could do a thing like that. It's like being out in space." Her drawings have received merit awards in newspaper competitions.

Her ability to verbalize discriminative judgments is probably unusually high as a result of her long period in treatment. She applies this ability equally to her inner and outer life. She recently volunteered the thought that she must have liked the smell of her rag dolly, because it smelled like her mother.

Swimming remains one of her favorite pastimes; she has won various badges, including one for lifesaving. On the whole, her activities tend to be solitary; in a group, she likes to take the role of instructor, telling stories or teaching others to swim. She has no particular interest in her appearance, though she dresses neatly and attractively. While her sexual fantasies involve boys in her class, they are tentative and not carried into action. She is contented at home and has no wish to leave her family. Susan looks forward to her future, but for the moment is quite content to be a little girl.

SUMMARY OF CONCLUSIONS

1. Susan's behavioral disturbance was first recognized after her hospitalization and anesthetization at twenty months. These events accentuated the passive-active conflict normally developing at the end of the second year. The fluidity of her instinctual organization and the immaturity of her ego at this age provided fertile soil for fantastic solutions in her assumption of gender role.

2. There was no timely suggestion that help could be made available for both parents and child. The parents' continued anxiety over her precocity added a special quality to Susan's object relations and complicated the problem of her identifications. The structuring of her narcissism was more than usually impeded, and her self-esteem became dependent on defensive fantasies involving her body image.

3. Fixation points induced by the quality of her earliest maternal care also predisposed her to continuous instinctual stimulation at all levels and partial ego regressions against which her primitive defense system could not be effective. Spitz (1954) emphasized that "it is the fixation point in the mother's personality which causes a disorganization in the orderly development of the child."

4. In the context of her later phallic (oedipal) development Susan's precocity and her ambivalent object relationships led her to see herself as a real rival to a mother with omnipotent powers of retaliation.

The fantasy of actual sexual rivalry with her mother, focused on the possession of secondary sex characteristics, accentuated her castration anxiety. The peculiar intensity and macabre quality of her fantasies owe much to the strength of these anxieties. But Susan's castration anxiety was also reinforced by a primitive fear of ego dissolution inherent in very early fixation points.

5. Susan's display of secondary sex characteristics functioned to aggravate the castration complex of the males in her environment, so that the quality of the consequent rebuff of her oedipal wishes intensified her tendency to regression.

In an impressive article,[1] Comfort (1960) suggests that at a time in human evolution prior to the development of the latency period, castration anxiety, which seems inappropriate to childhood in any known society, may have had the effect of restraining males from being competitive before they were mature. Avoidance of the sexually displaying female could serve to keep them out of the competitive struggle while still maternally dependent. The penis envy of the girl coming to normal adolescent expression in decorative symbols and cryptandric behavior would help in reversing the male anxiety response to the female genital and thus facilitate the expression of adult sexual drives.

6. The analysis afforded no evidence that Susan's physical precocity was accompanied by the quantitative increase in sexual drive that we associate with puberty. Her pathology is more readily explicable on other grounds. Identical pathological manifestations, involving phase agglutination, with marked passive features in all drive systems and ego regression, are observed in a group of cases in which early seduction and maternal frustration are common but which lack the feature of precocious puberty.

In analogy with what we know about the formation of neuroses, it might be assumed that the intensity of her pregenital relationship to her mother (accompanied as it was by manifestations of phallic exhibitionism) was in part the outcome of regression from an increased genital drive. The following facts argue against this view:

a. The main manifestation of conflict occurred in the area of Susan's narcissism; it was at this point in the analysis that her main regression, including regression to primary-process thinking, was evident (age four to five and a half years).

b. The onset of menstruation was not accompanied by a similar phenomenon (age six and a half years). Nor did any increase in defensive struggle which might have been a negative indicator of increased drive activity occur in relation to the onset of menstruation. It could scarcely be expected that an increase in genital drive would fail to exacerbate the genital anxieties of such a young child with so inadequate an ego. In the absence of increased inhibition or other evidence of increased defenses against sexuality, there is a

[1] My attention was drawn to the relevance of this article by Dr. Alfred Model, R.T.

very strong *prima facie* case for the hypothesis that Susan's precocious physical development resulted in no increase of psychic sexual drive.

c. Susan's development to the present shows none of the features of adolescence. She has reacted to her oedipal situation (the true oedipal phase) instinctually as a four-year-old, though with the added insight contingent on her long period in analysis. No wish is evident to break her object ties. At the height of her oedipal frustration, fantasies of street wandering similar to the prostitution fantasies of the adolescent were evident, but their outcome was only that Susan asked for more liberty to go about alone.

Analysis has contributed to the containment of her sexuality by the reorganization of her personality, and made possible the emergence of a true latency period.

7. The analysis affords overwhelming evidence that constitutional sexual precocity is a major problem for both the child and her family, in which psychological help for a considerable period may be needed. It is doubtful whether a true estimate of the child's internal disabilities can be gauged even by such intensive interviews as were undertaken by Hampson and Money (1955). In Susan's case the degree and nature of the impact of massive family defenses on the child's own defense system would have proved impossible to judge. Family casework over a long period by an analytically trained adviser, capable of eliciting and handling the transference manifestations of anxiety, would alone provide an adequate diagnostic plan.

BIBLIOGRAPHY

Beach, F. (1948), *Hormones and Behavior.* New York: Hoeber.
Benedek, T. (1950), Climacterium, a Developmental Phase. *Psa. Quart.,* XIX.
Comfort, A. (1960), Darwin and Freud. *Lancet,* II, No. 7142.
Di George, A. & Warkany, J. (1959), The Endocrine System. In: Nelson's *Textbook of Pediatrics.* Philadelphia: Saunders, 7th ed.
Fenichel, O. (1936), The Symbolic Equation: Girl = Phallus. *Collected Papers,* II. New York: Norton, 1954.
Ford, C. & Beach, F. (1952), *Patterns of Sexual Behavior.* London: Eyre & Spottiswood.
Freud, A. (1936), *The Ego and the Mechanisms of Defence.* New York: International Universities Press, 1946.
—— (1954), In: Problems of Infantile Neurosis. *This Annual,* IX.
Freud, S. (1900), The Interpretation of Dreams. *Standard Edition,* IV & V. London: Hogarth Press, 1953.
—— (1905), Three Essays on the Theory of Sexuality. *Standard Edition,* VII. London: Hogarth Press, 1953.

—— (1911), Formulations on the Two Principles of Mental Functioning. *Standard Edition*, XII. London: Hogarth Press, 1958.
—— (1914), On Narcissism. *Standard Edition*, XIV. London: Hogarth Press, 1957.
—— (1915), The Unconscious. *Standard Edition*, XIV. London: Hogarth Press, 1957.
—— (1923), The Ego and the Id. *Standard Edition*, XIX. London: Hogarth Press, 1961.
—— (1926), Inhibitions, Symptoms and Anxiety. *Standard Edition*, XX. London: Hogarth Press, 1959.
Greenacre, P. (1947), Vision, Headache and the Halo. *Psa. Quart.*, XVI.
—— (1952), Some Factors Producing Different Types of Pregenital and Genital Organization. In: *Trauma, Growth, and Personality*. New York: Norton.
—— (1954), In: Problems of Infantile Neurosis. *This Annual*, IX.
Hampson, J. & Money, J. (1955), Idiopathic Sexual Precocity in the Female. *Psychosom. Med.*, XVII.
Hampstead Clinic (1961), Index Manual of Hampstead Child-Therapy Clinic (unpublished).
Hartmann, H. (1939), *Ego Psychology and the Problem of Adaptation*. New York: International Universities Press, 1958.
Hubble, D. (1963), The Psyche and the Endocrine System. *Lancet*, II, No. 7301.
Jacobson, E. (1954), The Self and the Object World: Vicissitudes of Their Infantile Cathexes and Their Influence on Ideational and Affective Development. *This Annual*, IX.
Jolly, H. (1955), *Sexual Precocity*. Oxford: Blackwell.
Leuba, J. (1950), Women Who Fall. *Int. J. Psa.*, XXXI.
Lewin, B. D. (1933), The Body as Phallus. *Psa. Quart.*, II.
Loewald, H. (1951), Ego and Reality. *Int. J. Psa.*, XXXII.
Money, J., Hampson, J., & Hampson, J. (1955a), Hermaphroditism: Recommendations Concerning Assignment of Sex, Change of Sex and Psychologic Management. *Bull. Johns Hopkins Hosp.*, XCVII.
—— —— —— (1955b), Sexual Incongruities and Psychopathology: The Evidence of Human Hermaphroditism. *Bull. Johns Hopkins Hosp.*, XCVIII.
Novak, E. (1944), Female Precocious Puberty. *Amer. J. Obst. & Gyn.*, XLVII.
Paschkis, K., Rakoff, A., & Cantarow, A. (1958), *Clinical Endocrinology*. London: Cassell.
Reich, A. (1954), Early Identifications as Archaic Elements in the Superego. *J. Amer. Psa. Assn.*, II.
Spitz, R. A. (1954), In: Problems of Infantile Neurosis. *This Annual*, IX.
Symonds, E. M. (1960), Precocious Sexual Development. *Report of the Adelaide Children's Hospital*, III.
Wilkins, L. (1948), Abnormalities and Variations of Sexual Development During Childhood and Adolescence. *Advances in Pediatrics*, III.
—— (1957), *The Diagnosis and Treatment of Endocrine Disorders in Childhood and Adolescence.* Springfield: Thomas, 2nd ed.
Winnicott, D. (1953), Transitional Objects and Transitional Phenomena. *Int. J. Psa.*, XXXIV.
—— (1961), The Effect of Psychotic Parents on the Emotional Development of the Child. *Brit. J. Psychiat. Soc. Work*, VI.

CONTENTS OF PREVIOUS VOLUMES

VOLUME I, 1945

HEINZ HARTMANN AND ERNST KRIS—The Genetic Approach in Psychoanalysis
PHYLLIS GREENACRE—The Biologic Economy of Birth
RENÉ A. SPITZ—Hospitalism. An Inquiry into the Genesis of Psychiatric Conditions in Early Childhood
EDWARD GLOVER—Examination of the Klein System of Child Psychology
MARIE BONAPARTE—Notes on the Analytical Discovery of a Primal Scene
ANNA FREUD—Indications for Child Analysis
BERTA BORNSTEIN—Clinical Notes on Child Analysis
EMMY SYLVESTER—Analysis of Psychogenic Anorexia in a Four-Year-Old
KATE FRIEDLANDER—Formation of the Antisocial Character
DOROTHY T. BURLINGHAM—The Fantasy of Having a Twin
ELEANOR PAVENSTEDT AND IRENE ANDERSEN—The Uncompromising Demand of a Three-Year-Old for a Real Mother
HYMAN S. LIPPMAN—The Use of Dreams in Psychiatric Work with Children
MARGARETE RUBEN—A Contribution to the Education of a Parent
EMANUEL KLEIN—The Reluctance to Go to School
OTTO FENICHEL—The Means of Education
WILLIE HOFFER—Psychoanalytic Education
EDITHA STERBA—Interpretation and Education
ERIK HOMBURGER ERIKSON—Childhood and Tradition in Two American Indian Tribes
EDITH BUXBAUM—Transference and Group Formation in Children and Adolescents
FRITZ REDL—The Psychology of Gang Formation and the Treatment of Juvenile Delinquents
BERTRAM D. LEWIN—Gregory Bateson and Margaret Mead: Balinese Character, a Photographic Analysis
KATHERINE M. WOLF—Evacuation of Children in Wartime. A Survey of the Literature with Bibliography
LILLIAN MALCOVE—Margaret E. Fries' Research in Problems of Infancy and Childhood. A Survey
LAWRENCE S. KUBIE—Margaret A. Ribble: The Rights of Infants
KATHERINE M. WOLF—Edouard Pichon: Le Développement de l'Enfant et de l'Adolescent

VOLUME II, 1946

HEINZ HARTMANN, ERNST KRIS, AND RUDOLPH M. LOEWENSTEIN—Comments on the Formation of Psychic Structure
EDITH JACOBSON—The Child's Laughter
DOROTHY T. BURLINGHAM—Twins
JEANNE LAMPL-DE GROOT—The Pre-Oedipal Phase in the Development of the Male Child
RENÉ A. SPITZ—Hospitalism: A Follow-Up Report
MARGARET E. FRIES—The Child's Ego Development and the Training of Adults in His Environment

ANNA FREUD—The Psychoanalytic Study of Infantile Feeding Disturbances
MARGARET W. GERARD—The Psychogenic Tic in Ego Development
PHYLLIS BLANCHARD—Psychoanalytic Contributions to the Problem of Reading Disabilities
JENNY WAELDER HALL—The Analysis of a Case of Night Terror
BERTA BORNSTEIN—Hysterical Twilight States in an Eight-Year-Old Child
ANNY KATAN—Experience with Enuretics
ANNA MAENCHEN—A Case of Superego Disintegration
CHRISTINE OLDEN—Headline Intelligence
ELISABETH R. GELEERD—A Contribution to the Problem of Psychoses in Childhood
RENÉ A. SPITZ—Anaclitic Depression
WILLIE HOFFER—Diaries of Adolescent Schizophrenics (Hebephrenics)
KATE FRIEDLANDER—Psychoanalytic Orientation in Child Guidance Work in Great Britain
ERIK HOMBURGER ERIKSON—Ego Development and Historical Change
LILI E. PELLER—Incentives to Development and Means of Early Education
RAYMOND DE SAUSSURE—J. B. Felix Descuret

VOLUME III/IV, 1949

HEINZ HARTMANN, ERNST KRIS, AND RUDOLPH M. LOEWENSTEIN—Notes on the Theory of Aggression
ANNA FREUD—Aggression in Relation to Emotional Development: Normal and Pathological
BEATA RANK—Aggression
WILLIE HOFFER—Mouth, Hand and Ego Integration
DOROTHY T. BURLINGHAM—The Relation of Twins to Each Other
PHYLLIS GREENACRE—A Contribution to the Study of Screen Memories
RENÉ A. SPITZ with the collaboration of KATHERINE M. WOLF—Autoerotism. Some Empirical Findings and Hypotheses on Three of Its Manifestations in the First Year of Life
MARY LEITCH AND SYBILLE K. ESCALONA—The Reaction of Infants to Stress. A Report on Clinical Findings
J. LOUISE DESPERT—Dreams in Children of Preschool Age
BERTA BORNSTEIN—The Analysis of a Phobic Child. Some Problems of Theory and Technique in Child Analysis
EDITHA STERBA—Analysis of Psychogenic Constipation in a Two-Year-Old
ANNELIESE SCHNURMANN—Observation of a Phobia
AUGUSTA ALPERT—Sublimation and Sexualization. A Case Report
MARGARET SCHOENBERGER MAHLER—Psychoanalytic Evaluation of Tics: A Sign and Symptom in Psychopathology
ELISABETH R. GELEERD—The Psychoanalysis of a Psychotic Child
PAUL BERGMAN AND SYBILLE K. ESCALONA—Unusual Sensitivities in Very Young Children
BRUNO BETTELHEIM AND EMMY SYLVESTER—Physical Symptoms in Emotionally Disturbed Children
EMANUEL KLEIN—Psychoanalytic Aspects of School Problems
MELITTA SPERLING—Analysis of a Case of Recurrent Ulcer of the Leg
LYDIA JACOBS—Methods Used in the Education of Mothers. A Contribution to the Handling and Treatment of Developmental Difficulties in Children Under Five Years of Age
KATE FRIEDLANDER—Neurosis and Home Background. A Preliminary Report
AUGUST AICHHORN—Some Remarks on the Psychic Structure and Social Care of a Certain Type of Female Juvenile Delinquents
RUTH E. EISSLER—Observations in a Home for Delinquent Girls
EDWARD LEHMAN—Feeding Problems of Psychogenic Origin. A Survey of the Literature
BERTRAM D. LEWIN—Child Psychiatry in the 1830's

VOLUME V, 1950

HEINZ HARTMANN—Psychoanalysis and Developmental Psychology
WILLIE HOFFER—Development of the Body Ego
ERNST KRIS—Notes on the Development and on Some Current Problems of Psychoanalytic Child Psychology
RUDOLPH M. LOEWENSTEIN—Conflict and Autonomous Ego Development During the Phallic Phase
BEATA RANK AND DOROTHY MACNAUGHTON—A Clinical Contribution to Early Ego Development
RENÉ A. SPITZ—Relevancy of Direct Infant Observation
HEINZ HARTMANN—Comments on the Psychoanalytic Theory of the Ego
K. R. EISSLER—Ego-Psychological Implications of the Psychoanalytic Treatment of Delinquents
PHYLLIS GREENACRE—Special Problems of Early Female Sexual Development
EDITH JACOBSON—Development of the Wish for a Child in Boys
JEANNE LAMPL-DE GROOT—On Masturbation and Its Influence on General Development
M. KATAN—Structural Aspects of a Case of Schizophrenia
DAVID BERES AND SAMUEL J. OBERS—The Effects of Extreme Deprivation in Infancy on Psychic Structure in Adolescence: A Study in Ego Development
EDITH B. JACKSON AND ETHELYN H. KLATSKIN—Rooming-In Research Project: Development of Methodology of Parent-Child Relationship Study in a Clinical Setting
HANNA ENGL KENNEDY—Cover Memories in Formation
SELMA FRAIBERG—On the Sleep Disturbances of Early Childhood
MARTHA WOLFENSTEIN—Some Variants in Moral Training of Children
BRUNO BETTELHEIM AND EMMY SYLVESTER—Delinquency and Morality
HEDY SCHWARZ—The Mother in the Consulting Room: Notes on the Psychoanalytic Treatment of Two Young Children
LEO RANGELL—A Treatment of Nightmare in a Seven-Year-Old Boy
AUGUSTA BONNARD—The Mother as Therapist, in a Case of Obsessional Neurosis

VOLUME VI, 1951

ERNST KRIS—Opening Remarks on Psychoanalytic Child Psychology
ANNA FREUD—Observations on Child Development
DOROTHY T. BURLINGHAM—Present Trends in Handling the Mother-Child Relationship During the Therapeutic Process
MARIAN C. PUTNAM, BEATA RANK AND SAMUEL KAPLAN—Notes on John I.: A Case of Primal Depression in an Infant
VICTOR TAUSK—On Masturbation
ANNIE REICH—The Discussion of 1912 on Masturbation and Our Present-Day Views
ERNST KRIS—Some Comments and Observations on Early Autoerotic Activities
MILTON I. LEVINE—Pediatric Observations on Masturbation in Children
ANNA FREUD in collaboration with SOPHIE DANN—An Experiment in Group Upbringing
M. WULFF—The Problem of Neurotic Manifestations in Children of Preoedipal Age
PHYLLIS GREENACRE—Respiratory Incorporation and the Phallic Phase
MARJORIE HARLEY—Analysis of a Severely Disturbed Three-and-one-half-year-old Boy
CHARLES BRENNER—A Case of Childhood Hallucinosis
DOROTHY T. BURLINGHAM—Precursors of Some Psychoanalytic Ideas about Children in the Sixteenth and Seventeenth Centuries
RENÉ A. SPITZ—The Psychogenic Diseases in Infancy: An Attempt at Their Etiologic Classification
BERTA BORNSTEIN—On Latency
SELMA FRAIBERG—Clinical Notes on the Nature of Transference in Child Analysis
IVY BENNETT AND ILSE HELLMAN—Psychoanalytic Material Related to Observations in Early Development

SELMA FRAIBERG—Enlightenment and Confusion
MARTHA WOLFENSTEIN—A Phase in the Development of Children's Sense of Humor
JACOB A. ARLOW—A Psychoanalytic Study of a Religious Initiation Rite: Bar Mitzvah
LEO A. SPIEGEL—A Review of Contributions to a Psychoanalytic Theory of Adolescence: Individual Aspects

VOLUME VII, 1952

HEINZ HARTMANN—The Mutual Influences in the Development of Ego and Id
W. HOFFER—The Mutual Influences in the Development of Ego and Id: Earliest Stages
ANNA FREUD—The Mutual Influences in the Development of Ego and Id: Introduction to the Discussion
MELANIE KLEIN, S. NACHT, W. CLIFFORD M. SCOTT, H. G. VAN DER WAALS—The Mutual Influences in the Development of Ego and Id: Discussants
ANNA FREUD—The Role of Bodily Illness in the Mental Life of Children
JOHN BOWLBY, JAMES ROBERTSON AND DINA ROSENBLUTH—A Two-Year-Old Goes to Hospital
ELSE PAPPENHEIM AND MARY SWEENEY—Separation Anxiety in Mother and Child
MELITTA SPERLING—Animal Phobias in a Two-Year-Old Child
LUCIE JESSNER, GASTON E. BLOM AND SAMUEL WALDFOGEL—Emotional Implications of Tonsillectomy and Adenoidectomy on Children
MARIE BONAPARTE—Masturbation and Death or A Compulsive Confession of Masturbation
SELMA FRAIBERG—A Critical Neurosis in a Two-and-a-Half-Year-Old Girl
MARGARET L. MEISS—The Oedipal Problem of a Fatherless Child
MARGARET HARRIES—Sublimation in a Group of Four-Year-Old Boys
DAVID BERES—Clinical Notes on Aggression in Children
MARGARET BRENMAN—On Teasing and Being Teased: And the Problem of "Moral Masochism"
MARGARET SCHOENBERGER MAHLER—On Child Psychosis and Schizophrenia: Autistic and Symbiotic Infantile Psychoses
EMMY SYLVESTER—Discussion of Techniques Used to Prepare Young Children for Analysis
GERALD H. J. PEARSON—A Survey of Learning Difficulties in Children
CHRISTINE OLDEN—Notes on Child Rearing in America
EDITH B. JACKSON, ETHELYN H. KLATSKIN AND LOUISE C. WILKIN—Early Child Development in Relation to Degree of Flexibility of Maternal Attitude
ERICH LINDEMANN AND LYDIA G. DAWES—The Use of Psychoanalytic Constructs in Preventive Psychiatry

VOLUME VIII, 1953

ANNA FREUD—Some Remarks on Infant Observation
ROSE W. COLEMAN, ERNST KRIS, AND SALLY PROVENCE—The Study of Variations of Early Parental Attitudes
MARGARET E. FRIES AND PAUL J. WOOLF—Some Hypotheses on the Role of the Congenital Activity Type in Personality Development
BERTA BORNSTEIN—Masturbation in the Latency Period
PHYLLIS GREENACRE—Certain Relationships Between Fetishism and the Faulty Development of the Body Image
SYLVAN KEISER—A Manifest Oedipus Complex in an Adolescent Girl
CHRISTINE OLDEN—On Adult Empathy with Children
VICTOR H. ROSEN—On Mathematical "Illumination" and the Mathematical Thought Process: A Contribution to the Genetic Development and Metapsychology of Abstract Thinking
SAMUEL RITVO AND SALLY PROVENCE—Form Perception and Imitation in Some Autistic Children: Diagnostic Findings and Their Contextual Interpretation

MARTHA WOLFENSTEIN—Children's Understanding of Jokes
HEINZ HARTMANN—Contribution to the Metapsychology of Schizophrenia
K. R. EISSLER—Notes Upon the Emotionality of a Schizophrenic Patient and Its Relation to Problems of Technique
MARGARET S. MAHLER AND PAULA ELKISCH—Some Observations on Disturbances of the Ego in a Case of Infantile Psychosis
ANNA MAENCHEN—Notes on Early Ego Disturbances
ANNEMARIE P. WEIL—Certain Severe Disturbances of Ego Development in Childhood
GREGORY ROCHLIN—Loss and Restitution
BERTA BORNSTEIN—Fragment of an Analysis of an Obsessional Child: The First Six Months of Analysis
AUGUSTA ALPERT AND SYLVIA KROWN—Treatment of a Child with Severe Ego Restriction in a Therapeutic Nursery
SARA KUT—The Changing Pattern of Transference in the Analysis of an Eleven-Year-Old Girl
EMMA N. PLANK—Memories of Early Childhood in Autobiographies
GÉZA RÓHEIM—Fairy Tale and Dream
THOMAS A. PETTY—The Tragedy of Humpty Dumpty

VOLUME IX, 1954

ANNA FREUD—Psychoanalysis and Education
PROBLEMS OF INFANTILE NEUROSIS: A Discussion—Participants: Phyllis Greenacre, Anna Freud, Heinz Hartmann, Bertram D. Lewin, Sybille Escalona, Rudolph M. Loewenstein, Edith Jacobson, René A. Spitz, Robert Waelder, Charles Davison, Judith S. Kestenberg, Ernst Kris, Marianne Kris, Grace McLean Abbate, Mary O'Neil Hawkins, Anita Bell, Bela Mittelmann, Margaret S. Mahler, Gustav Bychowski
EDITH JACOBSON—The Self and the Object World: Vicissitudes of Their Infantile Cathexes and Their Influence on Ideational and Affective Development
PAUL KRAMER—Early Capacity for Orgastic Discharge and Character Formation
BELA MITTELMANN—Motility in Infants, Children, and Adults: Patterning and Psychodynamics
LILI E. PELLER—Libidinal Phases, Ego Development, and Play
OLIVE STEVENSON—The First Treasured Possession: A Study of the Part Played by Specially Loved Objects and Toys in the Lives of Certain Children. With a Preface by D. W. Winnicott
SELMA FRAIBERG—Tales of the Discovery of the Secret Treasure
AUGUSTA BONNARD—Some Discrepancies Between Perception and Affect As Illustrated by Children in Wartime
OTTO E. SPERLING—An Imaginary Companion, Representing a Prestage of the Superego
ILSE HELLMAN—Some Observations on Mothers of Children with Intellectual Inhibitions
EMMA N. PLANK AND ROBERT PLANK—Emotional Components in Arithmetical Learning As Seen Through Autobiographies
EDITH BUXBAUM—Technique of Child Therapy: A Critical Evaluation
AUGUSTA ALPERT—Observations on the Treatment of Emotionally Disturbed Children in a Therapeutic Center
RUDOLF EKSTEIN AND JUDITH WALLERSTEIN—Observations on the Psychology of Borderline and Psychotic Children

VOLUME X, 1955

HEINZ HARTMANN—Notes on the Theory of Sublimation
ERNST KRIS—Neutralization and Sublimation: Observations on Young Children
PAULA KRAMER—On Discovering One's Identity: A Case Report
K. R. EISSLER—An Unusual Function of an Amnesia

VICTOR H. ROSEN—Strephosymbolia: An Intrasystemic Disturbance of the Synthetic Function of the Ego

EDWARD LISS—Motivations in Learning

MAX SCHUR—Comments on the Metapsychology of Somatization

DOROTHY BURLINGHAM in co-operation with ALICE GOLDBERGER AND ANDRÉ LUSSIER—Simultaneous Analysis of Mother and Child

PHYLLIS GREENACRE—Further Considerations Regarding Fetishism

MARGARET S. MAHLER AND BERTRAM J. GOSLINER—On Symbiotic Child Psychosis: Genetic, Dynamic and Restitutive Aspects

RENÉ A. SPITZ—The Primal Cavity: A Contribution to the Genesis of Perception and Its Role for Psychoanalytic Theory

BELA MITTELMANN—Motor Patterns and Genital Behavior: Fetishism

SELMA FRAIBERG—Some Considerations in the Introduction to Therapy in Puberty

LAWRENCE S. KUBIE AND HYMAN A. ISRAEL—"Say You're Sorry"

DAVID CROCKER—The Study of a Problem of Aggression

ELINOR W. DEMAREST AND MURIEL CHAVES WINESTINE—The Initial Phase of Concomitant Treatment of Twins

LUCIE JESSNER, JOHN LAMONT, ROBERT LONG, NANCY ROLLINS, BABETTE WHIPPLE, AND NORMAN PRENTICE—Emotional Impact of Nearness and Separation for the Asthmatic Child and His Mother

ELIZABETH GERO-HEYMANN—A Short Communication on a Traumatic Episode in a Child of Two Years and Seven Months

MARTHA WOLFENSTEIN—Mad Laughter in a Six-Year-Old Boy

VOLUME XI, 1956

PHYLLIS GREENACRE—Experiences of Awe in Childhood

HEINZ HARTMANN—Notes on the Reality Principle

ERNST KRIS—The Recovery of Childhood Memories in Psychoanalysis

SEYMOUR L. LUSTMAN—Rudiments of the Ego

ELIZABETH R. ZETZEL—An Approach to the Relation between Concept and Content in Psychoanalytic Theory (With Special Reference to the Work of Melanie Klein and Her Followers)

AUGUSTA ALPERT, PETER B. NEUBAUER, AND ANNEMARIE P. WEIL—Unusual Variations in Drive Endowment

DAVID BERES—Ego Deviation and the Concept of Schizophrenia

L. BRYCE BOYER—On Maternal Overstimulation and Ego Defects

JUDITH S. KESTENBERG—On the Development of Maternal Feelings in Early Childhood: Observations and Reflections

ANNEMARIE P. WEIL—Some Evidences of Deviational Development in Infancy and Childhood

RUDOLF EKSTEIN AND JUDITH WALLERSTEIN—Observations on the Psychotherapy of Borderline and Psychotic Children

ERNA FURMAN—An Ego Disturbance in a Young Child

ELISABETH R. GELEERD—Clinical Contribution to the Problem of the Early Mother-Child Relationship: Some Discussion of Its Influence on Self-destructive Tendencies and Fugue States

LOUIS A. GOTTSCHALK—The Relationship of Psychologic State and Epileptic Activity: Psychoanalytic Observations on an Epileptic Child

WILLIAM G. NIEDERLAND—Clinical Observations on the "Little Man" Phenomenon

ELEANOR PAVENSTEDT—The Effect of Extreme Passivity Imposed on a Boy in Early Childhood

JOYCE ROBERTSON—A Mother's Observations on the Tonsillectomy of Her Four-year-old Daughter. With Comments by Anna Freud

LILI E. PELLER—The School's Role in Promoting Sublimation

MARTHA WOLFENSTEIN—Analysis of a Juvenile Poem

VOLUME XII, 1957

CHARLES BRENNER—The Nature and Development of the Concept of Repression in Freud's Writings

PHYLLIS GREENACRE—The Childhood of the Artist

EDITH JACOBSON—On Normal and Pathological Moods

JEANNE LAMPL-DE GROOT—On Defense and Development: Normal and Pathological

RUDOLPH M. LOEWENSTEIN—Some Thoughts on Interpretation in the Theory and Practice of Psychoanalysis

SEYMOUR L. LUSTMAN—Psychic Energy and Mechanisms of Defense

GABRIEL CASUSO—Anxiety Related to the Discovery of the Penis: An Observation. With an Introduction by ANNA FREUD

MARIANNE KRIS—The Use of Prediction in a Longitudinal Study

WILLIAM G. NIEDERLAND—The Earliest Dreams of a Young Child

ANNEMARIE SANDLER, ELIZABETH DAUNTON, AND ANNELIESE SCHNURMANN—Inconsistency in the Mother as a Factor in Character Development: A Comparative Study. With an Introduction by ANNA FREUD

PETER BLOS—Preoedipal Factors in the Etiology of Female Delinquency

ERNA FURMAN—Treatment of Under-Fives by Way of Parents

ELISABETH R. GELEERD—Some Aspects of Psychoanalytic Technique in Adolescents

BELA MITTELMANN—Motility in the Therapy of Children and Adults

NATHAN N. ROOT—A Neurosis in Adolescence

MARGARETE RUBEN—Delinquency: A Defense Against Loss of Objects and Reality

LISBETH J. SACHS—On Changes in Identification from Machine to Cripple

ROBERT PLANK—On "Seeing the Salamander"

PHILIP WEISSMAN—The Childhood and Legacy of Stanislavski

VOLUME XIII, 1958

PHYLLIS GREENACRE—The Family Romance of the Artist. *Discussion:* Leo Stone, David Beres, Robert C. Bak

LEO S. LOOMIE, VICTOR H. ROSEN, AND MARTIN H. STEIN—Ernst Kris and the Gifted Adolescent Project. *Discussion:* Bertram D. Lewin, Annie Reich, Margaret S. Mahler

SAMUEL RITVO AND ALBERT J. SOLNIT—Influences of Early Mother-Child Interaction on Identification Processes. *Discussion:* Rudolph M. Loewenstein, Jacob A. Arlow, Robert P. Knight

ANNA FREUD—Child Observation and Prediction of Development: A Memorial Lecture in Honor of Ernst Kris. *Discussion:* René A. Spitz, Heinz Hartmann, Robert Waelder

HEINZ HARTMANN—Comments on the Scientific Aspects of Psychoanalysis

ISHAK RAMZY AND ROBERT S. WALLERSTEIN—Pain, Fear, and Anxiety: A Study in Their Interrelationships

MAX SCHUR—The Ego and the Id in Anxiety

K. R. EISSLER—Notes on Problems of Technique in the Psychoanalytic Treatment of Adolescents: With Some Remarks on Perversions

ANNA FREUD—Adolescence

ELISABETH R. GELEERD—Borderline States in Childhood and Adolescence

LEO A. SPIEGEL—Comments on the Psychoanalytic Psychology of Adolescence

ANNIE REICH—A Character Formation Representing the Integration of Unusual Conflict Solutions into the Ego Structure

DAVID BERES—Vicissitudes of Superego Functions and Superego Precursors in Childhood

P. J. VAN DER LEEUW—The Preoedipal Phase of the Male

RENÉ A. SPITZ—On the Genesis of Superego Components

MARY E. BERGEN—The Effect of Severe Trauma on a Four-Year-Old Child

JOSEPH S. BIERMAN, ARTHUR B. SILVERSTEIN, AND JACOB E. FINESINGER—A Depression in a Six-Year-Old Boy with Acute Poliomyelitis
VIVIAN JARVIS—Clinical Observations on the Visual Problem in Reading Disability
WILLIAM G. NIEDERLAND—Early Auditory Experiences, Beating Fantasies, and Primal Scene
CHRISTINE OLDEN—Notes on the Development of Empathy
PHYLLIS GREENACRE—The Relation of the Impostor to the Artist
PHILIP WEISSMAN—Shaw's Childhood and *Pygmalion*
WRITINGS OF ERNST KRIS

VOLUME XIV, 1959

JAMES F. BING, FRANCIS MCLAUGHLIN, AND RUDOLF MARBURG—The Metapsychology of Narcissism
K. R. EISSLER—On Isolation
PHYLLIS GREENACRE—Play in Relation to Creative Imagination
LEO A. SPIEGEL—The Self, the Sense of Self, and Perception
GRETE L. BIBRING—Some Considerations of the Psychological Processes in Pregnancy
ANNA FREUD—Clinical Studies in Psychoanalysis: Research Project of the Hampstead Child-Therapy Clinic
EDITH JACOBSON—The "Exceptions": An Elaboration of Freud's Character Study
ALBERT J. LUBIN—A Boy's View of Jesus
AUGUSTA ALPERT—Reversibility of Pathological Fixations Associated with Maternal Deprivation in Infancy
RUDOLF EKSTEIN, JUDITH WALLERSTEIN, AND ARTHUR MANDELBAUM—Countertransference in the Residential Treatment of Children: Treatment Failure in a Child with a Symbiotic Psychosis
PAULA ELKISCH AND MARGARET S. MAHLER—On Infantile Precursors of the "Influencing Machine" (Tausk)
SIDNEY L. GREEN, HELEN SCHUR, AND MARVIN H. LIPKOWITZ—Study of a Dwarf
ANNY KATAN—The Nursery School as a Diagnostic Help to the Child Guidance Clinic
K. R. EISSLER—Notes on the Environment of a Genius
M. KATAN—Schreber's Hereafter: Its Building-Up (*Aufbau*) and Its Downfall
WILLIAM G. NIEDERLAND—The "Miracled-Up" World of Schreber's Childhood
LILI E. PELLER—Daydreams and Children's Favorite Books

VOLUME XV, 1960

JOHN BOWLBY—Grief and Mourning in Infancy and Early Childhood
ANNA FREUD—Discussion of Dr. Bowlby's Paper
MAX SCHUR—Discussion of Dr. Bowlby's Paper
RENÉ A. SPITZ—Discussion of Dr. Bowlby's Paper
JEANNE LAMPL-DE GROOT—On Adolescence
BELA MITTELMANN—Intrauterine and Early Infantile Motility
JOSEPH SANDLER—On the Concept of Superego
ROY SCHAFER—The Loving and the Beloved Superego in Freud's Structural Theory
PHYLLIS GREENACRE—Further Notes on Fetishism
ANNY KATAN—Distortions of the Phallic Phase
ANNIE REICH—Pathologic Forms of Self-Esteem Regulation
HAROLD BALIKOV—Functional Impairment of the Sensorium As a Result of Normal Adaptive Processes
EDITH BUXBAUM—Hair Pulling and Fetishism
HAROLD KOLANSKY—Treatment of a Three-Year-Old Girl's Infantile Neurosis: Stammering and Insect Phobia
PETER B. NEUBAUER—The One-Parent Child and His Oedipal Development
MARIE B. SINGER—Fantasies of a Borderline Patient

ILSE HELLMAN, OSCAR FRIEDMANN, and ELIZABETH SHEPHEARD—Simultaneous Analysis of Mother and Child

KATA LEVY—Simultaneous Analysis of a Mother and Her Adolescent Daughter: The Mother's Contribution to the Loosening of the Infantile Object Tie. With an Introduction by ANNA FREUD

PETER BLOS—Comments on the Psychological Consequences of Cryptorchism: A Clinical Study

ANDRÉ LUSSIER—The Analysis of a Boy with a Congenital Deformity

MARY A. SARVIS—Psychiatric Implications of Temporal Lobe Damage

VOLUME XVI, 1961

GRETE L. BIBRING, THOMAS F. DWYER, DOROTHY S. HUNTINGTON, AND ARTHUR F. VALENSTEIN—A Study of the Psychological Processes in Pregnancy and of the Earliest Mother-Child Relationship

DAVID L. RUBINFINE—Perception, Reality Testing, and Symbolism

ISIDOR SILBERMANN—Synthesis and Fragmentation

DOROTHY BURLINGHAM—Some Notes on the Development of the Blind

LISELOTTE FRANKL—Some Observations on the Development and Disturbances of Integration in Childhood

EDITH JACOBSON—Adolescent Moods and the Remodeling of Psychic Structures in Adolescence

ANNY KATAN—Some Thoughts About the Role of Verbalization in Early Childhood

SALLY PROVENCE AND SAMUEL RITVO—Effects of Deprivation on Institutionalized Infants: Disturbances in Development of Relationship to Inanimate Objects

JOHN BOWLBY—Note on Dr. Max Schur's Comments on Grief and Mourning in Infancy and Early Childhood

E. JAMES ANTHONY—A Study of "Screen Sensations." Discussion by PAUL KRAMER

SYLVIA BRODY—Some Aspects of Transference Resistance in Prepuberty

EDWARD D. JOSEPH AND JACK H. TABOR—The Simultaneous Analysis of a Pair of Identical Twins and the Twinning Reaction

MARJORIE R. LEONARD—Problems in Identification and Ego Development in Twins

BERTRAM D. LEWIN—Reflections on Depression

MARGARET SCHOENBERGER MAHLER—On Sadness and Grief in Infancy and Childhood: Loss and Restoration of the Symbiotic Love Object

EVELINE G. OMWAKE AND ALBERT J. SOLNIT—"It Isn't Fair": The Treatment of a Blind Child

EMMA N. PLANK AND CARLA HORWOOD—Leg Amputation in a Four-Year-Old: Reactions of the Child, Her Family, and the Staff

SHELDON R. RAPPAPORT—Behavior Disorder and Ego Development in a Brain-Injured Child

GREGORY ROCHLIN—The Dread of Abandonment: A Contribution to the Etiology of the Loss Complex and to Depression

ADELE E. SCHARL—Regression and Restitution in Object Loss: Clinical Observations

ALIZA SEGAL AND FREDERICK H. STONE—The Six-Year-Old Who Began to See: Emotional Sequelae of Operation for Congenital Bilateral Cataract

BENJAMIN SHAMBAUGH—A Study of Loss Reactions in a Seven-Year-Old

ALBERT J. SOLNIT AND MARY H. STARK—Mourning and the Birth of a Defective Child

HELEN D. WALLACH—Termination of Treatment As a Loss

I. HYMAN WEILAND AND ROBERT RUDNIK—Considerations of the Development and Treatment of Autistic Childhood Psychosis

VOLUME XVII, 1962

K. R. EISSLER—On the Metapsychology of the Preconscious: A Tentative Contribution to Psychoanalytic Morphology

HEINZ HARTMANN AND R. M. LOEWENSTEIN—Notes on the Superego

GEORGE S. KLEIN—Blindness and Isolation

JEANNE LAMPL-DE GROOT—Ego Ideal and Superego

JOSEPH SANDLER, MARIA KAWENOKA, LILY NEURATH, BERNARD ROSENBLATT, ANNELIESE SCHNURMANN, AND JOHN SIGAL—The Classification of Superego Material in the Hampstead Index

JOSEPH SANDLER AND BERNARD ROSENBLATT—The Concept of the Representational World

ANNA FREUD—Assessment of Childhood Disturbances

ILSE HELLMAN—Hampstead Nursery Follow-up Studies: 1. Sudden Separation and Its Effect Followed Over Twenty Years

ERNST KRIS—Decline and Recovery in the Life of a Three-Year-Old; or: Data in Psychoanalytic Perspective on the Mother-Child Relationship

SEYMOUR L. LUSTMAN—Defense, Symptom, and Character

JOYCE ROBERTSON—Mothering as an Influence on Early Development: A Study of Well-Baby Clinic Records

DAVID L. RUBINFINE—Maternal Stimulation, Psychic Structure, and Early Object Relations; with Special Reference to Aggression and Denial

RENÉ A. SPITZ—Autoerotism Re-examined: The Role of Early Sexual Behavior Patterns in Personality Formation

JOHN C. COOLIDGE, ELLEN TESSMAN, SAMUEL WALDFOGEL, AND MARY LOU WILLER—Patterns of Aggression in School Phobia

AARON H. ESMAN—Visual Hallucinoses in Young Children

JEROMA KAVKA—Ego Synthesis of a Life-Threatening Illness in Childhood

SAMUEL D. LIPTON—On the Psychology of Childhood Tonsillectomy

MARJORIE P. SPRINCE—The Development of a Preoedipal Partnership between an Adolescent Girl and Her Mother

MARTIN WANGH—The "Evocation of a Proxy": A Psychological Maneuver, Its Use as a Defense, Its Purposes and Genesis

M. KATAN—A Causerie on Henry James's "The Turn of the Screw"